GENESIS
TO ESTHER

TEACHER
GENESIS TO REVELATION SERIES
VOLUME 1

D1289786

ABINGDON PRESS

Nashville

ISBN 0-687-07259-X

Manufactured in the United States of America

This book is printed on acid-free paper.

97 98 99 00 01 02 03 04 05 06—10 9 8 7 6 5 4 3 2 1

GENESIS TO REVELATION SERIES
VOLUME 1
Table of Contents

HOW TO TEACH GENESIS TO REVELATION

Unique Features of This Bible Study

In Genesis to Revelation, you and your class will study the Bible in three steps. Each step provides a different level of understanding of the Scripture. We call these steps Dimension One, Dimension Two, and Dimension Three.

Dimension One concerns what the Bible actually says. You do not interpret the Scripture at this point; you merely take account of what it says. Your main goal for this dimension is to get the content of the passage clear in your mind. What does the Bible say?

Dimension One is in workbook form. The members of the class will write the answers to questions about the passage in the space provided in the student book. All the questions in Dimension One can be answered by reading the Bible itself. Be sure the class finishes Dimension One before going on to Dimensions Two and Three.

Dimension Two concerns information that will shed light on the Scripture under consideration. Dimension Two will answer such questions as

- What are the original meanings of some of the words used in the passage?
- What is the original background of the passage?
- Why was the passage most likely written?
- What are the relationships between the persons mentioned in the passage?
- What geographical and cultural factors affect the meaning of the passage?

The question for Dimension Two is, What information do we need in order to understand the meaning of the passage? In Dimension One the class members will discover what the Bible says. In Dimension Two they will discover what the Bible means.

Dimension Three focuses on interpreting the Scripture and applying it to life situations. The questions here are

- What is the meaning of the passage for my life?
- What response does the passage require of me as a Christian?
- What response does this passage require of us as a group?

Dimension Three questions have no easy answers. The task of applying the Scripture to life situations is up to you and the class.

Aside from the three-dimensional approach, another unique feature of this study is the organization of the series as a whole. Classes that choose to study the Genesis to Revelation Series will be able to study all the books of the Bible in their biblical order. This method will give the class continuity that is not present in most other Bible studies. The class will read and study virtually every verse of the Bible, from Genesis straight through to Revelation.

How many times have you stumbled over a biblical name or maybe even avoided discussing a person or place because you could not pronounce the word? While you are using the Genesis to Revelation Series, you may find a good Bible pronunciation guide helpful. These are available from any Christian bookstore. The *Harper's Bible Pronunciation Guide* (The Society of Biblical Literature, 1989, ISBN 0-06-068951-X) is one such guide.

Additional aids will be a glossary of terms in the back of some of the student books as well as biblical maps. The glossary will give definitions for the names and places that are mentioned in the student lessons. The maps will help with geographical clarification of the stories. An excellent additional resource is *Bible Teacher Kit* (Abingdon, 1994, ISBN 0-687-78006-3). It has both maps and a glossary.

Weekly Preparation

Begin planning for each session early in the week. Read the passage that the lesson covers, and write the answers to Dimension One questions in the student book. Then read Dimensions Two and Three in the student book. Make a note of any questions or comments you have. Finally, study the material in the teacher book carefully. Decide how you want to organize your class session.

Organizing the Class Session

Since Genesis to Revelation involves three steps in studying the Scripture, you will want to organize your class sessions around these three dimensions. Each lesson in the student book and this teacher book consists of three parts.

The first part of each lesson in the teacher book is the same as the Dimension One section in the student book, except that the teacher book includes the answers to Dimension One questions. These questions and answers are taken from the New International Version of the Bible.

You might use Dimension One in several ways:

1. Ask the group members to read the Scripture and to write the answers to all the Dimension One questions before coming to class. This method will require that the class covenant to spend the necessary amount of study time outside of class. When the class session begins, read through the Dimension One questions, asking for responses from the group members. If anyone needs help with any of the answers, look at the biblical reference together.

2. Or, if you have enough class time, you might spend the first part of the session working through the Dimension One questions together as a group. Locate the Scripture references, ask the questions one at a time, and invite the class members to find the answers and to read them aloud. Then allow enough time for them to write the answers in the student book.

3. Or, take some time at the beginning of the class session for group members to work individually. Have

them read the Dimension One questions and the Scripture references and then write their answers to the questions in the spaces provided in the student book. Discuss together any questions or answers in Dimension One that do not seem clear. This approach may take longer than the others, but it provides a good change of pace from time to time.

You do not have to organize your class sessions the same way every week. Ask the class members what they prefer. Experiment! You may find ways to study the Dimension One material other than the ones listed above.

The second part of each lesson in this teacher book corresponds to the second part of the student book lessons. The Dimension Two section of the student book provides background information to help the students understand the Scripture. Become familiar with the information in the student book.

Dimension Two of this teacher book contains additional information on the passage. The teacher book goes into more depth with some parts of the passage than the student book does. You will want to share this information with the group in whatever way seems appropriate. For example, if someone raises a question about a particular verse, share any additional background information from the teacher book.

You might raise a simple question such as, What words or phrases gave you trouble in understanding the passage? or, Having grasped the content of the passage, what questions remain in your mind? Encourage the group members to share confusing points, troublesome words or phrases, or lingering questions. Write these problems on poster paper or chalkboard. This list of concerns will form the outline for the second portion of the session.

These concerns may also stimulate some research on the part of the group members. If your study group is large enough, divide the class into three groups. Then divide the passage for the following week into three parts. Assign a portion of the passage to each group. Using Bible commentaries and Bible dictionaries, direct each group to discover as much as it can about this portion of the passage before the class meets again. Each group will then report its findings during the class session.

The third part of each lesson in this teacher book relates to Dimension Three in the student book. This section helps class members discover how to apply the Scripture to their own lives. Here you will find one or more interpretations of the passage—whether traditional, historical, or contemporary. Use these interpretations when appropriate to illumine the passage for the group members.

Dimension Three in the student book points out some of the issues in the passage that are relevant to our lives. For each of these issues, the student book raises questions to help the students assess the meaning of the Scripture for their lives. The information in Dimension Three of the teacher book is designed to help you lead the class in discussing these issues. Usually, you will find a more in-depth discussion of portions of the Scripture.

The discussion in the teacher book will give you a better perspective on the Scripture and its interpretation before you begin to assess its meaning for today. You will probably want to share this Dimension Three information with the class to open the discussion. For each life situation, the teacher book contains suggestions on facilitating the class discussion. You, as the teacher, are responsible for group discussions of Dimension Three issues.

Assembling Your Materials

You will need at least three items to prepare for and conduct each class session:
- A teacher book
- A student book
- A Bible—you may use any translation or several; the answers in this teacher book are taken from the New International Version.

One advantage of the Genesis to Revelation Series is that the study is self-contained. That is, all you need to teach this Bible study is provided for you in the student and teacher books. Occasionally, or perhaps on a regular basis, you might want to consult other sources for additional information.

HOW TO LEAD A DISCUSSION

The Teacher as Discussion Leader

As the teacher of this series or a part of this series, one of your main responsibilities during each class period will be to lead the class discussion. Some teachers are apprehensive about leading a discussion. In many ways, it is easier to lecture to the class. But remember that the class members will surely benefit more from the class sessions when they actively participate in a discussion of the material.

Leading a discussion is a skill that any teacher can master with practice. And keep in mind—especially if your class is not used to discussion—that the members of your group will also be learning through practice. The following are some pointers on how to lead interesting and thought-provoking discussions in the study group.

Preparing for a Discussion—Where Do I Start?

1. Focus on the subject that will be discussed and on the goal you want to achieve through that discussion.

2. Prepare by collecting information and data that you will need; jot down these ideas, facts, and questions so that you will have them when you need them.

3. Begin organizing your ideas; stop often to review your work. Keep in mind the climate within the group—attitudes, feelings, eagerness to participate and learn.

4. Consider possible alternative group procedures. Be prepared for the unexpected.

5. Having reached your goal, think through several ways to bring the discussion to a close.

As the teacher, do not feel that your responsibility is to give a full account or report of the assigned material. This practice promotes dependency. Instead, through stimulating questions and discussion, the participants will read the material—not because you tell them to but because they want to read and prepare.

How Do I Establish a Climate for Learning?

The teacher's readiness and preparation quickly establish a climate in which the group can proceed and its members learn and grow. The anxiety and fear of an unprepared teacher are contagious but so are the positive vibrations coming from a teacher who is prepared to move into a learning enterprise.

An attitude of shared ownership is also basic. Group members need to perceive themselves as part of the learning experience. Persons establish ownership by working on goals, sharing concerns, and accepting major responsibility for learning.

Here are several ways the teacher can foster a positive climate for learning and growth.

1. *Readiness.* A teacher who is always fully prepared can promote, in turn, the group's readiness to learn.

2. *Exploration.* When the teacher encourages group members to freely explore new ideas, persons will know they are in a group whose primary function is learning.

3. *Exposure.* A teacher who is open, honest, and willing to reveal himself or herself to the group will encourage students to discuss their feelings and opinions.

4. *Confidentiality.* A teacher can create a climate for learning when he or she respects the confidentiality of group members and encourages the group members to respect one another's confidentiality.

5. *Acceptance.* When a teacher shows a high degree of acceptance, students can likewise accept one another honestly.

How Can I Deal With Conflict?

What if conflict or strong disagreement arises in your group? What do you do? Think about the effective and ineffective ways you have dealt with conflict in the past.

Group conflict may come from one of several sources. One common source of conflict involves personality clashes. Any group is almost certain to contain at least two persons whose personalities clash. If you break your class into smaller groups for discussion, be sure these persons are in separate groups.

Another common source of group conflict is subject matter. The Bible can be a very controversial subject. Remember the difference between discussion or disagreement and conflict. As a teacher you will have to decide when to encourage discussion and when to discourage conflict that is destructive to the group process.

Group conflict may also come from a general atmosphere conducive to expression of ideas and opinions. Try to discourage persons in the group from being judgmental toward others and their ideas. Keep reminding the class that each person is entitled to his or her own opinions and that no one opinion is more valid than another.

How Much Should I Contribute to the Discussion?

Many teachers are unsure about how much they should contribute to the class discussions. Below are several pitfalls to avoid.

1. The teacher should remain neutral on a question until the group has had adequate time to discuss it. At the proper time in the discussion the teacher can offer his or her opinion. The teacher can direct the questions to the group at large, rechanneling those questions that come to him or her.

At times when the members need to grapple with a question or issue, the most untimely response a teacher can make is answering the question. Do not fall into the trap of doing the group members' work for them. Let them struggle with the question.

However, if the teacher has asked the group members to reveal thoughts and feelings, then group members have the right to expect the same of the teacher. A teacher has no right to ask others to reveal something he or she is unwilling to reveal. A teacher can reveal thoughts and feelings, but at the appropriate time.

The refusal to respond immediately to a question often takes self-discipline. The teacher has spent time thinking, reading, and preparing. Thus the teacher usually does have a point of view, and waiting for others to respond calls for restraint.

2. Another pitfall is the teacher's making a speech or extended comments in expressing an opinion or summarizing what has been said. For example, in an attempt to persuade others, a teacher may speak, repeat, or strongly emphasize what someone says concerning a question.

3. Finally, the pitfall of believing the teacher must know "the answers" to the questions is always apparent. The teacher need not know all the answers. Many questions that should be raised are ultimate and unanswerable; other questions are open-ended; and still others have several answers.

BIBLE TEACHER KIT (Abingdon Press, 1994, ISBN 0-687-78006-3)

This essential tool kit for teachers of Bible study classes is full of resources to enhance the learning process. The three-ring binder contains 160 resource pages featuring

- background articles
- charts
- a timeline
- a glossary of biblical terms
- ten one-color maps of Bible lands then and now

Many of the resource pages include photocopying privileges, so you can distribute additional copies to members of the class or photocopy onto transparencies.

The kit also includes

- eight 20" x 32" full-color maps of Bible lands
- a full-color video of Bible lands

GENESIS
Table of Contents

About the Writer

Dr. Walter Harrelson, the writer of these lessons, is distinguished professor emeritus of Old Testament at Vanderbilt Divinity School, Nashville, Tennessee, and adjunct professor in the Divinity School at Wake Forest University in Winston-Salem, North Carolina. He has written several books and many articles on the Old Testament as well as on religion and worship in Bible lands.

And God said, "Let there be light," and there was light (1:3).

—1—

Creation

Genesis 1–3

DIMENSION ONE:
WHAT DOES THE BIBLE SAY?

Answer these questions by reading Genesis 1

1. Who creates the heavens and the earth? (Genesis 1:1)

   God creates the heavens and the earth.

2. What is the earth like when God begins creating? (Genesis 1:2)

   The earth is formless and empty; darkness is over the surface of the deep.

3. What does God create on each of the first six days? (Genesis 1:3-27)

Day	What God creates on this day
One	*light*
Two	*expanse*
Three	*dry land, vegetation*
Four	*sun, moon, and stars*
Five	*living creatures of water and air*
Six	*animals and human beings*

4. What does God command the first creatures to do? (Genesis 1:22)

   God commands that they be fruitful and increase in number.

5. What position do the human beings occupy in creation? (Genesis 1:28)

   They rule over all living creatures.

6. After God creates the human beings on the sixth day, what does God think of creation? (Genesis 1:31)

   God sees everything that he has made, and it is very good.

Answer these questions by reading Genesis 2

7. What does God do to the seventh day? Why? (Genesis 2:3)

   God blesses it and makes it holy, because on this day he rests from all his work of creation.

8. From what does God make the first man? How does God give the man life? (Genesis 2:7)

   God makes man from the dust of the ground and breathes into man's nostrils the breath of life.

9. Where does God put the man? (Genesis 2:8)

   God puts the man in the garden God plants for him.

10. What command does God give the man when he places him in the garden? What will happen if the man disobeys the command? (Genesis 2:16-17)

    The man must not eat from the tree of knowledge of good and evil. If the man does, he will die.

11. When God decides that it is not good for the man to be alone, what does God do first? (Genesis 2:18-19)

    God forms animals and birds from the ground and brings them to the man to see what he will call them.

12. From what does God make the first woman? (Genesis 2:21-22)

    God makes the woman from a rib taken from the man's body.

13. According to God's instructions, what takes place when a man and woman unite? (Genesis 2:24)

    The man leaves his parents and is united with his wife. They become one flesh.

14. What does the serpent tempt the woman to do? (Genesis 3:1-5)

    The serpent tempts the woman to eat some of the fruit from the tree in the middle of the garden.

15. What knowledge comes to the man and the woman when they eat the fruit? (Genesis 3:7)

    They know they are naked.

16. When they hear the sound of God in the garden, what do they do? (Genesis 3:8)

    They hide among the trees.

17. Whom does God question first? (Genesis 3:9)

    God first questions the man.

18. What does God do to the serpent who tempted the woman? (Genesis 3:14)

    God curses the serpent and makes it crawl on its belly.

19. What is the woman's punishment? (Genesis 3:16)

    She will experience much pain in childbearing.

20. What is the man's punishment? (Genesis 3:17-19)

    He will toil hard to make a living from the earth.

21. What does God make for the man and the woman before sending them out of the garden? (Genesis 3:21)

    He makes them garments of skins.

DIMENSION TWO: WHAT DOES THE BIBLE MEAN?

Background Information on Genesis 1–3

As the student book suggests, many scholars think that Genesis 1–3 originated from distinct strands of tradition. These strands of tradition were then brought together by different individuals or groups in ancient Israel. Notice that the author of Luke's Gospel speaks of a similar process in Luke 1:1-4. He gathered together all of the available traditions about Jesus, weighed them, and put them together in a faithful way.

So also, ancient Israel had various ways of understanding the Creation. It seems likely that the people came to prefer two of these ways. The first tells the story in a straightforward, orderly way. It is based on the Hebrew view of the structure of the universe. It helped people understand that God was in charge of the whole process and carried it through in six days. Every act of God was good and complete. This story would have been of special value to the teachers of ancient Israel, the priests and theologians. Genesis 1 begins this story, which continues through Genesis 2:3.

The other tradition is a beautiful and sensitive literary account of the first man and woman. It tells of God's loving care for the first human beings, of their temptation and sin, and of God's leading them out into the kind of world that we know, outside the garden of Eden.

The stories fit together very well and complement each other. Indeed, they fit together so well that we cannot be certain that two accounts really exist. Perhaps we have a single account that presents the Creation in two ways. But most scholars today believe that at least two traditions lie behind the Genesis 1–3 account.

Genesis 1:16. The student book points out that the creation of light on the first day (Genesis 1:3)—before the sun, moon, and stars—was not a slip by the writer. The Israelites knew that the sun gave the basic light for earth. But they wanted their hearers and readers to know that God was not dependent upon the sun for light. Rather, the sun depended on God for its existence and power. Every creature in all the world was created by God and was good. While the sun was considered to be one of the high gods for the ancient Babylonians, Assyrians, and Egyptians, it held no power over Israel's God.

Genesis 1:26-28. This story of the Creation identifies the human race as consisting of male and female. When the writer says "man" he means "humankind," not the first male human being or only male human beings.

God prepares to create the first human beings, made in his own image. Yet before he does so, he reflects on the action as the heavenly host listen in. Most interpreters say that this poetic vision of God in heaven shows just how decisive a matter this act of creation is.

To be made in God's image and likeness says much about God as well as about human beings. In all of Creation, no other creatures are in God's image. We understand God to be a thinking, feeling, and willing being, just as we are. Since human beings are in the image of God, we share the divine likeness. For ancient Israel, being created in God's image meant that men and women were able to have communion with God, to share in God's purposes, to follow God's path.

Genesis 2:21-24. In the story of the first man and woman, God creates the man first. God charges the man to care for the garden. But Genesis 2, like Genesis 1, also knows that humankind consists of male and female persons, each helping to complete the existence of the other.

It is regrettable, therefore, that persons have used the Creation story throughout the centuries to show the superiority of men over women. Many have pointed out that God created the woman from the rib of the man, and that the man in ancient Israel was certainly understood to be superior in position and worth to the woman. In most ancient societies the woman occupied a position second to that of the man. Our story, not surprisingly, shows some of this understanding. But our story also gives a clear picture of the equality of male and female in God's sight.

Genesis 3:1. The serpent that speaks with the woman is a beast of the field, which God made. He walks, so to speak, and he talks. He is not a demon. He is sly and cunning, and he likes to deceive.

Throughout much of the ancient Near East, the serpent was a symbol of both deity and fertility. The headdress of the Egyptian pharaohs was crowned with the head of a cobra. The serpent plays a major part in many other stories, legends, and traditions from the ancient Near East. Many persons think of this creature as a kind of demonic being. Our story does not depict the serpent as a representative of Satan, but as one among God's many creatures.

Genesis 3:7. This verse shows that the man and the woman lived in the garden unclothed and knew no sense of shame at all—until they disobeyed the will of God. And the shame they discover is not so much their nakedness as their disobedience to God. The old communion between them and God is broken, and the clothing helps to hide them from God.

Genesis 3:9. God addresses the man first, since men were considered the leaders of the household. As noted in the student book, however, the story makes it clear that the man was present with the woman when she was tempted. He shared the temptation, but the serpent chose to tempt the woman.

In ancient Near Eastern society, the man was understood to have special responsibilities as head of the household. How, we might ask, could the man have let the conversation between the serpent and the woman go on in the way it did? Why didn't he stop the temptation? Clearly, this story shows that the man and woman share responsibility for sin.

Genesis 3:14-19. The curse that God places upon the serpent and the punishment that falls upon the man and woman are explanatory statements. These verses explain how it happens that human beings must toil so hard for the food they secure from the earth, and that women must endure pain in childbearing. In the case of the serpent, the story explains why this creature slithers along on its belly, why it eats dust, and why there is such hostility between snakes and human beings.

DIMENSION THREE: WHAT DOES THE BIBLE MEAN TO ME?

The class discussion of Dimension Three will concentrate on some or all of these areas: "The Bible and Science," "Personal Relationship With God," and "Original Sin."

Genesis 1:1–2:3—The Bible and Science

According to the student book, two attitudes prevail about the relationship between the Creation narratives and scientific theory. Many persons believe that the Creation accounts are not scientific at all, but are religious. Others believe that the biblical description of Creation opposes modern scientific theory. As the student book states, neither belief is quite correct.

Science tries to better understand the world and its operations. Creation stories can never be scientific in the full sense of the word, because we cannot prove them to be true or false. Creation stories are faith-claims. Ask the class members whether they have had problems reconciling the biblical account of Creation with scientific theories. Then ask them to talk about ways in which they have tried to resolve this conflict.

You might ask the class members why they think the Creation stories in Genesis were written. Creation stories all attempt to answer the question of how Creation could have happened at all. Was there not something there from which the world was formed initially? How do you create something from nothing? Creation seems to presuppose a prior substance, a prior space, a prior time.

The Creation account in Genesis does not resolve this problem. We read that God called into being everything that exists. But the story goes on to say that the initial form of the Creation was chaotic, unordered stuff that God ordered meaningfully. God surely must have called time into being, but Creation began at the very moment when God's action as Creator began.

The student book asks the class members to reflect on the statement, "God saw all that he has made, and it was very good." God calls the world he has made "good," and that says something about the nature of the created world. This affirmation opposes the widely held view in ancient cultures that the created world is only a shadow of the "real" and essentially good world of the gods. Genesis 1 tells us that our world, although marred by human sin, is good. We are to maintain God's good creation.

Genesis 1 affirms that God's creatures are created good. Each person is a creature of God. Therefore each person, each child of God, is good—sinful, yes, but not evil. God's creation is good.

Genesis 2:4-17—Personal Relationship With God

The student book talks about the differences between the two biblical accounts of Creation—one in Genesis 1 and one in Genesis 2. Although each of the stories emphasizes a different aspect of God's creation of the world, both stories concentrate on God's relationship with humankind.

The previous issue centered on the fact that God calls his creation "good." Ask the class members to read Genesis 2:4-17 again and discuss what new insights this passage offers us about our relationship to God. You might want to concentrate on two main areas in this discussion.

First, in Genesis 2:4-17, God creates the man before anything else. Unlike the account in Genesis 1, where the man and woman are the last to be created, here the man is the first of God's creatures. The remainder of Genesis 2 portrays the man as God's helper in the creation process.

Second, our narrative points out that God charges the man with responsibility for the rest of the created world (Genesis 2:15). The responsibility God gave to the first man tells us that all persons are responsible for the stewardship of God's world. While the world is for the use of human beings, it is not ours to exploit in any way we see fit. The class may draw other insights from this passage.

Genesis 3—Original Sin

The student book asks the question, "What is the sin of the woman and the man?" Some persons call this basic sin disobedience. The man and the woman disobeyed God's command. Augustine, one of the early saints of the church, called the sin in Eden pride. Ask the class to reflect on whether or not pride is involved in this story. Why is eating the fruit of the tree an act of pride? How do human beings transmit sin? As the student book indicates, Genesis 3 insists that sin arises both in the world outside human beings and within every human being. We freely choose to depart from the path that God lays out for us. A world already marred by sin encourages us to do so. The origin of sin is mysterious.

Ask your group if the term *sin* is always a religious term—a term that refers to a break in the relationship of human beings with God. We read of crimes against the state and against fellow citizens. We may deplore certain moral failings in ourselves and in others. But many persons think that sin is always sin against God. Is this statement true?

To prepare for this discussion on sin, you might want to look up "sin" in *The Interpreter's Dictionary of the Bible* (Abingdon, 1962). This book gives the range of meanings for the word *sin*. Or have someone in the class do this exercise during the class time.

The student book asks the class members to think about their interpretations of the story of Adam and Eve. You might ask the group if Genesis 3 ends with a sense of despair or with a deep sadness. If the latter, why is that? Is it because the story of the man and the woman's leaving the garden is a story as much marked by God's love and grace as it is by God's judgment? The mixture of divine grace and divine punishment that runs through these chapters appears often in the later stories in Genesis.

God clothes the first human pair as they go out to greet the world. God reaffirms his care in that the man may work, find food, earn a livelihood—although with great toil. God confirms the vocation of women as wives and mothers, but he also recognizes that women have great initiative and power of independent action. They suffer during childbearing, but they are indispensable in the peopling of God's entire creation.

And most important of all, God does not remain within the garden. God accompanies the first human pair as they leave, and the garden of Eden no longer figures in the story of humankind at all. The world awaits.

At the close of the session, ask the class members to think about what insights they have gained from studying this lesson on Genesis 1–3. What have they learned about sin? about their relationship to God and to others? about the Bible and scientific theory? You may want to list these insights on chalkboard or a large sheet of paper.

— 2 —
Cain and Abel

Genesis 4–5

DIMENSION ONE:
WHAT DOES THE BIBLE SAY?

Answer these questions by reading Genesis 4

1. What are the names of Adam and Eve's two sons? (Genesis 4:1-2)

   Cain and Abel are the sons of Adam and Eve.

2. What are the occupations of these two sons? (Genesis 4:2)

   Abel is a shepherd, and Cain is a farmer.

3. Whose sacrifice does God reject? (Genesis 4:5)

   Cain's sacrifice is rejected.

4. Who kills whom? (Genesis 4:8)

   Cain kills Abel.

5. What does Cain say to God about his brother? (Genesis 4:9)

   Am I my brother's keeper?

6. What does God do to Cain? (Genesis 4:11-12)

   He puts Cain under a curse and removes his source of livelihood by driving him from the ground.

7. How does God protect Cain? (Genesis 4:15)

   God marks Cain so that no one will kill him.

8. What is the name of Adam and Eve's third son? (Genesis 4:25)

   Seth is their third son.

Answer these questions by reading Genesis 5

9. How old is Adam when Seth is born? (Genesis 5:3)

   Adam is one hundred and thirty years old.

10. Excluding Abel, who lives for the shortest number of years? (Genesis 5:23)

    Enoch does.

11. Who walks with God? (Genesis 5:22, 24)

    Enoch walks with God.

12. Who is the oldest person to live before the Flood? (Genesis 5:27)

    Methuselah is the oldest person before the Flood.

DIMENSION TWO:
WHAT DOES THE BIBLE MEAN?

Genesis 4:1. This verse introduces a riddle that has never been satisfactorily answered: the meaning of the phrase "With the help of the LORD I have brought forth a man." The student book mentions that the name *Cain* is connected with the Hebrew verb *qanah*, which means "to get or acquire" or "to create or produce." We call this explanation of Cain's name an etymology.

The popular etymologies that fill the Bible were fascinating to ancient people. In ancient times, persons believed that names expressed the character and quality of the persons or objects named. Name and nature went together. The ability of the first man to name the animals indicates that he had considerable power over them. Eve's naming Cain makes Eve a partner with God in the bearing of the first children. For this reason, the unusual expression translated "with the help of the LORD"—which is the real mystery of this verse—probably expresses this collaboration with God in the birth of the first child on the earth.

The writer calls the child by the word *man.* This designation may point to the unusual event from the storyteller's point of view. This child is the very first ever born. The distinction between son and daughter comes later on. Cain is "man-child."

Genesis 4:3-7. The student book points out that in this passage, Cain and Abel stand for two ways of life—the farmer and the shepherd. The conflict between shepherds and farmers was a life and death struggle in ancient cultures. The ancient Israelites were primarily shepherds, but they lived on the fringes of settled land and grew some crops. They moved back and forth from the desert to the farm lands, but they were not fully a part of the settled society of Canaan. For this reason, a more positive attitude prevailed in ancient Israel toward the life of the shepherd than toward the life of the farmer.

Some persons identify Cain with the Kenites. The Kenites were desert folk who were metalsmiths by occupation. We know very little about these desert folk. Judges 4:11 tells us that the Kenites descended from Hobab (also known as Jethro), the father-in-law of Moses. Thus, they would have belonged to the tribe of the Sinai desert. According to 1 Samuel 15:6-7, King Saul was careful not to harm the Kenites because they were kind to Israel in early times.

Since the Flood brings an end to all the families except the family of Noah, how could Cain be connected with later descendants—either Canaanites or Kenites? We should remember that our writer is working with popular stories about the first human beings, weaving a picture of great power from these traditional materials.

This passage also tells us something about sin. We saw in Genesis 3 that the serpent stands for temptation to sin that lies outside the self. But a will to disobey arises within the man and the woman. The same is true here. Cain's face falls, and he is angry that God will not accept his sacrifice. The writer portrays sin as a demon that crouches like a lion, ready to spring upon human beings at any sign of weakness. The language that describes Cain's mastering sin reminds us of the language used in Genesis 3:16. There the woman's punishment is that she desires her husband, but he will rule over her.

In the story of Cain and Abel, sin tries to possess humankind, which is in turn charged to exercise rule over it. The desire of sin to undo human beings is the thing to be resisted. We resist by exercising rule over sin. This story is our earliest picture of how human beings can resist sin in the world. And we see God as a loving parent advising Cain to do so.

Genesis 4:8. No one knows for certain if the writer intends to show Cain as a murderer who had planned the deed from the beginning. The New International Version supplies the sentence, "Let's go out to the field." The Latin translation of Saint Jerome has simply, "Let us go outside." In all probability, the NIV gives the correct translation. If this is the case, Cain deliberately planned to murder his brother. The violence did not erupt suddenly as Cain and Abel discussed the matter of why God did not accept Cain's sacrifice.

Genesis 4:10-12. Here God confronts Cain with what he has done. For ancient Near Eastern people, a crime committed in a given place affects the very ground. One could lose the fertility of the soil because of the curse brought by the crime of murder. Deuteronomy 21:1-9 gives a ritual to free the land in the neighboring cities from any guilt of murder when the murderer is unknown.

Genesis 4:16. No one knows where the land of Nod is. The Bible tell us this land is east of Eden. Apparently, the writer of the story understands Cain to have settled far off in Mesopotamia. There he builds a city, marries, and has a family.

Many persons have wondered where Cain found his wife. Clearly, this question does not trouble the writer. He assumes that by this time other settlements exist in various parts of the earth.

Genesis 4:17-26. According to the student book, the genealogy at the end of Chapter 4 is similar to the genealogy in Genesis 5. Here is a comparison:

Chapter 4	*Chapter 5*
Cain	Kenan
Enoch	Mahalalel
Irad	Jared
Mehujael	Enoch
Methushael	Methuselah
Lamech	Lamech

What can we learn from this genealogy? First, the genealogy identifies various vocations. Lamech's sons by Adah and Zillah account for three of these vocations: Jabal initiates cattle-herding, Jubal is the first musician, and Tubal-Cain is the first metalworker. Ancient Near Eastern society believed that such vocations were brought from heaven to earth. They were a benefit to humankind that came from one of the friendly gods.

Second, we can learn from this genealogy a little about the biblical attitude toward longevity. In our literal-minded world, the question of whether persons actually lived these numbers of years is hard to escape. The student book mentions Mesopotamian lists in which the ages of the kings ran into the thousands of years. By comparison, the biblical personalities did not live long at all! The meaning of this pattern of long life before the Flood, followed by a decreasing life span after the Flood seems clear. The Bible, like other ancient literature, sees a "golden age" in the period of human life before the Flood. After the Flood, many things changed, including the normal length of human life. Psalm 90:10 tells us that the "normal" age of death is seventy years.

And yet, for the Book of Genesis the time before the Flood is not really a golden age. Wickedness increases on the earth so rapidly that God sends the Flood to cleanse the earth. That picture is entirely different from the golden age that we read about in ancient Mesopotamian literature.

The long lives of the pre-Flood people are not something we need to take literally. In this way, the biblical writers distinguish the two eras—before the Flood, a period that is gone forever; and after the Flood, which is our own kind of historical time.

From reading this genealogy in Genesis 4, we can also learn something about the importance of the individual and the family in ancient Hebrew culture. In contrast with the Mesopotamian list, the descendants of the biblical Adam are simply individuals, not kings. The form of government in Genesis is the family and the clan, or tribe. It is not a society made up of two classes of citizens—the rulers and the ruled. All are on the same level. We cannot even be certain that women were seen as inferior to men, although we have to recognize that men dominate the scene. Before the Flood, people live in families and in association with their ancestors or clan heads. We hear of cities, but not of kings and kingdoms.

A brief mention of Seth's birth follows the genealogy in Genesis 4. Seth's name is explained by a play on the Hebrew word that means "to appoint." Seth's son, Enosh, has a name that means "human being," just as the name *Adam* does. According to some ancient nonbiblical stories, the first man had the name *Enosh* instead of the name *Adam*.

We also read that at the time of the birth of Enosh, people began to call on the name of the Lord (that is, "Yahweh"). This mention of the name of Yahweh is somewhat surprising. In Exodus 6:2-3, God tells Moses that he has not previously revealed himself by the name Yahweh. Instead he has used the name *El-Shaddai*, translated "God Almighty" (Genesis 17:1).

Probably, we have two different traditions about when the name *Yahweh* was first used in Israel. The present Genesis story claims that even before the great Flood God was already revealing himself to humankind under this special personal name—long before Abraham and Moses appeared on the scene.

Genesis 5. Genesis 5:1 refers to a book of the generations of Adam. Many scholars believe that one of the sources or writers of Genesis used such a book of genealogies. Pieces of this book of genealogies appear throughout the Book of Genesis. The book covers many figures who are well known to us—Adam (5:1), Noah (6:9), the sons of Noah (10:1), Shem (11:10), Terah (11:27, which includes Abraham), Ishmael (25:12), Isaac (25:19), Esau or Edom (36:1, 9), and Jacob (37:2).

We learn from this story that God has organized humankind according to his own purposes. From the Creation forward, God's plan is working itself out.

DIMENSION THREE: WHAT DOES THE BIBLE MEAN TO ME?

The student book raises three issues in Genesis 4 and 5 that are relevant to our lives today. You may want to organize the class discussion of Dimension Three around these three major areas: "Dealing With Rejection," "Premeditated Murder," and "The Judgment and Grace of God."

Genesis 4:1-7—Dealing With Rejection

You might begin this session by supplementing the discussion in the student book of God's rejection of Cain's sacrifice. The Bible does not tell us the reason for God's rejection. The student book mentions some possibilities. In all probability, the author of the story deliberately does not explain why God accepts the offering of Abel and rejects Cain's offering.

God is in a position to accept or to reject as he sees fit. That does not mean that God is arbitrary or capricious. The writers of Genesis know that God fully understands the situation, and therefore the rejection of Cain's sacrifice was the correct decision. At the same time, the Bible does not object to our raising questions about such matters. Biblical faith becomes real for us as we struggle for answers to such questions.

As the student book notes, we cannot be certain whether the story wishes to portray Cain as a premeditated murderer or as a killer whose rage suddenly overcomes him. The fact that Cain rises up and kills Abel even after God reasons with Cain at such length suggests that Cain planned the deed. And the addition of the clause, "Let's go out to the field," seems to indicate that the writer sees Cain as a premeditated murderer.

However, no one knows Cain's motivation. The biblical evidence could lead us in either direction. You might want to ask the class members what they think.

The Hebrew text of Genesis 4:8 does not say, "Cain said to his brother Abel . . . ," but "Cain spoke with his brother Abel" (about the rejected sacrifice). Some Jewish interpreters understand the text in this way, pointing out that God's special care for Cain's life may be motivated by the fact that Cain killed Abel in a towering rage rather than having carefully planned it. When we read the passage, we can see in Cain a violence, a readiness to turn against his brother without adequate reason. We see Cain as one who takes out his anger at God on his innocent brother Abel. If Cain had deliberately murdered Abel, would God have protected him?

According to the student book, Cain's motivation for killing his brother Abel is related to his feelings of rejection by God. Ask the class members to think about the times in their lives when they have experienced rejection. Or, ask them to think about situations in which they have rejected others. Encourage them to talk about their feelings in these situations. Then ask the class members to reflect on whether or not they have ever felt rejected by God. How did they respond to God's rejection?

Genesis 4:9-24—The Judgment and Grace of God

The student book indicates that the story of Cain and Abel demonstrates both the judgment and grace of God at work. Begin this discussion by asking the class members to think about where in the story of Cain and Abel they see God's judgment. In Genesis 4 and 5, God's judgment on humankind is the direct result of Cain's violence.

Lamech's little poem (Genesis 4:23-24) shows us one consequence of Cain's act of violence against his brother. Lamech is not content with the sevenfold vengeance on anyone who harms Cain. No, Lamech maintains his honor and pride by vengeance that does not merely restore the balance. He avenges seventy-sevenfold. Violence breeds violence. Where will it end?

You might want to talk to the class a little about the view of sin in the story of Adam and Eve and then in the story of Cain and Abel. The sin of Adam and Eve is painted as an act of refusal to let God's commandments control their lives. God commands that the tree in the middle of the garden remain untouched. The man and the woman know that God's commandments are good and are for their own good.

In the case of Cain, the sin is an act of violence as well as disobedience. He presses his own desire for life and acceptance so hard that he takes the life of his brother. He will not let God set the terms of what is an acceptable offering but makes this decision on his own. Cain's disobedience also directly affects the life of his brother.

The consequences of Cain's sin are more severe than the consequences of the sin of Adam and Eve. From a religious point of view, the sin in the garden broke the intimate communion between God and humankind, a breach the Bible often deals with. Cain might not have killed his brother if that gap between human beings and God had not developed. We see in Genesis 4, verse 10, that God judges Cain because of his violence. Genesis 4:10 states, "What have you done? Listen! Your brother's blood cries out to me from the ground."

According to the student book, we see God's response to Cain's violence in Genesis 4:11-12. Ask the class members if they can recall how God judges Cain. God's judgment to Cain comes in two parts. First, God curses the ground, so it will no longer yield food for Cain. And second, Cain becomes a fugitive and a wanderer on the earth. Now ask the class members to consider how they have experienced God's judgment.

How do we experience God's grace in the story of Cain and Abel? As the student book indicates, when God pro-

nounces his judgment on Cain, Cain protests that the punishment is greater than he can bear. God then puts a mark of protection on Cain so he will not be harmed.

The student book also mentions that, in putting a protective mark on Cain, God avoids what in biblical times was almost an inevitable step. According to Old Testament law, a person who killed another person was automatically subjected to the death penalty. Exodus 21:14 states, "But if a man schemes and kills another man deliberately, take him away from my altar and put him to death." What does the story of Cain and Abel tell us about the death penalty?

As the class talks about this question, be sure the discussion remains in the context of Genesis 4 and 5. Emphasize that we cannot draw any general conclusions about the biblical views of capital punishment from this one passage; we can only discuss what this particular passage tells us about taking the life of a person who has taken the life of someone else.

In any group discussion of the death penalty there will be disagreements. Some say that the only way to eliminate the possibility of another crime by a murderer is to remove that person from society. But others find such a solution too drastic and not necessary or justified. It is correct to say that the Bible does not directly forbid capital punishment or the taking of human life. But the Bible does underscore the fact that life is a gift from God. Ask the class members to think about what we can learn from the story of Cain and Abel about capital punishment. Try to keep the discussion as specific as possible.

If you have the time, you might want to have the class discuss the meaning of Cain's question, "Am I my brother's keeper?" (Genesis 4:9). Cain's question implies that he does not want his own life and freedom troubled by care for his brother. He does not want to be challenged by any responsibility for others.

But the story shows that Cain cannot live alone. He cries out to God that to become a fugitive and wanderer, cut off from family and human companionship, is unbearable. If Cain cannot live a full life without community, surely he realizes his responsibility for the lives of other men and women. He is his brother's keeper, and has to be, even when he does not want to be.

We also are our brothers' keepers. We are tempted to see only our needs, untroubled by the needs of others. But every moment of our lives depends upon the gifts that others make to our lives. When we give to others, we also draw life from them.

Close the class session by asking the group members what insights they have learned about Genesis 4 and 5. List these insights on chalkboard or a large sheet of paper if time allows.

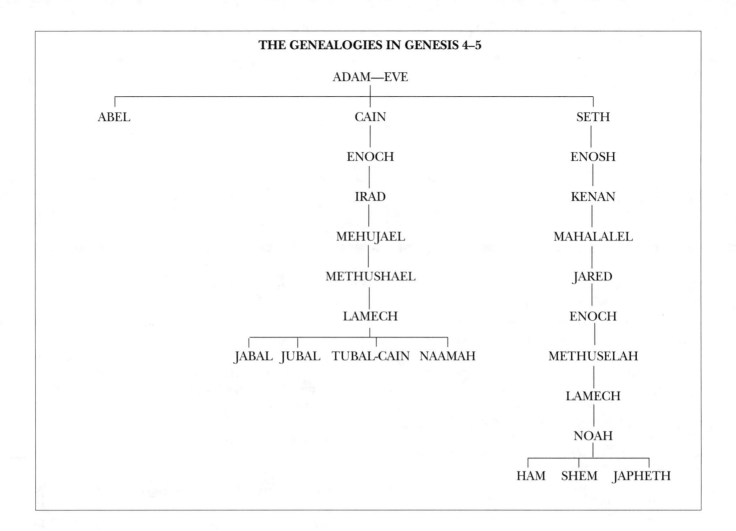

THE GENEALOGIES IN GENESIS 4–5

ADAM—EVE

ABEL   CAIN   SETH

ENOCH   ENOSH

IRAD   KENAN

MEHUJAEL   MAHALALEL

METHUSHAEL   JARED

LAMECH   ENOCH

JABAL JUBAL TUBAL-CAIN NAAMAH   METHUSELAH

LAMECH

NOAH

HAM   SHEM   JAPHETH

I am going to bring floodwaters on the earth to destroy all life under the heavens (6:17).

3

The Flood

Genesis 6–8

**DIMENSION ONE:
WHAT DOES THE BIBLE SAY?**

Answer these questions by reading Genesis 6

1. Whom do the sons of God take as wives? (Genesis 6:1-2)

   The sons of God marry the daughters of men.

2. What is the length of life to which God restricts people? (Genesis 6:3)

   One hundred and twenty years is the life span.

3. For what is God sorry? (Genesis 6:6)

   God is sorry that he made man on the earth.

4. Who finds favor with God? (Genesis 6:8)

   Noah finds favor with God.

5. What are the names of Noah's three sons? (Genesis 6:10)

   Shem, Ham, and Japheth are Noah's sons.

6. What does God decide to do about the sinful earth? (Genesis 6:13)

   He will destroy it.

7. What does God tell Noah to build? (Genesis 6:14)

   God tells Noah to build an ark of cypress wood.

8. How does God plan to destroy the earth? (Genesis 6:17)

   The earth will be destroyed with floodwaters.

9. Who among human beings is to enter the ark and be saved? (Genesis 6:18)

   Noah, his wife, his sons, and their wives will be saved.

10. How many of each kind of bird, animal, and "creature that moves along the ground" is Noah to take into the ark? (Genesis 6:19-20)

    He will take two of each kind.

Answer these questions by reading Genesis 7

11. How many pairs of clean animals and how many pairs of unclean animals is Noah to take into the ark? (Genesis 7:2)

    Seven pairs of all clean animals and one pair of animals that are not clean will enter the ark with Noah.

12. How long will the rain fall on the earth? (Genesis 7:4)

    Rain will fall forty days and forty nights.

13. Who shuts the entire group into the ark? (Genesis 7:16)

    The Lord shuts the ark.

14. How far above the high mountains does the water rise? (Genesis 7:20)

    The waters cover the mountains more than twenty feet.

15. How long do the waters cover the earth? (Genesis 7:24)

    Waters cover the earth one hundred and fifty days.

16. As the waters recede, where does the ark come to rest? (Genesis 8:4)

    The ark rests on the mountains of Ararat.

17. What bird does Noah send out first, and what happens to the bird? (Genesis 8:7)

    The raven flies about until the waters on the earth dry up.

18. Noah then sends out another bird three times, each time a week apart. What happens to this bird each time? (Genesis 8:8-12)

    The dove returns to the ark both the first and second times. The second time she carries an olive leaf in her mouth. The third time she does not return to the ark.

19. What does Noah do after he and his family and the animals leave the ark? (Genesis 8:20)

    He builds an altar to the Lord and makes burnt offerings on the altar.

20. What does God promise regarding the future of the earth? (Genesis 8:21-22)

    God promises that he will never again destroy every living creature as he has done, and that he will not upset the normal processes of nature.

DIMENSION TWO: WHAT DOES THE BIBLE MEAN?

Genesis 6:1-4. The student book explains a little of the background of this story about the sons of God and the daughters of men. The story here, like the one in Genesis 3, shows that sin arises from outside the human community as well as within the community and within the individual heart. The story seems to build upon the earlier reference to the tree of life in the garden of Eden. Once humankind ate of the tree of life, and thereby left the garden, immortality was not possible.

But human beings could live for very long periods of time. The beings born to the daughters of men and the divine beings might live longer yet, or even have immortality! God therefore radically reduces the lifespan of human beings. The longest persons can live will be one hundred and twenty years.

We learn in a later lesson that Moses dies at the age of 120. There are exceptions, however. Genesis 25:7 tells us that Abraham lives 175 years. According to Genesis 35:28, Isaac lives 180 years, and Genesis 47:28 tells us that Jacob lives to be 147 years of age.

In the mythology of many ancient peoples, the high gods and goddesses came down to earth, taking human partners and bringing forth or bearing semidivine beings. This activity is especially characteristic of ancient Greek religion. However, here in the Genesis account, the very existence of such beings is an embarrassment to the story-teller. These beings, born from the illegitimate union of the sons of God and the daughters of men, apparently perish in the Flood. Some persons identify these *Nephilim* with the giants who lived in the land of Canaan. See Numbers 13:28-33 where Moses' spies report about the giants who live in Canaan.

Genesis 6:6. This verse tells us that God is sorry for having made the earth, since sin has spread so widely and penetrated so deeply. Here the Bible shows God to be so closely caught up in events on earth that he is not impassive, unwilling to change his mind. In Numbers 23:19 we read that God is not a man that he should lie, or a mortal that he should repent. But the overwhelming biblical testimony is that God leaves the future open, even with regard to his own decisions. Human actions make a difference in the plans and actions of God, according to the Old Testament.

Genesis 6:6-13. In the student book, the writer underscores human responsibility for the coming of the Flood. God does not hate his creation. The Flood does not come because of the rebellion of the heavenly beings, but because of the spread of human evil. Human deeds, plans, thoughts, and emotions are all touched by evil. As the Bible says, "man's wickedness on the earth had become [great], and . . . every inclination of the thoughts of his heart was only evil all the time." We should notice that both men and women are included in this spread of sin. Women are taken as wives by the heavenly beings, but all the persons of the earth have corrupted their ways.

Genesis 6:14-22. The student book talks about other flood stories from the ancient Near Eastern world. Flood stories also exist in a number of cultures throughout world history, including the North American Indians and the Pacific Island societies. The memory of a great flood usually lies behind all stories of humankind's origin. Even today, floods are devastating events.

The symbolism of water includes both positive and negative elements. Water is life-bringing and life-sustaining, but water also is death-dealing and terrifying in its destructiveness.

The Flood story is not historical in the usual sense of the term. It is a story of beginnings, a story of how human beings developed on earth, the trials they endured, the sins they committed, and God's guidance of their destiny from the very beginning. The Flood story is true, because it lays out a great understanding and powerful truth.

Genesis 7. The writer calmly and objectively tells the story of Noah's gathering of the animals, birds, and creeping things; his loading them into the ark; and their being closed in by God. The story has a grandeur about it. It portrays Noah as making these preparations in clear view of all his neighbors. Probably they ridicule him for this foolish enterprise. According to Genesis 7:10, Noah and the inhabitants of the ark wait seven days before any rain falls. The Letter to the Hebrews describes this work of Noah as a great act of faith (Hebrews 11:7). The writer of Genesis gives no details about the destruction of humankind by the Flood.

Genesis 8. The student book talks about the Gilgamesh Epic—one of the best-known ancient Near Eastern flood stories. The Gilgamesh Epic parallels the biblical story of Noah and the Flood in many ways. In the Gilgamesh Epic, Utnapishtim builds a large boat. This boat is a perfect cube, certainly not a vessel that could have floated. In contrast, the biblical ark is much more like a ship, a structure that would float and hold an enormous cargo. However, the vast number of animals, birds, and creeping things that are known on earth is much too large to fit within the ark's dimensions.

In other matters, the writer of Genesis gives great attention to detail. For example, the waters rise twenty feet above the mountains (Genesis 7:20), so the ark can float over the highest of peaks without running aground. While we may not accept this story as historical in every detail, we should recognize that for the biblical writer, Noah was a part of the beginning of the new human race. In the story of the Flood, Noah and his family become the ancestors of all humankind.

At the end of the Flood story, Noah builds an altar to the Lord. This act symbolizes his thanksgiving for having been delivered from the Flood. The sacrifice of Noah is pleasing to God. The Gilgamesh Epic also contains a sacrifice, although in that instance the gods swarm around the sacrifice, since they had been without sacrifices the many days of the flood.

DIMENSION THREE:
WHAT DOES THE BIBLE MEAN TO ME?

The student book points to three basic theological issues that confront the reader of the Flood story. These issues are "The Spread of Sin," "Our Response to God," and "God's Forgiveness of Sin." The class discussion in Dimension Three will center on these three issues.

Genesis 6:1-8—The Spread of Sin

As the student book mentions, Genesis 6:1-8 tells us how sin spreads on the earth. The first human pair sins in the garden. The first child on earth kills his brother. Events on earth seem to go downhill. The sons of God become involved with the daughters of men, and God is sorry for ever having created humankind.

Genesis 6 pictures sin as spreading over the whole earth, beginning at the time the first human pair disobeys the will of God. Some persons think these early chapters of Genesis are extremely pessimistic. Clearly there is human failure, for humankind can never again serve God gladly and live joyously in the divine presence.

We experience the spread of sin in many ways. The student book mentions one way—a cycle in which one sin seems to lead to another. The student book asks the class members to reflect on the times in their lives or the lives of others when one sin seems to lead to another. The question is this: How was this cycle broken? Was God's help required? Ask the class members to think about and discuss this question now.

According to our story in Genesis, only God can put an end to the spread of sin. As a result of God's intervention, a positive dimension runs throughout these stories. Human life goes on, and the earth is peopled and settled. Cities are built, culture appears, arts and crafts develop. Just consider Noah's extraordinary act of building the ark!

The storyteller gives us a grim story, but the story is marked by the invention of sheep and goat herding, carpentry, metalwork, instrumental music, and agriculture (Genesis 4:19-22). Human life develops positively, but human beings keep departing from the way that leads to life. All of God's creation becomes tainted, and finally it has to be cleansed by divine action on a cosmic scale. Everything disappears. You might want to ask the class members whether they think the Flood story is basically optimistic or pessimistic.

Genesis 8:20—Our Response to God

"Then Noah built an altar to the LORD, and taking some of all the clean animals and clean birds, he sacrificed burnt offerings on it." In this verse, Noah celebrates God's act of deliverance. As the student book indicates, we also experience similar acts of deliverance. Ask the class members to think about times when they were delivered from distress. Have they always recognized God's part in these acts of deliverance? How have they responded to these acts of deliverance?

A response of thankfulness for God's deliverance involves some kind of communication with God. The Bible contains many examples of such responses to God. Suggest to the class members that Noah's response to God in Genesis 8:20—as well as other similar responses following God's acts of deliverance—remind us how we should react to God's deliverance.

Let's say a word about sacrifice. In Genesis 8:20, we read that Noah makes a sacrifice of some of all the clean animals and birds. Probably the writer does not want to make too much of this act of sacrifice, for the readers are given no details.

The Bible recognizes that God established sacrifices and offerings as part of worship and devotion. But sacrifices are never absolutely essential. While this act of sacrifice is significant, the writer hardly stresses it at all—and that can hardly be accidental.

We see the same uncertain attitude toward sacrifice if we read the Old Testament prophets. For the prophets, the making of sacrifices always included the devotion of heart. The prophets of Israel strongly urged the people of Israel to recognize that God wants public righteousness and mercy for the weak and oppressed much more than he wants sacrifices. You might ask someone in the class to read aloud Amos 5:21-24. This passage is a good example of the prophetic attitude toward sacrifice.

The sacrifices that Noah and his family make symbolize life before the Flood. In many ways, the world is the same after the Flood as it was before. Cities existed before the Flood and will soon reappear. Cain and Abel make sacrifices before the Flood, and now Noah and his family make sacrifices on an altar that Noah builds. The alternation of the seasons will continue. The natural rhythms of life and the historical and cultural arrangements are all reinstated following the Flood.

Genesis 8:21-22—God's Forgiveness of Sin

Genesis 8:21 emphasizes God's forgiveness of sin. This verse tells us that God will never again destroy every living creature by flood. Begin this discussion of God's forgiveness of sin by stressing the importance of Genesis 8:21. This verse is perhaps the most important in the entire Flood story. God will never again curse the ground or destroy the earth or disrupt the seasons. God will not do so because of the tendency toward sin that he knows is present in human hearts from the beginning.

God will hold the world secure in the face of human evil. In that way God keeps the evil of humankind in check, works upon it, and displays evil for what it is. This is the gospel of the Flood story, and it is a powerful gospel indeed.

The suggestion that the Flood story is not historical in every detail may disturb some members of the group. If you have time, you might want to ask the class to discuss the question of historicity. This issue is appropriate for the Flood story, as well as for many of the other stories in Genesis 1–11. Ask the class to discuss the following question: What is at stake in considering the Flood story as historical or not historical? How does it disturb our faith if some scholars want to consider this story as not historical?

The important reality is not whether the Flood is historical. The significant thing is that as we read the story we identify with Noah's struggle to preserve life. We identify with God's mercy for human beings who have failed and yet are ready to turn to God for help. If the story of Noah and the Flood is not historical in the ordinary sense of the term, it is historical in that it shows us God's searching love and concern for people even when they turn against him. The story shows us God's refusal to let wickedness continue on the earth forever without checking it.

Close the session by asking the class members to reflect on what new insights they now have about the Flood story. List these insights on chalkboard or a large sheet of paper for later reference.

—4—

Noah and His Descendants

Genesis 9–11

DIMENSION ONE:
WHAT DOES THE BIBLE SAY?

Answer these questions by reading Genesis 9

1. After the Flood, what creatures live in fear and dread of humankind? (Genesis 9:2-3)

   All the beasts of the earth and all the birds of the air, every creature that moves along the ground, all the fish of the sea live in fear of humankind.

2. God allows persons to eat the flesh of animals on what condition? (Genesis 9:4)

   Flesh may be eaten without its blood.

3. When a person kills a human being, what is to happen to the killer? (Genesis 9:6)

   The killer is to be killed.

4. With whom does God establish a covenant after the Flood? (Genesis 9:9-11)

   A covenant is established with Noah and his descendants as well as with all the living creatures on the earth.

5. What does God's covenant assure human beings about the world's future? (Genesis 9:11)

   God will never again destroy the earth by flood.

6. What is the sign of the covenant? (Genesis 9:12-17)

   The rainbow is the sign of the covenant.

7. Who is Ham's son? (Genesis 9:18)

   Canaan is Ham's son.

8. Who plants the first vineyard? (Genesis 9:20)

   Noah plants the first vineyard.

9. What happens to Noah when he drinks of the vine? (Genesis 9:21)

   He becomes drunk.

10. Who sees Noah in his drunkenness? (Genesis 9:22)

    Ham, the father of Canaan, sees Noah.

11. Who covers Noah? (Genesis 9:23)

    Shem and Japheth cover Noah.

12. Whom does Noah curse? (Genesis 9:25)

    Noah curses Canaan.

13. Whom does Noah bless? (Genesis 9:26-27)

    Noah blesses Shem and Japheth.

14. At what age does Noah die? (Genesis 9:29)

    Noah dies at the age of 950.

Answer these questions by reading Genesis 10

15. Which son of Noah is the ancestor of the maritime peoples? (Genesis 10:1-5)

    The maritime peoples decended from Japheth.

16. Which son of Noah is the ancestor of the Egyptians, the Cushites, and the Canaanites? (Genesis 10:6-20)

    These peoples decended from Ham.

17. What do the wanderers in the land of Shinar first make? (Genesis 11:1-3)

    They make bricks.

18. What do they plan to build? (Genesis 11:4)

    They plan to build a city and a tower.

19. Why do they want to build these? (Genesis 11:4)

    They want to make a name for themselves.

20. What does God do to prevent the people from continuing their work? (Genesis 11:7-9)

    He confuses their speech and scatters them over the face of the earth.

21. Who is the father of Abram? (Genesis 11:26)

    Terah is the father of Abraham.

22. Where does Abram's family live? (Genesis 11:27-28)

    They live in Ur of the Chaldeans.

23. Whom does Abram marry? (Genesis 11:29)

    Abram marries Sarai.

24. Do Abram and Sarai have children when they leave Ur? (Genesis 11:30)

    They do not.

25. Where do Terah, Abram, and other members of his family settle after they leave Ur of the Chaldeans? (Genesis 11:31)

    They settle in Haran.

DIMENSION TWO: WHAT DOES THE BIBLE MEAN?

Genesis 9:1-7. Genesis 1 tells us that in the garden of Eden, human beings ate fruit and plants (Genesis 1:29). In Genesis 9 God modifies his original command to say that human beings may now eat animal flesh, but not with its blood. "Everything that lives and moves will be food for you. Just as I gave you the green plants, I now give you everything. But you must not eat meat that has its lifeblood still in it" (Genesis 9:3-4).

After the Flood, however, God's kindness goes so far as to provide animal food for human beings. Later, God lets humankind eat any kind of animal food—even animals that are unclean. Leviticus 11 and Deuteronomy 14 list most of the animals that the Israelites are not permitted to eat.

Genesis 9:8-19. This section elaborates on Genesis 8:21-22. Genesis 8 emphasizes God's receiving of the sacrifice made by Noah and God's assurance that he will never again destroy the earth. Chapter 8 also gives God's promise that from the time of the Flood onward, he will hold the earth intact and allow the normal rhythm of changing seasons to continue.

Chapter 9 takes God's promises one step further. Here God makes a covenant with the whole human race. Covenants are binding agreements between two or more parties guaranteed by oaths, signs, promises, or (sometimes) special sacrifices or other religious acts.

We see two basic kinds of covenants in the Old Testament. The first is a covenant initiated entirely by God; guaranteed by God; and marked by grace, love, and goodness. We have such a covenant in the case of Abraham. (See especially Genesis 12:1-3 and Genesis 15.) This covenant of grace is also made by God with David and David's descendants (2 Samuel 7).

We see the other kind of covenant in the case of Moses. Moses and the people commit themselves to be God's people, to walk in God's ways, and to hold fast to the terms of the covenant. For his part, God will do what he promises to do, and the people can count on God.

The covenant with Moses, and other covenants of this type, binds both parties together in love and obligation. Exodus 19:3-6 is a good example of this kind of covenant. In Exodus 19, God promises the people of Israel that they will be his possession if they will obey him and keep the covenant. In Genesis 9, on the other hand, God's covenant of grace extends to every human being. No one is excluded from the covenant between God and Noah.

Genesis 9:20-29. The story of Noah's drunkenness is not to be set in a context of our problems today with drunkenness and alcoholism. Rather, we should view this story in the framework of an ancient society where wine was rarely plentiful enough to get persons drunk. In ancient Israel, wine was much less powerful than many of the alcoholic beverages used today.

Evidently the writer has left some details out of this story. These details would have related what the son of Noah did to his father, or what the father may have done to the son in his drunkenness. Emphasize that we do not need these details to understand the point of the story. The story tells about the conflict between Canaanites and Israelites, and between Egyptians (Hamites) and Israelites. The student book tells more about this conflict.

Noah's curse on Canaan makes Canaan "the lowest of slaves" (Genesis 9:25). That means that Canaan will serve at the bottom of the ranks of slaves, doing the most menial work. Many of the Canaanites in the Promised Land were made to serve the Israelites, but this curse is concerned more with the religious temptations the Canaanites posed to Israel.

Noah promises Japheth that he will live in the tents of Shem, with the Canaanites as his slaves. The people of Japheth are probably foreigners who lived within the land of Israel and worked with the Israelites—the Hittites, the Hivites, and the like.

Genesis 10:1-32; 11:10-32. These genealogies were tremendously important for the history of the Hebrew people. We receive some incidental information through the list, such as the word about Nimrod, Ham's grandson, who was a mighty hunter (Genesis 10:9). Some strange listings occur, like the identification of Cush as the ancestor of Babylonian descendants, while Cush is normally associated with what is today the Sudan, south of Egypt.

Notice that a grand freedom is at work in the arrangement that leads forward from Noah to Shem to Arpaxad to Shelah to Eber. Other branches of the family tree of Shem lead to the Assyrians and Elamites and Arameans, and so on. From Eber comes the Hebrew people, with a genealogy listed in Genesis 11:14-32.

The arrangement of the peoples as portrayed in this Table of Nations is a bit confused, but we can see that the author thinks of the descendants of Japheth as representing the Mediterranean island folk, those in Asia Minor, and in the northernmost part of the Middle East. The descendants of Ham, or Canaan, cover many lands and peoples, as do those of Shem.

The information in this table comes from the ancient book of genealogies that we spoke about in connection with Genesis 1–3, in the first lesson. This book of genealogies is broken up, and its parts appear in various places throughout Genesis 1–11.

Genesis 11:1-9. The story of the tower of Babel fascinates many persons. At the beginning of the story, the people seem to be wanderers who do not know where they are going. They are surprised to discover that they can make bricks from mud, and that bricks work as well as stone for building materials. These people all speak a single language and are apparently the only people on earth.

Perhaps this story was originally about the people who disembarked from the ark when it landed in the northern mountains of Mesopotamia. Possibly this is a fragment of the continued Flood story, which the biblical writer has woven into his own picture of the beginnings of humankind.

God scatters the people who are building and gives them independent languages. They now have to organize themselves by language-grouping. Evidently, the writer sees language as a development similar to the Fall in the garden of Eden. Originally, all people spoke one language, but because of sin, many languages are introduced.

Other writers have looked back to the time when there was only one language known on earth. Herodotus speculated on what that original language was, and he reports on experiments once made in ancient Egypt to discover the first language. A child was isolated from birth until he spoke his first word. That first word was identified as belonging to the Luvian language (an Asia Minor language). Other versions of this story exist as well. In any case, our author does not identify the original language as Hebrew.

Genesis 11:31-32. Later Jewish legends often speak about the life of Abraham in Ur of the Chaldeans. However, the Bible does not do so—not in Genesis 11:31 or anywhere else. These ancient legends sometimes portrayed Terah as a maker of idols who had a shop in Ur. Thus as a boy, Abraham came to see that idolatry was foolish and wicked.

According to these ancient traditions, Abraham begged his father to give up the business. Finally Abraham took steps to dispose of idolatry in Ur. Terah and his family had to flee for their lives to escape the irate citizens of Ur. That is how the legends explained Terah's move with his family to Haran. The biblical account is silent about the reason for the move. But it presupposes a divine initiative.

DIMENSION THREE:
WHAT DOES THE BIBLE MEAN TO ME?

The student book raises four issues based on Genesis 9–11 that have meaning for our lives today. These issues are "The Taking of Life," "Prejudice," "Striving for Fame," and "The Mystery of God." The class discussion of Dimension Three should center on several or all of these four areas.

Genesis 9:1-7—The Taking of Life

The student book asks the class members to think about the whole idea of taking animal life. You may want to think through your own views on this issue in preparation for the discussion of Genesis 9:1-7. The main emphasis is that the biblical writer wants to honor life as a gift from God, even animal life.

Sometimes we do not recognize the importance of animal life with regard to the lives of the animals on which we depend for food. Certainly human beings are more important than animals. Even so, there may be a connection between a casual attitude toward the lives of animals and a casual treatment of human beings whom we do not know. Genesis 9:1-7 speaks not only of the taking of animal life, but also talks about the taking of human life.

Genesis 9:6 is a real puzzle for many persons who look to the Bible for a definitive answer on the question of capital punishment. Read this verse aloud to the class and ask them to reflect on its meaning.

One meaning of Genesis 9:6 seems to be that we should not take human life without justification. How can we justify the taking of human life? The only justification for the taking of human life is when this act is in direct obedience to the will of God, and when it is the only way to be obedient to the will of God. Since God will require human life from our hands, we must be able to show that we have taken this human life in accordance with his will. How often can we make that justification today? Ask the class members to think of possible examples.

The basic protection of human life that this law to Noah offers is striking. God is the Lord and protector of human life, wherever life is found. We cannot casually take the life of another human being. Life is a sacred gift of the living God.

Genesis 9:20-29—Prejudice

The student book indicates that many persons have used this passage in Genesis 9 to promote racial prejudice. The student book then goes on to ask three questions: (1) What other prejudices exist aside from racial prejudice? (2) Are all prejudices misinformed prejudices? (3) How can we help to remove the prejudices of others?

Emphasize that this passage in Genesis 9 does not really have to do with prejudice at all. Rather, the story intends to explain how the nations are related to one another. However, since many persons have based their prejudices on this passage, this is an appropriate time to discuss that whole area. Ask the class members to consider and then discuss each of the three questions listed above.

Genesis 11:1-9—Striving for Fame

The student book asks the group members to think about the question, What is the motivation of the builders of the tower of Babel? Are they motivated by pride, or are they eager for new adventures? This discussion on the tower of Babel story involves the hunger of persons for transcendence—for the meeting of God. Desire to fulfill our potential can be a fine thing, but we can also be prompted by a driving anxiety to transcend our real limits. Are we to view the tower story in that way? Do we not sympathize with the tower builders, because we realize that they hunger both for community and for an undeserved place in that community? They want too much; they want to be at the center. They are not content where they are.

Once again, God's action both judges and delivers. God judges the people by confusing their language and scattering them over the earth. But God also gives them various languages, thereby creating the rich texture of human communication and artistic expression that language provides. God also makes language communities for them, enabling them to scatter over the earth and to settle it. Once they were wanderers, not knowing where they were going. Now they have communities, languages, and distinct cultures.

In Acts 1–15, we read of a kind of reversal of this division of the nations—especially in Acts 2. In Acts 2 all nations begin to hear the good news in their own languages. Separate languages continue, but the Spirit makes all languages into a means of universal human communication.

Now ask the class members to think about the meaning of the word *ambition*. Can we always characterize ambition as either positive or negative? Ask the class members whether their ambitions ever conflict with what they think God wants them to do. Then ask them for insights into how to handle such situations.

Genesis 11:1-31—The Mystery of God

In Dimension Two, we discussed the Bible's silence as to why Terah moved from Ur to Haran. We read only that Terah went forth from Ur of the Chaldeans, but we are not told why he left. Remind the class that there are many unexplained situations in the Bible. You might ask the class members to list the unanswered questions they have encountered so far in the study of the Book of Genesis. Then ask the group members to share examples from their lives when they have felt that God has moved in mysterious ways.

Close today's session by asking the class members to list the insights they have gained from studying Genesis 9–11. You might want to list these insights on chalkboard or a large sheet of paper for later reference.

Leave your country, your people and your father's household and go to the land I will show you (12:1).

—5—

Abraham Settles in Canaan

Genesis 12–15

DIMENSION ONE:
WHAT DOES THE BIBLE SAY?

Answer these questions by reading Genesis 12

1. What does the Lord promise Abram? (Genesis 12:1-3)

   God will make of Abram a great nation. God will bless him, make his name great, and protect him. All the peoples of the earth will be blessed through Abram.

2. Where does Abram stop first to build an altar in the land of Canaan? (Genesis 12:6-7)

   He stops at Shechem, at the tree of Moreh.

3. Where does Abram next stop and build an altar? (Genesis 12:8)

   He stops in the hills between Bethel and Ai.

4. What does Abram do when famine strikes the land? (Genesis 12:10)

   He goes down into Egypt.

5. What does Abram ask Sarai to tell the Egyptians about her relationship to him? (Genesis 12:13)

   He asks her to tell them that she is his sister.

6. What does the Lord do to Pharaoh because of his taking Sarai? (Genesis 12:17)

   He afflicts Pharaoh and his house with serious diseases.

7. What does Pharaoh do to Abram and his family and followers? (Genesis 12:20)

   He has his men send Abram and his family out of Egypt.

Answer these questions by reading Genesis 13

8. After leaving Egypt, where does Abram go in the land of Canaan? (Genesis 13:3-4)

   He goes to his former encampment between Bethel and Ai.

9. What causes the trouble between Abram and Lot and their herdsmen? (Genesis 13:5-7)

   The land cannot support the flocks and herds of both Abram and Lot. Conflict probably arises over the use of grazing and watering places.

10. How does Abram settle the trouble? (Genesis 13:8-11)

    He gives Lot his choice of any of the land.

11. Where does Lot settle with his family? (Genesis 13:12)

    Lot settles near Sodom.

12. Where does Abram go? (Genesis 13:18)

    Abram goes to the great trees of Mamre at Hebron.

Answer these questions by reading Genesis 14

13. Where does the battle between the four kings of the east and the five kings of Palestine take place? (Genesis 14:3, 8)

    The battle is in the Valley of Siddim.

14. What does Abram do when he learns that the four kings of the east have taken some of his family members captive? (Genesis 14:14-16)

    He pursues them with 318 trained men. He recovers the captives and the stolen goods.

15. What does Melchizedek, king of Salem, do? (Genesis 14:18-20)

He brings out bread and wine, as priest of God Most High. He also blesses Abram by God Most High.

16. What does Abram give Melchizedek? (Genesis 14:20)

Abram gives him one-tenth of everything.

Answer these questions by reading Genesis 15

17. Who does Abram intend to make his heir? (Genesis 15:2-3)

Abram will make Eliezer of Damascus, a slave, his heir.

18. What does God promise Abram about this person and about the number of Abram's descendants? (Genesis 15:4-5)

God promises that Eliezer will not be Abram's heir, and that Abram's descendants will be as numerous as the stars in the sky.

19. What does Abram do with the animals and birds he brings at the Lord's command? (Genesis 15:9-10)

He cuts all the animals, except the birds, in half and arranges each half opposite each other.

20. What passes between the animal pieces? (Genesis 15:17)

A smoking firepot with a blazing torch pass between the pieces.

DIMENSION TWO: WHAT DOES THE BIBLE MEAN?

Genesis 12:1-3. The name *Abraham* as well as the short form *Abram* are well-known names from the literature of ancient Near Eastern cultures. As the student book states, the name *Abraham* means "May the (divine) father be exalted!" The popular meaning in Genesis 17:5 assumes that the name *Abraham* means "father of a multitude."

Scholars are unsure about the proper translation of Genesis 12:3. We can translate the Hebrew verb for "to bless" in the passive tense, "be blessed." In this case, the verse is saying that all other families of the earth will somehow gain blessing for themselves through the blessing of God upon Abraham. We will speak more about that possibility later. The same Hebrew verb can also be translated as a reflexive verb, "bless themselves." This translation would mean that all families of the earth would use the name of the God of Abraham to pronounce blessings upon themselves.

Genesis 12:7-9. The writer tells us that Abram stops at Shechem and Bethel. Perhaps he intends to show that even though Abram's real home was at Hebron, he was also associated with places to the north, where Jacob was most at home.

In these verses, Abram is an individual, but he also stands for generations of early Hebrews associated with Hebron. The same is true for Isaac, associated especially with Beersheba, southwest of Hebron, and of Jacob, whose family is closely related to Shechem and Bethel.

Between Bethel and Ai, Abram builds another altar and again calls on the Lord. Bethel was an important Canaanite town. Ai was even more important and was older than Bethel. Notice that Abram does not settle at Shechem or at Bethel; he is moving south. The city of Hebron, located about thirty miles southwest of Jerusalem, is Abram's real home. Abram goes to Hebron when he returns from Egypt (Genesis 13:18).

Genesis 12:10–13:1. A stream of visitors probably came to Egypt when calamity struck in the countries of the north and east. Due to flooding on the banks of the Nile River every year, a basic grain crop was always possible in Egypt. So we can see why Abram moved to Egypt while Canaan experienced famine.

The Book of Genesis contains three stories of patriarchs who present their wives as their sisters: Genesis 12:10–13:1; Genesis 20:1-18; and Genesis 26:1-11. The latter two stories concern Abimelech, king of the city of Gerar, which is located southeast of Gaza. Possibly, a single incident has been told three times. The first time Abram, Sarai, and the pharaoh are the principal actors in the events.

Each of these three stories has its own features, as we shall see below. In the present story, the writer emphasizes how God quickly steps in to protect Sarai from harm. Plagues fall on the pharaoh's household, and the pharaoh sends Abram out of Egypt.

Genesis 13:10-11. Genesis 13:10 points out that before God destroyed Sodom and Gomorrah, the area south of the Dead Sea was very fertile and well settled. Archaeological evidence shows that the valley south of the Dead Sea was rather heavily settled around 2000 B.C. Lot's choice of the Jordan Valley is fully understandable in this context. The Jordan River provided water for the entire valley and thus offered the possibility of farming. The land around Hebron, in which Abram settles, is good for fruit, grapes, and cattle-grazing.

Genesis 14. This puzzling story in Genesis 14 seems to be connected with David's capture of Jerusalem much later on. In 2 Samuel 5 and 6, we learn that David is somehow able to penetrate the Jebusite city of Jerusalem and take it without much of a fight. He then brings the ark of the covenant to the city. Jerusalem is thereafter the center of David's kingdom and also central for the tribe of Judah.

David seems to have taken over a place of worship and perhaps even a priesthood (the priest Zadok and his family) when he captured Jerusalem. If so, this story of Abraham and Melchizedek could intend to show that even in Abram's time, the city of Jerusalem had shown its readiness to give blessing and honor to Abram and to the God of Abram. Abram's association with the god of Jerusalem, *El Elyon* ("God Most High") foreshadows the worship of Israel's God at Jerusalem.

What happened in David's time therefore had a precedent in the dealings of Abram and Melchizedek. We cannot know with certainty that such a purpose is served by Genesis 14. Some other scholars today believe that this rather unusual story, with its picture of Abram as a leader of a warrior-band, is historically reliable.

Genesis 15:1-6. God tells Abram that he is Abram's shield. This word may mean no more than that God protects Abram wherever he goes. On the other hand, it might relate to the name by which the God of Abram was known in some very early time. We hear later about the Fear of Isaac (Genesis 31:42) and the Mighty One of Jacob (Genesis 49:24). Possibly in early times, the patriarchs Abraham, Isaac, and Jacob worshiped God under these three distinct names: the Shield of Abraham, the Fear of Isaac, and the Mighty One of Jacob.

Genesis 15:1-6 discusses the problem of Abram and Sarai's childlessness. The fact that Abram thus far has no heir is the subject of Chapters 16–18 as well. In 15:3, we learn that Abram has apparently selected one of his household slaves as his heir. Although no Old Testament law regulates the situation, we do know that such a practice existed elsewhere in the Near East.

Genesis 15:6 states, "Abram believed the LORD, and he credited it to him as righteousness." Paul picks up this reference to Abraham's faith in Galatians 3:6-9 and Romans 4. The author of the Epistle to the Hebrews also refers to Abraham's faith in Hebrews 11:8-19. We can translate Genesis 15:6 literally as follows: "And he [Abram] believed the Lord, and he [the Lord] considered it a right thing for him [Abram] to do." That is, Abram places his trust in God, believing that God will find a way to give Sarai and him a son of their own.

Genesis 15:7-21. Apparently Abram is beginning to doubt whether he will ever settle in the land God has promised him. These verses represent God's assurance that he will fulfill his promise to Abram.

The dismembered animals in the covenant ceremony parallel ancient Mesopotamian practices of slaying donkeys in connection with the making of covenants. The practice as it is described here sounds like a very primitive one, assuring that both parties of the covenant will keep the agreement on penalty of death and dismemberment. In verses 13-16, God foretells the enslavement of the Israelites in Egypt.

In this particular covenant, God, rather than Abram, binds himself to the stipulations of the covenant. God promises that he will give the land between the Nile River and the Euphrates River to Abram and his descendants. The smoking firepot and blazing torch mentioned in Genesis 15:17 represent God, who walks between the pieces of divided animals.

In Genesis 15:18-21, God promises land to Abram's descendants. The list of descendants includes the name *Amorite.* This word is an overall term that refers to various Semitic peoples who settled in northern Mesopotamia, Syria, Phoenecia, and Palestine. The Canaanites were originally Amorites, who happened to settle in Canaan. The Jebusites were the settlers of the city of Jerusalem. According to Ezekiel 16:3 these settlers were a combination of the Hittites and the Amorites.

DIMENSION THREE: WHAT DOES THE BIBLE MEAN TO ME?

According to the student book, Genesis 12–15 raises at least two issues that are relevant for our life today: "God's Unconditional Love," and "Trust in God." You will want to organize your discussion time around these two topics.

Genesis 12:1-3—God's Unconditional Love

Before describing God's unconditional love for Abram (and his descendants), we need to review the promises God made in his threefold covenant with Abram:

1. "I will make you a great nation."
2. "I will bless you . . . so that you are a blessing."
3. "To your offspring I will give this land [Canaan]" (Genesis 12:7).

Why did God make his covenant with Abram? The student book indicates that the Bible gives us no reason for God's choice of Abram and his descendants to be God's chosen people. This choice of Abram's descendants as the people of God is central to the Bible, but it is very hard to explain. It was difficult for ancient Israel to understand, and the Christian community also had its problems in dealing with God's choice, or election, of a single people.

The Book of Deuteronomy contains efforts to avoid misunderstanding. According to the writer of Deuteronomy, God chose Israel not because of her greatness or her high morality. Israel was one of the least of the nations. Neither did God choose Israel because she was greater in number or stronger than other nations. Rather, God chose Israel to be his people simply because he loved them. God's reason is reflected in Deuteronomy 7:6-8, which you should study. You might want to read these verses aloud to the class.

For you are a people holy to the LORD your God. The LORD your God has chosen you out of all the peoples on the face of the earth to be his people, his treasured possession. The

LORD did not set his affection on you and choose you because you were more numerous than other peoples, for you were the fewest of all peoples. But it was because the LORD loved you and kept the oath he swore to your fore-fathers that he brought you out with a mighty hand and redeemed you from the land of slavery, from the power of Pharaoh king of Egypt.

God set his law upon Israel, and God made a promise to Abram. Those are the reasons, says Deuteronomy, that God made Israel his very own people and gave them a good land and a good heritage. Exodus 19:4-6, a short passage that is like a covenant-promise from God, reflects these same reasons. You should study this passage now and you might want to read this passage aloud to the class as well.

"You yourselves have seen what I did to Egypt, and how I carried you on eagles' wings and brought you to myself. Now if you obey me fully and keep my covenant, then out of all nations you will be my treasured possession. Although the whole earth is mine, you will be for me a kingdom of priests and a holy nation." These are the words you are to speak to the Israelites.

This passage helps us see what the theologians of ancient Israel most wanted the people to understand about God's choice of them. First, the people were to remember that God had come to them to help them, to bring deliverance to them, to provide protection, and to see to their needs.

Second, they were to understand that God genuinely loves and cares for them. God brings them to himself, bearing them up as if on the wings of eagles. No logical explanation exists for this love of God. It is not deserved, but it is real and unmistakable.

Third, this love carries an obligation. Genesis 12:1-3 does not stress Abram's responsibility, although verse 2 does indicate that the people are to "be a blessing." The Exodus 19 passage is conditional. Even though all the earth is God's, God will treat Israel as a special treasure, his very own possession, if Israel will obey the will and voice of God. This covenant in Exodus 19 calls for the people to commit their ways to God. It promises that if they do, God will hold them fast, love and care for them, and never let them go.

Fourth, Israel is to be a particular kind of people in the world, a people whose very life lends assistance to the lives other people lead. They are to be a "kingdom of priests." As a people they are to so order their lives that their lives will be a priestly service to others. Other people will learn something of who God is and what God requires by seeing how the Israelites live and how they keep the covenant.

The phrase *holy nation* means the same thing. The people are to embody the life of a people set apart to do God's will—practice justice, show mercy, and keep the covenant. As they do so, others will know that God is their God. God is making this faithfulness possible, and God is indeed the one God and Lord of creation.

A similar meaning must lie behind this short passage in Genesis. Genesis 12:1-3 asks Abram to leave everything on which his life depends—his larger family, his home and country, the customs and normal occupation of his life—to follow God's call to a land that is not even named. God requires Abram's complete trust as Abram sets out from Haran to a land that we know is to be the Promised Land itself. Such a life of faith, such a trust in God, is part of the blessing that Abram has to give to "all peoples on earth." Israel's blessing to the nations is faith in God, commitment to the covenant that binds God and people, and life in God's service.

Now ask the class members to describe what the phrase "unconditional love" means in their lives. Can we love others unconditionally? Can we love God unconditionally? What are the characteristics of unconditional love? Is God's love for us an unconditional love?

Genesis 12:8-13—Trust in God

Begin this discussion of trust in God by reminding the class members of the history of God's promise to the patriarchs. The early chapters of the story of Abraham, Isaac, and Jacob picture God's promise to the people of Israel as a promise that is endangered and threatened, but kept alive by God. The ancient storytellers masterfully show how dangers to God's people and to God's promise arise both within the people and from outside their community. Just as in the garden, where sin arose from within the first couple and also from the serpent, so also here danger arises from anxiety and lack of trust in God, and it arises from external forces.

The first danger is the famine in the land (Genesis 12:10). This famine is not sent by God, it just happens. But when it does, God arranges to protect Abram and Sarai from harm and also brings new blessing to them. Despite Abram's lie about who Sarai was, God protects Sarai and sees to it that Abram receives rich gifts from the pharaoh. Then the people of Israel return to Canaan.

The second threat to the promise is Lot's choice of the land. Abram is good and generous in letting Lot choose whatever part of the land he wishes. Abram endangers the promise by letting Lot choose, but God arranges that the choice will be in Abram's favor. At the same time, Lot's choice is a free one, not a choice forced upon him by God. Thus these Genesis stories show human freedom entirely intact, as God manages the flow of history so that the divine purpose is carried along toward fulfillment.

The third danger is posed by Lot's capture. God permits Abram to go and recover Lot and the goods. Abram is generous to the king of Sodom and will not enrich himself at the expense of the king. Abram is also generous with the king of Salem, Melchizedek. But Abram exposes the promise to great danger by pursuing the kings of the east. He could have lost his life and everything that belonged to him. The Bible does not tell us about God's special protection of Abram, but that is the way these stories unfold.

Human activity and divine guidance interweave. But this interweaving leaves the freedom of human beings intact, while God's purpose moves forward.

The promise is also endangered in the story of Abram's conversation with God about a descendant (Genesis 15:1-6). The danger is present when Abram chooses a slave to be his heir. Abram's sharp questioning of God ("What can you give me. . . ?" and "How can I know. . . ?" (verse 8) runs the risk of offending God. But God knows that Abram is faithful, and God graciously assures Abram that he and Sarai will have their own heir. God also assures them that they will come to occupy their own land of blessing.

From a literary point of view, these great stories of the beginning of Abram's life in the land of promise have great beauty and power. When we move further into the Book of Genesis, we will meet the best of Old Testament literary art.

After discussing with the class the trust that Abram has in God, ask the class members to think about their trust in God. When has their trust in God faltered? What circumstances cause them to lose their trust in God?

Close this lesson on Genesis 12–15 by asking the class members to share insights they have gained about this Scripture. If time allows, you might want to list these insights on chalkboard or a large sheet of paper.

—6—

Abraham Speaks With God

Genesis 16–19

DIMENSION ONE:
WHAT DOES THE BIBLE SAY?

Answer these questions by reading Genesis 16

1. Who arranges for Hagar to have Abram's child? (Genesis 16:2-3)

   Sarai does.

2. What is Hagar's attitude toward Sarai after Hagar becomes pregnant? (Genesis 16:4)

   She despises Sarai.

3. How does Sarai then treat Hagar, and what happens? (Genesis 16:6)

   She mistreats Hagar, and Hagar flees.

4. What does the angel promise Hagar? (Genesis 16:10-12)

   The angel promises Hagar that she will have descendants too numerous to count and that her son will be named Ishmael.

5. What name does Abram give Hagar's son? (Genesis 16:15)

   Abram names him Ishmael.

Answer these questions by reading Genesis 17

6. Why does God rename Abram? (Genesis 17:4-5)

   God renames him Abraham because God has made him the father of many nations.

7. From what age is circumcision to begin in accordance with the covenant? (Genesis 17:12)

   Males are circumcised when they are eight days old.

8. What name does God give Sarai? (Genesis 17:15)

   God calls her Sarah.

9. How old are Abraham and Sarah when God promises that they will have a child of their own? (Genesis 17:17)

   Abraham is one hundred, and Sarah is ninety years old.

10. What does God promise to Ishmael, the son of Hagar and Abraham? (Genesis 17:20)

    God promises to bless him, to multiply his descendants, and to make him a great nation.

11. How old are Ishmael and Abraham when they are circumcised? (Genesis 17:24-25)

    Ishmael is thirteen years old, and Abraham is ninety-nine years old.

Answer these questions by reading Genesis 18

12. Where is Abraham living when the Lord appears to him? (Genesis 18:1)

    Abraham is living by the great trees of Mamre.

13. What does Abraham do for the three travelers who call on him? (Genesis 18:2-8)

    He bows before them, has their feet washed, and gives them a place to rest. He prepares a large meal for them and waits on them himself.

14. What is the Lord's promise for Sarah? (Genesis 18:10)

    God promises she will bear a son.

15. What does Sarah do when she hears the promise? (Genesis 18:12)

    She laughs to herself.

ABRAHAM SPEAKS WITH GOD

33

16. What do Abraham and the Lord discuss? (Genesis 18:22-33)

They discuss the destruction of the righteous with the wicked in Sodom.

Answer these questions by reading Genesis 19

17. Who meets the angels at the city gate in Sodom? (Genesis 19:1)

Lot meets them.

18. What does Lot do for the strangers? (Genesis 19:2-3)

He invites them to his home and prepares a feast for them.

19. What do the men of the city demand of Lot? (Genesis 19:5)

They want the two men so that they may have sex with them.

20. Whom does Lot offer to turn over to the men of the city in place of the strangers? (Genesis 19:8)

Lot offers his two unmarried daughters.

21. What happens to the men of the city as they try to force their way into Lot's house? (Genesis 19:9-11)

They are blinded, so they cannot find the door to Lot's house.

22. What do the strangers do for Lot and his family? (Genesis 19:12-23)

They lead them out of Sodom and permit them to settle in the village of Zoar.

23. What happens to Lot's wife when she looks back at the burning city? (Genesis 19:26)

She becomes a pillar of salt.

24. Why do the daughters of Lot choose to lie with their father? (Genesis 19:30-32)

They want to preserve the family line through their father.

DIMENSION TWO: WHAT DOES THE BIBLE MEAN?

Genesis 16. Many persons believe that originally two separate stories existed of Hagar's rejection by Sarai. The other story comes in Genesis 21:1-21, which is part of next week's lesson. In that passage, Sarah forces Abraham to drive Ishmael and Hagar away after the birth of Isaac, Sarah's

own son. Notice that in Genesis 21:14, Ishmael is apparently a small child, carried by his mother.

Scholars who identify two different traditions in Genesis 16 and 21 also point to the different portraits of Hagar. In Genesis 16, Hagar is a proud Bedouin woman who knows how to confront any situation that develops, even in the desert. She is delighted when she gets pregnant, and Sarai remains barren.

In Genesis 21, however, Hagar seems not to know what to do in the desert, but wanders around the spring at Beersheba. Abraham recognized her inability to manage in the desert and provided carefully for her needs.

The differences in the two stories are considerable, and they probably do represent two different early traditions about Hagar. But we cannot consider one story historical and the other idealized. Both of these stories intend to portray the relationship among three personalities: Abram, Sarai, and Hagar.

Thus these two stories are basically tribal history. They are based on the relationship that existed between the ancestors of Israel and the desert tribes called the Ishmaelites, who were descendants of Ishmael. Israel's beginnings do not lie in one part of the ancient world only. Abram and his family settled in northern Mesopotamia, where most of the family remained. After that, Abraham journeyed into the land of Canaan, struck up relations with the inhabitants of central Palestine at Shechem, and also with the people who lived in the region of Hebron.

Some of Abram's family settled in Sodom, but then moved to the land of the Ammonites and Moabites. Still other family members were close to the people of the south. Isaac was closely identified with Beersheba as we shall see later on. The first-born son of Abraham, Ishmael, settled in the southeast, becoming the leader of the tribes there.

The prophet Mohammed knew the history of Ishmael in great detail. Mohammed's predecessors must have kept these stories of Ishmael alive and elaborated on them. The promise the angel of the Lord gives to Hagar (16:10) finds a remarkable fulfillment in the conquests and spread of Islam in the seventh century A.D. God repeats this promise about Ishmael to Abraham in Genesis 18. In fact, in Chapter 17 Abraham wants God to accept Ishmael, since Abraham is ready to abandon any hope of Sarah's bearing children.

Genesis 17:1. The name by which God identifies himself to Abraham is *El Shaddai*. This name reminds us of Genesis 14, where the name of the Lord is said to be *El Elyon*. These names for God that begin with "El" are part of the religion of the western Semitic people who were already in the land of Canaan when the Israelites arrived.

The tradition behind Genesis 17, which shows an interest in priestly concerns, shows the God of Israel claiming and taking over the power of the Semitic god El.

We do not know what the term *Shaddai* means. It may be connected with the eastern Semitic word for "mountains," in which case *El Shaddai* means something like "God of the mountains." Or the translation usually given—"God Almighty"—may be correct. However, the name *Yahweh* is not used in Israel until much later, in the days of Moses (Exodus 6:2-3).

Genesis 17 also tells us about the rite of circumcision. In the ancient world, other peoples and tribes practiced circumcision. It probably first developed as a puberty rite, marking the entrance of the males of the tribe into adulthood and membership in the tribe. The Israelites transformed the puberty rite into an act performed on male children when they were eight days old.

Genesis 18:1-8. The writer tells the story of the Lord's coming to Abraham at Mamre in such a way that hearers and readers know that one of the three "men" is actually the Lord in human form. The other two "men" go on to Sodom to lead Lot to safety, while the Lord stays and speaks with Abraham about the fate of the cities of the valley. For ancient readers this appearance of the Lord in the company of two traveling companions would not have been strange, but actually delightful.

Even the appearance of the travelers during the heat of the day would alert Abraham that these three travelers were not ordinary persons. In the desert land, and even in the hill country around Hebron, persons rested during the heat of the day and did their traveling either early or late. Abraham thus recognizes that the mission of these three persons must be especially urgent, or they would not be disturbing his rest.

Genesis 18:9-15. In ancient cultures, the man customarily served as host, and the woman of the household retired to the tent. The women were not around while the men ate and talked. But Sarah is intensely interested in what is going on and does not want to miss a word of the conversation. So she stands by the tent door.

Sarah's comment in verse 12 about the promise of a child can be translated literally, "Shall I have fun after I have grown old, and my husband is old?" Sexual relations were not understood to be for the purpose of procreation alone. It was natural for Sarah to raise the question of having pleasure with her husband, the result being the birth of a child.

The story also refers to the name *Isaac* when it speaks of Sarah's having fun or finding pleasure. The Hebrew verb *tsachaq* means "to laugh" or "to have fun." The name *Isaac* was probably connected with that verb, as the student book notes.

Genesis 18:16-22. Abraham meets with the Lord east of Mamre, which is not far south of Jerusalem. Abraham and the Lord stay by the path leading east to Sodom, while the other two "men" (angels) go on to rescue Lot.

Genesis 18:23-33. In these verses, God pays attention to Abraham's pleas for any righteous persons who still live in Sodom. Abraham's intercession on behalf of the city of Sodom is rooted in the political relationships between the people of Israel and the people of the region surrounding Sodom. Why do Sodom and Gomorrah have such an evil reputation in the Old Testament?

Sodom and Gomorrah were located in the region south of the Dead Sea. The Old Testament writers knew there was some connection between this region that encompassed Ammon, Moab, and Edom on the one side and the people of Israel on the other. This kinship developed into hostility between the Israelites and each one of these peoples later on. The relations with the Edomites were the most difficult, for they were apparently marked by a kind of intense hatred that was destructive for centuries. The Edomites were related to the Israelites through Esau, the elder son of Isaac. We will study that story later on.

Genesis 19. This chapter portrays the destruction of Sodom and Gomorrah. The destruction of these cities by fire from heaven reminds us of the instability of the region around the Dead Sea. This geological fault in the earth's surface resulted from some tremendous catastrophe in prehistoric times that broke open the surface of the earth. The surface of the Dead Sea is the lowest spot on the earth, almost 1300 feet below sea level. Probably, the story of the destruction of Sodom and Gomorrah is based on some natural catastrophe that occurred in ancient times.

DIMENSION THREE: WHAT DOES THE BIBLE MEAN TO ME?

The student book mentions three theological issues in Genesis 16–19 that are relevant to our lives today. Concentrate your class discussion around these areas: "Faith in God's Promises," "Commitment to the Community," and "The Mercy of God."

Genesis 16:1-7—Faith in God's Promises

God promises Abraham many descendants. Genesis 16:1 tells us that Abram and Sarai do not have any children. Sarai wants Abram to have a child, even if the child is born to another woman. Hagar is willing; but when she becomes pregnant, she cannot help but show her disdain for the barren Sarai. Sarai is unwilling to bear that added humiliation.

Sarai and Abram's decision to ask Hagar to bear a son for Abram is not a deliberate act of mistrust in God. But the act does endanger the promise of God. It is similar to Abram's other acts that jeopardize the divine promise. Abram has already taken three such actions: his trip to Egypt, his identifying Sarai as his sister rather than his wife, and his allowing Lot to choose any land he wishes.

The remarkable power of these stories is that they do not take away the freedom of human action. Yet they show an interplay of forces that goes beyond mere human actions. God is intimately associated with all of the happenings, but God does not control the history. God relates to the history, works within it, and guides the events to their appointed ends.

Ask the class members if they agree that Abram and Sarai's actions do not indicate a lack of trust in God. Then ask them to think about the times in their lives when their faith in God faltered. Ask the class members to share these situations with one another. Then see if you can discover any common bonds among these situations.

Genesis 17:9-14—Commitment to the Community

The rite of circumcision developed in Israel is a sign of membership in the people of God. After being circumcised, one was no longer able to choose not to be a member of God's people. The family confirmed the truth of one's membership by this rite, and thereafter it was impossible to separate oneself from the community.

The student book asks whether Christians experience this incorporation into the Christian community through the ritual of baptism. From early times, Christians have associated the act of baptizing infants with the incorporation of the infants into the family of God. Of course, Christian baptism does not carry with it the physical mark that circumcision involves. Yet, when baptism is treated seriously, individuals grow up recognizing that divine grace claims them totally. They cannot do a single thing to prepare for its coming. Confirmation reaffirms the grace of God that came with baptism.

Circumcision, too, is followed by the adult Jew's equivalent of confirmation, the *bar mitzvah*. In some Jewish communities, the *bar mitzvah* is matched by a *bat mitzvah* for girls. These rites occur at about the same age as Christian confirmation.

The student book also asks what advantages the Jewish community has in keeping a strong sense of community alive. Jews witness to the world by keeping God's commandments. The Christian community has the same sense of fellowship, and its identity is kept alive by its public witness to Jesus Christ. The Christian community has good news that has to be shared. Thus, the Christian community must be open for those who receive Christ's gracious invitation.

We cannot identify the Christian community as clearly as the Jewish community. Part of the glory of the Christian faith is its openness to persons—without respect to race, prior religious tradition, gender, nationality, or other human distinction. The price the church pays for this glory is its constant need to claim God's cleansing presence and power and to keep the church faithful, true to the baptismal vows of its members.

The class members might think for a short time about the whole idea of baptism. What does their baptism mean to them? Some members of the class may have had infants baptized. Ask them to share what that experience was like for them as parents.

Genesis 18:22-33—The Mercy of God

Abraham's bargaining with God is one of the most powerful scenes in the Book of Genesis. Abraham runs enormous risk in pleading with God for the wicked cities of the plain. Abraham does not plead in terms of God's mercy toward Lot and his family. Abraham is more concerned that God's judgment be discriminating. Surely, God does not wish to destroy a single righteous person. Yet, God cannot let wickedness go unchallenged. The outcry from these wicked cities is too great for God to be indifferent. However, our story makes it clear that God is quite ready to listen to Abraham. The writer justifies bold bargaining with God.

Our story tells us that even ten righteous persons in Sodom will guarantee the continued existence of that city. God will spare the cities rather than destroy the ten righteous persons. Abraham's cleverness in arguing with God was probably much appreciated by ancient readers. Abraham is polite; he knows that he has no right to ask these favors of God, but he does so anyway. Each time—without a single objection, and apparently without waiting to think things over—God answers that he will spare the city if there should be found the number Abraham proposes.

Abraham does not immediately come down from fifty persons to ten. He also speaks of the intervening numbers. Surely, says Abraham, God will not destroy a city if there are forty-five righteous persons in it. In a very subtle way, the narrator shows that Abraham can play the game of bargaining, while running the risk of offending God in doing so. Abraham is fighting for the life of Lot and his family, but he is also fighting for God's justice and honor.

The beginnings of what is called *theodicy*, the justification of God's governance of the universe, appear here for the first time in the Bible. In simple terms, the question theodicy raises is this: How can a just God allow evil to remain in the world? Another way to ask the question is, Why do innocent persons suffer? In verse 25 the story presses upon God the necessity to practice justice in the divine governance of the universe: "Will not the Judge of all the earth do right?" If we cannot count on God's justice, then how can we believe in justice at all?

Why does the story not carry the number of righteous persons below ten? The writer may have felt that any smaller number, below the number of Lot's family, should not be mentioned. But it also seems possible that the storyteller wished to leave the story unfinished, unresolved. How far would God have gone with Abraham? Would five righteous persons have been enough?

We know from the story's ending that only Lot, his wife, and their two unmarried daughters leave Sodom, and actually Lot's wife does not escape. Three persons do escape, but the other inhabitants of Sodom and the cities of the plain do not. Once Lot and his family left, apparently no righteous ones were there.

If ten righteous persons had been left in the city, aside from Lot and his family, then God would have spared the city and dealt with the wickedness another way. That is the remarkable thing about Abraham's bargaining with God. It could have led to the sparing of the cities of the plain. Just a few righteous persons could have saved the lives of thousands. The point of the story is that faithfulness to God affects the lives of others, contributes to the public good, and helps hold a society together.

This section in the student book on the mercy of God concludes with a number of questions about this passage. You might want to have the class discuss these questions. You can guide the discussion in light of the information given about this passage. Then ask the question: What is the limit to God's mercy?

Some persons think the closing verses of Genesis 19, which tell about Lot and his daughters, is such an immoral tale that it is best to pass it by in silence. It is certainly not a wholesome story. However, the class members will have read this passage along with the rest of Genesis 16–19, and they may have questions.

The story accomplishes two things, as mentioned in the student book. It shows the mixed origins of the people of Ammon and Moab, and thus criticizes them for not being what they ought to be. And the story also puts Lot in a bad light. Even after he left the wicked city, he was unwilling to join with the people of Abraham. Lot could have found his way back to his family and made a life for himself and his daughters. The daughters too, of course, act wrongly, but theirs is an act to which they feel driven. The writer seems to show a begrudging respect for their commitment to life and their cleverness in deceiving their father. Lot is the one who received criticism for not re-entering the community so that his daughters could also live in community.

However, the narrator of this scandalous story of the Ammonites and Moabites does not at all approve of the conduct of Lot and his daughters. Incest is looked upon with real horror in ancient Israel. See Leviticus 18 for the laws governing incestuous relationships.

Close today's session by asking the class members to share insights they have gained from this lesson on Genesis 16–19. List these insights on chalkboard or a large sheet of paper if the class is accustomed to doing so.

Take your son, your only son, Isaac, whom you love, and . . . sacrifice him there as a burnt offering (22:2).

7

Abraham and His Descendants

Genesis 20–24

DIMENSION ONE:
WHAT DOES THE BIBLE SAY?

Answer these questions by reading Genesis 20

1. What does God say to Abimelech about Sarah? (Genesis 20:3)

   He says that she is a married woman.

2. Does God accept Abimelech's claim of innocence? (Genesis 20:6)

   Yes, God knows that Abimelech is innocent of any wrongdoing.

3. How does Abraham explain his presenting Sarah as his sister? (Genesis 20:11)

   He says that he was afraid that he would be killed because of his wife, because there was no fear of God in the place.

4. What has God done to the women of the house of Abimelech because Abimelech took Sarah? (Genesis 20:17-18)

   God has closed their wombs so that they could not have children, but then God heals them so that they can have children.

Answer these questions by reading Genesis 21

5. What does Sarah ask Abraham to do with Hagar and her son? (Genesis 21:10)

   She asks Abraham to get rid of them and disinherit them.

6. How does trouble develop between Abimelech and Abraham? (Genesis 21:25)

   Abimelech's servants seize one of Abraham's wells.

7. What does Abraham name the place where he digs the well? (Genesis 21:31)

   He names it Beersheba, or "Well of the oath."

Answer these questions by reading Genesis 22

8. What does God command Abraham to do with his son Isaac? (Genesis 22:2)

   He commands Abraham to take Isaac to the region of Moriah and sacrifice him as a burnt offering.

9. Where does Abraham find the ram to offer as a burnt offering in place of his son? (Genesis 22:13)

   He finds the ram with its horns caught in a thicket.

10. What does God promise Abraham for not withholding Isaac? (Genesis 22:17-18)

    God promises to bless Abraham and make his descendants as numerous as the stars and sand. He also promises blessing for all nations on earth through Abraham.

Answer these questions by reading Genesis 23

11. How old is Sarah when she dies? (Genesis 23:1-2)

    She is one hundred and twenty-seven years old.

12. From whom does Abraham buy the cave of Machpelah as a burial place for Sarah? What is the purchase price? (Genesis 23:8-16)

    He buys the cave from Ephron the Hittite for four hundred shekels of silver.

Answer these questions by reading Genesis 24

13. What does Abraham make his servant swear not to do? (Genesis 24:3)

    Abraham must not take a wife for Isaac from among the Canaanites.

14. Who comes to the spring to get water as Abraham's servant waits and watches? (Genesis 24:15)

Rebekah, the daughter of Bethuel, comes to the spring.

15. What does Rebekah do for Abraham's servant after she gives him water to drink? (Genesis 24:19-20)

She waters his camels.

16. What is the name of Rebekah's brother? (Genesis 24:29)

Rebekah's brother is Laban.

17. What does Abraham's servant do before he takes food from Laban? (Genesis 24:33)

He tells why he has come.

18. What do Laban and his family ask Rebekah? (Genesis 24:58)

They ask if she will go with Abraham's servant.

19. What does Rebekah do when she knows the man in the field is Isaac? (Genesis 24:65)

She covers herself with her veil.

DIMENSION TWO:
WHAT DOES THE BIBLE MEAN?

Genesis 20:1. This verse tells us that after watching the destruction of Sodom and Gomorrah, Abraham begins his journey in the direction of the Negeb. The word *Negeb* means "southland" and refers to a valuable part of southern Palestine. In ancient times, this region was heavily settled because of advanced techniques of agriculture and irrigation. Today, the northern part of the Negeb is being rapidly settled, and as new homesteads and towns are built, evidence of earlier settlements becomes clear.

Genesis 20:2-18. Abimelech is one of the famous foreigners whose faith puts the people of God to shame. God addresses this foreigner in a dream, and the king reproaches Abraham for having deceived him. This idea of foreigners serving the interests of the God of Israel continues into New Testament times. See, for example, the faith of the Canaanite woman whom Jesus healed (Matthew 15:21-28; Mark 7:24-30).

This story in Genesis 20 does not follow a logical sequence. We discover in the last verse that Abimelech's family is barren because he took Sarah into his harem. The tone of the story also differs from that in the story of Abraham with the pharaoh (Genesis 12). This story shows an interest in dreams. The writer tries to show in verse 12 that Abraham does not really lie. And unlike Chapter 12, this story underscores God's concern for Sarah.

Genesis 21:1-7. These verses tell another story of the birth of Isaac and his circumcision on the eighth day. Genesis 17 tells the same story in more detail. This theme of Isaac and laughter comes up for a third time in Genesis 21. Here, it is a matter of persons poking fun at Sarah and ridiculing her when they see that such an aged person has had a child.

Genesis 21:8-14. Abraham is unhappy about Sarah's request that he dismiss Hagar and Ishmael from the household. However, God tells Abraham to do as Sarah asks. Once again, the writer's concern rests with Abraham's obedience to God, for God watches over him closely.

Genesis 21:22-24. Abimelech realizes that Abraham is unmistakably under the protection of a very powerful god. So Abimelech makes a covenant with Abraham insuring that their two peoples will show mutual respect for each other. Abraham swears to this covenant.

This swearing reminds us of the arrangement between Abimelech and Abraham at Beersheba. Here once more we have reference to an oath. Read Genesis 21:31-32 for the fuller story.

Genesis 22:1-2. As noted in the student book, we cannot be certain of the location of the mountains of Moriah. They are probably located somewhere around Hebron. Later tradition identifies the mountain in the land of Moriah with the mountain in Jerusalem on which Solomon's Temple was built. We find this association in 2 Chronicles 3:1. But the Samaritans maintained that the mountain was Mount Gerizim, just south of the city of Shechem, which was certainly a sacred mountain from early Israelite times.

Genesis 22:20-24. Abraham hears about the birth of children to his brother. In all, eight children are born to Nahor. This genealogy appears for two reasons. Abraham's departure has not left Nahor with so small a family that he cannot survive. On the contrary, God has been good to Nahor just as he has been to Abraham.

However, the chief reason for this genealogy is to let us know that Bethuel is a son of Abraham's brother Nahor, and that Bethuel, Abraham's nephew, has a daughter named Rebekah. Rebekah will appear in our story when we reach Genesis 24.

Genesis 23. Abraham has to have property within the land of Canaan that belongs to his own family. Otherwise, the burial of his dead wife will be on property that Abraham cannot care for or show proper respect for. The dead must be honored.

In the ancient world, burial of the dead was usually accompanied by a recognition that the spirits of the dead lived on and could assist or harm the living. Burial showed respect for the dead, but burial also helped set the spirits of the dead at rest. Ceremonies of veneration of the dead were common in most ancient cultures. The ancient Israelites probably also widely observed such ceremonies, although the early traditions prohibit any veneration of the dead through religious rites.

Abraham clearly arranges the ownership of the cave so that he will not endanger the rest of the dead at this place. Moreover, the Canaanites and Hittites might disturb Sarah's rest, if her burial site is not entirely in the custody of Abraham and his family forever.

In the actual bargaining, Ephron's offering Abraham the cave in the field for nothing is simply politeness. Buyers would not think of taking advantage of such an offer. Ephron goes from no price at all to a high one—again, the normal way merchants bargained in the ancient world.

In this cave, all the patriarchs will be buried: Abraham and Sarah, Isaac and Rebekah, Jacob and his wives and children. Joseph is buried in another location (Joshua 24:32), and so is Rachel, according to tradition (Genesis 35:19-20). The cave at Machpelah continues to be highly honored by Jews and Moslems as well, since Abraham and his descendants are as important to the Moslems as to the Jews.

Genesis 24:1-9. The opening scene in Genesis 24 seems to be a deathbed scene. Abraham is very old and wants to find a proper wife for Isaac before he dies. The servants' haste also seems to indicate that Abraham does not have long to live. We are surprised, therefore, to discover in Genesis 25:1-6 that Abraham has remarried and is rearing a new family.

Genesis 24:10-21. The prayer of Abraham's servant is that God will let him know the one God has selected to be Isaac's wife. The servant wants to be sure that the woman is industrious and generous of spirit. That is why he selects a woman who is willing to draw the water for his camels.

Springs are below the surface of the ground and camels require a lot of water. The drawing and carrying of water up the well steps for ten camels is no light undertaking. Rebekah shows herself equal to the task, while the servant gazes at her to see if she will tire and give up the job.

Genesis 24:62-67. In Genesis 24:63, we read that Isaac is meditating in the field when Rebekah and Abraham's servant arrive. Isaac may have been contemplating the return of his father's servant, wondering what his chosen wife will be like.

Rebekah turns out to be the right wife, for she comforts him over the loss of his mother Sarah. Rebekah becomes the head of the women in the household. She carries on the strong tradition of Sarah. The women of the Book of Genesis show a great deal of independence and strength, despite the fact that this is certainly, in most regards, a man's world.

DIMENSION THREE: WHAT DOES THE BIBLE MEAN TO ME?

The student book raises three issues in Genesis 20–24 that are relevant for our lives today. These issues are as follows: "Dealing With Moral Dilemmas," "Testing Our Faith in God," and "Courage to Face the Unknown." You will want to organize the class discussion around one or more of these three areas.

Genesis 20:1-7—Dealing With Moral Dilemmas

As the student book indicates, some persons think this story deliberately shows Abraham to be less morally upright than Abimelech. Abimelech, the king of Gerar, wants to take Sarah into his royal harem. The story shows that Abimelech is a man with integrity of heart, for he willingly restores Sarah to Abraham after learning of Abraham's deception.

This story does make it difficult to defend Abraham. However, is that not one of the marks of Old Testament heroes? None of its heroes are blameless. Even Abraham is sometimes fearful, sometimes deceitful, sometimes disobedient to the divine will. Abraham is not a saint, though he is a hero of faith.

Abraham's lack of consideration for Sarah is his striking flaw. Of course, God readily cares for Sarah, but Abraham exposes Sarah to mistreatment and abuse merely to protect himself from danger. Even when we allow for the fact that Abraham must stay alive as the heir of God's promise, the story is still unflattering to Abraham. Moreover, Sarah is to be the mother of all Israel. How can Abraham endanger her life, since she is the one through whom the lineage of the people of God is to be traced? In Israel, descent is traced through the mother, not the father.

Ask the class members to reflect on the character of Abraham. Can they excuse Abraham's behavior? Were there good reasons for Abraham's actions? Or, is Abraham simply immoral?

Now have the class members think about what it means to face a moral dilemma. We all face these dilemmas at certain times in our lives. To whom do we turn for help?

Genesis 22:1-14—Testing Our Faith in God

Before opening the class discussion on Genesis 22, you might ask someone to read verses 1-14 aloud.

Genesis 22 is the most important chapter in the Abraham story for later biblical theology. The Abraham we see in this chapter exemplifies a faith in God that defies imagination. God carefully words his demand: Abraham is to take his only son, whom he loves, and offer him as a sacrifice to the God who graciously gave Isaac to Sarah and Abraham in their old age. Abraham does not know that God is testing him and in fact will spare Isaac.

Abraham prepares to offer his son as a human sacrifice. He does not presume to question God. Silently he makes his way north, to the mountain identified as the place for the sacrifice. He has forgotten nothing: knife, fire, wood, and cord with which to bind Isaac's hands.

Father and son walk up the mountain, conversing. Abraham still affirms that God will provide what is required. What is required above all else is that God stop this deed and produce an animal suitable for the sacrifice. Or God could simply order Abraham to return to his tent with his son alive and safe.

However, for the unbearable period of time necessary for Abraham to kindle the fire, put the wood on it, place Isaac upon the altar, and raise the knife aloft, God does not intervene. No animal appears, and no voice from heaven speaks. Then, when Abraham can wait no longer and his heart is broken, the voice comes: "Abraham! Abraham!" What a blessed sound! Abraham now knows that Isaac will live. If the knife had had to fall, surely Abraham would not have lived much longer either.

God is faithful to his promise. Abraham is one who is ready to put not only his own life into God's hands, but even the life of his beloved Isaac, the son of the promise.

The story now rushes to its conclusion, for the tension is gone. Isaac is safe, and all that remains is to offer the ram, name the place, and go back down the mountain to the two young men who wait at the bottom. How different is the journey home!

Jewish tradition speaks of this event as the "binding" of Isaac. The Jews see in it a powerful and mystic act that relates God to Abraham and to his descendants forever. In the Christian tradition, Isaac portrays Christ's offering as the sacrificial lamb. The story in Genesis is clearly a test of Abraham's faith. In Christian understanding, it is quite a different event. In the case of the Son of God, the knife falls, but the blood means life for the sins of the whole world. And God brings the slain one to newness of life.

Ask the class members what other parallels they see between Abraham's offering of Isaac and Christ's offering of himself.

Genesis 24:52-61—Courage to Face the Unknown

When we read this story of Rebekah and Isaac, we cannot help but be impressed by Rebekah's courage. The choice of Rebekah seems right to us as we read the story. No one asks Rebekah if she wants to marry Isaac; the family arranges the marriage. But the servant forestalls what could have been a crisis by insisting on leaving for Canaan immediately. Rebekah's family gives her the choice to go or to remain. She freely chooses to go.

We see that women are not men's equals in that time and society. But women are not merely property or always dominated by the men in the family. Sarah comes through as a real personality, with independence and a will of her own. So also does Hagar. And certainly Rebekah makes her own decision to leave home and follow the path that Abraham once took—to Canaan and to the Promised Land.

Ask the class members to think a few minutes about how they would feel if they were in Rebekah's place. Could they say without hesitation that they would go with Isaac? We have all faced the unknown at various times in our lives. You might ask the class members to share some of these experiences. What specifically helped them get through these times in their lives?

Close the session by asking the class members to think about the insights they have gained from their study of Genesis 20–24. List these insights on a large sheet of paper or chalkboard. With today's lesson you have now finished half the lessons on the Book of Genesis. Take some extra time in this lesson to review with the class members what they have learned in the first seven lessons.

— 8 —

Esau and Jacob

Genesis 25–27

DIMENSION ONE:
WHAT DOES THE BIBLE SAY?

Answer these questions by reading Genesis 25

1. Whom does Abraham take as a wife? (Genesis 25:1)

   He takes Keturah.

2. How old is Abraham when he dies? (Genesis 25:7)

   Abraham is one hundred and seventy-five years old when he dies.

3. Where do his sons bury him? (Genesis 25:9)

   He is buried in the cave of Machpelah, east of Mamre.

4. To which of the twin sons does Rebekah give birth first? (Genesis 25:25-26)

   Esau is born first.

5. Which son does each parent favor? (Genesis 25:28)

   Isaac loves Esau, and Rebekah loves Jacob.

6. What does Esau give Jacob in exchange for some lentil stew and bread? (Genesis 25:29-34)

   He gives his birthright.

Answer these questions by reading Genesis 26

7. How does Isaac identify Rebekah to the people of Gerar? (Genesis 26:7)

   He identifies her as his sister.

8. What creates tension between the people of Gerar and Isaac's people? (Genesis 26:17-22)

   Tension is created by disputes over water.

Answer these questions by reading Genesis 27

9. Whom does Isaac ask to prepare special food for him as he draws near to death? (Genesis 27:1-4)

   He asks Esau, his older son.

10. Who actually prepares the food, and who brings it to Isaac? (Genesis 27:6-10)

    Rebekah prepares the food, and Jacob brings it to his father.

11. How does Jacob disguise himself as Esau? (Genesis 27:15-16)

    He puts on Esau's clothes and covers his smooth skin with goatskins.

12. What does Isaac's blessing include? (Genesis 27:28-29)

    It includes prosperity from the earth, high rank among the nations, and leadership over his brother.

13. When Esau brings food for Isaac, what does Isaac do? (Genesis 27:30-33)

    He trembles violently and asks who it was that he has already blessed.

14. What is Isaac's blessing upon Esau? (Genesis 27:39-40)

    Esau will live apart from the blessings of the earth. He will live by the sword and shall serve his brother, although he will someday break loose.

15. What does Rebekah advise Jacob to do in order to escape harm at the hands of Esau? (Genesis 27:43-45)

    She advises him to flee for safety to the home of her brother Laban in Haran.

DIMENSION TWO:
WHAT DOES THE BIBLE MEAN?

Genesis 25:1-6. One reason that Abraham takes another wife is the Israelites' belief that a man can continue to rule over the tribe and the family if he is still able to have children. Thus, this story intends to show that Abraham is still the head of the family. Despite the fact that he was almost on his deathbed when he sent his servant to get a wife for Isaac (Genesis 24:1-2), Abraham has evidently rallied and is still the head of the family in every sense.

Genesis 25:7-11. The writer mentions Abraham's death in a very matter-of-fact way. Abraham's death at a ripe old age, after a life marked by blessing, is not a tragedy in any sense. Premature death would be the real tragedy.

Genesis 25:12-18. The traditions about Ishmael show him to be a respected descendant of Abraham, the first-born of his father, and not in any way despised. Ishmael is the ancestor of the Arab desert-dwellers. Probably the Israelites always admired and respected some of the virtues of the Arabian people, their kinfolk. The Arabs are especially respected for their lives of freedom, their independence, and their hearty nature that enables them to survive in the desert.

Trading with Arab neighbors was regular and customary throughout the centuries. These close relations between the two peoples help us to realize that Ishmael is not being set aside or despised. Ishmael does not belong in the line that leads directly from Abraham to Isaac to Jacob.

In this passage, the writer lists Ishmael's descendants in detail, showing that God fulfills his promise to Ishmael, though God's favor follows Isaac. Ishmael, like the children of Keturah and their descendants, belongs to the desert rather than to the land of Canaan, which becomes the land of Israel. We cannot identify all the places mentioned in verse 18, but some of them are located in what is now northern Arabia.

In the religion of Islam, Ishmael—not Isaac—is the chief descendant of Abraham. The prophet Mohammed considered Abraham one of the greatest prophets and Ishmael the ancestor of all the Arabs. The Book of Genesis supports this belief, although God set Ishmael aside in favor of Isaac, for the people of Israel.

Genesis 25:19-26. This passage reflects the rivalry between Israel, represented by Jacob, and Edom, represented by Esau. In verse 23, the Lord tells Rachel that the two peoples born of her will be divided. God also says that the older, who is Esau, will serve the younger, who is Jacob (Israel).

The relations between Israel and Edom were not as congenial as those between Israel and the Ishmaelites, or Arabs. The kingdom of Edom, located to the southeast of Israel, was a brother-kingdom. But the hatred between the brothers was already a well-known fact by the time of Amos

(Amos 1:11-12). And this hatred continued through the centuries.

Relations became especially strained between the two countries when the Edomites helped the Babylonians gather Judean fugitives who had escaped the city of Jerusalem in 587 B.C. That dreadful act is the reason for the familiar attack on the Edomites found in Psalm 137:7-9.

Genesis 25:27-34. This part of the story of Jacob and Esau reveals great contempt for Esau. Esau thinks of nothing but his appetite. He despises his father's heritage and deserves to be set aside. However, we will see a more sympathetic picture of Esau later on in the Jacob story (Genesis 32–33).

Genesis 26:1-5. About 1200 B.C., a series of catastrophes decimated the populations of the eastern Mediterranean area. These catastrophes set in motion many groups of people who began migrating in search of a better life. Among these groups were the Sea peoples, also called the Philistines.

Genesis 26:6-33. This series of events connected with the wells that Isaac digs in the Negeb is credible. If a family is to prosper in such a land, it must control the watering places. Abimelech and his people see Isaac growing wealthy, both in crops and in herds. Finally Abimelech drives Isaac away.

Why does Isaac lie to Abimelech about his relationship to Rebekah? That is the main point of Genesis 26. The answer comes in 26:7—"He said, 'She is my sister,' because he was afraid to say, 'She is my wife.' He thought, 'The men of this place might kill me on account of Rebekah, because she is beuatiful.' "

The story's background is the rivalry between Isaac and Abimelech and their respective peoples. The real culprit is the lack of adequate water and Isaac's success in locating waterholes and in prospering so markedly. This region never has enough water. Even today, water is one of the chief points of contention between Israel and her neighbors in the Near East.

In Genesis 26:33, we learn that Isaac makes his headquarters at Beersheba. Beersheba is an important city in the Negeb, about eighteen miles southeast of Gerar. But the troubles continue between the two groups until they agree to a covenant. Here once more we have a wordplay, as we read of Isaac's digging a well at Beersheba (verses 32-33), and of the oath he and Abimelech make with each other (verse 31). As mentioned in an earlier lesson, Beersheba can mean "Well of the oath."

Genesis 27. The student book points out how important blessings are at the time of death in ancient Israel. The Bible contains a number of these blessings. For example, we have very long blessings from Jacob (Genesis 49) and Moses (Deuteronomy 33), and a brief and beautiful blessing from David (2 Samuel 23:1-7).

Blessings also occur frequently in the intertestamental literature, creating a whole body of literature called "testament." We have testaments from Abraham, Moses, the twelve sons of Jacob, and many more from that later period of time.

DIMENSION THREE: WHAT DOES THE BIBLE MEAN TO ME?

The student book mentions three issues from our study of Genesis 25–27 that are relevant for our lives today. You will want to discuss some or all of these three areas: "Polygamy," "The Importance of Family," and "Living With Deceit."

Genesis 25:1-6—Polygamy

According to the student book, having more than one wife was common practice in the ancient world. Certainly, the biblical stories do not condemn persons who have more than one wife. However, the marvelous portrayal of the relationship between the first man and the first woman is intended to be a model of life together at its best and most appropriate (Genesis 2). In Genesis 2, each partner completes the existence of the other, and each depends on the other.

Later on in Judaism and Christianity, having a single spouse becomes the accepted standard. A person must follow this standard especially if he or she aspires to special leadership within the religious community.

How do the class members react to Abraham's polygamy? Do they think his actions are justified in the context of his society? Can the class members justify polygamy under any circumstances today?

Genesis 25:29-34—The Importance of Family

Begin this discussion on the importance of family by outlining the relationships within Isaac's family. First of all, let us look at Jacob. One of the most difficult questions of interpretation in the story is how Jacob is to be understood.

The Book of Hosea struggles to show this patriarch in a good light (Hosea 12). But the Jacob stories in Genesis portray Jacob as clever, ruthless, wily, and deceitful.

On the other hand, we see Jacob so deeply committed to the struggle for the fulfillment of the divine blessing that we cannot simply consider him a scoundrel. Jacob is one who cares about life, about the future, and about his people. We should probably criticize Jacob when he goes too far. For example, Jacob goes too far when he deliberately deceives his father. We will see other instances later on of the Bible's double attitude toward Jacob and Jacob's instinct to fight for life and blessing.

And what can we say about Rebekah? We often hear that women in ancient Israel were not esteemed and were treated as property. Rebekah, on the other hand, emerges as an individual, ready to make her own decisions even while she still lives in Mesopotamia. When her father asks whether she is willing to go with Abraham's servant, her decision settles the matter (Genesis 24:58).

Now, in Genesis 25, Rebekah sees to it that her younger son Jacob is not prevented, by the mere accident of his having been born a few minutes later than Esau, from receiving Isaac's blessing. Rebekah knows that Jacob will make good use of Isaac's blessing. The actions of Rebekah go far beyond those of Jacob. Indeed, in this story the contest is really between Rebekah and Isaac to see which one of the sons will receive the blessing.

Rebekah also knows how to keep Esau from taking Jacob's life. Rebekah complains to Isaac about the Hittite women of the land. She could not bear Jacob to marry one of them. She might add, "as your favorite son Esau has already done!" Rebekah uses Isaac's own dissatisfaction with the marriages of Esau to secure Isaac's approval to send Jacob to Mesopotamia to get a proper wife.

Ask the class members what they think about the relationships within Jacob's family. Are such family relationships impossible today? Or does this kind of intrigue occur in some form in many families today? Ask the class members to share with one another situations in their lives or in the lives of others that compare to this picture in Genesis 25.

We all know or have heard of persons who, for one reason or another, renounce their family ties. Ask the class to think about what could cause persons to take such a step. Have the class members try to put themselves in Esau's place. What would they have done? What would they have done in Jacob's place?

Genesis 27:1-29—Living With Deceit

The issue of living with deceit is based on Jacob's ultimate deception of his father. Begin this discussion by asking the class members if they think Jacob went too far. What do they think would have happened if Isaac's blessing had fallen upon Esau?

Continue the discussion of Jacob's deception by retelling the story, emphasizing the human aspects. The Bible contains few stories with the artistry and power of this story of Jacob and Isaac. The nearly blind Isaac still has an ominous power of speech and power to determine the future. If only Rebekah and Jacob can work out a plan, they may be able to direct that awesome power to a person who would know how to appreciate it. Is it possible?

The day finally comes for Isaac to speak his final words of blessing. He sends his favorite son, the rough and ready Esau who loves the out-of-doors, to find some wild game for him. With this meal, and the strength it will give him, Isaac will be better able to pronounce the blessing. All is going in accordance with the plan.

Into the plan come a wily mother and her clever son, ready to do what is necessary. The story tells us that Jacob quickly locates an animal from the flock, and Rebekah prepares it. They think through the entire series of acts by which to deceive the father. Jacob must smell like Esau, and he must have, on the exposed parts of his body, the mat of hair that Esau sports. How is that to be arranged? No problem! The skins of animals will deceive the aging Isaac in a double way. Isaac will not be eating wild game; he will be eating food prepared by his wife, brought by the wrong son. And Isaac himself will be the one to say, after examination, "It is Esau after all!"

Jacob plays his part well, never hesitating to do his share in the deception. When Isaac asks, "Are you really my son, Esau?" Jacob is ready to lie to his father's face and say, "I am." The whole act of deception is sealed with a kiss (Genesis 27:26).

We have to remember that all of this family intrigue is concerned with nothing less than the future of Israel and the future blessing of God upon the human community. For on this promise of blessing to Jacob—intended for Esau—hangs Israel's future among the nations. Israel's future includes prosperity and her ability to be a blessing to other peoples of the earth.

Just as the blessing had been endangered by certain events in Abraham's life—the departure into Egypt, the readiness to let Lot choose the land he wished, the argument with God, and the test of faith that endangered Isaac's life—so here is another grave danger. This danger arises from the failings of everyone involved. Isaac is too old and too blind and too senile. He should have pronounced the blessing long ago, when he had greater strength. Jacob and Rebekah are too clever and sly and can outdo themselves with their skills in deception. Esau is just uncaring, although when he sees the blessing gone, how bitterly he longs for it!

None of these persons' actions is commendable. And yet, the blessing is passed along to the one who will make something of it. That is the great theological strength and power of this story in the Book of Genesis.

Genesis 27 emphasizes that deceitfulness is a human characteristic. The humanness of the persons involved is clear. Israel's beginnings are not painted in glowing colors. The feelings of the men and women involved stand forth; they are neither hidden nor overdramatized. God works with these human beings—these persons who see their responsibilities and often deliberately reject those responsibilities. God keeps the pressure on, but at the same time he shapes and directs the movement toward his desired goal.

The central understanding of the stories in Genesis involves the relationship between God and humankind. God guides history toward the fulfillment of the divine promise. But God also lets the human element have its full weight. Human beings are never automatons. They are flesh and blood—tempted, able to show remarkable generosity and largeness of spirit. But they are often all too ready to take advantage of other human beings, serve their own interests, and forget the cause of God.

God does not forget. God uses this group of fallible human beings. He nudges, directs, guides, and occasionally overrides them. But God sees to it that the people through whom the blessing is to come to the earth will have a future.

Do the class members agree that deceitfulness is a human characteristic? Do they think Genesis 27 supports this idea? Is deceit ever acceptable? Have they ever deceived someone else, or have they ever been deceived? Encourage the class members to share these experiences, as well as their reactions to these experiences.

Close the session by asking the class members to share any insights they may have gained from the study of Genesis 25–27. If time allows, list these insights on chalkboard or a large sheet of paper.

9

Jacob and Laban

Genesis 28–31

DIMENSION ONE:
WHAT DOES THE BIBLE SAY?

Answer these questions by reading Genesis 28

1. Where does Isaac send Jacob to find a wife for himself from his own family? (Genesis 28:1-2)

   Jacob goes to Paddan Aram to take one of Laban's daughters as a wife.

2. What does Esau do when he hears that Isaac will not let Jacob marry one of the Canaanite women? (Genesis 28:8-9)

   He weds Mahalath, the daughter of Ishmael.

3. What does Jacob name the place where he has the dream? (Genesis 28:19)

   He names it Bethel, or the "house of God."

4. What does Jacob promise to give to God if God blesses him on his journey? (Genesis 28:22)

   He promises one-tenth of all that God gives him.

Answer these questions by reading Genesis 29

5. Where does Jacob meet Rachel? (Genesis 29:2-9)

   He meets her at a well near Laban's house.

6. After Jacob serves seven years for Laban's daughter Rachel, whom does Laban give him to marry? (Genesis 29:23-25)

   He gives Leah to Jacob.

7. How long does Jacob wait before he receives Rachel as his wife? (Genesis 29:27-28)

   He waits one week.

8. How many additional years does Jacob serve Laban in payment for Rachel? (Genesis 29:30)

   He serves seven additional years.

9. Which of Jacob's two wives has the first child? (Genesis 29:31-32)

   Leah has the first child.

10. What are the names of Leah's first four children? (Genesis 29:32-35)

    They are Reuben, Simeon, Levi, and Judah.

Answer these questions by reading Genesis 30

11. What are the names of the sons born to Rachel's servant Bilhah? (Genesis 30:6-8)

    They are Dan and Naphtali.

12. What are the names of the sons born to Jacob and Zilpah, the servant of Leah? (Genesis 30:9-13)

    They are Gad and Asher.

13. What are the names of the additional two sons born to Leah and Jacob? (Genesis 30:18-20)

    They are Issachar and Zebulun.

14. What is the name of the daughter born to Leah and Jacob? (Genesis 30:21)

    She is Dinah.

15. What is the name of Rachel's first son? (Genesis 30:24)

    He is Joseph.

16. How does Laban attempt to cheat Jacob after Laban agrees to the distribution of the flocks? (Genesis 30:35-36)

He has his sons remove all the streaked or spotted male goats and female goats, as well as all the dark-colored lambs from the flocks.

Answer these questions by reading Genesis 31

17. Why do Leah and Rachel agree to return to Canaan with Jacob? (Genesis 31:14-16)

Their father regards them as foreigners and has spent their marriage money.

18. What does Rachel steal from her father before she leaves with Jacob? (Genesis 31:19)

She steals Laban's household gods.

19. What does Laban do when he hears that Jacob has left for Canaan? (Genesis 31:22-23)

He gathers his relatives and pursues Jacob for seven days.

20. What does the covenant between Laban and Jacob guarantee each of them? (Genesis 31:49-52)

It guarantees that they will observe the border between them, and God will keep watch over them when they go their separate ways.

DIMENSION TWO:
WHAT DOES THE BIBLE MEAN?

Genesis 28:1-9. In Genesis 28:2, we learn that Isaac sends Jacob to Paddan Aram to find a wife. Paddan Aram, located in Mesopotamia, was the homeland of Abraham and his family. According to ancient traditions, Abraham and his descendants were closely connected with this area in northwest Mesopotamia.

In Genesis 28:6-9, we read that Esau apparently realizes for the first time that his marriage to the Hittite women named Judith and Basemath (Genesis 26:34-35) grieved and angered his parents. Now, in order to make amends, he chooses a daughter of Ishmael, his half-brother, as an additional wife. The story shows Esau's effort to do what pleases his parents.

Genesis 28:10-22. Genesis 28:10-12 tells us that on his way from Beersheba to Haran, Jacob comes to "a certain place" to sleep. There he has a dream. We learn later, in verse 19, that the name of the place is Bethel. We have seen that Bethel was important for Jacob and the northern tribes, since it became the rival center of worship to the city of Jerusalem in later times.

The city of Bethel has been partially excavated, and we learn that it was an important Canaanite city long before the Israelites took over the territory. The biblical references to Bethel always indicate that the old Canaanite city was to the west of the place where Abraham and Jacob had their places of worship. Later on, in the days of Jeroboam I, this old Canaanite city was taken over by the Israelites. But the place of worship may have stayed where it was.

We learn from Genesis 28:11 that Jacob puts a stone under his head to use as a pillow. The use of stones as pillows is not as strange as it may appear. The stones would be covered with cloth to make them more suitable as pillows. This practice may reflect the ancient ritual of erecting stones at holy places to commemorate decisions made or vows taken in the presence of God. Long rows of such memorial stones have been found at ancient Gezer and also at the old city of Hazor.

Genesis 29:1-8. This episode takes place beside a well. This well was protected by a massive stone cover, which was removed only when enough people were on hand to do so. In this way, the water was protected from misuse by passersby. The flocks gathered at different times in the late afternoon to be watered. Only when enough physical strength was assembled could the stone be moved and the watering of the flocks begin.

As the student book notes, the story of Jacob's removing the stone by himself is designed to show what a strong man he was. The story also illustrates the way young men perform great feats of strength to impress their girlfriends.

Genesis 29:9-20. Jacob stays with Laban a month before any steps are taken regarding his employment or his suitability to marry one of Laban's daughters. This length of time is quite in line with ancient custom. Hospitality was extended for long periods of time with no one feeling offended. However, the time comes when it is necessary to get down to business. Apparently Jacob and Laban reach that point after a month has passed.

Laban asks Jacob to name his wages for service in Laban's household (verse 15). Jacob immediately says he will work seven years in exchange for Rachel as his bride. We may think it unusual that Jacob would agree to serve such a long time. Most commentators state that seven years is an enormous price for Jacob to pay.

The text makes it clear that Laban knows which daughter Jacob loves. Even so, he deceives Jacob when the time comes, claiming that the elder daughter must marry first. Such a custom probably did exist, but it could not have been an absolute law. Otherwise, Laban would not have agreed publicly to let Jacob have Rachel in exchange for seven years of labor.

Genesis 29:31-35. The names of the sons that Leah, Rachel, and their handmaidens bear, are all given explanations. These explanations show us that names in the ancient world were understood to have recognizable meanings.

The name *Reuben* was related to the Hebrew expression that can be translated, "Behold! A son!" Leah hoped to win the affection of Jacob with the birth of this son. Bearing one's husband a son was immensely important in the ancient Near Eastern world.

The name *Simeon* is incorrectly connected with the Hebrew term for "hate." *Simeon* is actually somehow related to the notion of hearing. Probably, the full name would have meant something like, "God has heard." Thus the name Simeon probably referred to God's having heard and granted the prayer for a child.

The other children's names have meanings as well. *Levi* is connected with the Hebrew verb for "to join," and the name *Judah* is related to the Hebrew verb for "to praise."

Genesis 30:1-8. Rachel's blaming her husband for her barrenness does not mean that she is saying Jacob is entirely at fault. She simply means to impress upon Jacob, who loves her dearly, that she must have children. The reproach of her barrenness is more than she can bear, especially when she sees how prolific Leah has been. But we can understand what Jacob means when he protests that he is not God; he cannot produce children at will.

Rachel gives her maidservant, Bilhah, to Jacob, so that Bilhah can bear sons to Jacob. Rachel names the two sons and takes them as her own. As with Leah's three children, Rachel gives explanations for the names of the two sons. *Dan* comes from the Hebrew verb for "to judge," and *Naphtali* means "I have wrestled."

Genesis 30:14-24. Notice that the story does not attribute the birth of Rachel's first child, Joseph, to the use of the mandrake plants. Rachel buys the mandrakes from Leah's son, Reuben, and must agree to Leah's sleeping with Jacob in exchange for the mandrakes. Leah has two more children, Issachar and Zebulun, before Rachel has Joseph. Perhaps during that time, Rachel is using the mandrake plants to aid her in removing the curse of infertility. Why does the storyteller not connect the use of the mandrakes too closely with the birth of Joseph? Because Joseph is too important a son to have come into the world through the use of an herb bought from a son of Leah!

Genesis 30:25-28. When Rachel bears Joseph, Jacob is ready to return home. Verse 26 tells us why Jacob wants us to return home: he no longer wants to be Laban's servant. Laban tells Jacob he can name his own wages if he will stay.

Genesis 30:31-43. The story of how Jacob and Laban contend to get the better of each other is full of popular folk humor. The story tells how the clever shepherd can always get the better of the owner of the sheep. Such stories were quite popular in the ancient world, and they are still popular in the Near East today.

Jacob proposes that he take all the speckled and spotted sheep and goats as well as the black lambs. The rest will remain with Laban. Laban agrees, but before the division, his sons gather all the animals that would otherwise go to Jacob. The sons take these animals a good distance away from the rest of the flock.

But Jacob is a match for the wily Laban. He arranges for selected breeding! The scheme includes the magical manipulation of striped, spotted, and speckled wooden branches at breeding time so that the animals born have these desired characteristics. The other part of Jacob's scheme is really more scientific. He sees to it that the animals with the desired characteristics and which are very robust, breed among themselves, leaving Laban the weak animals. Thus Jacob's prosperity abounds.

Genesis 31:1-16. In these verses, Jacob speaks to his wives and tries to persuade them to return to the land of Canaan. Laban kept trying to find a way to prosper with Jacob as his shepherd. But no matter what scheme he worked out for paying Jacob's wages, Jacob ended up getting most of the proceeds from Laban's flock. If Laban said, "You may have all the spotted kids and lambs," then all of the kids and lambs would be born spotted! Jacob simply could not lose. Seeing that, the wives of Jacob are ready to go with him to the land of Canaan.

Genesis 31:33-35. Rachel hides the household gods in a camel's saddle and sits on it. When Laban comes looking for the gods, she tells her father that she does not wish to rise because she is having her menstrual period. Thus Rachel assists Jacob by retaining the property taken from Laban, but she is also retaining her own stake in the property.

Rachel's theft is a very serious matter. These household gods were symbols of the gods worshiped by the family. They were objects of great worth to Laban.

DIMENSION THREE:
WHAT DOES THE BIBLE MEAN TO ME?

In the third dimension, the class will discuss how the Scripture is relevant today. As the student book indicates, Genesis 28–31 provides four issues for this discussion. These issues are as follows: "Receiving God's Blessings," "Bargaining With God," "Vocational Hardships," and "Honoring Our Agreements."

Genesis 28:12-17—Receiving God's Blessings

You might want to begin this discussion about God's blessings by talking to the class in general terms about God's blessing of Jacob. God's blessing to Jacob is more inclusive than God's blessing to Abraham. Abraham was not promised the land of Canaan. That came later. With Jacob, we see the concrete promise of land to the sons of Jacob. From Jacob, the entire people of Israel are descended. In fact, the term *Israel* comes to mean both Jacob himself (his second name is Israel) as well as the people who descended from Jacob's twelve sons. The people are never called the descendants of Moses or of David; they are the "children of Israel."

Genesis 28:17 tells us that when Jacob hears God's blessing, he is afraid. Why is Jacob so fearful when he realizes the Lord has come to him at Bethel? Does God's coming make persons fearful? Or does Jacob mean the place is awe-inspiring because the holy God appeared to him there? Ask the class members if they can put themselves in Jacob's place and decide why Jacob is so fearful. The class members may be better able to analyze Jacob's response to God's blessing if they think about the times in their lives when they have received God's blessings. How have they responded in these situations?

Genesis 28:20-22—Bargaining With God

Begin this discussion on bargaining with God by asking a class member to read this short passage aloud (Genesis 28:20-22). Point out to the class members that in this agreement between God and Jacob, Jacob is the instigator. That is, Jacob is the one who initiates the covenant with God, rather than the other way around. Ask the class members whether they think Jacob's action is appropriate.

Now ask the class members to think about their own bargains with God. In Jacob's bargain with God, Jacob promises to give a tenth of all that he has to God, if God will provide for his basic needs. Ask the class members: What kind of offers do you make when you bargain with God? What requests do you make of God in return? Ask the class members to share how they think God responds to their attempts at bargaining with him.

Genesis 31:36-42—Vocational Hardships

Open this discussion on vocational hardships by talking to the class about the background of this passage. The long list of the trials of the shepherd's life is a good antidote to our romantic view of the shepherd's existence. Even today, shepherds in the Middle East lead a rough existence. It is just as Jacob portrays it.

In our society today, we probably find it difficult to imagine what the life of a shepherd is really like. Few of us are exposed to inclement weather over long periods of time, and few of us are threatened by wild beasts in our work. But as the student book indicates, we can all identify with the idea of vocational hardships. You might ask the class members to share some of the hardships of their respective vocations.

Genesis 31:43-54—Honoring Our Agreements

Most persons are familiar with at least the basic conflict between Jacob and Laban. However, the events that take place at the close of this story are probably not as well known. Begin this discussion about honoring our agree-ments by briefly retelling the story of Jacob and Laban's parting from each other.

There is a kind of dignity in the ending of the story of Laban and Jacob that we ought not overlook (Genesis 31:51-55). These two arch rivals, who have fought so long and hard to outdo each other in the accumulation of wealth, finally make peace with each other and depart with no hostility.

Jacob and Laban eat a common meal, make their respectful good-bys, and the families go their separate ways. From this time forward, there will be no further journeys to Mesopotamia to find suitable wives for Jacob's descendants. From here on, Israel lives out her life in the land of Canaan. The Mesopotamian heritage of the patriarchs has drawn to a close. So Laban and Jacob, having fought each other for goods by every scheme they could devise, say their loving words of farewell to each other.

At this point, you might want to have someone in the class read Genesis 31:43-54 aloud. Ask the class to pay special attention to verse 49, which contains the "Mizpah Benediction."

Ask the class members if they are suspicious of either Jacob or Laban. Do they think that these two long-time enemies will honor this agreement? If we are suspicious of Jacob and Laban, it is probably because neither has proved to be absolutely trustworthy in the past. Ask the class members if, in their experiences, they have suspected persons who have been untrustworthy in the past. Do their commitments to agreements they make depend on the trustworthiness of the other person or persons involved?

At least two other issues arise in these chapters that are not covered in the student book. If time remains, you might use it to discuss these two additional issues.

The first issue concerns Jacob's dream at Bethel. When Jacob awakens from his dream and realizes that God has appeared and spoken to him, he is afraid. To what can we attribute Jacob's fear? Jacob was terrified when he realized that he had slept on ground that was holy. This was ground where angels of God had ascended to heaven and descended to earth on a ladder. Jacob is afraid because he appreciates the value of Bethel as a holy place. Places where the deity appears should be thought of as awesome. They are places at which a revelation occurs that can change the entire course of a person's life.

We live in a world that is much more crowded than Jacob's world. In our world, it is difficult to go off by ourselves to places we consider awesome. Ask the class members to talk about the places in their lives that have been holy places. What meaning do these places have for them?

The second issue not mentioned in the student book has to do with childlessness. In Genesis 30:1-2, Rachel attacks Jacob and demands that he give her children. Apparently Rachel thinks of herself as worthless because she has not had any children of her own. Notice that Jacob replies by saying that only God gives children.

Barrenness seems to be a frequent problem among Old Testament women. In 1 Samuel 1:8, Hannah's husband points out how much he loves Hannah despite her not having borne any children. So children were not the only basis for meaningful marriage, even though barrenness was a terrible disgrace in the eyes of the ancient Israelites.

Genesis 30 shows us that although one purpose of marriage was the bearing of children, that was not the only purpose. Rachel keenly felt the disgrace of having no children. Leah, on the other hand, keenly felt the disgrace of not being loved by her husband. Often in ancient Israel, persons married because they loved each other. Rachel and Jacob married for that reason. Rachel was the object of Jacob's love, and Jacob was willing to work for seven years to have her as his wife.

Women were not simply property in ancient times. They were not only instruments for producing children. Leah was a bitterly unhappy person despite her six sons and one daughter, for there was no bond between Leah and her husband Jacob.

Do we today consider the bearing of children as the purpose for marriage? Ask the class members to think of other purposes for marriage. How does our society today respond to childlessness? Does our society consider women who cannot bear children to be worthless? How does society react to women who have decided not to have children? Such a decision was foreign to Old Testament culture and values. Ask the class members: Do you see this movement toward free choice as progress? Why or why not?

Close today's session by asking the class members to reflect on any new insights they have gained from their study of Genesis 28–31. If time allows, list these insights on chalkboard or a large sheet of paper so that you and the class may refer to them at a later date.

For to see your face is like seeing the face of God (33:10).

— 10 —

Jacob in Canaan

Genesis 32–36

DIMENSION ONE:
WHAT DOES THE BIBLE SAY?

Answer these questions by reading Genesis 32

1. Whom does Jacob encounter on his way home? (Genesis 32:1)

   He encounters the angels of God.

2. What does Jacob do when he hears that Esau and his men are coming? (Genesis 32:7)

   He divides his people, flocks, and herds into two groups.

3. What does Jacob include in his present to Esau? (Genesis 32:14-15)

   He selected two hundred female goats and twenty male goats, two hundred ewes and twenty rams, thirty female camels with their young, forty cows and ten bulls, twenty female donkeys and ten male donkeys.

4. What happens when Jacob wrestles with the man until daybreak? (Genesis 32:25)

   Jacob's hip was wrenched.

5. What new name does God give Jacob at the Jabbok ford? (Genesis 32:28)

   Jacob is renamed Israel.

6. How does the wrestling match at the ford of the Jabbok River affect Jacob physically? (Genesis 32:31)

   Jacob limps because of his hip.

Answer these questions by reading Genesis 33

7. What is Esau's attitude toward Jacob when the two meet? (Genesis 33:4)

   Esau is delighted to see him and embraces him warmly.

8. Why does Jacob not choose to accompany Esau on his journey? (Genesis 33:13-14)

   Jacob's children are young and tender, and the many nursing animals will have to be driven slowly and carefully. Therefore Jacob, the people, and flocks will slow Esau down.

9. Where does Jacob go after Esau and his men disappear? (Genesis 33:17-18)

   Jacob goes to Succoth and then on to Shechem.

Answer these questions by reading Genesis 34

10. Who falls in love with Jacob's daughter Dinah? (Genesis 34:2-3)

    Shechem, the son of Hamor the Hivite, loves her.

11. What do the sons of Jacob demand that the men of Shechem do in order to intermarry? (Genesis 34:15-17)

    They demand that all the men be circumcised.

12. Which two sons of Jacob take the lead in attacking the men of Shechem? (Genesis 34:25-26)

    Simeon and Levi are the leaders.

Answer these questions by reading Genesis 35

13. Where does Jacob place the foreign gods of the people? (Genesis 35:4)

    He buried them under the oak at Shechem.

14. Where does Jacob bury Rachel? (Genesis 35:19-20)

    He buries her on the way to Ephrath, or Bethlehem.

15. How old is Isaac when he dies? (Genesis 35:28-29)

He is one hundred and eighty years old.

Answer these questions by reading Genesis 36

16. What are the names of Esau's five sons? (Genesis 36:4-5)

They are Eliphaz, Reuel, Jeush, Jalam, and Korah.

17. Where does Esau settle down with his family and possessions? (Genesis 36:8)

They settle in the hill country of Seir.

DIMENSION TWO: WHAT DOES THE BIBLE MEAN?

Genesis 32:1-8. In these verses we have two explanations of the meaning of the Hebrew word *Mahanaim.* In verses 1 and 2, the word means "two camps" (of angels). Verses 7 and 8 give us the second explanation of this place name. Jacob hears of Esau's coming to meet him and divides his people and goods into two camps. Jacob reasons that one of the two might escape if Esau attacks him. Genesis 33:8 mentions the word a third time. Here the reference is to the companies into which Jacob divides his possessions in order to impress Esau.

The student book mentions that Mahanaim is part of the territory of Gad, east of the Jordan River. Jacob's connection with the territory to the east of the Jordan River probably preserves an ancient tradition. Various peoples in the region often fought over the territory east of the Jordan, especially the very valuable land north and south of the Jabbok River.

Genesis 32:13-21. The details about Jacob's special arrangements of his family and his possessions make the story interesting to us. By his clever arrangements, Jacob intends to impress Esau and to turn him away from his anger. Jacob goes to great lengths to protect himself from Esau's wrath. Yet Esau will be generous and forgiving.

Genesis 32:22-32. In this trouble between Jacob and the "man" at the ford of the Jabbok River, we sense the power of this eerie scene. The man can strike Jacob dead in an instant. As Jacob struggles with the superhuman power to win his blessing, the man finally uses some of his own power. He merely touches Jacob's hip, and Jacob's hip is thrown out of joint!

On one level, this story is fascinating. On a deeper level, Jacob is struggling for the future of Israel, the people of God.

This story also explains why the ancient Israelites would not eat the sciatic muscle located on the hip socket. In later times we find no taboo in eating this part of an animal. Therefore, this story explains a taboo that did not influence the Israelites for long.

Aside from the place name *Mahanaim,* another word-play occurs in this passage as well. The name of the river, *Jabbok,* sounds similar to the Hebrew word "to wrestle." Thus, for the storyteller, the Jabbok River and Jacob's wrestling with God belong together.

Genesis 33:10. The word *Peniel* or *Penuel,* which means "the face of God," appears once more, this time in connection with Jacob's meeting Esau. Jacob says that seeing Esau is like seeing God's face. This remark refers to the place name *Penuel.*

Genesis 33:18-20. Jacob's early connections with the city of Shechem probably indicate that it was one of the places of origin of Israel as a community. Whether by peaceful or warlike means, the ancestors of the later twelve tribes of Israel were closely related to Shechem. Several of the Semitic tribes may have joined one another in a covenant with Shechem as their headquarters. In Judges 9:4 and 9:46 we learn that the god of the city of Shechem is called Baal-Berith or El-Berith by the city's inhabitants. *Berith* is the Hebrew word for "covenant."

In Joshua 24, Joshua calls all the elders to Shechem and makes his farewell address to them. On that occasion he refers to the fact that some of those present were worshipers of the gods in whose land they were then dwelling; others worshiped the gods of their ancestors; and yet others worshiped the Lord, the God of Israel. Thus, we understand Shechem's importance in early Israel as the headquarters for Israel's worship.

Genesis 35:1-4. We do not know when Bethel replaced Shechem as Israel's religious center. In the beginning of the divided monarchy, the people anointed Rehoboam king at Shechem, but he fled for his life when the people rebelled against his harsh leadership. From 1 Kings 12, which records this story, we also learn that Jeroboam made Bethel his religious capital, along with the northern town of Dan. But this story in Genesis 35 probably preserves a much older tradition than that of the tenth century B.C. (the time of the divided monarchy).

Genesis 35:16-21. The story of Benjamin's birth and of his mother's death is very old. Two different traditions exist about the location of Rachel's tomb. This passage tells us that Rachel was buried on the way from Bethel to Ephrath. The other tradition appears in Jeremiah 31:15. In this passage, Rachel's tomb is located near Ramah, a settlement north of Jerusalem in the territory of Benjamin. With Benjamin's birth, Jacob's list of descendants is now completed.

DIMENSION THREE:
WHAT DOES THE BIBLE MEAN TO ME?

The student book divides Dimension Three into three areas that have meaning for our lives today. These areas are "Appeasement or Bribery," "Encounters With God," and "The Cycle of Crime." In leading the class discussion of Dimension Three, you will want to organize your presentation around these three areas.

Genesis 32:1-21—Appeasement or Bribery?

Genesis 32 shows Jacob and his efforts to win the favor of his brother Esau. Although the class members have read this chapter in preparation for the lesson, you may want to review with them the events that take place.

The writer artfully presents the story of Jacob's preparing to meet his brother Esau. We see that Jacob wants to show Esau how wealthy he has become. Apparently, Jacob wants Esau to realize that he is in a position to share this wealth with him, who had lost the birthright.

But the word comes to Jacob that Esau is already on the way to meet him with four hundred men. To Jacob that can only mean that Esau is determined to get revenge on Jacob. Jacob knows that he cannot count on the mere promise of a rich gift to Esau. He must produce such a gift and hope for the best.

The first part of Jacob's plan is to divide his possessions into two parts. This way, if Esau comes with his army, one-half of the possessions and the family could probably escape. Apparently, Esau ruins this plan by not bringing his army across the Jabbok River.

During the night, Jacob devises another plan. He will send Esau a gift that will overwhelm him with its magnificence. The strategy is to tell Esau, as each of the gifts passes by, that it is a present to Esau from Jacob, and that Jacob is still to come. In Jacob's mind the person who sold his birthright for a bowl of soup and a bit of bread would surely be impressed by this grand gift.

This passage gives us insight into the character of Jacob. Ask the class members for their opinions on the character of Jacob. Do his actions anger them? Or is Jacob justified in what he does? Ask the class members to put themselves in Esau's place. What would they think when presented with such a gift? Would they consider it bribery? Or would they see Jacob as one who sincerely desired reconciliation?

Now ask the class members to apply this story personally. Ask them to think about the times in their lives when they thought they were being bribed. Or can they think of times when they have tried to bribe others? What results did such bribery bring about?

Genesis 32:22-32—Encounters With God

Before we discover Esau's reaction to Jacob's plan, we read about Jacob's meeting with a more formidable opponent than his brother Esau. Genesis 32:22-32 is the account of Jacob's meeting with God's angel, who is here simply called "a man." The powerful Jacob actually deals with this "man," who has unlimited power to do what he sees fit with Jacob, in a way that strikes the hearer as astonishing. How can Jacob possibly be so strong as to threaten even the messenger of God, requiring that the messenger ask Jacob for release?

We remember that Jacob single-handedly rolled the stone away from the well in Haran, but the Jacob we see here is even more powerful. This Jacob "struggled with the angel and overcame him" (Hosea 12:4). How are we to understand such power?

The most probable explanation is that Jacob is being tested by God just as Abraham was tested (Genesis 22). Jacob may be able to outwit his brother Esau and his uncle Laban. He may also be clever enough to placate the brother who is coming to meet him with four hundred men. But how will Jacob stand up to an encounter with God? Is Jacob prepared to re-enter the land of Canaan and become the father of the people of God?

That is the question being answered on the bank of the Jabbok, in a struggle that lasts all night. Jacob passes the test. He cares enough for his blessing that he is willing to endanger his own life. Wounded by the touch of this man, Jacob will not let go. A blessing simply must be forthcoming. We assume that the angel has only the night hours to carry out his mission.

The angel gives Jacob the new name *Israel* and with that new name, Jacob also acquires a new nature. The name *Israel* here means, "he who strives with God." This name itself is important to the early Israelite faith. The great Jacob, with all his faults, does not give up on God and on the blessing for God's people.

Jacob is a survivor—one who finds a way. Jacob turns this way and that. He considers alternatives, tries one scheme after another and will not be defeated. Jacob is committed to life and to a progress in life that gives dynamism to the faith of the early Israelite community. Jacob can go too far; he can be too clever for his own good. But he keeps coming back to God, demanding the blessing.

The student book asks whether Jacob is a changed person after the encounter with the angel. The class members may already have answers to this question. However, one way to approach the question is to look at what happens immediately after the encounter. You might want to review the reunion of Jacob and Esau with the class.

When morning comes, Jacob joins the company and begins to put into effect the plan to win over Esau. Picture a long line that includes 200 female goats and 20 male goats, 200 ewes and 20 rams, 30 camels and their young, 40 cows and 10 bulls, 20 female donkeys and 10 male donkeys, as well as all of Jacob's servants and family. Jacob, Rachel, and the children take their places at the end of the line.

However, Esau does not proceed according to Jacob's plan. He does not just stand by and watch the procession.

He rushes ahead, leaving his four hundred men, and finds his brother Jacob. Esau embraces his brother, showing that Jacob has miscalculated his brother's attitude. Esau is a changed person. He has not only found prosperity but also maturity. Esau asks about this large family and is pleased to learn they all belong to Jacob.

At first Esau rejects Jacob's gifts, saying he has all he needs. But finally, when pressed, Esau graciously accepts them. Probably, Esau then migrates to the south, expecting Jacob to follow him shortly.

Yet the story makes it clear that the Jacob who struggled with the angel and prevailed is in some respects the same old Jacob! He does not go with Esau to Seir, not even for a visit. Instead, he returns to Succoth, on the north side of the Jabbok River. He camps at Succoth for a short time and then heads for Shechem. Jacob is bound for the Promised Land, and he will not be detained any longer.

So Jacob returns from his flight to Haran with a large family, many possessions, good relations with Laban that assure no future trouble, and a peaceful relationship with his brother Esau. He has secured his fortune without a single military encounter. Jacob now re-enters Canaan and takes up his life there. God's favor rests upon him.

Jacob has worked hard for his blessing. But God has also seen that the blessing came Jacob's way. Human events were not dominated by divine activity, but God gave subtle direction and guidance to Jacob's enterprises.

Many persons think of Jacob as a scoundrel. What do the class members think about Jacob? If time allows, you might list on chalkboard or a large sheet of paper the positive and negative characteristics of Jacob. In this way, the class can come to a consensus about Jacob.

Now lead the class in a discussion of the whole area of personal encounters with God. Have the class members had encounters with God that have changed their lives? How would they describe these changes? Were the changes visible or were they from within?

Genesis 34:1-31—The Cycle of Crime

While momentous events were taking place in the life of Jacob, other events were taking place on the west side of the Jordan. In Canaan, events were running their course in such a way as to endanger once again the promise of God. The people of Shechem cooperate with Jacob by selling him land on which he builds an altar. This purchase of land is necessary, for it gives Jacob an undisputed land holding where he and his people may gather to worship the Lord.

Remember that God's promise to the patriarchs included a vast multitude of descendants and possession of the land of Canaan. Thus Jacob's acquisition of this land surrounding Shechem is a natural result of the promise made to the patriarchs.

Yet, events keep threatening this promise. Dinah goes out to visit the women of the land. We do not know why Dinah is not content to remain among her family members. Why does she expose herself to danger and the lustful eyes of Shechem? The story does not answer this question.

We read that Shechem "loved the girl and spoke tenderly to her." Hamor, Shechem's father, wants the sons of Jacob to allow Dinah to marry his son. He tells them, "My son Shechem has his heart set on your daughter."

However, Shechem takes advantage of Dinah. The story makes it clear that Dinah was unable to cry out for help. The ancient Hebrews had a law that governed the situation. An Israelite who raped a virgin in circumstances where her cries for help would do no good, was required to marry the virgin and pay a suitable sum to her family. If the woman was betrothed, then the man was stoned to death, and the woman was considered innocent of any crime. Deuteronomy 22 describes the law governing the situation.

But what happens in this case, since Shechem is not an Israelite but a foreigner? He has no right whatsoever to any relationship with a woman of Jacob's family. That is why Shechem's father immediately puts the problem into a larger perspective. If the two peoples can reach a general agreement that includes intermarriage, then the deed of Shechem can be justified after the fact. Dinah is not betrothed to anyone else. Shechem clearly loves the woman and is willing to do whatever is required in order to marry her.

The sons of Jacob agree that Shechem may have their sister Dinah in marriage if the men of Shechem will agree to be circumcised. However, the sons of Jacob have no intention of following through with the agreement. They intend to get vengeance on the Shechemites and nothing else. Their sister is to marry this foreigner under no condition.

The brothers seem more concerned about their own honor than they are about Dinah's. They never consult Dinah about their agreement. In fact, Dinah never speaks in this story. The men make all the arrangements. When her brothers, Simeon and Levi, come and kill the men of Shechem and take Dinah away, they still do not ask her what she wants to do. Their treatment of Dinah shows how personal interest can be set aside in favor of concern for justice.

And what is Jacob's part in this crime? He seems to be a more responsible person than his sons. True, he does not reproach his sons for their treachery and cruelty, only for their having endangered his life and the life of his people. Jacob's concern was that he had entered into a contract with these people, but was not permitted to honor this covenant.

The Israelites and Canaanites did intermarry and did share the land of Canaan for many centuries. The terms for intermarriage often included a readiness on the part of the ones entering Israel's community to undergo circumcision and to take up the requirements of the covenant law. This early venture into intermarriage was brought about by an act of violence against Dinah and was brought to an end by an act of violence by Jacob's sons. Sharing life with the Canaanites needed a more promising beginning than this!

In situations like these, where one crime follows another, it is often difficult to assess blame. Ask the class to think about the events in the story of Shechem, Dinah, and her brothers. Who was at fault? Was it Shechem? Dinah? Dinah's brothers? Jacob? Or were some or all of these persons at fault?

Such a cycle of crime is a common element of our society. Ask the class members to think of examples where one crime follows another. They can draw these examples from their personal lives or from the public domain. The American political scene is one place to look for such examples. Now ask the class members: How can such cycles of crime be broken? How could the cycle of crime in Genesis 34 have been broken?

Close this session by asking the class members to share the insights they have gained from studying Genesis 32–36. List these insights on chalkboard or a large sheet of paper.

— 11 —

Joseph's Journey to Egypt

Genesis 37–41

**DIMENSION ONE:
WHAT DOES THE BIBLE SAY?**

Answer these questions by reading Genesis 37

1. What garment does Joseph's father give him? (Genesis 37:3)

   He gave him a richly ornamented robe.

2. Why do Joseph's brothers hate him? (Genesis 37:4)

   They hate him because their father loves him best.

3. How do Joseph's brothers interpret Joseph's first dream? (Genesis 37:6-8)

   They believe that Joseph will rule over them.

4. What does Joseph's father understand the second dream to mean? (Genesis 37:9-10)

   He believes that he and his whole family will bow down before Joseph.

5. Which brother intervenes to save Joseph's life? (Genesis 37:21)

   Reuben intervenes.

6. Who proposes that the brothers sell Joseph to the Ishmaelites? (Genesis 37:26-27)

   Judah makes the proposal.

7. What do the brothers do to Joseph's robe? (Genesis 37:31-33)

   They dip the robe in goat's blood, and then send it to their father, leading him to believe that Joseph has been killed by a wild animal.

8. Who buys Joseph in Egypt? (Genesis 37:36)

   Potiphar, an officer of Pharaoh, buys him.

Answer these questions by reading Genesis 38

9. Whom does Judah choose for his eldest son Er to marry? (Genesis 38:6)

   He chooses Tamar.

10. After Er and Onan die, what does Judah ask Tamar to do? (Genesis 38:11)

    He asks her to remain a widow until his third son, Shelah, grows up and can marry her.

11. What does Tamar do in order to bear a child in memory of her husband, Er? (Genesis 38:14-19)

    She dresses herself as a harlot and tricks Judah into having relations with her so that he would father a child for her.

12. How does Tamar convince Judah that he is the father of her son? (Genesis 38:18, 25-26)

    She has his seal, cord, and staff in pledge that he would send her a kid goat.

Answer these questions by reading Genesis 39

13. How does Joseph fare in Potiphar's house? (Genesis 39:2-6)

    He does very well, eventually becoming Potiphar's overseer.

14. How does Joseph respond to his master's wife when she tempts him? (Genesis 39:8-10)

    He rejects her advances.

15. Whom does Pharaoh imprison with Joseph? (Genesis 40:1-3)

    He imprisons the chief cupbearer and the chief baker.

16. What are Joseph's duties while in prison? (Genesis 40:4)

    He attends the chief cupbearer and chief baker.

17. Who interprets the dreams of those imprisoned by the pharaoh? (Genesis 40:8-19)

    Joseph does.

18. What does the pharaoh do to the chief cupbearer and the chief baker? (Genesis 40:21-22)

    He restores the chief cupbearer to his assignment, and he hangs the chief baker.

Answer these questions by reading Genesis 41

19. To whom does Pharaoh first send to interpret his dreams? (Genesis 41:8)

    He sends for all the magicians and wise men of Egypt.

20. How does Joseph interpret Pharaoh's dreams? (Genesis 41:25-36)

    He interprets that Egypt will experience seven years of abundance, followed by seven years of famine.

21. Whom does Pharaoh place in charge of preparations for the time of famine? (Genesis 41:37-45)

    He chooses Joseph.

22. What does Joseph do during the seven years of plenty? (Genesis 41:47-49)

    He stores up grain in great abundance.

23. What does Joseph do when the people face famine? (Genesis 41:55-57)

    He opens all the storehouses and sells the grain to those who are in need.

DIMENSION TWO: WHAT DOES THE BIBLE MEAN?

Background Information on the Joseph Story

The story of Joseph's life takes up most of the rest of the Book of Genesis. This long tale of Joseph in Egypt strikes the reader as a different kind of literature than the series of stories about the lives of Abraham, Isaac, and Jacob that we have been studying since Genesis 12.

The story of Joseph parallels other literature that has been recovered from Egypt, especially "The Story of the Two Brothers." This story is a romance about Egyptian life in which the hero is the younger brother of a man whose wife tries to seduce him, but fails. The younger brother then flees for his life and undergoes various adventures. The younger brother is finally adopted as a son by the pharaoh and ascends to the throne of Egypt. The two brothers are reconciled at last.

The Joseph story is probably not dependent on this story, but the Egyptian story may have served as a model for the writer of Genesis 37–50. The writer of the Joseph story does use Egyptian expressions and shows considerable knowledge of Egyptian customs and terms.

No Egyptian sources prove that Joseph rose to be second in command to the pharaoh, or that Joseph and his brothers were in Egypt at all. However, available knowledge about Egypt indicates that the time Joseph spent there was probably somewhere between 1700 to 1300 B.C. We have no reason to doubt that western Semites like Jacob and his family could have made their way to Egypt and that one of their number could have come to great prominence in the court of the pharaoh.

Genesis 37:2-4. The story of Joseph begins with a brief description of Joseph—his age, his position in the family, and his relationship with his brothers. As the student book indicates, we cannot be certain of the nature of Joseph's role. However, it is obvious that Joseph is his father's favorite, much to his brothers' chagrin.

Genesis 37:5-11. Joseph's dreams also single him out. They present him as one who is to lord it over not only his brothers but also his father and mother. The story presupposes that Rachel, Joseph's mother, is still alive. But in the story as we now have it, Rachel died on the way to Bethlehem (Genesis 35:16-19).

Genesis 37:14. When the Joseph story opens, Jacob appears to be in the Hebron region, as Genesis 35:27 indicates. But the sending of Joseph on a long journey to Shechem to visit the other sons of Jacob seems strange. Therefore, it seems likely that in the early tradition, Jacob settled in the region of Shechem, rather than in Hebron as Genesis 37:14 states.

Genesis 37:15-28. These verses tell us that Joseph wanders in the fields for a while and decides to journey on to Dothan. The city of Dothan was an important town in early Canaan, with a major highway passing nearby. The account of a Midianite caravan passing by rings true. Although the practice was forbidden by law, Israelites were sold into slavery to foreigners.

It is clear from the contradictions regarding just who sold Joseph to the captain of the guard (the Midianites or the Ishmaelites) that our narrative is woven together from two slightly different versions of the Joseph story.

Genesis 38. The story of Judah and Tamar in chapter 38 is not related to the story of Joseph in Egypt. It seems to intrude into the middle of the Joseph story. We do not know for certain why this story of Judah and Tamar has been placed in its present location. As the student book points out, the main purpose of the story is to underscore the responsibility for heads of families to support the law of the levirate marriage (marrying the brother's widow). (See Deuteronomy 25:5-10.)

The story may also intend to show how dangerous it is to marry a Canaanite woman, as Judah does. Many problems arise after this marriage takes place. We remember that Isaac and Jacob found wives in Mesopotamia. Joseph, as we will learn, finds a perfectly acceptable wife in Egypt. But the Canaanite women are a different sort! They cause trouble, and the consequences of union with them can be as serious as they are for Judah.

Genesis 39. The story of Potiphar's wife tempting Joseph is similar to the tempting of the younger son by the wife of the elder son in the Egyptian story of the two brothers. Joseph is such a handsome man that he no doubt arouses the envy of his master and makes it possible for the master to believe his wife's story.

But Joseph is also portrayed as one to whom everything comes without effort. His life prospers, and it is no wonder that people both admire such a person and resent the favor from God that is his.

The narrator knows what effects Joseph's prosperity has upon people. Joseph's telling tales about his brothers and his dreams of his own future greatness angers his brothers and even annoys his doting father. But Joseph is also highly competent. He gets things done and has the gift of discerning the future. Joseph comes through as the kind of leader the people need.

The word *Hebrew* used to refer to Joseph (Genesis 39:14) apparently preserves an early term for the Israelites and other peoples who lived among the inhabitants of Canaan, but who were not a regular part of the Canaanite city-state system. The word may have had the meaning "outsider," in the sense that these residents of Canaan were non-Canaanite settlers within this society, lacking legal standing. Notice that Potiphar's wife refers to Joseph as a Hebrew. Strangely enough, the designation *Hebrew* was usually given to Israelites by non-Israelites.

Genesis 41:1-8. The pharaoh's dream, like those of his chief cupbearer and chief baker, represents important elements in the story. In ancient Israel, dreams allow the future to come into a person's life. During sleep, one is exposed to the power of the divine in a way that is not possible during waking hours.

DIMENSION THREE: WHAT DOES THE BIBLE MEAN TO ME?

According to the student book, this first part of the Joseph story in Genesis 37–41 raises three issues that have meaning for our lives today. You will want to center your class discussion on these three areas: "Sibling Rivalry," "Women's Rights," and "The Providence of God."

Genesis 37:1-11—Sibling Rivalry

Joseph's character and his relationship to God give us some clues about the problems that exist between Joseph and his brothers. Joseph is not at all sly or clever as his father Jacob was. Joseph is one of those persons who helps the blessing along with a kind of understanding and insight that are above average.

Joseph's ability to interpret dreams is presented as a gift and accomplishment, not as some mystical power. The same is implied by Joseph's use of the divining cup to read the future (Genesis 44:5). Joseph is no magician; he is a man of sound judgment, administrative talents, and hard work.

At the same time, God is with Joseph, seeing to it that the future comes out well for Joseph because so much depends on him. Not only is the future of God's people bound up with Joseph's success in Egypt, but the very life of Egypt itself depends upon Joseph. Egypt and its neighbors depend on Joseph's wise use of his personal gifts and of God's blessing upon him.

This combination of divine direction and human initiative appears throughout the Joseph story. Joseph knows full well how God's power and his own gifts and talents work together for good. That is what Joseph means when he says in 41:16, "I cannot do it . . . but God will give Pharaoh the answer he desires."

Joseph does not show the least hesitation before Pharaoh. Joseph says that the interpretation of dreams is not in himself. He flatly declares that God will give the interpretation of what the pharaoh asks—through Joseph. Joseph is not the least bit modest. He is entirely at home with the pharaoh, although he has just been released from prison. We realize that Joseph belongs in the household of the pharaoh. He is no keeper of sheep, no backwoods herdsman.

Joseph's responsibility for Pharaoh and the land of Egypt is clear at the close of his interpretation of the pharaoh's dream (Genesis 41:33-36). After he interprets the dream, Joseph does not wait to be asked how the pharaoh is to manage affairs in light of the dream. He tells the pharaoh exactly what to do! Joseph does not nominate himself for the post of chief overseer of the preparations for the famine. Yet, the description of what needs to be done seems so matter-of-fact, so clear in detail, that the pharaoh hardly has any choice at all. Joseph has for all practical purposes appointed himself to be the pharaoh's right-hand man!

After presenting this portrayal of Joseph's character, have the class think back to the beginning of the Joseph story. Remind them of Joseph's dream about his brothers, and his brothers' reaction to this dream. All the background information on Joseph's character prepares us for the brothers' deed against him. Knowing Joseph's character, we can certainly understand why the brothers acted as they did.

Joseph's dream was quite usual. Bales of grain and heavenly bodies were common images during Joseph's time. But the idea of Joseph's telling the dream and flaunting his future glory is not a pleasant thing. Joseph's actions endanger his own life by arousing his brothers' jealousy.

Now ask the class members to imagine living in a day-to-day situation with a person like Joseph. Consider all the aspects of Joseph's character that are brought out in Genesis 37–41. You might get a clearer picture of Joseph if you list some of these characteristics on chalkboard or a large sheet of paper.

Ask the class members how they might have reacted had they been one of Joseph's brothers. What does the Joseph story tell us about the issue of sibling rivalry? Some of the class members may remember such rivalry with their brothers and sisters. Other class members may have children who do not always get along. What can a child do about sibling rivalry? What can a parent do? Ask the class members whether they think sibling rivalry is inevitable when there are several brothers and sisters in a family.

Genesis 38—Women's Rights

According to the student book, the ancient Israelite law that governed the relationship between Tamar and Onan is called the *levirate law.* You might want to begin this discussion by presenting information on levirate law from a Bible dictionary or other reference source.

After this preparation, ask the class members to think about the place of women in the society that is reflected in this law. You might want to read the law aloud to the class—Deuteronomy 25:5-10. Ask the class members to put themselves in the place of either Tamar or Onan and talk about how they might feel in that situation. Does the levirate law protect women or take away their rights?

Genesis 39:1-6—The Providence of God

These verses tell us that Joseph progressed from a position of slavery to a position of great responsibility. How did Joseph accomplish this change in position? The writer is very clear on this point. Joseph accomplishes this feat with the help of the Lord (Genesis 39:2-3, 5).

What do we learn about Joseph's character from this passage? We read that Joseph is successful in the house of Potiphar. We also learn that Joseph is handsome. And God causes a blessing to fall upon everyone with whom Joseph comes into contact. Who could ask for more?

Have someone in the class read these verses aloud. Point out how often in these few verses the writer mentions the Lord's presence in Joseph's life. Contrast this description of God's intervention with our own situations. The providence of God in our lives is often difficult to see. Ask the class members how they recognize God's presence in their lives during the good times. Do they more readily see the presence of God in their lives during the good times than during the bad times? Why?

Now ask the group members if they know people who seem to be God's favorites. For some persons, everything seems to work out for the best in all situations. How do they account for such good fortune? Is God with them as he was with Joseph? Or do these persons work hard to see that their circumstances are always favorable?

Close today's session by asking the group members to reflect on what they have learned in their study of Genesis 37–41. If time allows, list these new insights on a large sheet of paper or chalkboard.

12

Joseph and His Brothers

Genesis 42–45

DIMENSION ONE:
WHAT DOES THE BIBLE SAY?

Answer these questions by reading Genesis 42

1. Why does Jacob not allow Benjamin to go to Egypt? (Genesis 42:4)

   He is afraid some harm will come to him.

2. What does Joseph give as the reason for his brother's coming into the land of Egypt? (Genesis 42:9, 12, 14)

   He accuses them of being spies.

3. Whom does Joseph keep as a hostage when he lets the brothers return to Canaan with grain? (Genesis 42:19, 24)

   He keeps Simeon.

4. How are the brothers to obtain the release of Simeon? (Genesis 42:20)

   They will obtain his release by returning with their youngest brother, and thus proving that they have told the truth.

5. How does Reuben's rebuke of the other brothers for their mistreatment of Joseph affect Joseph? (Genesis 42:24)

   He turns away from them and weeps.

6. What do the brothers discover in the tops of their bags of grain? (Genesis 42:27)

   They found the silver they had given for the grain.

7. How does Jacob respond to the demand that the brothers take Benjamin to Egypt? (Genesis 42:38)

   He refuses to let Benjamin go.

Answer these questions by reading Genesis 43

8. Why does Jacob send his sons to Egypt a second time? (Genesis 43:1-2)

   They return because they eat all the grain they brought from Egypt.

9. How does Judah get his father to agree to let the brothers take Benjamin with them? (Genesis 43:4-10)

   He convinces Jacob that Benjamin must go to Egypt, and he gives himself as guarantee for Benjamin's life.

10. How does Jacob try to prevent the Egyptians from keeping Simeon and Benjamin? (Genesis 43:11-14)

    He sends rich presents to be given to Joseph.

11. Why do the brothers think they are brought to Joseph's house? (Genesis 43:18)

    They think Joseph means to punish them for the money in their bags on the previous trip.

12. What does Joseph do when he sees Benjamin? (Genesis 43:29-30)

    He goes to his private room and weeps.

13. What kind of portion do the servants give Benjamin? (Genesis 43:34)

    Benjamin receives five times the portion of the others.

Answer these questions by reading Genesis 44

14. What does Joseph order his steward to place in Benjamin's bag along with the grain and the money? (Genesis 44:2)

    He has his own silver cup placed in the bag.

15. How do the brothers react when Joseph's steward finds the cup in Benjamin's sack? (Genesis 44:13)

They tear their garments, load their donkeys, and return to the city.

16. Who does Joseph say will be his slave? (Genesis 44:17)

He demands the man who possessed the cup.

17. What does Judah offer to do to free Benjamin? (Genesis 44:33)

He offers himself in place of Benjamin.

Answer these questions by reading Genesis 45

18. How does Joseph explain his brothers' deed? (Genesis 45:5, 7-8)

God used their deed to get Joseph to Egypt, where he would save their lives.

19. What does Joseph tell his brothers to do? (Genesis 45:9)

He tells them to go to their father and say that his son Joseph wants him to come to Egypt.

20. What is the pharaoh's reaction to the news that Joseph's brothers have come to Egypt? (Genesis 45:16-20)

He is pleased and he orders that the brothers, Joseph's father, and all their households come to Egypt and settle in the best of the land.

DIMENSION TWO:
WHAT DOES THE BIBLE MEAN?

Genesis 42:1-5. At various times in Egyptian history, Semitic people moved into the Nile delta region to buy grain in exchange for their goods or animals. We know of these migrations from Egyptian writings and also from wall-paintings in Egyptian buildings. Our story makes the point that many persons came to Joseph to buy grain during the famine. But part of the drama of our story is that with the famine, Joseph will soon meet his needy brothers and be able to teach them a lesson.

Genesis 42:6-8. The writer does not tell us how Joseph recognizes his brothers, or why they do not recognize him. Apparently, Joseph would have no trouble recognizing ten members of his family, even if the time since his departure was rather long. Moreover, he may well have heard them speaking Hebrew.

But the brothers could not dream that Joseph was still alive, and it would be beyond their wildest imaginings to find him in Egypt as the chief officer of Pharaoh. Until Joseph finally reveals himself to his brothers, they never once suspect that he is the brother they sold into slavery.

Genesis 42:9-14. As the student book points out, Joseph's charge that his brothers are spies seems absurd to us and must have seemed so to discerning readers or hearers of the story. During the time of Joseph, Egypt was far more powerful than Israel. These hungry shepherds could hardly pose a threat to Egypt.

Yet, Egypt did fear that the thousands of Semitic nomads that lived in the area might get together and, in a period of Egyptian internal weakness, sweep in and overwhelm the country of Egypt. This same thing had occurred in Mesopotamia more than once, and it may also have occurred in Egypt shortly before 2000 B.C., after the decline and fall of the Old Kingdom.

Genesis 42:15-24. The writer presents Joseph as an Egyptian through and through. Joseph even swears by the life of Pharaoh (verses 15-16). We can see why Joseph's brothers do not recognize him.

To test the truth of his brother's denial that they are spies, Joseph announces that he will imprison all the brothers but one. That one brother will go to Canaan and return with the youngest brother of whom the brothers spoke. Joseph is testing to see whether they are liars in what they have said about their family. Are they sons of a man named Jacob? Do they have one brother at home whose name is Benjamin? Are they the surviving brothers of one who "is no more" (Joseph)?

If what the brothers say is true, then they can be considered trustworthy in their denial that they have come down to spy out the land. The test serves the purpose of getting Benjamin to Egypt and in Joseph's possession, thus eventually exposing the crime of the brothers against Joseph.

We might ask why an all-powerful ruler like Joseph needs to spend any time or trouble over these hungry shepherds? If Joseph doubts their reliability, why doesn't he simply dispose of them? Joseph has no need of them!

However, for the Israelites who heard this story, it would be clear why Joseph was taking such trouble over these shepherds. He owed them plenty, and Joseph was not one to miss an opportunity for revenge. So the game continues. The brothers are entirely helpless before Joseph, required to do whatever he asks. They are unable to convince him of the truth of their visit; they are off balance, vulnerable, and afraid for their lives.

Genesis 42:25-38. Joseph gives his brothers grain and puts the money for the grain back into their sacks. This act heightens the brothers' anxiety; what will happen now? Will this Egyptian execute us? In the story as it is now told, the brothers discover their money twice. In verses 26-28, one of the brothers discovers that his money is in the sack along with the grain. These verses reflect a tradition in which all the brothers discover that the money had been returned to them for some unexplained reason at the first night's encampment.

In the other tradition, the brothers discover the money only when they get back to their father in Hebron (verse 35). These two traditions have been woven together fairly well in Genesis 42:26-28. Here only one brother discovers his money, and the others apparently are afraid to look into their bags for fear of finding their money also. This lack of action on the part of the brothers makes sense in the context of the story. Joseph has them in such a state that everything that happens to them simply indicates their powerlessness before this overwhelming Egyptian.

The bundles of money must not, of course, be thought of as rolls of paper money. The money presumably would have been in the form of silver tied up in cloth, or perhaps some other kind of precious metal or jewels. In biblical times, much of the buying and selling was accomplished by means of barter. But in a time of famine, one would use precious metal, the value of which was determined by its weight. Coins are not seen in the ancient Near East until about the sixth century B.C.

When Jacob sees the money in his sons' sacks of grain, he becomes distraught. He worries over the fate of his youngest son Benjamin. Reuben tries to assure his father than Benjamin will return safely (verse 37).

Again, we probably have two traditions. According to the first one, Jacob is given assurance by Reuben that Benjamin will return safely. The other tradition in 43:1-10, has Judah assuring Jacob of the youngest son's safety.

Jacob will not hear of a return to Egypt with Benjamin accompanying the other brothers, even though this means that poor Simeon must stay in Egypt indefinitely. Benjamin is too important to Jacob, as the youngest son and as the son of his favorite wife Rachel. Benjamin cannot be risked in Egypt now that Joseph (as Joseph supposes) is dead.

Genesis 43:1-15. The famine forces Jacob to do what he was desperately afraid of doing. He must send Benjamin to Egypt. Jacob sends a precious gift (precious to an Israelite shepherd), hoping to bribe the Egyptian into releasing Simeon and leaving Benjamin unharmed. Jacob probably knows that the present will not work. But what can he do? The famine shows no sign of easing, and all of them will soon be dead unless they can find food.

Again we see the element of the unequal partners in this struggle. Jacob and his sons and their simple life and simple needs are seen against Joseph the right-hand man of Pharaoh, who has everything and controls the lives of his father and brothers absolutely. Jacob tries to preserve the family and the one he loves, but he is no match for Joseph. At the same time, we know that Joseph is the one through whom deliverance comes to Jacob and his family. So Jacob fights against the very arrangement set up for his salvation.

Genesis 43:26-34. Before the banquet begins, Joseph speaks with the brothers about their father and inquires whether the person with them is in fact the youngest brother. Seeing Benjamin brings tears to Joseph's eyes. After going into one of the inner rooms of the house to cry, he washes his face and returns, ordering the banquet to begin. Nothing in Joseph's actions reveals his identity to his brothers, although they are amazed that Joseph knows enough about them to seat them according to age and rank.

The drama of the banquet scene is powerfully told. Joseph is in command—in the background of the action—but ordering every move. His servants put on the banquet, arrange for the separate tables, see to it that the Israelites have food suitable for them while the Egyptians have a proper menu for themselves. Everything is according to custom and tradition. The giver of the banquet pays attention to such details as the menu, the seating arrangements, and the comfort of the guests.

During the meal, the parties are carefully segregated. Egyptian dietary laws were probably as precise and strict as were the dietary laws of ancient Israel. And Joseph, actually the missing brother, sits in isolated splendor as an Egyptian host to these rude shepherd-guests.

Genesis 44:3-13. The brothers set out for home the next morning. When they are only a short distance from the city, Joseph's steward overtakes them and accuses them of stealing Joseph's cup. The brothers deny the charge, saying that the one who is found with the cup should be put to death and all the rest of them made slaves. The steward agrees, but changes the terms; only the one who has the cup will become a slave. When the steward finds the cup in Benjamin's sack, the brothers tear their clothing—a sign of mourning. Then they return to Joseph.

The money that is once more put back into the sacks of grain serves no real function. This time, the interest of the story is fixed on Joseph's silver goblet. Presumably, Joseph has the money put back in the sacks to further confuse and bewilder the poor brothers.

Genesis 44:15. Joseph asks them why they took his cup; do they not know that he is a diviner? Of course he would know that the goblet was stolen, and exactly who stole it and where it was hidden.

Genesis 45:1-8. Finally, Joseph can control himself no longer. He sends the Egyptians away and reveals himself to his brothers. The brothers are frightened because of what they have done. But Joseph explains that his brothers' deed was done under God's direction, to preserve life during these years of famine. Five years of famine remain, and God provides through Joseph for Jacob and his descendants.

DIMENSION THREE:
WHAT DOES THE BIBLE MEAN TO ME?

The student book mentions that the conclusion of the Joseph story in Genesis 42–45 provides at least two issues that are relevant for our lives today. You will want to concentrate the class discussion on the ideas of "Revenge" and "The Guidance of God."

Genesis 42:6-28—Revenge

When we read this part of the Joseph story, we recognize that Joseph is purposely getting revenge on his brothers. The student book describes in detail what this passage tells us about Joseph's vengeful character. Begin discussing this issue by reviewing all the ways Joseph gets revenge on his brothers in Chapters 42–45.

The story shows us a Joseph who almost outwits himself, almost goes too far, and comes close to falling into disfavor with God. The cat and mouse game with the brothers goes so far that it requires that Joseph break it off.

The next time we see Joseph and his brothers together, Joseph is hosting a meal for them (43:26-34). Throughout the elaborate banquet, the brothers are exposed to Joseph's lavish hospitality, but at the same time they are frightened within an inch of their lives. How can they tell what is coming next? The banquet runs its course, and the brothers spend the night unharmed. The next day they are permitted to leave unharmed. Is everything going to be all right after all? Have they come through the ordeal with Simeon and Benjamin and with their bags full of grain? Is it really possible that their good fortune can go so far?

Apparently, yes. The brothers begin the journey, and all seems well. Soon they see the dust of the pursuing Egyptians, and their hearts sink once more. What has gone wrong now? To their utter astonishment, they are accused of being thieves, despite their having returned the money for their previous bags of grain.

A search begins, and of course the silver cup is found in the very last bag searched—the one where it must not be found. Benjamin, the favorite of their father, surely is now marked for death or slavery. Back they go to Egypt. What can they do now?

Next we read Judah's beautiful speech in which he offers his own life in behalf of his brother Benjamin. This confession reminds us of Moses' pleas for the life of Israel and his readiness to sacrifice his own life so that God will not destroy a faithful people (Exodus 32:11-14, 31-34).

Judah readily confesses guilt for the deed on behalf of the brothers, even though he knows they have done nothing wrong. He offers himself and his brothers as slaves to Joseph. What use is resistance? Confess the deed and be done with it.

In Genesis 44:18-34, Judah retells the story of the events, beginning with their first meeting with this strange Egyptian. This is not an exact repetition of earlier happenings, but he sums up the story well. He finishes his speech by telling Joseph that Jacob's life is so bound up with the life of Benjamin that Jacob could not survive Benjamin's death.

Thus Judah pleads with Joseph to let him take Benjamin's place. Joseph may do with Judah what he wishes, but Benjamin must go free. Judah does not speak of his having used his own life to guarantee Benjamin's safety, for that is a matter between Judah and his father. He wants Joseph to see that he has nothing to lose by the substitution. Yet Jacob will lose everything if Joseph will not free Benjamin.

All the brothers know where Jacob's special affection lies. Yet they care so much for their father's welfare that they can act in this way toward Benjamin. We can see the nobility of these brothers. They have no illusions. They know their father loves them, but they also know their father has his favorite, Benjamin, who is loved even more now that Joseph is dead. They do not deny the situation, nor do they try to change it. They accept it and do not wallow in self-pity.

After Judah's confession, Joseph has finally had enough of the deception. He, too, knows the time has come for him to reunite with these brothers. He sends the Egyptians away and reveals himself to his brothers (Genesis 45:1-28).

Joseph's first words are about his father: Is Jacob really still alive? Is there any chance that he and Joseph might see each other again? Joseph hastens to give instructions to the brothers about what they are to do. He also explains that they should not be overcome with guilt by their mistreatment of him, for God worked through the events to preserve life.

The famine is to continue for five years. Joseph is in a position to see to it that Jacob and all his family come through the famine in good condition. Others will benefit also from God's decision to send Joseph to Egypt, but the direct purpose is to fulfill the promise of God to his people Israel.

When the pharaoh joins his voice with that of Joseph, it is clear that all will be well with Jacob and his family. Joseph is making no hollow promise, and he will no longer play with the brothers, tormenting them and then letting them go. Joseph has come as close to forgiving the brothers as he can come.

Joseph's plan to take revenge on his brothers is long and involved. As the student book indicates, the story shows that Joseph is a person with a long memory, who will go to great lengths to take revenge on his brothers. Ask the class members if they think Joseph was justified in his actions. Why or why not?

We have all been in situations when we were mistreated. Ask the class members to think about those times and to share their feelings about those situations. Did they feel like taking revenge after being mistreated? How did they act on these feelings? In retrospect, was revenge the right choice to make?

Genesis 45:1-15—The Guidance of God

In all Joseph's dealings with his brothers, he seems confident of his favored position with God, of his special wisdom and insight, and of his usefulness in keeping people alive during the famine. Joseph is a wise and resourceful person, a person upon whom God depends to fulfill the divine promise. Joseph has a special gift of discernment, but he also has the favor of God—God is with him at all times.

The story points out that God was behind all the events that took place in the Joseph story. This is especially clear when Joseph finally reveals himself to his brothers. Joseph says, "But God sent me ahead of you to preserve for you a remnant on earth and to save your lives by a great deliverance. So then, it was not you who sent me here, but God" (Genesis 45:7-8). Joseph is trying to say that the brothers' deed was really under the guidance of God. God's covenant with Abraham is still operative in the lives of his descendants!

Ask the class members if they have experienced God's guidance during the crises in their lives. Often we realize that something that seemed devastating at the time was for the best. Ask the class members whether they have had this realization. If so, when did they realize that God was at work?

Close today's session by asking the class members to think of the insights they have gained from their study of Genesis 42–45. They may find it difficult to separate the events of Chapters 37–41 from those in Chapters 42–45. You might want to review the list from last week's lesson. Then if time allows, list the new insights from Genesis 42–45 on chalkboard or a large sheet of paper.

I am God, the God of your father. . . . Do not be afraid to go down to Egypt,
for I will make you into a great nation there (46:3).

— 13 —

Jacob and His Family Reunited

Genesis 46–50

DIMENSION ONE:
WHAT DOES THE BIBLE SAY?

Answer these questions by reading Genesis 46

1. Including those who are born in Egypt, how many persons make up Jacob's household? (Genesis 46:26-27)

   They total seventy persons.

2. Why does Joseph tell his father and brothers to tell Pharaoh that they are shepherds? (Genesis 46:34)

   Shepherds are detestable to the Egyptians, and they will be able to settle in Goshen away from the Egyptians.

Answer these questions by reading Genesis 47

3. When the Egyptians have no more money to buy grain, what does Joseph first take from them in place of money? (Genesis 47:16-17)

   He takes their livestock

4. When their cattle and other animals are gone, what do the Egyptians next give to Joseph in exchange for grain? (Genesis 47:18-19)

   They sell themselves and their land into bondage.

5. What land does Joseph not buy up for the pharaoh? (Genesis 47:22)

   He does not buy the land of the priests.

6. What portion of the grain do the people give to Pharaoh? (Genesis 47:24-26)

   They give one-fifth of the grain.

7. What does Jacob make Joseph swear to do after Jacob's death? (Genesis 47:29-30)

   Jacob requests to be buried out of Egypt with his fathers.

Answer these questions by reading Genesis 48

8. What does Joseph do when he hears that his father is ill? (Genesis 48:1-2)

   He takes his sons, Manasseh and Ephraim, to see Jacob.

9. Which of Joseph's two sons receives the greater blessing from Jacob? (Genesis 48:13-20)

   Ephraim does.

Answer these questions by reading Genesis 49

10. Who is Jacob's first-born son? (Genesis 49:3)

    Reuben is the first-born son.

11. Why does Jacob curse Simeon and Levi? (Genesis 49:7)

    He curses them for their fierce anger and their cruel fury.

12. How will Judah's brothers treat him in the future? (Genesis 49:8)

    They will praise him.

13. Which of Jacob's sons receives the greatest blessing? (Genesis 49:22-26)

    Joseph does.

14. Where does Jacob demand that his sons bury him? (Genesis 49:29-31)

    The sons bury him in the cave of Machpelah, the plot of ground purchased by Abraham from Ephron the Hittite.

15. What does Joseph have done to his father's body in Egypt? (Genesis 50:2-3)

    He has the body embalmed.

16. Where do Joseph and the mourning party stop to weep for Jacob? (Genesis 50:10-11)

    They mourn at the threshing floor of Atad, near the Jordan River.

17. What do Joseph's brothers fear from Joseph after the death of their father? (Genesis 50:15)

    They fear his vengeance for their earlier mistreatment of him.

18. How does Joseph explain his brothers' mistreatment of him? (Genesis 50:20)

    Although the brothers meant evil, God meant their deed for good. Through this deed, God enabled many persons to live.

DIMENSION TWO: WHAT DOES THE BIBLE MEAN?

Genesis 46:1-4. This instance is the only one in the Joseph stories where a person offers an act of worship at an altar built by one of the patriarchs. God tells Jacob that it is all right to leave the land of Canaan to travel to Egypt. God will accompany him and will also bring him back to Canaan. God is promising that Jacob's descendants will return in the future and settle in the Promised Land again. The covenant with Abraham (Genesis 12) is being continued through his descendants.

This story of Jacob's stop at Beersheba ties together the Isaac and the Jacob traditions. Jacob honors his father Isaac, and he also shows his commitment to return to the land of Egypt when the famine is over. God identifies himself to Jacob as "the God of your father." The god of the patriarchs is one who guides them in their movements and who is almost like the head of the family. God does not engage in warfare nor does he lead the patriarchs in battle. Yet the Lord provides the protection they need, in all the situations they confront.

Genesis 46:8-27. This passage lists Jacob's descendants. Sisters and brothers count equally to make up the total number of seventy. And the children of the handmaids Bilhah and Zilpah count equally with the children of Leah and Rachel.

Genesis 46:28–47:12. As Jacob enters Egypt, he comes with sufficient riches and property to do adequate honor to Joseph. Joseph would have been humiliated if his father had arrived in rags or without sufficient signs of substance and wealth. The gifts sent by Pharaoh to Jacob (45:21-23) may be the pharaoh's effort to spare Jacob any embarrassment when he appears before Joseph.

Jacob sends Judah before him to let Joseph know that Jacob and his family are about to arrive. Joseph can therefore greet his father with the proper ceremony. Why does Jacob send Judah and not some other brothers? Judah seems to have a special place in Jacob's family, as we see from the special blessing Jacob gives him (Genesis 49:8-12).

From reading these verses it is difficult to understand why Joseph is so specific about instructing his family to present themselves to Pharaoh as shepherds. They are plainly arriving with significant numbers of livestock. Why discuss their occupation at all? Shepherds are detestable to the Egyptians, so possibly Joseph believes that his family will be better served in Goshen, an area near the border of Egypt specifically disignated for the grazing of herds. And the Egyptians would be equally happy to have them some distance away. Jacob follows Joseph's instructions and the plan to settle in Goshen comes about.

Genesis 47:13-26. This passage describes Joseph's land policies. Joseph uses the Egyptians' dependence on state-owned grain to gain all their individual possessions. Before the seven years of famine end, the pharaoh owns all the cattle, flocks, and other animals of the Egyptians. He also owns their land, as well as the Egyptians themselves as slaves. The Egyptians give the state one-fifth of all the goods they produce.

This reference to the pharaoh's retaining one-fifth of the grain of the tenant-farmers may also relate to Joseph's having used one-fifth of the grain during the years of plenty as a reserve against the coming years of famine (Genesis 41:34-35). The people had already become accustomed to the loss of this much grain.

Genesis 47:27-31. For five years Jacob lives in Egypt under famine conditions. Then he remains in the land of Egypt for another twelve years. The writer does not tell us why Jacob stays these extra years. Perhaps Jacob was such an old and feeble man, that he was unable to return to the land of Canaan. Perhaps Joseph was unwilling to let Jacob return to Canaan after the famine ended. In Canaan, Jacob would have to undergo the leaner and simpler life of a shepherd rather than the luxury of living in Pharaoh's court.

Genesis 48:1-22. As noted in the student book, the story of Ephraim and Manasseh is part of the tribal history of Israel. Ephraim and Manasseh are Joseph's sons by his Egyptian wife, Asenath. The Bible contains numerous lists of the twelve tribes of Israel. In some of the lists, Ephraim and Manasseh are named among the descendants of Jacob, rather than naming their father Joseph as a descendant. That practice is reflected here.

The tribe of Levi becomes a priestly tribe and does not inherit land. The five other sons of Leah (Reuben, Simeon, Judah, Issachar, and Zebulun), two sons of Zilpah (Gad and Asher), two sons of Bilhah (Dan and Naphtali), and three sons of Rachel (Manasseh and Ephraim [sons of Joseph], plus Benjamin) therefore complete the list of twelve. Quite a few variations in the listing of the twelve sons developed over the centuries.

Genesis 48:22 preserves a remnant of the story of Jacob's carrying out a battle against the Shechemites. Jacob promises Joseph a special inheritance of a *shechem*, which means "mountain slope." Jacob won this slope with his sword and bow. This reference is either to the city of Shechem itself or to the rich valley surrounding the city.

Genesis 49:1-27. These verses contain Jacob's blessing of his sons. Jacob praises Judah greatly and speaks of one who will take over leadership in Israel and secure the favor of the people (Genesis 49:8-12). Judah played an important role throughout the Joseph story. He advised his brothers to sell Joseph into slavery rather than killing him (Genesis 37:26). Judah also offered himself to Joseph as a replacement for Benjamin (Genesis 44).

Jacob's blessing also speaks in very positive terms about the tribe of Joseph, offering a large and glorious blessing from Jacob to this tribe (Genesis 49:22-26). Jacob's blessing of Joseph is beautiful poetry, but the Hebrew is especially difficult to translate. Since Joseph was the first-born son of Rachel, he is given a position of pre-eminence above the rest of Jacob's sons. In addition to his father's blessing, Joseph receives the blessing of God Almighty—a blessing that none of his brothers receive. Jacob's blessing for Joseph also blesses Ephraim and Manasseh, since the tribe of Joseph includes both of them.

The blessing neither criticizes nor praises Benjamin, calling him a ravenous wolf who devours the prey (Genesis 49:27). Jacob's blessing shows Benjamin's warlike qualities—qualities that could be good or bad, depending on their use.

Genesis 50:15-21. Joseph's brothers fear that Joseph will take revenge upon them after their father's death. They report a deathbed wish of their father that they heard, but that Joseph apparently did not hear. They say that their father asks Joseph to forgive them. And the brothers themselves ask for Joseph's forgiveness. Joseph forgives them.

Guilt plays a large part in this scene that takes place after Jacob's death. Here we realize that although the family is reunited, the brothers still feel guilty about what they have done. The first thing that occurs to them after Jacob's death is that Joseph might decide to pay his brothers back for what they did to him. But Joseph forgives them, and they fall down before him. Thus the Joseph story ends as his early dream foretold—with Joseph's brothers bowing down before him (Genesis 37:5-8).

DIMENSION THREE
WHAT DOES THE BIBLE MEAN TO ME?

The student book mentions three issues that call for our response. These issues are "Trusting in God's Promises,"

"The Importance of Possessions," and "Turning Evil Into Good." You will want to organize the class discussion around these three issues.

Genesis 46:1-4—Trusting in God's Promises

In Genesis 46:2-4, God reassures Jacob about going to Egypt. God's reassurance is an important theological point. The covenant is at stake. A move to Egypt would be a move away from the land that God promised Abraham, Isaac, Jacob, and their descendants. Only if God agrees to such a move is it safe for Jacob to leave Canaan. Isaac was forbidden to go to Mesopotamia to search for a wife; Abraham's servant did this for him. And Jacob went to Mesopotamia only because he had to escape from Esau.

God allows Jacob to remain in Egypt long after the famine ends, and he even allows Jacob to die in Egypt. Since Joseph has much to receive from Jacob—blessings upon his two sons—he can be counted on to get Jacob back to the land of Canaan.

The connection of the land of Canaan with the promise of God is of great importance for ancient Israel and also for contemporary Jews. Modern Jews still recognize their attachment to the land promised to their ancestors (Genesis 12:7, 17:8). Thus it is no small matter for Jacob to be leaving the land of Canaan for Egypt. God appears to him at Beersheba and authorizes a move that Pharaoh has commanded and that Joseph has prepared for.

Jacob wants nothing more than to see the face of the son he thought he had lost forever. But Jacob's priorities are in the correct order. First, he must receive word from the God of Abraham and Isaac that it is all right to leave the land of Canaan.

Ask the class members what they would do in Jacob's place. Jacob receives God's assurance after he offers sacrifices to God at Beersheba. But what if God had offered no assurance? Ask the class members, What would you do if you asked for, but did not receive, God's assurance?

Genesis 49:8-12—The Importance of Possessions

Jacob's blessing upon Judah (49:8-12) has a long history in the Christian community and later Jewish tradition. In this passage, later generations have found the promise of a king sent by God to bring the divine work on earth to its fulfillment. The messiah this passage promises does very earthly things. He establishes himself as a ruler and secures the allegiance and obedience of other nations.

The messiah's rule is marked by such prosperity that no one will want for anything. Judah will tether his donkey to the grapevine, letting the donkey eat all that he wants. After all, there are plenty more vines! Wine will be abundant and will be used even for the washing of clothes. Persons will have all the wine they wish. Because he will have food in abundance, the ruler will be handsome with dark eyes and white teeth. In short, the earth will have the food it needs, and no one will lack for anything.

The student book questions whether this picture of the future messianic age is too much tied to material blessings. Ask the class members if they think of the coming of the kingdom of God as a time when material possessions have such importance. Then guide the class into a general discussion of material possessions and the importance we attach to them.

If time allows, you might talk to the class about the importance of this passage in later Jewish tradition and in the Christian tradition. This is one of the oldest messianic passages in the entire Bible. In Genesis 49:8-12, we read for the first time about a coming ruler who will exercise a peaceful rule over a bountiful earth. The writer gives us a glowing picture of earthly fulfillment of divine promise. This promise lives on in Israelite tradition, and is modified and enlarged upon by later writers. The prophets Isaiah and Micah speak of a future king who is in the line of David, and whose coming means peace for Israel and for the nations. Later prophets carry this hope forward as Israel waits for the one who will crown her life with triumph. In Israel's future hope, God rules as acknowledged Lord and King. This messianic agent of God cooperates with God in establishing justice and peace over all the earth.

In the Christian community, the promise of this one called "Shiloh" (the one "to whom it belongs") is understood to have been fulfilled in Jesus of Nazareth. But Jesus' kingship is not marked by the public triumph of justice over injustice, by the end of warfare, or by bounty and plenty for all creatures. The Christian tradition finds fulfillment in this promise in a different way. The Messiah transforms the lives of human beings here and now. The Messiah invites persons into a new kind of communion with God and with one another. In this way, the world will move forward toward the day when the peace and plenty promised by God will appear for all to see.

Genesis 49:8-12 is, for Christians, both a future promise and a promise fulfilled. The fulfillment is real, for God calls into being the community of those transformed by the divine presence and power of Jesus Christ. This community has already experienced the fullness of life that God has promised. But more is to come—the world will know this glory. And we will see the community now living by faith become a community in which we recognize that God's promise of new life and blessing, truth and justice, are here to stay.

Genesis 50:15-21—Turning Evil Into Good

In these verses, we have one last look at Joseph and his brothers. After the death of Jacob, Joseph's brothers discuss their situation and consider how it may have changed after their father's death. Guilt overcomes them, and they now begin to worry about Joseph's revenge for what they have done to him in the past. As usual, Joseph appears as a person who is totally under the rule and guidance of God. Joseph says: "Don't be afraid. Am I in the place of God? You intended to harm me, but God intended it for good to accomplish what

is now being done, the saving of many lives" (50:19-20). Here Joseph reaffirms that God has directed all the past events in their lives. And God will continue to do so.

Given the picture of Joseph's brothers that we saw in the beginning of the Joseph story, we wonder whether they are telling the truth here. The brothers tell Joseph that Jacob, before he died, asked Joseph to forgive the brothers for what they did. Have the brothers made this story up in order to avoid Joseph's wrath? Ask the class members if they believe the brothers' story. Why or why not?

Joseph forgives his brothers. But—and this is the real question—can the brothers forgive themselves? According to our story, the brothers can forgive themselves when they realize that, although their motivation was not good, God turned their evil deed into something that benefited many people when the famine came to the land of Canaan. That is Joseph's message to his brothers in verse 20.

Ask the class members to think about situations in their lives that they thought were evil, but which God used to bring about good. Ask them to share these situations with the other members of the class. Then ask the class the question with which the student book closes: Can we say that God *always* brings good out of evil?

With this lesson on Genesis 46–50, we come to the close of our study of the Book of Genesis. We can now look back on this opening book of the Bible and see it as a storehouse of Israelite faith. From the creation of the universe to the death of Joseph, Genesis tells a story of faith. In Genesis we read about faith in a God who holds the entire world in his care and directs its affairs toward the appointed objective. God allows room for the free interplay of human activity, but still sees to it that the movement of the earth's people and of human history is in the direction of life and blessing.

The Genesis story tells of many setbacks. The world is not always necessarily better and better. But one thing is certain: God is the directing force in the world he has made, and all human activity is guided by God in subtle ways to further his objectives. Israel does not always know or understand God's objectives, and she does not always honor what she knows. But the covenant God remains with his people always—judging, coaxing, warning, guiding, loving, and forgiving. The end of the story is far ahead, but we have already learned that the One who leads Israel is both just and gracious, both powerful and gentle. God will not have his purposes set aside.

Close today's session by asking the class to list the insights they have gained from the study of Genesis 46–50. If time allows, list these insights on chalkboard or a large sheet of paper. At the end of the session, review what the class has learned from the past thirteen lessons. If time is too short in this class period, you might want to set aside time at a later date for reviewing the Book of Genesis.

EXODUS AND LEVITICUS
Table of Contents

About the Writer

Dr. Keith Schoville, the writer of these teacher book lessons, is professor emeritus in the Department of Hebrew and Semitic Studies at the University of Wisconsin-Madison. He is the author of *Biblical Archaeology in Focus*, an introduction to archaeology, and numerous articles in dictionaries and journals on archaeology and the biblical world.

Dr. Schoville has excavated at Tel Dan in northern Israel, Tel Lachish in the south-central region of the country, and Tel Aroer in the southern region. He is also president of the Near East Archaeology Society.

— 1 —

The Story of Moses

Exodus 1–5

DIMENSION ONE:
WHAT DOES THE BIBLE SAY?

Answer these questions by reading Exodus 1

1. What are the names of Jacob's sons who go with him into Egypt? (Exodus 1:1-3)

    Reuben, Simeon, Levi, Judah, Issachar, Zebulun, Benjamin, Dan, Naphtali, Gad, and Asher are the sons who go with him into Egypt.

2. Which of Jacob's sons does not go with him into Egypt? Why? (Exodus 1:5)

    Joseph is already in Egypt.

3. What do the Egyptians force the people of Israel to do? (Exodus 1:11, 14)

    The Egyptians force them to build store cities for Pharaoh and to work in the fields.

4. Why do the Egyptians come to dread the people of Israel? (Exodus 1:12)

    The people of Israel keep multiplying and spreading.

5. What command does the king of Egypt give to the Hebrew midwives? (Exodus 1:16)

    The king commands them to kill the baby boys of the Hebrews and to let the baby girls live.

6. Why do the midwives disobey the king of Egypt? (Exodus 1:17)

    The midwives fear God.

7. What command does the king of Egypt give to all his subjects? (Exodus 1:22)

He commands them to throw all the Hebrew baby boys into the Nile but to allow the baby girls to live.

Answer these questions by reading Exodus 2

8. To which tribe of the Israelites do the parents of the baby boy (Moses) belong? (Exodus 2:1-2)

    Moses' parents belong to the tribe of Levi.

9. How does the Levite woman attempt to save her son from death? (Exodus 2:3-4)

    She places him in a floating basket near the river's edge. She also has his sister keep watch at a distance.

10. Who nurses the baby boy for Pharaoh's daughter? (Exodus 2:8)

    The baby's mother nurses him.

11. Why does Moses kill the Egyptian? (Exodus 2:11-12)

    Moses kills the Egyptian because he is beating one of the Hebrews.

12. With what family does Moses dwell in Midian? (Exodus 2:16-21)

    Moses dwells with the family of the priest of Midian.

13. When God hears the groans of the people of Israel in their bondage, what does he do? (Exodus 2:24)

    He remembers his covenant with Abraham, Isaac, and Jacob.

Answer these questions by reading Exodus 3

14. Where does Moses lead the flock he is shepherding? (Exodus 3:1)

    He leads the flock to the far side of the desert—to Horeb, the mountain of God.

15. What makes the burning bush seem like a "strange sight" to Moses? (Exodus 3:2-3)

The bush is on fire, but it is not burning up.

16. Who does the Lord say he is? (Exodus 3:6)

The Lord says he is the God of Abraham, Isaac, and Jacob.

17. What name does God reveal to Moses at the place of the burning bush? (Exodus 3:14)

I AM.

18. What are the Hebrews to take with them when they leave Egypt, and where are they to get it? (Exodus 3:22)

The Hebrews are to take silver, gold, and clothing, which they receive from their (Egyptian) neighbors.

Answer these questions by reading Exodus 4

19. Moses wants proof that God has appeared to him. What three signs does God give him? (Exodus 4:2-9)

A staff that turns into a snake; Moses' hand, which God can turn leprous and then restore; and the power to change Nile water into blood when Moses pours it on dry ground.

20. What excuse does Moses give the Lord to avoid returning to Egypt? (Exodus 4:10-13)

Moses says he is slow of speech and tongue.

21. Who is Aaron? (Exodus 4:14)

Aaron is Moses' brother.

22. Who goes with Moses to Egypt? (Exodus 4:20)

Moses' wife and his sons go with him to Egypt.

23. What does Zipporah do when the Lord threatens Moses on the way back to Egypt? (Exodus 4:24-26)

Zipporah circumcises her son and touches the feet of Moses with the foreskin.

24. When Aaron speaks to the people of Israel, how do they respond? (Exodus 4:31)

They believe, bow down, and worship.

Answer these questions by reading Exodus 5

25. What is Pharaoh's response when Aaron and Moses ask him to let the people of Israel go? (Exodus 5:2)

Pharaoh says, "Who is the LORD, that I should obey him and let Israel go? I do not know the LORD and I will not let Israel go."

26. How does Pharaoh further oppress the people of Israel after Aaron and Moses visit him? (Exodus 5:6-8)

He requires the people to gather straw to make the bricks, which they had not done before, and still produce the same number of bricks each day as they had formerly done.

27. With what charge does Moses confront God after Pharaoh increases the burdens of the people of Israel? (Exodus 5:22-23)

Moses charges that God has not rescued his people at all.

DIMENSION TWO: WHAT DOES THE BIBLE MEAN?

Dimension Two attempts to discover what the Bible means. This meaning includes the originally intended meaning, the meaning of words and phrases within the passage, and the meaning given to the text by history and culture.

Background Information on Exodus

Exodus is the second of the five books of the Torah, the Law of Moses. These five books are also known as the Pentateuch. The English title of Exodus comes from the title used in the Septuagint and Vulgate versions of the Bible. The Hebrew title is "Names," the translation of *shemoth*, which is the most important word in the first sentence of the book. The Hebrews' way of naming a written work was in keeping with the ancient practice.

However, since the main theme of the book is the deliverance of the Hebrews from the bondage of Egypt, the Greeks chose the title "Exodus" rather than "Names." The Exodus was the most important event in the history of Israel. Jews remember it each year in the Feast of the Passover, just as Christians remember the resurrection of Jesus at Easter as the greatest event in history.

As with Genesis, some scholars think Exodus is the work of several authors. A careful reading of the English translation reveals variations in style and peculiar inconsistencies and breaks in the text. Differing traditions that come from different periods may explain these variations and inconsistencies.

We may also explain these peculiarities as the difference between the way ancient and biblical writings were produced and the way modern authors write. We should not judge ancient works by modern standards. We have no reason to doubt that much of Exodus contains authentic material from the time of Moses. Nor have we reason to doubt that later editors had a hand in shaping the book.

The inspiration of the book is not in question. We know of no time in which it was not considered the authoritative word of God. The biblical editors worked under divine guidance in the process that has given us the book as it is today.

Exodus was used in the liturgy of the Israelites. Since the book is a series of readings used in a religious setting, we can expect breaks in the text where one reading would end and another begin.

We can divide the book of Exodus into three main sections:

I. The Hebrews enslaved in Egypt and preparation for their deliverance (Chapters 1–12)
II. The Exodus and the journey to Mount Sinai (Chapters 13–18)
III. Israel at Mount Sinai (Chapters 19–40)

In Exodus 1–5, we find an introductory section that describes the Israelites' bondage in Egypt (Chapter 1), an account of the birth and infancy of Moses (Chapter 2), God's call of Moses (Chapters 3–4), and a narrative of the first encounter of Moses and Aaron with Pharaoh (Chapter 5).

Exodus 1:5. When Stephen mentions seventy-five family members who went down to Egypt in Acts 7:14, he is speaking to Jews from outside Palestine. These Jews were familiar with the Greek translation of the Bible called the Septuagint. In the Greek translation, the total of seventy-five family members resulted by including the three grandsons and two great-grandsons of Joseph in the total.

Exodus 1:7. Notice that the emphasis of this section is on the tremendous increase of Jacob's descendants from a mere seventy to a huge multitude. To persons in Bible times, many children were evidence of God's favor. This population explosion sets the stage for the enslavement of the Hebrews, for the cruel attempt of the Egyptians to limit the male Hebrew population, and for the birth of Moses. By limiting the number of males, the Egyptians could limit the number of men who might become warriors and fight against Egypt. (See Exodus 1:16.)

Exodus 2:1. Levi was the third son of Jacob and Leah. (See Genesis 29:34.) Levi joined his brother Simeon in a cruel act of vengeance against Shechem because he violated their sister Dinah. (See Genesis 34.) In his blessing, Jacob describes Simeon and Levi as violent and merciless. So their blessing becomes a curse. (See Genesis 49:5-7.)

The Levites later became priests in Israel. They never received a portion of the Promised Land as their territory. (See Joshua 13:14, 33.) They were assigned to the priesthood in place of each first-born Israelite male. (See Numbers 3:5-13.)

Exodus 2:1-10. The irony of the circumstances surrounding the way in which Moses came into the house of Pharaoh is amusing. Not only was Moses saved, but his mother became his nursemaid and received wages for raising him.

Exodus 3:6. Moses hides his face when he realizes that he is in the presence of Almighty God. Elijah acted similarly. (See 1 Kings 19:13.) No mortal eye is worthy to behold God. Exodus 33:20 tells us that no one may see God and live. Even the seraphim in Isaiah's vision covered their eyes in the presence of the Lord. (See Isaiah 6:2.)

Exodus 3:13-15. A name was more than an identifying label in the biblical world. A name expressed the basic character of the individual. As indicated in the student book, the name I AM reveals something of the character of God. He is the Eternal One. On one occasion Jesus referred directly to this name of God and associated it with himself. (See John 8:58.)

Exodus 3:17. God's promise is extraordinary. In the ancient world, a slave might escape bondage. However, if the slave was captured in a foreign country, he or she could be returned. Slaves might win freedom through an act of bravery on behalf of the master, or they might earn their freedom after a period of bondage. But for an entire people to be freed of slavery was unheard of. God's promise includes a complete reversal of circumstances for the Israelites. God promises that they will pass from the bitterness of bondage and poverty to the sweetness of freedom and plenty.

Exodus 3:21-22. We need to understand this "plundering" of the Egyptians in the light of Deuteronomy 15:12-15. There an owner is instructed to give liberally from his own property to the slave who is going out free after long years of service. The Israelites are to ask their neighbors for gifts in order to ensure that the parting will be in friendship and good will. Without these gifts, the Israelites would always remember the Egyptians as heartless enslavers. In Deuteronomy 23:7, the writer instructs the Israelites not to abhor the Egyptians.

DIMENSION THREE: WHAT DOES THE BIBLE MEAN TO ME?

The student book suggests four main themes as we apply the Scripture to our lives. They are "Dealing With Fear," "The Providence of God," "The Presence and Call of God," and "Dealing With Disappointment."

Exodus 1:1-22—Dealing With Fear

The problem of one segment of society fearing and mistreating another segment seems very modern. The new pharaoh did not know the Hebrew people. He and his close associates were not intimately acquainted with the Hebrews. All they knew about the Hebrews was that they were too numerous and that they could become a problem.

The Hebrews had been part of the Egyptian population for several generations before the new pharaoh came to power. In all that time they had not been considered a threat to the security of Egypt. But now they became suspect. They were no longer free and equal members of the society. The people in power did not attempt to know those whom they feared. They chose instead to oppress them.

Ask class members to think about current examples of oppression due to fear. Think in terms of our society or of social problems in foreign countries such as the problem of minority people from the old British Commonwealth who have migrated to England.

The student book suggests that love is the answer to problems of fear. What is love in practical terms? Consult 1 Corinthians 13. How can Christians keep the two great commandments Jesus taught in Matthew 22:36-40?

Exodus 2:1-25—The Providence of God

We will see the providential hand of God in later Scripture in this unit. The last section of Genesis contains the prophecy that God will bring his people into the land of promise. That land was occupied by other peoples. Only an army could conquer it. The multiplication of the Hebrews was God's method of enabling what was to follow.

Moses' mother took precautions for Moses' survival, but the hand of God brought him into the house of Pharaoh. In Moses' earliest years he was raised as a Hebrew. He also was reared as a prince in the royal household. Both of these elements contributed to his preparation as a leader of his people. Forced to flee Egypt, he became a desert man. That experience was to be vitally important for the survival of the Israelites in the desert.

Ask the group members to think of examples—in their own lives or in the lives of others—where they recognize the hand of God at work.

Exodus 3:1-12—The Presence and Call of God

Moses was about eighty years old when God called him for a special task. His life's experiences up to that time had prepared him for fulfilling God's purpose. Who contributed to Moses' preparation for his call and how? Can we identify persons who played a role in our becoming Christians? in our growth as Christians? Moses was a unique person called for a particular purpose. What does this mean for each of us as individuals? What does it mean in terms of God's purpose for our individual lives?

Exodus 5:4-23—Dealing With Disappointment

One way to deal with disappointment is to recognize that God is at work at times when we are unaware of it and in ways that we do not understand. Reread Exodus 2:23-25. God was aware of the plight of his people long before Moses and Aaron met with the elders of Israel. His providential hand had been at work in a number of ways behind the scene. The Hebrews simply were not aware of this. How can our study of the Bible help us deal with disappointment?

Close the session by asking the class members to reflect on the insights they have gained from their study of Exodus 1–5. You might want to have someone list these insights on chalkboard or a large sheet of paper. If you decide to use a sheet of paper and if you save each week's list, at the end of your study of Exodus and Leviticus you will have accumulated a handy summary of what your group has learned.

2

Moses and Pharaoh

Exodus 6–10

DIMENSION ONE:
WHAT DOES THE BIBLE SAY?

Answer these questions by reading Exodus 6

1. What does the Lord promise Moses that Pharaoh will do? (Exodus 6:1)

    He promises that Pharaoh will drive the people of Israel out of his land with a mighty hand.

2. By what name was the Lord known to Abraham, Isaac, and Jacob? (Exodus 6:3)

    The Lord was known as God Almighty.

3. What three things does the Lord promise to do for the people of Israel? (Exodus 6:6-8)

    He promises to bring them out from under the yoke of the Egyptians, to take them for his people, and to bring them into and give to them the land which he swore to give to Abraham, Isaac, and Jacob.

4. Why is Moses reluctant to go to the pharaoh again to tell him to let the people of Israel go? (Exodus 6:12)

    He is reluctant because the people of Israel have not listened to him.

5. What are the names of Aaron's wife and his sons? (Exodus 6:23)

    Elisheba is Aaron's wife. His sons are Nadab, Abihu, Eleazar, and Ithamar.

Answer these questions by reading Exodus 7

6. What effect will God's deliverance of the Israelites have on the Egyptians? (Exodus 7:5)

    The Egyptians will know that God is the Lord.

7. What miracle do Moses and Aaron perform for Pharaoh? (Exodus 7:8-10)

    Aaron casts down his staff, and it becomes a snake.

8. What does Aaron's staff do to the staffs of the Egyptians? (Exodus 7:12)

    Aaron's staff swallows the staffs of the Egyptians.

9. What is the nature of the first plague? (Exodus 7:17)

    The water of the Nile changes into blood.

10. How do the Egyptians suffer by this plague? (Exodus 7:18)

    The fish in the river die and make the water undrinkable.

11. What is Pharaoh's reaction to this plague? (Exodus 7:22-23)

    Pharaoh's heart becomes hard. He does not listen to Moses and Aaron, and he returns to his palace.

Answer these questions by reading Exodus 8

12. What is the nature of the second, third, and fourth plagues? (Exodus 8:2-21)

    They are plagues of frogs, gnats, and flies.

13. What do the magicians of Egypt say to Pharaoh when they are unable to duplicate the third plague? (Exodus 8:19)

    "This is the finger of God."

14. Why does the Lord keep the plague of flies away from the land of Goshen? (Exodus 8:22)

    God protects Goshen so that the Egyptians might know that God is the Lord and is present in the land.

15. Where will Pharaoh allow the Hebrews to sacrifice, and why might the Egyptians stone the people of Israel if they sacrifice to the Lord in Egypt? (Exodus 8:25-26)

He wants them to sacrifice within the land of Egypt. The Israelites might be stoned if they sacrifice things detestable to the Egyptians.

16. Where does Moses insist that the people of Israel go to sacrifice to the Lord? (Exodus 8:27)

Moses says that the people of Israel must go three days' journey into the desert to sacrifice.

Answer these questions by reading Exodus 9

17. What is the nature of the fifth plague? (Exodus 9:3)

It is a terrible plague on the livestock.

18. Why does Pharaoh send to see if any livestock of the Israelites died in the plague? (Exodus 9:4-7)

He sends to see because the Lord had promised that none of the Israelite livestock would die with the plague.

19. What is the nature of the sixth plague? (Exodus 9:9)

It is a plague of boils.

20. Why are the magicians of Egypt unable to stand before Moses this time? (Exodus 9:11)

They are unable to stand before Moses because the boils are on them as well as all the other Egyptians.

21. What is the purpose of the plagues? (Exodus 9:14)

The purpose is to teach the Egyptians that there is none like the Lord in all the earth.

22. Why does God not wipe the Egyptians off the earth? (Exodus 9:15-16)

God does not wipe the Egyptians off the earth so he can show them his power and so his name can be proclaimed in all the earth.

23. What is the nature of the seventh plague? (Exodus 9:18)

It is a plague of hail.

24. Where in Egypt does no hail fall? (Exodus 9:26)

No hail falls in the land of Goshen.

Answer these questions by reading Exodus 10

25. Why does the Lord harden Pharaoh's heart? (Exodus 10:1-2)

God hardens his heart so that (1) God might perform miraculous signs among the Egyptians, (2) the story of how God dealt harshly with the Egyptians might be told to Israelite descendants, and (3) Moses might know that God is the Lord.

26. What is the nature of the eighth plague? (Exodus 10:4)

It is a plague of locusts.

27. Why does Pharaoh let the people go to worship the Lord? (Exodus 10:7)

Pharaoh lets the people go because Egypt has been ruined for their sake.

28. What effect does the plague of locusts have upon Pharaoh? (Exodus 10:16-17)

Pharaoh confesses he has sinned against the Lord and asks Moses to forgive him and remove the plague from the land.

29. How does Moses end the locust plague? (Exodus 10:18-19)

Moses prays to the Lord, and the Lord brings a strong west wind that carries the locusts into the Red Sea.

30. What is the nature of the ninth plague? (Exodus 10:21)

Total darkness will spread over Egypt.

31. Why does Moses insist that the livestock go with the people of Israel to serve the Lord? (Exodus 10:26)

The livestock are to be used in worshiping the Lord, and the people would not know which to use until they got there.

DIMENSION TWO:
WHAT DOES THE BIBLE MEAN?

In this lesson on Exodus 6–10, we read about God's commissioning of Moses and Aaron (Exodus 6) and the first nine plagues on Pharaoh and the land of Egypt (Exodus 7–10). In order to help participants think of the nine plagues described in this lesson as real events, you might ask them to form small groups. Assign one or more of the plagues to each small group. Ask each group to discuss how the plague or plagues would have made them feel had they been living in Egypt at that time. Later, let each small group report its impressions to the entire group.

Exodus 6:1. Notice the connection between Exodus 5:22-23 and this verse. The chapter division should fall at the end of Exodus 5:21 rather than at 5:23. The division of the Bible into verses is relatively recent and is dated to about A.D. 900. The chapter divisions were apparently established a little later in the medieval period, in the thirteenth century. The original texts of the Old and New Testaments had no chapter and verse separations.

Exodus 6:2-3. This passage about the change of God's name has disturbed some readers through time. Yet, clearly the biblical writers were not bothered by the statement that God was known as *El Shaddai* (God Almighty) to the patriarchs and that he did not make himself known to them by the name *Yahweh* (Lord). The writers were sensible people, and they knew they had used the name *Yahweh* from Genesis 2 onward. In fact, they had used *Yahweh* more frequently than *El Shaddai*.

The most likely explanation for the new emphasis on the name *Yahweh*, which begins at this point, is that God now begins to reveal himself to the Israelites in a new way. From now on God begins to personally and actively deal with the descendants of Abraham to bring his promises to fulfillment. The name *God Almighty* spoke of a power that was recognized by Abraham and his descendants, but that power was not realized in redeeming acts of God. In Egypt, however, God sets events in motion that will fulfill his earlier promises. Yahweh means, "He who causes to be." (See Lesson 1 in the student book.) The change of name is quite appropriate for the new phase of God's relationship with the people of Israel.

Exodus 6:14-20. This partial genealogy repeats and expands upon the more complete listing of the tribes of Israel, which we read in Genesis 49. These verses only mention Reuben, Simeon, and Levi. (Compare Genesis 49:3-7.) These verses list the offspring of the three. Here the writer intends to get to Levi and ultimately to Aaron and Moses. Aaron and Moses, the two who speak to Pharaoh, are identified carefully by the genealogy.

The writer inserts this list of names into the account of events for a purpose, that is, to instruct those who will listen to the text being read. We find out in this way who Aaron and Moses are.

We pick up the story of Moses and the pharaoh in Exodus 6:28-30, which repeats the information given earlier in Exodus 6:10-13. Exodus is not a haphazard arrangement of various materials. It contains narratives, genealogies, and poetry; and each element plays its part in the whole story.

Exodus 7:17. Polytheism, the worship of many gods, assumes that many forces control the world. These forces are often manifestations of nature, and each of them is worshiped as a separate god. The Egyptians worshiped the Nile River since it was the source of all their food, providing fish for food, as well as water for their crops. Rain is practically unknown in most of Egypt. As Exodus 5:2 suggests, the pharaoh probably regarded the Lord as a god, but only as a previously unknown and minor god—much less powerful than the others. Moses' miracles dispel this notion by showing the Lord's power over what were really only parts of his creation.

Exodus 8:6-8. Although the Egyptian magicians also made frogs, the fact that Pharaoh has to call on Moses to remove them shows that his magicians are unable to do so. Perhaps Moses' ability impresses Pharaoh, although he does not keep his promise to let the people go.

Exodus 8:18-19. The magicians' remark implies that God has hindered their efforts so that they can do no more miracles. They attempt no further miracles.

Exodus 9:16. As this verse shows, God has always intended that all nations come to believe in him, even though large-scale evangelistic efforts were not begun until New Testament times.

Exodus 10:21-22. This plague again demonstrates the Lord's power over Egyptian gods. The sun was one of the most important gods of Egypt. Its name was Ra. Ra was later worshiped as the *aton*, or sun disk. Since the skies of Egypt are seldom cloudy, the sun was a prominent feature in the sky from morning until night. The benevolent rays of the sun were adored by the Egyptians. The fact that all of Egypt was in darkness while the Israelites had light emphasized the power of the true God in contrast to the Egyptian sun god. Christians may remember that Jesus said, "I am the light of the world. Whoever follows me will never walk in darkness, but will have the light of life" (John 8:12).

DIMENSION THREE: WHAT DOES THE BIBLE MEAN TO ME?

According to the student book, Exodus 6–10 offers two main ideas for discussion. These ideas are "The Significance of Names" and "The Power of God to Redeem." You may discuss either or both as time allows.

Exodus 6:2-8—The Significance of Names

Some evidence suggests that we are living today in a post-Christian world. In countries such as England, France, and the United States, the trend is away from belief in God and the moral life as taught in the Scriptures. In place of the traditional Judeo-Christian view of life, more and more people are satisfied to ignore God and to live completely secular lives. Some parents name their children after currently popular heroes of the mass media. Others, including earlier generations, give their children biblical names.

In discussing this trend, use the following questions as discussion starters:

1. Should Christian parents be encouraged to use biblical names for their children? Why or why not?

2. How might giving a child a biblical name later influence that child toward the Lord?

3. Every believer is a child of God and bears the name Christian. This name is as important as his or her own personal name. How can the honor of that name be built up so that the secular world respects it more? Is it important for Christians to work toward this end? Why or why not?

4. In what ways do Christians sometimes alienate themselves from the secular world?

5. What might Christians do or say to bring the secular world and Christianity together? (This question may be phrased in terms of the individual, the group, or the church.)

Exodus 9:13-16—The Power of God to Redeem

One problem people struggle with in our modern society is the inability to recognize the power of God at work in the world. Our world is complicated by technical developments. These developments can obscure God and elevate humanity. Scientific discoveries tend to overlook the Creator and to magnify human discoverers. Yet the Christian worldview is that God is the creator and sustainer of the universe. Christians and others who seek truth need to recover a biblical understanding of how God manifests his power.

The nine plagues presented in this lesson gave examples of God at work in a miraculous way. But the miraculous element was not completely supernatural. The psalmist tells that "the earth is the LORD's and everything in it" (Psalm 24:1). So God's power is often at work, even in miracles, within the natural laws. To discuss this idea of God's working within natural laws, consider the following:

1. When Aaron cast down his staff, it became a snake. This action was surely a miracle, but the staff became a natural creature rather than something never before seen upon the earth.

2. The Nile turned to blood—an extraordinary event. But both the people of Israel and the Egyptians were familiar with blood. They also were familiar with frogs, gnats, flies, disease among livestock, and boils. Hail was not common in Egypt, but it was a known natural event.

3. The stroke of Aaron's staff turned dust into gnats—an impossible feat for a man, but simple enough for God who created humankind from dust.

4. Locusts were well known in Egypt, both before and after the plague. The locusts arrived on an east wind and were carried away on a strong west wind. These winds were natural movements of the air.

The miraculous part of these plagues was that they occurred at the word of Moses and the actions of Aaron. Moses and Aaron acted at the word of God. But no Egyptians or Israelites had at any time seen God or heard his voice, except Moses and Aaron. The people knew only that they had experienced great difficulties over which they had no control. Only at the word of Moses did they know and understand that God existed and was at work in the world to accomplish his will.

How can we become more aware of God's personal blessings in our lives? Paul exhorted the Christians in Ephesus to live "for the praise of his glory," because that was God's purpose for them. (See Ephesians 1:12.) He told another group of Christians that as "grace . . . is reaching more and more people [it] may cause thanksgiving to overflow to the glory of God" (2 Corinthians 4:15).

Ask the class members to suggest ways we can become more aware of blessings in our lives. Do they see a connection between awareness and an increase in thanksgiving to God? How effective would expressions of thanksgiving to God in the presence of friends and associates be in helping them become aware of God? How can we help a secular world become more aware of God in a post-Christian age?

Close the session by listing on chalkboard or a large sheet of paper any new insights the class members have gained from their study of Exodus 6–10.

3

Passover and Exodus From Egypt

Exodus 11–14

DIMENSION ONE:
WHAT DOES THE BIBLE SAY?

Answer these questions by reading Exodus 11

1. What is the tenth and final plague? (Exodus 11:4-5)

   Every first-born Egyptian son and the first-born of the cattle will die.

2. Who will ask Moses and the people of Israel to leave Egypt? (Exodus 11:8)

   All of Pharaoh's government officials will ask Moses and the people of Israel to leave Egypt.

Answer these questions by reading Exodus 12

3. When is the community of Israel to select the lamb for the Passover? (Exodus 12:2-3)

   The selection is on the tenth day of the first month.

4. Who is to choose the lamb for a household? (Exodus 12:3)

   The man of the household chooses the lamb.

5. To be accepted for the Passover, what characteristics must a lamb have? (Exodus 12:5)

   The Passover lamb is to be a year old, without defect, and either a sheep or a goat.

6. What four things are the people to do as they eat the Passover meal? (Exodus 12:11)

   The people are to (1) tuck their cloak into their belt, (2) put sandals on their feet, (3) have a staff in their hands, and (4) eat in haste.

7. Why does God instruct the Israelites to put some of the blood of the Passover lamb on the sides and tops of their doorframes? (Exodus 12:7, 12-13)

   The blood will be a sign on the door so that the Lord will pass over the marked houses when he comes to slay the first-born sons and animals of Egypt.

8. Why does God instruct Israel to keep the Passover feast generation after generation? (Exodus 12:14)

   The Passover feast is to be a "festival to the LORD—a lasting ordinance."

9. What are the Hebrews to remember when they observe the Passover? (Exodus 12:17)

   The people are to remember that the Lord brought them out of the land of Egypt when they had the Feast of Unleavened Bread.

10. At the time of the Passover each year, how might an Israelite be cut off from Israel? (Exodus 12:15, 19)

    An Israelite can be cut off from Israel by eating anything made with yeast during the seven days of Passover.

11. How many days is the Feast of Unleavened Bread to last? (Exodus 12:15, 19)

    The Feast of Unleavened Bread lasts seven days.

12. In later generations when the Passover is kept and children ask what it means, what is the correct answer? (Exodus 12:27)

    "It is the Passover sacrifice to the LORD, who passed over the houses of the Israelites in Egypt and spared our homes when he struck down the Egyptians."

13. How does Pharaoh respond to the tenth plague? (Exodus 12:31-32)

    Pharaoh summons Moses and Aaron in the night and tells them to go worship the Lord with their people, their flocks, and their herds.

14. Who joins the people of Israel in the Exodus? (Exodus 12:38)

Many non-Hebrews join the people of Israel in the Exodus.

15. What does God require of a non-Israelite who wants to keep the Passover? (Exodus 12:48)

God requires that all alien males who want to keep the Passover be circumcised.

Answer these questions by reading Exodus 13

16. Of the males born in Israel, which are to be consecrated to the Lord? (Exodus 13:2)

All first-born males, whether human or animal, are to be consecrated to the Lord.

17. When does the Exodus begin? (Exodus 13:4)

The Exodus begins on the fourteenth day of the month of Abib.

18. Why are the first-born special to the Lord? (Exodus 13:15)

The first-born are special to the Lord because the Lord had slain all the first-born of Egypt when Pharaoh refused to let the people of Israel go.

19. Why does God not lead the people by way of the land of the Philistines? (Exodus 13:17)

God knows they will encounter war if they go that way, and the people of Israel will then return discouraged to Egypt.

20. Why does Moses take the bones of Joseph with him? (Exodus 13:19)

Moses takes Joseph's bones with him because Joseph had made the people of Israel vow to take his bones with them when they left Egypt.

21. How does God guide the people of Israel along the way? (Exodus 13:21)

The Lord guides in a pillar of cloud by day and a pillar of fire by night.

Answer these questions by reading Exodus 14

22. Why does the Lord want Pharaoh to think the people are trapped in the desert? (Exodus 14:3-4)

God wants the opportunity to gain glory over Pharaoh and all his army and to make them know he is the Lord.

23. What does Pharaoh do when he realizes the people have fled? (Exodus 14:5-8)

He changes his mind about letting them go and pursues them with his army.

24. Where are the people of Israel when Pharaoh overtakes them? (Exodus 14:9)

They are encamped at the sea by Pi Hahiroth, in front of Baal Zephon.

25. When the people see the approaching Egyptian army, what do they think will happen to them? (Exodus 14:11)

They think they will die in the desert.

26. What two things does Moses promise the frightened people? (Exodus 14:13)

(1) They will see the deliverance the Lord will bring them, and (2) they will never see the Egyptians again.

27. How does God prevent the Egyptians from overtaking the people of Israel? (Exodus 14:19-20)

The pillar of cloud moves between the Israelites and the Egyptians, bringing darkness to the Egyptians.

28. When Moses stretches his hand over the sea, how does the Lord divide the waters? (Exodus 14:21)

The Lord divides the sea with a strong east wind that blows all night.

29. How does the Lord slow the Egyptians as they pursue the Israelites into the sea? (Exodus 14:24-25)

The Lord slows the Egyptians by causing the wheels of their chariots to fall off so that they drive with difficulty.

30. Who dies in the sea? (Exodus 14:28)

The horsemen and all the army of Pharaoh who followed the Israelites into the sea die in the sea.

31. What effect does the miracle at the sea have on the people of Israel? (Exodus 14:31)

They fear the Lord, and they put their trust in the Lord and in his servant, Moses.

DIMENSION TWO: WHAT DOES THE BIBLE MEAN?

The Scripture for this lesson can be divided into three parts: (1) the narrative of the final plague (Chapter 11),

(2) the description of the first Passover (Chapters 12–13), and (3) the account of God's deliverance of the Israelites at the Red Sea (Chapter 14).

Exodus 11:4-6. The Lord's slaying of the first-born requires further explanation. In the biblical world, the first-born male was considered special. He was "the first sign" of his father's strength and evidence of both his physical and sexual power. (See Genesis 49:3.) The first-born, by right, inherited twice as much as every other son. (See Deuteronomy 21:17.) He ranked highest in the family after his father; and in the father's absence, he had authority over his younger brothers and sisters. (See Genesis 27:1-4.) The first-born of a king had the right to succeed his father on the throne.

This plague was a severe blow to Egypt, touching virtually every household. We must remember that it came only after a series of much less severe plagues had failed to convince Pharaoh to let God's people go. In Exodus 4:22 God instructs Moses to tell Pharaoh to let Israel go because Israel was the Lord's first-born son. Apparently the patience of God, the Creator, can be worn thin by rebellious persons such as the pharaoh.

Exodus 12:14-27. This passage mentions two separate feasts. The Passover Feast is connected with shepherding, while the Feast of Unleavened Bread is associated with agriculture. The Israelites were probably both shepherds and farmers, as well as forced laborers on Pharaoh's construction projects. The Feast of Unleavened Bread was probably not kept by Israel until after the conquest of Canaan, because the people lived a seminomadic life that was not connected with growing crops. Verse 19 also mentions removing the leaven from "your houses," rather than tents. The Israelites only began to live in houses in the land of Canaan after the conquest.

An alien, mentioned in verse 19, is someone who lives among another people, rather than a stranger who is unknown and only passing through. An alien could observe the feast if he were circumcised. A stranger who became an alien could also be circumcised and then participate in the feast. (See Exodus 12:48-49.) In this way, outsiders became a part of Israel.

Exodus 12:36. The plundering of the Egyptians was discussed earlier in connection with Exodus 3:21-22. This plundering was simply another way the Lord gained glory over Pharaoh. The silver and gold would be used later in the construction of the tabernacle.

Exodus 12:37-38. The huge number of people who went forth in the Exodus poses a problem. Adding a reasonable number of women and children and the "many other people" could bring the total to between two and three million. While not impossible, the number is not probable. Archaeological research indicates that the population at the time of the Canaanites was considerably less. Yet, Deu-

teronomy 7:7, 17, and 22 indicate that the Israelites were fewer in number than the Canaanites.

Apart from accepting the large number by faith as an example that "nothing is impossible with God" (see Luke 1:37), a reasonable explanation is that the large number was simply the writer's way of emphasizing the miraculous increase of Israel's descendants in Egypt. (See Lesson 1, Exodus 1.)

No one knows the actual number of people who left Egypt with Moses. The exact number is not nearly as important as the Exodus itself. The Exodus was the first and only time in recorded history when a large group of slaves left their master *en masse*. The biblical writers attribute the Exodus to God and Moses.

Exodus 12:40-41. The length of time that the Israelites spent in Egypt is much disputed. However, the traditional dating of the Exodus is about 1450 B.C.

Exodus 13:18. The Hebrew words *yam suph* are translated as Red Sea in the New International Version. Although its location is uncertain, this sea was probably in the Bitter Lakes region north of the present-day city of Suez and near the places named in the Bible. The marshy crossing was near the Desert of Shur, which the Israelites entered after the crossing. (See Exodus 15:22.)

Exodus 14:7. Pharaoh's army included over six hundred chariots. We know from other ancient historical records that this was a reasonable number. Many centuries later, King Ahab provided two thousand chariots for a battle against the Assyrians.

DIMENSION THREE:
WHAT DOES THE BIBLE MEAN TO ME?

Exodus 11–14 raises two issues that are relevant to our lives. These issues are "The Feast of Remembrance" and "The Problem of Faith."

Exodus 12:21-27—The Feast of Remembrance

Dimension Three in the student book draws attention to some of the connections between the Communion that Christians observe and the Passover that Jews keep. To prepare for the class discussion, use a Bible dictionary or encyclopedia for further information on both the Passover and the Lord's Supper.

The following ideas may add to the group discussion.

1. The Passover is an important point of contact between Christians and Jews. The spiritual roots of our faith reach back into Judaism, yet we are often unaware of these connections. Some Christians are ashamed of our spiritual roots and others simply ignore them. As Christians we may be guilty of having an anti-Jewish bias. What is a proper Christian attitude toward the Jewish faith?

2. Those who celebrated the Passover had to identify with the community of faith, the people of Israel. Males were required to be circumcised. Those who participated identified with the first Passover and with the Exodus. (See Exodus 12:26-27.) They saw themselves as participants in these events. The proper response to the question of the child who asked, "What do you mean by this service?" included the statement, he "spared *our* houses when he struck down the Egyptians" (italics added).

Who may participate in the Lord's Supper? How does an outsider become part of the community that keeps the Christian feast of remembrance? How can Communion become more meaningful personally?

Exodus 14:30-31—The Problem of Faith

The group may want to consider the way in which the people of Israel developed faith in the Lord. Exodus 14:31 records that the people finally "put their trust in [the Lord] and in Moses his servant." The New Revised Standard Version uses the word *faith* for *trust* in this verse. How did this trust/faith develop? It grew out of the long series of plagues.

You may wonder why the Lord took so long in bringing Pharaoh to the point of permitting the Israelites to leave Egypt. This time span allowed for a cumulative effect of the plagues, each one a little worse than the preceding one. Then with the death of the first-born males, Pharaoh was forced to let the people go. But the Lord could have forced Pharaoh to free Israel with Moses' first appearance. We do not know why he did not, but clearly the people of Israel had no faith in the Lord or in Moses at the beginning. Moses even had to explain to them who God was.

Moses came to his people with a report of God's appearance to him and the task that God had given to him. But the people had never heard God speak or seen him. Moses' first appearance before Pharaoh resulted in increased labor for the people of Israel. As each of the plagues came,

faith must have stirred in the Israelites, but still none of them had heard God speak nor had they seen him.

Even at the sea only Moses heard the Lord. The people depended upon Moses to report what God said. They heard of the death of the first-born in Egypt, while their own first-born lived. At the sea when Pharaoh's army approached, they saw a cloud come between them and the Egyptians, but at no time did they see God or hear his voice. They only heard the report from Moses.

At the command of Moses they crossed the sea on dry land. Even on the far side, when the sea returned to its bed, they had not seen God nor heard his voice. They had only heard Moses tell them what the Lord had said. But they knew they had been saved from their enemies.

The faith of the Israelites grew as they came to accept Moses' testimony about God, and as they experienced God's actions on their behalf. Israel did not suddenly believe in the Lord the first time Moses appeared in the land of Goshen. Israel's faith grew as the Israelites accepted the testimony and saw the works over a period of time.

Ask class members to discuss how our faith in God begins and grows today. (Consult John 17:20-21; Romans 10:17; 1 Thessalonians 2:13-15.) God moved in a miraculous way in the events leading to the Exodus, but his activities are not normally that spectacular. How may we increase our awareness of God's activities on our behalf today? As a Christian, when you are aware of something God has done for you, should you refrain from telling others or should you share it freely? Why or why not?

The story of the Exodus from Egypt illustrates the problem of faith. Ask the group to think of what this illustration means for winning people to Christ, for interesting others in this Bible study, or for helping the despondent. Encourage the class members to share their ideas in the group.

Close the session by asking the group members to share insights they have received from studying Exodus 11–14. List these insights on chalkboard or a sheet of paper.

4

The Desert Journey

Exodus 15–18

DIMENSION ONE: WHAT DOES THE BIBLE SAY?

Answer these questions by reading Exodus 15

1. To whom do Moses and the people of Israel sing this song? (Exodus 15:1)

   They sing to the Lord.

2. Why do the singers sing? (Exodus 15:2)

   They sing to praise and exalt the Lord.

3. How does the song describe the strong east wind that Exodus 14:21 mentions? (Exodus 15:8)

   The song describes the wind as a blast from the nostrils of the Lord.

4. What were the Egyptians thinking as they pursued Israel into the sea? (Exodus 15:9)

   "I will pursue, I will overtake them, / I will divide the spoils; / I will gorge myself on them. / I will draw my sword / and my hand will destroy them."

5. In what three ways do the people describe the Lord? (Exodus 15:11)

   The Lord is (1) majestic in holiness, (2) awesome in glory, and (3) working wonders.

6. What does the song promise that the Lord will do for his people in the future? (Exodus 15:17)

   The Lord will bring them in and plant them on the mountain where God established a sanctuary.

7. When Miriam takes a tambourine in her hand, what do all the women do? (Exodus 15:20)

   The women follow her, playing tambourines and dancing.

8. How long do the Israelites travel in the desert without water? (Exodus 15:22)

   They travel for three days without water.

9. Why do they name the place Marah? (Exodus 15:23)

   The waters are bitter at that place, and the word marah *means bitter.*

10. What three steps does Moses follow to turn the bitter waters sweet? (Exodus 15:25)

    He cries to the Lord. Then he takes the piece of wood the Lord shows him, and he casts it into the water. Then the water becomes sweet.

Answer these questions by reading Exodus 16

11. Why do the people of Israel grumble against Moses and Aaron in the Desert of Sin? (Exodus 16:3)

    They grumble against them because they thought that Aaron and Moses brought them into the desert to die of hunger.

12. Why does the Lord promise to bring bread from heaven to the hungry Israelites? (Exodus 16:4)

    He promises to do so in order to test whether the people will follow his instructions.

13. When the people grumble against Moses and Aaron, who are they really grumbling against? (Exodus 16:6-8)

    They are grumbling against the Lord.

14. How much of the bread from heaven is each Israelite to gather each morning? (Exodus 16:16)

    Each Israelite is to gather about an omer for each person in his tent.

15. Why does Moses become angry with some of the people? (Exodus 16:19-20)

He is angry because some of the people keep the manna overnight against his instructions, and it breeds maggots and begins to smell.

16. Why are the people who go out to gather bread on the morning of the seventh day disappointed? (Exodus 16:23-27)

They are disappointed because they find no manna.

17. Where does Moses tell Aaron to place the omer of manna? (Exodus 16:33-34)

Aaron is to put the manna in a jar and place it before the Lord.

18. When do the people of Israel stop eating manna? (Exodus 16:35)

They stop eating manna after forty years in the desert, when they come to the border of the land of Canaan.

Answer these questions by reading Exodus 17

19. What do the people grumble about at Rephidim? (Exodus 17:3)

They complain because there is no water to drink.

20. Why does Moses strike the rock at Horeb? (Exodus 17:6)

Moses strikes the rock at Horeb so that water could come out of it for the people to drink.

21. Why does Moses change the name of the rock to Massah and Meribah? (Exodus 17:7)

Moses changes the rock's name because the people quarreled and put the Lord to the test.

22. Who leads the Israelite men in their first battle against an enemy? Who is the enemy, and where does the battle take place? (Exodus 17:8-10)

Joshua leads the Israelites in their first battle. The enemy is the Amalekites, and the battle takes place at Rephidim.

23. What do Aaron and Hur do? (Exodus 17:12)

They hold up Moses' hands during the battle.

THE DESERT JOURNEY

24. What three things does Moses do to keep alive the memory of the battle with Amalek? (Exodus 17:14-15)

Moses keeps the memory of the battle alive by (1) writing the story in a book, (2) reciting the event to Joshua, and (3) building an altar.

Answer these questions by reading Exodus 18

25. Why does Jethro come to visit Moses? (Exodus 18:1)

Jethro comes to visit Moses because he hears how the Lord brought Israel out of Egypt.

26. Where is Moses when Jethro brings Zipporah and her sons to him? (Exodus 18:5)

Moses is encamped in the desert before the mountain of God.

27. How does Jethro express his faith in the Lord? (Exodus 18:12)

Jethro offers a burnt offering and other sacrifices to God and eats with the leaders of Israel.

28. Why does Jethro object to the way Moses judges the people? (Exodus 18:17-18)

Jethro thinks that Moses will wear out both himself and the people.

29. What kind of men should help Moses judge the Israelites? (Exodus 18:21)

Capable men who fear God, who are trustworthy, and who hate dishonest gain should help Moses judge.

30. In Jethro's plan, what are Moses' responsibilities? (Exodus 18:22)

Moses will judge only the difficult cases.

DIMENSION TWO: WHAT DOES THE BIBLE MEAN?

We can divide this lesson into two main parts: (1) A song of thanksgiving and praise after the crossing of the sea, and (2) The story of the journey through the desert to Sinai. Two types of literature appear in this Scripture. The song is written as poetry, and the account of the journey is written as historical narrative.

Exodus 15:1-18. The basic pattern of Hebrew poetry is parallelism. Notice the last half of verse 2:

He is my God, and I will praise him,
my father's God, and I will exalt him.

The ideas expressed in the two lines are almost exactly the same. The two lines are an example of synonymous parallelism. We can see other examples of this type of parallelism in verses 4, 5, and 6.

A second type is called antithetic parallelism. In this type, the first line states a theme, and the second line states the opposite. The song of Moses has no examples of antithetic parallelism, but some examples from Psalms and Proverbs follow:

For the LORD watches over the way of the righteous,
but the way of the wicked will perish. (Psalm 1:6)

A truthful witness does not deceive,
but a false witness pours out lies. (Proverbs 14:5)

A third type of parallelism is called synthetic. In this type the first line states an idea, then the next adds to it. The student book mentions verse 8 as an example, although it does not use the expression, "synthetic parallelism." Verse 9 provides another example. By looking closely at many of the psalms, you can distinguish these types of parallelism.

The first section of the poem (Exodus 15:1-12) pictures the Lord as a victorious warrior. This idea was expressed earlier in the words of Moses (Exodus 14:14) and in the words of the Egyptians in the midst of the sea (Exodus 14:25).

The second section of the poem (Exodus 15:13-18) tells of events after the crossing of the sea. The poet sees the people of Israel guided in the desert by the Lord. The people of Philistia (along the coast of the Mediterranean Sea), Edom (northeast of Sinai), Moab (in Trans-Jordan, east of the Dead Sea), and Canaan stood in the way of Israel's possession of the Promised Land. The mountain (verse 17) and sanctuary of the Lord probably refer to all the land of Canaan, since Israel later conquered and occupied the hilly part of that area.

Exodus 15:20-21. The writer calls Miriam a prophetess. This title is probably due to the song she sang in the fervor of the moment. First Samuel 10:5 associates song with prophecy. In other books of this Bible study series, you can meet other important women, such as the judge, Deborah.

Exodus 15:23. The name of this place reflects a characteristic of the water. Several other examples of names that reflect characteristics of an individual or a place or an event appear in our lesson. One of the names of the Lord is healer. (See 15:26.) Also notice the names of Massah and Meribah that mean "testing" and "quarreling." (See 17:7.) The names of the two sons of Moses, Gershom and Eliezer, are meaningful. (See 18:3-4.)

Exodus 16:33-36. The tradition of placing a jar of manna in the ark of the covenant ("the Testimony") begins as a direct quotation, "Take a jar and put an omer of manna in it. Then place it before the LORD to be kept for the generations to come." This command is followed by a historical note that speaks of Moses and Aaron in the third person. This third-person historical note suggests that the present tradition was instituted by someone other than Moses.

Exodus 17:8-13. As nomads, the Amalekites continued to raid Israel long after Israel had occupied Canaan. In this instance, Joshua defeats Amalek. A year later, after the Israelites refused to go into the Promised Land, they were defeated by Amalek at Hormah. (See Numbers 14:45.)

The Amalekites gave Israel trouble from time to time during the period of the judges. Samuel commanded Saul to totally destroy the Amalekites, but Saul failed to follow orders. (See 1 Samuel 15.) David fought the Amalekites. (See 1 Samuel 27:8; 30:1-20.) And in the days of the prophet Isaiah and of King Hezekiah, a force from Judah attacked a remnant of the Amalekites in the Trans-Jordan. (See 1 Chronicles 4:43.)

Exodus 18:27. The Midianites were descended from Abraham through Keturah. (See Genesis 25:1-6.) Jethro returns to Midian. Jethro was not the last contact Israel had with the region of Midian. Later Moses asked his Midianite brother-in-law, Hobab, to guide Israel through the desert. (See Numbers 10:29-32.) A short time later the Midianites began to oppose Israel. (See Numbers 22 and following.) Camel-riding Midianites became a threat to Israel in the period of the judges, but Gideon and his small band saved Israel. (See Judges 6–8.) The Midianites continue to crop up even later in Israel's history, but always as a minor enemy.

Finally, it is interesting to notice that Israel met two desert peoples shortly after the Exodus. The Amalekites fought with Israel; the Midianites ate with Israel. But in the course of time both of these groups dropped out of history while Israel continued on until the Exile. Even after the Babylonian experience, the Jews, descendants of the Israelites, continued on in history.

DIMENSION THREE:
WHAT DOES THE BIBLE MEAN TO ME?

The student book gives two possible emphases for this lesson. They are "Thanksgiving," and "Giving and Receiving Advice." Both emphases are worthy of thought, but the importance of giving thanks, both to God and to people, seems more significant.

Exodus 15:1-18—Thanksgiving

You might begin the discussion by asking if anyone in the group has ever done something for someone and received no word of thanks or acknowledgment of the favor. Most of us have had this experience from time to time. Ask these questions: How do you feel in this situation? Do we tend to change our attitude toward an individual who is ungrateful?

Another approach to thinking about gratitude is to ask if anyone in the group has ever felt especially happy after receiving a word of thanks or praise. Encourage group members to share such experiences with one another.

Now, lead the group into a discussion of how Israel expressed thanks to God for their miraculous delivery from the Egyptian threat. Emphasize that true thanksgiving is expressed in spoken words. The unspoken thought is not thanksgiving.

Draw attention to the content of praise and thanksgiving. The people sang to the Lord; yet they recounted what the Lord had done. They were certainly not telling him something of which he was unaware. Thanksgiving and praise then, describe to someone else a favor that he or she has done for you. But the description is stated in your own words.

The student book draws attention to two Scripture references on thanksgiving. You may want to use your concordance to find additional statements on this theme. Perhaps you could use the concordance in the group, giving a visible example of the usefulness of this Bible study tool. Look at these verses, and explore the ideas about thanksgiving. Notice that Christians are to give thanks in everything. (See Philippians 4:4-7.)

The student book instructs the group members to list three things for which they can personally give thanks to the Lord. Give everyone an opportunity to express thanks to God for one of the items on his or her list.

To complete the discussion on thanksgiving, have everyone read 2 Corinthians 4:15. In the time remaining, think together of how an increase in thanksgiving can bring glory to God.

Exodus 18:13-27—Giving and Receiving Advice

The student book asks the participants to analyze Exodus 18:13-27, which deals with Jethro's advice to Moses. Begin the discussion by asking how many of the group have ever received good advice that they never requested. Some humorous (or serious) examples may surface. If not, be prepared with an example from your own experience.

Then discuss the questions suggested in the student book. Move on to discuss how they might be able to improve their abilities to both give and receive advice based upon the examples of Moses and Jethro.

Probe the question, "As a Christian, should I give advice to others?" Do we have a responsibility to offer advice to friends and younger acquaintances? Discuss Titus 2:3-4, which talks about the role of older women as counselors. How does Philippians 2:4 offer some guidance about giving and receiving advice?

Exodus 16:1-8—Grumbling

The student book does not mention this subject, but you may wish to bring it to the group's attention. The text mentions grumbling in 15:24; then in 16:2-3; 16:6-12; and 17:2-3. The grumbling of Israel began in 14:11-12, a text in Lesson 3. We will meet this theme many times in the story of Israel's desert journey.

The grumbling began when the Israelites saw the approaching Egyptians and feared for their lives. After the miraculous crossing of the sea and the singing of the song, only three days later they grumbled because of thirst. Later hunger sparked the grumbling, then thirst again. Several times the people wanted to go back to Egypt. Why? Was it because these slaves could not imagine the goal of freedom in the land of promise? Or was it a lack of faith that the goal could be reached, even though they understood the promises of God to their fathers? Were they so concerned with material comforts that they were unwilling to suffer discomfort and inconvenience to attain the goal?

Ask each person to examine himself or herself. Is anyone a grumbler? What effect can grumbling have upon the church? How can the tendency to grumble and quarrel be stopped? How can a positive attitude of trust and support for church leaders be developed? What can each of us do to hinder grumbling?

Close the session with a prayer of thanksgiving to the Lord for the lessons learned from this study. You might also want to list on chalkboard or a large piece of paper any insights the class members have gained from their study of Exodus 15–18.

5

The Covenant at Sinai

Exodus 19–20

DIMENSION ONE:
WHAT DOES THE BIBLE SAY?

Answer these questions by reading Exodus 19

1. Where in the Desert of Sinai do the people of Israel encamp? (Exodus 19:2)

   The people encamp in front of the mountain.

2. What does God command Moses to tell the people of Israel? (Exodus 19:4)

   God carried them on eagles' wings and brought them to himself.

3. What does God ask the people to do so that they will be his own possession among all peoples? (Exodus 19:5)

   God asks the people to obey him fully and to keep his covenant.

4. How will the children of Israel be special to the Lord? (Exodus 19:6)

   The people will be a kingdom of priests and a holy nation.

5. How do the people respond when Moses reports what the Lord said? (Exodus 19:8)

   The people say, "We will do everything the LORD has said."

6. Why does God plan to come to Moses in a dense cloud? (Exodus 19:9)

   God will appear in a dense cloud so the people will hear when God speaks to Moses, and so they will put their trust in Moses forever.

7. How are the people to prepare for the coming of the Lord on Mount Sinai? (Exodus 19:10)

   Moses is to consecrate the people by having them wash their clothes.

8. What will happen to whomever touches the holy mountain? (Exodus 19:12)

   Whoever touches the mountain will be put to death.

9. Besides the washing of clothes, what additional requirement does Moses give? (Exodus 19:15)

   The people are to abstain from sexual relations.

10. What happens on the morning of the third day that causes the people to tremble? (Exodus 19:16)

    They tremble because of the thunder and lightning and the thick cloud over the mountain. They also hear a very loud trumpet blast.

11. What signs accompany God's appearance on the mountain? (Exodus 19:18)

    The mountain is wrapped in smoke, fire appears, and the whole mountain trembles violently.

12. What happens when Moses speaks? (Exodus 19:19)

    The voice of God answers.

13. After Moses warns the people and the priests, what is he to do? (Exodus 19:24)

    Moses is to bring Aaron—and only Aaron—up the mountain with him.

Answer these questions by reading Exodus 20

14. At the beginning of the Ten Commandments, how does the Lord identify himself? (Exodus 20:2)

    "I am the LORD your God, who brought you out of Egypt, out of the land of slavery."

15. What is the first commandment? (Exodus 20:3)

"You shall have no other gods before me."

16. To whom does God show love? (Exodus 20:6)

God shows love to those who love him and keep his commandments.

17. Why is the Sabbath day special to the Lord? (Exodus 20:11)

The Lord labored for six days to make heaven and earth, but on the seventh day he rested.

18. What promise does God make to those who honor their parents? (Exodus 20:12)

God promises that they will live long in the land that he will give them.

19. What two things does God command the Israelites not to do to a neighbor? (Exodus 20:16-17)

The Israelites are not to give false testimony against a neighbor nor to covet anything that belongs to a neighbor.

20. What do the people do while Moses draws near to God? (Exodus 20:21)

The people remain at a distance.

21. What two kinds of sacrifices may the people offer on the altar of the Lord? (Exodus 20:24)

The people may offer burnt offerings and fellowship offerings.

22. What benefits does God promise to the Israelites if they sacrifice to him? (Exodus 20:24)

The Lord promises to come and bless them.

DIMENSION TWO: WHAT DOES THE BIBLE MEAN?

This lesson brings us to the very heart of the Old Testament. Exodus 19–20 describes the establishment of a covenant between the Lord and Israel. God, through his servant Moses, has led to the foot of the holy mountain the company of slaves who were so miraculously freed from Egyptian bondage. His purpose is to establish a special relationship with them, one into which both parties freely enter. The heart of this covenant is the Ten Commandments.

Today's Scripture is connected closely with that of Lesson 6. The student book provides an outline of Exodus 19–24 (pages 38–39). Below is a similar, but slightly more detailed, outline.

The Covenant at Sinai

I. The arrival and encampment at Sinai (Exodus 19:1-2)
II. The Lord promises a covenant (Exodus 19:3-9)
  A. Concept of the covenant proposed (Exodus 19:3-6)
  B. Proposal accepted by the people (Exodus 19:7-8)
  C. Moses' special role is promised (Exodus 19:9)
III. Preparations for the covenant prior to the third day (Exodus 19:10-15)
  A. Instructions for two days of purification (Exodus 19:10-15)
  B. The people warned about the mountain (Exodus 19:12-13a)
  C. Declaration of the signal to approach the mountain (Exodus 19:13b)
  D. Moses completes the instructions (Exodus 19:14-15)
IV. Preparation on the third day and the appearance of the Lord on the mountain (Exodus 19:16-25)
  A. First signs of the Lord and the fear of the people (Exodus 19:16)
  B. Moses and the people approach the mountain (Exodus 19:17)
  C. The signs of the Lord increase (Exodus 19:18)
  D. Moses and God converse (Exodus 19:19)
  E. Moses called up the mountain for further instructions (Exodus 19:20-24)
  F. Moses carries the instructions to the people (Exodus 19:25)
V. The Ten Commandments declared (Exodus 20:1-17)
VI. Moses becomes a mediator (Exodus 20:18-21)
  A. The fearful request of the people (Exodus 20:18-19)
  B. The calming answer of Moses (Exodus 20:20)
  C. Moses becomes a mediator between God and the people (Exodus 20:21)
VII. The Book of the Covenant (Exodus 20:22–23:33)
VIII. Commitment to the covenant (Exodus 24:1-18)

Exodus 19:3-6. Draw the group's attention to the poetic nature of this announcement. Notice the parallel expressions: "house of Jacob/people of Israel," "carried you on eagles' wings/brought you to myself," "obey me fully/keep my covenant," "kingdom of priests/holy nation."

The student book contrasts the condition of the people of Israel three months earlier with what God promised them that they could become. Help the participants appreciate the difficulty these former slaves must have had in adjusting to the rapid changes taking place in their lives. Their forebears lived for four centuries in Egypt, with never

THE COVENANT AT SINAI

a word from God. Now the Israelites were confronted with God's mighty works time and time again. Previously, they lived in a settled land; in only two months they found it necessary to adjust to the difficult life of the desert. They were not warriors, yet they had to fight the Amalekites. No wonder the people trembled (see 19:16) and were afraid (see 20:18).

Exodus 19:15. Moses commands that the people refrain from sexual intercourse and that they wash their clothes. The Scripture does not say that sexual intercourse is evil or immoral. God made humankind male and female, and when God had finished his creation he said that it was good, very good. (See Genesis 1:31.) Yet what the Israelites are going to experience will be different from the usual events of life. So Moses requires them to separate themselves from things that are normally permitted. Then they will be prepared for this once-in-an-eternity event.

Exodus 19:16-19. God's presence on the mountain is signaled by thunder and lightning, clouds, fire, smoke, and earthquake. Some scholars believe this passage describes a natural volcano. But no volcanoes, recent or ancient, are found in the Sinai. The nearest active volcanoes are farther east, in Arabia. Although certain scholars believe that the holy mountain must have been in Arabia, we understand that these phenomena are supernatural evidences of the presence of God. We need not explain them by natural forces.

Exodus 20:3-17. The Decalogue was the basis of the covenant between Israel and the Lord. It was also the "constitution" on which the laws of Israel were based. One of the law codes that expands upon the Decalogue is the Book of the Covenant (Exodus 20:22–23:33; see the outline on page 87.) We know that these laws were necessary. Just before Israel received the law at Mount Sinai, Moses was busy trying to judge the cases of the people when they came to him with disputes. (See Exodus 18:13-26.)

The group may want to discuss the idea of covenant in order to understand and appreciate what happened at Mount Sinai. The following information should help you lead them in this discussion. You may want to use a Bible dictionary to supplement the information below.

Covenant

The Hebrew word for covenant is *berith,* as in B'nai B'rith, "the sons of the covenant." Our word *covenant* comes from *convenir,* a French word that means "to agree." Behind the French expression stands the Latin *convenire,* "to come together." A covenant is, therefore, a "formal, solemn, and binding agreement," according to *Webster's Ninth New Collegiate Dictionary.* Other words with meanings similar to *covenant* are *contract, pact, testament,* and *agreement.*

Each member of the study group has entered into some kind of contract or agreement. A credit card purchase slip represents a formal, solemn, binding agreement. The buyer has agreed to pay for the purchase; the seller has agreed to deliver the goods. This transaction is a type of covenant. Marriage vows made between a man and a woman represent another type of covenant. A covenant may be recorded on a document, but the covenant itself is a moral commitment between two parties.

The ancient world was full of covenants. Archaeology has provided us with several examples of covenants, or treaties, which were used in the Hittite Empire. These examples come from about 1400–1200 B.C., the period of Moses and the Exodus. The Hittite treaties are of two types: treaties made between equals (parity treaties), and treaties made between a great king and a lesser prince or king (suzerainty treaties).

We have a good example of a parity treaty in Genesis 31—the covenant between Jacob and Laban. On the other hand, the covenant between God and Israel fits the pattern of the suzerainty treaty. The main points of this type of treaty are listed below, along with similarities to the Sinai covenant.

1. The suzerain, or great king, considered himself king of kings and lord of lords. He identified himself as ruler over many kings. Exodus 20:2 identifies the Lord as God.

2. The suzerain described his gracious acts on behalf of the vassal, or lesser king. Exodus 20:2 reminds Israel of God's past favor in the Exodus. This part of the agreement was intended to obtain the vassal's obedience to the suzerain. This obedience was to come out of gratitude for the goodness of the overlord, rather than necessity.

3. The suzerainty treaty described the obligations of the covenant. One common requirement prevented the vassal from having anything to do with other great kings. The vassal was also expected to keep peace for the great king. The treaty usually included provisions for depositing the written treaty in a temple and for a regular public reading of its contents. The treaty called upon the suzerain and the vassal to be witnesses of the solemn agreement and listed curses on the vassal if he were to break the covenant. The treaty also listed blessings on the vassal for obedience to the terms of the agreement.

The Decalogue in Exodus 20:3-17 prohibits relations between the Israelites and other gods. They are to worship only the Lord. The last six commandments are concerned with the internal peace of Israel. God prohibits any activity that would set Israelite against Israelite—such as murdering, committing adultery, stealing, false witnessing, or coveting. Exodus 25:10-22 indicates that the commandments were to be put into the ark, a portable box, which was to be kept in a portable shrine. This box came to be called the "ark of the covenant." (See 1 Samuel 4:4.) Deuteronomy 28 lists the curses connected with the covenant; the blessings have already been mentioned. (See Exodus 19:5-6.) The covenant is conditional, that is, dependent upon keeping the commandments.

The similarities between Hittite treaties and God's covenant with Israel at Sinai help us understand God's ways with his people. But a political treaty cannot illustrate adequately God's love and grace. The Hittite kings acted out of selfish purposes. God acted toward Israel out of grace and love.

The covenant established at Sinai between God and Israel became the basis for what we call the Old Testament. We can speak of the Sinai covenant as "old" because centuries later God's prophet, Jeremiah, spoke of a "new" covenant. (See Jeremiah 31:31-34.) The new covenant was eventually established by Jesus Christ.

DIMENSION THREE:
WHAT DOES THE BIBLE MEAN TO ME?

The student book emphasizes two ideas. These are "The Priesthood of All Believers," and "The Ten Commandments and the Christian." The material below will help you guide the discussion of these topics so that the members of the study group may develop a deeper understanding of the relevance of this Scripture for their lives.

Exodus 19:4-6—The Priesthood of All Believers

Draw attention particularly to Exodus 19:5-6. Early Christians often identified themselves with Israel's experience at Sinai, and the discussion in the student book encourages the members of the group to seriously consider what this holy calling means for their lives. The questions they have been asked to consider are (1) How can we develop a sense of being set apart (consecrated) to the service of God? (Read Romans 12 as background for this question.) (2) If we actually begin to practice the idea of the priesthood of all believers, how will this practice affect our ideas of the clergy/laity distinctions in the church? (3) We often feel that the church demands too much of our time. Are these feelings the result of our being unaware of our calling to be priests to the Lord?

The New Testament gives us a number of details about the life of service to God. First, both deeds and words are holy tasks. (See Colossians 3:17.) Everything is to be done to serve the Lord and not persons. (See Colossians 3:23.) Each priest (believer) is gifted and should use that gift for the good of the entire body (the church). (See Ephesians 4:7-14.) Being holy is not a condition that is attained by our works; it is a gift of God through the Lord Jesus Christ. (See Romans 5:1-11.) Dedication to the Lord and to others must be a response to the saving grace of God rather than a means of gaining salvation.

Exodus 20:2-17
The Ten Commandments and the Christian

Because most of the Ten Commandments are phrased in the negative, "You shall not . . . ," many persons think they are basically restrictive. Suggest to the class members that a negative commandment forbids action in one area while leaving all other areas free. A positive law, "You shall . . . ," requires that all activities be limited to one area. This latter kind of law prevents freedom of decision and action to a much greater degree than does the negative commandment.

Jesus restated the law in a positive way—"You shall love" God and your neighbor. (See Matthew 22:34-40.) Does Jesus' law of love prevent freedom of decision and action? Examine the description of love given by Paul in 1 Corinthians 13, and then interpret the teaching of Jesus in the light of this definition. Can the Christian who fulfills the royal law of love (read James 2:8) also obey the Ten Commandments?

In closing, ask the group members to offer silent prayers of thanks to God for one new insight they have gained from this lesson. If time allows, list these insights on chalkboard or a large sheet of paper.

— 6 —

Covenant Laws

Exodus 21–27

**DIMENSION ONE:
WHAT DOES THE BIBLE SAY?**

Answer these questions by reading Exodus 21

1. To what kind of a purchased servant do the regulations in Exodus 21:2-6 apply? (Exodus 21:2)

   The regulations apply to a Hebrew servant.

2. To what three things is a female servant entitled if she marries her master? (Exodus 21:10)

   She is entitled to food, clothing, and marital rights.

3. What four offenses require the death penalty? (Exodus 21:12-17)

   a. Striking and killing another person
   b. Attacking one's father or mother
   c. Kidnapping a person
   d. Cursing one's father or mother

4. When does the law of an eye for an eye apply? (Exodus 21:22-24)

   The law applies when serious injury is caused to a person during a fight.

5. What is the penalty when a master strikes a servant and destroys an eye or a tooth? (Exodus 21:26-27)

   The master must let the servant go free.

Answer these questions by reading Exodus 22

6. What penalties are imposed upon a thief? (Exodus 22:1)

   A thief must make restitution many times over to pay for the theft.

7. If a thief steals borrowed property, what fine is required of him? (Exodus 22:7)

   A thief who steals borrowed property is required to pay double.

8. What obligations does a borrower have to the owner of the property that he borrows? (Exodus 22:14-15)

   The borrower must make restitution to the owner. If the owner is present, no restitution is required.

9. What must a man do who seduces a virgin? (Exodus 22:16-17)

   He must take her as his wife and pay the bride-price. If her father refuses to allow the marriage, the man must still pay the bride-price for a virgin.

10. What will happen to anyone who mistreats a widow or an orphan? (Exodus 22:24)

    God will kill that person with a sword.

11. When must a lender not charge a borrower interest? (Exodus 22:25)

    The lender cannot charge interest if the borrower is poor.

12. Why must a cloak taken in pledge be returned to its owner before nightfall? (Exodus 22:26-27)

    The cloak also serves as a cover for his body when he sleeps at night and he has no other.

Answer these questions by reading Exodus 23

13. In what way can persons pervert justice? (Exodus 23:1-2)

    Persons can pervert justice by malicious witnessing, whether by joining a wicked man or by siding with a crowd intent on evil.

14. Why is the prohibition against oppressing aliens especially important in Israel? (Exodus 23:9)

The people of Israel know what it is like to be an alien since they were aliens in Egypt.

15. During the harvest, what are the people to bring as an offering to the Lord? (Exodus 23:19)

They are to bring "the best of the firstfruits of your soil" as an offering to the Lord.

16. How are the Israelites to treat the gods of the Canaanites when they enter their land? (Exodus 23:24)

They are to demolish the Canaanite gods, and they are to break their sacred stones to pieces.

17. What are the boundaries of the land that Israel will possess? (Exodus 23:31)

The boundaries are from the Red Sea to the Sea of the Philistines, and from the desert to the River [Euphrates].

Answer these questions by reading Exodus 24

18. What do the people say when Moses tells them all the words of the Lord? (Exodus 24:3)

The people say, "Everything the LORD has said we will do."

19. Moses catches some of the blood from the sacrifices in bowls. What does this blood signify? (Exodus 24:6-8)

This blood is a sign of the covenant that the Lord has made with the people.

20. Why are the commandments engraved on tablets of stone? (Exodus 24:12)

The commandments are engraved on tablets of stone for the instruction of the people of Israel.

21. How long is Moses on the holy mountain? (Exodus 24:18)

Moses is on the mountain for forty days and forty nights.

Answer these questions by reading Exodus 25

22. Why are the people of Israel to give an offering to the Lord? (Exodus 25:1-8)

The offering will be used to build a sanctuary for the Lord.

23. What will Moses place in the ark? (Exodus 25:16)

Moses will place the Testimony (the Ten Commandments) in the ark.

24. God tells Moses to make everything after a pattern. Where does Moses get the pattern? (Exodus 25:40)

Moses gets the pattern from the Lord on the mountain.

Answer these questions by reading Exodus 26

25. With what materials is Moses to make the sides of the tabernacle? (Exodus 26:1)

Moses is to make the sides of the tabernacle of finely twisted linen and blue, purple, and scarlet yarn.

26. What material does Moses use to make a tent over the tabernacle? (Exodus 26:7)

Moses uses goat hair to make the tent over the tabernacle.

27. How is the tabernacle divided into two parts? (Exodus 26:33)

The tabernacle is divided into the Holy Place and the Most Holy Place by a curtain.

28. With what material is the altar to be constructed? (Exodus 27:1)

The altar is to be constructed of acacia wood.

29. With what materials is Moses to make the entrance to the courtyard of the tabernacle? (Exodus 27:18)

Moses is to make the entrance of finely twisted linen panels and bases of bronze.

30. Who is to provide the oil for the lamps, and who is to tend them? (Exodus 27:20-21)

The people of Israel are to provide the oil for the lamps, and Aaron and his sons are to tend them.

DIMENSION TWO: WHAT DOES THE BIBLE MEAN?

Exodus 21–27 includes three main types of literature. Chapters 21–23 contain a law code, Chapter 24 is a narrative that tells of the people's acceptance of God's covenant, and Chapters 25–27 record instructions on the building of the tabernacle. You will be able to distinguish these three types by the changes in subject matter.

A major section of this lesson deals with the statutes and ordinances in Chapters 21–23, the Book of the Covenant. Some of these laws are no longer meaningful in our society, but we can try to understand them in their ancient setting. Present the information below to the group. For additional material, consult a commentary on Exodus or an article on law in a Bible dictionary.

Background Information on Exodus 21–23

Two kinds of laws appear in the Bible. *Apodictic* laws are stated unconditionally, such as in the Ten Commandments, "You shall (not)...." Other apodictic laws are found in today's lesson in Exodus 22:18, 21, 28, 29, 30, and 31. The second type is called *casuistic* law. Casuistic laws are introduced by words like "if" or "when." These laws are intended to govern cases that are likely to arise again and again in a community. Exodus 21 contains examples of casuistic laws. In the student book, casuistic laws are called "case laws."

Both types of law were important and binding on the people of Israel. In a sense, the Ten Commandments functioned like the Constitution of the United States, providing a limited number of basic rules. The legal codes in the first five books of the Bible, including the Book of the Covenant, are similar to the various laws passed by Congress.

Some of the laws in this lesson reflect an agricultural way of life in a settled society, rather than a seminomadic life in a desert region. Neither vineyards, fields, nor houses were a part of Israelite life during the desert wandering. See, for example, the reference to a field and a vineyard in 22:5, or the mention of a man's house in 22:7. Possibly the Book of the Covenant came into being soon after the conquest and settlement of Canaan. But the laws are based on the Decalogue and are associated with God's word to Moses, the foundation of all Israelite law.

Exodus 21:1-11. This section of the Book of the Covenant contains slave (servant) laws. Slavery was an established social institution in Israel and throughout the ancient Near East. These laws require the humane treatment of slaves and prevent a lifetime of forced slavery. The slave is obligated to serve the master, but the master is also obligated to care for the needs of the servant.

A parallel passage in Deuteronomy 15:12-14 requires a master to free his slaves after six years of service. At this time, the master must liberally provide food and livestock to the servant who is being freed. Such a system had the advantage of giving economic security to the poor. The system also provided persons with a fresh start after a limited period of service, unless the individual chose to become a slave for life.

Exodus 21:12-17. These laws deal with offenses that are worthy of death in the Israelite community. They also reflect some of the ideas in the Ten Commandments, such as murder, honoring one's parents, and stealing. Exodus 21:13-14 distinguishes between planned and unplanned murder, or between murder and manslaughter. The actions covered in these laws were seen as direct threats to the life of the covenant community.

Exodus 21:18-36. These laws are concerned with actions that cause bodily injury. The person who causes an injury is responsible for compensating the injured party. Notice in verse 21 that the word *property* is "money" in the Revised Standard Version. Money as we know it did not develop until much later, in the seventh century B.C. In a very real sense, these laws answer "Yes" to Cain's question, "Am I my brother's keeper?" (See Genesis 4:9.)

Exodus 22:1-17. These laws deal with damage to property. Notice in verse 3 that the slaying of a thief in broad daylight would make the defender guilty of bloodshed. *Bloodshed* ("bloodguilt" in the New Revised Standard Version) means that the family of the thief could avenge his or her death by killing the slayer. But a thief killed at night does not require bloodshed. This law assumes that a thief might be killed accidentally at night, but a thief should not be killed on purpose.

Exodus 22:16-17 speaks of the bride-price, given in exchange for a virgin. A daughter was the property of her father until another man purchased her as a wife or a servant. The bride-price, or marriage present, was the amount paid by the groom for a bride. So the man who seduced a virgin had to compensate the father for the price of the bride, whether the father permitted the marriage or not.

Exodus 22:18-31. These laws treat various social, moral, and religious matters. They require the death penalty for sorcery, bestiality, and idolatry. (See verses 18-20.) These practices were all part of the pagan society of Canaan. Notice that the poor are not to be exploited. In any society the poor are the most vulnerable. Exploitation is a form of coveting, and to covet is to break the tenth commandment.

Exodus 23:1-9. This legislation calls for equal treatment for each Israelite, rich or poor, and the resident alien as well. These laws are based on the ninth commandment against giving false testimony. (See Exodus 20:16.) In the New Testament, James 2:1-13 also calls upon Christians to refrain from showing partiality.

Exodus 23:10-19. These regulations are concerned with worship. The seventh (sabbatical) year was a test of Israel's faith in God. By not sowing crops, one had to depend on God's providential care for food. To appear before the "Sovereign LORD" (verse 17) meant to go to the sanctuary where the Lord was worshiped.

Exodus 23:20-33. This appendix emphasizes the relationship between obedience to the Sinai covenant and possession of the Promised Land. Although angels play a larger role in the New Testament, they do appear in the Old Testament. Here they serve as divine agents of the Lord. Notice the emphasis upon serving the Lord, the one true God. The idea of one, supreme power was unheard of in the surrounding pagan world.

DIMENSION THREE: WHAT DOES THE BIBLE MEAN TO ME?

Dimension Three in the student book is limited to a single topic, "Justice Versus Vengeance." Read the material in the student book, and have the group read the Scripture reference aloud. Then lead a discussion of the questions contained in the last paragraph of the student book (see page 50).

Justice versus vengeance is but one of several insights that may be gained from this lesson. Below are other ideas for group discussion.

Exodus 24:3-8—The Blood of the Covenant

The covenant between God and Israel was a mutual agreement, freely entered into by both parties. When the Lord stated the basis of the covenant (read Exodus 19:3-6), the people's first response was, "We will do everything the LORD has said." Then the Lord gave Moses all the ordinances and the words that were to be part of the covenant. Now, in Exodus 24:3, Moses repeats them to the people. The covenant is affirmed with blood sacrifices as the people pledge, "We will do everything the LORD has said; we will obey." (Exodus 24:7).

The blood of this sacrifice is called the blood of the covenant. Likewise in Genesis 15 God sealed the covenant between himself and Abraham with a sacrifice. The blood of the covenant was shed.

In the New Testament, the Letter to the Hebrews discusses the establishment of the Mosaic covenant. The letter states that Christ, the mediator of a new covenant, established it through his own blood. (See Hebrews 9:11-28.) Jesus, when instituting the Lord's Supper, referred to the cup of wine as "my blood of the covenant, which is poured out for many for the forgiveness of sins" (Matthew 26:28; see also Mark 14:24; Luke 22:20). Paul refers to the Christians in Corinth who drank of the Communion cup as participating in the blood of Christ. (See 1 Corinthians 10:16.)

Share these references with the class members, and then ask them to consider the following questions. How is the blood of Christ essential to the individual who wishes to be a part of the covenant community (the church)? (See also Romans 5:6-11.) The blood of the covenant allowed each Israelite to have a personal relationship with the Lord. How does Christian baptism make our relationship with God a personal one under the new covenant? (See Romans 6:1-11.)

Exodus 24:12—The Importance of Instruction

In this verse, God commands Moses to ascend the mountain and receive God's instruction for the people. From the beginning of his ministry, Jesus called people to be his disciples. (See Luke 14:25-33.) A disciple is a learner, one who receives instruction. How important is this activity for a Christian? Consider the words of Jesus in John 8:31: "If you hold to my teaching, you are really my disciples."

Ask the group to think about various ways they receive religious instruction (sermons, retreats, camps, personal Bible study, radio and television, small study groups, Christian literature). Consider with the group the particular value each of these forms of instruction may provide.

Discuss aids to learning such as Bible dictionaries, atlases, commentaries, concordances, and study Bibles. Ask each member of the group to plan a personal program of study. The group members could share ideas about what such a personal study might include. A variety of learning possibilities enhances any personal study program.

Exodus 25:8—The Dwelling Place of the Lord

The tabernacle, here called the sanctuary, was to be the dwelling place of the Lord in the midst of his people. Later Solomon built a house for the Lord, the first Temple in Jerusalem. (See 1 Kings 5–8.) This building took the place of the tabernacle. The Babylonians destroyed Solomon's Temple in 587 B.C. After the Babylonian Exile, the people built a second Temple in Jerusalem. This second Temple was in turn destroyed by the Romans in A.D. 70.

From the earliest days of the church, before the second Temple in Jerusalem was destroyed, Christians have believed that God was in Christ (see 2 Corinthians 5:19) and that "in Christ all the fullness of the Deity lives in bodily form" (Colossians 2:9). But the church also teaches that the dwelling of God today is in each believer. (See 1 Corinthians 3:16.)

Ask the group members to consider what it means in practical terms to be a dwelling place for God. Encourage them to think of the idea as a privilege. Ask them to give some thought to the responsibilities that such a relationship with the Lord requires of us. How might this idea affect our style of living?

In closing, ask persons to thank to God for something they have learned in this lesson that they consider important to them personally. List these items on chalkboard or a sheet of paper, then pray a brief closing prayer of appreciation.

THE ROUTE OF THE EXODUS

The Great Sea

Nile Delta

GOSHEN

BAAL-ZEPHON

SUCCOTH

BITTER LAKES

desert of Shur

MARAH

NILE RIVER

E G Y P T

Gulf of Suez

S I N A I

P E N I N S U L A

desert of sin

MT. SINAI OR MT. HOREB

C A N A A N

LAND OF MIDIAN

Gulf of Aqaba

Red Sea

Then the LORD relented and did not bring on his people the disaster he had threatened (32:14).

7

Cultic Instructions

Exodus 28–34

DIMENSION ONE:
WHAT DOES THE BIBLE SAY?

Answer these questions by reading Exodus 28

1. Whom does God designate as Israel's priests? (Exodus 28:1)

   God designates Aaron and his sons to be Israel's priests.

2. What are the colors of Aaron's priestly garments? (Exodus 28:5)

   They are gold, blue, purple, and scarlet.

3. What is Moses to do with the onyx stones, and where is he to place them? (Exodus 28:9-12)

   Moses is to engrave the stones with the names of the twelve sons of Israel. He is to place them on the shoulder pieces of the ephod.

4. Why are bells and pomegranates attached to Aaron's robe? (Exodus 28:33-35)

   They are attached so that Aaron can be heard when he walks in and out of the Holy Place and will not die.

5. Besides tunics, sashes, and headbands, what does God require priests to wear? (Exodus 28:42)

   Priests also have to wear a linen undergarment, reaching from the waist to the thigh.

Answer these questions by reading Exodus 29

6. What is the final act in the ordination of Aaron and his sons? (Exodus 29:7)

   Moses anoints their heads with oil.

7. What is the purpose of the sacrifice that follows the ordination of Aaron? (Exodus 29:10-14)

   It is a sin offering.

8. Why does Moses sprinkle the blood of the ram upon Aaron and his sons? (Exodus 29:21)

   Moses sprinkles the blood of the ram on Aaron and his sons so they will be consecrated.

9. What does Moses do with the fellowship offering? (Exodus 29:27-28)

   He gives the breast that was waved to Aaron and his sons.

10. What does God require as a repeat burnt offering? (Exodus 29:38-39)

    God requires two lambs each day as a repeat burnt offering, one in the morning and the other at twilight.

11. What happens at the door of the Tent of Meeting? (Exodus 29:42)

    God meets Moses and speaks with him there.

12. What does the tabernacle, or Tent of Meeting, signify to the people? (Exodus 29:43-46)

    The tabernacle signifies the dwelling of God among the people of Israel.

Answer these questions by reading Exodus 30

13. From what material is the altar made, and what are its dimensions? (Exodus 30:1-2)

    The altar is made of acacia wood. It is one cubit long, one cubit wide, and two cubits high.

14. What does God tell Aaron to do on the altar? (Exodus 30:7-8)

God tells Aaron to burn fragrant incense every morning and at twilight.

15. Who among Israel is to give a half shekel to the Lord, and what is the purpose of the half shekel? (Exodus 30:13-15)

Everyone twenty years old and upward gives a half shekel. The offering is for the purpose of atonement.

16. What is the purpose of the bronze basin? (Exodus 30:17-21)

The bronze basin contains water to be used by Aaron and his sons, to wash their hands and their feet before entering the Tent of Meeting or approaching the altar.

17. What restrictions does God place upon the use of the holy anointing oil? (Exodus 30:32)

The priest must not pour the oil on ordinary men.

Answer these questions by reading Exodus 31

18. What duties does God give to Bezalel? (Exodus 31:2-5)

God fills Bezalel with the Spirit of God so that he can design and work with gold, silver, bronze, stones, and wood.

19. Why is a person who works on the Sabbath subject to death? (Exodus 31:14)

The Sabbath is holy, and to work on the Sabbath is to desecrate it.

20. What does the Sabbath signify for Israel? (Exodus 31:17)

The Sabbath is a reminder that the Lord labored six days to create the heaven and earth, and on the seventh day he rested.

21. At the end of the conversation on the mountain, what does God give Moses? (Exodus 31:18)

God gives Moses the two stone tables of the Testimony, inscribed by the finger of God.

Answer these questions by reading Exodus 32

22. Why do the people ask Aaron to make gods for them? (Exodus 32:1)

The people think Moses will never return.

23. What words do the people say to honor the idol cast as a calf? (Exodus 32:4)

"These are your gods, O Israel, who brought you up out of Egypt."

24. What rituals do the people perform before the calf? (Exodus 32:6)

They offer burnt offerings and fellowship offerings; and they eat, drink, and indulge in revelry.

25. How does the Lord describe the Israelites to Moses? (Exodus 32:9)

The Lord calls the Israelites a stiff-necked people.

26. What does Moses ask God to remember? (Exodus 32:13)

Moses reminds the Lord of his promise to Abraham, Isaac, and Israel.

27. What does Moses do with the golden calf? (Exodus 32:20)

Moses burns the golden calf, grinds it into powder, scatters the powder in water, and makes the people drink the mixture.

28. How many Israelites do the Levites kill at the command of Moses? (Exodus 32:28)

The Levites kill about three thousand people.

29. What does Moses ask God to do if he refuses to forgive the people? (Exodus 32:32)

Moses asks God to blot out his name from the book God has written.

Answer these questions by reading Exodus 33

30. Why do the people mourn when they hear that they will go to the land of promise? (Exodus 33:3-4)

They mourn because God says he will not go with them.

31. When Moses goes out to the Tent of Meeting, how do the people know that the Lord is speaking? (Exodus 33:9)

When Moses enters the tent, the pillar of cloud descends and stands at the door of the tent.

32. Why does the Lord agree to go with the people? (Exodus 33:17)

God agrees to go because God is pleased with Moses.

Answer these questions by reading Exodus 34

33. How does God describe himself to Moses? (Exodus 34:6-7)

God describes himself as compassionate and gracious; slow to anger; abounding in love and faithfulness; forgiving wickedness, rebellion, and sin; but punishing the guilty.

34. When the people of Israel enter the Promised Land, what warning does God give them? (Exodus 34:12)

God tells them not to make a treaty with those who live in the land.

35. After his second visit to the mountain, what strange thing do the people notice about Moses? (Exodus 34:29-30)

They notice that the face of Moses is radiant because he has been talking with God.

DIMENSION TWO: WHAT DOES THE BIBLE MEAN?

The Scripture for this lesson continues the instructions God gave to Moses during the forty days and nights Moses spent atop the holy mountain. In the previous lesson we read the instructions for making the tabernacle. This lesson includes three topics: regulations for the priestly ministers of the tabernacle, Israel's breaking of the covenant by making the golden calf, and the renewal of the covenant.

Begin this portion of the lesson by asking the participants whether they have any questions about the material in Chapters 28–31. After discussing questions from the first section, continue into Chapters 32–34. The material provided below will supplement the information in Dimension Two of the student book.

The group may enjoy the description of the high priest that is found in the Book of Ecclesiasticus (Sirach), Chapter 45:6-24. This book of the Apocrypha is also known as The Wisdom of Jesus ben Sirach. It can be found in a Catholic Bible if you do not have access to a copy of the Apocrypha.

Exodus 28:30. Urim and Thummim have traditionally been translated as "lights and perfections," but the exact meaning of the two words is unknown. When Saul sought God's direction using Urim and Thummim, the answer was apparently either "Yes" or "No." (See 1 Samuel 14:41-42.)

After the time of David, the Bible does not indicate that anyone used Urim and Thummim to obtain oracles. In Jewish tradition, the priests did not use Urim and Thummim after the Babylonian Exile. Ezra 2:63 states that no priest was to handle Urim and Thummim. (See also Nehemiah 7:65.) The use of lots as an indication of God's will occurs in the New Testament. After the death of Judas, Peter and his followers selected Matthias by lot to fill his place. (See Acts 1:15-26.)

Exodus 28:35. The ringing of the bells must have served as a kind of protection for the high priest. The end of this verse mentions the specific reason for the ringing of the bells: "so that he will not die." In his priestly duties Aaron passed through the doorway of the sanctuary, and the entrance to a temple was thought to be especially subject to deadly power. (See 1 Samuel 5:5.)

Exodus 30:13. The shekel is a weight of silver rather than a coin. Coinage began in Palestine only in the seventh century B.C. In 1979 the shekel was established once again as a measure of money in the modern State of Israel. It is the basic money measure, as the dollar is in the United States.

Exodus 31:12-17. This commandment about the Sabbath occurs also in Exodus 16:22-27. There Moses tells the people not to collect manna on the Sabbath. Here in Exodus 31, God emphasizes that work on the tabernacle should stop on the Sabbath.

For the ancient Babylonians, the seventh day represented a quarter of the moon's phase. In Israel, the Sabbath was connected with God's creative activity rather than the phases of the moon. The Sabbath was a day of rest, refreshment, and joy. It also reminded Israel of the Lord's covenant with his people in which he set them apart for his work.

Exodus 32:1-6. Some scholars maintain that this story is based on the golden calf worship that Jeroboam I established in Israel. (See 1 Kings 12:26-33.) They believe that the story circulated in order to oppose the religion of the Northern Kingdom and that it was added to this account when Exodus took its final form (during the Exile, in their view). However, we have no reason to doubt that the incident of the golden calf occurred at Mount Sinai at the time the covenant was established.

Draw attention to the attitude of the people of Israel. Their attitude is reflected in what they say and how they say it. The Hebrew original indicates that they gather themselves more against Aaron than to him (as they will do later to both Moses and Aaron in Numbers 16:3).

Aaron may intend the calf to be a symbol of the Lord's invisible presence. At least he announces a feast to the Lord, Israel's God, rather than to another god. But Aaron still comes off in a bad light. Moses left him in charge of the camp, but the people actually are in charge. Aaron is weak and fearful. Here is an example of the straightforward manner in which the Bible presents people, without attempting to cover up sins or weaknesses. Surprisingly, God makes Aaron the high priest.

CULTIC INSTRUCTIONS

97

Exodus 32:7-14. Notice that in verse 7 the Lord speaks to Moses and mentions Israel as "your people" and proclaims their corruption. In verse 11, Moses speaks to the Lord still about "your people." But here Moses defends the people before God. In a similar way, Abraham interceded before the Lord on behalf of Sodom and Gomorrah. (See Genesis 18:23-33.)

Exodus 32:32-33. References to a book in which names are written also occur in Psalm 69:28; Daniel 12:1; and Revelation 20:12; 21:17. Moses offers to give up his life to redeem Israel from sin and guilt. Here he foreshadows Jesus Christ who gave his life "as a ransom for many" (Matthew 20:28). Paul also was willing to be accursed and cut off from Christ for the sake of the people of Israel. (See Romans 9:1-5.)

Exodus 34:11-16. In the last half century, archaeological excavations in Israel, North Africa, and Syria have recovered new information about the Canaanite religion. Apparently few religious differences existed among the groups mentioned in verse 11. They all believed in many gods who represented the forces in nature that were beyond the control of the Canaanites.

The "sacred stones" (verse 13) were probably plain standing stones, erected in honor of the god Baal, the storm god. The "Asherah poles" were wooden objects that symbolized the goddess Asherah, goddess of love and war. We do not know exactly what these objects looked like.

Exodus 34:29-35. Medieval artists often painted pictures of Moses with horns. This portrayal was due to a mistranslation of the Hebrew word *qaran* in the Latin Bible. The word appears three times in this passage. *Qaran* means "to shine" and is similar in spelling to another Hebrew word, *qeren*, which means "horn." The similarity confused the translators. Actually, the face of Moses was changed and reflected the glory of God because of his experience with God. Matthew 17:2 records a similar transfiguration of Jesus on a mountain, together with Moses and Elijah, which was witnessed by Peter, James, and John. In 2 Corinthians 3:7-18, Paul refers to the veiled face of Moses and emphasizes that God is in the process of transforming Christians through the Spirit.

DIMENSION THREE: WHAT DOES THE BIBLE MEAN TO ME?

Exodus 32:1-14; 34:6-9—A New Beginning With God

In the student book, this dimension considers the idea of a new beginning, based on the sin of Israel (see Exodus 32:1-14) and the re-establishment of the covenant (read Exodus 34:6-9). Because of their sin, the Israelites deserved certain death under the law. But instead God provided forgiveness and a new beginning. Israel's experience is a powerful example of the awful reality of sin, but also of the grace of God. Believers in Christ have a much greater reason for hope than the Israelites had under the law. We are confident that the blood of Jesus Christ cleanses us from all sin. In him we are assured of a new beginning.

Check the student book for the Scripture references and the questions. You may wish to present one or more of the following ideas to the group as well.

Exodus 28:2—Garments of Glory

Aaron's priestly vestments were glorious garments. No other mortal could hope to wear clothes of such rich ornamentation and beauty. Moses, on the other hand, wore no special dress. But God clothed him with a heavenly radiance. (See Exodus 34:29.) Jesus was clothed similarly with God's glory in the Transfiguration. (See Matthew 17:2.)

How should Christians dress? Jesus taught his disciples not to be anxious about what to put on, for life is more than food and clothing. (See Matthew 6:25.) The New Testament does not give specific rules for outer dress, although modesty should prevail. (See 1 Timothy 2:9.) This same writer urges Christian women to adorn themselves with good deeds (verse 10).

Revelation 3:5 pictures the saints of God clothed in white garments. Revelation 19:8 calls these white robes the righteous acts of the saints. Believers should be clothed in love and good works.

If we actively considered "how we may spur one another on toward love and good deeds" (Hebrews 10:24), how would this affect the amount of money we spend for clothing? How could living a simpler lifestyle (for example, dressing less expensively) affect the number of good deeds we could do? How might the words of James 2:14-17 enter into our judgment about buying clothes and adornments?

Exodus 32:1—The Importance of Patience

Israel became very impatient while Moses was on the mountain. The people had spent years in slavery, but they could not spend forty days waiting on the Lord. They were determined to go their own way.

How can we develop patience? Consider the words of Jesus in Luke 21:19, which he spoke to believers in the last days. Are these words also true for the present time? What dangers are hidden in an impatient attitude? Ask the group to consider these Scriptures: Romans 12:12; Hebrews 10:36; James 1:4; 5:7.

To close this session, lead the group in a simple prayer of thanksgiving to God for his grace and the opportunities in Christ for new beginnings. If time allows, ask the class members what insights they have gained from this lesson and write them on chalkboard or a piece of paper.

— 8 —

Instructions Carried Out

Exodus 35–40

DIMENSION ONE:
WHAT DOES THE BIBLE SAY?

Answer these questions by reading Exodus 35

1. When Moses begins his instructions, what is the first requirement he places on the people? (Exodus 35:1-2)

   Six days shall work be done, but on the seventh day you shall have a holy Sabbath of rest to the Lord.

2. From the Israelite community, whom does Moses ask to give an offering to the Lord? (Exodus 35:5)

   Moses asks everyone who is willing to bring an offering to the Lord.

3. Whom does Moses ask to come and make the tabernacle, its furnishings, and the priestly garments for Aaron? (Exodus 35:10)

   Moses asks everyone with a skill to come and make all that the Lord has commanded.

4. Who actually brings offerings for the Lord? (Exodus 35:21)

   Everyone who was willing and whose heart moves him, brings offerings for the Lord.

5. Why is Bezalel such a great craftsman? (Exodus 35:31)

   He is a great craftsman because he is filled with the Spirit of God, with skill, ability, and knowledge in all kinds of crafts.

6. Who is the main coworker of Bezalel? (Exodus 35:34)

   Oholiab is the main coworker of Bezalel.

Answer these questions by reading Exodus 36

7. Why does Moses restrain the people from bringing any more offerings for the sanctuary? (Exodus 36:6-7)

Moses restrains them because the items they had already brought were more than enough for the job.

8. How are the acacia wood frames of the tabernacle decorated? (Exodus 36:34)

   The frames are overlaid with gold.

Answer these questions by reading Exodus 37

9. With what metal is the tabernacle overlaid, within and without? (Exodus 37:2)

   It is overlaid with pure gold.

10. What material does Bezalel use to make the atonement cover and the cherubim? (Exodus 37:6-7)

    Bezalel uses pure gold for the atonement cover and hammered gold to make the cherubim.

11. What vessels of gold are to be upon the golden table in the tabernacle? (Exodus 37:16)

    The vessels for the table are plates, dishes, bowls, and pitchers.

Answer these questions by reading Exodus 38

12. What utensils of bronze are used with the bronze altar? (Exodus 38:3)

    The utensils are pots, shovels, sprinkling bowls, meat forks, and firepans.

13. What is the source of the bronze that Bezalel uses to make the basin? (Exodus 38:8)

    The bronze comes from the bronze mirrors of the women who minister at the entrance to the Tent of Meeting.

14. How is the golden thread made that is used to embroider the holy garments for Aaron? (Exodus 39:3)

    Gold leaf is hammered out and cut into strands for the embroidery.

15. How is the ephod attached to the breastpiece on the priestly garments of Aaron? (Exodus 39:20-21)

    Two gold rings are attached to the shoulders of his ephod. A blue cord connects the rings on the ephod to the rings on the breastpiece.

16. What two things are used for the fringe on Aaron's robe? (Exodus 39:24-26)

    Bells and pomegranates are used for the fringe on Aaron's robe.

17. What inscription is written on the plate of the sacred diadem of pure gold? (Exodus 39:30)

    The inscription reads, " HOLY TO THE LORD."

18. Why does Moses bless the people when they finish working on the tabernacle? (Exodus 39:43)

    Moses blesses them because they have done all the work just as the Lord commanded.

Answer these questions by reading Exodus 40

19. When is the tabernacle first set up? (Exodus 40:17)

    The tabernacle is first set up on the first day of the first month of the second year (after the Exodus).

20. Who sets up the tabernacle after it is finished? (Exodus 40:18)

    Moses sets up the tabernacle.

21. How does Moses finish his work? (Exodus 40:33)

    Moses sets up the courtyard around the tabernacle and puts up the curtain at the entrance.

22. After the consecration of the tabernacle, why can't Moses enter it? (Exodus 40:35)

    Moses cannot enter because the cloud is upon it, and the glory of the Lord fills it.

23. How do the Israelites know when to break camp and move on during their journeys in the desert? (Exodus 40:36)

    Whenever the cloud is lifted from the tabernacle, the Israelites go onward.

24. How do the people know that the glory of the Lord is in the tabernacle at night? (Exodus 40:38)

    They know that the glory of the Lord is in the tabernacle at night because they can see the fire in the cloud.

DIMENSION TWO: WHAT DOES THE BIBLE MEAN?

In Exodus 25–31 we read God's instruction to Moses on Mount Sinai. However, the carrying out of the instructions was delayed by the sin of the people in worshiping the golden calf. But God was gracious to Israel and forgave the people. The covenant was renewed, and after another forty days and nights on the mountain (read Exodus 34:28), Moses returned again to the waiting people. This time they had not fallen into idolatry. They were now ready to carry out the instructions of the Lord.

You may want to review Lessons 6 and 7. Much of the Scripture in today's lesson is almost word for word repetition of Exodus 25–31. You will want to consult the notes in your teacher book for these lessons.

Notice that in Exodus 25–31 God gave the plan for the tabernacle privately to Moses. In today's Scripture Moses repeats the details of the construction to the people, and they build the tabernacle. The failures of the past, when the people used their jewelry to construct a golden calf, are now followed by complete success. They follow God's instructions exactly and enthusiastically, and both Moses and the Lord are pleased with the results. Moses blesses them, and God takes up his abode among them in the sacred tent that their hands had made.

Assured of the presence of the Lord in their midst, the people prepare to march forth to the Promised Land. The story of that journey awaits us in the Book of Numbers. In this lesson we reach the end of the Book of Exodus. But because the final event recorded in Exodus is the construction and dedication of the tabernacle, the details of the cultic and sacrificial ritual connected with it are given in the next book of our study, the Book of Leviticus.

At least a week before the group's study of this lesson, ask a small group (two or three people will do) to find out the weight of an Old Testament talent. Ask them to compute the total weight of gold, silver, and bronze used in the construction of the tabernacle. (The number of talents for each metal used is given in Exodus 38:24-31.)

A Bible dictionary or encyclopedia will provide the weight of a talent. Suggest that they look under the heading "Weights and Measure" or "Money." Ask them to also compute, at current prices, the value of the gold that was used in the tabernacle. (Information on the current price of gold is available in the financial section of major newspapers, or a local jeweler should know the price.) The group should be prepared to report its findings to the whole group.

Since this is the last lesson in Exodus, you may want to return to the outline given in Lesson 1 for a brief review. This review will give the participants a sense of accomplishment in having completed their study of the book.

Also you may set the stage for the study of the next lesson, the first in the series of lessons on Leviticus. Do this by explaining why the writers inserted Leviticus between the account of the building of the tabernacle and the continuation of Israel's journey toward the Promised Land, in the Book of Numbers. (See the idea given above.)

This lesson falls into three sections: preparation of materials and craftsmen (Exodus 35:1–36:7), the construction (Exodus 36:8–39:32), and the work completed and consecrated (Exodus 39:33–40:38).

Exodus 35:3. The prohibition against lighting a fire on the Sabbath appears here for the first time. In Exodus 16:23, Moses commands the Israelites to prepare the food for the Sabbath by cooking it on the previous day. This prohibition against lighting a fire has led some Jewish sects to refrain from any use of light or fire on the Sabbath. However, rabbinical teaching only prohibits cooking and baking.

Exodus 35:5, 21-22. The writer emphasizes the people's desire to give. Verse 5 mentions the generous person willing to bring an offering. Verse 21 refers to everyone whose heart moved him. Verse 22 mentions the willing person. The men and women freely contribute their ornaments and thus show their enthusiasm for the project.

Exodus 38:8. This reference to women who minister at the entrance to the Tent of Meeting poses a problem, since the Tent of Meeting, or tabernacle, had not yet been built. The mirrors were made of burnished bronze, and the women who gave them for the service of the Lord before the tabernacle was built, continue their devout service after it was built.

We do not know what kind of service such women performed. Tradition says they came to pray. First Samuel 2:22 refers to women and the sanctuary, but the women mentioned there are involved in unseemly acts.

Apparently women had a place in Israelite worship. The Temple in Jerusalem had a Women's Court. And the New Testament indicates that a devout widow, Anna, practically lived in the Temple. (See Luke 2:36-37.)

Exodus 39:1. The phrase, "as the LORD commanded Moses," appears seven times in this chapter. Long ago Jewish rabbis noticed the similarities between this section of Exodus and the Creation account in Genesis. Creation took seven days,

the building of the tabernacle took seven months, and the building of the Temple took seven years.

The repetition of this phrase emphasizes how well the people had done the work. Earlier, they had failed in their allegiance to the Lord and Moses. But now they were devoted to the work. The blessing of Moses comes at the end rather than at the beginning of their efforts. Tradition tells us that Moses composed Psalm 90 on this occasion. The concluding verse of the Psalm states,

> May the favor of the Lord our God rest upon us;
>   establish thou the work of our hands for us—
>   yes, establish the work of our hands.

Exodus 40. Notice that the sanctuary was erected beginning with the Most Holy Place (the ark of the Testimony) and working outward. The presence of God was localized in the Most Holy Place. Here only gold was used. God's great glory was worthy of only the most precious and purest of metals, gold.

The Book of Exodus closes with the fulfillment of the promise that God gave to Moses in Exodus 29:43, 45. God's presence dwells with the people.

The Tent of Meeting accompanied the Israelites in their wanderings in the desert. After the conquest they established it at Shiloh. (See Joshua 18:1.) During the time of Samuel, the Tent of Meeting was at Nob (see 1 Samuel 21:1-6), east of Jerusalem. David moved it to Gibeon (see 1 Kings 3:4), and Solomon had it brought to Jerusalem (see 1 Kings 8:4). From this point in history, the location of the Tent of Meeting is lost. It is possible that it was retained within the Temple of Solomon and destroyed with it by the Babylonians in 587 B.C.

DIMENSION THREE: WHAT DOES THE BIBLE MEAN TO ME?

This lesson encourages the group to consider the level of participation God's people should attain in carrying out worthy projects. Dimension Three in the student book directs the individual to consider the idea of "Gifts of and for God." Read the material in the student book, and draw upon the additional ideas below to develop the discussion.

Exodus 35:20-35; 36:1
Gifts of and for God

The participation of the people in the project was at two levels: (1) the generous contributions of material gifts, which were brought to the project by every part of the community, and (2) the work of the gifted individuals who did the actual crafting of the Tent of Meeting.

You could ask the participants to form two groups. Each group will discuss one of the levels of participation mentioned above. Appoint one person in each group to report the results of the discussion to the entire study group. After

INSTRUCTIONS CARRIED OUT

a five- to seven-minute period of discussion, bring the two groups together and have the reporters summarize the discussions of their groups.

You may want to emphasize the generosity of the people. Compare their generosity to that of the early Christians, recorded in 2 Corinthians 8:1-5. The project mentioned there was to provide relief for the Christians in Jerusalem. See also 2 Corinthians 9:6-15.

The group might want to consider what are fitting projects for a congregation of committed Christians. The building of a sanctuary was the project in today's lesson, and building facilities for educational purposes and for worship engage many congregations. Such building projects, although they may be within the will of the Lord, cannot be compared to the building of the tabernacle. To Israel, the Tent of Meeting was a visible symbol of the presence of God in the midst of his people. For Christians, no building can fulfill that function. The presence of the Lord is in the hearts of his people. (See 1 Corinthians 3:16; 6:19; 2 Corinthians 6:16; Ephesians 2:19-21.) The church existed for two or more centuries before actual church buildings were constructed.

James 1:27 suggests another project—meeting the needs of the widow and orphan. They represent the weakest and most vulnerable elements in a Christian community. Paul instructs Christians as follows: "Therefore, as we have opportunity, let us do good to all people, especially to those who belong to the family of believers" (Galatians 6:10).

Do government-sponsored social welfare programs relieve the local Christian community of the responsibility to meet human needs? Ask the group to identify unmet needs in your community. How might those needs be met in a community?

The talents that individuals possess are gifts from God, spiritual gifts. Christian communities often honor highly gifted preachers, singers, and musicians. Do we often overlook less visible gifted members of our communities? Recall Tabitha. (See Acts 9:36-43.) Her sewing skills were certainly a gift of God that met the needs of the widows in Joppa. Ask the group members to consider what unrecognized talents exist within the group and/or church. How can we help people realize that their talents are from God and are useful to his purpose?

Before closing, point out that Moses blessed all the people, not just Bezalel, Oholiab, and their assistants. The entire community is blessed when it engages in godly projects.

Close the session with a prayer of thanks for all individuals in the group and for the contribution that their gifts from God make to the church. On chalkboard or a large sheet of paper, list any insights the class members may have gained from their study of Exodus 28–34.

It is a burnt offering, an offering made by fire, an aroma pleasing to the LORD (1:17).

— 9 —

Instructions for Sacrifices

Leviticus 1–5

DIMENSION ONE:
WHAT DOES THE BIBLE SAY?

Answer these questions by reading Leviticus 1

1. From what place does the Lord speak to Moses about the offerings that the Israelites are to bring? (Leviticus 1:1-2)

   God speaks to Moses from the Tent of Meeting.

2. What qualities does God require in an animal to make it acceptable for a burnt offering? (Leviticus 1:3)

   The animal must be a male without defect.

3. Where is the burnt offering to be offered? (Leviticus 1:3)

   It is to be offered at the entrance to the Tent of Meeting.

4. Why must the person bringing the burnt offering lay his hands on the head of the animal? (Leviticus 1:4)

   The person lays his hands on the animal's head because the animal will be an atonement for him.

5. Who kills the bull of the burnt offering? (Leviticus 1:5)

   The person offering the sacrifice kills the animal.

6. Who is to sprinkle the blood of the sacrificial bull against the altar and lay the pieces on the altar? (Leviticus 1:5-8)

   The priest is to do these things.

7. Where is a sheep or goat, taken from the flock for a burnt offering, to be killed? (Leviticus 1:11)

   The animal is to be killed on the north side of the altar before the Lord.

8. Besides a bull from the herd or a ram from the flock, what other animals will God accept for a burnt offering? (Leviticus 1:14)

   Doves or young pigeons are also acceptable for a burnt offering.

9. Who kills burnt offerings of birds? (Leviticus 1:15)

   The priest kills birds brought as burnt offerings.

10. Where does the priest place the ashes of the sacrifice? (Leviticus 1:16)

    He places the ashes on the east side of the altar.

Answer these questions by reading Leviticus 2

11. When an Israelite brings a grain offering to the Lord, what does he bring to the priests? (Leviticus 2:1)

    He brings fine flour, oil, and incense.

12. What happens to the part of the grain offering that is not burned? (Leviticus 2:3)

    The remainder is for Aaron and his sons.

13. How may the grain offering be prepared? (Leviticus 2:4-7)

    Grain offerings may be baked in the oven, made on a griddle, or cooked in a pan.

14. What two elements does God not permit in a grain offering, and what element does God absolutely require? (Leviticus 2:11-13)

    God does not permit yeast or honey, but he requires salt in a grain offering.

15. How is a grain offering of firstfruits to be prepared? (Leviticus 2:14-15)

The grain head is to be crushed, roasted with fire, and offered with oil and incense.

Answer these questions by reading Leviticus 3

16. For what kind of sacrifice can persons use either a heifer or a bull? (Leviticus 3:1)

Either can be used for a fellowship offering.

17. What parts of the sacrificial animal are burned on the altar for a fellowship offering? (Leviticus 3:3-4)

The fat from the inner parts, the kidneys with their fat, and part of the liver are burned.

18. Why does God not permit the Israelites to eat fat or blood? (Leviticus 3:16-17)

Fat and blood belong to the Lord.

Answer these questions by reading Leviticus 4

19. For what kind of sin does the anointed priest offer a young bull without defect? (Leviticus 4:2-3)

The offering is for unintentional sins.

20. What does the anointed priest do with the blood of the bull offered for a sin offering? (Leviticus 4:6-7)

He sprinkles part of the blood before the curtain of the sanctuary seven times, places some on the horns of the fragrant incense altar, and pours the rest at the base of the altar of burnt offering.

21. What does the priest do with the parts of the bull that are not used in the sacrifice? (Leviticus 4:11-12)

The priest carries them outside the camp to a ceremonially clean place and burns them.

22. What is an acceptable sin offering for a leader who sins unintentionally? (Leviticus 4:22-23)

The correct offering is a male goat without defect.

23. What is an acceptable sin offering for one of the members of the community who sins unintentionally? (Leviticus 4:27-28)

The member of the community brings a female goat without defect.

Answer these questions by reading Leviticus 5

24. For what four offenses does God require a person to present a guilt offering? (Leviticus 5:1-4)

  a. *failure to testify as a witness*
  b. *touching a ceremonially unclean animal*
  c. *touching human uncleanness*
  d. *thoughtlessly taking an oath*

25. If a person guilty of a sin cannot afford to offer a female lamb from the flock as an offering, what else can he offer? (Leviticus 5:7)

He can offer two doves or two young pigeons.

26. Besides offering a ram, what else must a person do who has committed a violation? (Leviticus 5:16)

He must make restitution for the violation and must add a fifth of the value of the offering to give to the priest.

27. Is a person guilty who commits a sin unintentionally? (Leviticus 5:17-19)

Yes, the person is guilty.

DIMENSION TWO: WHAT DOES THE BIBLE MEAN?

The group may benefit from the following information about Leviticus. This information supplements the information given in Dimension Two of the student book.

Genesis is the book of beginnings, while Exodus is the book of redemption. These two books lead into Leviticus, which can be considered as a book of communion and priestly worship. While the book emphasizes worship in the tabernacle, controlled by the priests who were from the tribe of Levi, the intention of Leviticus is to set down regulations that will produce a holy people.

Leviticus can be outlined as follows:

  I. Instructions for sacrifice for individuals, the congregation, and the priests (Leviticus 1–7)
  II. Consecration of priests and the beginning of sacrifices (Leviticus 8–10)
  III. Laws for purification and atonement (Leviticus 11–16)
  IV. Holiness laws (Leviticus 17–26)
  V. An appendix on vows and tithes (Leviticus 27)

In this lesson, Chapters 1–3 deal with the offerings of individuals, Chapter 4 with the offerings for a priest and the whole congregation, and Chapters 5–7 give rules for various kinds of offerings.

After the class members have completed Dimension One, take a few minutes to discuss this outline of Leviticus. You might want to write this outline on chalkboard or a large sheet of paper.

To supplement this outline, examine the titles of Lessons 9 through 13 in this unit. The titles give a general indication of the content of the lessons, and the progression of the titles through Lesson 13 provides an idea of the content of the book.

To complete the overview, read with the participants Leviticus 1:1 and 27:34. These passages establish the fact that in this book the Israelites travel no further. Leviticus contains very little action, and what little action there is, centers on the sanctuary. Israel's journey to the Promised Land only begins anew in the Book of Numbers, after the rules and regulations of Leviticus have been fully presented.

In Exodus 33:16-17 God promised his presence on their journey; and in Exodus 40:34-35, the glory of the Lord filled the newly erected tabernacle. But before the journey toward Canaan continued, Israel had to receive instructions on how to live with a holy God in their midst. That is what the study of Leviticus is all about.

The student book provides considerable background information. Additional material is provided below.

Leviticus 1:2. Jewish commentators draw attention to the expression, "any of you" (Hebrew, *adam*), in this verse. It indicates that even a heathen can bring an offering to the Lord if moved to do so, and it will be accepted.

Leviticus 1:16. An interesting interpretation notes that the inner parts [crop] of the pigeon were thrown away while inner parts of the animals were washed and burned (see verses 9, 13). The explanation is that the ox or sheep is fed by its master, while the bird finds its own food. Some of its food may have been stolen, and that would make it an unacceptable sacrifice.

Leviticus 2:3. The portion of the offerings given to the priests is classified as "holy" or as "most holy." The most holy food could be eaten only by the priests within the tabernacle enclosure. The holy food could be eaten by the families of the priests outside the sanctuary in any clean place; for example, in their homes.

Leviticus 4:2-3, 13-14. This chapter no longer focuses on "any of you" but on the offering of the anointed (high) priest (see verses 2-12) and on the whole community. The leaders of the community make up the assembly. (See Exodus 18:21-26.) The assembly offers the sin offering on behalf of all the people.

Leviticus 5:1-13. This section deals with special cases that require a sin offering. No distinction is made here between sins committed intentionally or unintentionally. In verse 3, human uncleanness implies contact with a dead body. In

verse 4, the person apparently took an oath to do something and then forgot to do it. Later he became aware of his thoughtless oath.

Leviticus 5:15. A shekel is a weight of silver, since coinage had not yet been invented. Exodus 30:13 establishes the shekel of the sanctuary as twenty gerahs. Twenty gerahs is about four-tenths of an ounce of silver.

Leviticus 5:17. The phrase, "though he does not know," means "while not sure of it." The person is in doubt as to whether he has broken a law that requires a sin offering.

DIMENSION THREE: WHAT DOES THE BIBLE MEAN TO ME?

Leviticus 5:1-13—The High Cost of Sin

The student book suggests that the group consider "The High Cost of Sin." The main ideas expressed are these:

1. God intends that his people be holy
2. Sin is the transgression of God's will
3. The cost of sin is high
   a. In terms of material costs
   b. In terms of social or community costs

Point out that sin is "missing the mark" of God's will for our lives. Rather than aligning one's life with the will of God, the sinner departs from that divine will. The result is separation from God. The person that sins shall surely die. (See Genesis 2:16-17; Romans 5:12.) The sentence of death can only be removed by the death of the guilty person or by the substitution of an innocent victim. The blood of the sacrifice provides atonement.

Animal sacrifice began in Genesis 3:21, where God made Adam and Eve garments of skins to clothe their nakedness. Abraham offered sacrifices to God, and in time the complicated sacrificial system about which we are studying was established in Israel by Moses under God's direction.

This system continued until the atoning death of Christ on the cross reconciled all persons to God. (See 2 Corinthians 5:14-21; 1 Peter 1:18-20.) In Jesus, God provided a substitute for each of us, his only begotten son who was without spot or defect.

To become a Christian one must recognize the reality of personal sin and accept the atonement by Jesus Christ in faith. Recall the words of John the Baptist, "Look, the Lamb of God, who takes away the sin of the world!" (John 1:29).

In light of God's plan of salvation for humankind, have the group consider the following questions:

1. How has our modern, secular society obscured the reality of sin? To be convinced of the reality of sin, people must be convinced of the reality of God. How has modern

life dulled our sense of the divine? What should Christians do to make society aware of the reality of God? Has your local church been negligent in this respect? If so, what can you as individuals or as a group do to change the situation?

2. The church is called to be the community of the redeemed and the committed. How effectively do the churches in your area demonstrate this redemption?

3. The Bible is God's revelation to all. How important is Bible study in your life? What can be done to extend the influence of the Bible in your church and/or community?

You might want to have the group discuss the idea of acceptable worship. Read Leviticus 1:1-2 aloud. Recall that the regulations for worship in today's lesson were addressed to the people generally. Acceptable worship for the Israelites required them to bring sacrificial animals and offerings to the tabernacle. The purpose of these activities was to maintain ritual cleanness and to receive remission of sins through the substitutionary death of the animal that was offered. What is acceptable worship today? Consider various aspects of public worship.

Consider such factors as the location of worship. Why do we call the buildings in which we meet *churches*, rather than *tabernacles* or *temples*? How do church buildings differ in function from a temple or a tabernacle? In what way or ways are they similar? Is it proper to call a building a church?

What is a *church*, based on the New Testament usage of the word? (You might use a Bible concordance to examine the passages in which the word appears.) What did Jesus mean in Matthew 16:18 when he said, "On this rock I will build my church, and the gates of Hades will not overcome it"?

Consider the form of worship. Do some of the group prefer a liturgical service, while others prefer a less formal meeting? What direction can we find in the New Testament? Is Ephesians 5:18-20 helpful in this respect? What can we learn from Paul's words in 1 Corinthians 14:26-40?

What about music? What music is acceptable to God? How open are we to variations in the music we associate with worship?

Close the session by offering a brief prayer of thanksgiving for the opportunity to study God's word with this group of persons. If time allows, list any insights the class members may have gained from their study of Leviticus 1–5.

So Aaron and his sons did everything the LORD commanded through Moses (8:36).

10

Cultic Worship

Leviticus 6–10

DIMENSION ONE:
WHAT DOES THE BIBLE SAY?

Answer these questions by reading Leviticus 6

1. In what four ways can a person deceive a neighbor? (Leviticus 6:1-3)

   a. *in a matter of something entrusted to him*
   b. *through stealing*
   c. *by cheating of lost property*
   d. *by swearing falsely*

2. Anyone guilty of mistreating a neighbor must offer a guilt offering in order to be forgiven. What else does God require? (Leviticus 6:4-5)

   God requires full restitution plus one-fifth to the person wronged.

3. To whom does Moses give the law of the burnt offering? (Leviticus 6:8-9)

   Moses gives the law to Aaron and his sons.

4. What will Aaron do with the fire on the altar at night? (Leviticus 6:9)

   Aaron will keep the fire on the altar burning throughout the night.

5. After the priest takes away the ashes of the evening burnt offering, what does he do? (Leviticus 6:12)

   He keeps the fire on the altar burning and makes offerings on it.

6. How long should the fire on the altar burn? (Leviticus 6:13)

   The fire should burn continuously.

7. Who among the Israelites may eat the priest's portion of the grain offering? (Leviticus 6:18)

   Any male descendant of Aaron may eat of the priest's portion.

8. On the day Moses anoints him, what does the high priest offer to the Lord? (Leviticus 6:20-22)

   He offers a grain offering.

9. Who must eat the sin offering that an Israelite brings? (Leviticus 6:26)

   The priest who offers it must eat it.

10. How do the priests prepare the meat of the sin offering? (Leviticus 6:28)

    The priests boil the meat in a clay pot or bronze pot.

Answer these questions by reading Leviticus 7

11. How are the guilt offering and the sin offering alike? (Leviticus 7:7)

    Both of the offerings are given to the priest who offers them.

12. If a person is unclean and eats of the meat of a fellowship offering, what happens? (Leviticus 7:20-21)

    That person is cut off from the people.

13. What two parts of a sacrificial animal may the people not eat? (Leviticus 7:22-27)

    They may not eat the fat or the blood of a sacrificial animal.

14. Which priest receives the right thigh of an animal offered as a fellowship offering? (Leviticus 7:32-33)

    The priest who offers the fellowship offering receives the right thigh.

Answer these questions by reading Leviticus 8

15. Besides assembling the people and priests, what things does Moses assemble for the consecration of the priests? (Leviticus 8:2)

    Moses also assembles the garments, the anointing oil, the bull, the two rams, and the basket of bread made without yeast.

16. Who offers the first sacrifices in the new tabernacle? (Leviticus 8:15-16)

    Moses offers the first sacrifices in the tabernacle.

17. What does Moses do with the blood from the ram of ordination? (Leviticus 8:23-24)

    He puts some of it on the right ears, thumbs, and big toes of Aaron and Aaron's sons, and he sprinkles the remaining blood on the altar.

18. How long does the ordination ceremony of Aaron and his sons last? (Leviticus 8:33)

    The ordination ceremony lasts seven days.

Answer these questions by reading Leviticus 9

19. How is the glory of the Lord shown to the people? (Leviticus 9:23-24)

    The glory of the Lord is the fire that comes forth and consumes the offering on the altar.

20. How do the people react when they see the glory of God? (Leviticus 9:24)

    The people shout for joy and fall facedown.

Answer these questions by reading Leviticus 10

21. Why does the fire devour Nadab and Abihu? (Leviticus 10:1-2)

    They offered unauthorized fire before the Lord.

22. What does Moses warn Aaron, Eleazar, and Ithamar not to do? (Leviticus 10:6-7)

    He warns them not to let their hair become unkempt, not to tear their clothes, and not to go out from the Tent of Meeting.

23. Besides offering sacrifices, what other function does God require of the priests? (Leviticus 10:11)

    God requires the priests to teach the people all the decrees of the Lord given to Moses.

24. What part of the sacrificial meat may the daughters of Aaron eat? (Leviticus 10:14)

    They may eat the breast and thigh from the fellowship offerings.

25. Why does Moses become angry with Eleazar and Ithamar? (Leviticus 10:16-17)

    They burn the goat of the sin offering rather than eating it.

DIMENSION TWO: WHAT DOES THE BIBLE MEAN?

The specific regulations for this entire sacrificial system are so foreign to us that these lessons in Leviticus are some of the most difficult in our study of the Bible. Nevertheless, it is important for us to have a general understanding of the system. After the Temple of Solomon was built, the sacrifices (ordinarily made at various shrines) were made at the Temple. This practice continued until the Temple was destroyed in 587 B.C. The Temple was rebuilt in Jerusalem in 520 B.C., and the sacrificial system continued until the destruction of the second Temple in A.D. 70 by the Romans.

The sacrificial system was good preparation for the coming of Jesus and his sacrificial death. To appreciate fully what God has done for humanity in Christ, a general understanding of the sacrificial system instituted by Moses is useful. This study can provide that understanding.

This lesson divides into three main parts: Chapters 6–7 are addressed to the priests and discuss certain sacrifices. Chapters 8–9 describe the ritual observed at the consecration of the priests to their office, and Chapter 10 records a major priestly sin, which is followed by supplementary instructions.

Because Chapter 10 records the bizarre death of Nadab and Abihu, the participants may want to spend the most time discussing that section of the lesson.

All the information about sacrifices in Lesson 9 was addressed to "the people of Israel." (See Leviticus 1:2; 4:2.) Today's lesson begins with words addressed to Aaron and his sons—the priests. Part of the lesson contains further instructions for the people. (See Leviticus 7:11-38.) Chapter 8 contains an account of the anointing of Aaron. Chapter 9 describes Aaron as he offers his first sacrifice in the new tabernacle. The tenth chapter provides a dramatic example of how carefully persons were to observe the sacrificial system.

Leviticus 6:9. The previous chapters were addressed to the people. This section is addressed to the priesthood and concludes with a summary statement in 7:37-38. The content is concerned with instructions to the priests about offerings.

The word "regulation" is a translation of the Hebrew word *torah*. Literally, the word here means, "direction, instruction."

The burnt offering described here is a sacrifice made every morning and evening on behalf of Israel. (See Exodus 29:38-42.)

Leviticus 6:10. The ashes of the sacrifice were treated with great reverence, since they were the remnant of holy things. The morning preparation of the altar for the sacrifices of the day was a sacred ritual. Even though it was a physically dirty task, the priest in charge dressed in ceremonial robes while cleaning the surface of the altar. The ashes and charred bones were carefully removed and placed beside the altar. After changing into ordinary clothes, the priest took the ashes to a clean place outside the camp.

Leviticus 6:13. The perpetual fire on the altar meant that the law against lighting a fire on the Sabbath did not apply to the sanctuary. (See Exodus 35:3.) In the time of Jesus, a special day was set apart when everyone was to bring wood for the altar so that it would never lack for fuel.

Leviticus 6:14-23. Two separate rituals concerning grain offerings are given here. The first (verses 14-18) accompanies the daily burnt offerings. The second (verses 19-23) concerns a grain offering made by a priest on the day of his ordination. The grain offering of a priest is completely burned; no one is to eat any part of it.

Leviticus 7:7-8. "The priest who makes atonement" is the officiating priest of the day. A number of priests were required daily for the services in the tabernacle, but one was charged as the officiating priest. (See Luke 1:5-10.)

The main interest here is in establishing the share of the sacrifice allotted to the officiating priest. The skin of the animal was of value not only for the manufacturing of leather products but also for the making of scrolls upon which to write.

Leviticus 7:16-18. Apart from the religious requirements, this regulation would prevent the eating of meat that had been cooked and then kept three days without refrigeration. To have eaten it would probably have caused gastric poisoning.

Leviticus 7:22-27. The prohibition against eating fat and blood occurs several times in Leviticus. (See 3:17; 17:10-14.) It lies behind the marketing of modern kosher meat. Kosher meat is slaughtered by a specialist who bleeds the animal rapidly. The remaining blood is extracted by means of washing and salting the meat. All fat, except that covered by flesh, is removed.

Leviticus 8:10. This activity was carried on in conjunction with the consecration of the tabernacle described in Exodus 40. This account of the consecration of Aaron and his sons is separated from Exodus by several chapters of regulations on sacrifices. Yet logically, the prescriptions for the priesthood would be stated before it began to function.

Not only did Moses instruct Aaron and his sons, he demonstrated how sacrifices should be made. Moses was of the levitical family, but Jewish tradition notes that he was a priest only for the seven days connected with Aaron's consecration.

Leviticus 8:23. The sanctified blood, which Moses applied to Aaron's right ear, thumb, and big toe, probably symbolized Aaron's need to hear the instruction of the Lord, to have a hand ready to carry out his will, and to have feet ready to walk in the path outlined in the covenant.

Leviticus 10:1-20. This extraordinary incident marred the dedication of the sanctuary and the ordination of the priesthood. It was long remembered in Israel. Twice, the Book of Numbers (see 3:4; 26:61) attributes the death of Nadab and Abihu, Aaron's oldest sons, to their use of unauthorized fire.

The meaning of "unauthorized fire" is unclear, but scholars have suggested various possibilities. Because verses 8-9 stipulate that priests abstain from intoxicating liquor before performing their sacred duties, some have suggested that Nadab and Abihu had been drinking when they made their fatal error. On the other hand, perhaps the fire was said to be unauthorized because the sons of Aaron did not consult Moses and Aaron before offering the fire. Failure to consult with their elders could have been a deliberate attempt to usurp the authority of Moses and Aaron.

Some scholars have suggested that an "unauthorized fire" was one that was not taken from the altar, the only legitimate place from which fire may be taken. The fire on the altar was lighted by the Lord and was sacred. There were other fires in the enclosure of the tabernacle; perhaps Nadab and Abihu took their fire from one of these non-sacred fires.

Leviticus 10:2 tells us that "fire came out from the presence of the LORD" and consumed the sons of Aaron. Fire from the presence of God would have come from the Most Holy Place. The origin of the fire that devoured these men suggests that they may have entered the Most Holy Place, and thus the presence of God. No one was permitted there except the high priest.

Priestly regulations were very specific about the making of incense. (See Exodus 30:34-38.) Perhaps the incense that Nadab and Abihu used was improper, and the improper incense made the fire "unholy." The important phrase is found at the end of verse 1: "contrary to his command." Whatever the precise meaning of "unauthorized," Nadab and Abihu acted in disobedience to God and were punished.

While death came to Nadab and Abihu suddenly and without warning, they had no excuse. As leaders and priests, they had received full instructions. Their actions represented a change from what was required. The event certainly served to impress Israel with the sacredness of everything that pertained to the Lord and his worship. Moses uses their deaths to illustrate the oracle in verse 3: "Among those who approach me / I will show myself holy; / in the sight of all the people / I will be honored." When the Lord is honored by those who are near him, the effect will be that all the people will glorify him.

DIMENSION THREE: WHAT DOES THE BIBLE MEAN TO ME?

The student book focuses on "The Problem of Sin." The following ideas will supplement those given in the student book.

Leviticus 9:7-16—The Problem of Sin

Draw the group's attention to Matthew 15:1-20. Here Jesus teaches that sin is more than wrong or inappropriate actions. How a person thinks determines what he or she is before God. Notice also Matthew 12:33-37. There Jesus states that "out of the overflow of the heart the mouth speaks," and "by your words you will be acquitted, and by your words you will be condemned."

Point out that while Christians are not free of the tendency to sin, they are dedicated to living a life free from sin. Read Romans 6:1-14. How is the desirable end about which Paul speaks possible? First, no Christian bears a burden of guilt for past sins. Repentance, confession, and commitment are parts of the Christian life. Paul can say "There is now no condemnation for those who are in Christ Jesus" (Romans 8:1). One who believes in Jesus has confidence in his or her salvation.

Leviticus 10:1-20 describes the consequences of sin and the importance of serving the Lord according to the rules he established. We serve no altar, nor is our service confined to a sacred enclosure as was that of the Mosaic priesthood. Yet in Romans 12:1-2, Paul uses sacrificial terms to exhort Christians to lead lives of dedicated service. These words remind us of the Communion ritual, which you might read aloud to the group. The remainder of the chapter (12:3-21) provides a "ritual list," so to speak. With the group, consider such questions as, "How am I (or, How are we) doing in respect to letting love be genuine, being aglow with the Spirit, rejoicing in hope," and so on.

To close the session, list any insights the class members have gained from their study of Leviticus 6–10. Then ask one of the group to lead in prayer, asking God for his support in overcoming our tendency to sin.

I am the LORD your God; consecrate yourselves and be holy, because I am holy (11:44).

— 11 —

Laws of Cleanness and Uncleanness

Leviticus 11–16

DIMENSION ONE:
WHAT DOES THE BIBLE SAY?

Answer these questions by reading Leviticus 11

1. Among the animals, which group can the people of Israel eat? (Leviticus 11:3)

   They can eat animals that have a completely divided hoof and chew the cud.

2. What types of water creatures does God forbid the people of Israel to eat? (Leviticus 11:9-12)

   They may eat any sea animals that have fins and scales.

3. How many different birds does God forbid the people of Israel to eat? (Leviticus 11:13-19)

   God forbids them to eat twenty different birds.

4. What four types of insects may the people of Israel eat? (Leviticus 11:20-21)

   They may eat the locust, katydid, cricket, and grasshopper.

5. Under what conditions can certain rodents and other "things that move along the ground" make an Israelite unclean? (Leviticus 11:31)

   One who touches these dead things becomes unclean.

6. When can contact with a clean animal make a person unclean? (Leviticus 11:39)

   When the animal is dead, touching it makes a person unclean.

7. What is the basic reason for these laws concerning cleanness and uncleanness? (Leviticus 11:45)

   God expects Israel to be holy because he, her God, is holy.

Answer these questions by reading Leviticus 12

8. How many days is a woman considered unclean after the birth of a son? of a daughter? (Leviticus 12:2-5)

   She is unclean for seven days if she has a son and fourteen days if she has a daughter.

9. What two offerings does God require of a woman after the days of her purification from childbirth? (Leviticus 12:6-8)

   God requires a lamb for a burnt offering and a pigeon or dove for a sin offering.

Answer these questions by reading Leviticus 13

10. By what symptoms can a priest identify an infectious skin disease? (Leviticus 13:1-3)

    An infectious skin disease may be detected when there is a swelling, or a rash, or a bright spot on the skin.

11. For how many days is a person suspected of having an infectious skin disease isolated? (Leviticus 13:4)

    The suspected person is isolated for seven days.

12. How does the priest know when a person who has an infectious skin disease is healed? (Leviticus 13:16-17)

    When raw flesh turns white, the person is healed.

13. Is a bald person unclean? (Leviticus 13:40-41)

    No, a bald person is not unclean.

14. What must a person with an infectious skin disease do to warn others that they are approaching a diseased person? (Leviticus 13:45)

    The person must wear torn clothes, let his or her hair be unkempt, cover the lower part of his or her face, and cry out, "Unclean! Unclean!"

15. How are persons with an infectious skin disease separated from healthy Israelites? (Leviticus 13:46)

They live alone outside the camp of Israel.

16. How must priests destroy contaminated garments? (Leviticus 13:52)

The priests must burn them.

Answer these questions by reading Leviticus 14

17. Who decides whether a person with an infectious disease is actually cured? (Leviticus 14:1-3)

The priest makes the decision.

18. What does a person who has been healed of an infectious skin disease do as a symbol of cleansing? (Leviticus 14:9)

He shaves off all the hair on his body and bathes himself and washes his clothes.

19. How does the priest use oil in the atonement ritual for a person cured of an infectious skin disease? (Leviticus 14:15-18)

He sprinkles some of the oil before the Lord and applies some of it to the right ear, thumb, and big toe of the person.

20. What does a poor man substitute for the usual sacrificial animals? (Leviticus 14:21-22)

A poor man offers one male lamb, a tenth of an ephah of fine flour, a log of oil, and two doves or two young pigeons.

21. What does a mildewed house look like? (Leviticus 14:37)

A mildewed house has greenish or reddish depressions on its walls.

22. How does a priest purify a house that harbored a mildew? (Leviticus 14:40-42)

The priest removes the infected stones and clay and plaster and replaces them with new.

Answer these questions by reading Leviticus 15

23. A person who comes into contact with someone who has a bodily discharge becomes unclean. How can that person become clean again? (Leviticus 15:5)

The person must wash his or her clothes, bathe, and be unclean until evening.

24. How can a person with a discharge willfully make someone else unclean? (Leviticus 15:8, 11)

He or she can do this by spitting upon someone or touching someone with unwashed hands.

25. For a person cured of a bodily discharge, how many days of purification are required? (Leviticus 15:13)

The purification rites take seven days.

26. An emission of semen makes a man unclean. What procedure must he follow to become clean again? (Leviticus 15:16)

He must bathe in water and be unclean until the evening.

27. Following her monthly period, for how many days is a woman unclean? (Leviticus 15:19)

She is unclean for seven days.

28. If a woman has an abnormal discharge, how can she become clean again? (Leviticus 15:28-30)

She waits seven days, and on the eighth day she presents a sin offering and a burnt offering.

29. What will happen to those who come to the tabernacle in an unclean state? (Leviticus 15:31)

They will die.

Answer these questions by reading Leviticus 16

30. What must Aaron do with two male goats? (Leviticus 16:9-10)

One goat is a sin offering for the people, and he sends the other into the desert.

31. What sacrifice must Aaron make for himself and his household before entering the holy place behind the curtain? (Leviticus 16:11)

Aaron must offer a bull as a sin offering with fragrant incense.

32. What happens to the goat dedicated to be the scapegoat? (Leviticus 16:21-22)

Aaron offers it to the Lord as atonement and sends it away into the desert.

33. How often does Israel observe this statute? (Leviticus 16:34)

Israel observes this statute of atonement once every year.

DIMENSION TWO:
WHAT DOES THE BIBLE MEAN?

This lesson begins with laws forbidding the consumption of certain animals. Chapters 12–15 are concerned with personal defilement and purification. The lesson concludes with a chapter on the Day of Atonement, the most holy day in the religious calendar of the Law of Moses. As you study the lesson, notice the emphasis on personal cleanness and holiness. These regulations show God's deep concern for the welfare of his people. They are to be a holy people. (See Leviticus 11:44.)

To begin the discussion of the text, ask the participants if they have any questions about Chapter 11. Since this chapter is concerned with the problem of clean and unclean animals, treat it separately.

Next, handle any questions on Leviticus 12:1-8, which deals with the purification of women after childbirth. Class members may be reluctant to talk about this subject. Encourage them to deal forthrightly, as the Old Testament does, with natural life processes.

The largest section of the lesson covers the problem of infectious skin diseases or leprosy and bodily discharges and secretions (Chapters 13–15). (*Leprosy* is the translation used by older Bible versions. Modern medicine doubts that leprosy was actually the condition mentioned.)

The last chapter of this lesson is on the Day of Atonement. Many calendars indicate the date on which Yom Kippur, as the day is called, falls. Usually it occurs sometime in late September. Make a note of the date for this year and ask your students to be aware of the day when it arrives. It is a part of what Jews call the high holy days. This season includes the Jewish New Year.

Leviticus 11:1. These regulations are addressed not only to Moses but also to Aaron. It was the priests' responsibility "to distinguish between the holy and the common, between the unclean and the clean" (10:10). The distinction between clean and unclean was important because God wanted his worshipers to be clean.

Leviticus 11:8. Any dead body was considered defiling, be it person or beast. Clean animals that had been properly slaughtered for food or for sacrifice did not cause uncleanness. But a clean animal that died naturally would cause uncleanness if touched. (See Leviticus 11:39-40.)

Leviticus 11:27. This verse includes dogs and cats. Touching them while alive did not confer uncleanness, but touching their dead bodies would.

Leviticus 12:1-8. Uncleanness connected with birth was due to the bodily discharges of the birth process. The child itself was not considered unclean. The reference to menstruation indicates that the discharge was the source of uncleanness.

No apparent reason exists for the distinction between the birth of a boy and that of a girl, as pertains to the length of time for purification. The symbolism of the sacred number seven may be at work here. Notice the use of seven and its multiple. Forty (seven days plus thirty-three days) was also a sacred number, and its multiple, eighty, (fourteen days plus sixty-six days) also occurs here. For further information on the symbolic use of numbers, look under "Number" or "Numerology" in a Bible dictionary.

Leviticus 13:1-8. Older versions of the Bible use the word *leprosy.* We can trace the English word *leprosy* back to the Latin Vulgate Bible and to the Greek Septuagint. The word does not adequately translate the Hebrew, for in ancient times *leprosy* was incurable. An *infectious skin disease* is more accurate.

In all these cases, the priest simply determines whether the person with symptoms is ritually unclean. At no time is the priest like a doctor, trying to cure the disease. Almost without fail the uncleanness was the result of a discharge from the body. Anyone with such a condition was ineligible to participate in the sacred rites of the tabernacle, either to bring an offering or to partake of the sacrificial food.

Leviticus 13:9-17. The diagnosis of an infectious skin disease apparently hinges on the presence of raw flesh.

Leviticus 13:26-28. An isolation period of seven days would result in major healing for sores not related to infectious skin disease. But a serious infectious skin disease would show little change and would probably spread.

Leviticus 13:29-37. This case appears to be one of ringworm.

Leviticus 13:45-46. Serious infectious skin disease was considered a living death. The person suffering from it was cut off from the congregation of Israel and from the sanctuary. The person suffering from infection was required to adopt the customs and clothing of someone in deep mourning. After recovery, the person must go through a service of ritual cleansing. Leviticus 14:1-32 describes this procedure.

Leviticus 13:47-49. The greenish or reddish patches probably refer to mold or mildew. Once a problem was suspected, the priest determined if the clothes were clean or unclean. If he was unable to determine the purity immediately, the item was placed in isolation for the usual seven days. After that time, if the growth had enlarged, it was judged unclean. If there was no change, the article was washed and again laid aside for seven days. If washing did not remove the evidence of growth, the item was declared unclean and destroyed.

Leviticus 14:2-7. We do not really understand the reason for these procedures. They may represent restoration to life and society of the person with infection. Notice the emphasis upon "living" birds and "fresh" water. The slain bird could represent the leper's former state, while the living bird that is released into the open field would represent the freedom of the healed person to return to the camp of Israel.

Leviticus 14:33-53. As in the case of a fungus infection on clothes, the Israelites did not understand the growth of lichens, dry rot, and the sort. Again, they thought in terms of human diseases. The priest followed the procedures for a person suspected of having an infectious skin disease. He closed up the house for a seven-day period. After seven days, if the mildew had spread, the infected walls and plaster were replaced. If the mildew reappeared in the newly repaired house, the entire structure was torn down and cast away. For a repaired house in which the problem did not reappear, the priest used the same ritual for cleansing the house as he used for cleansing the person cured of an infectious disease.

Leviticus 15. This chapter deals with bodily secretions, both normal—such as male semen and female menstruation— and abnormal, such as running sores. Keep in mind that most bodily secretions were considered unclean, although some produced only short-term uncleanness. Notice that anyone who touched anything unclean became unclean also. The main purpose of the chapter is stated in verse 31—the prevention of the defilement of God's tabernacle by anyone or anything that was ritually unclean.

Leviticus 15:25. This regulation helps us understand the desperate situation of the woman with the flow of blood whom Jesus healed. (See Matthew 9:20-22; Luke 8:43-48.) Her flow of blood made her ritually unclean.

Leviticus 16:2. God's holiness is so great that even the high priest can be endangered in his presence. Aaron and his successors were limited to entrance before the ark of the covenant only once each year—the Day of Atonement. There the high priest was to make atonement for the entire nation, including himself.

We read about the Day of Atonement in Exodus 30:10, but Leviticus 16 presents the institution of the ceremony in full. The regulations for the great annual day of purification follows the earlier chapters on purification for individual problems.

DIMENSION THREE: WHAT DOES THE BIBLE MEAN TO ME?

In the student book, Dimension Three centers on "The Biblical Idea of Holiness." Read the information provided in the student book, and discuss with the class members the questions found there. In addition, you may decide to discuss with them the theme of dietary restrictions.

Leviticus 11:1-47—Dietary Restrictions

The purpose of these dietary restrictions was clearly religious in intent—to establish Israel as a peculiar people, separate and distinct from the surrounding nations. Nevertheless, many commentators point to the value of the laws for good health. For example, it is common knowledge today that the disease trichinosis is transmitted to humans through improperly cooked pork.

While the dietary laws are no longer in force for the Christian, how careful should a Christian be about the diet? Do we have a responsibility toward God to eat only wholesome, nourishing foods?

Does Paul's statement in 1 Corinthians 6:19-20—that we are to consider our bodies temples of the Holy Spirit— apply to our eating habits? Should Christians be concerned about excessive weight, particularly in light of the close relationship between obesity and heart disease? How can we make persons in the local church aware of this problem without hurting the feelings of some and causing resentment in others? Or should we ignore it?

Close the session by asking the class members to think about any new ideas or insights they have gained from studying today's lesson.

— 12 —

Laws for Everyday Living

Leviticus 17–21

DIMENSION ONE:
WHAT DOES THE BIBLE SAY?

Answer these questions by reading Leviticus 17

1. To whom does God address this series of laws? (Leviticus 17:1)

    God addresses these laws to Aaron, his sons, and all the people.

2. Where must persons kill animals? (Leviticus 17:3-4)

    They must kill the animals at the entrance to the Tent of Meeting.

3. What is the punishment for a person who does not bring a sacrifice to the Tent of Meeting for an offering to the Lord? (Leviticus 17:9)

    That person will be cut off from the people.

4. What part of an animal does God forbid the people to eat? Why? (Leviticus 17:10-11)

    The people cannot eat blood because the animal's life is in its blood, and blood is the atonement for their lives.

5. When Israelites go hunting and kill a game bird or animal, what must they do with the blood? (Leviticus 17:13)

    They must drain out the animal's blood and cover it with earth.

Answer these questions by reading Leviticus 18

6. God does not want the Israelites to imitate the practices of what two nations? (Leviticus 18:3)

    These two nations are Egypt and Canaan.

7. To whom do these ordinances apply? (Leviticus 18:26)

    These ordinances apply to the native and to the alien.

Answer these questions by reading Leviticus 19

8. Why does God require Israel to be holy by keeping these laws? (Leviticus 19:2)

    The Lord is a holy God who demands a holy people.

9. What penalty do Israelites suffer when they eat meat from a sacrifice on the third day after it is offered? (Leviticus 19:5-8)

    They are cut off from their people.

10. Why must a farmer leave gleanings from his crops? (Leviticus 19:9-10)

    The gleanings are a source of food for the poor and the alien in Israel.

11. How can persons profane the name of God? (Leviticus 19:12)

    Swearing by God's name falsely profanes the name of the Lord.

12. How does God show concern for persons with handicapping conditions? (Leviticus 19:14)

    God prohibits persons from cursing those who do not hear or putting a stumbling block before those who are blind.

13. In what two ways can a person commit an injustice in judgment? (Leviticus 19:15)

    A person commits an injustice in judgment by showing partiality toward the poor or favoritism to the great.

14. How must Israelites treat their neighbors? (Leviticus 19:18)

They must love their neighbors as themselves.

15. Why are a man and a female slave who have sinful sexual relations not put to death? (Leviticus 19:20)

They are not put to death because the slave girl is not free.

16. When in the life of a fruit tree may the owner begin to eat its fruit? (Leviticus 19:23-25)

The owner may eat the fruit in the fifth year.

17. Why must the Israelites observe these practices? (Leviticus 19:25, 30, 31)

They must observe these practices because God is the Lord.

18. How must the Israelites treat aliens living with them? Why? (Leviticus 19:33-34)

They must treat aliens like native-born Israelites because the Israelites were once aliens in Egypt.

Answer these questions by reading Leviticus 20

19. Chapter 20 establishes penalties for violations of holiness. With a word or two, list some of the violations that require the death penalty. You may add others to the list.

(Leviticus 20:2) offering a child to Molech
(Leviticus 20:6) consulting mediums or spiritists
(Leviticus 20:9) cursing one's mother or father
(Leviticus 20:10) committing adultery
(Leviticus 20:11-12) sexual intercourse with a father's wife or a daughter-in-law
(Leviticus 20:15-16) sexual relations with animals

20. How is Israel distinct from the other nations? (Leviticus 20:26)

God has separated Israel from other nations.

Answer these questions by reading Leviticus 21

21. Which dead persons may a priest touch without profaning himself? (Leviticus 21:1-3)

He may touch his mother, father, son, daughter, brother, or an unmarried sister.

22. Why does God place special restrictions on what a priest can do and whom he can marry? (Leviticus 21:7)

Priests are holy to God.

23. What requirements does the bride of a high priest have to meet? (Leviticus 21:13-15)

She must be a virgin, she must not have been divorced or defiled, and she must not be a prostitute.

24. What restrictions does God place on priests who have physical defects? (Leviticus 21:16-21)

A priest who has a physical defect may not approach the altar to offer sacrifices to God.

DIMENSION TWO: WHAT DOES THE BIBLE MEAN?

Biblical scholars call Leviticus 17–26 the "Holiness Code" or "The Law of Holiness." These chapters emphasize the holiness of God several times, along with the demand that the people of Israel also be holy. (See Leviticus 19:2; 20:26.) The purpose of the laws was to separate Israel's practices from the practices of the Canaanites and the surrounding pagan peoples.

Leviticus 17 is concerned with the sacredness of blood and the slaughter of animals for food. Leviticus 18 deals with the sanctity of marriage and with sexual behavior. Leviticus 19 is a collection of various rules of conduct. Chapter 20 lists transgressions that are punishable by death. The last chapter in this lesson discusses the holiness of the priesthood.

The laws in the Holiness Code describe how Israel should act in order to maintain fellowship with a holy God. These laws are an outgrowth of God's statement in Exodus 19:4-6 in which he promised that Israel would be a holy nation. For Israel to be his special people, she had to live separately and differently from the nations round about who were guilty of gross immorality and abominable practices. Therefore the theme throughout the Holiness Code is the demand that Israel be holy for the Lord God is holy.

Approach these chapters in three segments. The first consists of Chapter 17 only. In a way, it supplements the first part of Leviticus, making the point that animals slaughtered for food must be free of any idolatrous taint. Chapters 18–20 form the second segment of the lesson. This section deals with proper conduct among God's people. Personal conduct should be marked by a level of morality that reflects the holiness of God. The third segment, or Chapter 21, focuses on rules for the priests. Those rules are continued in Lesson 13. Deal primarily with the second segment, but allow enough discussion of Chapters 17 and 21 to resolve any questions the students may raise.

Leviticus 17:1-8. The requirement that every animal be slain at the Tent of Meeting applied only while Israel was encamped in the desert. During that time the Lord provided manna for food. In addition, meat from certain of the sacrifices was eaten by the Israelites. In this situation, probably little slaughtering solely for food was carried out. Later, when Israel was about to enter the land of Canaan where they would be living in cities and widely scattered from the sanctuary, this law was modified. It allowed slaughter for food consumption away from the sanctuary. (See Deuteronomy 12:20-28.)

Animal sacrifice to various deities and demons was common in pagan nations around Israel. The sacrificial system was retained in Israel as a manner of worship, but the worship was directed to the one, true God. The sacrifices were not beneficial to God, as they were thought to be in pagan worship. Rather, they were for Israel's benefit, that she might maintain a relationship with a holy God.

Leviticus 17:11. The Hebrews believed that when the blood was drained from a living creature, the life was also gone. The life, and thus the blood that contained life, was sacred and belonged to God. The early church also recognized the sanctity of blood. The Jerusalem Council ended with a communication to Gentile churches in which the Christians were exhorted to "abstain from food sacrificed to idols, from blood, from the meat of strangled animals" (Acts 15:29).

Leviticus 18–20. While the earlier chapters in Leviticus dealt with ritual uncleanness, these chapters are concerned with moral uncleanness. Among the concerns is sexual relations between family members related either by blood or by marriage. While such activities are common among the pagan populations of ancient Canaan, these laws raise marriage and the family to a sacred level. Christians inherit these moral truths and should treat family relationships with the utmost respect. (See Ephesians 5:21–6:4; 1 Thessalonians 4:1-7, for example.)

Leviticus 19:26, 31; 20:6, 27. These statements against mediums and spiritists indicate that occult practices were a real source of temptation to Israel. Behind such practices is the pagan idea that one can, through magical incantations or symbolic actions, obtain knowledge about the future and control it. Pagans thought in terms of many different forces that might cause bad or good in their lives. They tried to control these forces, or gods. For Israelites who professed belief in one all-knowing, all-powerful God, turning to pagan ways was utter folly and a reproach to Almighty God. No one who believed in the Creator of the universe should dabble in the occult. It was sheer pagan foolishness to do so. Isaiah called upon Israel to look "to the law and to the testimony!" (Isaiah 8:20).

Leviticus 19:29. The prohibition against selling a daughter into prostitution indicates (a) that such a thing was practiced, and (b) that a father owned his children as property and could sell them if he chose. (See Deuteronomy 23:17-18 also.) The use of the word *degrade* here is worthy of notice, for it indicates that womanhood was considered sacred.

Leviticus 19:32. Respect for the older community members is a mark of civility that was the rule.

Leviticus 19:33-34. The alien mentioned is a non-Israelite who lives among them and has adopted their religious customs and practices. Such a person, though a minority, was still treated with respect.

Leviticus 20:1-5. The identification of Molech is uncertain. First Kings 11:5, 7 identifies Molech with Milcom, a god of the Ammonites. At other times he is equated with Baal. Both Ahaz and Manasseh, kings of Judah, sacrificed their sons to Molech. (See 2 Kings 16:3; 21:6.) Child sacrifice took place in Jerusalem in the valley of Hinnom, just west and south of the city. The Hebrew word for valley, *gey*, was joined to *Hinnom* to become *Gehenna* in the New Testament. It became a symbol for hell.

Leviticus 21:16-24. The text lists twelve bodily defects that could bar a priest from serving in the sanctuary. They did not remove him from the priesthood nor deny him the normal share of the priestly families in the holy food. It seems strange that these conditions could be used against a man since no one could be blamed for having them. But the work of a priest actually required considerable physical strength. A priest had to be someone of robust physical health.

The prohibition, however, is religious rather than physical. It was not intended to point out specific defects in particular persons. Rather, it was intended to emphasize the perfect holiness of God. This aspect of the law also teaches spiritual truths in preparation for the fuller revelation of God in Christ. A large part of Jesus' ministry was given to healing physical (as well as spiritual) defects in people and emphasizing the love of God.

DIMENSION THREE: WHAT DOES THE BIBLE MEAN TO ME?

The student book suggests that we consider several of the moral and ethical teachings in Chapter 19 as they relate to our lives today. Perhaps you can collect newspaper clippings that will illustrate several of the suggested discussion topics.

Leviticus 19:1-37—God's Ethical Demands

The student book indicates that we no longer live under law, but under grace. Yet Christians may sense an obligation to the moral teachings of the law while ignoring the ritual obligations. For the Christian, the law of Moses has been fulfilled in Jesus Christ. As he said, "Do not think that I have come to abolish the Law or the Prophets; I have not come to abolish them but to fulfill them" (Matthew 5:17). Jesus taught that the law could be reduced to two commandments: " 'Love the Lord your God with all your heart and with all your soul and with all your mind.' This is the first and greatest commandment. And the second is like it: 'Love your neighbor as yourself.' All the Law and the Prophets hang on these two commandments" (Matthew 22:37-40).

The atoning death of Jesus was a perfect and final sacrifice, so we have no further need for animal sacrifices. (See Hebrews 9:12-28.) The death of Jesus instituted the new covenant in his blood by which the law of God is written on our hearts and minds. Those who believe in him may live to the praise of his glory as a part of the church.

Peter can thus apply to the church the statement that "you are a chosen people, a royal priesthood, a holy nation, a people belonging to God, that you may declare the praises of him who called you out of darkness into his wonderful light. Once you were not a people, but now you are the people of God; once you had not received mercy, but now you have received mercy" (1 Peter 2:9-10).

Even the dietary restrictions have been removed for Christians (see Acts 10:14-15; Colossians 2:16; 1 Timothy 4:3-4) because the atoning work of Christ fulfilled all the symbolism of the ceremonial laws.

Read the passages in the next column and consider the question that follows each passage.

Leviticus 19:11. What examples of these prohibited activities do you see in our society today? (See also Revelation 21:8.)

Leviticus 19:15. Most of us are not judges, but are you aware of partiality in the community where you live? List examples of such partiality.

Leviticus 19:17-18. Is it all right for a Christian to suffer an injury at the hands of another Christian, and then to nurse the hurt and not discuss it with the other Christian? When has this happened in your Christian community or group?

Leviticus 19:31. Are spiritualists, astrologers, and mediums harmless individuals? Why or why not?

Leviticus 19:35-36. What shady business practices exist in your community? Does this moral principle apply, for example, to filing an income tax return?

Close today's session by listing the new insights of the class members on a chalkboard or a large sheet of paper. Here is a suggested prayer for closing: "Thank you, God, for the freedom from the law, which we have in Christ and for the freedom to choose to seek and do your will in Christ. Bless each of us with a deep hunger to live according to your holy will; in the name of Jesus. Amen."

I will walk among you and be your God, and you will be my people (26:12).

— 13 —

The Priests and Their Duties

Leviticus 22–27

DIMENSION ONE:
WHAT DOES THE BIBLE SAY?

Answer these questions by reading Leviticus 22

1. Why do the priests want to be ritually cleaned? (Leviticus 22:7)

   The priests want to be ritually clean so they can eat of the sacred things.

2. What outsiders are not allowed to eat of the holy things? (Leviticus 22:10-13)

   Guests of the priests, hired servants of priests, and a daughter of a priest who marries a nonpriest cannot eat of them.

3. What are the requirements for an acceptable freewill offering? (Leviticus 22:18-20)

   Certain male animals—bulls, sheep, or goats—without defect are acceptable as a freewill offering.

4. What is the minimum age required for a sacrificial lamb? (Leviticus 22:27)

   A lamb must be at least a week old to be acceptable for sacrifice.

Answer these questions by reading Leviticus 23

5. What feast do the Israelites observe in connection with the Passover? (Leviticus 23:5-6)

   The Feast of Unleavened Bread immediately follows the Passover.

6. What three offerings must precede the eating of the harvest? (Leviticus 23:12-14)

   God requires a burnt offering of a lamb, a grain offering, and a drink offering of wine.

7. During a sacred assembly, what else does God require of the Israelites? (Leviticus 23:21)

   During a sacred assembly, the Israelites must refrain from all work.

8. If an Israelite fails to observe the Day of Atonement, who sees to his punishment? (Leviticus 23:28-30)

   God will destroy any person who fails to observe the Day of Atonement.

9. Why must the people of Israel dwell in booths during the Feast of Tabernacles? (Leviticus 23:42-43)

   They must dwell in booths because the people lived in booths when God brought them out of Egypt.

Answer these questions by reading Leviticus 24

10. Who receives the week-old bread that is removed from the golden table? (Leviticus 24:9)

   The bread is for Aaron and his sons to eat.

11. What error does the son of Shelomith commit? (Leviticus 24:10-12)

   He blasphemes the Name of God and curses.

12. What does the statement "If anyone curses his God, he will be held responsible" mean? (Leviticus 24:15-16)

   Whoever curses God will be stoned to death.

Answer these questions by reading Leviticus 25

13. How do the people keep a sabbath to the Lord? (Leviticus 25:2-4)

   The people do not sow their fields or prune their vineyards.

14. How often does Israel observe a Year of Jubilee, and when does this year begin? (Leviticus 25:8-9)

Every fiftieth year is a Year of Jubilee. It begins on the Day of Atonement.

15. How must the Israelites observe the fiftieth year? (Leviticus 25:10-12)

They must return to their family property and must not sow, reap, or harvest the untended vines.

16. Why does God not permit the Israelites to sell their land permanently? (Leviticus 25:23)

The land belongs to the Lord.

17. If a poor Israelite must sell a part of his property, how can he later reclaim it? (Leviticus 25:28)

It will be returned to him in the Year of Jubilee.

18. Houses can be redeemed at any time in which cities? (Leviticus 25:32)

In the cities of the Levites, houses can be redeemed at any time.

19. What is the permanent possession of the Levites? (Leviticus 25:34)

The pastureland belonging to their towns is their permanent possession.

20. How must an Israelite deal with poor countrymen? (Leviticus 25:35-37)

An Israelite must lend money without interest and sell food without profit to poor countrymen.

21. What people may the Israelites buy as slaves? (Leviticus 25:44-45)

Israel may buy slaves from surrounding nations and from the temporary residents who live among the Israelites.

Answer these questions by reading Leviticus 26

22. How does God promise to bless the land if Israel remains faithful? (Leviticus 26:12)

God promises to be Israel's God, and Israel will be his people.

23. What does God promise to an unfaithful Israel? (Leviticus 26:18)

God promises to punish them seven times over for their sins.

24. Why are wild beasts such a threat to Israel? (Leviticus 26:22)

Wild beasts destroy children and cattle, causing Israel to become few in number.

25. What further warning does God give to the people? (Leviticus 26:33)

God will scatter the people and destroy their land and cities.

26. An unfaithful Israel can make amends to the Lord by doing what three things? (Leviticus 26:40-42)

They must confess their sins, humble their hearts, and pay for their sins.

27. What promise of the Lord will provide hope even to those Israelites in the land of their enemies? (Leviticus 26:45)

God promises to remember his covenant with their ancestors.

Answer these questions by reading Leviticus 27

28. If a poor man wishes to make a religious vow, who determines the value of the vow? (Leviticus 27:8)

The priest determines the value of the vow.

29. How can an Israelite who has dedicated his house to the Lord redeem it? (Leviticus 27:14-15)

After the priest establishes the value of the house, the man pays that amount plus an additional fifth of the value.

30. In Israel, who possesses property that has been dedicated to the Lord? (Leviticus 27:16-21)

The priests possess property dedicated to the Lord.

31. Why can an Israelite not dedicate a firstborn animal to the Lord? (Leviticus 27:26)

The firstborn of animals already belong to the Lord.

32. What part of all produce of the land and increase of the flocks belongs to the Lord? (Leviticus 27:30-32)

The tithe of all the land and the flocks and herds belongs to the Lord.

DIMENSION TWO:
WHAT DOES THE BIBLE MEAN?

In this closing session of your study of Exodus and Leviticus, you will want to accomplish two main goals. The first of these is to study Leviticus 22–27. The second goal is to help the participants draw all the lessons together in a general overview. Only then can you and the group sense the real accomplishment in having completed this unit of study.

To accomplish the second goal, plan to present a brief overview of the thirteen lessons in the last five minutes allotted to Dimension Three. For further suggestions, see Dimension Three below.

In this final lesson of our study of Leviticus, Chapters 22–26 continue the Holiness Code that we began in Lesson 12. Chapter 22 provides rules for the priests about the holy offerings. Chapter 23 contains a calendar of Israel's religious feasts. Chapter 24 deals with the light in the tabernacle, the bread of the Presence, and the penalty for blasphemy. The sabbatical year, the Year of Jubilee, and the law of the redemption of property make up Chapter 25. Chapter 26 lists rewards and punishments, and Leviticus 27 is an appendix on vows and tithes.

Leviticus 22:1. This chapter continues the listing of rules and regulations for the priests that began in Chapter 21. The emphasis is on the ritual purity required of the priests. The rules for the holiness of the people were given earlier in Leviticus. The demands of holiness required of the priests were even stiffer than those required of the people.

Leviticus 22:17-25. For an acceptable sacrifice, both the priest and the sacrificial animal have to be without blemish. These requirements set the stage for the ultimate sacrifice, the atoning death of Christ on the cross. He was a perfect priest as well as a sacrifice, without spot or blemish. (See 2 Corinthians 5:21; Hebrews 4:14-16; 8–10; and 1 Peter 1:19.)

Leviticus 23:1-44. Deuteronomy 16 contains a similar calendar of the religious feasts. The feasts of Passover/Unleavened Bread, Pentecost, and Tabernacles were closely related to the agricultural year in the Middle East. In the Mediterranean climate, grain harvest begins in March and April—about the time of Passover. Pentecost marks the end of the grain harvest. The fall grape harvest occurs in late September or early October, at the time of the Feast of Tabernacles. Shortly thereafter the early rains of fall soften the summer-hardened ground to mark the beginning of another season of sowing and reaping.

Leviticus 23:15-16. Jewish tradition connects Pentecost with the giving of the Law on Mount Sinai, just as it connects the Passover with the Exodus. Pentecost became, in a sense, a festival of revelation. Pentecost in the New Testament marks the beginning of the church. The gospel of salvation through Jesus Christ was first publicly proclaimed by Peter on that day. (See Acts 2.) Peter's sermon was a new revelation to his audience. Thus the church's observance of Pentecost as the festival of revelation is in line with ancient tradition.

Leviticus 24:9. The holy bread is reserved for the priests, but in 1 Samuel 21:1-6 we read of the incident where David and his men ate it. Jesus referred to this incident when his disciples were accused of profaning the Sabbath. (Read Matthew 12:1-8.) Jesus justified his followers' actions by stating that "the Son of Man is Lord of the Sabbath."

Leviticus 24:13-14. Exodus 22:28 commands, "Do not blaspheme God," but gives no penalty. These two verses establish the penalty. The New Testament lists Hymenaeus as a blasphemer whom Paul "handed over to Satan." Blasphemers reject conscience and make shipwreck of their faith. (See 1 Timothy 1:19-20.) Hymenaeus's blasphemy is connected with his rejection of the coming resurrection. (See 2 Timothy 2:17-19.) Jesus taught that every sin could be forgiven except blasphemy against the Holy Spirit. (See Matthew 12:31-32.)

Leviticus 25:9-10. The word *jubilee* comes from the Hebrew word *yobel.* It means literally "a ram's horn." The blast from such a horn ushers in the fiftieth year in which Hebrew slaves and their families are freed. All property reverts to the families to whom it had originally been given.

Leviticus 25:35-38. The early church practiced the moral equivalent of this law. (See Acts 2:44-45 and 4:32-37.)

Leviticus 26:3-33. Notice that the blessings God promises in verses 3-13—abundant food, freedom, security, and his presence in their midst—are balanced by the punishments listed in verses 14-33. The punishments include poverty, oppression, and fear. God promises to use the sword to desolate the land.

If Israel proves faithless and does not observe the sabbatical years, then God promises to empty the land so that it will naturally be at rest, with none to sow or reap.

Leviticus 27:2-8. A vow is a voluntary pledge. It is a dedication of oneself or something one owns to the Lord. A person might make a vow in haste at a moment of crisis or joy. A man could dedicate another person who was under his control, say a child, a slave, or a wife, to the Lord. He then had to redeem that person since he or she could not serve the Lord in the sanctuary, for that role was left to the priests.

Vows were extremely sacred and binding. Recall that Jephthah's daughter had to die because of her father's vow. (Read Judges 11.) The Book of Ecclesiastes warns against making hasty vows. (See Ecclesiastes 5:4-5.)

Leviticus 27:30-33. The law of the tithe again points to God's ownership of all and the stewardship role of humankind. This same idea appeared in Leviticus 25:23.

DIMENSION THREE:
WHAT DOES THE BIBLE MEAN TO ME?

You will use a part of the time allotted to this dimension to summarize the Exodus and Leviticus study, so discussion time for this lesson is limited. The student book raises the issue of what are acceptable offerings to the Lord. Use one or two of the questions from the student book to begin discussion, or ask the group members to suggest related questions that interest them.

The wide variety of ideas in this lesson suggests other topics. The group might want to consider one of the following questions as an alternative discussion topic:

(1) The Israelite feasts were connected with the agricultural cycle, but more significantly they were associated with the saving acts of God. By contrast, no feasts are ordained in the New Testament, except the institution of Communion at the Last Supper. How does Communion serve the same purposes as the feasts in the Old Testament?

(2) Leviticus 25:35-37 requires Israelites to help one another in economic ways. As a result of this law, every organized Jewish community pools its financial resources to advance interest-free loans to the poor. How can Christians respond to the poor within the church? outside the church? Or should Christians respond? Has our society's stress on individualism blinded Christians to responsibilities within their churches and communities?

Exodus and Leviticus in Retrospect

Begin a review of Exodus and Leviticus by asking the class members to list new insights from today's lesson. Then review the insights from previous lessons, if you have kept a record of them.

Commend the class members for their accomplishment. They have read sixty-seven chapters in this unit as compared to fifty chapters in Genesis! Remind them, too, that while the stories in Genesis are filled with human interest, as are the first few chapters in Exodus, most of the texts we have read in the unit are filled with rules, regulations, and descriptions of cultic utensils and structures that are strange to us.

Yet the stories of the Exodus and of the establishment of God's covenant with Israel—along with the building of the tabernacle and the stipulations on how Israel is to become a holy people—are as important to our understanding of the Bible as are the stories about beginnings with patriarchs. All these things were written and lived out in Israel to set Israel apart from the nations so that God's purposes could be worked out through them. Through Abraham's descendants (Israel), all nations of the earth were to be blessed. So the apostle Paul could say, "The law was put in charge to lead us to Christ that we might be justified by faith" (Galatians 3:24).

Our study of the Pentateuch is not yet completed. The books of Numbers and Deuteronomy remain. At the end of this unit, Israel is still encamped at Mount Sinai; but now the preparations are complete. The trek of Israel toward the Promised Land begins in the opening lesson of Numbers.

Close the session, if time permits, with brief prayers by those in the study group who wish to do so. Encourage prayers of thanksgiving for the completed study and for each person in the group. Let your prayer be the closing prayer.

NUMBERS AND DEUTERONOMY
Table of Contents

About the Writer

The writer of these lessons is Dr. Wayne Barr. Dr. Barr is a retired professor of Old Testament at United Theological Seminary, Dayton, Ohio.

— 1 —

Moses and Aaron Number the People

Numbers 1–4

With this lesson we begin the study of the Book of Numbers. Its thirty-six chapters open with the census of the Israelites while they are still at Sinai, where God had revealed the covenant law to Israel. The book then recounts the events of the long desert wandering and ends with the people of God on the plains of Moab, making preparation for entrance into the Promised Land. In addition to its narrative, Numbers includes instruction and legal regulations about such varied topics as the numbering of Israel, the Tabernacle, strategy for encampment, Levites and priests, offerings, and holiness.

The book is divided into three parts. The first, Chapters 1–9, deals with the situation while Israel is still at Sinai. The second, Chapters 10–21, tells of the wandering in the desert. The third, Chapters 22–36, recounts the arrival at the plains of Moab, across the Jordan from Jericho. Numbers is not a straightforward, flowing narrative. It is a combination of story and legal regulation.

The book's name, derived from the term used in the Septuagint (an early Greek translation of the Old Testament), is somewhat misleading. The name refers to the census activity found only in Chapters 1–4 and again in Chapter 26. The Hebrew title, "in the desert," more fully describes the life and experience portrayed in Numbers.

DIMENSION ONE:
WHAT DOES THE BIBLE SAY?

Answer these questions by reading Numbers 1

1. Where are the children of Israel when Numbers begins? (1:1)

   They are in the Desert of Sinai.

2. Where does God speak to Moses? (1:1)

   God speaks to Moses in the Tent of Meeting.

3. What does the Lord tell Moses to do? Why? (1:1-3)

   God tells Moses to take a census in order to discover the number of men able to go to war.

4. Moses numbers twelve groups. What are the names and the count given for each group? (1:20-46)

Group	Name	Number
One (1:20-21)	*Reuben*	*46,500*
Two (1:22-23)	*Simeon*	*59,300*
Three (1:24-25)	*Gad*	*45,650*
Four (1:26-27)	*Judah*	*74,600*
Five (1:28-29)	*Issachar*	*54,400*
Six (1:30-31)	*Zebulun*	*57,400*
Seven (1:32-33)	*Ephraim*	*40,500*
Eight (1:34-35)	*Manasseh*	*32,200*
Nine (1:36-37)	*Benjamin*	*35,400*
Ten (1:38-39)	*Dan*	*62,700*
Eleven (1:40-41)	*Asher*	*41,500*
Twelve (1:42-43)	*Naphtali*	*53,400*

5. Which important tribe is omitted? Why? (1:47-53)

   The Levites are omitted because they are appointed to the care of the Tabernacle.

Answer these questions by reading Numbers 2

6. Where are the Israelites to camp? (2:2)

   They are to camp around the Tent of Meeting.

7. The twelve tribes are divided into four groups of three tribes each. Which tribes are located in each of the directions below?

East (2:3-9)   *Judah*
                Issachar
                Zebulun

South (2:10-16) *Reuben*
                Simeon
                Gad

West (2:18-24) *Ephraim*
                Manasseh
                Benjamin

North (2:25-31) *Dan*
                Asher
                Naphtali

8. The Tent of Meeting is in the middle of the camp. Who encamps closest to it? (2:17)

The Levites encamp closest to the tent.

Answer these questions by reading Numbers 3

9. What is the work of the Levites? (3:5-8)

The Levites perform duties for Aaron and for the congregation, minister before the Tabernacle, and have charge of all the furnishings of the Tent of Meeting.

10. For whom are the Levites a substitute? (3:11-13)

The Levites substitute for the first-born males of Israel.

11. How does the numbering of the Levites differ from the general census described in 1:3? (3:15)

All males over one month are counted, whereas in the general census only those over twenty years of age were included.

12. The three Levite groups are assigned places around the Tabernacle and responsibilities for its maintenance. What are the location and work of each group?

Name	Location	Responsibility
Gershonites (3:21-26)	*West of Tabernacle*	*Tent, coverings door curtain, court curtain, ropes*
Kohathites (3:27-31)	*South of Tabernacle*	*Ark, table, lampstand, altars, sanctuary articles, and curtain*
Merarites (3:33-37)	*North of Tabernacle*	*Frames, cross-bars, posts, bases, and equipment*

13. Who camps east of the Tabernacle? (3:38)

Moses, Aaron, and Aaron's sons camp east of the Tabernacle.

Answer these questions by reading Numbers 4

14. Who is Moses to count in the third census? (4:2-3, 22-23, 29-30)

He is to count all males from thirty to fifty years old who work in the Tent of Meeting.

15. What is the special work of the sons of Aaron? (4:5-14)

They dismantle and cover the most holy things (ark, altar, vessels, and so on) in preparation for travel.

16. What does the Lord specify about holy things? (4:15, 18-20)

No one except the sons of Aaron shall touch or look upon them.

17. Each group of the Levites is to carry certain things when the Israelites travel. Are these the same as those indicated in Chapter 3? (4:4, 25-26, 31-32)

Yes, the areas of responsibility are the same as those in Chapter 3.

DIMENSION TWO: WHAT DOES THE BIBLE MEAN?

Background Information on Numbers 1–4

Some Bible students conclude that the Book of Numbers contains at least two major accounts of the ancient Israelite traditions. The earlier account probably took shape in the reigns of David and Solomon and addressed the issues in Israel's establishment of a monarchy. The second major account is usually attributed to the time of the Exile, when it spoke to the questions precipitated by the fall of Judah in 587 B.C. Interpreting and reshaping old traditions, the writers address the issues of Israel's survival and the nature of its future. This writing is done in a time when all the institutions (kingship, Temple, nationhood) have been destroyed, Jerusalem is in ruins, and many of the ablest people are captive in a strange land. The basic emphases are the Temple, the priesthood, and the proper practice of worship. Together these emphases address the question of how Israel can survive and look with hope to the future as the people of God.

The dating of Old Testament material involves two aspects. The first is to determine when the reported events occurred. The second is to define when the story was written. While these dates may coincide in some cases, to ignore the possible difference in times may result in the

Bible student's missing one of the most distinctive characteristics of the Old Testament. This characteristic is the use of a traditional story from ancient times to make a significant point that is crucial at a later period.

Stories are powerful witnesses to the nature and responsibilities of God's people in the new and different situations during successive periods of their turbulent history. The constant element is faith in the action of God. Israel's traditions are shaped and reshaped to articulate this faith. The resulting narratives are appropriate and relevant to the widely varied conditions and cultures that Israel encountered.

Numbers 1:1. The Sinai setting for the events of these chapters continues that of Exodus 19–40 and all of Leviticus. Sinai is the location of God's central revelation of covenant law. This includes the Ten Commandments (Exodus 20:1-17); the Covenant Code (Exodus 20:21–23:19); the detailed instructions for making the Tabernacle (most of Exodus 24–40); and the legal regulations pertaining to worship, priesthood, and sacrifice (Leviticus).

The Sinai revelation is the focus of one of the main traditions in the Old Testament. It includes such prominent elements as covenant, revealed law as the specification of covenant responsibility, and emphasis on the action of a sovereign God. Moses is the central figure in this tradition.

In contrast to God's earlier revelation at Sinai, which was given to Moses on the sacred mountain (see especially Exodus 20–40), the revelation recorded in Numbers comes to him in the Tent of Meeting. While the Book of Numbers always identifies this setting with the Tabernacle, interesting references elsewhere (for example, Exodus 33:7-11) indicate that the Tent of Meeting is outside the camp. It serves primarily as a place where the Lord gives oracles to Moses, and apparently is open to others beside Moses.

The Tabernacle in Exodus and Numbers is identified with this Tent of Meeting. The Tabernacle, however, is located in the middle of camp, functions as the worship center with priesthood and altar, is much larger and more elaborate, and may only be entered by members of the priesthood. Perhaps the Tabernacle with its emphasis on specific detail is an anticipatory model of Solomon's temple. If, as some scholars believe, Numbers 1–4 was written during the Exile, then the Tabernacle functions in the account to show the centrality of worship for Israel. This message is particularly timely for a nation whose existence is severely challenged. The people of God, stunned by the tragedy of exile, are trying to discern the shape of their future. Numbers sets forth the Temple, the sacrificial system, and the priesthood as a focus for discovering what is asked of God's people in exchange for their survival and fulfillment of their divine destiny.

The Tabernacle, while perhaps elaborating on a simpler Tent-of-Meeting model, is an authentic symbol of the meaning of the desert experience for the exiles: God is in their midst, and they are called to respond in faithful worship.

Numbers 1:2. God's command to Moses to "take a census of the whole Israelite community" sets the theme of the opening chapters of the book. Moses takes a general census (Chapter 1), numbers all the Levites above the age of one month (Chapter 3), and takes a second count of Levites between thirty and fifty years old (Chapter 4). In addition to the census described in Chapter 1, a second general census is taken thirty-eight years later on the plains of Moab (Chapter 26). The idea of numbering a people is not strange in the ancient Near East. The Mari texts of the eighteenth century B.C. make specific reference to such a census in a tribal confederation. In Numbers, the census serves the purpose of external organization and is considered acceptable to God.

The census idea gets quite a different reading in 2 Samuel 24. (See also 1 Chronicles 21.) David's counting the people is seen as a violation of God's will and results in severe punishment. Although the reasons for the different view are not clear, we can surmise that David's census went against ancient tribal concepts and was regarded as the king's usurpation of divine right and power.

Chapter 1 and Chapter 26 indicate no such struggle between tribe and king. These chapters present the census as a desirable step in organizing the people of God.

Numbers 1:20-46 and 2:1-34. The student book discusses the importance and meaning of the tribal list in Israel's recounting of history. In addition, you may wish to compare the list and groupings in Chapters 1 and 2 with the geography of the tribal settlements in Palestine. Most Bible atlases will include a territorial map that gives this information. (Good examples may be found in *Oxford Bible Atlas*, edited by H. G. May, and in *Westminster Historical Atlas to the Bible*, edited by G. E. Wright and F. V. Filson.)

Numbers 3:1-10, 14-43; 4:1-33. The Old Testament references to the Levites, their place in Israel, and their relation to the Aaronite priests are somewhat varied. An early story in Judges 17–18 speaks of a Levite who functioned as a priest and established a worship center in Dan, where his descendants were priests until 721 B.C. In the time of Josiah's reform (621 B.C.) the Levites were considered as full priests.

In exilic times, however, a sharp distinction develops, and the Levites are regarded as subordinate to the Aaronite priesthood. Ezekiel 44:10-16 describes the Levites as inferior temple servants, condemned to this status because of their infidelity in pre-exilic worship. The books of Chronicles reflect this same status for Levites but do not view their position as punishment. In later times the Aaronites occupy a central position. They alone are given full priestly function in the worship of Israel.

DIMENSION THREE:
WHAT DOES THE BIBLE MEAN TO ME?

Dimension Three encourages group members to discover ways they can understand and apply the Bible to life situations for insight and guidance. Discussion topics for this session are as follows: "The Israelite Census," "Family Ties," "Pilgrimage," and "Clergy and Laity."

Numbers 1:2-4, 17-19—The Israelite Census

The discussion of this topic in the student book focuses on the fact that the Bible contains two quite different numberings of the Israelite people. Moses takes the census in Numbers at the command of God and with the approval of God. Many years later, however, David's numbering of the Israelites results in God's wrath and punishment.

Have the class members compare these two numberings. (You may use either the 2 Samuel 24 account or the one found in 1 Chronicles 21). Ask them to consider such questions as, Who takes the census? At whose command is the census taken? Where and how is the census taken? What is God's reaction?

Numbers 1:20-46—Family Ties

Chapters 1 and 2 focus on the careful organization of God's people. On the brink of disorder and threatened by enemies, they want to establish a way to understand themselves and to achieve fullness of life as a people. The story begins with a census—an all-out effort that emphasizes tribal identification as well as total numerical strength.

By taking a census, the Israelites are struggling for survival by seeking a focal point for identity. Throughout the history of God's people, this identity has been a recurring need. It was true for Israel in the desert era, in the later period of growth from the simplicity of the judges to the complexity of the monarchy, and in the time of the Exile. Likewise, the church has felt a need for identity at many times in its history.

Encourage the class members to focus on the idea of identity, both individual and with respect to family. How can we as a part of the church community develop and maintain our personal identity? What contributes to our identity as a community of faith?

Numbers 2—Pilgrimage

The instructions in Chapter 2 provide for movement, an element that is as important as order in the life of Israel. Their tribal locations and groupings are those of a camp, and they imply readiness to decamp and move out. The record in Chapter 2 (and also in Chapter 4) makes it clear that God's will for Israel includes a central provision for marching.

The account of Israel's organization recognizes the necessity for pilgrimage. The people cannot fulfill their destiny unless they are ready to move.

The need for pilgrimage has significance for the church. How can we prevent our concern for organization and self-preservation from making us resistant to movement and change? On the other hand, how can we provide for orderliness, for marshaling of strength, and for a conscious sense of identity while we are on pilgrimage? How do we do what God wants us to do as a church?

You can approach these questions by asking group members to share and compare their responses to the questions in Dimension Three of the student book. You may facilitate this discussion by dividing the group into teams of three or four members. Ask the team members to consider how they arrived at their answers and how Chapter 2 helped them in this process. Encourage them to talk about the differences in their responses.

Numbers 1:47; 2:17; 3:1-51; 4:11-33
Clergy and Laity

A primary theme of Chapters 3 and 4 is the selection of the Levites to carry out special responsibilities in Israel's worship. A particular group among them (the sons of Aaron) had an even more specialized role—that of officiating in the rites of worship.

This theme raises the question of why the Israelites, a chosen and special people, should have a group delegated from among them for a particular role in worship. The question of priesthood and holy orders has long been a concern of religious people. All religions make some provision for persons who deal in distinct ways with what is considered holy by that religion. In Judaism, this institution takes on a special dimension because of Israel's explicit sense that God has chosen her as a whole people.

The Levites and priests act in a representative way for Israel. They are given a special place, but they are never considered separate from the rest of Israel in any ultimate way. While their role may be complex and may differ in different Old Testament accounts, they are always part of Israel. This permanent relationship is instructive to us as we deal with the church and its ministries.

In our day, issues surrounding the role of ordained ministry, of clergy's relation to laity, and of lay ministry's role are all important.

Why is a specialized ministry necessary for the church? How does this specialized ministry relate to every member's ministry?

The group's discussion of "Clergy and Laity" might begin by your asking for words that describe the Levites and Aaronites in Chapters 3 and 4. These should be recorded on a chalkboard or a large piece of paper. What characteristics predominate in those descriptions?

Next, the question of ministry's place in Israel and in the church might be raised. Ask the class what Chapters 3 and 4 contribute to our view of church and ministry.

(Other sources useful in consideration of these questions of ministry are H. R. Niebuhr, *The Purpose of the Church and Its Ministry,* and *Consultation on Church Union 1967.*)

If time allows, you might ask group members to list characteristics of outstanding ministries they have observed. When they have done this for five minutes, ask them to compare these lists with the responsibilities given the Levites and priests in Numbers. After they have presented their findings, discuss how the Bible applies to the make-up of an outstanding ministry.

Close the session by asking a few volunteers to identify in a sentence something new they have learned about the Book of Numbers. If time allows, list these new insights on a chalkboard or a large piece of paper.

— 2 —
Laws and Regulations

Numbers 5–9

DIMENSION ONE:
WHAT DOES THE BIBLE SAY?

Answer these questions by reading Numbers 5

1. Who are the people of Israel to remove from camp? Why? (5:1-3)

   They are to remove people with infectious skin diseases or with discharges and those who are unclean through contact with the dead so the camp will not be defiled.

2. How does one make restitution for wrongs done to others? (5:5-8)

   One makes restitution by confessing and returning all that was taken plus one-fifth the value.

3. What does a husband do if he suspects his wife of unfaithfulness? (5:11-15)

   He brings her to the priest along with the required offering for jealousy.

4. What does the priest make the suspected wife do? (5:18-22, 26)

   The priest unbinds her hair and makes her take the oath of the curse. He then makes her drink the bitter water from the offering.

5. How is the guilt or innocence of the wife known? (5:27-28)

   If the water of bitterness causes her pain, swelling, and miscarriage, she is assumed guilty. If such symptoms do not occur, she is judged innocent.

Answer these questions by reading Numbers 6

6. What are the three conditions of the Nazirite vow? (6:1-8)

   They are abstinence from all products of the grape, avoidance of contact with a dead body, and no cutting of the hair.

7. What offerings is a Nazirite to bring when he completes his vow? (6:13-15)

   He brings a male lamb for a burnt offering, a ewe lamb for a sin offering, a ram as a fellowship offering, a basket of unleavened bread, and grain and drink offerings.

8. What does the Nazirite do with his hair? (6:18)

   He shaves it off at the door of the Tent of Meeting and puts it in the fire under the fellowship offering.

9. What does the wave offering include? (6:19-20)

   It includes the boiled shoulder of a ram, one unleavened cake, and one unleavened wafer.

10. With what words are Aaron and his sons to bless Israel? (6:22-26)

    The LORD bless you and keep you:
    the LORD make his face shine upon you and be gracious
       to you;
    the LORD turn his face toward you and give you peace.

Answer these questions by reading Numbers 7

11. What offerings do the tribal leaders bring to the Tabernacle? What is their use? (7:1-5)

    Six covered carts and twelve oxen are presented for the Levites' use in the service of the Tent of Meeting.

12. What gifts does Nahshon of the tribe of Judah bring on the first day? (7:12-17)

    He brings a 130-shekel silver plate and a 70-shekel silver sprinkling bowl, each filled with fine flour mixed with oil for a grain offering; a 10-shekel gold dish filled with incense; a young bull, a ram, a male year-old lamb for a burnt offering; a male goat for a sin offering; two oxen, five rams, five male goats, and five male year-old lambs for a fellowship offering.

13. The other eleven tribal representatives bring identical gifts on successive days. In what order do the tribes come? (7:18-83)

   Issachar, Zebulun, Reuben, Simeon, Gad, Ephraim, Manasseh, Benjamin, Dan, Asher, and Naphtali.

14. When Moses speaks with the Lord, where is the voice of the Lord located? (7:89)

   It comes from above the atonement cover on the ark of the Testimony, from between the two cherubim.

Answer these questions by reading Numbers 8

15. How is Aaron to set up the lamps? (8:1-3)

   The lamps must give light in front of the lampstands.

16. What are the Levites to do in the ritual of cleansing? (8:5-9)

   They are to have the water of cleansing sprinkled on them, shave their whole bodies, wash their clothes, cleanse themselves, and bring one bull for a sin offering and another with grain for a grain offering.

17. What kind of offering are the Levites themselves? (8:10-11)

   They are a wave offering.

18. Why are the Levites the Lord's own? (8:14-18)

   They replace all the first-born of Israel in being wholly consecrated to do the Lord's service.

19. What are the years of service for a Levite? (8:23-26)

   A Levite serves from twenty-five to fifty years of age.

Answer these questions by reading Numbers 9

20. When is Israel to observe the Passover? (9:2-3)

   The Passover is at twilight on the fourteenth day of the first month.

21. How are those absent or "unclean" at that time to observe the festival? (9:6-12)

   They are to observe it fully on the fourteenth day of the second month.

22. What is the provision for aliens among them? (9:14)

   An alien may keep the Passover in the same way as an Israelite.

23. How do the children of Israel know when to make camp and when to set out? (9:15-17)

   They are to travel when the cloud over the Tabernacle is taken up and to make camp when the cloud settles down.

DIMENSION TWO: WHAT DOES THE BIBLE MEAN?

Background Information on Numbers 5–9

The unique contribution of Numbers to the biblical story is its account of Israel's journey from Sinai to the threshold of the land of Canaan. The actual departure from Sinai is not recorded until Chapter 10. The first nine chapters are occupied with preparations for setting out on the journey.

Chapters 5–9 may be divided into two sections: 5–6 and 7–9. In Chapters 5–6, the rules governing various aspects of life are set forth. In this section, the divine commands do not call for specific single actions. The primary theme, stated in Numbers 5:3, is concern for the purity of the people of God since God dwells among them. The particular ways in which this concern is elaborated reflect the Israelites' understanding of purity in their world. Judged in their setting, God's people show a high regard for worship, morality, and ethics.

Chapters 7–9 turn more explicitly to preparing the Israelites for their imminent desert sojourn. The account returns to the narrative form of Chapters 1– 4. When God gives the instructions, the account tells us how Moses, Aaron, and Israel carry them out.

Numbers 5:1-4. This is the first of a series of laws introduced by the words, "The LORD said to Moses." This phrase occurs in Chapters 1– 4 with some frequency, but there we read each time that the instruction is implemented. In Chapters 5–6, the same phrase is used but without reference to fulfillment of the instruction. The content of these two chapters is more general in its prescriptions about Israel's life and does not deal with matters that can be accomplished by a single action.

The regard for purity in the camp concentrates on those unclean because of infectious skin disease, discharges, and contact with the dead. The concern is not primarily hygienic but is based rather on a concept of purity that regards corpses and certain diseases as defiling.

Many older Bible versions translate the Hebrew word as "leprosy." But it should probably be understood more broadly. Our New International Version renders it more appropriately "infectious skin disease."

Numbers 5:5-10. The meaning of this passage is that wronging another human being constitutes breaking faith with God. Here, as elsewhere in the Pentateuch, ethical conduct is a central element in piety.

Numbers 5:16-31. The meaning of the term translated "holy water" in verse 17 is unclear. The term probably refers to water kept in the sanctuary for worship purposes. This water is mixed with dust from the floor of the place of worship, another ingredient included because of its association with the holy place. The third component is the curses written down and washed into the water to be drunk. The guilt or innocence of the woman is determined by the effect, particularly on fertility and childbearing, of the potion when it is drunk.

Verse 31 underscores the fact that the woman bears the burden of proof in this law. The man is not punished for any accusations that turn out to be unfounded. Nor is the man ever subjected to such a test in the event his faithfulness is suspect. Indeed, in the patriarchally oriented world in which Israel lived, faithfulness as we define it was not required of the husband. (He was, of course, liable to severe punishment if caught in adultery with another man's wife.)

Numbers 6:1-21. The Hebrew word *nazir* means one who is consecrated, devoted, or separated. Becoming a Nazirite involves a person's "separating" himself or herself from wine (or any other grape product), from cutting the hair, and from contact with the dead. Taking this vow does not seem to imply withdrawal from society.

This passage is the only treatment of the Nazirite vow in the Pentateuch. The regulations define the commitment as voluntary and temporary and prescribe certain rituals and offerings for completing the vow.

The most familiar example of the Old Testament Nazirite is Samson. Samuel is probably also a Nazirite. In those cases, the vow appears to be lifelong and to include a certain charismatic quality.

The emphasis in both cases in on consecration to the Lord and the demonstration of this dedication by certain abstentions. The seriousness of the vow is measured by the variety and quantity of offerings given at the conclusion of the Nazirite period.

Numbers 6:22-27. This classical blessing is specified as a priestly function, spoken in the setting of public worship. Second Samuel 6:18 and 1 Kings 8:54 recount occasions when the king performs this priestly function. Leviticus 9:22 and, in the Apocrypha, Ecclesiasticus 50:19-20, relate the more typical formal blessing by the priest at the close of public worship services.

The form of Aaron's blessing here is striking. The three-line benediction builds to a climax in a stair-step fashion. While this progression is noticeable in English, it is even more impressive in the original Hebrew. Each line contains two verbs, the first having the Lord as its subject. The object of all six verbs is "you," understood to be Israel. The force of the repetition is heightened by the increase in length (in Hebrew) from three words (verse 24) to four words (verse 25) to five words (verse 26). The threefold use of the divine name and the total effect of lengthening sentences lends an aura of stateliness and movement to this terse expression of a central element in Israel's worship.

Numbers 7:1-88. Here we turn from the legal prescriptions of the previous two chapters to the regulations related more directly to Israel's preparation for leaving Sinai. It is instructive to read this passage in connection with the accounts of temple dedications in 1 Kings 8 and 2 Chronicles 5:2–7:10 (first temple); Ezra 6:16-18 (second temple); and 1 Maccabees in the Apocrypha 4:52-58 (rededication of the second temple with its new altar). In each case, the celebration includes extensive offerings of various kinds.

Numbers 7:89. This rather enigmatic verse appears to be detached from a larger story. The reference is to Moses' being instructed to build the ark with "atonement cover" and cherubim (Exodus 25:18-20). He is promised that when the Tabernacle and ark are completed the Lord will speak with him from above the ark. This verse notes the fulfillment of that directive and promise.

The ark has a cover on which two cherubim, wooden figures overlaid with gold, face each other. Probably this represents the throne of God and the cherubim that support it. (For this image see Psalm 80:1; 99:1; Isaiah 37:16.)

Numbers 8:5-26. Chapters 3 and 4 define the Levites' special position as the Lord's own because they act as substitute for all first-born, who belong to God. Although Chapter 8 reiterates this concept (verses 16-19), the new and more striking understanding of their particular place in Israel is their description as an offering of the people to God. This new dimension is particularly evident when the people lay their hands on the Levites (verse 10) just as the Levites lay their hands on the bulls that are to serve as burnt offerings (verse 12).

The Levites are offered as a wave offering (verse 11). Some commentators suggest that the action involved extending the offering toward the altar and then bringing it back toward the priest and worshiping congregation. Such a gesture expresses the most likely meaning of the offering—that it is offered to God and then God gives it back for use by the priests. The wave offering often designates the priest's portion of the sacrifice.

The wave offering has deep significance for our perception of the way Israel viewed the Levites. The Levites are offered to God, who in turn gives them back to the priesthood for service in Israel's worship.

Numbers 9:1-14. The regulations for observing Passover appear in Exodus 12. The new element here involves the case of those who cannot keep the festival at its appointed time. What are they to do?

Moses presents the question to God and asks for a decision. God's answer is that the festival may be observed in full a month later by those who have a valid reason for missing the regular observance.

Verse 14 reiterates an inclusive note that occurs often in the Pentateuch. The alien (the Hebrew word is better translated "resident alien") who resides in Israel is included in the community of worship. Such a person enjoys the full rights of a citizen, but Exodus 12:48-49 indicates that he must submit to circumcision in order to participate in Passover.

DIMENSION THREE: WHAT DOES THE BIBLE MEAN TO ME?

Underlying the early chapters of the Book of Numbers is the question of what it means to be the people of God. You will want to prepare for discussion of the following related topics: "Responsibility in Relationship," "A Special Commitment," "The Blessing of God," and "Preparation for Pilgrimage."

Numbers 5:1-31—Responsibility in Relationship

Basic to the life of the church is the sense that God's presence is among us. That awareness should make a difference in the way we live together. The particular way in which Israel viewed the presence of God in regard to health and death is not particularly useful to us, except as it emphasizes that Israel took the call to purity seriously. Do we respond to the questions of quality of life with the same degree of commitment as did ancient Israel?

Numbers 5:5-8 brings us the significant insight that wrongs done to other human beings injure our relationship with God. Remedy must include confession to God, mending of relationship with the person wronged by return of property, and restoration of the relationship with God by a public act of worship. Our tradition tells us it is not enough to be scrupulous in our personal dealings, although that is essential. Today's Christian must address areas in our social order that deprive people of opportunity for livelihood, growth, and redress for wrong.

You might ask class members to identify examples of deprived people in your community. What can be done to remedy their situations? What responsibility do we as Christians have to them?

Numbers 5:11-31, which provides a procedure for dealing with a wife suspected of unfaithfulness, is most difficult to apply to our lives today. The woman must prove her innocence in such a case, but no provision is made to deal with the possibility of a husband's unfaithfulness. How can this law apply to use in our relationships?

First, in interpreting a difficult biblical passage, we cannot simply pick it up and apply it directly to our lives. To do so is to ignore the fact that its content was formulated to address the life of another time and place. Such an approach also ignores the advances in social and religious thought made since that time in human history. The result is that the word of God becomes an abstraction, a word unrelated to human experience.

Second, we need to examine the time from which the passage comes to get a fuller sense of its meaning in that setting. In addition to understanding what it said to its own time, we also begin to see the direction in which it points.

Further study of Numbers 5:11-31 shows us that in dealing with the case of unfaithfulness within worship, Israel has already begun to develop greater humaneness by modifying a common practice of neighboring cultures. God calls us to continue the process of transformation in our interpretation so that the Bible can speak to us with full relevance.

In the class setting, you might stop at this point to ask the students to discuss the following questions.

1. How do you think this instruction of God to Israel is related to our times? Can it be used literally? How does the passage represent the divine will for us?

2. How can we use this passage? If we take the passage literally, how can we provide for the specified practices in our church life? If we do not take Scripture literally, how is it instructive for our lives?

3. What is the underlying concern of the passage as it addresses the situation of its time? Is this concern valid today? How can this Scripture be interpreted so that it does not discriminate against women?

Numbers 6:1-21—A Special Commitment

The provision for the Nazirite vow is another indication of Israel's sense of what it means to be God's people. Any individual who wishes can become a Nazirite by adopting certain stringent regulations. Becoming a Nazirite expresses a true measure of special commitment, and the desire to serve God within the life of Israel.

Ask the class members to reflect on the Nazirite vow and its regulations. Ask them to draw parallels between the Nazirite vow and vows of commitment that persons make today. How can the church include provisions for special consecration?

Numbers 6:22-27—The Blessing of God

Aaron's blessing in this passage points to a significant Old Testament concept—the concept of blessing. Israel's understanding of God's action includes the double aspect of deliverance and blessing.

The classic statement in Numbers 6:22-27 makes three important points: God is the source of blessing, God is motivated by good will in relation to humankind, and we experience the result of this good will within our day-to-day living.

If we take this view of God seriously, we must modify our whole outlook on life. We see creation as fundamentally good and its creator as well-intentioned and effective. How does this view affect our faith? Where does this emphasis appear in our worship and living?

Numbers 7–9—Preparation for Pilgrimage

After extensive attention to setting Israel in order, Chapters 7–9 turn more definitely to the preparation for leaving Sinai. The first of these, the Tabernacle's completion, provides a focus for the community. The story of the offerings in Chapter 7 points out the centrality of worship in Israel.

Worship still serves a unifying function in our lives. Ask class members to consider the value of worship to them and to the church. How does worship unify the church? How does worship direct the life of the church? In light of its important function, at what points should our worship be modified? What elements need stronger emphasis?

A second aspect of readying Israel for leaving Sinai is the special ritual by which the people "offer" the Levites to the Lord (Chapter 8). They are given to the Lord who then gives them back for service and use in worship.

In all independent churches and fellowships, and denominations today, several steps of examination by leaders and officials precede a person's recommendation for ordination as clergy. You might want to share with the class the information about ordination from your church or denomination. What is the relationship between the ritual of the Levites and the process of granting clergy credentials today?

The third element in these preparatory chapters is the Passover. Pilgrimage people need to know who they are. The primary aspect of the Passover festival is remembrance, the re-experiencing of Israel's deliverance from the Egyptians and of her becoming a covenant people.

Let your class consider and discuss these questions. Which Christian festivals are most important to us? Why is celebration of these events important? What function do they serve?

The fourth element in Israel's preparation is the cloud that covers the Tabernacle. This symbol of the Lord's presence signals when the Lord wants Israel to set forth and when they are to make camp.

How does the church decide when to launch out on pilgrimage and when to stay in camp? What constitutes our sense of divine guidance as we decide on policy and program?

Perhaps each phase in preparation is an integral part of God's guidance. Attention to Israel's story may make us more fully aware of the divine will and enable us to be the people of God in our time.

Close today's session by asking the class members what new insights they have gained from their study of Numbers 5–9. List these insights on a chalkboard or a large piece of paper, if time allows.

3

The Long Journey Begins

Numbers 10–14

Chapters 10–14 record the Israelites' departure from Sinai and the beginning of their journey to the Promised Land. One of the most important themes of the Pentateuch—the grumbling or complaint tradition—begins here. The tensions of pilgrimage and Moses' agonies as leader are portrayed in realistic terms. The account of Israel's first opportunity to enter Canaan takes up the two concluding chapters. Throughout these chapters is the question of how God's people respond to responsibility, adversity, and opportunity.

DIMENSION ONE: WHAT DOES THE BIBLE SAY?

Answer these questions by reading Numbers 10

1. What does God tell Moses to make? For what are these to be used? (10:1-10)

   God tells Moses to make two silver trumpets and use them to call the community together and signal them to break camp.

2. How do the people know they are to move from Sinai? (10:11-12)

   The cloud is lifted from above the Tabernacle.

3. When the Israelites set out from Sinai, where do the Levites march? What is their task? (10:14-21)

   The first Levites are to march between the first and second groups, while the second Levites are placed between the second and third groups. The Levites carry the Tabernacle and the holy things.

4. What goes before the children of Israel when they leave Sinai? (10:33)

   The ark of the covenant of the Lord goes before them.

Answers these questions by reading Numbers 11

5. How does the Lord respond to the people's complaining? (11:1)

   The Lord becomes angry and sends a fire that burns the outer parts of the camp.

6. What do the Israelites crave? Why? (11:4-6)

   They crave a variety of foods because they are tired of manna.

7. Why is Moses troubled? (11:10-15)

   He feels the burden of the people's complaints.

8. What does the Lord promise Israel? (11:18-23)

   God promises meat for a whole month.

9. When the seventy elders go with Moses to the Tent of Meeting, what happens to them? (11:24-25)

   The Lord puts some of Moses' spirit upon them, and they prophesy.

10. What meat does God provide for Israel? What happens as they eat? (11:31-33)

    God provides quails. The anger of the Lord is kindled against the people, and a plague falls on them.

Answer these questions by reading Numbers 12

11. Who raises questions about Moses' leadership and why? (12:1-2)

    Miriam and Aaron question Moses' leadership. They do not approve of his Cushite wife, and they are jealous of his status.

12. What makes Moses different from other prophets? (12:6-8)

    The Lord speaks to him face to face and clearly.

13. What happens to Miriam? (12:9-10, 13-15)

Miriam is punished with a skin disease. She is healed through Moses' intercession.

Answer these questions by reading Numbers 13

14. Where does God tell Moses to send the twelve representatives of the tribes of Israel? (13:1-15)

He sends them to explore the land of Canaan.

15. What are the explorers to find out? (13:17-20)

They are to find out whether the land is a good land and how strong its defenses are.

16. What is the explorers' report when they return? (13:27-28)

The land is a good land, flowing with milk and honey; but the people are strong, and the cities are large and well fortified.

17. What is Caleb's advice? (13:30)

Caleb urges the people to go into Canaan and possess it.

18. What do the other explorers say? (13:31-33)

They counsel against attempting to take the land because of the strength of the people there.

Answer these questions by reading Numbers 14

19. How do the people of Israel react to this report? (14:1-4)

They grumble against Moses and Aaron and want to return to Egypt.

20. What happens when Caleb and Joshua urge the Israelites to go into Canaan? (14:6-10)

The people are so aroused that they want to stone them.

21. When God threatens to destroy Israel, what does Moses do? (14:13-19)

Moses intercedes for the people, prevailing on divine mercy and urging the Lord to spare them.

22. What punishment does God place upon Israel? (14:20-35)

All will wander in the desert for forty years; and all above twenty years of age except two people will die there.

23. Who are the exceptions? (14:30, 38)

Caleb and Joshua are the exceptions.

DIMENSION TWO: WHAT DOES THE BIBLE MEAN?

Background Information on Numbers 10–14

In Lesson 1, we mentioned that some students of Numbers think the book includes material from at least two major Israelite traditions. Most of Chapters 1–9 is believed to come from the later exilic account. With Chapter 10, however, we come to material attributed to the earlier account, dated in the time of King Solomon. The presence of two sources is believed to be especially evident in the spy story of Chapters 13–14. In addition to this, some of the most ancient poetry in the Old Testament—the ark sayings in 10:33-36—is found in this segment of the book.

Desert tradition is central in Israel's life over a long period of time. It stands alongside the deliverance and conquest themes in importance. The three themes together constitute a saga that is much more than a recounting of past events. Telling and retelling their story, the Israelites maintain their identity in the midst of difficult and challenging circumstances. Their story reminds them that God is their sovereign, that they are marked for a particular place and mission in the divine purposes, and that God's will is worked out in the realities of human history.

Numbers 10:1-10. The final step in the preparation for marching toward Canaan is the making of two silver trumpets with which to signal the encamped hosts of Israel. In this passage, two distinct trumpet sounds are noted—one, a battle alarm, and the other, a call to assembly. The latter is used in the rituals of public worship while the former signals Israel to break camp and march forth. The original Hebrew employs two different words for the two sounds, but is not certain what the distinction was between them. *Tekiah* can be translated as the assembly and worship signal (verses 3-4, 7, 10) and *teruah* can be translated as the war and marching sound (verses 5-6, 9). Our NIV translation does not make a literal distinction, but shows them in their proper use.

Numbers 10:29-32. The name of Moses' father-in-law is something of a puzzle. In Exodus 2:18, he is called Reuel; but in Exodus 3:1 and 18:1, he is Jethro. The meaning of our passage is not quite clear. The question is whether "Moses' father-in-law" in verse 29 refers to Reuel the Midianite or to Hobab, his son. The former agrees with Exodus 2:18, but the latter is given some support by a reference to Moses' father-in-law as Hobab the Kenite in Judges 4:11 in some Bible translations. The NIV calls Hobab Moses' brother-in-law. In the presence of varying traditions, we can conclude that the name was remembered differently and the identification as Midianite or Kenite (a subgroup of the Midianites) was not exact. Beyond this confusion, however, lies the solid fact that Israel had a close relation from earliest times with at least the Kenite branch of the Midianites. We may also conclude that these Kenites played a significant part in Israel's early religious development.

Numbers 10:33-36. The ark, probably a wooden chest of some sort, has been variously interpreted. Later traditions emphasized it as a depository of tablets containing the Decalogue. The wording used in verse 33, "ark of the covenant," supports this idea.

The poetry of verses 35-36, however, makes a somewhat different implication. These two ancient sayings address the ark as if it were God. This is not idolatry; but it does emphasize the ark as an extension of the divine, deeply symbolic of the Lord's presence in leading the people as they wander between Egypt and Canaan.

Numbers 11:4-34. A clear understanding of Chapter 11 depends on our ability to separate the two story lines that appear within it. These are closely related but emphasize different themes. The first, found in verses 4-9, 18-23, and 31-35, tells of Israel's complaining about desert conditions in general and the lack of meat in particular. A similar story in Exodus 16 records the people's grumbling against God immediately after their deliverance at the sea. In that case, they complained about lack of food and the Lord sent both manna and quails. In Numbers 11, the people ("the rabble with them") cry out for meat because they are tired of manna.

The manna described here is small, gummy, and sweet-tasting. Such a substance is found in the Sinai Peninsula where an excretion from a particular kind of tamarisk tree falls to the ground in the early summer months. (See also the description of manna in Exodus 16:31).

The Lord brings quails in abundance in answer to their request. This story provides a remembrance of a regular occurrence in the Sinai Peninsula, during which large flocks of quails settle down to rest as they migrate along the eastern shore of the Mediterranean.

The outcome of the story is anticipated in verses 19-20. The complaining of the people brings meat, but their action amounts to rejection of God. The greed and faithlessness of the people are answered by a devastating plague. The second story line in this chapter, found in verses 10-17 and 24-30, tells of Moses' difficulties in bearing the burden of his office in the face of Israel's constant complaining. As he cries out to God, the images he uses for God's expectations of him are very significant. In verse 12, Moses says in effect that he did not conceive or bear the Israelites. How then can God expect him to nurse them? He is not their mother and therefore cannot be expected to care for them as a mother does. Some commentators see ground in this for interpreting this verse as a reference to the maternal qualities in God's relation to Israel.

God addresses Moses' problem through the sharing of the spirit of Moses with seventy chosen elders. These elders are empowered to help him carry the leadership burden. The reference to prophesying reflects an early view in which ecstatic frenzy was a part of prophetic activity. The slightly later stories about Saul and his unusual behavior when around bands of prophets (1 Samuel 10:10-13; 19:20-24) give us a clear picture of the meaning of prophesying in those early times.

The curious story about Eldad and Medad manifests a picture of Moses as a man who rises above jealousy and narrowness to the acceptance of all prophetic activity, however far outside usual channels it may fall.

Numbers 12:1-16. The meekness of Moses, noted in the account of Miriam and Aaron's attack on him, is a quality of humility and modesty. He is not self-assertive, is not quick in coming to his own defense. In this passage, God presents his case, while Moses refrains from speaking of himself.

The Lord's punishment of Miriam is usually pictured as leprosy, although it may have been any one of a number of similar skin diseases. In any case, she is healed through Moses' intercessions. But, according to legal custom in such matters of cleansing, she must remain outside camp for seven days. (See also Leviticus 14:1-8).

Numbers 13:1-33. One of the central stories in the desert narrative is the explorer account in Chapters 13–14. From their location in Paran in central Sinai the explorers are sent to the Negeb, a dry wasteland on the southern edge of Canaan, and northward to the hill country around Hebron. Later tradition expanded the territory to include all of Canaan from the Desert of Zin (just south of the Negeb) to Rehob in the far north. The explorers' activity, however, centers around Hebron, an ancient city about twenty miles south of Jerusalem. Hebron, earlier known as Kiriath Arba, is the central location in the Abraham stories and burial place of all three patriarchs as well as Sarah, Rebekah, and Leah.

After forty days the spies return to report to Israel that the land is indeed fertile but is inhabited by many people with strong fortifications. Archaeological excavations have shown us that some Canaanite cities had walls fifteen feet thick and over thirty feet high. Among the people the explorers report finding there are the Anakim, known in the Old Testament as giants. Mentioned in verses 22 and 28, they are identified as descendants of the Nephilim in verse 33. The Nephilim are mentioned elsewhere only in Genesis 6:4, where they are described as the offspring of "the sons of God" and "the daughters of men." In Hebrew, *Anakim* denotes "long-necked ones." Thus they came to be regarded as exceptionally tall persons or giants.

Other groups mentioned as inhabitants include the Amalekites, a nomadic tribe who were bothersome enemies of Israel at least until the time of Saul (1 Samuel 15). The Hittites and Amorites mentioned are evidently remnants from earlier periods when they established themselves in power throughout this area. The Jebusites, also mentioned in the explorers' report, are to be identified with ancient Jerusalem (Jebus). Second Samuel 5:5-9 tells us that they held Jerusalem until David captured it and made it his capital.

Numbers 14. The account of the explorers leads into another rebellion story in Chapter 14. Israel's mounting restiveness expresses itself in plans to seize control from their leaders and return to Egypt. Once again they complain that conditions in the desert are too difficult. They plot to overthrow Moses, Aaron, and their supporters, Joshua and Caleb. God pronounces a sweeping judgment upon Israel's faithless rejection of the divine purpose.

DIMENSION THREE: WHAT DOES THE BIBLE MEAN TO ME?

These chapters contain at least five themes: "God's People on the Move," "Order in Our Lives," "The Problems of Freedom," "A Leadership Model," and "Realism, Faith, and the Future."

Numbers 10:1-10—God's People on the Move

The student book discussion of this topic emphasizes the idea of remembrance (verse 10). The trumpets that God commands Moses to make are symbols of God's presence with the people. Have one or more persons in the class look up the word *remembrance* in a Bible concordance. Then have the class members read other verses that use this word. Ask the class to discuss the other contexts in which the word *remembrance* is used, and identify similarities in these contexts.

How do we incorporate the idea of remembrance into our worship today? Ask the class to list items they can think of that we use as symbols of God's presence.

Numbers 10:11-28—Order in Our Lives

The first nine chapters of Numbers concentrate on matters of order and organization. Groups are numbered, places in camp allotted, particular persons designated for special duties, and regulations clarified. The writer is certain that the structures of life and worship of God's people need to be specific and visible. When we reach Numbers 10:11, however, the account turns to the primary point of the whole desert story—Israel's pilgrimage from Sinai to Canaan.

The progression from organization to movement has implications for the life of the church today. Many churches today are constantly self-examining, working earnestly with organizational questions, and making modifications. Worship patterns continually receive careful study, as do program direction and missional strategy. Church leaders obviously believe that structure and order are important components in the life of the church.

Our term for the movement of the church is *mission.* In mission, we venture beyond our walls and the security of familiar relationships. How is mission related to structure? Most Christians meet and experience this issue in the context of the local church. Perhaps you can approach this question by asking the group to list the qualities that best define your church. What worship and organizational characteristics describe your congregation?

Then the class might compile a similar list of things the church needs to do in the community. The most important part of the exercise is comparing the two lists and discussing the points at which they interfere with each other and those at which they support one another. (For example, does the necessary maintenance of the building help or hinder mission outreach? How do matters of organization come to receive more attention than mission? How can this imbalance be prevented?)

Numbers 11:1-6—The Problems of Freedom

The complaint theme, so prominent in the desert stories, occurs several times in Chapters 10–14 (11:1-6; 12:1-2; 14:1-4.) The people, faced with a difficult life after their deliverance from their Egyptian oppressors, immediately begin grumbling against Moses and God. They grumble about their misfortunes, demand a more varied diet, recall with nostalgic fondness the life of Egypt, and finally plan a rebellion. Israel's action grows from the people's unwillingness to face the problems that come with freedom. Wherever this theme occurs, such conduct is displeasing to God and stands under divine judgment.

The New Testament use of these passages (and a similar one in Psalm 95:7-11) further emphasizes God's displeasure. The writer of Hebrews looks to the past and cites the condemnation of God's people for their rebellion (Chapter 3). Pointing to the desert experience as a warning, the writer exhorts Christians to avoid falling away from the faith in disloyalty and disobedience.

Have the class members discuss the "Egypts" in their individual lives. Ask persons to share experiences in which they outgrew their pasts but felt pulled back to them because the new stage they entered brought greater responsibility and uncertainty. What conditions in our lives interfere with growth? Does the Bible's emphasis on God's continuous call to move forward and face ever-growing responsibilities apply to us? How does God work to move us toward change and growth?

Numbers 11:10-17, 24-30; 12:1-16 A Leadership Model

Two quite different stories about Moses' leadership are related in Numbers 11:10-17, 24-30, and 12:1-16. The first story emphasizes the weight of the leader's burden and God's provision for distributing this burden among appropriate persons. The second, however, stresses Moses' authority and uniqueness.

If we bring this combination to bear on the issues of religious leadership, we can gain insight in a crucial area of our church life. What do the themes of shared leadership and unique individual gifts mean when applied to our situations?

One way to deal with this question would be to ask half of the class to list the qualities of Moses they see in these two stories. Some suggestions of things to look for are Moses' humility (12:3), his asking God for help (11:14), his openness to unexpected sources of strength and help (11:26-29), his striking use of unusual images for understanding God's concern (11:12), and his caring intercession for one who has caused him problems (12:13).

You could ask the other half of the class to list problem areas they see in church leadership. When the lists are compared, discuss whether Moses is a relevant model for church leadership today. If so, what specific points in Moses' leadership can apply to us today?

Numbers 13:1-33—Realism, Faith, and the Future

Repeatedly in the Bible we see people who regard difficult situations as opportunities within the providence of God. What we sometimes miss is the fact that this interpretation grows out of Israel's faith. It is a reading based on the assumption that God is at work for good in the realities of history.

The biblical faith expressed in Numbers 13–14 sees the possibilities of God's action within human affairs. Can we bring the biblical reading of events and conditions into the understanding of our times? In considering this question, ask each student to identify a critical situation in today's world. This situation may come from an international, a national, or a local setting. Consider the explorer story with its report of the positive and negative aspects of Canaan, and then identify similar elements in the contemporary situations described. Discuss what course of action a Caleb or a Joshua would urge Christians to take in such settings. Finally, ask the class to think about what in our biblical faith can make us as bold as Caleb as we face the future and attempt to discover our mission.

At the close of today's session, list on a chalkboard or a large piece of paper any new insights the class members have after studying Numbers 10–14.

Aaron's staff . . . had not only sprouted but had budded, blossomed and produced almonds (17:8).

4

The Perilous Journey Continues

Numbers 15–21

Chapters 15–21 continue the story of Israel's journey through the desert. We read of Israel's first victories and land acquisitions across the Jordan from Canaan. In these chapters, the generation that left Egypt dies, two serious rebellions against Moses and Aaron are quelled, the complaining of the people continues, Aaron and Miriam die, and Israel arrives on the threshold of the Promised Land.

Included in the narrative are regulations concerning offerings, portions due priests and Levites, and provisions for making water to cleanse Israel from impurity. In addition, three pieces of ancient poetry are incorporated into the story. All the elements that distinguish this book are here as Israel moves from desert wandering to the Promised Land.

DIMENSION ONE:
WHAT DOES THE BIBLE SAY?

Answer these questions by reading Numbers 15

1. What is to accompany Israel's animal offerings? (15:1-11)

   A grain offering and a drink offering accompany animal offerings.

2. When the people sin unintentionally, what is the community to do? (15:22-25)

   They shall offer one young bull for a burnt offering with accompanying grain and drink offerings and one male goat for a sin offering.

3. How is the congregation to treat the man who gathers sticks on the sabbath? (15:32-36)

   They are to stone him to death outside the camp.

4. Why are the Israelites to wear tassels on the corners of their garments? (15:37-40)

   The tassels remind them to do the Lord's commandments.

Answer these questions by reading Numbers 16

5. What charge do Korah and his supporters bring against Moses and Aaron? What does Moses tell the Korahites to do? (16:1-3, 16-19)

   Moses and Aaron have exalted themselves above the rest of the people. The Korahites must appear before the Lord with fire and incense in their censers.

6. Why are Dathan and Abiram punished, and what happens to them? (16:12-15, 25-33)

   Dathan and Abiram rebel against Moses' authority. The Lord opens the earth; and these men, their households, and their belongings are swallowed alive.

7. How does God punish the Korahites? (16:20-24, 35)

   He consumes them by a fire.

8. When the Lord punishes Israel for her constant grumbling, what keeps the plague from destroying all of Israel? (16:41-48)

   Aaron takes his censer and, standing between the living and the dead, makes atonement for the people.

Answer this question by reading Numbers 17

9. How does the Lord make known his choice of Aaron? (17:1-11)

   When twelve staffs are placed in the Tent of Meeting, Aaron's staff sprouts, blossoms, and produces almonds overnight.

Answer these questions by reading Numbers 18

10. Since the priests have no inheritance, what is their portion? (18:8-20)

    The Levites have the grain, sin, guilt, and wave offerings, and the first fruits of the flocks and herds. In addition, the redemption money for human first-born (five shekels of silver) belongs to them.

11. What do the Levites receive? (18:21-24)

The Levites receive the people's tithes.

Answer these questions by reading Numbers 19

12. How do the priests produce the ashes that are used in the water for impurity? (19:1-9)

An unblemished red heifer that has never been yoked is slaughtered and burned completely. Cedar wood, hyssop, and scarlet wool are also burned.

13. Who is unclean, and how are they cleansed? (19:14-19)

Anyone who comes into or is present in the tent when a man dies, every open vessel in that tent; anyone who touches a person slain with a sword, or a dead body, a human bone, or a grave is unclean. Those who are unclean are cleansed by being sprinkled with water mixed with the ashes of the purification offering.

Answer these questions by reading Numbers 20

14. Where is Miriam buried? (20:1)

She is buried in Kadesh, which is in the Desert of Zin.

15. After the people are given water from a rock at Meribah, what judgment does the Lord pronounce on Moses and Aaron? (20:2-13)

They will not be allowed to bring Israel into Canaan.

16. What do the Israelites request of the king of Edom, and what is his answer? (20:14-21)

They request free passage through the land of Edom. The king refuses permission.

17. When Aaron dies, who succeeds him? How is this signified? (20:23-29)

His son Eleazar succeeds him. Moses strips Aaron of his priestly garments and puts them on Eleazar.

Answer these questions by reading Numbers 21

18. What happens when the people complain against God and Moses? (21:4-6) What saves them? (21:7-9)

Venomous snakes attack them and they die. Moses makes a bronze snake and sets it up on a pole. Those bitten who look at it live.

19. What king do the Israelites defeat, and what territory do they occupy as a result? (21:21-30)

They defeat Sihon, king of the Amorites, and occupy the Amorite territory as far as the Arnon River.

20. What other king do they defeat? (21:33-35)

They defeat Og, king of Bashan.

DIMENSION TWO:
WHAT DOES THE BIBLE MEAN?

Background Information on Numbers 15–21

Numbers 15–21 continues the themes and forms of the preceding chapters but arranges them in a new way. Chapters 1–9 consist almost entirely of regulations and instructions. Chapters 10–14, on the other hand, are in story form. They tell of events in the period immediately following Israel's departure from Sinai. Chapters 15–21 are distinctive in their mixture of regulation and narrative.

In these chapters, the rebellion and murmuring themes continue, as does the emphasis on the role of the priests and Levites. In Chapter 21, the conquest theme appears for the first time. In these chapters Israel makes the transition from wandering in the desert to movement toward the Promised Land.

Numbers 15:1-16. Grain offerings can be offered alone, but when animal offerings are given they are to be accompanied by grain and drink offerings. This passage defines the kinds of grain and drink offerings that are to accompany the animal offerings.

Numbers 15:22-31. The offerings deal only with unintentional sins. One who sins intentionally cannot be protected in this way. The NIV, accurately reflecting the original Hebrew, calls him a person "who sins defiantly." The reference is to a hand raised in defiance and denotes one who acts arrogantly toward God and the divine commandments.

Numbers 15:32-36. This anecdote is an example of defiant sin. The regulation is not yet fully developed, so the case awaits a word from the Lord. Such instruction is called *torah.* Once given, the instruction becomes *mishpat*—a precedent governing similar cases.

Numbers 15:37-41. In other cultures, tassels may have been used in a kind of magical practice. For Israel, they serve as a reminder to observe the commandments. The Hebrew word is rendered "tassels" by most translations but as "fringes" in a few. We do not know whether the word refers to a tassel or a continuous fringe along a garment.

NUMBERS AND DEUTERONOMY

In Judaism, this instruction uses the fringes of the prayer shawl. In Matthew 23:5, Jesus condemns the religious leaders because they show their piety by making "the tassels on their garments long." Many Jews still wear a fringe of tassels on their prayer shawls. The fringed stole worn by some Christian clergy when leading worship has its origin in this tradition.

Numbers 16:1-35. Verses 1-35 tell of two challenges to Moses, two places where judgment takes place, and two kinds of judgment. Most scholars see two separate rebellion accounts that have been interwoven.

The Korahite rebellion, involving two hundred and fifty followers from among Israel's leaders, challenges the authority of Moses' and Aaron's religious leadership. The rebellion is settled by having the rebels appear before the Lord in a specific religious role (carrying censers with incense). They are consumed by fire from the Lord, thus demonstrating that they have performed this priestly function without proper authority.

On the other hand, Dathan and Abiram say that Moses lords it over them. Their rebellion is focused on political leadership rather than religious authority.

The separation of these stories is supported by Numbers 27:3, which mentions only Korah and his company. In Deuteronomy 11:6 and Psalm 106:17, only Dathan and Abiram appear in references to rebellion in the desert.

Numbers 18:1-20. The priests "bear the responsibility for offenses against the sanctuary." This means they are responsible for any wrongs done in the holy place. Some commentators, linking these words to 17:12-13, interpret them to mean that the priest and Levites take the risk, on behalf of the congregation, of approaching and handling holy things.

The "covenant of salt" (verse 19) implies a permanent covenant and a continuing obligation. The term is found elsewhere only in 2 Chronicles 13:5, in which the Lord speaks of making a covenant of salt with David's house.

Numbers 19:1-22. The ritual of the red heifer cannot be compared with any other Old Testament ceremony. The rabbis puzzled over the ritual's mystery, even devoting a whole section of the Talmud to its interpretation. They did conclude that the rules of this ritual were instituted not to be understood, but to test the unquestioning obedience of Israel.

The color specified is probably to be identified with the color of blood, which was regarded as particularly effective in cleansing (Leviticus 4:7). This identification is in keeping with the ritual's purpose to provide a way to deal with defiling contact with the dead.

The addition of cedar, hyssop, and scarlet wool is due to their cleansing properties. In Leviticus 14:6-7, all three are used in the rite of purification for a person with severe skin diseases.

Numbers 20:1-13. Because Moses "did not trust in me [the Lord] enough to honor me as holy in the sight of the Israelites," he is not allowed to enter Canaan. Scholars have made a number of suggestions concerning the exact nature of Moses' sin.

One notes that Moses strikes the rock (verse 11) when he is instructed to tell the rock (verse 8) to yield its water. This shows a lack of trust and a failure to obey. Another observes that Moses speaks angrily to Israel (verse 10) and thus his leadership is flawed under pressure. A third suggestion, based on Moses' words, "must we bring you water out of this rock?" (verse 10), points to an improper claim on Moses' part that he is responsible for the miracle of water from the rock. Still another scholar notes Moses' stunned immobility and lack of effective response (verse 6) when the people, after forty years, repeat their charges against him and God. Lacking faith in God's continuing power to fulfill the divine promise, Moses is incapable of providing effective leadership and must give way to another.

Numbers 20:14-21. In verse 14, "your brother Israel" points to the tradition that Israel's and Edom's ancestors were the twin brothers, Jacob and Esau. The greater part of the two peoples' history is a story of enmity. Kings of Judah gauged their strength by their ability to keep Edom subservient. Edom was among Judah's neighbors who despoiled her at the time of Jerusalem's fall. In the postexilic period, both Obadiah and Malachi reflect Judah's bitter hatred of Edom. Even in New Testament times, Herod the Great, an Idumean (a Greek term for "Edomite"), was despised by the Jews, in part for his origins.

The incident recorded in these verses marks the point at which God's people put their long desert sojourn behind them and begin the final stages of their journey to the Promised Land.

Numbers 21:10-35. This section records Israel's movement from Mount Hor, near Kadesh, to the plains of Moab. The stations along the way are named, but most of them cannot be identified with certainty. The general route is indicated by the phrase "that faces Moab toward the sunrise" (verse 11). If we assume that the travel route is on the east side of Moab, then one part of the journey is determined. The only segment that is not clearly located is the route around Edom after the people are refused passage through that land. Numbers 21:4 suggests that the route went around the south end of Edom and up along its east side.

The tentative identifications of the places mentioned in verses 10-11 lead many scholars to suggest a different route. In their view, Israel travels eastward on Edom's northern boundary between Moab and Edom. You may want to trace these routes on a map of the Promised Land.

This passage includes three pieces of ancient poetry. The first (verses 14-15) is a quote from the Book of the Wars of the Lord, an early collection of poetry mentioned only this one time in the Old Testament. The second piece of poetry is a song celebrating the appearance of water in a new well (verses 17-18). The third is the ballad singers' song telling of an Amorite victory over Moab (verses 27-30). The song tells of Sihon whom Israel defeated.

The accounts of two Israelite victories (verses 21-32, 33-35) are significant because they represent Israel's first steps in the conquest of the Promised Land. Although outside Canaan, these are the first territories Israel occupies permanently.

DIMENSION THREE: WHAT DOES THE BIBLE MEAN TO ME?

Chapters 15–21 are as varied in theme as they are in form and content. These chapters include a wide variety of subjects, ranging from garment tassels and the Levites' tithe to a red heifer and a bronze snake. In examining the meaning of this Scripture for us, our focus will be on the themes: "The Abundance of Offerings," "Crisis in Leadership," "The Red Heifer," "The Bronze Snake," and "From Preparation to Action."

Numbers 15:1-31—The Abundance of Offerings

The number and variety of offerings in Israel's worship strike us as strange and difficult to understand. However, if we understand Israel's purposes in her worship, new meanings begin to emerge.

Israel's elaborate provision for various offerings grows out of a desire to express loyalty to the God who called her to be a people in covenant. The offerings represent a significant part of her response. The offerings also represent a commitment to relationship with God. This commitment is grounded in the faith that God has delivered them, has made them a people, and continues to offer them life and destiny.

We identify ourselves as the people of a new covenant. We believe God has acted in grace to establish this relationship with us. What shall we use to symbolize our response to divine love? How are we to express loyalty and devotion?

Israel's covenant religion calls her to obey the commandments God has given her. An important aspect of Israel's worship, therefore, is the provision for sin offerings to handle unintended violation of commandments.

What aspects of our worship deal with our shortcomings? How do we express our desire to restore the covenant bond, which our sin impairs?

At this point you might ask the class members (individually or in groups of two) to list the various parts of the worship service and what they perceive to be the purpose of each part. Which parts are responses to God's love in extending life in covenant to us? Which parts address the brokenness caused by disobedience? How seriously do we take these expressions?

Numbers 16—Crisis in Leadership

The rebellions against Moses' leadership (Chapter 16) are the most serious recorded in the desert story. The common complaint in both rebellions, although one is religious and the other secular, is that Moses has claimed too much authority for himself. The questions surrounding leadership and the exercise of power are difficult in any society.

The question is no less acute today. One need only reflect on political campaigns or populist protests to be convinced of this problem. And the issue is as significant in the life of the church as it is in the political arena.

Leadership is a necessity in any movement or organization. However, individuals who possess it are always tempted to abuse it by seeking to guarantee its continuance or to exploit it for personal gain. On the other hand, whenever a significant decision is involved, the occasion arises for jealousy and resentment on the part of those affected.

What qualities characterize positive leadership in the church? How can a leader do what is necessary for the good of all and still be respected by those who are in opposition?

What are the signs of a leader's trying to hold on to office for its own sake? What part does the leader play in a Christian concept of group organization?

Numbers 19:1-10—The Red Heifer

In the Old Testament, and particularly in the later legal material, contact with the dead is taboo. Touching a corpse is defiling. The ritual of the red heifer provides a means for cleansing.

This account, while not mentioned again in the Old Testament, is used by the writer of Hebrews (9:13-14) to interpret Christ's sacrifice as superior in removing sin from human lives. Ask the class members what connection they see between Numbers 19:1-10 and the Crucifixion.

What situations in our lives create a need for cleansing? How does the church's worship help us to understand and to experience liberation from sin in Christ's death?

Numbers 21:4-9—The Bronze Snake

The snake was a part of many religions of the Near East in ancient times and was regarded as having extraordinary wisdom and recreative powers. Its image has turned up in many plaques, amulets, and shrines recovered from excavations in pre-Israelite Canaan. Even place names, such as Bethshan, are associated with snakes.

Numbers' account of the bronze snake, however, is no mere repetition of a common mythology. The image possesses no healing powers of its own, but serves as the instrument by which God provides healing and safety to Israel in the midst of the desert peril of poisonous snakes.

When we are desperate and threatened, we look for deliverance and protection. Faith tells us that ultimate deliverance comes from God. When we find a way out of difficulty, we tend to latch onto the means by which relief came. It is easy to confuse the instrument of healing with the source from which healing comes.

In the history of this story, which moves from snakes with magical powers to Jesus on a cross, we see how to avoid idolatry. The final step points to the symbol of deliverance in Jesus' death, the ultimate sign of God's love and healing (John 3:14).

At this point you could ask the class to list areas in which secondary agents of growth, deliverance, or sustenance are confused with their source. What resources in modern life may act as instruments for salvation, betterment, or deliverance as long as they are not confused with the provider of those resources? How can we use our Christian understanding to cope with common idolatries?

Numbers 21:10-35—From Preparation to Action

Numbers 20–21 signals the end of an era in Israel's life. Miriam and Aaron die; God tells Moses he cannot enter Canaan. The people still complain, but a new emphasis is unfolding in the story.

The generation-long wandering is nearing an end. God's promises and purpose are coming to fulfillment, not in a stroke of magic that transports the people of God into the land of Canaan, but in the succession of historical events.

These events begin with Edom's refusing "transit rights" to the Israelites. As a result, they are forced to circumvent Edom and are later led to victories in the area north of Moab. These victories give them territory of their own, and part of Israel settles here permanently.

We too experience times of aimless wandering and times of purposeful movement in the life of the church. How does the modern church's experience compare with the Israelites' desert sojourn? What can we learn from such times?

What parts of our church life today seem to represent achievement, fulfillment, goal realization, and conquest? How are desert and conquest related?

Close the session by asking the group members to list new insights they have gained from studying Numbers 15–21. If time allows, list these insights on a chalkboard or a large piece of paper.

5

Balaam and the Moabites

Numbers 22–27

Chapters 22–27 begin with the story of Balaam, the seer who refused to curse Israel. Following this story is Israel's first defection to Baal worship, the account of the second census, a legal narrative on inheritance by daughters, and the designation of Joshua as Moses' successor. The Scripture is varied in form, but all of it pertains to Israel's preparation for moving from desert to Promised Land.

DIMENSION ONE: WHAT DOES THE BIBLE SAY?

Answer these questions by reading Numbers 22

1. What is the Moabite reaction to the Israelites? (22:1-3)

   Their reaction is terror and dread.

2. Why does Balak send for Balaam? (22:4-6)

   He wants Balaam to come and put a curse on Israel.

3. Why won't Balaam come at first? (22:7-13)

   God tells him not to go.

4. What is the Lord's instruction when he allows Balaam to go? (22:15-20)

   He must do only what God tells him to do.

5. How is Balaam's life saved as he travels? (22:21-35)

   The donkey on which Balaam is riding refuses to move forward when it sees the angel of the Lord standing before them.

6. When Balaam arrives in Moab, on what condition will he speak? (22:36-38)

   He tells Balak he must speak only what God puts in his mouth.

Answer these questions by reading Numbers 23

7. Does Balaam curse the Israelites for Balak? What does Balaam say about them? (23:1-10)

   No. He says that he cannot curse those whom God has not cursed.

8. In his second oracle, what does Balaam say about God's relationship to Israel? (23:18-24)

   The Lord is with Israel, has brought the people out of Egypt, and has made Israel a nation as strong as a lion.

Answer these questions by reading Numbers 24

9. What is Balaam's vision of Israel's future? (24:3-9)

   He envisions Israel as an exalted kingdom, one that will prevail over her enemies.

10. How does Balak respond to Balaam's vision? (24:10-11)

    He is angry and tells Balaam to leave.

11. How does Balaam's fourth oracle describe the future relationship between Moab and Israel? (24:15-17)

    Israel will crush Moab.

Answer these questions by reading Numbers 25

12. What does Israel do that causes God to punish her? (25:1-5)

    The men indulge in sexual immorality with Moabite women and worship the Baal of Peor.

13. What is Phinehas's reward for his bold action against Zimri and Cozbi? (25:6-15)

    The Lord gives him a covenant of peace—a covenant of lasting priesthood.

Answer these questions by reading Numbers 26

14. What are the census totals for each tribe listed below? (26:1-50)

Reuben—*43,730* Manasseh—*52,700*
Simeon—*22,200* Ephraim—*32,500*
Gad—*40,500* Benjamin—*45,600*
Judah—*76,500* Dan—*64,400*
Issachar—*64,300* Asher—*53,400*
Zebulun—*60,500* Naphtali—*45,400*

15. How many people from the first census are counted in the later one? (26:63-65)

None. Only Caleb and Joshua entered the Promised Land.

Answer these questions by reading Numbers 27

16. What decision is reached concerning the inheritance of Zelophehad's five daughters? (27:1-11)

Since they are the only children of their father, they are entitled to his inheritance ahead of their father's brothers.

17. Whom does the Lord select as Moses' successor? What is Moses to do to him? (27:12-19)

God selects Joshua. Moses is to lay his hands upon him and commission him in the presence of Eleazar the priest and all the community. Then he is to give Joshua some of his authority.

DIMENSION TWO: WHAT DOES THE BIBLE MEAN?

Background Information on Numbers 22–27

At the beginning of Numbers 22, Israel makes camp on the plains of Moab. This is their location until they cross the Jordan to enter Canaan, an event recorded in Joshua 3. The six chapters of this lesson tell of Balaam, Israel's sin with the Baal of Peor, a second census, Zelophehad's daughters' inheritance rights, and Joshua's commissioning.

Numbers 22:1. This reference to Jericho is the first in the Bible. The city, well-known in the Old Testament because of its destruction by the Israelites under Joshua (Joshua 6), is one of the oldest cities in the world. Extensive archaeological excavations indicate that it dates back to at least 7000 B.C., and that it has a significant culture from that time until Israel enters Canaan.

Numbers 22:2-20. Israel's success in battle strikes fear into the hearts of the Moabites. Balak, king of Moab, decides to take strong measures to defend his country. The reference in verse 4 and verse 7 to "the elders of Midian" is somewhat puzzling since the Midianites were a separate people from

the Moabites. Their presence in the story may be due to a later event concerning Balaam (Numbers 31:8) in which the Midianites are centrally involved. Some evidence indicates that Moab was part of a Midianite empire at this time.

The Balaam stories reflect a double tradition about him. Numbers 22–24 tells of a far-off seer enlisted by Moab to curse Israel. He refuses to do so because God has blessed them, and Balaam is unable to curse what God has blessed. This view is reflected in Deuteronomy 23:4-5, Joshua 24:9-10, and Micah 6:5. Another tradition is found in Numbers 31:8, 16, however. These verses regard Balaam as a Midianite who is responsible for seducing Israel into defection at Peor. This view also appears in Joshua 13:22 and is the basis for three New Testament references to Balaam—2 Peter 2:15-16; Jude 11; and Revelation 2:14.

The location of Balaam's home is "Pethor, near the River" (22:5). References to the *River* in the Old Testament are generally to the Euphrates River. In inscriptions from the ninth century B.C., a northern Mesopotamian town called Pitru is mentioned.

The difficulty with this site is its distance from Moab. Efforts have been made to establish Balaam as coming from the nearby Ammonites on the basis of the literal Hebrew text which reads that Balak sends to Balaam "in the land of the children of his people." By adding one letter to the Hebrew word for his people ('ammo) it becomes 'ammon. This solves the problem of distance, but most interpreters regard the solution as somewhat forced and believe the evidence favors the northern Mesopotamian site.

Balaam is a diviner with a reputation for effective blessings and curses. In the thought of that day, words of blessing and cursing had power. The person who pronounced them set in motion a power that had a life of its own.

The overall theme of the story is set in verses 12 and 20. Balaam's powers are subject to God's will, and God has blessed Israel. What the Lord has blessed, Balaam cannot curse.

Numbers 22:21-35. The episode of Balaam and his donkey, an excellent example of the Hebrew art of storytelling, raises a question about its relationship to the rest of the story. God gives Balaam permission to go to Moab (verse 20). In verse 22, however, we are told God is angry because Balaam is going. How can we reconcile these verses?

One explanation is that this story comes from a source different from that of the preceding verses. Most scholars regard the Balaam story as a combination of two different accounts. The story as it now stands, however, emphasizes a significant tension that is basic to its meaning. The contradictions serve to heighten the tension.

The struggle reflected in the story pertains to the question of whether a seer with a reputation for powerful blessings and curses can put a curse on the people whom God intends to bless. Underneath this is the question underlying all of the pentateuchal narrative—the question of the power of God in the face of other powers. The inconsistencies in the Balaam story insure that the fundamental issue is fully addressed before it is settled at the story's end. Thus, the solution is not a superficial one but one that has dealt with all the questions the hearers have.

Numbers 22:41–23:12. From the first it is apparent that Balaam cannot curse Israel, whom God has blessed. Balaam tells Balak to build seven altars, and they offer a bull and a ram on each. Here the intention is to set the stage for a revelation from God. Balaam speaks "what God puts in my mouth" (22:38), that is, an oracle God intends for Balak.

The first oracle introduces the theme of Israel's prosperity and blessing. The reference to Israel's dwelling alone indicates that the people occupy a special place among the nations. A comparison with the blessing of Moses (Deuteronomy 33:28) indicates that the idea of security may also have been involved.

Balak is understandably frustrated, but Balaam repeats the theme that runs throughout the account. He can only say what the Lord gives him to say.

Numbers 23:13-26. Balak tries again by moving Balaam to another vantage point. Once more the oracle emphasizes Israel's favored position. The story refers to their freedom from misfortune and adverse divination.

Numbers 23:27–24:9. The third oracle follows a slightly different pattern. It begins by stating that Balaam receives what he speaks in a state of ecstasy, under "the Spirit of God" (24:2). The theme of Israel's blessing is expanded to emphasize reference to power and prosperity. The oracle ends with words of blessing which repeat God's promise to the patriarchs (Genesis 12:3; 27:29).

Numbers 24:10-19. This final oracle further emphasizes that Balak has not been deceived. Balaam has said from the beginning that what he speaks depends on what the Lord gives him to say. The fourth oracle concerning Israel reiterates the emphasis of the first three, but in a more explicit fashion. This oracle introduces a specific figure as the "star [that] will come out of Jacob" (24:17), that is, Israel. This image probably refers to the coming Davidic kingship. Moab and Edom succumb to David's power and become part of his empire.

The puzzling use of the word *Sheth* in verse 17 may refer to the *Seth* of Genesis 4:25-26 and 5:3, 6-8. If so, the reference may be to all humankind, as an early version suggests. The usual poetic parallelism, however, would suggest that the word should refer in a more limited way to Moab, as does the preceding line. A tradition may link Seth to Moab, as Cain was connected with the neighboring Kenites; but no such connection is known anywhere else in the Old Testament.

Numbers 24:20-25. Three short oracles are attached at the end of the Balaam story. The Amalekites are a people who occupy the territory south of Palestine. They are enemies of Israel in their early history (Numbers 13:29) until Saul defeats Agag, king of the Amalekites (1 Samuel 15). Even after this, they remain bothersome to Israel on her southern border until David is able to subdue them (2 Samuel 8:12).

The Kenites (verses 21-22) are familiar to us from past references in the desert story. They are a people friendly and helpful to Israel. The "nest . . . in a rock" (verse 21) is a pun. The Hebrew *ken* (nest) sounds like *Keni*, the Hebrew form for Kenite. The word play is carried further because *ken* sounds similar to *Cain*. Cain is the traditional ancestor of the Kenites.

Numbers 25:1-5. After the Balaam account, the ongoing story of Israel's movement toward the Promised Land resumes with the Baal of Peor incident. This is the first instance of defection to another god. Israel is drawn into immoral and idolatrous practices through sexual entanglement with the Moabites.

The incident at Peor is the beginning of a long struggle between Israel's covenant faith and the allurements of the fertility cults. This tension lives on in Israel through the time of the eighth century prophets, and even beyond that to the Exile.

The drastic punishment indicates the serious threat the actions presented to Israel's continued life. Without doubt the act of leading Israel into involvement in the worship and practices of baalism is a capital offense.

Numbers 25:6-18. This story intends to support claims of Phinehas's descendants to the priesthood (verses 12-13). The story credits Phinehas with stemming the tide of apostasy and preventing Israel's destruction.

Numbers 26:1-65. The second Israelite census follows the same order and shows the same pattern as the one at Sinai (Chapter 2). Three differences are evident, however. In the Moab census, each tribal listing adds the second generation clans, with further personal notes being given in three instances (Dathan and Abiram, Er and Onan, and the daughters of Zelophehad). The order of Manasseh and Ephraim is reversed. Three tribes (Manasseh, Benjamin, and Asher) increase significantly while three others (Simeon, Ephraim, and Naphtali) show a substantial loss in number.

The Levite census is taken separately in both accounts, with the account in Chapter 26 being briefer. But the account does include a genealogy for Moses, Aaron, and Miriam. In this same section, a reference to Nadab and Abihu, sons of Aaron, points back to the story of their deaths due to improper priestly actions (Leviticus 10:1-7).

The numbers of the census have been variously interpreted. One scholar has suggested that the Hebrew word *'eleph,* which meant "thousand" in later usage, should be

NUMBERS AND DEUTERONOMY

understood as "unit" of fighting men. If we take the word in this way, Reuben, for example, would number forty-three units made up of seven hundred thirty men.

Verses 52-56 speak of land allotment and give a reason, in addition to determining fighting strength, for taking the census.

Numbers 27:1-11. Land inheritance in Israel is predominantly through the male line. In cases where there are no sons at the time of the husband's death, a brother is to marry the widow and attempt to father sons in the dead man's name (Genesis 38). This is called *levirate marriage.* The story of Zelophehad's daughters, however, gives a different answer to the line of inheritance in sonless families. God gives a law in which daughters are given first inheritance rights in such cases.

Numbers 27:12-23. As Moses prepares for his death, provision is made for his successor, Joshua. Throughout his career, Moses has received word directly from God. But Joshua will need the help of the priest and the Urim (elsewhere denoted as Urim and Thummim) in determining God's will. The object mentioned here is the sacred lot and is evidently kept in the breastplate of the priest's robe (Exodus 28:30; Leviticus 8:8). One interpreter suggests that this may have been two stones of different colors, one for "yes" and the other for "no," which were withdrawn to ascertain the divine will in difficult decisions.

DIMENSION THREE: WHAT DOES THE BIBLE MEAN TO ME?

The stories in Chapters 22–27 raise several significant issues for our thought and life today. The three themes selected for further exploration are these: "A King's Will and God's Purposes," "Realism and Faith," and "From One Generation to Another."

Numbers 22–24—A King's Will and God's Purposes

The relationship between Moab and Israel has a long and eventful history. Even though they knew themselves to be related (Genesis 19:36-37), their geographical nearness frequently threw them into conflict.

The story of Balak and Balaam treats this relationship at the point where Moab, already established as a nation, seeks to dispose of Israel, still a wandering people, before she becomes a greater threat.

The account is grounded in the view that blessing and curse possess objective power. Once pronounced, a curse (or blessing) is believed to have power to come to fulfillment. A person skilled in such pronouncements is seen as having special powers. Balaam is such a person, renowned for his ability to pronounce effective blessings and curses.

The issue this story presents for us concerns our belief that ultimate power resides in human affairs. In the story, Balaam is a man caught between two forces in conflict. Will he be used as an instrument of blessing, or as a tool of cursing? The conflicting forces are not Moab and Israel, but rather Moab and the Lord. Israel is the people of God, and as such, her fortune is the measure of divine effectiveness in history. The real struggle is between Balak, who wills to destroy Israel, and the Lord, who seeks to bless this chosen people.

This battle is portrayed frequently in the Old Testament. Sometimes the line is drawn between Israel and an enemy nation. Sometimes the battle is within Israel, between the king and his subject (as in the case of David and Uriah or Ahab and Naboth). In the prophets, the conflict is between the oppressive rich and the Lord's concern for the welfare of the poor and defenseless. The question in all cases is, Does God act in history to effect the divine will for justice, righteousness, and freedom?

Always, as exemplified in the person of Balak, the visible, immediate, and human power seems invincible. The Balaam story, however, witnesses to the fact that all human powers are subject to the divine will. Balaam, however skilled he may be, cannot curse what God blesses.

The application of this truth to our times is the responsibility of the church. Ask the class members to give specific cases of wrongs they see being done to powerless persons by those in authority. As they share their examples, ask them whether we as Christians believe God can act in these situations to bring justice. If so, how does justice come about?

Numbers 25:1-5—Realism and Faith

In the immediate aftermath of the great climax in the Balaam story, God's people fall into sin and disloyalty. In their first encounter with the fertility cults in the vicinity of Canaan, they give way to the alluring attraction of the nature deities. Is this the end of their life as the blessed people of God?

Although severe and drastic punishment falls upon the Israelites, the story goes on. The Lord continues to entrust the divine purposes to a people prone to immorality, defection, and rebellion.

The biblical faith is realistic. God cannot be defeated by insensitive and willful wrongdoing. God is aware of the full range of human conduct. The amazing thing is his radical and continuing commitment to work in real-life, human experiences.

We can find many examples of this faith in the biblical record. Our question is, How do we see God functioning in our world today?

The place to begin is with the "Peors" of our lives. What other gods do we go after? In what areas does the church fail to serve God?

After the class members have considered the church's shortcomings, ask them to discuss ways God continues to work through an imperfect institution.

Numbers 26—From One Generation to Another

When the second census is compared with the first (Chapter 2), the numbers are similar, the totals very nearly identical, and the order and grouping of tribes almost the same. The changes in setting and the passage of time, however, give new significance to the second enumeration. Israel has held her own as the people of God. From Sinai through the uncertainties and short-comings of the desert sojourn to the threshold of the Promised Land, the people of God exhibit a certain continuity. The purposes of God are holding their own in human history.

However, the crucial point to note is that the second census deals with a whole new generation (verses 63-65). The question then arises, How are the faith and vision of the people of God communicated from one generation to the next? The story gives us few hints.

Two elements may be significant. One is the impressive leadership of Moses and his trust in God's leading. The other element may lie in the sense of covenant, the consciousness of belonging to God and of being responsible for obedience within that relationship. This awareness of belonging and responsibility is based on the remembrance of God's deliverance of Israel at the sea of reeds (Red Sea).

The problem of continuity is also addressed in the story of Moses and Joshua in Numbers 27:12-23. Leaders who have been as involved as Moses do not let go of their responsibilities easily. This remarkable story reflects a Moses who requests the appointment of a successor and who then, on God's instruction, commissions Joshua and then shares his authority with him. It is little wonder that Moses is remembered for his selflessness.

The central point of these two accounts—that the faith and mission of God's people can survive the crisis of transmission from generation to generation—is instructive for the church today. Ask the class to list the elements in the life of the church that enable it to continue from one generation to another. When they have shared their lists, ask them to compare their points with the biblical emphasis on God's part in this continuity. In light of what we have studied and learned, what can we do to insure that the faith will continue in the next generation?

Close the session by asking the class members to share their new insights on Numbers 22–27.

— 6 —

Preparing for the Promised Land

Numbers 28–36

With these chapters we close our study of the Book of Numbers. Throughout these nine chapters Israel remains encamped on the plains of Moab. The main interest in this section is Israel's preparation for entrance into Canaan.

DIMENSION ONE:
WHAT DOES THE BIBLE SAY?

Answer these questions by reading Numbers 28

1. What animal offerings are the people to make daily? What is to accompany these? (28:3-5, 7)

   They are to offer two lambs a year old, accompanied by a grain offering of a tenth of an ephah of fine flour mixed with a fourth of a hin of pressed olive oil, and a drink offering of one-fourth hin.

2. For what other occasions does the Lord specify offerings? (28:9, 11, 16-19, 26)

   Offerings are to be made on the sabbath, on the first of every month, the Passover, the festival of Unleavened Bread, and the Feast of Weeks.

Answer these questions by reading Numbers 29

3. In addition to the two sacred assemblies mentioned in Chapter 28 (verses 18, 26), what three occasions call for sacred assemblies in Israel's religious calendar? (29:1, 7, 12)

   The first, tenth, and fifteenth days of the seventh month are occasions for assembly.

4. How long does the third festival last? How does it end? (29:12-38)

   It lasts eight days and ends with an assembly.

Answer these questions by reading Numbers 30

5. How does the vow of a woman still in her father's house differ from that of a man? (30:1-5)

   Her vow is subject to her father's approval.

6. How does marriage affect a woman's vows? (30:6-8, 10-12)

   A married woman's vow is subject to her husband's approval.

7. How do widowhood and divorce affect a woman's vows? (30:9)

   The vows of a widow or of a divorced woman are binding.

Answer these questions by reading Numbers 31

8. Against whom do the Israelites go to war? (31:1-2) What is the outcome? (31:7-11)

   They fight the Midianites. They slay every man, take their women and children captive, take cattle and goods as plunder, and burn all their towns and camps.

9. Whose counsel does Moses blame for Israel's sin at Peor? (31:16) What happens to the one blamed? (31:8)

   Balaam is blamed, and he is slain.

10. How are the spoils from the battle with the Midianites divided? (31:25-27) What levies does Moses take from each half? (31:28-30)

    It is divided evenly between the soldiers and the community. The soldiers are levied one part in five hundred, for the priests; the people of Israel, one part in fifty, for the Levites.

Answer these questions by reading Numbers 32

11. What tribes ask for land east of the Jordan? (32:1-5)

   Reuben and Gad request the land.

12. What do they agree to do before settling down? (32:6-7, 16-27)

   They agree to lead the rest of the tribes into Canaan.

Answer this question by reading Numbers 33

13. What is the starting point of Israel's journey, some of its most memorable stopping points, and the location of the final encampment before Canaan? (33:5, 8, 15, 36-37, 48)

   The starting point is Rameses. Stopping points are Succoth, the sea, the Desert of Etham, the Desert of Sinai, Kadesh, and Mount Hor. The final encampment is in the plains of Moab.

Answer these questions by reading Numbers 34

14. What information does God relay to Moses? (34:1-12)

   God gives the boundaries of the land of Canaan, Israel's inheritance.

15. How many tribes does Moses include in the division of the land of Canaan? (34:13-15)

   He includes nine and one-half tribes.

Answer these questions by reading Numbers 35

16. What is Israel to provide for the Levites? (35:1-8)

   Israel is to provide forty-eight towns with their pasturelands.

17. What purpose do the cities of refuge serve? (35:9-15)

   They are to be places of refuge from the avengers for any person who kills another accidentally.

18. What is the distinction between murderer and the one who is to be spared from the avenger of blood? (35:16-28)

   The former kills with malice and intent.

Answer this question by reading Numbers 36

19. Why must the daughters of Zelophehad marry within their own tribe? (36:1-9)

   Their inheritance must stay within their tribe.

DIMENSION TWO: WHAT DOES THE BIBLE MEAN?

Background Information on Numbers 28–36

The preparation theme underlies most of the material in Chapters 28–36. The subjects in these nine chapters seem to be unrelated to each other, but they all deal with things Israel needs to know or do in order to carry out the conquest and to settle in Canaan as the people of God.

The chapters are a mixture of narrative and law that characterizes the Book of Numbers. In a larger sense, this combination of story and regulation is typical of the whole Pentateuch. It expresses Israel's conviction that the ordered life and historical experience are two elements of the existence of God's people.

Numbers 28:11-15. The observance of "the beginning of months" is added to the daily and sabbath offerings. The Hebrew word translated *months* may also be rendered *new moons,* making it clear that Israel used a lunar calendar. Modern Judaism still follows the lunar calendar with regard to observances. The year consists of twelve lunar months, which leaves it shorter than the solar year by eleven days. To compensate, an extra month is inserted about every three years, seven times within a nineteen-year cycle. Although the Old Testament gives no clear evidence of such an orderly pattern, the early rabbis mention it explicitly.

Numbers 28:16-25. The early spring festival is a combination of Passover and Unleavened Bread. It is not clear when these were combined. Passover is evidently of nomadic background, reflecting rites used when flocks were moved to new pasture for spring and summer. Unleavened Bread is an agricultural festival marking the entrance into a new harvest year by starting a new lump of dough, as yet unleavened.

At some point in Israel's worship, these festivals were put together to commemorate Israel's exodus from Egypt. In the Israelites' annual celebration of deliverance, they relived the emancipation of their ancestors and took their place among the people of God.

"The first month" reflects one of the Old Testament views of calendar. Evidence indicates that Israel used two new year dates at different times in the biblical period. The numbering of the months always starts in the spring, but it is also clear that Israel had a fall new year in the monarchical period, perhaps even earlier. Under Babylonian domination, in the exilic period, Israel adopted the Babylonian spring new year. In post-biblical times, when the Jewish observance of Rosh Hashanah developed, it grew out of the fall festival.

Numbers 29:1-11. Most Old Testament references to the major festivals mention only one, Booths (or Ingathering), in the fall. This reference and two in Leviticus (16:29-34;

23:23-25) are the only places in the Scriptures that split the fall observance into three parts. Some scholars believe the fall festival included a covenant renewal element or some other turn-of-the-year aspects. When the atonement rites are developed and set into the fall worship calendar, the result is a three-part observance—one, the first; another, the tenth; and the original festival, the fifteenth.

As time goes by, the new year festival and the day of atonement observance become so important that Ingathering, once one of the two most significant observances, gradually becomes of less importance. This situation still exists.

Numbers 30:1-16. Two words, *vow* and *pledge*, figure prominently in this passage. The former is the more general term. In later times, the term is restricted to a binding promise to give something. *Pledge* refers to a negative vow, a serious promise to abstain from something.

In this passage, verses 6-8 appear to cover the same situation as verses 9-12. The difference is indicated by the phrase "living with her husband" in verse 10. The first case is that of a betrothed woman who is still in her father's house but under the law is treated as already married. The second involves the situation in which the marriage has taken place.

Underlying the restrictions of this passage are the conditions of status and ability to hold property in a patriarchal society. Since women do not command resources or power to make good on vows, their vow-making capacity is restricted. Perhaps restriction is for their own protection, since a vow once pronounced must be fulfilled. That wives would have so few rights today are now seen as untenable. We must work through the meaning of this passage in light of a new set of relationships, making greater allowance for equality and respect.

Numbers 31:25-54. Following the account of the holy war against the Midianites, who are held responsible for Israel's defilement at Peor, is a section on disposal of plunder. The unusual sharing between warriors and people is found one other place in the Old Testament. First Samuel 30:24-25 tells of a similar decision and practice carried out by David. This became a precedent in Israel.

The most distinctive element in the Midianite story is the levy that is to provide for priests and Levites. This levy is not found anyplace else in the Old Testament.

Numbers 33:1-48. The list of stages in the desert journey is a summary of all that has happened to this point since the Israelites left Egypt. The summary is evidently included here to indicate the closing of the desert chapter and to emphasize the turning to the future task, the conquest of Canaan.

The places listed total forty-two. Half of these places are unknown elsewhere in the Old Testament. Most are found in verses 18-29, which may indicate that the writer had an independent source for the section covering the journey from Sinai to Kadesh. An overview of the list shows Israel going from Rameses, in Egypt, to Sinai (eleven stages, one year); from Sinai to Kadesh (twenty-one stages, thirty-eight years); and from Kadesh to the plains of Moab (ten stages, one year).

Numbers 34:1-12. This is the clearest and most detailed of several boundary descriptions found in the Pentateuch. The southern boundary runs from the lower end of the Dead Sea west to the Mediterranean, which then forms the western boundary. The northern line is difficult to locate, but it seems to run east some one hundred miles from a point above Byblos in northern Lebanon. The northern section of the eastern boundary is also somewhat obscure until it reaches the Sea of Chinnereth (Galilee). From there the boundary follows the Jordan to the Dead Sea.

Numbers 35:1-8. In the Pentateuch, the Levites are described as without inheritance, that is, without territory of their own. The rest of Israel gives them their livelihood through tithes connected with the Levites' function in worship and service in the Tent of Meeting. In this passage, however, God provides for the other tribes to give them forty-eight towns and adjoining pastureland. (A fuller account is found in Joshua 21). The cities of the Levites include the six cities of refuge.

Numbers 35:12. The word *avenger* means a person who functions in a variety of ways in Israelite society. The word is usually translated *redeemer* and refers to responsibility to reclaim lost land, to buy the freedom of a family member who is enslaved, or to avenge the slaying of a relative. The basic function of the avenger is to restore the fortune of the family or tribe.

The term is also used for God's gracious activity toward Israel, particularly in the references to restoration from exile. The implication is that God is concerned about Israel's welfare and works in history to redeem Israel's fortune when she is in dire need.

Numbers 35:15-25. The distinction in types of homicide is based in Israel, as in other societies, on intent. If the slaying was accidental, the slayer may claim protection in the city of refuge. Terms used to describe one who kills another accidentally are "accidentally" (verse 15), "without hostility" (verse 22), and "without seeing him" (verse 22). On the other hand, the terms "with malice," "intentionally," and " in hostility" (verses 20-21) indicate a murderer, who is given over to the blood avenger to be put to death (verse 21).

Numbers 36:4. The meaning of the reference to the Year of Jubilee is not clear. The law of jubilee, an observance of the fiftieth year, is recorded in Leviticus 25:8-34. The regulation there, however, applies only to land that is sold and does not appear to cover inheritance.

Numbers 36:13. The book's concluding sentence applies to the whole section of regulations in Numbers 27–36. Note the similarity of this text to the closing words of Leviticus.

DIMENSION THREE:
WHAT DOES THE BIBLE MEAN TO ME?

The class discussion of Dimension Three will concentrate on some or all of these areas: "Festival and Offering," "The Dilemma of God's People," "Following Through," "Murder and Society," and "Freedom and Limitation."

Numbers 28:16-31; 29:1-16, 35-38
Festival and Offering

When we want to understand another religion we are likely to ask about its beliefs. We learn more about its vitality and motivation, however, if we ask what it celebrates.

The Israelite festivals are observed on an agricultural calendar, which comes from the surrounding cultures who use it in the fertility rites of the nature religions. Israel, however, adapts the festivals so that their internal meaning is quite different from the magical, baalistic worship of their neighbors.

The worship of Israel is not intended to insure that the fertility cycle will repeat itself, a major purpose of festival observance in agricultural religions. In the Old Testament, worship is geared to the praise of the God of history and the remembrance of divine actions that produced the people of Israel. In so remembering, each generation of Israel enters once more into relationship with God.

Within this relationship Israel has certain responsibilities which, at times, are spelled out in terms of ethical conduct and moral obedience. The other aspect of responsibility, however, resides in worship, including its specification of offerings, proper ritual, and particular personnel. Numbers 28–29 emphasizes this aspect.

The worship of God is a time of celebration and remembrance. It is also a time that calls for offering and service on the part of the worshiper. Only as we give the latter full weight do we understand the total meaning of Israel's life and worship.

This passage calls us to accountability in the area of offering, that is, what we bring to God in worship. The passage asks us what we do to express the devotion and loyalty to God, which Israel shows through these offerings.

One way to address this issue concretely is to think of those things in our present worship that take the place of animal and grain offerings. Ask the class to identify the specific elements in worship that express our response to God's action in Christ. What implication does our response have for stewardship?

Numbers 31:1-20; 33:50-56
The Dilemma of God's People

The story of Israel's victory over the Midianites in Numbers 31:1-20 strikes us as extraordinarily violent and harsh. In the same vein, the instructions to drive out all the Canaanites (33:50-56) from the Promised Land raise serious questions for us. The identification of these attitudes with the will of God is a challenge to our understanding of divine love.

Within the Old Testament there are other voices, such as that of Hosea, who condemn the bloody religious revolution that had taken place at Jezreel one hundred years before his time (Hosea 1:4-5). The Book of Jonah speaks of God's forgiveness of the repentant Assyrians, a nation that was one of Israel's worst enemies.

As Christians, we can hardly believe that the God who is revealed in Jesus could have ordered such an inhuman disposition of captives as we find in Numbers 31:17. How can we maintain a faithful relationship with the biblical record and at the same time take seriously what our Christian tradition tells us about God's love?

This story was probably written to address the problems of a later time, perhaps the Exile. Although the story tells us that the Midianites were completely destroyed, a later account in Judges 6–8 indicates that the Midianites continued to give Israel great difficulty. The primary point of the account of the Midianite war is that Israel must keep herself free from involvement with pagan cults. For us the important of the passage is its insistence on clarity of moral decision and the importance of unwavering constancy to the God we know.

Ask the class how we can stand for the things that matter in our faith and express them in the midst of a culture that has different values. Where do Christian values of justice, love, and righteousness clash with the practices and purposes of our society? How should we relate to those who are committed to other values and ends?

Numbers 32:1-7, 16-27—Following Through

The request of Gad and Reuben (and later of half of Manasseh) that they be allowed to settle east of Jordan seems to be a reasonable one. Moses, however, is aware of the extreme importance of a "full Israel" for the conquest of Canaan. He presses these tribes to support the interests of the rest of Israel. They sense their responsibility to the whole people of God and promise their full support.

The incident suggests that we should go beyond an individualistic view of salvation to a greater concern for our sisters and brothers in the church and in the world. Perhaps, like Gad and Reuben, we are called to involvement beyond ourselves for the sake of the church and those whom it serves.

Ask the class to think of concrete ways in which we as individual Christians need to commit ourselves beyond the concerns for our private religious experience.

Numbers 35:9-34—Murder and Society

God's provision for cities of refuge is a most interesting phenomenon in Israelite society. The regulation of homicide is first handled by a kind of private punishment, the work of the avenger, which grows out of tribal organization. The avenger-redeemer, next-of-kin to the slain person, is responsible to right the imbalance between tribes by taking the life of the slayer.

The cities of refuge act as a curb, however, on the free exercise of the avenger role. These verses express an acute sense of human values, which, even in the presence of the terrible fact of homicide, tries to distinguish motives and deal justly with the slayer. The passage also expresses the conviction that any human killing has a profound effect on the whole of Israelite society.

Society had to compensate for the family member's loss on the quality of family life. Israel was also concerned for the rights of the accidental slayer, and knew the serious effect of homicide on the whole community's relationship with God. So dealing with homicide was a delicate and complicated matter. For Israel the primary concern was God's evaluation of human life. All of these elements were given attention in expressing that concern.

Ask the class to think of how homicide is handled in our culture and legal system. They might briefly list the aspects of our system that provide for redress to the victim's family, for guaranteeing the rights of the person charged, and for the damage done to society as a whole. How does every violent taking of human life affect society? What methods of dealing with homicide do our biblical tradition and Christian faith suggest?

Numbers 36:1-12—Freedom and Limitation

The second episode in the story of Zelophehad's daughters reminds us that no significant change can be made in social order and regulation without affecting other aspects of society.

Justice calls for sensitivity and change in the face of new issues and emerging needs. However, simple change is not enough. When we make adjustments to right wrongs, we must deal responsibly with the effects of such adjustments.

To make this issue more concrete, ask class members to consider and identify areas in which change has taken place in the community in recent years, particularly when action was taken to give deprived people their rights. What adjustments has such change required?

Close the session by asking group members to list new insights they have gained from today's lesson. If time allows, list these insights on a chalkboard or a large piece of paper.

7

Moses Recounts God's Acts

Deuteronomy 1–3

Our study now turns to the Book of Deuteronomy. This book consists mainly of words that Moses spoke to Israel on the plains of Moab. Within its thirty-four chapters are included a brief historical summary, an extended exhortation, a distinctive body of law with accompanying blessings and curses, Moses' last words, and the account of his death.

DIMENSION ONE: WHAT DOES THE BIBLE SAY?

Answer these questions by reading Deuteronomy 1

1. Where does Moses speak to all Israel? (1:1-5)

   He is beyond the Jordan in the Desert of the Arabah; in the land of Moab.

2. What does Moses report that God said at Horeb? (1:6-8)

   Israel has stayed long enough at the mountain. The people are to journey to the hill country of the Amorites and take possession of the Promised Land.

3. Why does Moses appoint other leaders? (1:9-18)

   He cannot bear the burden of leadership alone, due to the number of the Israelites and their burdens.

4. What do the children of Israel ask Moses to do at Kadesh Barnea? (1:22-23)

   They ask Moses to send explorers to the Promised Land.

5. Why do the Israelites refuse to go into the Promised Land? (1:26-28)

   They have heard that the people are larger than they and that the cities are heavily fortified.

6. What is the Lord's reaction to their refusal? (1:34-40)

   The Lord is angered and swears that no one of this generation (except Caleb) shall go into the land.

7. Why does Israel fall in the later attempt to fight the Amorites as the Lord commanded? (1:41-46)

   The Lord is not with the Israelites.

Answer these questions by reading Deuteronomy 2

8. Who has given Seir to the descendants of Esau? (2:1-5)

   The Lord has given them Seir.

9. What are the Israelites to do as they pass through Seir? (2:6)

   They are to avoid conflict and pay for the food and water they use.

10. Where do the Israelites go after this? How are they to treat the inhabitants there? (2:8-10)

    They go into Moab. They are to avoid war.

11. With whom does Israel do battle? What is the result? (2:24-36)

    Israel fights Sihon, the king of Heshbon, and completely defeats his forces.

12. What country does Israel avoid? (2:37)

    Israel avoids the land of the Ammonites.

Answer these questions by reading Deuteronomy 3

13. What is the result when Israel goes to war with Og of Bashan? (3:1-7)

    Israel defeats Og and destroys all the inhabitants of Bashan.

14. Of what group is Og a remnant? What shows his size? (3:11)

    Og is a remnant of the Rephaites, as can be seen by the size of his bedstead.

15. To whom does Moses give the conquered territory? What does the half-tribe of Manasseh receive? (3:12-17)

Manasseh receives the northern half of Gilead and all of Bashan. The remaining conquered land is given to Reuben and Gad.

16. What does Moses expect these tribes to do? (3:18-20)

They are to send their fighting men along with the other tribes of Israel when the latter enter Canaan to possess it.

DIMENSION TWO: WHAT DOES THE BIBLE MEAN?

Background Information on Deuteronomy

The language and style of the Book of Deuteronomy are distinctive and uniform. The preference for a full, somewhat repetitious way of saying things and the characteristic use of certain words (for example, *commandments, statutes,* and *ordinances*) set the fifth book of the Pentateuch apart from the first four.

Deuteronomy's form is determined by the fact that Moses is the speaker throughout. These chapters, marked by a sermon style, can be divided internally into three addresses or sermons (Chapters 1–4; 5–28; 29–30) with an appendix (31–34). Their prevailing tone is hortatory.

Deuteronomy addresses Israel as a holy people and focuses on the covenant between God and the people. The covenant theme is accompanied by an emphasis on obedience to covenant law.

Since the time of Jerome (late fourth century A.D.), scholars have suggested a connection between Josiah's reform in 621 B.C. (2 Kings 22–23) and Deuteronomy. The actions of the reform, based on a book found in the Temple, closely parallel the regulations of Deuteronomy 12–26. Other characteristics of Deuteronomy point to a date of authorship in the seventh century B.C.

The issues facing Judah in the days prior to the Exile are addressed by looking at them from the perspective of Israel's life just before the people enter Canaan. Israel stands between promise and fulfillment on the plains of Moab. In the seventh century, Israel still lives in the tension between past and future, trying to work out her identity and purpose.

Those who study Deuteronomy have noticed the similarity of its structure to Near Eastern (particularly Hittite) treaty forms. These treaty documents are usually written to spell out the conditions between conquering monarch and subject people. The standard pattern consists of five sections: identification of the king giving the treaty, historical preamble, stipulations of the conditions, listing of witnesses, and blessings and curses. Deuteronomy reflects a similar structure and may represent an adaptation of the form in order to express the covenant relationship between God and Israel.

Deuteronomy 1:1-8. The most characteristic statement of the Book of Numbers is "The LORD said to Moses . . . ." The opening of Deuteronomy immediately tells us of the difference in emphasis in this book. The distinction is one of focus rather than theology. While both books cite a divine basis for their words, Deuteronomy places Moses in the forefront to a greater degree.

In verse 5, we read that Moses "began to expound this law." The word for "expound" appears only three times in the Old Testament. The other occurrences (Habakkuk 2:2; Deuteronomy 27:8) describe some kind of clarification, in both cases associated with writing. Some have concluded that this verse refers to written material, although the context does not support such a meaning. It is clear, however, that Moses' function is to clarify all that follows.

In verse 6, Moses launches into a recital of the events from Horeb to the plains of Moab as a preface for the instruction to follow in the core of the book. He begins with the Lord's admonition to set out from Horeb for the land of Canaan. From a strict historical standpoint the term *Amorite* (verse 7) refers to a larger group of Semitic peoples who inhabited the Near East early in the second millennium B.C. Hammurabi and the other rulers of the First Babylonian Dynasty came from this ethnic group. In the Pentateuch, however, the term is often used to refer specifically to the Canaanites.

Deuteronomy 1:9-18. Two other passages in the Pentateuch refer to the appointment of persons to help Moses meet the demands of leadership. Exodus 18:13-27 tells of Jethro's advice to his son-in-law, Moses, who is trying to arbitrate all the disputes within Israel. On Jethro's recommendation, Moses appoints rulers to decide cases for which there is precedent. Only the major matters still come to Moses for counsel and decision.

In Numbers 11:16-17, 24-30, Israel's complaining and the task of providing food for the people overwhelm Moses. When he cries out for help, the Lord tells him to appoint seventy elders, whom the Lord then endows with some of the spirit that is upon Moses.

Deuteronomy's account is a summary that draws on both other accounts of the appointments of subleaders. The double reason for the appointments—the numbers of people to deal with and Israel's complaining—combines those given in Exodus and Numbers respectively. The term *commanders* in verse 15 is the same word in Hebrew as the officials of Exodus 18:21.

The term *officials* in verse 15, which also appears in Numbers 11:16, has legal, military, and administrative meaning. The other official title used in this passage (verse 16) is *judges.* Although these various titles may indicate three sets of officials, we do not have enough information to be sure. It is more likely that the terms describe the various duties of one group, who carries administrative and judicial responsibilities.

Verses 9-18 comprise the first of seven episodes chosen to summarize Israel's experience in the desert. The other six are found in the remainder of Chapters 1–3.

Deuteronomy 1:19-46. The second event in the condensation of the Israelite desert experience is the explorers' story, which we have previously considered in Numbers 13–14.

In Deuteronomy, greater emphasis is laid on the contrast between the Lord's gracious giving of the land and Israel's refusing to go up and conquer it. Deuteronomy's version, while generally similar to the longer Numbers account, heightens the faithlessness of Israel in their refusal to go into Canaan.

Both versions close with the Israelites' ill-fated attack on the hill country. Having disobeyed the call of the Lord to go up against Canaan, they attempt to right matters by deciding on their own to attack. However, because the Lord is not with them, the result is disaster. Deuteronomy adds a poignant note, lacking in Numbers, about Israel's outcry to the Lord and the Lord's refusal to listen to her pleas.

Deuteronomy 2:5, 9, 19. Deuteronomy recounts Israel's dealings with Edom (Seir), Moab, and the sons of Ammon. In each case, God instructs Israel to be careful in her dealings, avoiding anything that appears to be aggressive. This note is important to Deuteronomy's view of history. Israel is to respect the holdings of these three nations because the Lord has given them territorial rights.

In verses 20-23, God's sovereignty over all history is further emphasized in the statement that God has removed the previous inhabitants from certain areas to make a place for the Edomites and Moabites. Deuteronomy sketches Israel's possession of a promised land on the broader historical canvas of the Near East. The other nations have been given their places by the same historical action of God that gives Israel her Promised Land.

Deuteronomy 2:26-37. The story of the struggle with Sihon is understood in somewhat the same way the record of the confrontation with Pharaoh in Egypt is interpreted. This similarity is particularly clear in verse 30.

The reference to complete destruction in verse 34 indicates that the war with Sihon is governed by the ban. The clearest illustration of the meaning and force of the ban in the Old Testament is the story of Achan's violation when Jericho fell to the Israelites (Joshua 7).

Deuteronomy 3:1-11. The sixth episode in Deuteronomy's historical summary tells of the defeat of Og, king of Bashan. These verses are very similar in form to the preceding passage about the victory over Sihon. We obtain little new information except for the location of territory and the explanatory note in verse 11 linking Og to the giants of the past.

The action in this passage is located in the north. The victory over Og, joined to the conquest of Sihon's territory, gives Israel most of the territory east of Jordan from the Arnon River to the area east of Galilee.

While little is known about Og and Israel's victory over him, he is mentioned with Sihon in Psalm 135:11 and Psalm 136:19-20.

Deuteronomy 3:12-22. Verses 12-13 give the basic account of Moses' distribution of the east Jordan territory. The tribes of Reuben and Gad receive the land from the Arnon River, Moab's north boundary, to the Jabbok River, which cuts Gilead in two. These two tribes thus hold the southern half of Gilead. The half-tribe of Manasseh is given the part of Gilead north of the Jabbok River plus Bashan, the fertile land farther north. The following verses (14-17) provide a further explanation of the distribution, dividing Manasseh's holdings into two parts.

Verses 18-20 sum up the longer story of Numbers 32, which addresses the responsibility of the east Jordan tribes to actively join in the conquest. Here, as in Numbers, the condition for these two and one-half tribes receiving their territory is their full participation with the rest of Israel when she goes into Canaan.

Verse 20 refers to the conquest of the land as the Lord giving rest to Israel. The term *rest* is essentially a theological term, rather than a physical one. The rest of the Lord refers to the blessings of security and settlement in one's own land.

Deuteronomy 3:23-29. In the final segment in the historical introduction to Deuteronomy, Moses asks God to be allowed to enter Canaan but is denied. The Lord is angry with him because of Israel's faithlessness. The words "because of you the LORD was angry with me" (3:26) are quite significant and suggest that Moses' punishment is a substitute for what all of Israel deserves. In contrast to the Numbers account, in Deuteronomy the judgment on Moses is due to Israel's sin rather than to his own.

The place to which Moses goes to look at Canaan has various names in the Pentateuch. Numbers 27:12 uses *Abarim.* In Deuteronomy 32:49, Abarim designates the range of mountains that includes Mount Nebo. Both Nebo and Pisgah appear in Deuteronomy 34:1. The general area is the same in all cases. The difference in name is probably due to the variety of traditions.

DIMENSION THREE:
WHAT DOES THE BIBLE MEAN TO ME?

Class discussion for Dimension Three should focus on one or all of the following topics: "Moses and God's Revelation," "Distorted Vision," "Living With the Consequences," "God and the Nation," and "Relinquishing Leadership."

Deuteronomy 1:1—Moses and God's Revelation

The first verse of Deuteronomy points to Moses' role in God's revelation to Israel. Numbers usually says that the Lord instructed Moses and that Moses carried out the instruction. Deuteronomy, on the other hand, consistently focuses on what Moses says. In a few places, we are told that his words come from God. This is no doubt of the underlying assumption, but the attention is on Moses and his addresses.

We sometimes overlook this biblical theme that human beings act in a substantial way as the channels of God's revelation. Revelation does not take place in a vacuum. It comes through human instruments and is clothed in human personality.

The presence of men and women as agents of divine communication suggests something of the degree of human potential. At the same time, it opens the possibility of limitation in the expression of God's will. The biblical view combines a faith in human ability to understand the meanings of God and a recognition that all divine-human communication takes place in finite time and space.

When we think of revelation in our time, we usually think of the Holy Spirit. The class members might consider areas in which they believe the Spirit is at work today. After thinking about this question they might discuss how such a process involves human beings. What roles do particular persons play? How is the total person involved?

Deuteronomy 1:19-33—Distorted Vision

A significant note in Deuteronomy's version of the spy story (compare Numbers 13–14) is found in 1:27. Under the pressure of a call to risk everything in an invasion of Canaan, Israel responds in fear and refuses to go. Anxiety not only clouds Israel's perception, but actually inverts it, so that Israel regards the promises and blessings of God as signs of enmity. The moment of opportunity is poisoned by the fear that makes trust impossible, just at the point when it is most essential.

Looking at our own situations, can we identify the faith-testing challenges that beckon us in the church? in our individual lives? What threats in our lives can we turn into opportunities by approaching them with adventurous faith and a trust in God's providence?

Deuteronomy 1:41-46
Living With the Consequences

The spy story ends with a surprising twist (1:41-46). The Israelites, having refused to go into Canaan, are punished by God for their faithlessness. When the people realize they will not be allowed to go into Canaan at all, they admit they have sinned. They then decide to "go up and fight, as the LORD [their] God commanded [them]." Contrary to what we might expect, their act of seeming repentance ends in

disaster. The story tells us that the Lord is not with them and they suffer a resounding defeat.

The biblical message elsewhere agrees with the outcome of this story in dispelling false hopes of averting punishment. In the early chapters of Genesis, humanity goes through a series of judgments. These include expulsion from the garden of Eden; Cain's condemnation to a life of wandering; destruction by the Flood; and confusion of languages, with the resulting dispersal of peoples.

Although God's judgment is not reversed in any of these cases, God's grace is evident in each one. God clothes the first man and woman when they leave the garden of Eden; God gives Cain a mark of protection to ward off attackers; God makes new promises to Noah and his family, the lone survivors of the Flood; and God calls Abraham as the first of a chosen people, whose experience will witness in a divided world to the sovereignty and grace of God. God's grace in every instance is forward-oriented. It does not go back to reestablish former conditions nor does it dwell on lost opportunities. God's grace deals with the future and keeps the door open to new possibilities and continuing relationships.

We seldom get a second chance to right a wrong decision. However, the power of the grace and forgiveness of God lies in furnishing us with the resources for going on, for seeing the potential for redemption in later experiences and events. Second chances are seldom duplicates of former situations. They usually involve accepting the consequences of past mistakes and maintaining faith in the openness of life under God to live God's will fully in the present and future.

The class might think together about incidents and life experiences involving recognized mistakes that cannot be undone. When these are shared, consider how our Christian faith and hope enable us to rise above past sins and to make new commitments in the present and future. What role does acceptance of judgment for our past errors play? How does the biblical view of forgiveness open up life's fuller possibilities?

Deuteronomy 2:1-6, 8-9, 16-19—God and the Nation

This account of Israel's wandering includes a striking universal note. The people of Moab, Edom, and Ammon possess their lands by God's action in history. Israel's possession of Canaan as a gift of the Lord is to be understood in the larger context of God's sovereign action in all of history. Although this theme is found elsewhere in the Old Testament (see, for example, Amos 9:4-5; Isaiah 40–55) it is especially impressive in Deuteronomy.

The primary emphasis of Deuteronomy is on the internal quality of Israel's life. Maintaining this quality depends on separation from the nations whose wickedness is corrupting. Despite this, the realization that God's purposes are larger than the welfare of a single nation breaks through in this passage. This realization in turn affects Israel's conduct toward the nations with whom she is in contact. Even though the message of Deuteronomy is mixed overall, the international dimension of God's rule in history is definitely present.

How do we visualize the roles of other nations in the purposes of God? As we think of God at work in history, can we see a role for nations that are threatening to us? You might focus this question on specific nations that threaten world order and peace today. What place do we see for them in God's will? To what degree do our national interests dictate our understanding of God's will in international affairs?

Deuteronomy 3:23-28—Relinquishing Leadership

Moses' request to go into Canaan is based on his desire to see the outcome of God's working with Israel. He feels that he has not seen the best part, which is still to come; and he pleads with God to be allowed to be a part of the story's climax in Canaan.

God's answer is no. Moses, as a member of the faithless Exodus generation, must share their fate in spite of his indispensable contribution to the freedom of God's people. The most he can hope for is an opportunity to look across the Jordan into the land of promise.

Human beings participating in great movements often have difficulty recognizing their limitations. Creative geniuses quite frequently accomplish the nearly impossible in establishing a great organization or in getting a significant movement underway. Often they jeopardize the very things they care most about (their greatest contributions) by refusing to share the leadership or to provide for the kind of stability they cannot supply. It is difficult for anyone with deep commitment to a cause to relinquish control and to trust it to others.

This story and others like it teach us the finiteness and mortality of leadership. The implications are important but not easy to see in the complexities of our society.

A discussion of questions surrounding retirement might be helpful at this point. What does this biblical story about a leader's limitations say to the issue? Does the story downgrade the worth of older people? Does it encourage ageism? On the other hand, what sense of responsibility and awareness of limits does the story call for in those who lead?

One of the issues of congregational leadership is limitation of tenure. What does the biblical story say about external term limitations on all church leadership? What does this passage teach us about exercising our leadership responsibilities?

Close the session by listing on a chalkboard or a large piece of paper any new insights gained from this study of Deuteronomy 1–3.

I am the LORD your God, who brought you out of Egypt (5:6).

— 8 —
Moses Recalls the Covenant

Deuteronomy 4–5

DIMENSION ONE:
WHAT DOES THE BIBLE SAY?

Answer these questions by reading Deuteronomy 4

1. What is Israel to follow? for what purpose? (4:1)

   Israel must follow the decrees and laws that Moses gives in order to live in and take possession of the Promised Land.

2. Who survives Baal Peor? (4:3-4)

   The Israelites who hold fast to the Lord their God survive Baal Peor.

3. What two things does Israel have? (4:7-8)

   Israel has a God who is near when called and righteous decrees and laws.

4. When the Israelites stand at the foot of Mount Horeb, what does the Lord declare to them? (4:13)

   God declares the covenant; that is, the Ten Commandments.

5. Against what activities does Moses warn the Israelites? (4:15-19)

   He warns them against making idols and worshiping the sun, moon, and stars.

6. What will happen to Israel if the people makes idols? (4:25-28)

   Israel will perish from the Promised Land and be scattered among the nations.

7. Will God forget the covenant? (4:29-31)

   No, not even when Israel is scattered.

8. What two great things have happened to Israel? (4:32-35)

   Israel heard the voice of God speaking out of fire and was taken as a nation out of Egypt with signs, wonders, war, and great and awesome deeds.

9. Where does Moses set the law before Israel? (4:44-46)

   He sets the law beyond the Jordan in the valley opposite Beth Peor, in the land of Sihon.

Answer these questions by reading Deuteronomy 5

10. With whom does God make the covenant at Horeb? (5:1-3)

    God makes the covenant with the generation of Israel present as Moses speaks on the plains of Moab.

11. Who gives these laws? (5:5-6)

    The Lord, Israel's God, gives these laws.

12. What three commandments deal with God? (5:7-11)

    You shall have no other gods. You shall not make an idol. You shall not misuse the name of the Lord your God.

13. Why is Israel to observe the sabbath? (5:12-15)

    On that day the Israelites are to remember that they were servants in Egypt and that the Lord brought them out with a mighty hand.

14. What is the result of honoring one's parents? (5:16)

    They will have a long and successful life in the land that God gives them.

15. The last five commandments concern human relationships. Summarize them by completing this sentence. You shall not

(a) *murder* (5:17)
(b) *commit adultery* (5:18)
(c) *steal* (5:19)
(d) *give false testimony* (5:20)
(e) *covet* (5:21)

16. What does the Lord tell Moses after the people go to their tents? (5:30-31)

God tells Moses all the commands, decrees, and laws he is to teach the people.

DIMENSION TWO: WHAT DOES THE BIBLE MEAN?

Background Information on Deuteronomy 4–5

The core of the Book of Deuteronomy is Chapters 12–26, where the covenant stipulations are located. Preceding this part are two introductions, Chapters 1–4 and 5–11. The former, as we have seen in Lesson 7, contains a historical summary of Israel's desert experience. The latter covers a number of topics, but its main theme is exhortation to observe the covenant and its law.

Chapters 4 and 5 provide an important connection between two main sections of the book. They tie together the first addresses of Moses. Chapter 4 draws the history to focus on obedience to the covenant. Chapter 5 states the Ten Commandments and sets the stage for Moses' expansion on the Decalogue.

Deuteronomy 4:1-8. History for Israel is always recited for the lessons it brings to current questions and decisions.

Most of the terms for *law* that appear regularly in Deuteronomy are found in verse 1. They have distinct meanings but their use here is to indicate the importance of the whole law rather than its separate parts.

Deuteronomy associates the observance of the law with wisdom and understanding (verse 6). Among the Old Testament sages, wisdom is regarded as a life-giving gift from the Lord. Similarly, Deuteronomy regards the law as God's gift to Israel, a gift that contains life.

Deuteronomy 4:13-14. The revelation at Horeb, God's covenant with the people, is specifically identified with the Ten Commandments in verse 13. The Hebrew for this revelation, "the ten words," occurs only three times in the Old Testament (Exodus 34:28; Deuteronomy 10:4).

Although the explicit combination of Horeb, covenant, and ten commandments is significant, verse 14 is even more important as an indication of the source of Deuteronomy's law. Moses says that the law he is about to impart

to them in his Moab sermons was given to him at Sinai, just after Israel received the Decalogue. In a real sense, verse 14 is the charter of the Book of Deuteronomy.

Deuteronomy 4:15-24. The prohibiting of images applies not only to images of the Lord but to other idols as well. In verse 19, the proscription is extended to include worship of the heavenly bodies, a common practice in nearby cultures.

Verse 20 refers to the "iron-smelting furnace" in Egypt. The term is also used in Solomon's dedicatory prayer in 1 Kings 8:51 and in Jeremiah's reference to covenant obedience in Jeremiah 11:4. The furnace image of the Egypt experience regards it as a time of ordeal and testing.

The description of God as "jealous" in verse 24 is used to undergird the demand for Israel's exclusive loyalty. It refers primarily to God's intolerance of the worship of other gods.

Deuteronomy 4:25-31. "I call heaven and earth as witnesses" (4:26) is a familiar statement in the Old Testament. It is also used regularly in the Near Eastern treaties of the second millennium B.C. In that context the natural powers are understood as gods. They are invoked to enforce the faithfulness of the two parties to the agreement. In Israel's use, however, heaven and earth are not supernatural. They are elements of creation, which owe their existence to the creator God. They have no power apart from God. Nevertheless, their use in witnessing lends force and seriousness to what God is doing.

This passage regards the covenant as still in effect even after Israel is sent into exile. The characterization of God's relationship with Israel emphasizes the importance of obedience. It also allows for continued access to divine resources even for a prostrate nation under judgment. This view provides a great hope for an exiled people as they raise serious questions about their future.

Deuteronomy 4:32-34. The giving of covenant law and the deliverance from Egypt are two astounding events in human history. The law is a gift of God's grace, fully as impressive as the central saving event in Israel's history.

Deuteronomy 4:41-42. Moses implements Numbers 35:9-15 by appointing three specific cities of refuge in the territory Israel now controls east of the Jordan (compare Joshua 20:1-9).

Of the cities listed, only Ramoth is mentioned outside this passage and the related sections in Joshua 20–21. Ramoth is a fortified border city that was involved in the Israel-Aram wars of the ninth century B.C. (1 Kings 22 and 2 Kings 8–9.) The Moabite Stone, which carries a ninth century B.C. inscription of King Mesha of Moab, mentions the rebuilding of Bezer.

Deuteronomy 4:44-49. The "law" is a term that includes testimonies, decrees, and commands. As noted earlier,

NUMBERS AND DEUTERONOMY

these terms are probably synonyms whose use together is meant to denote the fullness and richness of the Torah.

Deuteronomy 5:1. Moses' second address, which continues through Chapter 28, begins here. Made up of the Deuteronomic law (12–28) and a hortatory introduction (5–11), the Horeb Decalogue opens the address.

Deuteronomy 5:6. The preamble to the Ten Commandments identifies the lawgiver. The act of deliverance is the central point of God's identity for Israel. The lawgiver is first a deliverer.

Deuteronomy 5:7-10. In the first two commandments God speaks in the first person. God's prohibition against serving other gods is the primary commandment in Israel's faith. She must give exclusive loyalty to the God who is Lord of all.

The second commandment is an extension of the first. Indeed, in the Jewish, Roman Catholic, and Lutheran traditions, the two are counted as one. The content is distinctive, however, in its insistence on avoiding idolatry. Idols and images serve to represent deity and manifest divine presence. Israel's long-standing prohibition of images is unique in the ancient world. It grows out of her sense of the sovereignty of God, which makes all creatures of the creator God inadequate as divine representations.

Deuteronomy 5:11-16. The next three commandments speak of God in the third person. They complete the first half of the Decalogue, which deals with worship and piety.

The third commandment has often been understood as applying to profanity. While such trivializing of the divine name probably falls under this prohibition, to limit it to this alone is to underestimate the range of this commandment.

The import of the prohibition is to prevent the use of God's name in the service of empty or worthless ends. It warns against using the divine name—trying to enlist God's power—for causes and interests not in keeping with the divine purposes.

The divergence of Deuteronomy's Decalogue from that in Exodus 20:1-17 appears first in the fourth commandment. Deuteronomy uses "observe" where Exodus has "remember," a difference which, while small, represents a somewhat different emphasis. Deuteronomy also includes animals in its list of those who are to abstain from work—an indication of Deuteronomy's sensitivity to the welfare of all creatures. The biggest difference, however, is in the rationale for keeping the sabbath. Exodus finds the reason in creation and God's rest on the seventh day, while Deuteronomy grounds its observance in God's act of deliverance and in the need for rest from work.

The fifth commandment is oriented toward human relations. However, because it involves piety more than ethics it is most appropriately linked with the first four. The commandment addresses Israelite adults who live in an extended family, that is, in the same household as their parents and even grandparents. Recognition of and respect for the authority of the older generation provides a way the religious tradition can be passed along in a living form. Ephesians 6:2-3 quotes this passage as an admonition for early Christians and then adds a reciprocal responsibility for parents not to "exasperate [their] children" (6:4).

Deuteronomy 5:17-21. The last five commandments deal with ethical conduct in human relationships.

The word *murder* (verse 17) comes close to the original meaning, since the Hebrew verb does not refer to war, capital punishment, or killing of animals. *Murder*, however, does not completely cover the Hebrew meaning, which also includes accidental killing (4:42). The focus appears to be on killing within the covenant community.

The prohibition of false testimony (verse 20) pertains to court cases. Elsewhere two witnesses are required to appear in such cases. Evidently witnesses are not under oath, and their burden of proof of innocence lies with the person accused. These factors heighten the importance of truth in testimony. An extreme example of the kind of miscarriage of justice that can occur when this commandment is ignored is the execution of Naboth in 1 Kings 21.

Some interpreters have suggested that the Hebrew word rendered *covet* describes not only attitude of unwarranted desire but also the action of appropriation. Other scholars argue that covet should be limited to "strong desire." Whatever one concludes, the word denotes unbridled desire that is likely to lead to improper action.

Deuteronomy 5:22-33. These verses clarify the relationship between the Decalogue and the rest of Deuteronomy. All Israel hears the Ten Commandments, the basic words of the covenant. Fearful of further exposure to the fire of God's glory and greatness, they ask that Moses be delegated to hear the rest of God's revelation. After they leave, God gives Moses "all the commands, decrees and laws" that he will teach the Israelites (5:31), thirty-nine years later as they prepare to enter Canaan. The instruction, identified as the substance of Deuteronomy, also includes the exhortation to obey the law that is revealed.

DIMENSION THREE: WHAT DOES THE BIBLE MEAN TO ME?

Topics for class discussion in Dimension Three include the following: "Adding to the Word," "Idolatry," "Misusing the Name of the Lord," and "Observing the Sabbath."

Deuteronomy 4:1-8—Adding to the Word

At the beginning of Chapter 4, the law that Moses is about to teach Israel takes center stage. Moses warns Israel not to add to or take from the word he is about to give them. This admonition is one that appears in legal and wisdom material from many times and places. It occurs in Deuteronomy 12:32 as part of a command to keep all of the law. Similar expressions are also present in Jeremiah 26:2, Ecclesiastes 3:14, and Proverbs 30:6. The most striking parallel is found in Revelation 22:18-19.

On the basis of such expressions, the early church fathers admonished the church not to tamper with the unchangeable text. But the writer of Deuteronomy did not use this exhortation in the rigid sense that it later came to have.

The force of the admonition is that Israel must take the covenant word seriously and deal with it in fullness and honesty. The word must not be made to conform to Israel's wishes. It must not be expanded or compressed so that it is easier to observe. Adjustment is not obedience.

One of the contested issues in the church today is the question of what constitutes God's word and how we should handle it. Some insist that only in a literal treatment of each word of the Bible do we avoid adding to or subtracting from the word. Paul, however, says that the letter kills and the spirit gives life (2 Corinthians 3:6). And John, in writing of Jesus, says "the Word became flesh" (John 1:14). Jesus himself quoted the Old Testament and then said, "But I tell you" (Matthew 5:17-44). These passages seem to indicate that God's word is a dynamic reality, which cannot be confined to words on a page or to precise definitions in a particular theological position. Others believe that the truth of God must be found wholly within the resources of our own time, if it is to be relevant.

Most of us find ourselves somewhere between these two poles. We believe in the truth of the biblical word, interpreted in its own setting and interacting with the real situation of our day. In the midst of this complexity, between the absolute interpretation of objective words and the rootless ignoring of the Bible, we hear "Do not add to what I ocommand you and do not subtract from it." And we ask ourselves how we may take this charge seriously, how we may deal with the word directly and honestly.

Ask the class to discuss areas in which they see the church failing to live out what the biblical message defines as Christian. Where have elements that do not relate to the meaning of the word of God been added? Where is conformity with the values of modern culture evident? How do we relate the developments of our day to the biblical word without taking that word less seriously?

Deuteronomy 4:15-24; 5:7-10—Idolatry

Israel, alone among all the nations, observes a thorough prohibition of images and idols. She possesses such a strong sense of God as creator and all else as creature that nothing in nature can adequately represent the God of greatness and power.

Meaning and value come from God. Anything else has meaning only as God gives it. Ascribing ultimate and independent value to anything else constitutes idolatry.

Ask the class to name idols people give allegiance to in this day. As they share their views, ask them to determine what makes something an idol. How can we respect technology and knowledge advances without giving them inordinate power and control in our lives?

Deuteronomy 5:11—Misusing the Name of the Lord

In the ancient world, to know another's name was to possess a powerful weapon that may be used against that person. When a divine name is known, the magical employment of divine power is a distinct possibility. The third commandment may have arisen to combat this idea. Israel comes to see such use as manipulative and presumptuous, a misunderstanding of the nature and freedom of her God.

The prohibition comes to focus on those who wrongfully claim the divine name for purposes unworthy of God and out of keeping with divine ends.

The third commandment has continuing relevance for the church and modern Christians. Those who claim God's approval and assume divine support for any program or movement need to take it seriously.

To make this relevance more concrete, have class members cite examples in which divine backing has been asserted for unworthy causes. Stimulate their thinking by reminding them of historical events, such as the children's crusade, persecution of the Jews, and massacre of native peoples.

In addition to listing examples, you might have the class discuss how to determine where the invocation of God's name is warranted. Discuss whether the following are Christian or have God's involvement in them: "nationalistic" militias; prayers in schools; a foreign policy that maintains American interests at the expense of Third World peoples; violence against abortion providers. What criteria are helpful in determining the fitness of the use of God's name?

Deuteronomy 5:12-15—Observing the Sabbath

Scholars have long been interested in the origins of the sabbath. Their study has not as yet produced a clear picture of the beginning of this institution in Israel. All we can say with certainty is that it came to occupy an important place at an early period. It is found in the earliest law codes, the Ten Commandments, and the ritual decalogue (Exodus 34:21). Use of the sabbath was intensified in the Exile as a distinctive mark of Jewish identity.

Exodus 20:8-11 and Deuteronomy 5:12-15 give us important insight into the meaning of the sabbath. Exodus indicates that the sabbath plays an important part in God's creative activity. Deuteronomy asserts that it is a reminder of freedom from bondage and responsibility to treat humanely all of God's creation. The sabbath combines elements of worship of God and concern for human welfare and, at the same time, becomes a mark of Israelite identity.

The shift from sabbath to Sunday observance took place early in the Christian church. Every Sunday celebrates the Christ's resurrection. The fact is, however, that the Christian Sunday has appropriated many aspects of the Old Testament sabbath observance and that a certain continuity exists between them, even though their meanings are different.

In today's Christian church our practices and attitudes about the sabbath go from complete abstinence from normal activity to full participation in regular activities. What does it mean for us to keep the sabbath holy?

The class could sharpen its thinking about this question by listing the purposes of Sunday in a Christian context. What distinct values can it have? How do elements of rest, recreation, worship, and acts of service belong together?

As they discuss this question and compile their list, ask them to consider what activities foster the uses they have included. Do other activities interfere with a proper sabbath observance?

The outcome of this exercise might be a class statement on biblical resources for Sunday observance, the purposes of Sunday for us in our heritage and culture, and the ways in which these purposes can best be expressed in our time.

If time allows, list on a chalkboard or a large piece of paper the new insights from today's lesson.

See, I am setting before you today a blessing and a curse (11:26).

9

Moses Exhorts the People

Deuteronomy 6–11

**DIMENSION ONE:
WHAT DOES THE BIBLE SAY?**

Answer these questions by reading Deuteronomy 6

1. What is Israel to hear? (6:4)

   The Lord their God is one Lord.

2. How is Israel to love God? (6:5)

   The people are to love God with all their heart, with all their soul, and with all their strength.

3. What are the Israelites not to forget when they enter Canaan? (6:12)

   The people are not to forget the Lord who brought them out of Egypt.

4. When a son asks about the meaning of the law, what answer is to be given? (6:20-25)

   The Lord brought the Israelites out of slavery in Egypt by showing great signs and wonders against Pharaoh. God has given them the land and has commanded them to keep the law.

Answer these questions by reading Deuteronomy 7

5. What nations will God clear out before Israel? How is Israel to treat the sacred objects of these peoples? (7:1, 5)

   God will clear out the Hittites, Girgashites, Amorites, Canaanites, Perizzites, Hivites, and Jebusites. Israel is to break down their altars, smash their sacred stones, cut down their Asherah poles, and burn their idols.

6. Why has the Lord chosen Israel? (7:8)

   The Lord loves Israel and is keeping an oath sworn to Israel's ancestors.

7. What is the basis of the Israelite's hope when they enter the Promised Land? (7:17-21)

   The Lord who brought Israel out of Egypt is in their midst.

Answer these questions by reading Deuteronomy 8

8. Why does the Lord feed Israel with manna? (8:3)

   God feeds the people so that they may learn that they do not live by bread alone but by every word that comes from the mouth of the Lord.

9. What does Moses warn the Israelites not to do when they settle in the affluence of Canaan? What will happen if they do? (8:11-20)

   They must not forget the Lord who brought them out of Egypt or they will be destroyed.

Answer these questions by reading Deuteronomy 9

10. What arouses the Lord's anger against Israel? (9:11-19)

    The people sin against the Lord by casting a molten calf.

11. What is the basis of Moses' appeal when he intercedes? (9:26-29)

    Israel is the Lord's people, and her destruction will cause the Egyptians to say that the Lord was not able to bring her into the Promised Land.

Answer these questions by reading Deuteronomy 10

12. What is on the second pair of stone tablets? Where does Moses put the tablets? (10:1-5)

    The Ten Commandments are on the tablets. He puts them in the ark of acacia wood that he has made.

13. What kind of God does Israel worship? (10:17-18)

Israel worships a great, mighty, awesome, and impartial God, who defends the cause of the fatherless and the widow and who loves the alien.

14. What does Moses command Israel to do in response to God? (10:19-20)

Israel is to love the alien and fear the Lord, serving and holding fast to God and taking their oaths by his name.

Answer these questions by reading Deuteronomy 11

15. What past events is Israel to consider? (11:2-6)

The people are to consider the signs and wonders in Egypt; the destruction of the Egyptian army, horses, and chariots in the waters of the sea; the desert events; and the judgment on Dathan and Abiram when the earth swallowed them.

16. Where are the blessing and the curse to be set? What determines which one falls on Israel? (11:26-29)

The blessing is on Mount Gerizim and the curse is on Mount Ebal. Obedience to the commands of the Lord determines Israel's fate.

DIMENSION TWO: WHAT DOES THE BIBLE MEAN?

Background Information on Deuteronomy 6–11

Deuteronomy is unique as a book of law. No other code gives as much attention to motivation and rationale. Chapters 6–11 are devoted mainly to explaining the basic understandings of God's covenant with Israel and to urging Israel's commitment to obey the law of the covenant. These chapters give the book its distinctive flavor.

The persuasive sermon is dominant in this section. The only narrative (9:7–10:11) included is used to teach the importance of obedience and the action of God in restoring covenant.

The main themes of Chapters 6–11 are the demand that Israel serve the Lord exclusively; the necessity of destroying the nations and cults already in the land; the warning against forgetting God in the affluence of Canaan; the breaking and restoration of covenant; and the profound importance of obedience in determining Israel's success in the land. All of these together form an introduction to the law of the following chapters. These themes set the stage for the law by emphasizing the importance of willing obedience on Israel's part.

Deuteronomy 6:4-9. These verses are the first section of the *Shema.* According to early rabbinic law, the Shema is to be recited in the morning and evening. It is still regarded as the central expression of Jewish faith.

The Shema was first confined to Deuteronomy 6:4, to which 6:5-9 was then added. Later, Deuteronomy 11:13-21 and Numbers 15:37-41 were attached. All this Scripture is technically defined as the Shema, although in popular use, Deuteronomy 6:4-5 often goes by this title.

The term *shema* comes from the first word of verse 4. It is an imperative form of the Hebrew verb meaning *to hear.* In Mark 12:29-31, Jesus quotes these verses (along with Leviticus 19:18) when he is asked to state the greatest commandment.

The reference to "heart," "soul," and "strength" (verse 5) deals more with the total person than with separate personal components. In Hebrew thought, the heart is the seat of intellect and will, while the soul denotes something like personal force or personality—here these terms indicate that the whole person is to be involved in steadfast loving obedience.

Verses 6-7 express the importance of this injunction. The words of the Lord's covenant are to be taught to the children and are to affect all of life's activities.

The references in verses 8-9 were probably intended to be understood metaphorically. As time passed, however, Judaism made concrete signs out of them and created *phylacteries.* These are little boxes, containing in four compartments the words of Deuteronomy 6:4-9, 11:13-21, and Exodus 13:1-10, 11-16. Phylacteries are bound to the forehead and left arm during prayer to remind the worshiper of the whole Torah. The *mezuzah,* a container holding some of the same Scripture, developed in a similar manner. The mezuzah is attached to the door frame of a house to keep its inhabitants aware of the covenant law.

Deuteronomy 6:10-15. The list of good things God will give Israel in the land of Canaan emphasizes the fact that the gifts they receive are undeserved. Their labor will not have produced them. Similar lists (cities, houses, wells, vineyards, olive trees) occur in Joshua 24:13 and Nehemiah 9:25, with the theme of unmerited gift present in both. These elements and this emphasis form part of the continuing tradition concerning the possession of the land.

Jesus quotes from verse 13 in answering the temptations to worship Satan (see Matthew 4:10; Luke 4:8).

Deuteronomy 6:16-19. The reference to Israel's testing of the Lord does not occur elsewhere in Deuteronomy. The same emphasis is found in connection with the Massah story in two other places, Exodus 17:1-7 and Psalm 95:8-9.

In Matthew 4:7 and Luke 4:12, Jesus' response to the temptation to throw himself down from the highest point of the Temple is to quote Deuteronomy 6:16.

Deuteronomy 6:20-25. Exodus 12:26-27 gives a form in which an adult answers a child's question about Passover observance. The intent there and in this passage is to provide a regular occasion, insuring that traditions are passed to the next generation.

The word *righteousness* (verse 25) refers to being in a right relationship with God. It is not intended to convey sinlessness. Such a relationship depends on Israel's willingness to accept responsibility for keeping the law. The covenant relationship is kept in proper order through obedience.

Deuteronomy 7:1-5. Moses expresses concern that the inhabitants of Canaan will turn Israel away from the Lord to the worship of other gods. To insure against this temptation, his instructions, based on the concept of the ban, demand utter destruction of these people and their places and objects of worship. Verse 3, however, indicates that the ban was observed more in theory than in practice. Had it been practiced widely, there would have been no need for the prohibitions concerning intermarriage. It seems more probable that referring to the ban functioned as an effective way of expressing abhorrence of Canaanite religious practices and their corruptive influence.

Deuteronomy 7:12-14. The heavy emphasis on fertility in the list of blessings for an obedient Israel is purposeful. The Canaanites believe Baal is the source of fertility. The real question when Israel enters Canaan is whether the Lord, who delivered them from Egypt and sustained them in the desert, has any power in the agricultural land of Canaan. The struggle between the adherents of Baal and the followers of the Lord went on for centuries. We can see this by consulting the stories of Elijah or the books of Hosea and Jeremiah.

The unequivocal assertion in Deuteronomy is that God, the deliverer and the source of law and covenant, is also the giver of land and fertility.

Deuteronomy 8:1-6. Two elements in this passage are distinctive in their interpretation of the desert experience. The first is the understanding of manna as a lesson in dependence on God's word. The issue is between human self-sufficiency and trust in God's creative and sustaining power. The words of verse 3 are quoted by Jesus as an answer to the temptation to turn stones into bread (Matthew 4:4; Luke 4:4).

The second somewhat unique emphasis is on the particular expression of God's sustenance of Israel (verse 4). Occurring once more in Deuteronomy (29:5) and once in Nehemiah (9:21), it is evidently an independent tradition since it does not appear in the stories of the desert.

Deuteronomy 8:7-20. Canaan's blessings are extolled in almost hymn-like form. The word *land* occurs five times, in parallel phrases. It is followed each time by a series of nouns or clauses signifying blessing. The passage moves successively through water, grain and fruit, olives and honey, abundance of food, and minerals. Praising the land is intended to encourage proper response from Israel. The following verses (11-20) deal with the temptations such blessings bring and a warning against forgetting the Lord.

Deuteronomy 9:7–10:11. As in Chapters 1–3, Deuteronomy resorts to first person narrative. The purpose is to illustrate that Israel has been a rebellious people since the day she came out of Egypt.

The story of the golden calf is chosen to make the point (Exodus 32). In contrast to the Exodus version, in Deuteronomy Moses tells the story from his own viewpoint.

The narrative moves from covenant-making (9:9-10) to Israel's breaking of the covenant (9:11-17), ending with the breaking of the stone tablets. Following this comes Moses' atoning action—fasting, praying for Aaron, grinding the molten calf to dust, and throwing it in the running stream (9:18-21), and his intercessory prayer for Israel (9:25-29). These actions lead to the renewal of the covenant (10:1-5) and the resumption of the journey toward the Promised Land (10:10-11). Although God's covenant can be broken by disobedience, it can also be renewed and the life of God's people resumed in history.

Deuteronomy 11:2-9. The summary of Israel's salvation history selects four elements from the larger story. These are the plagues in Egypt, the deliverance at the Sea, the wandering in the desert, and the punishment of Dathan and Abiram. This particular selection emphasizes God's power over natural forces and is probably connected to the following theme, God's blessing through the rains (verses 13-17). The use of history in these verses supports the case for life-giving obedience.

Deuteronomy 11:18-20. Perhaps this repetition of 6:6-9 is intended to serve as a bracket for the whole introduction. The repetition reminds us that everything included in between is to be integrated into all of life.

Deuteronomy 11:26-32. Deuteronomy regularly sets out life's alternatives in unmistakable terms. This passage is one example. Similar expressions may be found in 27:11-26 and 30:15-20.

The geography of verse 30 is somewhat puzzling. Gilgal is an ancient worship center near Jericho. The Arabah refers to territory near the Jordan. The biblical traditions, however, clearly locate the "great trees of Moreh" some distance away in Shechem (Genesis 12:6, 35:4; Joshua 24:26).

The name *Moreh* comes from the root meaning to instruct. Perhaps the trees were renowned as place to receive oracles, a site where teaching was disseminated.

The message of this concluding passage is consistent and clear. Everything supports the imperative that Israel "be careful to do all the statutes and the ordinances" Moses is about to set before them.

DIMENSION THREE: WHAT DOES THE BIBLE MEAN TO ME?

Topics for class discussion in Dimension Three include these: "Love and Law," "Affluence and Forgetfulness," "Curse and Blessing," and "Scripture and Temptation."

Deuteronomy 6:4-9—Love and Law

Deuteronomy 6:4-5 plays a central role in Judaism. Jesus cites verse 5, along with Leviticus 19:18, as the great commandment. What are we to do with this statement? The first question that arises is the specific meaning of verse 4. Is this verse a declaration of monotheism, a statement on the unity of God, or a call to Israel for exclusive loyalty to the Lord? Each of these interpretations has been put forth as the correct understanding. While all three possibilities probably have some truth in them and each adds a dimension to the rich meaning of the verse, we have in Dimension Two expressed some preference for the second alternative. The verse speaks an important word to the people of Israel as they settle in a culture in which each community has its own shrine and local god. In this situation, there is a risk that God will be understood as fragmented and the divine will as divided.

Verse 5 insists that love is the proper attitude toward God. We think of Old Testament law as external, rigid, and little concerned with relationship with the lawgiver. Such oversimplification can cause us to miss much in the Old Testament that is important to our faith. The Book of Deuteronomy is particularly concerned to show that the whole person is involved in living in covenant by keeping the law.

The Hebrew word used here for "love" has a wide range of meanings in the Old Testament. The word can apply to love between woman and man or between friends. It is also used to describe God's action toward Israel in choosing her, delivering her from Egypt, and giving her the Promised Land. In addition, the word can be employed here as to describe the human attitude toward God.

In Deuteronomy, love is responsible, that is, aware and responsive to God's prior love and accountable in its expression to God's covenant, with its strong sense of social concern. Law is the guide for love; love is the motivation for observance of law within covenant.

Deuteronomy challenges the understanding of love in our culture. We tend superficially to identify love with feeling and emotion. We suppose that the only authentic action is that which we have a strong desire to do. The individualistic emphasis of our western culture leads us to identify love with self-gratification and love's expression toward God as a private matter.

The whole question of ethical substance in the Christian gospel is at stake in this consideration. Is Deuteronomy's concept of love useful to us as twentieth-century Christians?

Ask the class to think about love and list its various meanings in our day. After sharing these briefly, consider how Deuteronomy's understanding of the love of God applies to us as Christians. To what does our love respond? Since we believe that grace supersedes law in the gospel, what can we say about the expression of our love of God? How does our response within the new covenant involve us with others?

Deuteronomy 6:10-12; 8:7-20 Affluence and Forgetfulness

Deuteronomy's writer is concerned about Israel when she enters the Promised Land. Two passages (6:10-12 and 8:7-20) expand on the theme of the goodness of the land. Deuteronomy 6:10-11 points to the cities, houses, wells, vines, and trees Israel will inherit when she comes into the Promised Land. Each term in this list has a qualifying cause, "which you did not build" (or dig, plant, and so on). Israel will receive the rewards of others' labors when God brings her into Canaan.

Once the people have become affluent, however, they must be careful not to forget the giver and the circumstances of acquisition: "Be careful that you do not forget the Lord. . . ." (6:12). The marks of remembering are fear, service, and use of the Lord's name in the making of oaths (6:13).

Deuteronomy 8:7-20 describes the conduct that characterizes loss of grateful memory. Verses 12 and 13 describe the success and prosperity that lead to forgetfulness. The God they come to ignore is the one who delivered them from Egypt and protected them in the desert. No matter how much they owe to God's goodness, they come to believe they have earned and deserve all they have.

The empty boast in verse 17 is familiar to every reader. Human conduct does not change greatly from one era to another. No one is exempt from the corrupting temptation to claim sole credit for achievement and wealth. We too need to ponder the nature of our forgetfulness. Do our lives reflect the ingratitude and insensitivity about which God warns Israel?

Think about the attitudes and actions of the middle-class toward the poor in America. Do our typical responses express a lack of concern? If so, in what ways is this true? What is the meaning of our relative affluence?

On the international scene, how can we as a nation show that we recognize that some of our power and wealth has come to us from sources beyond ourselves? that circumstances of history have favored us with resources and opportunities? Discuss the effect such an understanding of our wealth could have on our relations with poorer nations. Has America forgotten God in her dealings with the underdeveloped nations?

Deuteronomy 11:26-32—Curse and Blessing

One of the most prominent characteristics of Deuteronomy's thought is its insistence that actions have consequences. This conviction is set out pointedly in 11:26-32, where life is described in terms of blessing and curse. The blessing comes to those who obey the Lord's commands and the curse to those who are disobedient. The statement appears to be too simplistic. Life does not always fit neatly into the scheme of retribution, in which the righteous prosper and the wicked suffer.

Making full allowance for the complex realities of life, we still have to realize that when faced with decisions, we must choose the path to take. And our choice has significant consequences.

Ask the class to think of conduct that has direct and immediate consequences. Can we thus explain all suffering? all prosperity?

If we know of cases of unjustified suffering or profitable crime, what use can we make of Deuteronomy's retribution concept? Are all blessings and curses objective and obvious? How can we discern them in particular situations?

Deuteronomy 6:13, 16; 8:3
Scripture and Temptation

Because Jesus quoted Deuteronomy in the stories of his temptation (Matthew 4:1-11; Luke 4:1-13), we will look at the Old Testament text as it is used in a New Testament setting.

The striking fact about the temptation stories in Matthew and Luke is that Jesus' answer to each of the three temptations is from the Book of Deuteronomy. Significantly, in each Gospel, this event is placed at the critical beginning point in Jesus' ministry. Both Matthew and Luke locate Jesus' temptation in the desert between his baptism and the beginning of public ministry.

The New Testament use of Deuteronomy shows us how dynamic this book is for those who know it from within. They experience it as a resource in the midst of their life crises. Jesus exhibits an awareness of his heritage when he remains true to the integrity of God's purpose by calling on the deepest understandings of his ancestors in the faith. His internalizing of Deuteronomy's faith produces new understandings for his time. It also gives us a gospel that remains contemporary in every generation.

What can we learn from Jesus' sense of heritage and his use of its resources? Ask the class to consider how Jesus used Scripture. What determines his choice of passages? How do these passages fit his needs at the time of temptation? What does this story teach us concerning our use of Scripture?

At the close of the session, ask the class members to share new insights they have gained from their study of Deuteronomy 6–11. List these insights on a chalkboard or a large piece of paper.

— 10 —

Statutes and Ordinances

Deuteronomy 12–19

DIMENSION ONE:
WHAT DOES THE BIBLE SAY?

Answer these questions by reading Deuteronomy 12

1. Where is Israel to bring her offerings, sacrifices, and tithes? (12:5-11)

   Israel is to bring them to the place the Lord will choose to put his name and make his dwelling.

2. Where may the Israelites slaughter and eat meat? What are they to do with the blood? (12:15-16)

   They may slaughter within any of their towns. They must pour blood out on the earth like water.

Answer these questions by reading Deuteronomy 13

3. When are the people to ignore the words of a prophet? (13:1-5)

   The people are to ignore a prophet when he advises following other gods and worshiping them.

4. What are persons to do when a close relative or friend counsels apostasy? (13:6-10)

   They are to stone him or her to death.

5. What will happen to a town that worships other gods? (13:12-18)

   The inhabitants and their animals will be slain, and the town with all its plunder will be burned. It will not be rebuilt.

Answer these questions by reading Deuteronomy 14

6. What characteristics make an animal acceptable for eating? (14:6) What fish are clean? (14:9)

   Persons may eat animals with a split hoof and that chew the cud. Fish that have fins and scales are clean.

7. What are the Israelites to do with their tithes if the sanctuary is too far away from them? (14:22-27)

   They are to exchange them for silver, take the money to the place the Lord chooses, and there buy whatever they wish to eat before the Lord.

8. Who receives the third-year tithe? (14:28-29)

   The Levite, the alien, the fatherless, and the widow receive it.

Answer these questions by reading Deuteronomy 15

9. What is the creditor to cancel in the seventh year? (15:1-2) What attitude are persons to show to the poor? (15:7-11)

   He is to cancel whatever has been loaned to an Israelite. They are to show a generous attitude that freely lends them as much as they need.

10. What is the length of service for a Hebrew slave? (15:12) What if the slave wishes to stay? (15:16-17)

    A slave serves for six years. An awl is thrust through his ear lobe into the door and he becomes a servant forever.

Answer these questions by reading Deuteronomy 16

11. What festival are the Israelites to observe in the month of Abib? (16:1) With what is the festival sacrifice to be eaten? (16:2-4)

    They are to observe the Passover. The sacrifice is to be eaten with unleavened bread.

12. What other festivals are they to keep during the year? (16:10, 13)

    They are to keep the Feast of Weeks and the Feast of Tabernacles.

STATUTES AND ORDINANCES

13. If a case arises that is too difficult for local decision, what is the person to do? (17:8-13)

The person is to go to the place the Lord chooses and consult with the Levitical priests and the judge.

14. What four things must a king not do? (17:16-17)

He must not acquire many horses for himself, send people back to Egypt to acquire more horses, take many wives for himself, or accumulate much silver and gold for himself.

15. What is the king to consult daily throughout his reign? (17:18-20)

He consults a copy of the Deuteronomic law.

Answer these questions by reading Deuteronomy 18

16. What right does a Levite from any town have at the place which the Lord chooses? (18:6-7)

He may minister there in the name of the Lord with equal rights to other Levites.

17. How can Israel tell the difference between a prophet who speaks God's word, and one who has a false word? (18:19-22)

The word of the one who has a false word does not come to pass.

Answer these questions by reading Deuteronomy 19

18. Who may use the cities of refuge? (19:1-7)

Anyone who kills another unintentionally may use them.

19. What is the punishment for a false witness? (19:15-20)

The punishment is whatever the witness had meant to do to the one charged.

DIMENSION TWO: WHAT DOES THE BIBLE MEAN?

Background Information on Deuteronomy 12–19

With Chapter 12 we come to the central part of the book. Chapters 12–26 are the law section, the heart of Deuteronomy. Bible scholars have long identified Deuteronomy 12–26 with the book that furnished the basis for Josiah's reform in 621 B.C. (2 Kings 22–23). The themes of Deuteronomy's legislation are quite similar to the empha-

ses of Josiah's reform. Distinctive elements such as centralization of sanctuary, purification of worship, unification of Passover observance at the Temple, reward for loyalty, and punishment for disobedience are found in both places.

Deuteronomy 12:1-12. The admonitions to destroy all the Canaanite centers of worship reflect the continuing struggle of Israel's covenant religion with the Canaanite nature cult. When the Israelites move into Canaan, they take over many of the native shrines (high places). In the process, they tend to assimilate much of the baal worship practiced there. As a result, Israel's religious leaders attempt to destroy the high places. The conflict continues long after Israel enters the land. Josiah's thoroughgoing reform (621 B.C.) is the culmination of the long battle, although Israel regresses even after this.

Verse 5 introduces the basic regulation, which calls for a single sanctuary. This regulation is related to the destruction of the Canaanite high places. The centralization of worship is the means by which Israel can maintain purity in worship.

At the place the Lord chooses, the divine name will dwell (verses 5, 11). The formula "to put his Name there" or the variant to "choose as a dwelling for his Name" is found in Deuteronomy 12:11, 21; 14:23-24; 16:2, 6, 11; and 26:2. This phrase indicates the presence of the Lord without confining the deity to a specific location.

Verse 12 lists the various people who are to celebrate at the sanctuary. Specifically included in worship are daughters and maidservants, reflecting the relatively high status women are given in Deuteronomy.

Deuteronomy 12:13-28. In the ancient world, killing animals is regarded as a serious matter. For the early Israelites, any meat that is eaten comes from animals first sacrificed to God.

Deuteronomy, in stipulating a centralized sanctuary, creates a problem. Must all Israel now go to a distinct sanctuary to slaughter meat? In characteristic fashion, Deuteronomy introduces a sensitive and innovative modification—secular slaughter.

The discussion of blood is in harmony with the consideration of the subject elsewhere in the Old Testament. The agreement made with Noah after the Flood (Genesis 9:4) provides for eating meat but specifies that no blood should remain in it. As the carrier of life, blood belongs to God. Thus worship regulations stipulate that the blood is to be poured on the altar. In Deuteronomy's secularizing of slaughter, the blood still occupies a special place. Although the blood can now be poured on the ground instead of on the altar, this act is probably conceived as another way of returning the life to God.

The prohibition against eating meat with blood in it is retained in the agreement worked out in the early church concerning which laws Christians should observe (Acts 15:19-20). This stipulation is still observed today in Judaism's kosher food practices.

Deuteronomy 13:1-18. Three instances of temptation to apostasy, the gravest of sins, are presented in this passage. Sign-fulfillment is generally respected in the Old Testament. A sign is usually an ordinary event or condition whose appearance at a particular time or place validates what has been said. Examples are found in Moses' call (Exodus 3:12), in Isaiah's discussion with Ahaz (Isaiah 7:11, 14), and in the angel's word to the shepherds at Jesus' birth (Luke 2:12). In the case of temptation to apostasy, however, even the sign that comes to pass cannot authenticate a prophet who counsels such a course.

Relatives and special friends may also try to entice persons to defection. The sin is the same, and Deuteronomy insists on the death penalty in both cases.

A third instance is the apostasy of a whole town that has yielded to the suggestion of "wicked men." It might also be rendered "sons of worthlessness." The Authorized Version (King James) renders the term "children of Belial." In 2 Corinthians 6:15, Belial is synonymous with Satan.

Deuteronomy 14:1-2. The practices prohibited here are probably those used in Canaanite religion to mourn the dying fertility god.

Deuteronomy 14:3-21. A list of clean and unclean animals similar to the one that appears here is found in Leviticus 11. One apparent criterion Israel uses for delegating animals to the prohibited list is association with other religions. Such a judgment is undoubtedly responsible for the puzzling stipulation in verse 21. The practice of boiling a young goat in its mother's milk seems to be related to a Canaanite fertility rite. A fourteenth century B.C. text from Ugarit in northern Syria contains a reference to a similar practice.

Deuteronomy 15:1-11. Exodus 23:11 provides for land to lie fallow in the seventh year. The extension of this regulation to loans and debts may indicate a desire to deal with an inequity in the original stipulation. As a money economy developed, the stipulation that the land not be planted would pose an uneven burden on the peasant. This law may be an attempt to compensate for such an imbalance.

No law is completely free of unintended consequences. In this case, a humane regulation can be counterproductive for the poor. Persons can become more tightfisted as the seventh year approaches and they know debts are soon to be forgiven. As a result, the needy will encounter difficulty in obtaining funds. Verses 7-11 anticipate this problem and counsel generosity. This kind of law demonstrates the unusually insightful concern of Deuteronomy.

Deuteronomy 16:18-20. These verses begin a long section (16:18–18:20) that treats various offices in the life of Israel. The reference to local judges and officials raises a question about their relation to the elders at the city gate. The latter

are portrayed throughout the Old Testament as making judicial decisions in the towns. The local judges are mentioned only here and in 2 Chronicles 19:5. The Hebrew word for judge has connotations that extend beyond judicial matters, possibly including administrative responsibility. Whatever the name and role, responsibility for impartial justice is clearly emphasized.

Deuteronomy 16:21-22. The Asherah pole and the sacred stone are associated with the nature religion of Canaan, the former representing the chief goddess and the latter the male fertility deity.

Deuteronomy 17:14-20. The only consideration of kingship in the Pentateuch views the institution as initiated by the people rather than as ordained by God. This view is related to one of the two views of monarchy found in the story of Saul's anointing (compare 1 Samuel 8:5, 20 and 10:24). The king, however, is to be chosen by the Lord.

Verse 18 speaks of "a copy of this law," which refers to Deuteronomy. The king is to consult the book so that he may keep the covenant and live. The Septuagint, an early (third century B.C.) Greek translation, renders this term "this second law." From this somewhat inaccurate translation, we get the name Deuteronomy.

Deuteronomy 18:1-8. Deuteronomy's view is that the priests and Levites have equal standing and responsibility. We have only to remember how sharply the Book of Numbers differentiates priests from Levites to recognize that Deuteronomy's view finds little agreement elsewhere in the Pentateuch. In the postexilic period, the difference in status between the two groups widens even more.

Deuteronomy 18:9-22. The treatment of the prophets begins with a prohibition of all practices that attempt to ascertain the future by magical manipulation. No type of occult practice escapes condemnation.

Divination is an inclusive word used to cover all the others that follow. The terms used include all aspects of such activity—from pronouncing incantations and reading omens to casting spells and consulting the dead. Magical attempts to control such extraordinary knowledge infringe on God's sovereignty.

The God of the covenant reveals the purpose and course of events on a divine agenda. This revelation is not subject to human demand. When such information is disclosed, it comes through the prophets.

Deuteronomy 19:1-13. Chapter 19 begins a new section (19:1–21:9), the principal theme of which is homicide and war. The stipulations concerning the cities of refuge indicate that they are provided for the benefit of those who have killed accidentally and without malice. A fuller treatment of the cities of refuge is found in Numbers 35.

Deuteronomy 19:14-21. Verse 18 indicates that a verdict is reached, but we are left to guess how "thorough investigation" and decision are carried out. It may involve casting lots, some new word of priestly instruction, or some other means of ascertaining the will of God.

The passage closes (verse 21) with a statement of the law of retaliation, which appears two other places in the Old Testament (Exodus 21:23-25; Leviticus 24:17-21). The law is not applied literally here, since the case of false witness does not involve physical injury. Rather, it expresses the judgment that when persons are wronged, proper compensation must be made.

DIMENSION THREE: WHAT DOES THE BIBLE MEAN TO ME?

Class discussion for Dimension Three should focus on one or more of the following themes: "The Unity of God's People," "The Seriousness of Disloyalty," "God and the Poor," "King and Covenant," and "True and False Prophets."

Deuteronomy 12:1-4—The Unity of God's People

Israel's problem, as Deuteronomy perceives it, arises from external forces that foster corruption and internal conditions that produce division and weakness. The solution is to unify worship and to get rid of all corrupting extraneous elements.

Unity of worship grows out of Deuteronomy's insistence that God is one. This oneness is expressed in theology, worship, and law. The covenant is with one God, proper worship is located at one place, and Israel is one as the covenant people of God.

The progression of Deuteronomy 12:2-19 shows the significance of Israel's unity in worship. This unity performs the function of purifying the worship of the people of God. It also functions to clarify the worship of a people when they are unsettled and disunited. In addition, Deuteronomy's code reflects responsible sensitivity about the impact of its effects on everyday life.

Understanding the idea of unity lets us see Deuteronomy's important contribution to the religious life of Israel. But what does this unity mean for us? Recent thought and discussion in the church make us aware of the value of pluralism. We are not sure that we trust unity. We have discovered that commitment to unity can turn into demand for uniformity. When this happens, what the majority considers normative may stifle minority voices and contributions. Some kinds of unification are tools of racism and sexism. As a result, the more sensitive we are to Christian responsibility, the more likely we are to distrust superficial unity as a proper means of Christian expression. This attitude touches on theology, worship, and standards of conduct.

A careful look at Deuteronomy will lead us to fuller appreciation of the dynamics of Deuteronomy's unity. These chapters combine the value of unified focus with a genuine concern for what the focusing does to people involved. The values on both sides of this coin—the clarity in unity and the awareness of the needs of all in their participation—are equally important. They must be provided in whatever theology and worship we live by in our time.

Ask the class to think of examples in which worship practices shut out some people's expressions and needs; list things Christian worship should provide for all Christians. How can we worship the same God together in ways that are expressive of the aspirations and sensitive to the needs of each of us?

Deuteronomy 13:1-18 The Seriousness of Disloyalty

Deuteronomy's assertion that apostasy is a capital crime raises a serious question for us. Other parts of the Old Testament tell us that this view is not the whole of Israel's thought and that divine truth is more evident in broader scope.

Deuteronomy speaks to us clearly and significantly about the seriousness of apostasy. Obedience to our fullest understanding of God's will is just as important today as ever.

A crucial question concerns the nature of loyalty. Is loyalty always measured by adherence to the past? Does obedience allow for thinking? How can we define commitment and concern so that they allow us as Christians full range for our best thought and the fullest investment of our personal gifts?

Deuteronomy 15:1-18—God and the Poor

The treatment of the sabbatical year in Deuteronomy extends its stipulations beyond the use of land into matters of money and wider economic issues. This extension expands the sensitive spirit of the former stipulations into the fuller economy of a later period. Social concern is updated so that it represents the caring expressed in past practices. Thus Deuteronomy has a heightened sense of responsibility for the poor, those outside the mainstream of economic benefit.

Ask the class what the writer of Deuteronomy would say to us about the poor as we consider national budget and programs, economic values and priorities, and social responsibility.

Deuteronomy 17:14-20—King and Covenant

The role of the king receives much attention in the Old Testament. Deuteronomy 17:14-20, however, is the only place in the Pentateuch where kingship is discussed.

Israel's unique view of monarchy is represented clearly. In contrast to general Near Eastern patterns, Israel asserts that the king, powerful but far from absolute, is subject to the judgment of God. In Israel's covenant understanding, this makes him amenable to the best interests of all of Israel, including the humblest peasant.

The provisions of this passage warn against apostasy and pride. To counteract the corrupting pressures of the office, Deuteronomy prescribes for the king a lifelong reading of the Deuteronomic law book. This reading will remind him of the sovereignty of God and the responsibility of the whole covenant people.

Since we do not have a monarchical form of government, we must adapt the concerns of these verses to our form of social and political organization. However, the temptations of power and the responsible exercise of leadership are issues for any era, including ours.

Ask the class to rephrase the three stipulations of this passage so that they speak to political leaders today.

Deuteronomy 13:1-5; 18:15-22
True and False Prophets

Deuteronomy addresses the issue of false prophecy in two passages: 13:1-5 and 18:15-22. The latter passage reiterates the importance of heeding the prophets who bring the Lord's word. Following this admonition, two tests of the true prophet are provided. The first test is whether the word spoken comes from God. This may be determined by whether the word is fulfilled. The second test is loyalty to God. No prophet who speaks for other gods can be a true prophet. Deuteronomy 13:1-5 indicates that this latter point takes precedence over sign fulfillment.

The age-old problem of reading the meaning and course of events is ours also. How are we to discern whose counsel is right about a course of action we should take? What values should determine our interpretation of the times? Which voices are authentic among all those who seek to guide us?

Our questions about Christian discernment of our times are many. Where can we turn in Deuteronomy for help in our dilemma?

Ask the class to identify areas in which Christian voices differ in our time. Which "secular prophets" raise issue with traditional Christian interpretations? After considering the areas where the range of difference is greatest, have the class consider the tests of Deuteronomy. How can these tests be applied now? How does the history of prophetic concern and criticism help us to recognize the "true word?" What does covenant loyalty mean to Christians today?

Close the session by asking the class to share new insights into Deuteronomy 12–19. List these insights on a chalkboard or a large piece of paper if time allows.

— 11 —

A People Holy to the Lord

Deuteronomy 20–26

DIMENSION ONE:
WHAT DOES THE BIBLE SAY?

Answer these questions by reading Deuteronomy 20

1. Why is Israel not to fear when she goes to war? (20:1)

   The Lord her God is with her.

2. Who is exempt from war service? (20:5-8)

   Exempt is the one who has built a new, undedicated house, who has planted a new vineyard, who has betrothed a wife, or who is fearful.

3. If a city refuses Israel's offer of peace, what are the Israelites to do? (20:10-14)

   They are to lay siege to it and when it surrenders, slay all the men, and take everything else as plunder.

4. Why are the Israelites to completely destroy the nearby cities? (20:15-18)

   They are to destroy the cities so that they may not teach Israel their detestable worship.

Answer these questions by reading Deuteronomy 21

5. How does the nearest city deal with unsolved murders? (21:1-9)

   The elders of the city shall take a heifer that has never been worked, bring it to an unsown valley with running water, and break its neck. Then the elders shall wash their hands over the heifer while vowing innocence and praying for forgiveness.

6. When an Israelite man marries a captive foreign woman, what must he not do? (21:10-14)

   He must not sell her for money or treat her as a slave.

7. Where must parents take a rebellious son for judgment? (21:18-19)

   They must take him to the elders at the town gate.

Answer these questions by reading Deuteronomy 22

8. What must persons do when they see a neighbor's ox or sheep go astray? (22:1-2)

   They must take it back to its owner.

9. If a man is proved wrong when he makes irresponsible charges against his wife, what is his punishment? (22:13-19)

   He is given a fine of one hundred shekels of silver.

10. Why is the woman treated differently when suspected adultery takes place in the open country rather than in the city? (22:23-27)

    Though she cries for help, there is no one to rescue her.

Answer these questions by reading Deuteronomy 23

11. Why are Ammonites and Moabites excluded from the assembly of the Lord? (23:3-4)

    They are excluded because they did not give Israel bread and water when Israel came out of Egypt and because they hired Balaam to curse Israel.

12. Why must the Israelites maintain a holy camp? (23:14)

    The Lord their God moves about in the camp.

13. What does the Lord detest? (23:18)

    God detests shrine prostitution (both male and female) and bringing a prostitute's earnings into the house of the Lord to pay a vow.

Answer these questions by reading Deuteronomy 24

14. Who does the Lord command the Israelites to protect? (24:17)

The alien, the fatherless, and the widow are protected.

15. When the Israelites overlook produce in harvesting, for whom shall they leave it? (24:19-22)

They shall leave it for the alien, the fatherless, and the widow.

Answer these questions by reading Deuteronomy 25

16. How many lashes are allowed as punishment for a crime? Why? (25:1-3)

Forty lashes are allowed. More than this would be degrading.

17. When a man dies without sons, his brother must marry the widow. What happens if he refuses to marry her? (25:5-10)

She pulls off his sandal, spits in his face, and says, "This is what is done to the man who will not build up his brother's family line."

Answer these questions by reading Deuteronomy 26

18. When the people bring the first fruits to the altar, what do they say God did for them? (26:8-9)

God brought them out of Egyptian bondage into a land flowing with milk and honey.

19. What does Israel declare concerning God? (26:17)

Israel says that the Lord is Israel's God; that the people will walk in the Lord's way, keeping the Lord's decrees, commands, and laws, and obeying God.

20. What does God declare about Israel? (26:18-19)

God declares that Israel is the Lord's own treasured possession and that he will set Israel high above all nations.

DIMENSION TWO: WHAT DOES THE BIBLE MEAN?

Background Information on Deuteronomy 20–26

Chapters 20–26 are the second half of the central legal section of Deuteronomy. While none of Chapters 12–26 evidences a particularly logical order, the second half (20–26) is much more miscellaneous than the first. There is little internal organization, the number of topics is large, and their range is quite broad. The main subjects addressed are: war and murder (20:1–21:9); marriage and family relationships (21:10–22:30); and purity and humane conduct (23:1–25:19). Chapter 26 contains two liturgical confessions, one for presentation of first fruits (verses 1-11) and the other for the third-year tithe (verses 12-15). The chapter closes with a covenant summary (verses 16-19).

Deuteronomy 20:1-20. The laws concerning warfare are unique to Deuteronomy. They have a particular relevance to the Deuteronomic insistence on destruction of the Canaanites for threatening to corrupt Israel.

The setting of verse 2 is Israel's entrance into war. The Hebrew word *'am* means "people," but here it describes a military force as it prepares for battle. NIV renders this word *army*. This army—a militia, or a people's army—contrasts with the standing army of the monarchy, which exists apart from the rest of the nation. The Deuteronomic army is representative. In a real sense, it is the people of Israel.

The reasons for exemption (verses 5-8) from service appear in other Near Eastern cultures. In other societies, such people are regarded as particularly subject to harmful influences, and therefore, as dangerous to the well-being of the army as a whole. In the Deuteronomic explanation, however, the writer substitutes concern for the welfare of the persons themselves.

The second half of the chapter treats the methods of warfare. The application of the ban to Canaanite cities (verses 16-18) reflects the Deuteronomic view that everything Canaanite must be destroyed lest it corrupt Israel.

Verses 19-20 express an unusual sense of the value of food-producing trees. The concern for provision of food in the aftermath of war shows a vision rarely present in time of war.

The siege works that require wood (verse 20) are probably siege towers, ladders, and battering rams, all of which appear in ancient Near Eastern representations of warfare.

Deuteronomy 21:1-9. Murder is believed to bring bloodguilt on the people and pollution to the land unless something is done to expiate the condition. The most direct way of doing this is to take the life of the murderer (compare Numbers 35:33).

The case of an unknown slayer presents a difficult problem. In this instance, the elders of the city nearest the murdered person slay a young heifer in a remote place outside the city and transfer the guilt onto their victim.

Deuteronomy 21:10-17. This passage stands at the beginning of a new section, primarily devoted to matters affecting family life. Verses 10-14 provide a safeguard for the foreign captive who marries an Israelite husband. If the man later divorces her, he may not reduce her to slavery. She is protected from further subjection to the whims of her husband.

A similar curb on caprice is expressed in verses 15-17, which guarantee the right of the firstborn.

Deuteronomy 22:13-30. The rest of Chapter 22 is concerned with marriages and sexual relations.

The first of six laws in this section deals with charges of unchastity against a bride. The procedure seems to ask the accused to take an undue amount of responsibility for proving innocence. Seen against the background of previous practice, the provision here is an advance. The procedure makes it possible for the bride to prove her innocence. When she does, the man is fined and forbidden to divorce her. The assessed fine goes to the bride and her family.

Verses 22-29 deal with three cases of adultery and a closely related case of seduction. Adultery is defined in the ancient world as illicit relations with and by a married woman. Reflecting the patriarchal structure of society, the law did not affect the man equally, except when the woman with whom he was involved was married. In the fourth instance (verses 28-29), the man who seizes a woman and lies with her must pay her father the normal price of the bride, since he has taken the daughter's virginity. He must marry her and can never divorce her.

The regulation of the concluding verse is also found in Leviticus 18:8 and 20:11. In Leviticus, it is only one element in a much fuller list. It is not clear why Deuteronomy only mentions one of the several relationships forbidden in Leviticus.

The person involved in this law is the stepmother. The general principle in categorizing relationships is that sexual relations between people in the same household (the extended family) are forbidden.

The Bible mentions at least two cases of such activity: Reuben with Bilhah, Jacob's concubine (Genesis 35:22), and Absalom with David's concubines (2 Samuel 16:21-22). In early times, it was probably customary for the heir to inherit his father's concubines. The actions of Reuben and Absalom are declarations of premature claim of inheritance.

Deuteronomy 23:15-25. Among this section's laws regarding asylum for slaves, shrine prostitution, interest charges, and respect for a neighbor's crops is a general admonition concerning vows. Its didactic flavor suggests that it may have wisdom origins (compare Ecclesiastes 5:4-5).

Deuteronomy 24:5-13. The various laws in this passage find a general focus in concern for the needs of certain people. The most impressive element in this material is its regulations concerning debtors' pledges. Verse 6 forbids taking a millstone since the debtor's livelihood depends on it. In a regulation that is unusually sensitive to the dignity and the need of the debtor, the creditor is required to wait outside the latter's house until he brings his pledge out. He may not enter the debtor's house to get it (verses 10-11). The cloak taken in pledge must be returned before sundown because the debtor may have no other cover for sleeping (verses 12-13). Amos charges Israel's upperclass with violation of this understanding (2:8).

Deuteronomy 25:1-3. Deuteronomy is even sensitive to the person who is judged worthy of public beating. This law limits the number of lashes to prevent abuse and degradation. The practice is to give one less than the limit to avoid violating the law through error. In 2 Corinthians 11:24, Paul says that he received "the forty lashes minus one" five times.

Deuteronomy 25:4. The ox is used to trample or pull a threshing sled over the grain to thresh it out. The prudent thing to do is to prevent the animal's eating any of the grain. Typical of the spirit of Deuteronomy, however, the ox is allowed to eat as it wishes. Concern for animals that serve is part of the covenant with God.

Deuteronomy 25:5-12. Levirate marriage is most clearly illustrated in the story of Judah and Tamar in Genesis 38, where this practice is taken with great seriousness. Onan's sudden death is understood as punishment because he refused to consummate the marriage with his dead brother's widow and to raise up children for his brother, Er.

Verses 11-12 address the same basic issue, the provision for procreation and the severe treatment of any action that threatens it.

Deuteronomy 25:13-19. Weights and measures are important elements in Israel's life. One of the prophets' prime targets is the person who falsifies weights in commercial transactions (Amos 8:5).

The Amalekites (verses 17-19) were a nomadic tribe who lived in the northern part of the Sinai desert. They attack the Israelites soon after they leave Egypt (Exodus 17:8-16), but Israel defeats them. The Amalekites continue to be enemies even in the time of the monarchy (1 Samuel 15:1-9).

Deuteronomy 26:1-11. Some scholars regard this passage as the credo of early Israel, the confession of faith around which the saga of God's people takes shape. Others see it as a later summary. Whether it is origin or summary, its value as a focal statement of Israel's life and thought is unquestioned. Their sense of the past actions of God in history is combined with the realization that each generation is a part of Israel and can claim as its own the mighty acts of God.

Deuteronomy 26:16-19. The closing verses of the law summarize the terms of the covenant. Israel has agreed that the Lord is her God and that she will live in obedience to the covenant. God, on the other hand, has agreed that Israel is his own possession, that she will be exalted, and that she is a holy people by his action.

DIMENSION THREE:
WHAT DOES THE BIBLE MEAN TO ME?

Topics for class discussion in Dimension Three include the following: "God and War," "Hiding From Need," "Advancing Toward Justice," "Attitude Toward the Poor," and "Tradition and Identity."

Deuteronomy 20:1-20—God and War

The presentation in Deuteronomy 20 of the laws of warfare is the only such explicit treatment of the subject in the Pentateuch. The factors underlying the regulations for holy war are the perception of difference between Israel's covenant religion and the nature cults, the awareness of God's requirement of exclusive loyalty, the sense of call and chosenness in Israel's self-understanding, and the insistence on God's sovereign activity in history.

The focus on holy war presents problems for twentieth-century religious thought. Modern Jewish interpreters of this passage raise serious questions about its relevance. For many Christians the concept of God who calls for annihilation of a whole people is very difficult to accept. The revelation in Christ of God as love can hardly be reconciled with a militant God who calls followers into warfare to root out whole peoples.

Experiences with war have taught us that the issues in international conflict are more often rooted in conflicting economic and political interests than in moral issues. Furthermore, war cannot accomplish the victory of right over wrong. Engagement in warfare is itself brutal and requires adoption of some of the very behavior against which it is directed.

Our best theology and our most acute perceptions of war lead us to raise questions about the concept of God expressed in Deuteronomy 20. How are we to handle the questions of biblical interpretation?

One option is to dismiss Deuteronomy 20 as obsolete. But how can we decide that biblical passages can be ignored? How can we avoid creating a Bible that reflects only what we already believe?

Another option is to insist that Deuteronomy's view of holy war is viable, even though it conflicts with Christian thought today. This interpretation demands that we impose a norm on ourselves without regard for the present realities of life. In the process we may "save the Bible," but we lose contact with life and we risk making our faith artificial.

A third option asks us to look at the biblical text in its own setting, amidst the conditions of its own time. This assumes that God speaks to people in the midst of human experience, and that we can understand a faith witness best when we understand its life-setting.

Have the class think about Deuteronomy 20 and decide what underlying concerns it expresses. How does this passage remind us of concerns for Christians today? How should we oppose evil? How can we express our faith that God works in history?

Deuteronomy 22:1-4—Hiding From Need

Much of the material in Chapters 20–26 serves to make us more conscious of our social responsibility. One passage, Deuteronomy 22:1-4, suggests that awareness of social needs is not enough. Its phrase of admonition (verses 1, 3-4), "do not ignore it," points to a reflexive form of the Hebrew verb *to conceal*. Concealing oneself in the face of need is a familiar pattern of avoidance.

Deuteronomy not only prods Israel and us to greater ethical sensitivity. It also warns us not to shield ourselves from what we know we should do. What are some of the ways we "conceal ourselves" in the face of need?

Deuteronomy 22:13-21—Advancing Toward Justice

The strongly patriarchal overtones of the law in Deuteronomy 22:13-21 strike us as putting unfair burden on the woman to prove her innocence. It is important to see, however, that the situation before us is a definite advance over what preceded it. In a society where only men could initiate divorce, and that without explanation, it is important to understand that the law before us places a significant curb on male freedom to raise questions of suspicion. These questions must be presented in court where they can be subjected to critical examination and where the accused has opportunity to answer. The outcome still seems somewhat crude and one-sided to us. We are not asked to imitate their solution, but rather to emulate their concern for providing fuller redress of injustice with progressively better law.

When we see the stipulation in this way, we turn from judging its inadequacy to judging the quality of our handling of justice in our society.

What instances of injustice are apparent in our legal system? What groups need fuller access in our system of justice? What is our Christian responsibility with respect to injustice in our society?

Deuteronomy 24:10-13, 19-22
Attitude Toward the Poor

Many passages in Deuteronomy remind the Israelites of responsibility for the welfare of the poor and defenseless in their society. Deuteronomy 24:10-13 reflects unusual sensitivity to debtors. The creditor is not allowed to enter the house of the debtor to obtain the object given as security for the loan. He must wait outside for the debtor to bring it to him. This law guards the dignity and personhood of the debtor.

Are we as sensitive in our society? Are the dignity and the privacy of those who ask for help guarded as well in our day? What of welfare recipients and the personal information they must furnish? Is there any way of giving adequate help that would be more humane and Christian?

Deuteronomy 24:19-22 requires that Israel should harvest in such a way that needy people have access to food. In an agrarian society, this is not a peripheral matter. Landowners and harvesters are to conduct their activities with concern for the needy and powerless.

In recent years an organization called Senior Gleaners has been formed by a group of people in Sacramento, California. Concerned that so much food is wasted in the production, harvesting, and distribution system of American agriculture, they ask for food, formerly left to spoil because it was not profitable to harvest it with highly mechanized equipment. They deliver this food to centers for distribution to persons who need it. Positive and effective action of this sort comes from a combination of ethical concern about "hidden" hunger problems and imaginative tapping of unused resources created by our advances in agriculture.

What does our attitude toward the poor motivate us to do? Is our attitude as sensitive as that of Deuteronomy? How can we develop ways in our social and economic system for creative ethical action?

Deuteronomy 26:5-10—Tradition and Identity

Many biblical scholars have seen the liturgy of 26:5-10 as a basic credo, a summation of Israel's salvation history.

These verses focus Israel's faith in a terse, pointed statement of essentials.

Although the Israelites follow the calendar and observe the harvest festivals of their neighbors, they give these their own meaning. While other religions serve nature gods, Israel witnesses to the mighty acts of God in history.

The location of the action and revelation of God in history has significant implications. It means that Israel's religion is not a cycle of creation and chaos, and it does not see natural forces as deities with independent power. God's relationship to human beings is not located in natural phenomena but in human experience in history. The words of 26:5-10 are used in worship as a memory exercise, a remembrance that creates anew the experience of covenant events in each worshiper.

Ask the class members to say what they think tradition means. While sharing their ideas, have them consider what Christian tradition is. How do we get in touch with tradition?

How does worship help us to experience our tradition? What part does awareness of history play in worship? How can we, as the people of God, experience our past as living tradition?

Close the session by listing on a chalkboard or a large piece of paper the new insights from today's lesson.

See, I set before you today life and prosperity, death and destruction (30:15).

12

Blessings and Curses

Deuteronomy 27–30

DIMENSION ONE:
WHAT DOES THE BIBLE SAY?

Answer these questions by reading Deuteronomy 27

1. What does Moses command Israel to do at Mount Ebal? (27:4-5)

   Israel must build an altar of fieldstones on which to write the law, and sacrifice burnt offerings and fellowship offerings.

2. Have the Israelites become God's people because they obey the law or must they obey the law because they are God's people? (27:9-10)

   They must obey the law because they are God's people.

3. Which tribes are to stand on Mount Gerizim? Which on Mount Ebal? To do what? (27:11-13)

   On Mount Gerizim: Simeon, Levi, Judah, Issachar, Joseph, and Benjamin stand to bless. On Mount Ebal: Reuben, Gad, Asher, Zebulun, Dan, and Napthali stand to curse.

Answer these questions by reading Deuteronomy 28

4. What will happen to the Israelites if they obey God? (28:1-2)

   God will set them high above the nations.

5. If Israel obeys the Lord, what will be blessed? (28:3-6)

   The fruit of their body, ground, and beasts; their basket and kneading trough; their going out and their coming in will be blessed.

6. If Israel does not obey, what will be cursed? (28:16-19)

   She will be cursed in the city and in the fields; her kneading troughs; the fruit of her womb, land, and livestock; and in her going out and her coming in.

7. How will the Lord smite the disobedient people? (28:22)

   God will smite them with wasting disease, fever, inflammation, scorching heat, drought, blight, and mildew.

8. What will happen to Israel's fields, vineyards, and olive trees? (28:38-41)

   Locusts will eat the crops, worms will eat the grapes, and olives will drop off the trees. Sons and daughters will be taken captive.

9. What will the enemy do to Israel? (28:49-52)

   They will eat all Israel's food and besiege the cities.

Answer these questions by reading Deuteronomy 29

10. What is the purpose of the sworn covenant the Lord makes with Israel? (29:10-13)

    God makes the covenant in order to establish Israel as God's people and so that the Lord may be Israel's God.

11. When the nations ask why the Lord has made the land a desolation, what is the answer? (29:24-26)

    The answer is that Israel abandoned the covenant and worshiped other gods.

Answer these questions by reading Deuteronomy 30

12. If Israel has a change of heart and returns to the Lord while in exile, what will the Lord do for her? (30:1-3)

    God will gather Israel from wherever she has been dispersed, bring the people back to the Promised Land, and restore all Israel's fortunes.

13. What will happen when the Lord circumcises the heart of the people? (30:6)

    The people will love the Lord with all their heart and soul.

14. What two ways does Moses set before the people? (30:19-20)

Moses sets life and death, blessings and curses before the people.

DIMENSION TWO: WHAT DOES THE BIBLE MEAN?

Background Information on Deuteronomy 27–30

We may look at the four chapters of Deuteronomy before us in a number of ways. From the viewpoint of the book's structure, they include the last two chapters of Moses' second address (Deuteronomy 5–28) and all of his third address (Deuteronomy 29–30). From the standpoint of the central law code (12–26), they are a concluding section.

Chapter 28 is the focal chapter of this lesson. It deals with blessings and curses, the consequences of faithfulness or unfaithfulness to the covenant and its law. Those who see the influence of treaty forms in Deuteronomy point to this section as evidence. The characteristic ending of the Near Eastern suzerainty treaty includes blessings and curses that spell out the consequences of treaty observance or nonobservance. Whether treaty influence is direct or indirect, Deuteronomy makes significant use of blessings and curses to emphasize the necessity of obedience and the consequences of disobedience.

The curses in Chapter 28 indicate that a covenant broken by disobedience is irreparable. The covenant people will go into exile as the curse for disobedience is fulfilled. Chapters 29–30 (Moses' third address) deal with the reality of this situation and speak of hope for an exiled nation.

Deuteronomy 27:1-8. Chapter 27 is composed of four parts, which do not fit together in any logical way. However, they do share a common connection with Shechem, a prominent worship center in central Palestine during the time of Solomon (Joshua 24).

Moses (verse 1) is referred to in the third person only four places in Deuteronomy outside this chapter (1:1-5; 4:41; 5:1; 29:1-2). Three of these references stand at the beginning of his addresses. The reference to the elders in conjunction with Moses appears just this one time in the book.

Mount Ebal and the adjoining Shechem area are some twenty miles from the Jordan River. The account states that the activities around Shechem are to take place on the day the Israelites pass over the Jordan. This reflects a strong concern that the covenant be activated immediately after entering Canaan.

Deuteronomy 27:9-10. This terse statement of one of the fundamental tenets of biblical faith is more closely related in thought to the covenant formula in 26:16-19 than it is to

anything in Chapter 27. In verse 1, Moses is associated with the elders, but here the Levitical priests join him in speaking to Israel.

Deuteronomy 27:11-13. The full meaning of the division of tribes and their placement on adjoining mountains is not completely clear. Exactly how the ceremony took place is not clear from the Scripture. We seem to have a fragment of a blessing-curse ritual placed here because of its relation to the general blessing-and-curse theme of the following section (verses 14-26) and Chapter 28. The content of verses 11-13 is probably related to the reference to Ebal and Gerizim in Deuteronomy 11:29.

Deuteronomy 27:14-26. The differing role of the Levites indicates that this passage is not a continuation of the preceding verses. Here the Levites fill a priestly role, while in verses 11-13 they are one tribe among twelve of equal standing and function.

In this list of twelve curses, the first and last curses stand apart from the rest. Within the ten remaining, the first four relate to social misdeeds and the following four address sexual offenses.

The sin of sexual union with an animal is the only offense of this type mentioned in the Covenant Code (Exodus 22:19). Perhaps this activity was practiced in some neighboring cults as a means to achieve physical union with the deity, represented by a sacred animal. (Baal, for example, was characterized as a bull in Canaanite mythology.)

The other three sexual regulations come from a different source. The original prohibition forbids sexual relations with anybody in the same household of the extended family. This prohibition is expanded here to include other relatives, such as mother-in-law (verse 23), who would not be in the same residence. Similar but longer lists are found in Leviticus 18:6-23 and 20:11-21.

The last two curses deal with murder and bribery to have someone murdered. The use of the word *secretly* in verse 24 (*in secret* in verse 15) may point to a particular characteristic of all the laws. Some interpreters see this list as a catalogue of secret sins. These sins can best be handled within worship. The litany of curses could address such a situation very effectively. If a person guilty of one of these sins participated in the ritual, his "Amen" would give his assent to the imposition of the curse and he would be punished.

The curses in this passage do not specify their accompanying punishment, but the use of the word 'arur denotes harmful consequences. The word implies, at the very least, exclusion from normal community worship and ordinary relationships. In some cases, the curse may even require capital punishment.

Deuteronomy 28:3-6, 16-19. The subject throughout Chapter 28 is blessings and curses, with the latter in the majority. The blessings and curses are set forth as the respective consequences of obedience and disobedience. The chapter's location at this point is a natural outgrowth of Deuteronomy's law and of covenant thinking. In this sense, it directly continues Chapters 12–26.

The two sections that anchor the discussion are blessings (verses 3-6) and curses (verses 16-19). Matching almost exactly in both language and form, they may well be parts of an old covenant ceremony.

Deuteronomy 28:7-14. All of the blessings in Chapter 28 are found in verses 3-6 and 7-14. Everything else relates to curses.

Deuteronomy 28:15. The whole chapter pivots on verses 14-15. Verse 14 is the close of the section on blessings, and verse 15 is the opening of the extended passage on curses. The basis of the change is more important that its location. Obedience to covenant commandments, including exclusive loyalty to the Lord, characterizes all that precedes, while disobedience is the theme from this point on.

Deuteronomy 28:20-46. This list of curses is quite extensive. In addition to physical disease, plague, and drought, there is defeat by enemies, madness, and death without burial.

Interestingly, the list of frustrations in verse 30 is the same as the set of situations that furnished a basis for exemption from military service (20:5-7).

The curses move on finally to exile (verses 36-37), a theme that is more fully developed later in the chapter. Verses 45-46 close this section by reiterating the prevailing theme. Disobedience has brought Israel to this state.

Deuteronomy 28:47-57. Expanding on the theme of Israel's defeat at the hands of her enemies, verses 47-57 describe the horror of the siege and the extreme measures to which people inside the walls resort in their desperation.

Deuteronomy 28:58-68. In the concluding section, the force of the curse mounts. Such terms as "fearful plagues" (verse 59), "all the diseases of Egypt" (verse 60), and "terror that will fill your hearts" (verse 67) underscore this threat. Verse 63 even asserts "it will please him [the Lord] to ruin and destroy you," a statement that measures Deuteronomy's horror as the results of Israel's sin. Exile holds no peace or rest. It brings only a trembling heart, a languishing soul, and constant dread.

The use of the term "in ships" (verse 68) to describe the way by which Israel will get back to Egypt is puzzling. It may refer to slave boats, but the implication otherwise is that the journey will be over land. *The Revised English Bible,* making a slight emendation in the Hebrew text that changes "ships" to "sorrow," reads "bring you sorrowing back to Egypt."

Deuteronomy 29:1-9. Verse 1 makes a distinction between the Sinai covenant and a covenant made in the land of Moab. The question, which is also raised in Chapter 5, is the relationship between Sinai's Decalogue-based covenant and the covenant law "preached" by Moses on the plains of Moab. Chapter 5 makes it clear that both covenants come from Sinai. The former was revealed while Israel was present to hear, and the latter is an explanation of the former, revealed to Moses to be given to the people later. The two covenants are thus regarded as having equal weight and authority. This is probably the fact to which verse 1 refers.

Verse 2 introduces Moses' third address. The address, which continues through Chapter 30, begins with a historical prologue (verses 2-8). It follows the form of the first address in which Chapters 1–3 are used as a historical introduction. The short account in these verses tells of the struggle with Pharaoh, the Lord's leading and sustenance in the desert, the victories over Sihon and Og, and the settlement of two and one-half tribes in the territory east of the Jordan.

Deuteronomy 29:10-15. All of Israel is party to the covenant. This concept is socially inclusive, encompassing leaders, women, children, and aliens. Verse 15 implies that the covenant is also historically inclusive, since it incorporates the coming generations.

The sworn covenant (verse 12) combines two Hebrew words, *covenant* and *oath.* Literally, the sentence reads, "That you may enter into the covenant of the Lord your God and his oath."

Deuteronomy 29:16-21. The individual Israelite who secretly defects to other gods is a person dangerous to the community. He spreads poison among the people of God. The covenant law becomes a curse for that person.

Deuteronomy 29:22-28. The effect of the Exile will be a punishment so severe that it will remind people of legendary destruction. The references to the condition of the land in verse 23 indicate that it is sown with salt and sulphur, making it unfit for future use.

Sodom, Gomorrah, Admah, and Zeboiim are listed as neighboring cities of the same region (Genesis 10:19). They also appear among a list of places in Genesis 14:2, 8. Although these cities are all situated in the same region, only the first two are mentioned in the destruction described in Genesis 19. Hosea refers to Admah and Zeboiim as places whose names denote destruction (11:8), while Amos remembers Sodom and Gomorrah in the same way (4:11). Evidently all four cities were involved in the same event in the story of Genesis 19. Deuteronomy pulls varying traditions together to list the names of these cities that traditionally symbolize complete annihilation. They evoke in the hearers a stark picture of what is to happen to Israel.

Deuteronomy 29:29. The contrast between "secret things" and "things revealed" refers to the body of human knowledge and its limits. Matters of the future reside with God. The Israelites know the law, and it is sufficient to teach them how to live in peace and enjoy the blessings of God. Their problem is not lack of knowledge but stubbornness of will.

Deuteronomy 30:1-14. The unique message of these verses is that even in exile, when the judgment of God has fallen, all is not lost. If Israel returns to God, the relationship will be restored. God will even circumcise their hearts, an action that will bring their hearts into the covenant and make them capable of loving the Lord. This action is similar to that described in Jeremiah's new covenant (Jeremiah 31:31-34). The new element in the new covenant is God's action, which internalizes the covenant and empowers human beings to keep it. The covenant remains in effect by God's grace. God now gives Israel a new ability to live by the covenant.

Deuteronomy 30:15-20. At the end of his third address Moses sets the issue before the Israelites in categorical terms. Only two ways are available. Obedience to the covenant, which is now fully before them, leads to life and blessing. Disobedience and defection are the way to death. Moses calls heaven and earth to witness that everything necessary has been done to set the covenant.

The issue is clearly before the people. They have all the resources necessary to live in obedience to God's will. All that remains is their choice.

DIMENSION THREE: WHAT DOES THE BIBLE MEAN TO ME?

Class discussion of Dimension Three will include some or all of the following topics: "Grace and Ethics," "Blessing and Curse," "Eyes That Do Not See," and "Choose Life!"

Deuteronomy 27:9-10—Grace and Ethics

Almost everything in Chapter 27 is related to Shechem and the ceremonies of blessing and curse enacted on the nearby mountains, Ebal and Gerizim. Verses 9 and 10 are the exceptions. In terms of content, they are somewhat isolated from the rest of the chapter.

When we look for a logical place to put 27:9-10, our attention is drawn to 26:16-19. Both passages use the word *today,* and both witness to Israel's place as God's people and her responsibility to "obey the Lord your God."

The use of the word *today* may well indicate a worship setting for both passages. The first passage brings the covenant assumptions into clear focus. Worship functions to bring the past into the present. The essential quality is "nowness," the sense that the relationship with God is real in a moving way in the present moment.

This same sense characterizes Deuteronomy 27:9-10. The Israelites "today" become the people of the Lord. This fact puts them under responsibility to obey the Lord by keeping the commandments and statutes.

These verses establish two points. The first is that the covenant relationship with God already exists. Second, the establishment of covenant brings with it the expectation of obedience. Obedience to the will of God is based on God's grace. Religion has always struggled with "faith and works," the question of whether divine relationship is earned by our best efforts or whether it exists by the action of God and we claim it by faith.

The other side of this issue is the question of motivation for ethical conduct. Are we doing good because we want God's favor or because we are responding in gratitude to what God has already done?

Deuteronomy's statement is clear on where the matter stands for Israel. God's covenant is in effect. Obedience, though essential, is not a prerequisite. Responsibility for righteousness is inescapable within the covenant relationship, but it is always a response to the relationship God has already established.

Christians have always questioned the relationship between grace and law. How can we put them in proper perspective?

Can we trust ourselves and others to do the right thing if God does not require it to earn approval? Does grace excuse us from ethical responsibility? Can we believe that God's love accepts us before we do anything to deserve it?

Deuteronomy 28:1-6, 15-19—Blessing and Curse

The rewards of obedience and the punishment for disobedience are the themes of Deuteronomy 28:1-6, 16-19. These two passages are the basis for the rest of the chapter. They contain a parallel, matching series of blessings (verses 1-6) and curses (verses 16-19).

These portions from a longer treatment of blessings and curses set the main issue before us. Deuteronomy's consistent viewpoint is that righteousness is rewarded and wrongdoing is punished. Deuteronomy states the retribution concept in terms of obedience or disobedience to covenant law. This is the basis on which blessing or curse enters life. Deuteronomy's witness is that quality of life is determined by the degree of obedience to God and to covenant law.

Two things must be remembered when dealing with Deuteronomy's statement of retribution. First, Deuteronomy's witness is primarily directed to the nation of Israel, rather than to individual lives. Retribution is expected in national life and fortune. Deuteronomy probably does not assume that each person could expect specific and immediate results.

Second, the concept is an answer to an essentially magical view of life, which leaves results to divine whimsy. Deuteronomy insists that the covenant understanding of life connects ethical conduct and the course of human affairs. The book is essentially a philosophy of history.

After the time of Deuteronomy, Israel begins to apply retribution to individual experience. When this happens, numerous Old Testament wisdom expressions (for example, Job, Ecclesiastes, Psalm 73) raise questions about the idea of individual retribution. There is too much righteous suffering and wicked prosperity to maintain an oversimplified retribution theology.

How are we to regard Deuteronomy's theology on this point? Ask the class to consider areas of our experience in which the idea of rewards and punishments seems valid and accurate. Can we agree with Deuteronomy that life as a whole is moral? What problems are raised when retribution is applied individually? How does retribution relate to discipleship and Christian suffering?

Deuteronomy 29:2-4—Eyes That Do Not See

In characteristic fashion, Moses' third address begins with a look at history as a prelude to consideration of covenant. While rehearsing the great things God did for Israel in Egypt, the passage notes that the people's "eyes have seen" the signs and wonders (verse 2). However, verse 4 laments that the Israelites do not understand the meaning of these signs. They fail to see the divine love at work in history and what their response to that love should be. Their failure shows in their apostasy and their refusal to observe the law.

Our understanding of the meaning of what is happening around us influences the way we live. Like the Israelites, we often do not see the deepest meanings of history and experience.

Ask the class members to identify a recent event (election, uprising, terrorist episode) that has received more than one interpretation. How can we decide which interpretation is accurate? How does our Christian faith affect our interpretation of these events?

Deuteronomy 30:15-20—Choose Life!

At the end of Moses' final sermon (30:15-20), Deuteronomy brings all its themes together and expresses them in a straightforward, categorical call for decision from Israel. As Moses concludes, he says, "This day . . . I have set before you life and death, blessing and curse. Now choose life." (30:19).

Is Deuteronomy's view that there are only two ways in life a valid view? How can the two ways help us make decisions in the complex realities of modern life?

To close the session, ask the class members to think back over their study of Deuteronomy 27–30 and list any insights they have gained. Have them share these insights and compile, if time permits, a list of the most important points.

13

Epilogue

Deuteronomy 31–34

DIMENSION ONE:
WHAT DOES THE BIBLE SAY?

Answer these questions by reading Deuteronomy 31

1. How does Moses encourage Israel when he says he will not be going to Canaan? (31:3-7)

   He encourages the people by assuring that the Lord is going with Israel, that the nations will be destroyed before them, and that Joshua will lead them.

2. What does Moses instruct the priests and elders to do with the law? (31:10-11)

   They are to read Deuteronomy before all Israel at the Feast of Tabernacles every seventh year.

3. Where does the Lord tell Joshua to go? (31:23)

   The Lord tells Joshua to lead Israel to the Promised Land.

4. Where does Moses tell the Levites to put the Book of the Law? (31:24-26)

   They are to put it by the side of the ark of the covenant.

5. What does Moses expect to happen after his death? (31:27-29)

   He expects Israel will act corruptly and turn aside from the way that Moses has commanded them.

Answer these questions by reading Deuteronomy 32

6. In Moses' song, who does he say is the Lord's portion and allotted heritage? (32:9)

   The Lord's portion is his people, Jacob his allotted inheritance.

7. What response does Moses say that Israel made to God? (32:15-18)

   Moses says Israel abandoned God, went after other gods, and made sacrifices to demons and strange gods.

8. What prevents God from bringing punishment on Israel? (32:26-27)

   God does not punish Israel because her enemies will think she, rather than the Lord, accomplished Israel's downfall.

9. What will the Lord do for Israel? (32:36)

   The Lord will judge Israel and have compassion on her.

10. Where does the Lord tell Moses to go? What will Moses do there? (32:48-50)

    The Lord tells Moses to go to Mount Nebo to view the land of Canaan and die.

Answer these questions by reading Deuteronomy 33

11. What is Deuteronomy 33? (33:1)

    This chapter is Moses' blessing on the Israelites.

12. What persons are mentioned in the poem? (33:6, 7, 8, 12, 13, 18, 20, 22, 23, 24)

    Reuben, Judah, Levi, Benjamin, Joseph, Zebulun, Issachar, Gad, Dan, Naphtali, and Asher are mentioned.

13. What responsibilities does Moses give to Levi? (33:10)

    Moses tells Levi to teach Israel God's law and officiate at the Lord's altar (put incense before God and whole burnt offerings upon God's altar).

Answer these questions by reading Deuteronomy 34

14. What does the Lord show Moses from the mountain top? (34:1)

   The Lord shows Moses the whole land, promised to Abraham, Isaac, and Jacob, and soon to be given to Israel.

15. Where is Moses buried? (34:5-6)

   Moses is buried in the valley in the land of Moab opposite Beth Peor, in a place no one knows.

16. How old is Moses when he dies? How long does Israel mourn for him? (34:7-8)

   Moses is one hundred twenty years old. Israel mourns thirty days.

17. What marks Moses as a unique prophet? (34:10-12)

   The Lord knew him face to face. He was also greater in deeds, signs, and wonders performed than any prophet before or since.

DIMENSION TWO: WHAT DOES THE BIBLE MEAN?

Background Information on Deuteronomy 31–34

The last four chapters of Deuteronomy are an appendix to the main part of the book. They have little to do with law and covenant, the main themes of Deuteronomy. The purpose of including these chapters is to complete the story of Moses and to provide for a leadership succession that will connect with the conquest events recorded in the next book.

The chapters contain several narrative sections and two extended poems. The narrative has three main themes: final instruction about the law (31:9-13, 24-29; 32:45-47); installation of Joshua as Moses' successor (31:7-8, 14-15, 23; 34:9); and Moses' death (32:48-52; 34:1-8, 10-12).

The poems are quite different in form and content. The first one (32:1-43) is like a psalm in form. It considers the Lord's grace toward Israel, Israel's waywardness and God's punishment, and the Lord's rescue of Israel from exile. The second (33:2-29) is Moses' blessing of the twelve tribes—a collection of individual pieces of varying length about each tribe of Israel. This whole poem is couched in the form used for a patriarch's blessing of his children just before he dies (compare Genesis 49).

Deuteronomy 31:1-8. Moses is near the end of his life. Having completed the addresses in which he gives Israel the covenant law, he begins to prepare Israel for her future.

"You shall not cross the Jordan" (verse 2) repeats the words of the Lord from Deuteronomy 3:27. The effect is to tie the closing narrative to the earlier narrative in Chapters 1–3. Moses' entreaty to enter Canaan in 3:23-27 has been refused, and the later story continues that theme.

Moses encourages Israel as she prepares for the conquest of Canaan. Using assurances from the holy war tradition, Moses assumes the role of a leader of holy warfare.

The main point of this passage appears in verses 7-8, as Moses gives Joshua his charge as "leader-elect" before all Israel. Thus continuity of leadership is provided, and the story turns towards its next chapter.

Deuteronomy 31:9-13. In addition to providing for his successor, Moses also has three more instructions that relate to the law. The first occurs in this passage.

Having written the Deuteronomic law, Moses entrusts it to the priests and elders, that is, to the religious and civil leaders. He goes one step further to provide for a covenant renewal festival every seventh year at the fall festival. Near Eastern treaty specifications call for the treaty terms to be put in writing and recited at regular times. If Israel is consciously using this form, she makes it over for her own purposes in describing the covenant.

Deuteronomy 31:24-29. The second instruction concerning the law indicates the important of Deuteronomy's law. Moses tells the Levites to place it beside the ark. The Decalogue is in the ark, and the placement of Deuteronomy (probably Chapters 5–26) beside it indicates its equal authority.

Deuteronomy 32:1-6. The song of Moses, extending through verse 43, begins with this summons to instruction and ascription of praise to the Lord's name. The contrast that runs throughout the poem—the greatness and faithfulness of God compared with the perversity and disloyalty of Israel—begins in this first section.

The Hebrew word translated "Creator" in verse 6 is the same word used in Proverbs 8:22 to describe wisdom's place in creation. Other similarities to wisdom words and expressions in this section of the poem may indicate wisdom influence on its composition.

Deuteronomy 32:7-14. The term "sons of Israel" (verse 8) is rendered "sons of God" in the Revised Standard Version. the word *God* is based on a reading in the early Greek translation called the Septuagint. A fragment of a text from the caves at Qumran supports the Septuagint reading. "Sons of gods" means that at the beginning of history each of the nations is assigned to a heavenly being for protection and care. This applies to all peoples except Israel, which the Lord chooses and blesses in special ways. This picture of election is unique in the Old Testament.

EPILOGUE

185

Deuteronomy 32:15-18. In spite of all these blessings, Jeshurun (Israel) defects to alien gods and strange worship practices. Verse 18, speaking of God's relationship with Israel, uses verbs that denote a mother's giving birth to a child—a striking figure for the God-Israel relationship in the Old Testament.

Deuteronomy 32:19-25. Reflecting the same theme we find elsewhere in Deuteronomy, the Lord's judgment falls on Israel's apostasy. The punishment is to come through those who are "not a people" (verse 21), a reference to some enemy nation, perhaps Babylon.

Deuteronomy 32:26-35. Verses 26-27 are a turning point in the poem. The Lord had previously decided on punishment for the people of God because of their sinfulness. In a remarkable turnaround, the divine purposes change from judgment to vindication. The change hinges on God's realization that the other nations will misunderstand the defeat of Israel. They will interpret Israel's demise as their triumph and completely miss the fact that God is using them to judge Israel. From this point on the Lord becomes Israel's vindicator and champion.

Deuteronomy 32:43. Typical of the style of a hymn, the poem concludes with a general call to the nations to praise God. Psalms of praise regularly end with a call to praise. Praise in this case is motivated by the Lord's protection of the people from their adversaries.

Deuteronomy 32:45-47. In Moses' third reference to the law, he urges the Israelites to take the law seriously and to teach it to their children. He supports this command with a plea that they understand the true important of the law as the source of life.

Deuteronomy 32:48-52. The theme of Moses' approaching death appears in the narrative at this point, connecting the account in Numbers 27:12-14 with the story of Moses' actual death in Deuteronomy 34:1-6. This passage, like the Numbers account, cites Moses' sin at Meribah as the reason he is not allowed to go into Canaan. Deuteronomy's version usually blames the sins of the people.

Deuteronomy 33:1-5, 26-29. Moses' blessing on the twelve tribes is regarded as having particular weight. More than good wishes, the blessing is a word with power to effect what it contains. In addition, these words of the great leader Moses have special import because he is near death.

Deuteronomy 33:6-25. This collection of tribal sayings is similar to the one in Jacob's blessing in Genesis 49. The tribe of Simeon which disappears through absorption into Judah at an early period, is not included among the twelve tribes listed here. The number of tribes is kept at twelve by counting both Joseph tribes and by including Levi, which is usually omitted because of its special priestly status.

The Judah blessing (verse 7) expresses a plea to "bring him to his people," indicating separation from the rest of Israel. This points either to the period of the judges when Judah will be somewhat separated from the rest of Israel, or to the time of the divided kingdom, when Judah alone will remain loyal to the Davidic dynasty.

The section on Levi (verses 8-11) is one of the two longest sections in the poem. Expressed in prayer form, it asks that the Urim and Thummim be given to the Levites. These were objects through which the divine answer to questions could be supplied. They were used by priests and evidently were capable of giving a yes or no answer. Verse 10 defines Levi's role as teaching the law and officiating at the altar, the two chief responsibilities of the priest.

The other long section belongs to Joseph and includes the tribes of Ephraim and Manasseh. Verses 13-17 take the form of a blessing. The theme throughout is the fruit of the land, the blessing of fertility. The reference in verse 16 to the one "that dwelt in the bush" must point to God's role in Moses' call (Exodus 3:2-6).

The other tribes receive shorter notices and the forms are quite varied. Some are prayers (verses 7-11), some blessings (verses 13-17, 24). Still others are simple statements (verse 12), direct addresses (verse 18), wishes (verse 24), and tribal sayings (verses 22-23).

Deuteronomy 34:1-6. The double name for the mountain to which Moses goes indicates a double tradition about the name. Deuteronomy regularly uses Pisgah for the site of Moses' death, while Numbers speaks of the place as Nebo. The two traditions are joined in verse 1.

At the top of the mountain, the Lord shows Moses the whole land Israel is to possess. It runs from Dan in the north to the Negeb in the south and from Gilead and the Jordan Valley on the east to the western (Mediterranean) sea on the west.

Verse 4 is a reminder that the promise made to the patriarchs centuries earlier is about to be fulfilled in their descendants.

Deuteronomy 34:7-12. The picture of Moses in verse 7 is somewhat different from the one in 31:2, where Moses describes himself as old and feeble. The words in 34:7 are probably intended more as a tribute to the greatness of Moses than as an exact description of his physical prowess.

The passage and the book close with a reference to Joshua's assuming leadership, and a final tribute to Moses as a unique prophet. When we think of Moses' career we are reminded of the many roles he filled and of the outstanding quality of his leadership.

DIMENSION THREE: WHAT DOES THE BIBLE MEAN TO ME?

In the Dimension Three portion of the lesson, you will want to concentrate on these topics: "The Meaning of Tradition," "Affluence and Waywardness," "Trifle or Word of Life?" and "Giants Die; Life Goes On."

Deuteronomy 31:9-13—The Meaning of Tradition

Deuteronomy presents Moses as the proclaimer of covenant law. The whole book is organized around his addresses in which he sets out decrees and laws and exhorts Israel to observe them as the people of God. Now that activity is complete. The full revelation of Horeb has been given to Israel. Moses, knowing his death is near, wants to assure continuance of knowledge and respect for the covenant and its law.

Deuteronomy 31:9-13 recounts Moses' next step. He writes the law and gives it to the levitical priests and the elders. All three elements in this action are significant.

Writing the law is a major shift in the story. Moses, mediator of the Horeb revelation, has completed his preaching responsibility. He now commits the law into writing where it will live on after his death.

Entrusting the written law to the priests, the carriers of the religious tradition and instruction, is an important contribution to their body of teaching. It also releases the law into the mainstream of tradition.

The involvement of the elders who order and judge everyday civil life, means that the law is to be put into practice in life situations. The combined effort of the two groups, priests and elders, will assure Israel's continued awareness of covenant and observance of its law.

However, even this is not enough for Moses. He provides for Israel's regular exposure to the law by commanding that Deuteronomy be read at the sanctuary during the fall festival every seventh year. The whole congregation is to gather for this occasion to hear the law. One purpose is to raise the consciousness and to renew the memory of the people. A second objective is to enable the children to learn the law. This practice strikes us as a good way to keep the law alive in the covenant community. How do we keep the law alive in our Christian community? What can we learn from Moses' traditions?

Ours is a culture of newness and experimentation. We do not put great value on the past and are impatient with repetition. We tend to regard regularity as routine. In such an environment, what can we accomplish by reading old documents and going through all-too-familiar worship exercises?

Our impatience with repetitions and rehearsals of the past can cause us to lose touch with who we are. Our heritage slips away from us. Much of value, even something of ourselves, is lost.

What is central and essential to us as the church? To be the church, what do we need to keep alive among us? How does worship keep us in touch with our tradition?

Ask the class to list the elements they would include if they were planning a renewal service for your church.

Deuteronomy 32:15-18—Affluence and Waywardness

The song of Moses presents in poetic form the whole life of Israel. In the section that treats the blessings of life as the people of God, a familiar theme is sounded. In verse 15, a prosperous Jeshurun (Israel) is pictured settling down in Canaan, where the people then abandon God and scoff at the Rock of salvation. In this one verse we have a summary of Israel's history before the Exile, at least as it is viewed by the prophets and Deuteronomy.

The prophets speak frequently to this same point. Blessings enjoyed in Canaan have corrupted Israel and have caused the people to forget the source of their blessing. This forgetfulness has led to defection and the worship of other gods. It has also produced a society that does not know or practice the concerns for justice and righteousness that stand at the center of their tradition.

We may easily agree with a people's harsh judgment of themselves but find it more difficult to look at ourselves objectively. We can see how the Israelites went wrong and where their conduct showed ingratitude and callousness. How does this passage speak to us?

We do not need to look far to see that ingratitude continues to produce insensitivity. Human nature still interprets blessing in such a way that it leads to selfishness and callousness, rather than to humility and righteousness.

In our time, many religious voices promise blessings as a reward for turning to God. While this is certainly a part of the biblical message, the more crucial concern for us is what we do with the blessings of affluence. What kind of people do we become when we prosper? How should we relatively affluent American Christians regard and handle prosperity?

Deuteronomy's warnings are relevant to us today. What do we need to remember as we enjoy the blessings of life? Deuteronomy reminds us that the Israelites ran into trouble when they forgot the source of their blessings. But remembering that source is more than calling a name to mind. Remembering is worshiping God and living in obedience to God's will.

Ask the class members to give examples in which wealth has produced disdain for God or insensitivity to the needs of others. Does this attitude apply to America's conduct in the world today? What does it mean for our relations with underdeveloped countries? What is the effect of prosperity on our personal way of living?

The church in its history has not been immune to the temptations of wealth. Where in the life of the church does prosperity cause us to forget who we are? How do our decisions about programs and facilities reflect God's concern for righteousness and justice? How do our decisions ignore these concerns?

Deuteronomy 32:45-47—Trifle or Word of Life?

One of the major issues in history and individual life is knowing what is important. Moses addresses this concern in Deuteronomy 32:45-47. In verse 47, he says of the law, "They are not just idle words for you—they are your life." The great revelation, the covenant law itself, is in danger of being dismissed as empty words.

Moses has insisted throughout that the words he is revealing to Israel are life-giving. Here he says they "are your life." Living by the covenant law will enable the people to live long in the Promised Land.

How many times the people of God pass by or spurn the life-giving word! One outstanding example is Israel's refusal to listen to the prophets. As a result, she goes into the "death" of exile.

Deuteronomy's concern in 32:45-47 is that the word of life may be overlooked as inconsequential. The problem, then and now, is in discerning what is important. The Bible and the church serve to remind us of the crucial words in life, the ones that require our response.

Ask the class to discuss how the word of life comes to us as Christians today. In what ways do we treat that as an "idle word"? What kind of response is called for? Is our response a matter of life and death?

Deuteronomy 34—Giants Die; Life Goes On

Few people would deny that Moses is a truly significant figure in our religious history. Deuteronomy 34, while recounting his death, indicates something of the measure of his person and leadership. Verse 7 speaks of Moses in terms of his remarkable vigor up to the time of his death. Verses 10-12 go farther by pointing to his uniqueness in knowing God face to face. He accomplishes great things as God's agent in the struggle with Pharaoh; and, at the end, he is even credited with "mighty power and . . . [and] awesome deeds" before all Israel. The tribute is the measure of the man.

Chapter 34 also records Moses' death. The fact that the chapter does not end here is a lesson in itself. In verse 9, we read that Joshua, whom Moses had commissioned as his successor, was "filled with the spirit of wisdom" and that the people obeyed him, carrying out the Lord's will. This points to the continuity of history and to the source of that continuity in the purposes of God.

Ask the class to give examples of crises produced by the deaths of great leaders. What happens afterward? How does life go on? How are divine purposes involved in the continuity of life and history?

Ask the class to think back over the highlights of Israel's experiences in Numbers and Deuteronomy. What themes are most important in holding the story together?

Close the session by having the class share new insights into Deuteronomy 31–34. At the end of the session, review what the class has learned from the past thirteen lessons. If time is short, you might set aside time at a later date for reviewing Numbers and Deuteronomy.

JOSHUA, JUDGES, AND RUTH
Table of Contents

About the Writer

The writer of these lessons is the Reverend Ray Newell. He is the pastor of Westland United Methodist Church in Lebanon, Tennessee. For several years, Mr. Newell taught Bible and religion at Mount Union College, Alliance, Ohio.

"Get ready to cross the Jordan River into the land I am about to give to . . . the Israelites" (1:2).

— 1 —

Entering the Promised Land

Joshua 1–3

DIMENSION ONE: WHAT DOES THE BIBLE SAY?

Answer these questions by reading Joshua 1

1. Who takes over the leadership of Israel when Moses dies? (Joshua 1:1-2)

   Joshua the son of Nun takes command.

2. What part of the land the Israelites are about to enter will God give to them? (Joshua 1:3)

   Every place they set their foot will be given to them.

3. What does the Lord promise to Joshua? (Joshua 1:5, 9)

   The Lord promises to be with Joshua wherever he goes.

4. What condition does God lay down for the success of the coming conquest? (Joshua 1:7)

   Israel must be strong, courageous, and must strictly follow the law that Moses gave her.

5. What is Joshua to do with the Book of the Law? (Joshua 1:8)

   He shall meditate on it day and night and do everything that is written in it.

6. What does Joshua order the Reubenites, the Gadites, and the half-tribe of Manasseh to do? (Joshua 1:12-15)

   All the fully armed fighting men from these tribes shall cross over the Jordan and help the other tribes possess the land.

7. How do these tribes respond to Joshua's command? (Joshua 1:16-17)

   They will do whatever he commands and go wherever he sends them.

Answer these questions by reading Joshua 2

8. Where do the two spies go? (Joshua 2:1)

   They go to the house of Rahab, the prostitute, in Jericho.

9. How does Rahab reply to the king of Jericho's command to turn over the two men? (Joshua 2:4-5)

   She says the men left at dusk as the city gate was closing.

10. Where are the two spies? (Joshua 2:6)

    Rahab has hidden them under the stalks of flax on her roof.

11. What does Rahab request of the two Israelite men? (Joshua 2:12-13)

    She asks them to swear to save the lives of her father's house because she showed kindness to them.

12. How do the two men respond to Rahab's request? (Joshua 2:14)

    If Rahab will aid them, they promise to deal kindly and faithfully with her.

13. What sign do the spies tell Rahab to display in order to save her family from death? (Joshua 2:18)

    They tell her to tie a scarlet cord in her window.

14. What do the spies report to Joshua? (Joshua 2:24)

    They know that the Lord has given them the land because the people who live there are melting in fear of Israel.

Answer these questions by reading Joshua 3

15. What will lead the Israelites into the Promised Land? (Joshua 3:3)

    The people will follow the ark of the covenant into the land.

16. How do the people prepare to cross the Jordan River? (Joshua 3:5)

They consecrate themselves.

17. Where does Joshua say the living God will be? (Joshua 3:10)

Joshua says that the living God will be among the Israelites.

18. Joshua says the waters will stop flowing when? (Joshua 3:13)

The river will stop flowing as soon as the priests carrying the ark of the Lord set foot in the Jordan.

19. What time of year does Israel cross the Jordan? (Joshua 3:15)

The people cross during harvest time, when the Jordan is at flood stage.

20. Where is the ark of the covenant while the people pass over the Jordan on dry ground? (Joshua 3:17)

Priests carrying the ark are standing on dry ground in the middle of the Jordan.

DIMENSION TWO: WHAT DOES THE BIBLE MEAN?

Background Information on Joshua 1–3

The Book of Joshua is one part of a larger literary work called the Deuteronomic history. This history runs from Deuteronomy all the way through Second Kings and charts the history of Israel from the conquest of the land to the fall of Jerusalem. The Book of Ruth was not originally part of this work.

The final form of the Deuteronomic history was written during the Exile, about 550 B.C., to explain why God's people were in exile. When Jerusalem fell in 586 B.C., the Israelites felt that God had broken the promise to give them the Promised Land and make them a nation. No doubt the Israelites had many questions about God's faithfulness when they did not get all the things they expected. The Deuteronomic history was written in response to these questions to explain that God had not broken the covenant with the people of Israel. The Israelites were the ones who had broken their promise to obey God's laws.

Beginning with these laws of God (Deuteronomy), the Deuteronomic history shows how Israel continually acted against God's will. In Deuteronomy, God promises Israel success if the people obey the laws. If they go against God's will, they will be punished. The history shows that God is not at fault for Israel's suffering. Israel alone bears the burden of guilt. In fact, the books of Joshua and Judges tell how God continuously shows mercy to Israel when she should have been punished.

Throughout Israel's history, God commands the Israelites to be loyal. But finally God can no longer ignore the sins of the people. Judgment must fall. They must be sent into exile in order to shock them back to their primary loyalty to God. The Deuteronomic history chronicles this interaction of God's law, judgment, prophetic word, and mercy with Israel's continual disobedience. The history's final purpose is to call the people back to God by reminding them that the Lord is a merciful God. If Israel turns to God in faith, God will surely restore the covenant with the people.

As we look at Joshua and Judges we are told of Israel invading and securing the Promised Land. We need to keep in mind that the end of the Deuteronomic history is the story of the loss of the land through the people's disobedience. Joshua, Judges, and First Samuel portray God graciously giving the land to an Israel that does not deserve it. Second Samuel and First and Second Kings record how God passes judgment on Israel.

Joshua 1:1-4. You can set the stage for this unit by showing the borders of the Promised Land as they are described in verse 4. (Use a map of the ancient Near East. You will find one in the back of many Bibles, or perhaps your Sunday school has wall-size maps available.) You may also want to pinpoint Mount Nebo, where Moses died; Shittim, where the Israelites camp while the spies go into the land (Joshua 2:1); and Jericho (Joshua 2:1).

Joshua 1:5-9. In these verses God promises to be with Joshua during the conquest. God says, "As I was with Moses, so I will be with you." We can note, then, that the idea of Immanuel—God with us—belongs to the earliest sections of the Bible. In the Deuteronomic history, however, the continued presence of God depends on how humans respond. The proper human response consists of being strong, courageous, and obedient to "all the law my servant Moses gave you" (verse 7). The importance of the Book of the Law is emphasized in verse 8. Following the law is a response to God's grace and the way of maintaining the already promised presence of God, but not a requirement for receiving God's grace.

Joshua 1:12-18. You might want to review the story of the conquest of land east of the Jordan (Numbers 32) and the story of how this land was given to the tribes of Reuben, Gad, and the half-tribe of Manasseh (Deuteronomy 3:12-20). Although this land is given by God to these tribes, it does not stand within the boundaries of Canaan, the Promised Land (see Joshua 22:19).

Joshua 1:18. The tribes emphasize Joshua's new absolute authority over them. His position as God's spokesman is assumed in the statement that anyone who disobeys his commands shall be put to death.

Joshua 2:1. Joshua's action of sending the spies into the land is ironic considering the admonition in 1:18 to "be strong and courageous!" The Israelites had once before sent out spies after God had promised a land to them and said, "Do not be afraid; do not be discouraged" (Deuteronomy 1:21-40). The first time spies were sent out, Israel became afraid and rebelled against God's command. This distrust in God's ability to fulfill the promise is why God did not allow any from this generation (except Joshua and Caleb) to enter the Promised Land. Deuteronomy 1:22 explains that after God has already given them the land, sending spies reveals a weakness of faith. Here Joshua, Moses' successor and God's spokesman, wavers in his total trust of God's word.

Jericho, named after the Semitic moon god, was one of the oldest inhabited cities in the world. People have lived there since 8000 B.C. After walls were built, about 6800 B.C., Jericho became the earliest known fortified town in human history. Jericho's major periods of habitation were from 2900 to 2300 B.C. and from 1750 to 1560 B.C. At the end of both of these periods, Jericho's defensive walls were destroyed. For the period of Joshua's invasion (1250–1225 B.C.), we have very little archaeological evidence about Jericho.

Rahab, the prostitute who became faithful to the Lord, was one of the four most beautiful women in the world, according to Jewish tradition. She is believed to be an ancestor of eight prophets (including Jeremiah and Ezekiel) and one prophetess, Hulda.

Rahab is also important in the New Testament. According to Matthew 1:5, she is an ancestor of Jesus, being the mother of Boaz who married Ruth. James 2:25 claims Rahab was justified by works in her kindness to the Israelite spies. Hebrews 11:31, on the other hand, says her welcome to the spies revealed her faith.

Joshua 2:2-11. Rahab chooses loyalty to the Lord, the God of Israel, over loyalty to her city and people. This primary loyalty demanded by God above all other human loyalties is demonstrated over and over in the Bible. Abraham leaves his native land and family to follow God (Genesis 12:1) and even chooses God over his beloved son Isaac (Genesis 22:2). Jesus proclaimed faithfulness to God took precedence over faithfulness to family (Luke 18:28-30).

Rahab also reveals that her faith in the Lord is stronger than Israel's. She states in verse 9, "I know that the LORD has given this land to you." Where Joshua and Israel timidly send spies to discover if God has truly given them the land, Rahab knows already this is what God has done. That one of Israel's enemies trusts God's power more than Israel does, is ironic. Rahab gives the statement of faith Israel should have given! Israel sends spies out of weak faith; Rahab acts decisively out of her sure faith in God.

Joshua 2:12-14. The two spies promise to spare Rahab and her family for the kindness she has shown them by hiding them from her king. Interestingly, by swearing to protect her, the two spies go beyond God's command that no one who is defeated in the Promised Land shall live. By promising to let Rahab and her family live, the spies are breaking the letter of the law. Perhaps the point of this story is that the spirit of the law calling for loyalty and faithfulness to God takes precedence over slavishly following the letter of the law.

Joshua 2:15-21. We see here the importance of an oath for Israel. When one swears to do something in the name of the Lord, one is obligated to carry it out. Breaking the oath calls down God's judgment upon one's unfaithfulness. For this reason, one of Israel's commandments demands that persons not misuse the name of the Lord (Deuteronomy 5:11). Once an oath has been made—even if it goes against God's law (as here), even if one had been tricked into it (Joshua 9:19-21), even if it was made rashly without full realization of its consequences (Judges 11:30-36)—it has to be fulfilled! For these reasons the limits of Israel's obligations to Rahab and her family are strictly detailed by the spies.

Joshua 2:22-24. Compare this report from the spies with the earlier report of the first-generation spies found in Numbers 13:27-33 (also Deuteronomy 1:22-33). Where fear and unfaithfulness resulted from the first spying adventure, this second one results in faith. Joshua's spies do not bring back military information on the nature of Jericho's defenses. Rather, they repeat Rahab's statement of faith that the Lord has already given the land into Israel's hands. An outsider's faith in the Lord restores Israel's faith in her God.

Joshua 3:3-6. Review for class members the descriptions of the ark of the covenant found in Exodus 25:10-22. You can find the war cries of Israel associated with the ark's presence in battle in Numbers 10:35-36. Israel conceived of holiness as raw power that had to be handled with special care. The ark, the most holy of objects, could bring blessings; but if mishandled, it could bring disaster. (The ark brought death to Uzzah, but brought blessing to Obed-Edom in 2 Samuel 6:6-7, 9-11).

Joshua 3:7-13. We see in this section one of the reasons for the miraculous crossing of the Jordan. Through the crossing the Lord will exalt Joshua so Israel knows God is with him as with Moses.

Joshua reports God's words in an interesting way. Verses 7-8 contain God's statement that Joshua will be exalted and God's command that the priests bearing the ark stand still when they come to the brink of the Jordan. In verse 9, Joshua calls the people to hear the words of the Lord. Then in verses 10-13, Joshua says nothing about his personal exaltation, but rather states that the upcoming miracle is a sign so Israel will know God will drive out the inhabitants of the land. He commands the selection of one man from each tribe for some unspecified task. He transmits God's command to the priests carrying the ark.

Joshua on his own, not God, tells the people that the waters of the Jordan will be stopped from flowing and will stand up in a heap. Joshua, as God's chosen leader, apparently receives the power to interpret and extend God's word.

The names of people in 3:10 show the number of different ethnic groups living in the Promised Land. Many migrations of people into Canaan, as well as conquests by great empires, had occurred before the tribes led by Joshua arrived. The Bible uses both *Canaanites* and *Amorites* as general names for all the pre-Israelite inhabitants of the land. More specifically, *Canaanites* usually refers to those people living in the coastal areas. The Amorites migrated into Palestine about 1900 B.C. and lived in the hill country.

The Hittites originated in the area of modern Turkey. Only a few decades before Joshua, the Hittites had successfully fought with Egypt for control over Syria, just north of the Promised Land. Apparently they were able to set up colonies in Palestine as Egyptian control weakened. The Hivites and the Hurrians are probably the same. Widely scattered throughout the ancient Near East, the Hivites (Hurrians) reached the height of power between 3000 and 2000 B.C. The Jebusites are the native residents of Jerusalem. Nothing is known about the Perizzites and the Girgashites.

Joshua 3:14-17. Here the water stops just as Joshua says it will. Compare this section with the story of the crossing of the Red Sea in Exodus 14:21-29. Although there appear to be some parallels between the accounts, there are more differences than similarities.

Differences

1. Moses' hand over the sea begins the action	1. Priests bearing ark step in water to begin miracle
2. Wind divides waters	2. Water stops flowing
3. Wall of water visible on both sides of people	3. Water stopped out of sight to the north
4. Egyptians chase Israelites	4. No opposition

Similarities

1. God ultimate cause	1. God ultimate cause
2. Wall of water	2. Water heaped up
3. People pass over on dry ground	3. People pass over on dry ground

This section ends with an interesting image that contrasts the movement of the people with the immobility of the ark. This image emphasizes that the movement of God's people through life depends on the eternal stability and rest of God.

DIMENSION THREE: WHAT DOES THE BIBLE MEAN TO ME?

Joshua 1:1-18—Passing on Leadership

The Bible constantly calls persons to various forms of loyalty. The Hebrew word that is usually translated *steadfast love* is the primary biblical word for this concept. One is supposed to be loyal to, or show steadfast love toward, family, friends, and of course, God. But the Bible realizes that loyalties often conflict. Many stories deal with problems of conflicting loyalties and how persons should choose between them. Abraham must choose God over his beloved son Isaac (Genesis 22:1-19). Jesus warns us that we might have to choose God over our family (Matthew 10:21-22). Jonathan was forced to choose his friendship to David over his loyalty to his father Saul (1 Samuel 20:30-42).

The problem of loyalty to the political leadership of the state is dealt with differently at different points in the Bible. In 2 Samuel 17:1-23 we find that a rebellion against God's chosen David fails. Ahithophel, David's rebellious counselor, realizing the revolt is marked for failure, commits suicide. On the other hand, the prophet Elisha sends a representative to anoint Jehu to rebel against the current ruling house (2 Kings 9:4-7). The Bible stresses loyalty toward leaders (see Romans 13:1-7), but only if they maintain their loyalty to God. Jesus' statement, "Give to Caesar what is Caesar's and to God what is God's" (Mark 12:17), emphasizes the point that our ultimate loyalty must go to God.

Joshua 2:1-14—God's Unattractive People

To prepare for this section you might want to examine Jesus' interesting habit of using disreputable people as examples in his parables. The clearest example is the parable of the shrewd manager in Luke 16:1-9. The manager, who is about to lose his job, does what he must to prepare for the future. He cheats his boss, and for this he is commended. Rahab's story is similar. As a native of the land she should die, but she betrays her people and is saved by affirming her faith in the Lord.

The Samaritan (Luke 10:29-37), the unrighteous judge (Luke 18:1-7), the tax collector (Luke 18:9-14), and Lazarus (Luke 16:19-31) were all unsavory people in Jesus' day, yet he uses them as heroes in his stories. As Matthew 11:19 affirms, Jesus' reputation was that of "a glutton and a drunkard, a friend of tax collectors and sinners."

Perhaps the best story from Jesus' ministry that deals with the questions raised in this section is that of the sinful woman who anoints his feet (Luke 7:36-50). Jesus' words in this story should help class members understand why the irreligious rather than the religious respond to God's call.

Joshua 3:1-6—Sanctity and Wonders

You might want to concentrate on the questions in the student book for this section. Ask for specific answers from the group and stress practical answers to the last two questions. Perhaps the class members can give helpful suggestions to one another on how to prepare to encounter God daily and in the church.

Joshua 3:7-17—Effects, Not Miracles

To prepare for this discussion, you might want to look at Jesus' views toward what we call miracles, but what the Bible calls signs. Jesus refused to use miracles to prove who he was. When people asked him to do so, he rejected them, sometimes violently: "A wicked and adulterous generation asks for a miraculous sign" (Matthew 12:39).

Jesus saw that miracles might result in the wrong response. In John 6:26, Jesus accuses the crowd of seeking him, not because they saw in his actions signs pointing to God, but "because you ate the loaves and had your fill." In Jesus' confrontation with the doubting Thomas, we see most clearly that a faith built only on miracles is weaker than a faith built on trust alone. "Blessed are those who have not seen and yet have believed" (John 20:29).

Close today's session by listing on chalkboard or a large sheet of paper any new insights the class members share from their study of Joshua 1–3.

2

The Battle of Jericho

Joshua 4–6

DIMENSION ONE:
WHAT DOES THE BIBLE SAY?

Answer these questions by reading Joshua 4

1. What does the Lord tell Joshua he wants the twelve men, one from each tribe, to do? (Joshua 4:3)

   They are to take up twelve stones from the riverbed and carry them over to their camp.

2. What is the purpose of the stones? (Joshua 4:6-7)

   The stones will be a sign for Israel's children to remember how the Lord cut off the waters of the Jordan.

3. What does Joshua set up in the midst of the Jordan? (Joshua 4:9)

   Joshua sets up twelve stones in the midst of the Jordan.

4. How do the people feel toward Joshua after the crossing? (Joshua 4:14)

   The people revere Joshua, just as they revered Moses.

5. What happens after the priests bearing the ark come up out of the riverbed? (Joshua 4:18)

   The waters of the Jordan return to flood stage as before.

6. Where do the people camp after crossing the Jordan? (Joshua 4:19)

   The people camp in Gilgal on the eastern border of Jericho.

7. Why does Joshua set up the twelve stones? (Joshua 4:20-24)

   Joshua sets up the stones as a sign to Israel that God dried up the Jordan and as a sign to all the peoples that the hand of the Lord is powerful.

Answer these questions by reading Joshua 5

8. How do the kings of the Amorites and Canaanites react after they hear about the Israelites crossing the Jordan? (Joshua 5:1)

   Their hearts melt and they no longer have the courage to face the Israelites.

9. Why does Joshua circumcise all the male Israelites at this time? (Joshua 5:3-5)

   None of the people who had been born in the desert after the Exodus have been circumcised.

10. Why is the place of the Israelite camp called Gilgal? (Joshua 5:9)

    The place receives its name because that is where the Lord "rolled away the reproach of Egypt" from Israel.

11. What religious festival do the Israelites keep at Gilgal? (Joshua 5:10)

    They celebrate the Passover on the fourteenth day of the month.

12. What happens the day after this festival? (Joshua 5:11-12)

    The manna ceases and the Israelites eat the produce of the land.

13. Whom does Joshua meet when he is near Jericho? (Joshua 5:13-14)

    Joshua meets the commander of the army of the Lord.

Answer these questions by reading Joshua 6

14. What does the Lord say to Joshua about Jericho? (Joshua 6:2)

    The Lord says Jericho, its king, and its mighty men are delivered into Joshua's hand.

THE BATTLE OF JERICHO

15. What part do the priests play in taking Jericho? (Joshua 6:4)

Seven priests, each blowing a trumpet of a ram's horn, will go ahead of the ark on its march seven times around Jericho.

16. How do the people participate in Jericho's capture? (Joshua 6:5, 20)

After the seventh circle of Jericho on the seventh day, the priests make a long blast with their horns. The people then shout and go over the fallen walls.

17. Where is the ark of the Lord during the march around the city? (Joshua 6:12-13)

The ark of the Lord holds the central position with priests and armed men before it and the rear guard following it.

18. What does Joshua command the people to do after the seventh circle of Jericho on the seventh day? (Joshua 6:16-17)

The people are to shout and then destroy all that is within the city except Rahab and her household.

19. What does Joshua warn will happen if anyone takes something devoted to destruction? (Joshua 6:18)

He or she will bring trouble upon the camp of Israel.

20. What do the Israelites do when Jericho's walls fall down flat? (Joshua 6:20-21)

They utterly destroy every living thing in the city, human and animal.

21. Who survives Jericho's fall? (Joshua 6:22-23)

Rahab, the prostitute, and all who belong to her survive the destruction of Jericho.

22. How do the Israelites complete their conquest of Jericho? (Joshua 6:24)

They burn the city and all within it, sparing only the silver, gold, bronze, and iron articles for the treasury of the Lord's house.

23. What curse does Joshua speak over Jericho's ruins? (Joshua 6:26-27)

Joshua curses whoever would rebuild Jericho with the loss of his children.

DIMENSION TWO:
WHAT DOES THE BIBLE MEAN?

Joshua 4:2-7. This section shows the contrast between God's command and how Joshua carries out the command. God simply orders the twelve tribal representatives each to carry a stone from the riverbed to that night's camp. Joshua communicates God's command to the people. Then, as we have seen before, he goes beyond the words God speaks and explains the reason for God's command. Here we find the third reason for the crossing (compare last week's lesson on 3:7-13). The crossing is not just for this generation, but for all generations of Israelites. The reasons for collecting the stones is so that Israel will have a visible monument forever to remind her of what God did for her. Later in verses 21-24 of this chapter, Joshua will extend the meaning of the monument and add a fourth reason for the crossing.

Joshua 4:9. Joshua sets up a second monument of twelve stones in the riverbed to eventually be covered by water. Strangely, no reason is given for this monument. Perhaps Joshua erects this monument as a further extension of God's commands. The reasons for the monument in the camp, then, also apply to the monument in the waters.

This verse makes the point that this set of stones in the river is still in place "to this day." Scholars call a notation that explains an object's or custom's origin an *etiology*. The Book of Joshua contains several etiologies (see 6:25; 7:26; 8:28; 10:27).

Probably by the time the Book of Joshua was written (about 550 B.C.) there was no longer a sanctuary or monument at Gilgal. Only the monument in the Jordan River remained. After discovering the Book of the Law of God in 621 B.C., King Josiah destroyed all places of worship outside of Jerusalem in an attempt to reform the religious customs in his kingdom. (See 2 Kings 22–23.) So the significance of the original monument at Gilgal is transferred to the stones set up in the Jordan.

Joshua 4:10-13. After all the people cross over, the priests carrying the ark move again into the lead. The tribes of Reuben, Gad, and the half-tribe of Manasseh lead the people up out of the riverbed and into the Promised Land.

A unified Israel participates in the conquest, including those tribes that had already gained their land. An emphasis on unity is important in the Deuteronomic history, since by 550 B.C. when the history was written many of Israel's original twelve tribes had been destroyed. The northern tribes disappear after the fall of the Northern Kingdom in 722 B.C. Only the tribe of Judah, part of Benjamin, and part of Levi remained, and they were scattered outside Palestine after the fall of Jerusalem in 587 B.C. The other tribes are called the ten lost tribes of Israel, since no one knows exactly what happened to them. In a time when disunity reigned, the Deuteronomic history proclaims the unity of all who worship Yahweh.

Joshua 4:18. After the crossing, the waters return to their seasonal flooding. Several indirect references are made to springtime at the beginning of the conquest: the drying flax on Rahab's roof (2:6), the flooded Jordan and the mention of harvest time (3:15), and the return to flooding after the crossing (4:18). Flax is harvested in March and April. Spring is also the normal time for military campaigns to begin. The crossing and the conquest are symbolically tied to Passover, the central spring festival (see 5:10-11). God's grace shown in the crossing and the conquest is paralleled with God's greatest act of grace for Israel—freedom from slavery in Egypt.

Joshua 4:19-20. In 5:9 *Gilgal* will be tied with the Hebrew word for "roll, turn over." However, scholars think Gilgal originally meant "circle" (obviously related to the word *roll*) and referred to the twelve stones set up in a circular pattern. Gilgal apparently stood on the eastern edge of the territory surrounding the city-state of Jericho. Gilgal will remain the base of operations throughout the conquest, even though Israel would be expected to choose a more central location in the land after her initial victories.

Joshua 4:20-24. Finally we arrive at the event that is receiving so much emphasis—setting up the stones at Gilgal. Notice the interesting way the story has developed to this point. In 3:12 twelve men, one from each tribe, are chosen; but there is no explanation of what they will do or why. Later in 4:2-7, the "what" (they will take twelve stones from the riverbed) and the "why" (the stones will be a sign to the children of Israel) are divulged. In 4:8 the men take the stones to Gilgal. Finally, in 4:20-24, Joshua finishes the task by setting up the stones and again explains their meaning. Still another addition is made when Joshua says that the monument is not only a sign for Israel, but for all the peoples of the earth. The story begins with a hint about some task to be done, then states what will be done and why, and finally the reason for the action is emphasized and extended.

Joshua proclaims that the stones carry a double significance. The stones are to remind Israel of God's saving grace shown in the fulfillment of the promise and to remind other nations of God's power over the world. Fear, in the sense of reverence and awe, results for both Israel and the people of the world. The monument will force them to remember God's saving power in the crossing of the Jordan.

Joshua 5:1. The crossing accomplishes God's purpose. The Amorites and the Canaanites, inhabitants of the land, lose their courage. You might note how closely this parallels Rahab's words in 2:9, 11.

Joshua 5:4-9. You might want to review with the group the origin of circumcision for Jews. Genesis 17:9-14 explains that circumcision is the sign of the covenant between God and the Jews. Any descendant of Abraham who is not circumcised is separated from his people and has broken God's covenant. Exodus 12:43-49 requires circumcision of all who would participate in Israel's celebration of the Passover.

In light of this strong tradition that all descendants of Abraham be circumcised, it is surprising to discover that no males born in the desert had been circumcised. Although this tradition is given as the explanation for why Joshua had to circumcise all the men before they could participate in Passover, it does not explain why the men had not been circumcised when they were eight days old.

Perhaps the reason is evident in the Israelites' understanding of their desert experience. Those who witnessed the destruction of the Egyptian army still did not trust God enough to be certain of their victory in the Promised Land. Numbers 14:3-4 states they were even ready to return to Egypt. Because of their lack of faith, God condemned the people to wander in the desert for forty years until this first generation had died.

For Israel, then, the desert was a place of sin and a sign of her breaking faith with God. Perhaps because they were born in a time when their relationship with God was broken and they were being punished, those born in the desert were not circumcised. Only when the punishment was past and God again began to fulfill the promise of land did it seem appropriate for the men to take on the sign of the covenant their parents had broken. In the crossing of the Jordan, God signals continuance of the covenant with Israel. In response, the Israelites too perform a sign. They again accept their covenant obligations.

Joshua 5:10-12. Now that the covenant is fully restored, the people participate in the first Passover held in the Promised Land. The Bible encloses Israel's total experience in the desert with a sort of symbolic parenthesis formed by the celebration of Passover. In the first Passover, God acts to free the Israelites from slavery. They are led out of Egypt, and the dramatic crossing of the Red Sea reveals God's power to save. Now the end of the period in the desert comes with crossing the Jordan River at full flood. Now Israel again accepts her obligation of faith and celebrates the Passover.

Joshua 5:13–6:5. Joshua encounters the commander of the Lord's army and receives instructions on how the people may participate in the destruction of Jericho. Before he knows who confronts him, Joshua asks the man whether he is "for us or for our enemies."

God's commands to Israel make it clear that Jericho will not be taken by military means. The divine commander does not communicate strategy or tactics. Rather, he tells Israel how to share in the divine act. God has already promised the city will be given to them. The people are primarily called upon to witness what God does.

Two ritual aspects of the crossing reappear here—the priests and the ark. Two additional elements appear—the rams' horns and the use of the number seven. Trumpets of rams' horns are primarily signaling instruments, rather than musical instruments. (The Hebrew word is the same for both.) They announce the beginning of important religious times like new moon and full moon (Psalm 81:3) and the Year of Jubilee (Leviticus 25:9). They serve an important function in the holy war tradition here and elsewhere (see Judges 3:27; 7:20, 22).

Joshua 6:17-25. Most modern readers of the Bible have trouble dealing with the aftermath of the fall of Jericho. The devotion of all captured people and goods to God by destroying them (the ban) strikes many of us as barbaric. Since this element of holy war will be so predominant in the books of Joshua and Judges, we must clearly understand what is happening with the ban. Perhaps by understanding (1) what ancient culture's attitude toward defeat in war meant, (2) the biblical reasons for enacting the ban, and (3) the element of mercy that overrides the ban, the group can better deal with this difficult tradition.

(1) In the warfare of this period, defeat usually meant death. Archaeologists have found many pictures of Egyptian and Assyrian kings ritually killing defeated and captured enemies. A king of Moab, Israel's southeastern neighbor, left an inscription boasting that he totally destroyed several Israelite cities.

Apparently, the whole ancient Near Eastern culture held the belief that defeat meant death. So in part, Israel's destruction of her defeated enemies was an idea shared with the wider pagan culture and was not unique to Israel.

(2) Israel, unlike her neighbors, believed that defeat and death in war came as the result of sin. Deuteronomy 9:4-5 clearly explains that God uses Israel in the conquest to punish the wickedness of those people living in the land. Wickedness calls for judgment, according to the Bible. So God does not arbitrarily call for the destruction of the Canaanites. God calls for their destruction as just punishment for their evil.

To complete our understanding of the moral judgment enacted in the ban, we need to look beyond the Book of Joshua to the whole Deuteronomic history. According to the literary work of which Joshua is only a part, Israel will not escape the same judgment as the Canaanites before her. As Deuteronomy warned and as the rest of the Deuteronomic history portrays, wickedness on Israel's part will result in the same defeat and destruction experienced by the original inhabitants. Second Kings 17:1-23 and 25:1-21 explain how the Northern Kingdom of Israel and the Southern Kingdom of Judah are destroyed because of their immorality and unfaithfulness to God. The Bible sees the ban as God's totally just punishment for evil done by human beings.

(3) In the Bible, God's final word is not judgment, but mercy—even in the stories of the ban found in Joshua and Judges. The total destruction called for by Deuteronomy 20:16-18 never occurs! Not all the inhabitants of Jericho die. Rahab and her family, although officially marked for death, are saved through her faith. This salvation by faith is stressed in the Deuteronomic history. Joshua 2 and 6 devote more space to Rahab's salvation than to Jericho's destruction. The importance of God's mercy rather than judgment is noted by the fact that Rahab's family still resides in Israel "to this day." Her family becomes a living sign of God's mercy, just as the stones in the Jordan stand as a sign of God's grace.

DIMENSION THREE: WHAT DOES THE BIBLE MEAN TO ME?

Joshua 4:1-7, 19-24—Signaling God's Deeds

You might want to go through the questions in the student book and concentrate on practical answers. Stress the things we do and say that reveal our faith. We must be cautious about our actions and words that appear religious but do not reveal concern for others. Then pursue the question of whether acts of piety show our faith to others. Jesus warned us against being "like whitewashed tombs, which look beautiful on the outside but on the inside are full of dead men's bones and everything unclean" (Matthew 23:27). How can we truly signal the love we experience for others?

Joshua 5:2-12—Old Signs and New Signs

Many of us like to hold on to the familiar in our lives and often hesitate to accept new ideas or new ways of doing things. "But that's the way we've always done it!" greets almost any attempt to change established practices in any church. In contrast to this view, the Bible says there are times to leave behind even the past revelations of God. Think of Jesus' attacks on the laws concerning the sabbath (Mark 2:27), divorce (Mark 10:11-12), and revenge (Matthew 5:38-39). Building on Jesus' work, Paul proclaims that the law was but a temporary custodian until the coming of Christ (Galatians 3:24-25).

The Bible often portrays the life of faith as a growing process, a journey from spiritual milk to spiritual solids (see Hebrews 5:11-14). Twentieth-century Christianity follows this biblical understanding in its emphasis that the experience of grace is only the starting point for a growing faith relationship with God. Our task now is to "go on to perfection," to strive toward the total sanctification of our lives.

As we grow in our faith, those things that supported our faith in its infancy must be put aside. As we become more mature in our faith we must give up childish ways (see 1 Corinthians 13:11). In John 6:31-33, the people demand that Jesus give them manna from heaven. Jesus rejects this demand, saying the time for old signs is past. In light of this biblical understanding of faith as growth or movement, you might want to discuss with the group ways to see God's ever new revelations.

Joshua 6:15-21—Devoted to the Lord

You will probably want to explore in depth the group's feelings toward holy war. As the leader, try to help them avoid misunderstanding what the Bible says. Much of the information in Dimension Two on Joshua 6:17-25 should help you at this point.

Once you think the group has an understanding of the reasons for the ban, you might want to explore the questions about whether or not we are religious for gain. In Matthew 6:2-6, Jesus implies that those who are religious for public display have missed the true reward from God. In the parable of the sheep and the goats, those who are rewarded had not been seeking reward for their good deeds (Matthew 25:31-46).

Paul also insists that even the greatest acts of faith done for the wrong reason are worthless (1 Corinthians 13:1-3). The Bible affirms that we are called to absolute loyalty to God alone. All selfish thoughts or barriers to this total commitment to God must be removed from our lives (see Mark 10:21).

Joshua 6:21-25—Mercy in the Face of Judgment

Although many in your group may disagree with the way Jericho is judged for its wickedness, you may want to explore how often we also harshly judge those with whom we disagree. The story of Jericho emphasizes the mercy shown to Rahab because of her present faith, not judgment on her past life. We find this theme quite often in the stories about Jesus. Although he condemned divorce (Mark 10:11), when he meets a divorced woman he does not condemn her (see John 4:16-18). When the woman taken in adultery is brought to him, he explicitly states, "Neither do I condemn you" (John 8:11). How often do we truly show mercy as Jesus did? When have we forgotten his injunction, "Do not judge, or you too will be judged" (Matthew 7:1)? God's final word is mercy, even in judgment. How can we visibly extend mercy to those we have judged?

Close the session by asking the group members what new insights they have learned about Joshua 4–6. List these insights on chalkboard or a large sheet of paper if time allows.

3

The Sin of Achan

Joshua 7–8

**DIMENSION ONE:
WHAT DOES THE BIBLE SAY?**

Answer these questions by reading Joshua 7

1. Why does the Lord's anger burn against the people of Israel? (Joshua 7:1)

   The people of Israel have broken faith. Achan took some devoted things.

2. Where does Joshua send the spies? (Joshua 7:2)

   He sends them to Ai, which is near Beth Aven, east of Bethel.

3. What do the spies report to Joshua? (Joshua 7:3)

   They report that only two or three thousand men are necessary to attack the few people in Ai.

4. What is the outcome of the first attack on Ai? (Joshua 7:4-5)

   Thirty-six Israelites are killed, and the remainder flee before the men of Ai.

5. What does Joshua ask the Lord after the attack? (Joshua 7:7-9)

   He asks why God brought Israel over the Jordan to be destroyed by the Amorites.

6. How does the Lord answer Joshua? (Joshua 7:11-12)

   The Lord says Israel cannot stand before her enemies because of her sin of stealing devoted things.

7. What does the Lord command the Israelites to do the next day? (Joshua 7:13-14)

   After consecrating themselves, the Israelites shall be brought before the Lord who will then choose first the guilty tribe, then family, then household, and finally the guilty person.

8. What will happen to the person who has taken devoted things? (Joshua 7:15)

   The person and all that he has shall be destroyed by fire.

9. Who is identified as the guilty person? (Joshua 7:18)

   "Achan son of Carmi, the son of Zimri, the son of Zerah, of the tribe of Judah" is identified as the guilty person.

10. What does Joshua ask Achan to do? (Joshua 7:19)

    Joshua asks Achan to give glory to the Lord God of Israel and to confess what he has done.

11. How is Achan punished? (Joshua 7:24-25)

    Achan, his family, his goods, and the stolen things are all stoned; and then they are burned.

12. What happens after Achan is punished? (Joshua 7:26)

    The Lord turns away from "his fierce anger."

Answer these questions by reading Joshua 8

13. After the punishment, what does the Lord say to Joshua? (Joshua 8:1-2)

    Joshua should not be afraid. He should take all the fighting men up to Ai and do to it as he did to Jericho.

14. What does Joshua tell the mighty men of valor to do? (Joshua 8:3-8)

    The men will lie in ambush behind the city. The others will approach the city and flee from the men of Ai. Then those in ambush will seize the city and set it on fire.

15. How does Joshua signal the moment of ambush? (Joshua 8:18)

    Joshua holds out his javelin toward the city of Ai.

16. Why don't the men of Ai flee when they see their city on fire? (Joshua 8:20-21)

They cannot flee because they are caught between their captured city and the people they were chasing.

17. How is the ban applied to Ai? (Joshua 8:25-27)

Israel destroys all the inhabitants of Ai, but keeps the livestock and plunder.

18. What does Joshua do with the king of Ai? (Joshua 8:29)

Joshua hangs the king of Ai on a tree until evening, then buries him under a large pile of rocks at the entrance of the city gate.

19. Where does Joshua build an altar to the Lord? (Joshua 8:30)

Joshua builds an altar to the Lord on Mount Ebal.

20. What does Joshua write on the stones of the altar? (Joshua 8:32)

Joshua writes upon the stones a copy of the law of Moses.

21. Where do the people stand to receive the blessings from the priests? (Joshua 8:33)

Half of Israel stands on one side of the ark of the covenant in front of Mount Gerizim; the other half stands on the other side of the ark in front of Mount Ebal.

22. What does Joshua do in the presence of all the people? (Joshua 8:34)

Joshua reads all of the law written in the Book of the Law.

23. Who hears all the words read by Joshua? (Joshua 8:35)

All the assembly of Israel, including the women, the children, and the aliens, hear Joshua read.

DIMENSION TWO: WHAT DOES THE BIBLE MEAN?

Joshua 7:1. This verse, an introduction to the story of Achan, serves several narrative functions. First, it ties this story with what has gone before. This verse also reminds us of the warning in 6:18 against stealing things devoted to God and bringing trouble upon Israel. By relating that Israel breaks the covenant because of Achan's theft, this verse also signals the reader early why the defeat at Ai takes place in 7:2-5. Finally, naming Achan in this way foreshadows the events that will be described in 7:14-18.

Joshua 7:2-5. The defeat at Ai reveals the results of human action without God's guidance. Joshua and Israel act without first waiting for the Lord to speak. They do not even consult God. On his own, Joshua sends spies to Ai, which again reveals a certain lack of faith. (Note the comments on Joshua 2:1 [first paragraph] in Lesson 1 of this teacher book.) These spies return with the human military assessment of the situation that only two or three thousand men will be needed to take the city.

Rather than depending on God's guidance and actions, Israel depends on her own resources. The result is defeat. The men of Ai easily drive off the Israelites. While the loss of thirty-six men is not that great out of a force of three thousand, the unexpected experience of defeat shatters Israel's confidence. Now their hearts melt as the hearts of the natives of the land had melted previously (see 2:11; 5:1).

Because of the detailed discussion of geography found in 7:2 and 8:10-15, we can locate Ai with certainty at the modern site of *et Tel.* This name means "the ruin" in Arabic and Hebrew. Archaeological excavations at Ai have uncovered evidence that proves troubling to many persons. There was a town on the site of Ai from about 3300 to 2400 B.C. From that time on, no one lived at Ai until some Israelites settled there between 1100 and 900 B.C. No evidence has been found that anyone lived at Ai during the period of Joshua (1250–1225 B.C.). The place was indeed just a ruin when those tribes under Joshua entered the land.

Explaining the story of Ai in relation to the archaeological data is difficult. Some scholars have suggested that the story of Ai really tells about nearby Bethel. Archaeological studies have shown Bethel was destroyed during the time of Joshua (see Judges 1:22-26). However, the description of the ambush really fits only Ai's location. Other scholars have risked saying that no real battle took place at Ai, the ruin. They suggest that later Israelites saw this great ruin and asked how it became destroyed. Having heard stories about the destruction of many cities during the conquest, the Israelites assumed this ruin also resulted from Joshua's actions. Remembering that the Book of Joshua was not written down until 700 years after the events, perhaps we need to be open to the possibility that these stories are not always as accurate about events and locations as we would wish.

Joshua 7:6-9. Although he is the successor to Moses' leadership, Joshua does not share Moses' strength of faith. Here Joshua accuses the Lord of trying to destroy Israel. His words here are similar to the words spoken by the people, in Deuteronomy 1:27-28, when they first hear about the inhabitants of the Promised Land. You might want to read these verses from Deuteronomy aloud so the group can see the relationship.

In Deuteronomy, Moses tells the people to trust in God when they speak these words (Deuteronomy 1:29-31). On the other hand, Joshua, the Lord's chosen leader, declares the words of unfaithfulness himself. Ironically, Joshua's name means "Yahweh is salvation."

Joshua 7:10-18. God refuses to accept the blame for the defeat, claiming to have upheld the covenant. Israel cannot assume that God has let her down and cannot plead ignorance. The people were warned ahead of time about the consequences of taking objects devoted to destruction (6:18). Israel has broken the covenant.

Israel believed that guilt for an evil act extended beyond the individual responsible. Each Israelite saw herself or himself as part of a larger whole, a cell in a larger organism. If asked who they were, Israelites would give their name, but they would also explain to which family, clan, tribe, and people they belonged. Where we find our identity in what sets us apart from others, Israelites found theirs in what bound them together. Israel believed very real bonds tied the individual to the group and the group to the individual. So the consequences of a person's acts never affected only that individual. Others were always affected.

Another important belief of Israel is that God's power is vividly real. We discussed earlier, in relation to the ark of the covenant, Israel's belief in holiness as raw power. (See Lesson 1 on Joshua 3:3-6.) Any unprepared person who came in direct contact with a holy object was drawn into the object's purpose. Achan, by stealing things that were given over to God for destruction, becomes a thing for destruction and causes all of Israel to become a thing for destruction, too. Only by isolating and destroying the stolen goods and the thief will Israel be cleansed.

Although this concept may be difficult to understand, it was Israel's way of affirming that God is to be taken seriously. The Lord is real, holy, and powerful. The person who does not act accordingly cuts himself or herself off from God and the community.

Verses 14-18 describe a process of judging the guilty party from among all the people. As the people processed by, dice were used to determine who was guilty. The guilty is "taken." The idea that a person's life could depend on dice may also strike us as strange. Many of us would see throwing dice to determine the guilty person as only a matter of blind chance. Israel sees nothing arising from chance, but believes that ultimately God directs everything. Thus for Israel, the sacred lot (dice, probably two colored stones called the Urim and Thummim) cast by God's appointed priest shows the direction of the Lord.

For Israel, God uses the lot mainly to reveal those things hidden from human eyes. Many deeds, especially evil deeds, are done in secret. Therefore, only God, who knows all secrets, can know what happened. (See Deuteronomy 29:29; Jeremiah 23:24; Psalm 44:21; Hebrews 4:12-13.) God alone can ensure that evil deeds do not go unpunished. (See Ecclesiastes 12:14; Romans 2:16.) By the lot, God reveals what was done in secret so that the people can make the appropriate response. In conclusion, the sacred lot declares Israel's faith that God not only directs her but intervenes when necessary to make sure justice is done.

Joshua 7:19-22. Joshua calls upon Achan to give glory and praise to the Lord for bringing his secret deed to light. Asking the sinner to give glory to God for discovering and punishing his sin seems cruel. However, Israel sees the request as an opportunity for the guilty person to proclaim God's faithfulness even to the sinner. God shows loyalty to Achan, not by ignoring his evil deed, but by exposing it. No favor is done by letting a person get away with doing wrong. Only exposing and punishing the wrong action can counter the evil done to the covenant community. Achan, as part of the community, praises God for separating evil from Israel, even when that evil is himself.

Joshua 7:23-26. As we have seen before, a visible sign—a large pile of rocks—marks "to this day" where Achan and his family are buried in the Valley of Achor. The Promised Land seems studded with monuments. Here the stones are a sign proclaiming God's justice, just as the stones from the Jordan reveal God's grace, and Rahab's family, God's mercy.

Joshua 8:1-2. You might want to point out to the group the standard phrases from the holy war tradition that appear here: "Do not be afraid," "Do not be discouraged." (see Deuteronomy 20:3; Joshua 1:9; 10:8, 25; 11:6), and "I have delivered [it] into your hands" (see Joshua 2:24; 6:2; 10:8, 19; Judges 3:28). These phrases reveal the kind of faith God calls Israel to have—total trust in the Lord.

As the student book notes, here is a departure from the total imposition of the ban. (You might want to review Lesson 2, page 198, on Joshua 6:17-25 for the meaning of the ban in Israel.) Through the first several encounters with the natives of the land, we can notice a movement away from the total destruction called for in Deuteronomy 20:16-18. At Jericho everything and everybody was destroyed except Rahab and her family. Now at Ai, the people are killed, but the livestock and goods are spared. In the encounter with Gibeon (Chapter 9), people, livestock, and goods will all escape destruction.

The ban, for Israel, symbolizes the tension she experiences between God's judgment and God's mercy. We tend to think in either-or terms; God either punishes or forgives. Israel, on the other hand, saw God's justice and mercy as bound mysteriously together. For Israel it was a matter of both. Israel knew the reality of God's punishment of the sinner, and also God's forgiveness of the evildoer. Primarily in her experience of the ban, Israel came to understand the unity of punishment and forgiveness. God declared total destruction as just punishment on the wicked inhabitants of the land and even the wicked in Israel. But Israel also knew the ban was never totally carried out. Some of the wicked received mercy. To bring together these two apparently contradictory truths, the Bible affirms that God is merciful when just and just when merciful.

Joshua 8:3-27. The battle for Ai contrasts starkly with the taking of Jericho. At Jericho, God was the only real actor. At Ai the Lord goes underground. On the surface, humans act and win the victory. God participates by blinding the warriors of both Ai and Bethel to the ambush they go through (verse 17) and telling Joshua when to raise his arm (verses 18 and 26). You might want to have the group compare and contrast the battles of Jericho and Ai.

Similarities

	Jericho	*Ai*
Cause:	God's direction (6:2-5)	God's direction (8:1-2)
Leader:	Joshua (6:6-7, 16-19)	Joshua (8:3-8)
Victory:	Total victory (6:20-21)	Total victory (8:24-26)
Outcome:	Some spared (6:25)	Some spared (8:26-27)

Differences

	Jericho	*Ai*
Agent:	Ark and priests (6:6)	Best fighting men (8:3)
Means:	Religious ritual (6:8-15)	Human military acts (8:9-17)
Signal:	Trumpets and shout (6:20)	Joshua's javelin (8:18)
Victory:	Walls fall down (6:20)	Successful ambush, entrapment (8:19-22)
Outcome:	People spared (6:21-25)	Livestock, plunder spared (8:26-27)

Clearly, these two battles have more differences than similarities.

Joshua 8:28-29. Here we read of double monuments: the heap of ruins as the sign of the destruction of Ai, and a large pile of rocks at the entrance to the city marking the grave of its king. Ask the class members what they believe these monuments signify. In light of the parallel with the great pile of rocks in the Valley of Achor, Ai and its king's grave may signify God's justice.

Joshua 8:30-35. Here the action suddenly shifts to Mount Ebal, twenty miles north of Jericho. You might want to trace on a map Israel's movements in these two chapters. The account begins at Jericho. The spies go to Ai and return. Then part of Israel goes up to Ai and is driven back to Jericho in defeat. Then all of Israel goes south of Jericho to the Valley of Achor to bring judgment on Achan. Now, with the covenant restored, 30,000 Israelites go up again against Ai. They capture and destroy the city. Upon achieving this victory, they journey north from Ai to Mount Ebal. All together, well over 100 miles are covered in the space of these two chapters. The beginning of the next chapter finds Israel back at Gilgal, a couple of miles east of Jericho (9:6).

Review for the group the background for these verses, found in Moses' commands in Deuteronomy 27:4–28:6. You might want to look especially at the curses found in Deuteronomy 27:15-26. Note how strongly these curses emphasize God's judgment on evil done in secret. Our major discussion of this ceremony is in Lesson 7. The ceremony is repeated in greater detail in Joshua 24.

DIMENSION THREE: WHAT DOES THE BIBLE MEAN TO ME?

Joshua 7:1-5, 24-26—Evil Affects Others

The comments in Dimension Two on Joshua 7:10-18 should help you in preparing for the discussion on these verses. Work through the questions in the student book with the group, and then shift the discussion toward the positive side of Israel's understanding of the relationship between the individual and the group.

Christianity depends heavily upon this concept for its understanding of the work that Christ accomplishes. Just as one person can pull down the group, so one person can lift the group. Paul stresses this relationship in his comments in 1 Corinthians 15:21-22: "For since death came through a man, the resurrection of the dead comes also through a man. For as in Adam all die, so in Christ all will be made alive." Later, Paul developed this idea further in Romans 5:12-18. Christianity affirms that through the humility, obedience, and death of one man, Jesus Christ, salvation comes.

Paul's image of the church as the body of Christ also depends heavily on this biblical understanding that the individual never stands alone, but always in relationship to others. In his discussion with the Corinthian church over spiritual gifts, Paul stresses that like parts of the body, each Christian contributes his or her gifts to the good of the whole (1 Corinthians 12:12-27). In Ephesians, we find this emphasis again that the faithful are all knit strongly together into one whole, because "we are members of his

[Christ's] body" (Ephesians 5:30). We always remain part of a greater whole and what we do affects that whole.

Joshua 7:6-13—God's Responsibility or Our Own?

From Jesus' ministry we can see the danger of not accepting responsibility for what we do. We cut ourselves off from God and others. The Palestine of Jesus' day was fractured into various groups, each claiming to be right and accusing the others of preventing God's kingdom from coming. The Pharisees believed that if every Jew would keep the law for one day, God would send salvation. Because they were so sure that people like Jesus, who broke the law (see Mark 3:1-6), were to blame, the Pharisees were blinded to their own opposition to God's will (see Mark 7:8-13).

The Sadducees thought things were satisfactory as they were, so it was better "that one man die for the people than that the whole nation perish" (John 11:50). By blaming Jesus for their problems they missed seeing who Jesus was. Jesus tried to counter this human tendency to blame outside causes for all evil and uncleanness by pointing out: "For from within, out of men's hearts, come evil thoughts, sexual immorality, theft, murder, adultery, greed, malice, deceit, lewdness, envy, slander, arrogance and folly. All these evils come from inside and make a 'man unclean' " (Mark 7:21-23). Only by assuming responsibility for evil can we hope to cleanse ourselves and tear down the barriers that separate us from God and others.

Joshua 8:14-29—Ambushed by God

You might want to develop the discussion along one of two lines—personal or theological. With the first, have the group discuss the dangers of each person's racial, sexual, or social prejudices. You might research whether your church or denomination has an official position on these issues and if so present it to the group. How do they feel about these positions?

Theologically, you might want to develop the question of whether we get so comfortable with the gospel through the long hearing of it that we miss its power to shock. Are we so sure we know what Jesus meant, that we actually miss the sharpness of some of his statements? In the end, we cannot really blunt such words as "it is easier for a camel to go through the eye of a needle than for a rich man to enter the kingdom of God" (Luke 18:25), or "let the dead bury their own dead" (Luke 9:60), or "anyone who loves his father or mother more than me is not worthy of me; anyone who loves his son or daughter more than me is not worthy of me" (Matthew 10:37).

Even as longtime church-goers, we need to watch for God's will expressed in unexpected ways. We need to remember that Jesus did not come as the Messiah everyone expected. As Paul says, he came to the cross as "a stumbling block to Jews and foolishness to Gentiles. . . . For the foolishness of God is wiser than man's wisdom, and the weakness of God is stronger than man's strength" (1 Corinthians 1:23, 25). Ask the class members to share their experiences of God that came in unexpected ways. Emphasize that we need to be conscious of the weakness of our own prejudices so that we do not stumble over God's will for us.

Close today's session by asking the class members to reflect on any new insights they have gained from their study of Joshua 7–8. If time allows, list these insights on chalkboard or on a large sheet of paper so you and they may refer to them at a later date.

These are the kings of the land whom the Israelites had defeated . . . thirty-one kings in all (12:1, 24).

— 4 —
Joshua Defeats the Kings

Joshua 9–12

DIMENSION ONE:
WHAT DOES THE BIBLE SAY?

Answer these questions by reading Joshua 9

1. What do the kings in the hill country and the coastlands do? (Joshua 9:1-2)

   The kings gather together to fight Joshua and Israel.

2. How do the inhabitants of Gibeon act when they hear what Israel did to Jericho and Ai? (Joshua 9:3-6)

   The Gibeonites go to Israel's camp at Gilgal deceitfully dressed in worn-out clothes with dry and moldy provisions.

3. What do the Gibeonites ask Israel? (Joshua 9:6)

   They ask Israel to make a treaty with them.

4. How do the Gibeonites trick Israel? (Joshua 9:9-13)

   They claim they are from a distant country. They show their worn-out clothes and their old provisions and say they were new and fresh when they left home.

5. How does Israel respond to the Gibeonite request? (Joshua 9:14-15)

   Without asking direction from the Lord, Israel makes a peace treaty with Gibeon.

6. Why don't the Israelites kill the Gibeonites when they learn about the trick? (Joshua 9:18-20)

   They do not kill the Gibeonites because they have sworn an oath to them.

7. How does Joshua curse Gibeon? (Joshua 9:23)

   He declares that they shall always be woodcutters and water carriers for the house of God.

8. How do the Gibeonites explain their deceit? (Joshua 9:24)

   The Gibeonites know the power and will of God and are afraid of the Israelites.

Answer these questions by reading Joshua 10

9. What does Adoni-Zedek, king of Jerusalem, do when he hears about Jericho, Ai, and Gibeon? (Joshua 10:1-5)

   He unites with four other Amorite kings to attack Gibeon.

10. How does Israel respond to Gibeon's call for help? (Joshua 10:7-9)

    Israel's army marches all night to come to Gibeon's rescue.

11. What happens to Adoni-Zedek's army when Joshua's army appears at Gibeon? (Joshua 10:10)

    The Lord throws Adoni-Zedek's force into a confusion and the Israelites defeat them.

12. What happens as they flee? (Joshua 10:11)

    The Lord throws large hailstones from the sky on them and they die.

13. How does the Lord mark the day the Amorites are given over to the men of Israel? (Joshua 10:12-14)

    The Lord has the sun stand still and the moon stop.

14. Where do the five kings go after they are defeated? (Joshua 10:16-18)

    The five kings flee to the cave at Makkedah where they are trapped by Joshua.

15. After slaughtering the enemy soldiers, what does Joshua do to the five captured kings? (Joshua 10:24-26)

    After the army commanders put their feet on the necks of the kings, the kings are killed and hung on five trees.

16. What are the names of the towns Joshua captures after the battle at Gibeon? (Joshua 10:28-39)

Joshua captures Makkedah, Libnah, Lachish, Eglon, Hebron, and Debir.

17. What is the outcome of Joshua's campaign in the southern part of the Promised Land? (Joshua 10:40-42)

Joshua defeats the whole land and all its kings.

Answer these questions by reading Joshua 11

18. How do the kings in the northern hill country respond to Joshua's victories in the south? (Joshua 11:4-5)

They come out with all their troops and join to fight Israel.

19. What happens by the Waters of Merom? (Joshua 11:7-9)

Joshua suddenly attacks the army of the northern kings and slays them all.

20. How is Hazor treated differently from the other northern cities captured by Joshua? (Joshua 11:13)

While all the cities are destroyed, only Hazor is burned with fire.

21. Why does the Lord harden the hearts of the natives of the land? (Joshua 11:20)

The Lord hardens their hearts so they will fight Israel and be destroyed.

22. What is the outcome of all of Joshua's conquests in the Promised Land? (Joshua 11:23)

Joshua takes the entire land as commanded, and the land has rest from war.

Answer these questions by reading Joshua 12

23. How many kings do the people of Israel defeat east of the Jordan? (Joshua 12:2, 4)

Israel defeats two kings east of the Jordan, Sihon and Og.

24. How many kings do Joshua and the people defeat west of the Jordan? (Joshua 12:24)

They defeat thirty-one kings west of the Jordan.

DIMENSION TWO: WHAT DOES THE BIBLE SAY?

In the next three lessons we will encounter many place names. You can locate them on a map of Old Testament Palestine found in the back of most Bibles. Or your classroom may have a map of Palestine. Or check your church library for an atlas of the Bible. The class members will understand the movements involved better if they can see them on a map.

Joshua 9:1-2. For information on this list of natives of the Promised Land see the notes on Joshua 3:10 in Lesson 1 of this teacher book (page 193).

Joshua 9:3-7. To save themselves from death, the Gibeonites try to trick the Israelites. By making Israel believe they come from another country, the Gibeonites hope Israel will make a treaty with them. Earlier, Rahab, another native of the land, had become part of the covenant community through her kind deeds. The Gibeonites, perhaps mimicking Israel's trickery at Ai, try to fool Israel into allowing them to live.

You might want to remind the group of other deceits in Israel's history. Abraham tricks Pharaoh and Abimelech into believing his wife Sarah is his sister. Then after receiving many goods from these kings, Abraham reclaims his wife with God's help (Genesis 12:10–31:1; 20:1-18). Isaac also used the same trick on Abimelech (Genesis 26:6-11). Jacob, who was renamed Israel and became father of the twelve tribes, is the trickster *par excellence.* His very name means "the supplanter" or "the trickster." This roguish patriarch tricks his brother Esau out of his birthright (Genesis 25:29-34). He even fools his blind old father into giving him the blessing that Isaac intended for Esau (Genesis 27:1-45). Perhaps Gibeon thinks that Israel, who had tricked so many others, would ultimately accept a people who gained entrance into her ranks through trickery.

Joshua 9:8-11. The type of treaty Gibeon offers Israel parallels the type Israel has with the Lord. As you will probably remember, at Mount Sinai the Lord's claim to rule over Israel was based on God's saving her from Egyptian slavery. Israel, in response, took on the role of a servant people dedicated to following God's will (see Exodus 19–20).

Scholars are familiar with this type of agreement from various ancient treaties. They call it a *suzerainty covenant,* because it involves a suzerain, or overlord, and a vassal, or servant. This type of covenant takes place between a dominant party and an inferior party.

Joshua 9:12-15. The offer of bread and wine to seal the treaty comes from the Gibeonites. The meal seals the treaty. This meal between Gibeon and Israel parallels the type of covenant meal found in Exodus 24:9-11. Accepting food from someone results in an obligation to protect that person. The Lord's acceptance of the sacrifice at Sinai signals acceptance of all the obligations in being Israel's God. Likewise, Israel's eating of Gibeon's bread and wine marks her acceptance under oath of the role of Gibeon's defender.

Joshua 9:16-27. You will want to review Lesson 1 (teacher book, page 192) on Joshua 2:15-21 on the importance of oaths in Israel. You might use a map or atlas to show the group the positions of Gilgal and Gibeon.

Israel discovers Gibeon's lie; we do not know how. We do see how the community of Israel is affected—unity is strained. The people murmur against their leaders, blaming them for being fooled. Interestingly, Joshua is not singled out as being responsible.

This disruption results from Israel's refusal to ask direction from the Lord. The Bible emphasizes over and over that, when people turn from depending on God to depending on themselves, human relationships suffer. This problem is portrayed right at the beginning of the Bible with the story of Adam and Eve. The man's first reaction to God's question whether he had eaten from the tree was to separate himself from Eve and pass the blame on to "the woman you put here with me" (Genesis 3:12). Here the outcome of disobedience is a broken relationship not only with God, but with other persons as well.

The story of the tower of Babel graphically portrays this same theme. The people try to build a tower to heaven to guarantee their unity. However, the result of their act was that God confused their language and "scattered them from there over all the earth" (Genesis 11:8).

This motif is also a dominant one in the stories of the desert wandering. In the desert, Israel's lack of trust in the Lord resulted in constant grumbling against Moses' leadership (see Exodus 15:22-24; 16:1-35; 17:1-7). This same community breakdown is evident in the story of Israel's defeat at Ai (Joshua 7). And here in Chapter 9 we again meet a long-standing biblical emphasis: the attempt by persons to depend on themselves disrupts all relationships, human and divine.

The trickster also suffers for his trick. Israel honors her oath and does not destroy Gibeon, but refuses to allow Gibeon full entrance into her covenant community. Joshua applies Gibeon's offer of servanthood literally. The Gibeonites do not totally escape the ban, because Joshua reduces them to slavery and dedicates them to service in God's house.

The Bible notes that the Gibeonites still serve God, even "to this day." You might point out that we have here another monument. However, instead of a physical monument we have a living monument, like Rahab's family. You might note that living monuments, like Rahab's family and the Gibeonites, appear to symbolize God's mercy. Physical monuments, on the other hand, usually point to God's justice.

Joshua 10:1-5. Locate these cities on a map for the group. They are south of Gibeon.

The Book of Joshua portrays the conquest in these stages: (1) a slashing attack into the middle of the country (Chapters 6–9), (2) an assault on the south (Chapter 10), and (3) the overthrow of the north (Chapter 11). The conquest of the south and north are described much more concisely than the conquest of the central section of the country.

Joshua 10:6-14. In response to the call for help, Joshua leads Israel to the defense of the Gibeonite cities. The Lord sanctions this defense as a holy war under divine guidance. The conquest of the south occurs under the greatest signs of the Lord's power portrayed in the book. Each sign becomes more visible and powerful. We barely notice the first sign—the rapid march from Gilgal to Gibeon. Moving an army twenty miles over very mountainous terrain in one night is an astonishing military feat. We can understand why when we compare the three days it took to do the same thing in Joshua 9:17. But this marvelous feat, comparable to Elijah's running seventeen miles before Ahab's chariot (1 Kings 18:41-46), goes unstressed. God's use of power at first goes unnoticed.

The second sign is more visible. The enemy troops are thrown into confusion. The Bible says God caused this. Although it is a typical holy war motif, the confusion could result from something besides God's work. The surprise attack launched by Israel against the Amorite kings by itself could have caused the panic. This second sign, although more visible, requires much faith to credit it to God.

With the third sign, we move much more obviously into the area of divine action. The hailstones from the sky that kill only Israel's enemies are difficult to explain as a natural phenomenon. The comment that more of the enemy died from the stones than from Israel's sword takes this event further into the realm of acts of God.

Next, the Bible describes an even greater sign. The greatest sign the Lord has ever performed is the sun standing still in the sky for a whole day. This is the most open and undeniable sign of God's power. To emphasize the trustworthiness of this report and to counter those who would doubt the actuality of this event, the Book of Jashar is cited. This book was apparently well enough known in Israel that the mere mention of it carried authority.

With the sun standing still, the series of signs reaches a dramatic climax. We have moved through a holy battle in which God's actions have progressively revealed themselves ever more clearly and powerfully. In the space of a few short verses, we see God's acts move from the nearly invisible to the undeniably visible.

To understand the purpose for describing this progression, we need to remember the situation when this part of the Bible was written. The Deuteronomic history was written for a people in exile. They were in a strange land, wondering how they could find God, let alone worship the Lord (see Psalm 137). Many of the exiles doubted the Lord's power or ability to save them. In this situation, the description of the battle at Gibeon contains a special message. It says that in the past God's activity was at first hidden and difficult to see. But God's power did not remain hidden. The Lord progressively revealed this power so that Israel's enemies, and ultimately the whole world, could not deny that the God of Israel controlled all creation and protected the chosen people. What God did once, can be done again, and all the world will see it.

Another reason for the emphasis on the final sign also lies in the exilic situation of the time this book was written. In Babylon, where the exiles were located, the sun and moon were important gods. By proclaiming the Lord's power over these bodies, the writer proclaims that Israel's God is more powerful than Babylon's gods. In the Exile, where many might interpret Judah's defeat by Babylon as the defeat of the Lord by the gods of Babylon, this becomes an important faith statement. The sun and moon themselves now become monuments of hope to God's saving power instead of alien gods.

We have looked very carefully at this passage describing the events at Gibeon because they are fascinating for many modern readers—especially the description of the sun standing still. Perhaps the group will be interested in discussing whether such an event could happen. If so, you will want to use the information given in the special section at the end of this lesson, entitled "Can the Sun Stand Still?"

Joshua 10:15-27. This section emphasizes the destruction of the five kings who attacked Gibeon. Some scholars suggest that the conquest was more an attack on the institution of kingship in Canaan than an attack on the land or the people. This section and Chapter 12, with their emphasis on the destruction of kings rather than places or populations, supports this view.

Canaanite kings held absolute power over their subjects. They claimed the right to exploit their subjects and used their military power to enforce their demands. In Israel's religion, however, only the Lord could claim absolute power and authority. No human ruler could demand total loyalty from his subjects. Even when kingship later arrives as an institution in Israel, the kings never have the power the earlier Canaanite kings had. The Israelite king always stands under God's law, just like any other Israelite.

In this context, we may be able to understand better why Rahab would exchange her loyalty to her king for loyalty to the Lord. Israel's proclamation that only the Lord deserved absolute loyalty was a revolutionary message for the oppressed peasants of Palestine.

Joshua 11:1-15. These battles for the north include no great miracles. Perhaps the writer, who was from the south, could not believe that the conquest of what later became the heretical Northern Kingdom (see 1 Kings 12:25-33) could have been as dramatic as the conquest of the south.

You might want to locate some of the northern cities on a map. Archaeological excavations at Hazor confirm that it fell in the thirteenth century B.C. Since verse 13 states that only Hazor was completely destroyed with fire, archae-ological confirmation of the capture of these other cities would be difficult to attain.

Joshua 11:16-23. This passage concludes the account of the conquest of the Promised Land. The Bible makes clear in verse 18 that this conquest took "a long time." It did not occur as quickly as the bare record might lead us to assume. Verse 23 states that Joshua also took "the entire land." Later, however, the writer will continually give evidence that Joshua did not, in fact, completely conquer the land and clear it of native peoples (see Joshua 13:1-6; 15:63; 16:10; 17:16; and especially Judges 1).

Joshua 12:1-24. This list of cities conquered by Israel under the leadership of Moses and Joshua concentrates on the kings who were defeated.

DIMENSION THREE: WHAT DOES THE BIBLE MEAN TO ME?

Joshua 9:3-15—Being Deceptive

The questions in the student book deal mainly with the problem of hypocrisy, or pretending to be what we are not. You may want to work through these questions with the group, perhaps by asking persons to share stories of their own personal experiences. Ask them if pretending to be someone they are not is hypocrisy, and if they ever see themselves as hypocrites.

You might want to read Jesus' teaching on hypocrisy found in Matthew 6:1-6, 16-18; 23:13-36. Jesus speaks harshly of hypocrites in these passages. Why? Are we in the church ever guilty of doing what Jesus accuses the Pharisees of doing? Perhaps you could concentrate on discussing ways we Christians can keep from being hypocritical.

Joshua 9:18-27—Oaths Are for Keeping

An excellent way of discussing the questions in this section would be to look at either the vows for confirmation and membership in your church or denomination or the marriage vows. You might discuss with the class members whether, looking back, they feel they really understood the meaning of these vows when they took them. Do they feel they truly understand them now? You might have them reflect on specific things they have done or are doing to remain loyal to these vows.

Joshua 10:1-5—Attacking the Wrong Problem

All denominations have some sort of written documentation of its rules and policies and positions on a variety of social issues—many of them are controversial. One way you could approach the questions in the student book is to look at what your church believes and practices concerning sexuality and homosexuality, racism, women's rights, abortion, or gambling.

Ask the class members whether these stands and actions deal effectively with difficult problems. If they say "yes," ask them why they feel this way. If they say "no," ask them how the church could do better. They may even want to discuss specific ways they could help the church tackle these problems.

Close the session by asking class members to share any new insights they have gained from studying Joshua 9–12. List these insights on chalkboard or a large sheet of paper.

Joshua 10:12-13
Can the Sun Stand Still?

The ancient reader had no trouble believing that the sun could stand still. For the ancient Israelite, the earth was the center of the universe. The sun and moon were lights moving across the firmament. However, since that time we have discovered that the sun does not circle the earth. The apparent movement of the sun and moon across our sky results from the rotation of the earth. We realize today that for the sun to stand still in the sky would mean the earth would have to stop turning.

If this should happen, a physicist friend informs me, the energy involved in the earth's rotation would immediately be transferred to every loose thing on the planet's surface. This would throw everything into the air, like stones slung from a whirling sling. Although we would not escape gravity, everything and everyone on earth would move. How can we come to grips with what the Bible says happened and what science says would happen?

Perhaps the best place to begin discussing this question is with the historian's source, the Book of Jashar, probably a poetic work. The quotation from it found in Joshua 10:12-13 follows typical Hebrew poetic form. Hebrew poetry, rather than rhyming sounds, rhymes thoughts and concepts. The common way for Old Testament poets to work is first to picture an idea, then to restate the idea using different words. In our present poem, the sun standing still is balanced in the second line by the moon standing still. The sun and moon are parallel. This form of poetry is called parallelism.

> "O sun, stand still over Gibeon,
> O moon, over the Valley of Aijalon."

The poetic picture of the son and moon standing still may originally have been a poetic image suggesting the great length of the battle. However, this image fit in so well with the writer's desire to proclaim God's visible power over creation, that the writer took literally what was intended to be taken as poetic imagery. A literal reading of this poetic image makes two points: (1) the Lord controls other gods, and (2) God once revealed the power to save Israel and will again. Perhaps we can understand the author's meaning even if we are not certain we can accept the reality of the event.

"Be sure to allocate this land to Israel for an inheritance" (13:6).

— 5 —

Joshua Divides the Territory

Joshua 13–17

DIMENSION ONE:
WHAT DOES THE BIBLE SAY?

Answer these questions by reading Joshua 13

1. What does the Lord say to Joshua? (Joshua 13:1)

   The Lord says, "You are very old, and there are still very large areas of land to be taken over."

2. What does God command Joshua to do? (Joshua 13:6-7)

   God commands Joshua to allot the mountain regions to Israel for an inheritance.

3. Which tribes receive land east of the Jordan? (Joshua 13:8)

   Reuben, Gad, and the half-tribe of Manasseh receive their inheritance east of the Jordan.

4. Within each tribe, how is the inheritance divided? (Joshua 13:15, 24, 29)

   Each tribe's land is allotted according to its clans.

Answer these questions by reading Joshua 14

5. Who distributes the inheritance of the land west of the Jordan? (Joshua 14:1)

   Eleazar the priest, Joshua the son of Nun, and the heads of the tribal clans distribute the inheritance.

6. How is this distribution of the land made for the nine and one-half tribes? (Joshua 14:2)

   The distribution of the land is made by use of the lot.

7. Into how many tribes are the "sons of Joseph" divided? (Joshua 14:4)

   The "sons of Joseph" are two tribes, Manasseh and Ephraim.

8. What happens when the people of Judah come to Joshua? (Joshua 14:6-8)

   Caleb reminds Joshua of the words Moses had sworn to him in the desert and of their exploration into Canaan.

9. What had Moses sworn to Caleb? (Joshua 14:9)

   Moses swore that the land Caleb had walked on during his spy venture would be his and his children's forever.

10. How many years have passed since Moses spoke the Lord's word to Caleb? (Joshua 14:10)

    Forty-five years have passed since the Lord made this promise.

11. What land does Caleb receive for his faithfulness? (Joshua 14:13-15)

    Joshua gives Hebron to Caleb.

Answer these questions by reading Joshua 15

12. What does Caleb offer to any man that captures Kiriath Sepher? (Joshua 15:16)

    Caleb offers to give his daughter Acsah as wife to whomever captures Kiriath Sepher.

13. Who captures Kiriath Sepher? (Joshua 15:17)

    Othniel takes the city.

14. What does Caleb's daughter ask of him? (Joshua 15:19)

    She asks for springs of water to go along with the land her father gave her in the Negev desert.

15. Who are the people of Judah unable to drive out? (Joshua 15:63)

    The people of Judah are unable to drive out the Jebusites, the inhabitants of Jerusalem.

16. Who is the tribe of Ephraim unable to drive out? (Joshua 16:10)

The tribe of Ephraim is unable to drive the Canaanites out of Gezer.

Answer these questions by reading Joshua 17

17. What happens to the daughters of Zelophehad during the distribution of the land? (Joshua 17:3-4)

They receive an inheritance along with the male members of their tribe.

18. What are the sons of Manasseh unable to do? (Joshua 17:12)

The sons of Manasseh are unable to take possession of the cities inhabited by the Canaanites.

19. What do the people of Joseph ask Joshua? (Joshua 17:14)

The people of Joseph ask why they are given only one allotment and portion.

20. How does Joshua respond to the question of Joseph's people? (Joshua 17:15)

Joshua says if they are so numerous they can go up to the forest and clear land there.

21. What keeps the people of Joseph from moving beyond the bounds of their original allotment? (Joshua 17:16)

The Canaanites have iron chariots where Joshua tells the people of Joseph to go.

22. How does Joshua encourage the house of Joseph? (Joshua 17:17-18)

Joshua emphasizes the power of the house of Joseph to possess its land and drive out the Canaanites.

DIMENSION TWO: WHAT DOES THE BIBLE SAY?

Background Information on Joshua 13–17

This lesson and the next one primarily contain descriptions of the boundaries of the various tribal lands. Basically these are lists of cities or descriptions of terrain that delineate the various areas. This may be difficult reading for the group.

Remind group members that when the Deuteronomic history was written, Israel no longer possessed the land. They were in exile in Babylon. In this context, the full description of the Promised Land that Israel received from God becomes a provocative way of emphasizing some of the major points of the history. It drives home the reality that Israel's disobedience to God's law has cost her a homeland. It also serves to remind the new generation being born in Babylon that their primary tie is not with Babylon, but with the Promised Land of Canaan, the land given to their ancestors. These lists focus the thoughts of the exiled Jews on what they have lost and what they should try to regain.

Joshua 13:1-6. The land described in these first six verses basically comprises the coastal region of Palestine. This level area is some of the best land in the country. You might especially want to point out on a map the Philistine city-states along the southern coast. As we continue into the books of Judges and First Samuel, the Philistines will gradually become the Israelites' greatest enemy. The Philistines' powerful threat to Israel's independence is a primary reason Israel asks the Lord for a king (see 1 Samuel 8:19-20).

The Philistines apparently originated in the general Aegean area, perhaps Crete. They first tried to settle in Egypt, but were repelled by the pharaohs Merneptah and Ramesses III. They consequently settled on the southwestern coast of Canaan about the same time Joshua and the Israelites were entering the land from the east. The Philistines gave their name to the country. The name *Palestine* ultimately derives from *Philistine*.

Joshua 13:22. You might recall the story of Balaam in Numbers 22–24. Although Balaam's oracles were favorable to Israel, his participation in trying to lead Israel astray at Peor brought about his death.

Joshua 14:6. Caleb's name (*Dog*) and his tribe mark him as an outsider. The first one to claim any of the land promised to Abraham is not an Israelite. Those outside the bounds of the chosen people (note Rahab and Gibeon) still receive a place in Israel and a portion of the land. Caleb's claim to land has priority over any of the tribes of Israel.

Joshua 14:7-9. Of those who had gone on the spy mission recorded in Numbers 13–14, only Caleb and Joshua retained their trust in the Lord's power to give them the land. For that reason, Joshua and Caleb did not die in the desert. Because of his faith, Caleb was promised a share in the land and he now comes forward to make his claim. Interestingly, Caleb has to remind Eleazar and Joshua of the Lord's promise to him.

Joshua 15:1-12. The first tribe to receive an allotment of land is Judah. Although this tribe was not the first-born of

Israel, the Deuteronomic historian perhaps mentions it first because this writer comes from the Southern Kingdom of Judah. Also, the description of the boundaries of Judah is noticeably more detailed than any of the other tribal boundaries (compare, for example, Joshua 16:1-3).

Joshua 15:13-14. Caleb here receives credit for capturing Hebron, later the capital of the tribe of Judah. Earlier, however, we read that Joshua captured Hebron (Joshua 10:36-39). Perhaps what has happened here is that, as the leader, Joshua received credit for what was accomplished by his subordinate, Caleb.

Most Americans think of George Washington as the general who won the Revolutionary War. But Washington was not present at some of the most significant victories in that war (for example, the battles of Bunker Hill, Saratoga, Kings Mountain, and Cowpens). In the summary lists, such as we find in Chapters 10 and 12, tradition may have simply given credit to Joshua, the commander of all Israel's armies, rather than mentioning each individual commander who captured a city.

Joshua 15:15-19. This passage is repeated almost verbatim in Judges 1:11-15. You might want to read the Judges version to the class members and let them compare it with the wording in Joshua. The Judges version, though, is set in the context of land taken after Joshua's death (see Joshua 24:29). Earlier, however, we read that Joshua captured Debir (see Joshua 10:38-39; 12:13). We have, then, three biblical accounts of the capture of Debir, suggesting three different times for its conquest: once while Joshua commands the armies, once by Othniel when Joshua is an old man, and once by Othniel after Joshua's death. The two nearly identical accounts of Othniel's capture argue against the idea that Debir had been continually recaptured by Canaanites, thereby necessitating repeated conquests by Israel.

Perhaps all we can conclude from these time discrepancies is that the books of Joshua and Judges may not always recount events in sequence. The Deuteronomic historian may not have been concerned with specific historical order. Or maybe 700 years later the writer could no longer be sure of the order of events. After all, how many of us remember what happened in the Middle Ages? Rather than try to determine exactly when these events happened, the writer may have just included all the various recountings of them. We cannot simply assume that the order of the stores in these two books automatically matches the time sequence of the events.

In verse 17 Caleb and Kenaz are not blood brothers, and Othniel is not the cousin of his bride Acsah.

Joshua 15:20-62. This list of cities is divided into twelve districts. Many scholars believe these districts correspond to the administrative divisions in the later kingdom of Judah. The final numbers of cities in each district does not always match the number of cities named. Perhaps new cities were simply added to the lists without revising the final number.

Joshua 16:1–17:13. Compared with the description of the land given to Judah, the description of the land given to the two major tribes of the north is much less detailed. This could result from two factors. First, in 922 B.C., the north rebelled against rule by the Davidic kings from Judah. The historian considers this action by the north as rebellion against God's will (see 1 Kings 12:25-33). As we have noted elsewhere (see Lesson 4 in this teacher book on Joshua 11:1-15), this religious judgment by the writer may influence the portrayal of the capture of the north. (See also the negative view of these tribes in Joshua 17:14-18). Secondly, the Northern Kingdom was destroyed by the Assyrians in 722 B.C., almost 200 years before Joshua was written. No doubt time blurred the memory of these northern tribal boundaries.

Joshua 17:3-6. In the story of Zelophehad's daughters, we again find an account of someone normally outside the bounds of Israel's number being included in the community. Usually land was only passed down through male descendants. As we will see in the Book of Ruth (Lesson 13), even a widow was not granted her husband's land. She had to unite with a male kinsman to gain a male heir for the land. Israel was an extremely male-oriented society. Only men were required by the law to appear before God on a regular basis. Of course, the sign of initiation into God's covenant, circumcision, is limited to males.

With the ancient Israelite attitude that women were basically outside God's covenant, this story of the granting of land to Zelophehad's daughters stands as a striking example of God's insistence that women too share in the promise to Abraham. The Deuteronomic historian highlights women as people God cares for and uses in significant ways. For example, Deborah (Judges 4:4–5:30) and Huldah (2 Kings 22:12-20) appear at crucial moments in Israelite history as bearers of God's word. Like Caleb, Zelophehad's daughters must remind Eleazar and Joshua of God's promise to them. This suggests that they cannot assume the religious and political leaders will remember their rights.

Joshua 17:14-18. The demand of the Joseph people for more land casts them in an unfavorable light. Perhaps they hope to gain a more favorable lot from Joshua, a member of their own tribe of Ephraim. Joshua suggests they utilize their land more effectively by clearing the forests. The Joseph people then explain that the hill country is not large enough for them, and they are afraid to move out into the plain because of the Canaanite military power. Joshua points to their number and says they can clear the forests and drive out the Canaanites. Although they witnessed God's repeated power over Israel's enemies, the Joseph people evidently still do not have enough faith in God.

DIMENSION THREE:
WHAT DOES THE BIBLE MEAN TO ME?

Joshua 14:6-15—Outsiders Before Insiders

You might want to examine with the class members our feelings toward people who are not part of our group. You might especially want to elicit feelings about persons who do not attend church. Do we ever feel superior toward them? Should we?

You may want to examine those verses where Jesus speaks about how the expectations of religious people will be reversed by God. This theme of the first being last and the last being first can be found in the parable of the Pharisee and the tax collector (Luke 18:9-14), in Mark 9:33-35, and in Matthew 19:27-30. You might ask the class members where they see themselves in these stories. Do we ever miss or oppose God's intention to bring all people to God through Christ?

Joshua 15:1-12, 20-61—Pictures of Home

Ask the class members how many of them have kept pictures of former homes. You might want to explore their reasons for doing this. You might then want to build on this discussion and talk about the importance of memories in our lives. You could then discuss the place of memory in our religious faith.

Remembering is important to our religion. Much of the reason for our studying the Bible has to do with the high value we place on memories. We believe it is worth remembering what God has said and done in the past.

Our faith, our hope, and our life together as Christians are based on remembrances. On the night he was betrayed, Jesus broke bread and passed a cup to his disciples, telling them to "do this in remembrance of me." We continue to remember what Jesus did for us when we take Holy Communion. On Easter morning, the women understood the meaning of the empty tomb when "they remembered his words" (Luke 24:8).

Even our hope for a close relationship with God is based on remembering. When Jeremiah proclaims the promise of the new covenant, he speaks in the name of the Lord: "I will forgive their wickedness / and will remember their sins no more" (Jeremiah 31:34; see Hebrews 8:12). Many Christians remember the moment God's grace flowed into them. Perhaps the group members would like to share with each other important memories of their relationship with God. You might conclude this discussion by asking why memory is so important for our religious faith.

Joshua 17:3-6—The Weak Must Remind the Strong

After working through the questions in this section in the student book, you might want to lead the group in a survey and discussion of your own local church or denomination. What minority groups are present? Are minorities actually welcomed? Are they part of the leadership of the church? Are women included in the leadership of the church beyond the areas of education and mission? Does your church or denomination have or welcome women as clergy?

Have the group discuss your church's performance in support of minority groups and women in light of the Scriptures they have read.

To close this session, ask class members to share new insights on Joshua 13–16. List these insights on chalkboard or a large sheet of paper, if time allows.

"After you have written descriptions of the seven parts of the land, . . . I will cast lots for you" (18:6).

— 6 —

Seven Portions Remain

Joshua 18–21

**DIMENSION ONE:
WHAT DOES THE BIBLE SAY?**

Answer these questions by reading Joshua 18

1. Where does the whole congregation of Israel now gather? (Joshua 18:1)

   The whole congregation gathers at Shiloh.

2. How many tribes have yet to receive an inheritance? (Joshua 18:2)

   Seven tribes have yet to receive an inheritance.

3. What does Joshua ask the Israelites? (Joshua 18:3)

   He asks them how long they will wait before taking possession of the land given them by the Lord.

4. What are the three men from each tribe to do? (Joshua 18:4-5)

   They are to survey the land, write a description of it all, and divide it into seven parts.

5. After the report of the tribal representatives, what does Joshua do? (Joshua 18:9-10)

   Joshua casts lots for them in Shiloh before the Lord and distributes the land by tribal division.

6. Where does the lot of the tribe of Benjamin fall? (Joshua 18:11)

   It falls between the tribe of Judah and the tribe of Joseph.

Answer these questions by reading Joshua 19

7. Where does the tribe of Simeon receive its inheritance? (Joshua 19:1)

   Simeon's inheritance lies within the territory of Judah.

8. Why does the tribe of Simeon receive part of Judah's territory? (Joshua 19:9)

   Simeon receives territory in the land of Judah because the portion given to Judah is more than Judah needs.

9. Which tribes receive the third, fourth, fifth, and sixth allotments? (Joshua 19:10, 17, 24, 32)

   The tribes of Zebulun, Issachar, Asher, and Naphtali receive these allotments.

10. What does the tribe of Dan do after failing to capture its territory? (Joshua 19:47)

    After its failure, the tribe of Dan goes up and captures Leshem, renaming it Dan.

11. After the distribution of the territories, what do the people of Israel do for Joshua? (Joshua 19:49-50)

    The people of Israel give Joshua Timnath Serah for his promised inheritance.

Answer these questions by reading Joshua 20

12. What purpose do the cities of refuge serve? (Joshua 20:3)

    These cities protect anyone who kills another unintentionally.

13. When may a slayer return home? (Joshua 20:6)

    A slayer may return home after facing a trial and until the death of the high priest at the time.

14. What three cities west of the Jordan does Israel set apart as cities of refuge? (Joshua 20:7)

    Israel sets apart Kedesh, Shechem, and Kiriath Arba (Hebron) as cities of refuge west of the Jordan.

15. What three cities east of the Jordan does Israel set apart as cities of refuge? (Joshua 20:8)

East of the Jordan, Israel sets apart Bezer, Ramoth, and Golan as cities of refuge.

Answer these questions by reading Joshua 21

16. Why do the heads of the Levites come to Eleazar, Joshua, and the tribal leaders? (Joshua 21:1-3)

The Levites come before these leaders to ask for towns to dwell in.

17. What are the three groups into which the Levites are divided? (Joshua 21:4, 6, 7)

The Levites are divided into Kohath's descendants (Kohathites), Gershon's descendants (Gershonites), and Merari's descendants (Merarites).

18. How many towns do the Levites receive? (Joshua 21:41)

The Levites receive forty-eight towns.

19. After the tribes take possession of their land, what does the Lord do for them? (Joshua 21:44)

The Lord gives Israel "rest on every side."

20. What happens to all the Lord's promises to Israel? (Joshua 21:45)

Every promise the Lord made to Israel is fulfilled.

DIMENSION TWO: WHAT DOES THE BIBLE MEAN?

Joshua 18:1. Now that the Promised Land has been secured, Israel can leave her old battle camp at Gilgal and move to Shiloh, which means "place of tranquility." This move also serves as a transition between the allotment of land to the great tribes of Judah, Ephraim, and Manasseh and the allotments assigned to the remaining smaller tribes.

Shiloh remains, for about 150 years, the central sanctuary where the ark of the covenant is contained. About 1050 B.C., the Philistines capture the ark at the battle of Ebenezer (1 Samuel 4). Archaeological excavations at Shiloh suggest the Philistines also destroyed Shiloh about this time (see Jeremiah 7:12).

Perhaps the Tent is mentioned here to emphasize that the conquest is over, since the ark of the covenant is normally the center of interest. The ark, which primarily symbolizes the Lord's presence in battle, returns to its proper place of rest in the Tent's Most Holy Place (see Exodus 26:33-34). According to Exodus 33:11, Joshua served as the guardian of the Tent of Meeting under Moses.

Joshua 18:2-9. Joshua tells Israel to form a committee with equal representation from all the tribes. These men will survey the land yet to be assigned. The committee is to present a written report of its findings so Joshua can act on it. You might enjoy pointing out to the group that committees can use this text as a biblical sanction for their existence.

Joshua 18:10. Joshua takes the central position in this casting of lots at Shiloh. Those who had earlier participated in the allotment at Gilgal, Eleazar and the tribal leaders (see Joshua 14:1), do not appear. Joshua alone casts the lot at Shiloh (see verses 6 and 8). We are not sure why. This different method of dividing the land may be another way to distinguish between the two allotments. Perhaps, since Joshua is so clearly tied to the Tent of Meeting earlier in the Bible (see above on 18:1), his central role is emphasized now that the Tent of Meeting has been set up. (Note that the Tent of Meeting had not been erected at Gilgal.) Whatever the intention, the Bible emphasizes that Joshua not only led Israel in time of war, but he continues to lead the people in times of peace.

Joshua 18:11-18. Indicate on a map the location of the land given to Benjamin. You will probably want to do this as well for the other tribal areas we will discuss in this lesson. For the description of the southern boundary of Benjamin, the northern boundary of the tribe of Judah (see 15:5-9) has apparently been adapted. However, in this way, Jebus, or Jerusalem, is included within the land of Benjamin. The northern boundary of Judah passed south of Jerusalem. Nowhere else, except in this chapter, does the Bible place Jerusalem within Benjamin's boundary. We know from elsewhere that Jerusalem remains an island of Canaanite culture between the tribes of Benjamin and Judah until David's time (2 Samuel 5:6-9).

Joshua 19:1-9. In 18:5, Joshua directed the tribal representatives to exclude the territories of Judah, Joseph, and Manasseh from their description of the land still to be divided. However, here we find that the area for which the second lot is cast comes from Judah's territory. In verse 9, this is justified because Judah has more land than it needs. Nevertheless, Simeon's allotment contrasts strikingly with Joshua's original charge to the committee.

Simeon's territory lies in the southern part of Judah's original allotment, in the Negev Desert. Many of the cities listed in verses 2-7 already appeared in Judah's city lists (see 15:21-32, 42-44).

Simeon's existence as a separate tribe is difficult to trace in the Bible. Apparently, it soon lost its dependent existence and became part of the greater tribe of Judah. This may be why the Deuteronomic history, written several centuries later, has difficulty separating Simeon's land from that of Judah.

Joshua 19:10-16. The first lot cast at Shiloh had been for territory in the center of the Promised Land. Benjamin's territory covered the area first penetrated by Israel under Joshua's leadership. With the second lot, we shift to the south, into territory captured by Israel after the central section of the country had been secured. Now, with the third and subsequent lots, we move to the northern section of the Promised Land—the area of Palestine conquered last by Israel. This suggests that the allotment of land at Shiloh by Joshua intentionally follows the order of the conquest led by Joshua. This may give us another clue as to why Joshua figures so preeminently in the casting of lots at Shiloh (see page 215 on 18:10). He who conquered the land, divides the land.

Now that we are back in the area of the northern tribes, we find again that we are given a much less detailed description of the tribal territories. See Lesson 5 (page 212) on Joshua 16:1-17:13, for an explanation of why we are given less information about the northern tribal boundaries. This region, however, holds more interest for most Christians. The territory of Zebulun and Issachar, along with that portion of Naphtali on the western border of the Sea of Galilee, is the area where Jesus carried out much of his ministry. Nazareth, the city in which Jesus grew up, falls within the boundaries of the ancient tribe of Zebulun, given in these verses.

Joshua 19:40-48. With the seventh lot we appear to move back to the central part of the Promised Land. Dan's portion lies west of Benjamin's, between Judah and Joseph. Dan is ultimately driven from this land. According to Judges 1:34, the Amorites drive the Danites away from the coastal plain, back into the hills. The Samson stories of Judges 13–16 (see Lesson 11) find their setting in Dan's original territory. But these same stories witness to the great pressure this tribe came under from the Philistines.

Judges 18:1 (see Lesson 12) says Dan never received an inheritance. They finally migrate to the far northern region of Palestine, capture the city and territory of Laish (the same as the Leshem of Joshua 19:47), rename it Dan, and settle there. (See Judges 18:27-29.) Dan, therefore, stands at the far northern boundary of the Promised Land. The expression "from Dan to Beersheba" (see Judges 20:1; 1 Samuel 3:20) becomes a popular way for Israel to describe the northern and southern limits of her territory.

Joshua 19:49-50. Giving Joshua a portion of land completes the formal division of the land. Of the original spies sent by Moses to Canaan, only Caleb and Joshua returned believing the Lord could give Israel this land held by such powerful peoples (see Numbers 14:6-9). As a reward for his faithfulness, Caleb received territory of his own at the beginning of the land distribution (Joshua 14:13-15). Joshua receives his at the end. In this way the Deutero-nomic history frames the giving of the land to all Israel with the receiving of territory by persons who had held absolutely to their faith in God. The lands assigned to Caleb and Joshua join the list of other monuments to God's dealings with Israel. These two portions of land remind Israel that possession of the Promised Land depends on Israel's faithfulness to God.

Joshua 20:1-6. This may be a difficult passage for the group to understand. The views of life, death, vengeance, and legal procedure found here are, for the most part, different from our own.

The early Israelite tribes believed that any person responsible for the death of another person should die. "Whoever sheds the blood of man, by man shall his blood be shed . . ." (Genesis 9:6). Israel believed that the blood of a murdered person cried out for vengeance (see Genesis 4:10; Job 16:18), and only by shedding more blood could things be balanced. (See Exodus 21:23; Deuteronomy 19:11-12; Leviticus 17:11; Hebrews 9:22.) Consequently, the murderer had to be killed to cancel the great wrong he had done. In Israel, a society with no police or formal judicial system, the nearest kinsman of the victim was duty-bound to seek vengeance. The avenger was obligated to track down the killer and execute him or her.

A distinction develops in Israelite law between intentional killing (murder) and unintentional killing (manslaughter) (see Exodus 21:12-14). Judgment should not occur on the basis of the act alone. The motive behind the act must also be considered. With this understanding, the system of cities of refuge is set up as a way of taking into account the reason behind the killer's act.

You will find the original command to set up the cities of refuge in Numbers 35:9-34 and Deuteronomy 19:1-13. These cities are places where the unintentional killer can flee to escape the avenging kinsman. As Numbers 35:16-25 explains, the killer has to stand trial in the city of refuge to which he or she has fled. If it is proved that he or she has indeed committed premeditated murder, the killer is handed over to the avenger for execution. If the refugee can show there was no premeditation, he or she can remain a resident of the city of refuge.

The city-of-refuge system does not do away with the older system of blood vengeance. Rather, it supplements the older beliefs. The avenger of blood still attempts to slay the killer. The city of refuge serves only as a protective place. If caught outside the city limits, the killer may be slain. Another old belief, a life for a life, also remains. For this reason, the slayer must stay in the city of refuge until the life he or she has taken has been accounted for by another life.

This balancing of life for life occurs with the death of the high priest. Apparently the life of the high priest replaces the life of the killer as far as the demands of vengeance are concerned. The high priest's death serves as a type of sacrifice by which the killer's debt to his or her victim is paid. The avenger's duty is also canceled. Only when the demands of justice have been met by another may the killer return safely home.

Joshua 20:7-9. All six cities of refuge appear to have been sacred Israelite cities. Shechem, in the middle of Palestine, goes back to the time of Abraham and Jacob. Israel went there after the conquest of Ai to satisfy God's covenant in the Promised Land (Joshua 8:30-35). In Chapter 24 (see next week's lesson), Shechem is the site for a major covenant renewal ceremony.

The patriarchs are buried at Kiriath Arba, or Hebron, in the south. Kedesh lies in the far north. Since its name means "holy," we can be sure it too was a sacred place. We know little about the cities east of the Jordan. Since they also appear, like their three western counterparts, on the list of cities assigned to the priests, they too are probably sites of Israelite holy places.

This designation of sacred sites as cities of refuge suggests that the whole justice system is tied with the ancient right of sanctuary. In the ancient world, it was believed that a person who had committed a crime could go to a sacred site to come under the protection of the god worshiped there. Once in sacred territory, the person could not be assaulted or arrested. With Israel's understanding that the motive behind the act should decide the degree of criminality, the right of sanctuary was limited to those who had committed their crime unintentionally. Persons who had committed their crimes intentionally could not seek the Lord's protection. The guilty person could be dragged from the altar to receive punishment fitting the crime (see Exodus 21:14). The cities-of-refuge system also suggests that a person who commits manslaughter could only go to one of these six cities to claim sanctuary. Nowhere else could he or she seek safety from the avenger of blood.

Joshua 21:1-3. All the land has been apportioned to the tribes. Now the climax of the division takes place. The people take part of what they have received from God and dedicate it to the service of God. The Levites, the Israelite tribe that serves God as priests, now receive land from the other tribes. We need to remember that at this period of history, Israel did not have a monetary economy. The only pay priests who attended God's altar (or anyone) could receive was food and a place to live. The establishment of levitical cities becomes a way the priests are guaranteed a place to live.

You might want to compare this system with the parsonage system used by modern churches. The main difference between the parsonage system and the levitical cities is that the Levites were granted sole ownership of these cities. The growing practice in many churches today of giving the minister a housing allowance so he or she may buy a house more closely resembles the practice we see in this passage.

Joshua 21:8-42. The levitical cities are not evenly distributed over all of the Promised Land. They appear almost solely in areas that presented problems to Israelite religion. The Levites are given cities in places where there is a continual presence of non-Israelite peoples. Since these non-Israelites often continued their old religious practices, the places where they lived could always become sources of possible contamination for Israel's religion. Consequently, Israel places the Levites where the greatest threat to Israelite faith could arise. This practice is entirely appropriate, especially when we remember the Levites were given the priesthood because of their zeal for the Lord during the golden calf incident. (See Exodus 32:26-29.)

Joshua 21:43-45. For the Deuteronomic history, the final goal of the conquest is now reached. The Lord has fulfilled all the promises to Israel. The Israelites have the land and are now at rest.

This goal of rest is important and mentioned several times (Deuteronomy 3:20; 12:10; 25:19; Joshua 1:13, 15; 11:23). Rest is more than just the end of warfare. Rest includes peace, well-being, and security. Rest does not mean the cessation of work, for work is part of what God intends humans to do (see Genesis 2:15). But rest does mean the end of unsatisfactory or unfruitful labor. To achieve rest means to experience God's care and blessing, to feel satisfied with what you do, and to be at peace with yourself and others.

DIMENSION THREE: WHAT DOES THE BIBLE MEAN TO ME?

Joshua 2:1-6—Judge the Motive, Not the Act

As you work through the questions in the student book with the group, you might want to discuss some parts of Jesus' ministry that speak to these issues. Jesus often pointed out to the Pharisees that the motives prompting their pious acts were hypocritical (see especially Matthew 23). Although they were doing the right things on the outside, their impure motives condemned them. Jesus also saw that persons could use the letter of the law to bypass the spirit of the law: the love of God and neighbor (see Mark 12:28-31). Mark 3:1-6 vividly recounts Jesus' anger and grief at the Pharisees' condemnation of him for healing someone on the sabbath. According to the law, healing was work and therefore not allowed.

Jesus sees the reaction of the Pharisees as an excuse for not fulfilling our duty to our neighbor. According to the Gospel of Matthew, Jesus calls us to follow a way of higher righteousness that goes beyond just doing the right thing, but also intending to do the right thing (Matthew 5:20). In Matthew 5:21-28 Jesus says the angry intent brings us into judgment, whether or not we carry through and kill the one we are angry with. The motive of lust brings us into judgment, whether or not we follow through with the act of adultery. Jesus appears to say that God is more concerned with why we do or do not do something than with what we do or do not do.

Joshua 21:1-3—God's Servants Deserve a Portion

You and the class members may feel uncomfortable discussing the questions in this section. Often we in the church hesitate to discuss money. Many Christians feel we should not be concerned with such worldly matters. However, as we see in this chapter, as well as elsewhere in the Old Testament, the compensation of God's ministers is pictured as a special concern of the Lord. God is portrayed as affirming that priests should receive an ample portion of the people's gifts.

This active concern for ministerial pay continues into the New Testament. Jesus himself says to his chosen ones, "the worker deserves his wages" (Luke 10:7). Paul seconds this view in 1 Corinthians 9:14: "the Lord has commanded that those who preach the gospel should receive their living from the gospel." Rather than being outside the concerns of faith, the Bible asserts that the subject of ministerial salaries is an important one for religious people to reflect upon.

You could use the questions in this section as a way for the group to develop a theological base for compensating clergy. You might want to explore why the Bible finds it necessary to mention this subject. Do class members see clergy salaries as a way to express our Christian concerns and stewardship? Do they feel clergy are paid too much or too little? Why do they feel the way they do? If the class members feel uncomfortable with this subject, they might find it valuable to pursue the reasons for these feelings. As a group, you might want to develop concrete ways the church can express its beliefs about compensating its clergy.

Joshua 21:43-45—Rest Is an Active State

In preparing for the discussion of these questions on the biblical notion of rest, you might find if helpful to read Hebrews 4. This New Testament author states that Joshua did not bring his people into God's rest. Only Jesus can do that. This affirmation on the writer's part carries special meaning when we remember that *Joshua* and *Jesus* are the same name. For the Christian, the second Joshua/Jesus fully accomplishes what the first Joshua/Jesus could do only in part. He brings his people into God's presence where they share the rest of God. This chapter of Hebrews should help you and the class members formulate Christian answers to the questions in the student book.

To close this session, ask the class members to share insights they have gained in their study of Joshua 18–21. If time allows, list these insights on chalkboard or a piece of paper.

On that day Joshua made a covenant for the people (24:25).

7

Joshua Prepares to Die

Joshua 22–24

DIMENSION ONE:
WHAT DOES THE BIBLE SAY?

Answer these questions by reading Joshua 22

1. What does Joshua tell the tribes of Reuben, Gad, and the half-tribe of Manasseh? (Joshua 22:4-5)

    Joshua tells them to return to their homeland, and to follow the Lord's commands and law.

2. What do these tribes do when they reach the region around the Jordan? (Joshua 22:10)

    The tribes build an imposing altar by the Jordan.

3. How do the people of Israel react to the news of what these tribes have done? (Joshua 22:12)

    The whole assembly of Israel gathers at Shiloh in order to make war against them.

4. Who does Israel send to the land of Gilead? (Joshua 22:13-14)

    Israel sends Phinehas, the son of Eleazar the priest, and ten chiefs, one from each tribe.

5. What do these representatives accuse the eastern tribes of doing? (Joshua 22:16)

    They accuse the eastern tribes of breaking faith with God by building the altar.

6. How do the Reubenites, the Gadites, and the half-tribe of Manasseh answer the charges against them? (Joshua 22:22-23)

    They swear by the Lord that they have not built the altar to turn away from God or to make offerings.

7. What reason do these eastern tribes give for building the altar? (Joshua 22:25-27)

    The eastern tribes claim that because the Jordan River keeps them from the sanctuary, they built the altar as a witness that they too serve the Lord.

8. How do the representatives of Israel respond to the words of the eastern tribes? (Joshua 22:30-31)

    Phinehas and the chiefs are pleased with these words.

Answer these questions by reading Joshua 23

9. What does Joshua tell Israel that God will do to the nations remaining in her midst? (Joshua 23:5)

    Joshua says the Lord will drive the remaining nations out so that Israel can possess the land.

10. In response to what God will do for her, what does Joshua command Israel to do? (Joshua 23:6)

    Israel should respond to what God does for her by strictly keeping the Law of Moses.

11. What will happen if the Israelites turn back from God and join the nations left among them? (Joshua 23:12-13)

    God will not continue to drive out the nations before Israel. Rather, the nations will become a trap for Israel until she perishes from the land.

Answer these questions by reading Joshua 24

12. Where does Joshua assemble all the tribes of Israel? (Joshua 24:1)

    Joshua assembles all the tribes at Shechem.

13. What does the Lord say concerning their forefathers? (Joshua 24:2)

Their forefathers lived beyond the River (Euphrates), and they worshiped other gods.

14. What did God do to Abraham? (Joshua 24:3)

God led Abraham through Canaan and gave him many descendants.

15. What happened at the sea when God brought Israel out of Egypt? (Joshua 24:6-7)

The Lord made the sea come over the Egyptian chariots and horsemen and cover them.

16. What does the Lord say happened at Jericho? (Joshua 24:11)

God says the citizens of Jericho and all the Canaanites fought against Israel, and God gave them "into your hands."

17. What did God send before Israel to drive out the inhabitants of the land? (Joshua 24:12)

God sent the hornet before Israel to drive out the inhabitants.

18. In light of what God has done for Israel, what does Joshua command the people to do? (Joshua 24:14)

Joshua commands the people to fear the Lord and to throw away other gods.

19. No matter what Israel chooses, what does Joshua vow he will do? (Joshua 24:15)

No matter what Israel chooses, Joshua vows he and his household will serve the Lord.

20. How do the people respond to Joshua's command? (Joshua 24:16-18)

The people affirm that they will not serve other gods. They will serve the Lord.

21. Does Joshua believe that the people will serve the Lord? (Joshua 24:19)

Joshua doubts that the people can serve the Lord who is a holy and jealous God.

22. After the people affirm their loyalty a third time, what does Joshua do? (Joshua 24:25-27)

Joshua makes a covenant for the people at Shechem, writing down the words in the Book of the Law of God. He also sets up a large stone as a witness against Israel.

23. How old is Joshua when he dies? (Joshua 24:29)

Joshua dies at the age of 110 years.

24. How long does Israel serve the Lord? (Joshua 24:31)

Israel serves the Lord during the lifetime of Joshua and of the elders who outlived him.

25. Who is buried at Shechem by the people of Israel? (Joshua 24:32)

The people of Israel bury "Joseph's bones" at Shechem.

DIMENSION TWO: WHAT DOES THE BIBLE MEAN?

Joshua 22:1-4. You might want to review for the group the place of the tribes of Reuben, Gad, and the half-tribe of Manasseh in the conquest. (See Joshua 1:12-18; 4:12-13.) Point out the portion of land given to these tribes east of the Jordan. If you have a map that shows the tribal allotments, this would be an excellent time to point them out to the class members. In that way class members will have a good grasp of the positions of all the tribes in relation to one another.

Joshua 22:5. Here Joshua repeats the main item of faith in the Deuteronomic history. You might want to read this commandment in its full form as found in Deuteronomy 6:5. The group may recognize it as the commandment Jesus gives in answer to the question, "Of all the commandments, which is the most important?" (See Mark 12:28-30.)

Joshua 22:10. Since most Israelite altars were small structures of stone a few feet high, this "imposing altar" may have looked like a military tower or fortress. The eastern tribes also built the altar on the western side of the Jordan River, on territory not their own. Both these characteristics probably added to the offense the western tribes took at this structure.

Joshua 22:11. After hearing about the altar, the western tribes assume the worst about the tribes to the east. The westerners believe the easterners have rebelled against God's commandment that there be only one altar to the Lord in Israel. You might want to read this commandment, found in Deuteronomy 12:10-14. Although Israel did not always follow this rule, it was a major test by which to judge her loyalty to God.

Joshua 22:12. The tribes not involved in building the altar gather in order to purge from their midst what they perceive to be a rebellion against God. As we discussed previously in Lesson 3 concerning Achan's sin, Israel believed that sin extended beyond the individual and affected the whole group. Therefore, the sinner must be called into judgment, or all will suffer for what he or she has done. In the present passage, the tribal delegation refers to the results of Achan's sin as a basis for their concern and action (see verse 20).

Joshua 22:13-14. To help the class understand Phinehas's zeal for the Lord, read aloud the account of his action found in Numbers 25:6-8.

Joshua 22:19. The ideal boundaries of the Promised Land did not include the territory where the eastern tribes lived. The Jordan River was the eastern boundary. In this verse, the western tribes suggest to those tribes living outside the land that, if their place of residence causes them to turn away from the Lord, they should come back into the land of Canaan. Perhaps the Israelites in exile had these words in mind when they asked, "How can we sing the songs of the LORD / while in a foreign land?" (See Psalm 137:4.)

Joshua 22:22-23. The eastern tribes swear that they have not turned away from the Lord. They affirm that, if they have rebelled, God should destroy them. These words certainly affirmed the belief of many exiles that living outside the Promised Land did not cut them off from knowing the God of Israel.

Joshua 22:24-29. The eastern tribes explain that they built the great altar as a monument to remind those who live in the Promised Land that those who live outside the land also belong to Israel. Remind the group of other monuments that the Deuteronomic history mentions (see Joshua 4:9, 20, for example). This account of a monument to a relationship is similar to the story of the stone set up to mark the relationship between Jacob and Laban (see Genesis 31:43-54).

Joshua 22:30-34. The affirmation of loyalty to the Lord by Reuben, Gad, and Manasseh keeps Israel from suffering from God's judgment for apostasy. The giant altar is not a way of turning away from the Lord, but a witness to the faithfulness of those people who serve the Lord while living outside the Promised Land.

Joshua 23:1-2. These verses introduce Joshua's last testament to Israel. Because Israel believes that the spoken word carries its own power, the words of a dying person carry special meaning. They embody the total life-power of the person speaking them. Consequently, the Old Testament contains several testaments uttered by persons about to die. We can read the testaments of Abraham (Genesis 24), Isaac (Genesis 27), Jacob (Genesis 49), and Joseph (Genesis 50:25). The whole Book of Deuteronomy takes the form of the last testament of Moses to Israel.

In Joshua 23, the aged leader sets down the alternatives Israel now faces. Loyalty to the Lord brings blessing; disloyalty brings curse.

Joshua 23:12-13. Intermarriage with non-Israelites was a threat because of the important place the mother had in religious training. She was responsible for a child's earliest religious instruction. If the woman was not a worshiper of the Lord, she would not teach her children the commandments of God and the history of Israel.

Joshua 23:14-16. Joshua explains that God's promise had a negative as well as a positive side. God's promise regarding the land has already been fulfilled. Now it is up to Israel to choose how she will respond to this gift. After all, Israel did not really have to do anything to get the land. The Lord gave it to her. In other words, Israel did not earn her relationship to God. But now that Israel has said "yes" to God, she must work to keep this relationship strong. Failure to be loyal to the covenant partner will destroy the relationship.

Covenants and relationships are always two-way arrangements. A gift of love calls for a response of love. If no response comes forth, it means the gift has been rejected, along with the giver. The Promised Land reveals God's love for Israel. The proper response to this gift is loving service to the Lord. If Israel turns away from God and serves other gods, the relationship with God is severed. The result will be loss of Israel's closeness with the Lord and loss of God's gift of the land.

Joshua 24:1. Shechem (the name probably means "shoulder" or "slope") guards the pass between Mount Gerizim and Mount Ebal in central Palestine.

Shechem's importance for Israel's history is hard to overrate. The main roads of the country converge there. Abraham built his first altar in the Promised Land at Shechem. (See Genesis 12:6-7.) Joseph was buried there (Joshua 24:32). Shechem was the site for the first experiment in kingship in Israel (see Lesson 10 on Judges 9). When the northern tribes later revolt against the house of David, they establish their first capital in Shechem. (See 1 Kings 12:25.)

Joshua 24:1-11. This summary of Israel's history with the Lord parallels other summaries found in the Deuteronomic history (for example, see Deuteronomy 26:5-10). These statements, which give the history of God's relationship with Israel, are often called *creeds*. As such, they are similar to the creeds that we recite as part of our worship. Interestingly, none of these creeds mentions Sinai or the laws given there. We do not know why this event that is so central for Israel's self-understanding finds no expression in these summaries of Israel's history.

We have noted before that the Deuteronomic history often points to living monuments as signs of God's mercy and to material monuments as symbols of God's justice.

Perhaps, since these creeds are living words repeated by the people, they speak only of God's merciful acts on Israel's behalf. The law, with its emphasis on judgment, receives its monument in the stone Joshua erects as a witness against Israel's pledge of faithfulness (see verses 26-27).

Joshua 24:12. As the student book notes, the hornet probably symbolizes the fear and helplessness the Lord brings upon the natives of the land. We also find this image in Exodus 23:28 and in Deuteronomy 7:20, both times within similar contexts. The hornet stings its prey, causing paralysis. Then the hornet sucks out the vital fluids from its victim. Similarly, the Lord stings Israel's enemies, causing their impotence. Like a hornet with its paralyzed victim, so is Israel in its conquest of the demoralized inhabitants of the Promised Land. The metaphor emphasizes that the conquest is God's doing, not Israel's.

Joshua 24:14-15. Joshua now switches from summarizing Israel's history with God to calling for a decision on the part of the people. He tells the people that the only proper response to all these signs of God's love and mercy is reverence, sincere service, and faithfulness to the Lord. This response can occur only if Israel abandons all the other gods she has worshiped through time. Persons cannot give full loyalty to more than one thing. They must choose either the Lord, who continually guides and saves them, or those things that call for loyalty but cannot give us life. Joshua affirms that, no matter what others do, he and his family will remain faithful to the Lord.

Joshua 24:16-24. The people respond to Joshua's call by promising to serve the Lord. Joshua doubts their ability to serve a God who claims absolute loyalty from followers. He warns them of the consequences if they do not remain faithful. The people again swear their service to God. Joshua calls upon them to become a living monument of their own promise to God, and they accept this position of witness. The people of Israel themselves become the sign of their relationship with God. No material monument can signify a living relationship. Israel herself now declares by her own existence her closeness to God.

Affirmation of loyalty is not enough. Israel must now act on her vow of loyalty and deny all other gods to whom she has tried to give the faithfulness due to the Lord alone. With a third affirmation of service and obedience, Israel turns away from all that pulls her from absolute obedience to the Lord.

Joshua 24:25-27. Joshua now makes a covenant with the people. This covenant was probably renewed continually. The detailed instructions in Deuteronomy 27–28 concerning this ceremony suggest that Israel regularly gathered together at Shechem to renew her covenant with the Lord. This renewal probably occurred every seven years (see Deuteronomy 31:10-13). Shechem is an especially appro-

priate place for a covenant ceremony, since it had a long tradition as a center for worship and ritual.

Joshua 24:29-33. The deaths of Joshua and Eleazar mark the end of the generation of the conquest. A new generation that has not witnessed God's gift of the land to the people will now arise.

DIMENSION THREE: WHAT DOES THE BIBLE MEAN TO ME?

Joshua 22:10-14—Excluding the Affected Party

This issue may be a personal one for many in the group. Most of us have, at some time in our lives, either been excluded from a meeting dealing with us or have been involved in a meeting discussing someone else. You may want to concentrate on the feelings aroused by both of these situations. Then try to explore with class members the reasons we are afraid to confront conflict situations. Most of us know that more people are hurt from such behind-the-back attacks than from direct confrontations.

You might point out the direct means by which Jesus dealt with conflict (see, for example, Matthew 21:12-17). Jesus was not afraid to disagree openly with others, yet he still loved them. Do we think disagreement or conflict with another keeps us from loving him or her? Jesus' words in Matthew 5:43-47 suggest that persons can disagree openly and still love one another.

Joshua 22:21-29—Misinterpreting Others' Actions

These questions call for personal opinions on topics of concern to most people. Your main function as a teacher is to help the class members concentrate on specific ways they can overcome false perceptions of Christianity. Have the group suggest some concrete methods to show concern for persons.

Have someone in the class read aloud Matthew 12:46-50. What does Jesus mean to say about family in this passage? How easily can Jesus be misunderstood? Have the class discuss how easily something said can be misinterpreted.

Joshua 23:5-13 God's Positive and Negative Promises

This section deals with the positive results of a relationship with God and the negative results of a refusal to accept God's love. The Bible repeatedly shows that God does not judge us, but rather we judge ourselves. Jesus' parable of the last judgment shows this truth. (See Matthew 25:31-46.) By our refusal to respond in love to the love we receive, we cut ourselves off from God.

Encourage the class members to talk about specific ways we reject God's will for us. Ask persons to share experiences where they have turned away from the Lord and suffered the consequences. How did they reaffirm their loyalty to God? Have the group discuss concrete ways we can show our love for God.

Joshua 24:19-24—Can We Serve a Jealous God?

The Bible often asserts that God receives our first loyalty. This is the primary meaning of the first commandment: "You shall have no other gods before me" (Exodus 20:3). Loyalty to God even precedes loyalty to family. This assertion is perhaps most poignantly expressed by Abraham's offering of Isaac. Jesus also stressed that family and friends come second to the call of God. (See Matthew 10:34-37.)

With Jesus' attacks on the Pharisees, we see that loyalty to religion can come between persons and God. (See Mark 7:9-13.) Paul attacked Christians who wanted to put their loyalty to one preacher or group ahead of their loyalty to the Lord. (See 1 Corinthians 1:12-13.) Jesus affirmed that we cannot serve more than one master (Matthew 6:24). The choice always stands between the Lord and other gods or loyalties. No matter how difficult it may be for us, God always comes first.

Close the session by asking the class members to share insights they have gained from their study of Joshua 22–24. If time allows, list these insights on chalkboard or a large sheet of paper.

— 8 —

The Lord Raised Up Judges

Judges 1–3

DIMENSION ONE:
WHAT DOES THE BIBLE SAY?

Answer these questions by reading Judges 1

1. What happens when Joshua dies? (Judges 1:1-2)

   The people of Israel ask God who will lead them against the Canaanites. God answers that Judah will lead them.

2. What kind of agreement do Judah and Simeon have? (Judges 1:3)

   They agree to help each other capture their allotted territory.

3. What do Judah and Simeon do to Adoni-Bezek when they capture him? (Judges 1:6)

   They cut off Adoni-Bezek's thumbs and his big toes.

4. What happens when the men of Judah fight against Jerusalem? (Judges 1:8)

   The men of Judah capture Jerusalem and destroy it.

5. How successful is Judah in taking the allotted territory? (Judges 1:19)

   Judah takes possession of the hill country, but cannot drive out the people from the plains.

6. Who are the people of Benjamin unable to drive out from their land? (Judges 1:21)

   Benjamin cannot drive out the Jebusites who live in Jerusalem.

7. What other tribes are unable to drive out all the inhabitants of their territories? (Judges 1:27, 29, 30, 31, 33, 34)

   Manasseh, Ephraim, Zebulun, Asher, Naphtali, and Dan are unable to drive out all the inhabitants.

Answer these questions by reading Judges 2

8. How does the angel of the Lord explain Israel's failure to capture all her land? (Judges 2:1-3)

   The angel explains that Israel has made covenants with the people of the land. Therefore, God will leave them as "thorns in your side and . . . , a snare to you."

9. What do the Israelites do after hearing the angel's message? (Judges 2:4)

   The people of Israel weep aloud.

10. What happens after the death of the generation that had experienced the conquest? (Judges 2:10)

    Another generation grows up that does not know the Lord or what he has done for Israel.

11. Which gods do the people of Israel serve when they turn away from the Lord? (Judges 2:13)

    The people of Israel serve the Baals and the Ashtoreths.

12. How does God respond to the people's rejection? (Judges 2:14-15)

    The Lord becomes angry and hands Israel over to plunderers and sells them to their enemies.

13. After God punishes Israel for a time, what happens? (Judges 2:16)

    The Lord raises up judges to save Israel from the raiders.

14. Why does God still act to save the sinful people? (Judges 2:18)

    The Lord is compassionate to Israel's oppression.

15. What happens when a judge raised up by God dies? (Judges 2:19)

Whenever a judge dies, Israel becomes more corrupt than before.

Answer these questions by reading Judges 3

16. What nations does the Lord leave in the land to test the Israelites? (Judges 3:3)

The Lord leaves the Philistines, the Canaanites, the Sidonians, and the Hivites to test the Israelites.

17. What happens when the Lord's anger burns against Israel? (Judges 3:8)

The Lord sells Israel into the hands of Cushan-Rishathaim.

18. Who does God raise up as a deliverer for Israel? (Judges 3:9)

God raises up Othniel to deliver Israel.

19. What happens when Israel's first deliverer dies? (Judges 3:12)

God places Eglon king of Moab over Israel, because Israel was doing evil in the eyes of the Lord.

20. How is Ehud different from other people? (Judges 3:15)

Ehud is left-handed.

21. How does Ehud prepare himself to meet the Moabite king? (Judges 3:16)

Ehud makes a double-edged sword and straps it on his right thigh under his clothes.

22. What message from God does Ehud deliver to Eglon? (Judges 3:20-22)

Ehud thrusts his sword so deeply into Eglon's belly that the fat closes over it.

23. What does Ehud do after his escape? (Judges 3:27-28)

Sounding a trumpet, Ehud leads the Israelites to the Jordan to possess Moab.

24. Who kills six hundred Philistines with an oxgoad? (Judges 3:31)

Shamgar the son of Anath performs this deed.

DIMENSION TWO: WHAT DOES THE BIBLE MEAN?

Background Information on the Book of Judges

As we begin to study the Book of Judges, you may want to remind the class members that Judges is not a totally separate book. It is part of a larger work, written about 550 B.C., which we call the Deuteronomic history. The books of Deuteronomy and Joshua constitute the first two volumes of this seven-volume work, which runs through Second Kings (minus Ruth). For your own purposes, you might find it helpful to review the comments on the Deuteronomic history found in this teacher book at the beginning of Dimension Two, Lesson 1 page 191.

Although it continues the story we found in Joshua, the Book of Judges tells of a new stage in Israel's relationship to God. In the Deuteronomic history, the period of the judges marks the beginning of Israel's defection from the Lord, and tells of God's response to this defection. After the death of Joshua and his generation, the Israelites begin to give their loyalty to the gods of the land where they have settled. But God's promise to maintain Israel in the land depends on her loyalty to the Lord alone.

In an attempt to bring the people back, God disciplines them by placing them under foreign powers. The people cry out to God for help. They do not repent of their disloyalty; they just call to God for deliverance from their suffering. The Lord is unable to ignore their cries of torment. God empowers different men and women to save Israel.

However, as soon as Israel's pain is alleviated by the work of a divinely appointed deliverer, the people return to their former ways. God again punishes them and the cycle of apostasy, punishment, cry for help, and salvation appears to start over. But the cycle never becomes exactly circular. Israel's condition never returns to its original state of faithfulness to the Lord. Rather, after the death of each judge or deliverer, the situation among the Israelite tribes and their relationship to God becomes worse. The completion of each cycle carries Israel one step further from the goals of loyalty to God and good intertribal relations demanded by the covenant.

The structure of the Book of Judges, then, exhibits a downward spiral. The book's beginning portrays a united Israel, faithful to the Lord, trying to decide what to do now that Joshua has died. But this initial loyalty and unity quickly disappear.

After telling about the work of twelve deliverers, the book ends with a vivid picture of a fragmented Israel living in anarchy. The tribes feel little loyalty toward one another, let alone toward God. No single leader guides Israel. Each person does what is right in his or her own eyes. This conclusion of the Book of Judges sets the stage for the rise of the kingship under Saul and David, described in First and Second Samuel. The period of time encompassed by the Book of Judges is from 1200 B.C. to 1050 B.C.

The name for the book comes from the reference in Judges 2:16 to the Lord's raising up judges to save Israel from "the hands of these raiders." In many Bible versions we find the verb rather than the noun form of this word (for example, "Jephthah judged Israel," in 12:7, Revised Standard Version). The New International Version (NIV) notes this use of the word *judged*, but replaces it with *led* to show the broader function of the judges.

Indeed, the Hebrew word that we translate *judge* has a wider meaning than just the maker of legal decisions. In some passages the word is parallel to the term *deliverer* (see Judges 3:9-10). The role of judge in ancient Israel encompasses the roles of military leader, tribal administrator, and legal functionary. Judges are not elected by the people, nor do they inherit their positions. Israel believes that only God can properly call up a judge or deliverer. The Lord empowers this chosen person to do the job God wants to be done. Victory in battle, deliverance from an oppressor, or successful legal administration all confirm for Israel that this person must indeed be called by God.

Judges 1:1-3. After Joshua's death, the Lord does not immediately appoint a successor. The people inquire of God, either through the use of the lot or through a prophet, who shall now lead them. The answer they receive is not the name of an individual, but a tribe. The Deuteronomic history, which comes from the area of Judah, records that God gave this tribe leadership over all Israel. This idea of Judah's leadership becomes explicit in the rise of David, from the tribe of Judah, to the kingship over Israel.

Now, Judah spurns its divinely appointed role as leader. It joins only with its brother tribe—Simeon—to capture its own land. This move by Judah to help another tribe only in order to get help for its own tribal needs signals the temporary end of unified Israelite action. Israel will not act again as a fully united body until the battle of Ebenezer in about 1050 B.C. (see 1 Samuel 4:1-11). A major theme of the Book of Judges is this descent of Israel into anarchy.

Judges 1:7. Adoni-Bezek describes the justice of his situation. What he has done to others, now happens to him. You might want to remind the group that the Deuteronomic history understands Israel to be an agent of judgment by which God punishes the evil done by the nations of the land.

Judges 1:8. This account of the capture and destruction of Jerusalem by the tribe of Judah contrasts with the assertion in Joshua 15:63 that Judah could not drive out Jerusalem's inhabitants. In verse 21 of Judges 1, we read that because Benjamin cannot capture Jerusalem, the Jebusites still live there. Later, 2 Samuel 5:6-7 tells us that Jerusalem remains an independent non-Israelite city until David takes it.

The reason for this discrepancy is not clear. Perhaps we are seeing a pattern in which David follows in the steps of

his tribe and completes its appointed task. In this opening chapter of Judges, Judah—designated by God as leader over the tribes—rejects its role. Perhaps the Deuteronomic history is suggesting that, with David's kingship and his capture of Jerusalem, the tribe of Judah finally accepts leadership over Israel.

Judges 1:9-15. These verses repeat the incident found in Joshua 15:13-19. (See Lesson 5 in this teacher book.) Perhaps the reason the story is retold is so that Caleb, the only other faithful Israelite from the desert period besides Joshua, can be mentioned again before Israel descends into another period of unfaithfulness.

Judges 1:16-18. If you have a map of Palestine, point out the location of these cities to class members.

Judges 1:22-26. Bethel lies about a mile west of Ai, whose capture we read about in Joshua 7–8. Archaeological research at Bethel indicates that the city was destroyed about 1250 B.C. This story of the capture of Bethel has some parallels with the story of Rahab. (See Joshua 2:1-21; 6:22-25.) You might want to ask the class members to recall the main events in the Rahab story. Then discuss any parallels they see between the two stories.

The land of the Hittites referred to here is probably the region of north Syria. The city of Luz commemorates the betrayal by its builder, since its name means "deception."

Judges 1:27-36. In contrast to earlier statements that Israel acquired all the land promised her by God, this list emphasizes the land and people over which the tribes do not gain control. We find several different relationships here between the Israelite tribes and the native peoples. You might ask the class members what types of relationships they can find.

Although they are unable to drive out all the natives, Manasseh and Zebulun eventually grow strong enough to enslave them. However, Ephraim cannot even do this and must accept independent Canaanite enclaves in the midst of its territory. The situations of Asher and Naphtali are even worse. Their conquests are so unsuccessful that they are described as living among the Canaanites, rather than vice versa (see verses 32-33). The people of Naphtali eventually succeed in forcing Beth Shemesh and Beth Anath to labor for them. Dan, on the other hand, does not even gain its territory. The Amorites drive Dan back from its allotted territory, and the people must seek new land.

Judges 2:1-5. We do not know of a sanctuary called Bokim ("weepers"). Bokim may be another name for Bethel, since Genesis 35:8 tells us that an *Allon Bacuth* ("oak of weeping") is located there.

You might want to have the group compare this angelic appearance to Israel with that of the Lord's commander in Joshua 5:13–6:5. They will easily see the positive content of

JOSHUA, JUDGES, AND RUTH

the Joshua passage versus the negative content of the Judges one.

You might review this Joshua passage (see Lesson 2 in this teacher book, page 197), since the angel of these verses in Judges answers Joshua's question, "Are you for us or for our enemies?" (Joshua 5:13). Because Israel has disobeyed God, the angel says that the inhabitants of the land are now God's appointed adversaries against Israel. Just as the Lord used Israel to punish the evil of the land's natives, God now uses the inhabitants of the land to punish the Israelites for their unfaithfulness.

Judges 2:6-10. These verses repeat Joshua 24:29-31, but with an important addition. This passage in Judges makes explicit what was only implicit earlier. When Joshua and his generation die, a new generation appears that knows neither the Lord nor the Lord's work. The Book of Judges may repeat Joshua's death notice in order to reemphasize his theme that a new, dark age of unbelief has begun for Israel.

Judges 2:11-23. The history now sketches the course of Israel's downward spiral. Israel turns away from the Lord and serves the gods of the land (verses 11-13). In response, God punishes Israel by having Israel's enemies plunder and defeat the tribes (verses 14-15).

Out of pity for Israel's suffering, the Lord raises up judges to save Israel from her enemies (verses 16 and 18). Although the judges save the people from their oppressors, they do not succeed in restoring Israel to a right relationship with God (verse 17). When each judge dies, Israel turns even further away from her loyalty to the Lord (verse 19), starting the cycle over again at a still lower stage (verses 20-23).

This outline emphasizes Israel's rejection of God's judgment and mercy. In later versions of this outline, another element is inserted between the punishment by God and the raising up of judges: the people's outcry to God. (See Judges 3:9, for example.) Since these outcries do not contain words of true repentance, their presence should not be overemphasized. They serve only as occasions for the expression of God's mercy; they do not guarantee it. Israel does not earn grace by calling out to God in pain. God saves the people out of pity for them, not on the basis of their repentance.

Judges 3:1-6. This section mentions another reason why God leaves nations in Israel's midst—to teach warfare to the new generation of Israelites. You will find a description of these ethnic groups in this teacher book, Lesson 1, on Joshua 3:7-13, pages 192–193.

A new people appears in this Judges list—the Sidonians. They are Phoenicians who live in Sidon, on the Mediterranean coast northwest of the tribal possessions. The five cities of the Philistines—Gaza, Ashkelon, Ashdod, Gath, and Ekron—are located on Palestine's southwestern coastal plain. Since the Philistines and Sidonians appear prominently later in the book, find and point out their territories on a map of Palestine.

Judges 3:7-11. The events surrounding the rise of the first judge over Israel—Othniel—show the cycle of disobedience most clearly: (1) Israel's sin, (2) God's punishment, (3) Israel's cry to God, and (4) God's deliverance. Othniel first appears during Joshua's lifetime (Joshua 15:16-19) and again in a repetition of the same event after Joshua's death (Judges 1:11-15).

With this short story of Othniel's deliverance of Israel from Cushan-Rishathaim, we encounter another major theme of the Book of Judges. The deliverers God calls to lead the people are persons normally excluded from Israelite society. Othniel is not even an Israelite! He is from the Kenites, a nomadic tribe that claims descent from Cain, the first murderer. As a Kenite, Othniel is not even included in Israel's covenant with the Lord. Yet it is by the hand of this outsider that God delivers Israel.

All the other major judges also stand either on the edge of the Israelite community or totally outside it. As we will discover in our reading, Ehud is left-handed, and therefore superstitiously excluded from society by the majority, the right-handers. Shamgar is not only a non-Israelite, he probably worships a god other than the Lord. As a woman, Deborah would normally be excluded from participating in war and politics. Gideon is a fearful man always needing assurance from God before going to battle. As the son of a concubine, Abimelech should be denied a leadership role, and Jephthah is an illegitimate son of his father and a prostitute who by law cannot even attend the worship of the Lord.

These judges are persons we would least expect God to choose; yet they are exactly the people the Lord picks to deliver Israel. This theme of God's salvation coming through those least expected to be deliverers is important for the Book of Judges. Later this theme becomes central to the New Testament understanding of the role of Jesus in God's salvation. (See 1 Corinthians 1:18-25.)

Judges 3:12-30. To help understand Ehud's position as an outcast from society, ask whether any left-handed people can tell the group what it is like to be left-handed in a world designed for right-handers. Older left-handed persons can probably tell about being forced to use their right hands or of being held in suspicion by others. Many cultures in the history of the world have seen left-handed persons as being on the side of evil rather than good. However, we discover that Ehud is on God's side.

This story of Ehud is a good example of Hebrew narrative style. Only the details necessary to the story are here: Ehud's left-handedness, Eglon's obesity, the small roof chamber, the locked door, and the sword's double edge.

The final detail about the sword is more noteworthy than we would normally suppose. During this period in Israel, there are two types of swords. The main battle sword—designed for slashing—resembles a sickle, but with the cutting edge on the outside of the blade's curve. Its pronounced curve would be difficult to conceal under clothing. The second type, a double-edged sword, is used only for stabbing. Its handle is strong enough for cutting. Also, this sword would lie flat along a person's leg, making it hard to detect under a garment.

With Ehud, then, we meet a trickster who works God's will by deception. He uses his left-handedness, his role as a tribute bearer, and Eglon's curiosity about a secret message to maneuver the Moabite king into a situation where he can be killed.

Judges 3:31. As the student book notes, Shamgar is not only a non-Israelite, but probably also a nonworshiper of the Lord. Worship of God is not a necessary prerequisite for the Lord's use of a person. The prophets will often see God working for Israel's good in the actions of foreign kings and nations. The Book of Isaiah even calls the Persian king, Cyrus, anointed (see Isaiah 45:1).

An oxgoad—a pole about five or six feet long with a pointed metal end—is usually used to prod cattle.

DIMENSION THREE:
WHAT DOES THE BIBLE MEAN TO ME?

Judges 2:6-10
Each Generation Must Know the Lord

You might turn your class discussion into a workshop on experience. Ask the class members to share personal experiences of God and what they have learned from their own and from experiences with God shared by others. At the end of the class time, ask the members to reflect on the stories they have just shared and what insights they have just gained from others. You can then point out the value of the process, both for the early Israelites—and for themselves.

Judges 2:11-18—God's Grace, Not Human Acts

With this discussion topic, we are at the heart of Christianity's message. We are saved by what God does through grace and mercy, not by anything we do. Ephesians 2:1-10 (especially verses 8-9) states this view most clearly. Paul works this concept out in great detail in his discussion of faith versus works of the law (see Romans 3:21-31). This biblical understanding that we do not earn our salvation in any way, that deliverance is a pure gift based on God's love and mercy for us, is so crucial for Christian faith that it cannot be overemphasized.

Judges 3:15-23
The Double-edged Sword of Judgment

To open this discussion, you might read aloud Hebrews 4:12-13, which speaks about God's word in terms of a double-edged sword that penetrates and judges each person. Revelation 1:16 describes the son of man by saying that "out of his mouth came a sharp double-edged sword." These passages will help put the story of Ehud in a wider biblical perspective. You might want to discuss with the group the meaning of the Bible's use of the double-edged sword as a symbol for God's word of judgment. How is the double-edged sword an effective image for us today?

In the remaining time, ask the class members to share new insights from today's lesson on Judges 1–3. List these insights on chalkboard or a piece of paper.

9

Deborah and Gideon

Judges 4–8

DIMENSION ONE:
WHAT DOES THE BIBLE SAY?

Answer these questions by reading Judges 4

1. Who leads Israel after Ehud's death? (Judges 4:4)

   Deborah, a prophetess, leads Israel after Ehud's death.

2. How does Barak respond to the Lord's command given through the prophetess? (Judges 4:8)

   Barak says he will not go unless Deborah goes with him.

3. What does Sisera do when he hears the tribal armies of Zebulun and Naphtali have formed? (Judges 4:12-13)

   Sisera calls out his 900 chariots of iron and all his men.

4. What is the outcome of the battle? (Judges 4:15-17)

   The Lord routs Sisera, all his chariots, and all his army. Sisera escapes on foot while all his army is killed.

5. Why does Sisera flee to the tent of Jael? (Judges 4:17)

   Sisera flees to Jael's tent because there is peace between his king and Jael's husband.

6. What does Jael do to Sisera? (Judges 4:21)

   Jael hammers a tent peg into Sisera's temple while he is asleep in her tent.

Answer these questions by reading Judges 5

7. Who composes the song in Chapter 5? (Judges 5:1)

   Deborah and Barak compose the song.

8. Which tribes participate in the battle? (Judges 5:14-15, 18)

   Ephraim, Benjamin, Makir [son of Manasseh], Zebulun, Issachar, and Naphtali participate in the battle.

9. Which tribes are condemned for not taking part in the battle? (Judges 5:15-17)

   Reuben, Gilead, Dan, and Asher are condemned for not taking part.

10. What happens during the battle at Taanach by the waters of Megiddo? (Judges 5:19-21)

    The stars fight against Sisera, and the river Kishon sweeps them away.

Answer these questions by reading Judges 6

11. Where does the angel of the Lord appear to Gideon? (Judges 6:11)

    The Lord's angel appears to Gideon under the oak in Ophrah.

12. What does Gideon say in response to the angel's command to save Israel from the hand of Midian? (Judges 6:15)

    Gideon asks how he can save Israel since his clan is the weakest of his tribe and he is the least in his family.

13. Why does Gideon go at night to replace Baal's altar and the Asherah pole with an altar to God? (Judges 6:27)

    Gideon destroys these objects at night because he is afraid of his family and the men of his town.

14. Why does Gideon gain the new name *Jerub-Baal*, "Let Baal contend"? (Judges 6:32)

    He gains this new name because he broke down Baal's altar.

15. What signs does Gideon demand from God to show that God will indeed save Israel? (Judges 6:36-40)

First, Gideon asks that dew fall only on the fleece, and not on the ground. Then Gideon asks that the ground be wet while the fleece remains dry.

Answer these questions by reading Judges 7

16. Why does God want Gideon's army to be smaller? (Judges 7:2)

God wants a small army so that Israel will not claim the glory for herself, but recognize God as the victor.

17. How does God tell Gideon to reduce his force to only 300 men? (Judges 7:3-7)

Gideon first sends home everyone who is afraid. Then he takes the remaining force to the water and chooses only those who lap water with their tongues.

18. What does Gideon overhear when he goes down to the Midianite camp? (Judges 7:13-14)

He overhears a man telling a comrade about a dream he had in which a barley cake strikes down a tent. The dreamer's comrade interprets the dream to mean that God has given them into Gideon's hand.

19. What do Gideon's men do at the outskirts of the Midianite camp? (Judges 7:19-21)

The men blow their trumpets, break the jars containing torches, and cry, "A sword for the LORD and for Gideon!"

20. What does the Lord do to the Midianites? (Judges 7:22)

The Lord causes the Midianites to turn against one another and causes them to flee.

Answer these questions by reading Judges 8

21. How do the men of Succoth and Peniel respond to Gideon's request for food? (Judges 8:6, 8)

They refuse to give him food because he has not yet captured the two Midianite kings.

22. After Gideon captures those he was pursuing, what does he do to Succoth and Peniel? (Judges 8:16-17)

Gideon flails the elders of Succoth with thorns and briers. He breaks down the tower of Peniel and kills its men.

23. Who did Zebah and Zalmunna kill? (Judges 8:19)

Zebah and Zalmunna kill the brothers of Gideon.

24. Why does Gideon reject the offer of the men of Israel to rule over them? (Judges 8:23)

Gideon rejects the role of ruler because only the Lord rules over Israel.

25. What does Gideon make with the golden earrings his men took as plunder? (Judges 8:24-27)

Gideon makes an ephod that he places in his town, Ophrah.

26. What name does Jerub-Baal give to his son by his concubine in Shechem? (Judges 8:31)

Jerub-Baal names this son Abimelech.

DIMENSION TWO:
WHAT DOES THE BIBLE MEAN?

Judges 4:1-3. The cycle of obedience and disobedience begins again. Upon the death of the judge, the people do evil. God punishes them for their unfaithfulness, and the people cry out to the Lord. This introduction sets the stage for the story of Deborah.

Judges 4:4-5. Deborah's seat of judgment lies between five and twelve miles north of Jerusalem. As a prophetess, Deborah stands in good company. Miriam, the sister of Moses, was a prophetess (see Exodus 15:20). Huldah was the third Old Testament prophetess. She is the person whom the high priest asks whether the book found in the Temple is really God's law (see 2 Kings 22:14). Her word of affirmation begins the great reform movement under King Josiah. While female prophets are unusual in the Old Testament, the prophet Joel saw the day coming when all men and women would receive God's spirit of prophecy (Joel 2:28-29). Quoting Joel, Peter proclaims that the day has already arrived with the coming of the Spirit at Pentecost. (See Acts 2:17-18.)

Judges 4:6-10. On a map of Palestine, either in the back of a Bible or on a wall map in your classroom, locate these places for group members. All are found in the northern area of Palestine. A Bible atlas can be especially helpful to you for this lesson and the rest of the lessons on Judges, since an atlas often gives detailed maps of each movement and battle from a particular Bible period.

As a prophetess, Deborah calls upon Barak to summon the armies of Naphtali and Zebulun to fight against Sisera. Barak refuses to go unless Deborah goes with him. His reasons for this demand are unclear, although it apparently was customary in Israel for a prophet to accompany the army to war. (See 2 Kings 3:9-20.) Perhaps the presence of a prophet or prophetess shows that the Lord is with Israel's soldiers. However, because Barak demands her presence, Deborah foretells that he will not receive the glory for killing the enemy commander. Since Barak demanded the presence of a woman, Sisera shall fall by the hand of a woman.

Judges 4:11. Normally the Kenites roamed through the southern or middle part of the Promised Land. However, Heber has journeyed to the far north to camp near the city of refuge, Kedesh in Naphtali. (See Lesson 6, on Joshua 20:7-8.) The NIV note says that *brother-in-law* might also be *father-in-law.* Elsewhere, Moses' father-in-law is said to be a Midianite called Jethro (Exodus 3:1) or Reuel (Exodus 2:18).

Judges 4:13. Iron chariots gave the Canaanites a technological advantage over Israel on the battlefield. The period of the judges occurred during the transition from the Bronze Age to the Iron Age. Bronze swords and spears work against iron armor and chariots about as effectively as bullets work against tanks.

Judges 4:14-16. This account of the battle gives no details as to how the Israelite infantry succeeded against Canaanite chariots. The poetic version of the battle suggests a rainstorm and flash flood caught the chariots in mud and water (see 5:20-21).

Judges 4:17-22. Sisera comes to the tent of a nomad with whom his king is at peace. He expects both hospitality and sanctuary. Among ancient peoples, and especially among desert nomads (even into the modern age), the protection of a guest is a sacred duty. If necessary, the host must sacrifice even his most valuable possession to protect the honor and life of a guest. (See Genesis 19:2-8; Judges 19:16-24.)

This custom of hospitality and sanctuary developed as a way to guarantee the possibility of travel in a land with no law enforcement agencies. If you protect those who travel across your territory, then they will protect you when you move through their land. If everyone along the way protects the guest, travelers can make their journeys without fear of being attacked.

At first Jael appears to offer Sisera such protection, and he feels safe. Jael helps to put Sisera further at ease by giving him more than he asks. He asks for water, she gives him milk. He seeks sleep; she gives him eternal rest. By killing her guest, Jael breaks one of the most sacred customs of her world. Yet, as we have seen with Rahab (Joshua 2:1-21) and the people of Gibeon (Joshua 9:3-15), all customs and loyalties—no matter how honorable or hallowed—take second place to loyalty to the Lord. Although they are non-Israelites, the Kenites worship Yahweh. Therefore, Jael's first responsibility is not to protect her guest, but to carry out the will of God.

Judges 5:1-31. The Song of Deborah contains a very ancient form of Hebrew that uses archaic grammatical constructions and rare words. The language of this poem is very different from the language of the rest of the Deuteronomic history. Also, the language of all the Old Testament is distant in time from our language. If you can find a copy of Chaucer's *Canterbury Tales* in the original Middle English language, read some of it to the group. It will sound both foreign and strangely familiar at the same time. Some of it will be unintelligible. In the Song of Deborah, scholars are not always certain what the Hebrew means.

You can do an exercise with the class members to show them the problems involved in translating this song. Using different translations of the Bible, have the students read aloud various sections of the poem. Verses 2, 10-11, and 13-16 are especially difficult. Ask them to compare and contrast how the different versions translate these sections. (Note also what the footnotes of the translations say.)

You might want to write these differences on a chalkboard or on a sheet of paper. Use parallel columns, one for each version. Does the group see any substantive differences among the translations?

With the repetition in poetry of the events we have just read about in prose in Chapter 4, we come across a fairly rare phenomenon in the Old Testament. We have two versions of the same event (see also Exodus 14 and 15). You might want to have the group compare the prose version in Chapter 4 with the poetic version in Chapter 5. Some similarities and differences are listed below. The class members may come up with other ideas.

Similarities

1. Deborah and Barak identified as Israel's leaders (4:14; 5:12)
2. Sisera identified as leader of the Canaanite army (4:2; 5:20)
3. Banks of Kishon River as site of battle (4:7; 5:21)
4. Defeat of Canaanite chariots by Israel (4:15; 5:21-22)
5. Sisera asks for water, is given milk (4:19; 5:25)
6. Jael identified as Sisera's killer (4:21; 5:26-27)
7. Tent peg and hammer as instruments of death (4:21; 5:26)

Differences

1. In Judges 4, Jabin is identified as the king of Hazor (4:2); in Judges 5 he is not mentioned.
2. Judges 4 notes that two Israelite tribes participated in the battle (4:6); Judges 5:14-18 mentions Ephraim, Benjamin, Makir, Zebulun, Issachar, and Naphtali.
3. Judges 4:14 says the battle took place at the foot of Mount Tabor; in Judges 5, Taanach is the location of the battle (5:19).

4. The specific cause of victory is an Israelite attack in Judges 4:15 and a rainstorm and flash flood in Judges 5:20-21.
5. In Judges 4, Sisera dies after Jael drives a tent peg through his head while he is sleeping (4:21); in Judges 5 he is awake (5:26-27).

The feminine perspective of the Song of Deborah is an element well worth emphasizing to the group. The poem looks at the events through the experiences of the women involved. Verses 2-23 speak about the events in which Deborah is most involved—the summoning of the tribes and the battle itself. Jael's murder of Sisera is described from her perspective, especially the dramatic, slow-motion description of Sisera dropping from her blow. (See 5:26-27.) The poem's last scene takes place in the royal harem, where no men are allowed. The mother's worry and the women's explanation reflect feminine experience. That the author of this poem is a woman may seem to be an obvious conclusion, but many people are surprised at this possibility.

Judges 6:7-10. This is the only appearance by a male prophet in the books of Joshua, Judges, and Ruth. Notice how he appears after Deborah and how he remains anonymous.

Judges 6:11-24. This call of Gideon to the Lord's service shares the same general pattern as other divine summonses. The elements are (1) a divine commission or appearance, (2) a claim by the chosen person to be unfit to do the job, (3) a rejection of that claim by God and God's promise to be present, and (4) a sign given to demonstrate God's power. We find this pattern in the calls of Moses (Exodus 3–4) and Jeremiah (Jeremiah 1).

This call of Gideon reveals much about Gideon's character. The angel of the Lord finds him hiding from the Midianites. All through the story of Gideon, the theme of fear continually reappears (see Judges 6:15, 27; 7:10; 8:20). Rather than a strong, courageous warrior, God chooses a coward to lead the people. There is probably some irony present when the angel addresses Gideon hiding in the pit of the winepress: "mighty warrior" (verse 12). This irony could explain Gideon's own sarcastic retort that, if the Lord is with Israel, why is Israel suffering so much? The presence of God is supposed to bring persons strength and courage. Fright and dismay show a lack of faith and trust in the Lord. Gideon's fearful nature is not dispelled by God's promise and presence.

Judges 6:25-32. The first acts the Lord commands Gideon to do are to tear down the altar of the Canaanite god Baal and to cut down the tree or wooden pole representing the goddess Asherah. The Israelites would have seen some humor in this story of Gideon using a bull to tear down the altar of Baal, who, because of his fertility association, is known as "the bull." Gideon does what God commands; but because of his fearful nature, he does it at night.

This story explains why one of the great judges of Israel had the name of a Baal worshiper. Jerub-Baal would normally be an affirmation of Baal's power, not a challenge that he prove himself a god if he can. Considering both Gideon's opening comment to the Lord's messenger and the fact that the altar he tears down is his own father's, there is a good chance Gideon was raised in the worship of Baal.

Judges 6:36-40. Gideon's fear leads him to test God. The Deuteronomic law declares, "Do not test the LORD your God" (Deuteronomy 6:16). However, Gideon demands a more dramatic, miraculous sign before he proceeds.

Judges 7:1-3. Ironically, after showing his continued lack of courage in his demand for signs, Gideon leads his troops into camp at the spring of Harod, which means "fear." There God tells him to whittle down his army's size by invoking the rule of holy war that all men who are afraid should return home. (See Deuteronomy 20:8.) How little Israel still trusts the Lord's power is seen in the return home of over two-thirds of Gideon's force. Gideon does not stand alone in his fear.

Judges 7:4-8. As the student book notes, no satisfactory answer has been given as to how the two modes of drinking set the two groups of warriors apart. Class members might want to make their own suggestions. Perhaps the method of selection is based on alertness. Those who kneel with their faces to the water are not alert for danger. Those who lapped with their hands to their mouths were in a posture ready to fight at any time. However, as we soon learn, these 300 brave and trusting Israelite warriors are led by a man who is afraid and still does not quite trust the Lord.

Judges 7:9-14. The Lord tells Gideon that the victory is already secure. But, if Gideon is still afraid, if he does not yet trust God's promise, he should go down to the Midianite camp. Note that he is told to go down to the camp only if he is still afraid. By his reconnaissance, Gideon shows that he does not yet trust God. Only after hearing the Midianite's dream and its interpretation—that God has given Midian into Gideon's hand—does Gideon believe in the victory. Here we have the startling portrait of an Israelite judge who trusts the word of his enemy more than he trusts the word of the Lord. Again, we see someone we would least expect chosen to accomplish God's purposes.

Judges 7:16-23. In the defeat of Midian, Israel demonstrates her presence and God does the fighting. All Israel does is pursue the Midianites after the Lord's victory.

Judges 8:4-9. The growing deterioration of Israelite communal unity and loyalty are clearly evident in this passage. In the Song of Deborah, we saw that not all the tribes responded to Deborah's summons to battle. Here in Judges 8 two Israelite towns reject outright any aid to God's chosen leader. As we soon find out, they may have a good reason for this refusal, since Gideon is turning the Lord's army into an instrument of personal revenge. Still, their refusal of aid and Gideon's promise of revenge show us that Israel not only has been turning away from the Lord in her cycles of disobedience but has also been turning against herself.

Judges 8:13-17. Verse 14 suggests that the knowledge of writing was widespread in ancient Israel. The invention of the alphabet in the region of Aram [Syria] and Palestine only a few centuries before the conquest made reading and writing easy so that many more people could learn them.

Gideon uses the information given to him by the young man to fulfill his threat on Succoth. He also destroys Peniel, the place where Jacob had wrestled God (see Genesis 32:22-30). Whereas earlier some attempt was made to arbitrate difficulties within Israel before resorting to war, now we see an Israelite leader destroying Israelite cities for not going along with his personal vengeance.

Judges 8:18-21. We now learn that in order to achieve personal vengeance, Gideon continued his pursuit of the Midianites well after the victory had been won. In a polygamous society, a person's first loyalty would be to the brothers and sisters of his own mother, then to his half-brothers and half-sisters by the same father but different mothers. Zebah and Zalmunna had slain Gideon's full brothers. By custom, Gideon was indeed required to seek revenge for their deaths. However, he does not have the right to use the army selected by God to achieve his vengeance.

Gideon's request that Jether slay the two Midianite leaders is an honor for Jether but a dishonor for the kings. By executing them, Jether would proclaim his solidarity with his family. On the other hand, being killed by a mere boy would bring shame on the warrior leaders. Like father, like son! Jether is too afraid to slay his uncle's murderers. Zebah and Zalmunna goad Gideon into living up to his name, which means "hacker," by killing them himself. To die at the hands of a warrior is not shameful.

Judges 8:22-28. In one way, Gideon shows his loyalty to the Lord by rejecting hereditary kingship over Israel. Then he immediately turns away from God by using a portion of the plunder of battle to make an ephod. Although scholars do not know exactly what an ephod is in this case, this passage emphasizes that it perverts Israel as well as Gideon and his family. In his last official act, Israel's deliverer sets up something that will turn Israel even further away from her God.

Judges 8:33-35. With Gideon's death, the cycle begins again. The name Baal-Berith means "lord of the covenant." The people of Israel turn from their covenant with the Lord and enter into a covenant with Baal. Not only do they not remember the Lord, they also forget what Gideon and his family have done for them.

DIMENSION THREE: WHAT DOES THE BIBLE MEAN TO ME?

Judges 4:4-9—A Woman's Place in Peace and War

The place of women in today's world, let alone in the church, is hotly debated. In Judges 4 we see a woman accepted in the roles of prophetess of God's word, maker of legal decisions, and participant in war. These roles, which many people would deny to women today, were accepted by the Israelites over 3,000 years ago!

To deal with this issue of a woman's place in the world from a Christian perspective, we need to take seriously the fact that the Gospels often portray Jesus treating women as equal to men. For example, he broke the customary taboos against speaking to women publicly (John 4), and he even accepted women sitting at his feet listening (Luke 10:39), clearly one of the roles of discipleship.

Peter declares, in his Pentecost sermon, that the age of the prophetic spirit coming upon men and women has dawned with the resurrection of Christ (Acts 2:17-18). And Paul speaks of two women, Euodia and Syntyche, who labor beside him in the gospel (Philippians 4:2-3).

Almost everyone has heard the passages in 1 Corinthians 14:33-36 and 1 Timothy 2:9-15 that speak against female participation in the church. How far we can press these passages is a dilemma. First Corinthians 14 contradicts both Paul's practice of using women for the spreading of the gospel and his earlier statement that, when women speak out in the church, they should do so with their heads covered. (See 1 Corinthians 11:5.) Consequently, many scholars believe these verses in 1 Corinthians 14 may have been inserted later by someone trying to gain apostolic authority for a more traditional view of women.

The issue, then, of a woman's place in the community is complicated even in the Bible. According to Genesis 3:16, woman's subjection to man occurs as punishment for her disobedience in the garden of Eden. However, with the coming of God's kingdom this curse is lifted and women are restored to full equality with men as originally intended by God. (See Acts 2:17-21.) The main question Christians must ask is, Do we participate now in the kingdom, or is it totally future? An answer of yes to the first question suggests that women are equal now to men. Yes to the second question indicates the view that women are still under the curse of subjection.

One of the major themes of Judges is that God is responsible for the selection of leaders, and often God's choices appear illogical. Normally, in Israel and perhaps even today, persons do not expect a woman prophet, judge, or warrior. But God does not work on the basis of human expectations and desires. Instead, God acts on the basis of divine purposes. If God calls a woman to deliver the word of God, to political leadership, or even to military leadership, should we not be able to accept God's choice?

Judges 6:25-32—Afraid to Contend for the Lord

Jesus' statement in Matthew 10:16-23 that his disciples should "be as shrewd as snakes and as innocent as doves" might contribute to this discussion. In this passage, Jesus tells his disciples what they can expect to receive from those who hear their witness. You might read this passage to the group as a model for how we should speak out for the Lord. These verses suggest that we are not supposed to seek confrontation for conflict's sake, but we must still witness publicly to what we believe, no matter what the consequences.

Judges 8:4-21—Using God for Our Own Purposes

The student book speaks about Gideon's use of God's power to achieve his own purposes. A more contemporary parallel can be found with Jim Jones and the mass suicide at Jonestown in November of 1978. Many of the class members have probably heard or read about the incident. Some may even have seen the television movie broadcast on Jim Jones's life.

Evidence suggests that Jones started out his ministry with a strong sense of calling and a strong desire to help others. As time passed and more people became loyal to him, he centered his followers' faith more and more upon himself. Finally, he asked them to kill themselves out of loyalty to him. Ask the group to think of other examples of persons who used God for their own purposes.

Close today's session by listing on chalkboard or large sheet of paper any insights the class members have gained from their study of Judges 4–8.

— 10 —

Abimelech and Jephthah

Judges 9–12

DIMENSION ONE:
WHAT DOES THE BIBLE SAY?

Answer these questions by reading Judges 9

1. How does Abimelech appeal for the leadership of Shechem? (Judges 9:2)

   He asks it if would not be better to be ruled by one son of Jerub-Baal than by seventy.

2. How does Abimelech use the money given him by the men of Shechem? (Judges 9:4)

   He hires reckless adventurers to follow him.

3. What happens to Abimelech's brothers? (Judges 9:5)

   Abimelech slays all seventy of them except for Jotham, who hides himself.

4. What do the citizens of Shechem and Beth Millo do to Abimelech? (Judges 9:6)

   The citizens crown Abimelech king.

5. Who are the main characters in the story that Jotham tells from Mount Gerizim? (Judges 9:8-15)

   The main characters in Jotham's story are the olive tree, the fig tree, the vine, and the thornbush.

6. What curse does Jotham level against Shechem, Beth Millo, and Abimelech? (Judges 9:20)

   Jotham says that if they have not acted honorably then Abimelech and the two cities shall destroy each other with fire.

7. How does God intervene in the relationship between Abimelech and Shechem? (Judges 9:23)

   God sends an evil spirit to separate Abimelech and the citizens of Shechem.

8. How does Abimelech react to the treachery of Shechem? (Judges 9:43-45)

   He kills its citizens, destroys it, and scatters salt over it.

9. How does Abimelech destroy the tower of Shechem? (Judges 9:48-49)

   He and his men place branches against the stronghold and set it on fire.

10. What happens to Abimelech when he leads an attack against the tower of Thebez? (Judges 9:52-53)

    A woman throws down an upper millstone that cracked Abimelech's skull.

11. What does Abimelech ask his armor-bearer to do? (Judges 9:54)

    Abimelech asks his armor-bearer to kill him and prevent his death by a woman.

Answer these questions by reading Judges 10

12. Who arose after Abimelech? (Judges 10:1, 3)

    Tola and Jair appear after Abimelech.

13. What do the Israelites say to the Lord? (Judges 10:10)

    The Israelites confess that they have sinned against God by serving the Baals.

14. How does the Lord respond to Israel's cry for help? (Judges 10:11-14)

    God rejects Israel's cry and tells her to call upon the other gods she has chosen to save her.

15. Who are Jephthah's parents? (Judges 11:1)

Jephthah's father is Gilead, and his mother is a prostitute.

16. What do Jephthah's half-brothers do to him? (Judges 11:2)

Jephthah's half-brothers drive him out of their father's house and deny him any inheritance.

17. What do the elders of Gilead promise Jephthah if he goes with them to fight the Ammonites? (Judges 11:8-10)

The elders of Gilead promise that they will make Jephthah head over them if he defeats the Ammonites.

18. Who does Jephthah declare will decide the issue between Israel and Ammon? (Judges 11:27)

Jephthah declares that the Lord will decide between Israel and Ammon.

19. What vow does Jephthah make to the Lord? (Judges 11:30-31)

Jephthah vows that if the Lord gives him victory, he will sacrifice whatever comes out the door of his house to meet him when he returns.

20. Who comes forth from Jephthah's house to meet him? (Judges 11:34)

Jephthah's only child, a daughter, comes out to meet him.

21. What happens for the next two months? (Judges 11:38)

For two months Jephthah's daughter and her friends go to the hills to weep because of her virginity.

Answer these questions by reading Judges 12

22. Why do the men of Ephraim threaten to burn Jephthah's house with him in it? (Judges 12:1)

The men of Ephraim threaten Jephthah because he did not call them to go fight the Ammonites.

23. How do the Gileadites trick the Ephraimites trying to escape across the Jordan? (Judges 12:5-6)

The Gileadites make those who want to cross the Jordan try to say the word Shibboleth. If they mispronounce it, they are killed.

24. Who are the next three judges after Jephthah? (Judges 12:8, 11, 13)

The next three judges are Ibzan, Elon, and Abdon.

DIMENSION TWO: WHAT DOES THE BIBLE MEAN?

The rise of Abimelech to leadership shows that Israel's relationship with God has slipped yet another notch. Abimelech does not wait for the Lord to choose him to lead Israel. He chooses himself! The story of Abimelech tells what happens to someone who usurps God's right of leadership. That person quite literally destroys himself.

Judges 9:1-6. Apparently, after Gideon's death, his sons continued in some sort of leadership role. Abimelech, as the son of a concubine—a sort of second-class wife—would have no place in this leadership role. He goes to the city of his mother and argues that it would be better for the citizens of Shechem to be ruled by one than by many. He also notes his blood relationship to the Shechemites. Since at this time in history Shechem is still basically a Canaanite town, rule by a man directly related to the Shechemites would be better than rule by the full-blooded Israelite sons of Gideon.

Abimelech uses the funds given to him by Shechem to create his own private army. He then goes to Ophrah and destroys all potential rivals to the throne by slaying his seventy half-brothers. Slaying them on one stone suggests that he slew them in the manner of a sacrifice, perhaps to Baal-Berith (the Canaanite god in Shechem). Some scholars suggest that the reason Abimelech slays his brothers on a stone is so their blood will not spill on the ground and cry out for vengeance.

Judges 9:7-15. Jotham's fable concludes with an image that is both ludicrous and serious. The idea of great trees seeking shade and protection from a thornbush is ridiculous, but the threat of destruction that the bramble makes is not funny. The thornbush is a main source of kindling in Palestine, since it makes a very hot fire. The thornbush king cannot protect his towering subjects, but he can destroy them. The fable warns that the dangers of having a king far outweigh any possible advantages.

Judges 9:16-21. Jotham now utters a curse against Abimelech, Shechem, and Beth Millo. Since he is the last of his family and has just escaped death, his words carry special power. If the people have faithfully honored Gideon and his family, then the cities' relationship to Abimelech will go well. But if—as is obvious—the people have not acted in good faith by making Abimelech king, then all parties to the agreement will destroy one another.

Jotham's final act clearly shows that he is a son of Gideon. He runs away because he was "afraid" of Abimelech (see last week's lesson). Gideon's sons take after their father. Either they are afraid, like Jether (Judges 8:20) and Jotham (9:21), or they use their power for their own purposes, like Abimelech (9:4-6).

Judges 9:22-25. This passage suggests that Abimelech's kingship over Shechem actually extends to all of Israel. However, Abimelech's leadership does not come from God, but from his own ambition. So God enters into the story by sending an "evil spirit" to separate Abimelech and the citizens of Shechem. Elsewhere in the Book of Judges, God's spirit is a positive force empowering God's chosen leader to accomplish his or her task. (See the note on Othniel in 3:10, and the note on Samson in 14:6.) However, here in Judges 9 God sends his power as a negative force to destroy a self-appointed leader. This story is one of defeat rather than success—defeat of the one who tries to usurp God's right to designate Israel's judges.

Judges 9:26-29. Apparently, Gaal is a full-blooded Canaanite and therefore claims an even closer relationship to the Shechemites than Abimelech, who is only half Canaanite. By participating in their Canaanite festival for the grape harvest, Gaal shows his full unity with the citizens. During this celebration Gaal drinks a lot of wine. Under its influence, he boasts that he can defeat Abimelech.

Judges 9:34-41. Zebul, the governor, says that the men Gaal thinks are coming are only the shadows of the mountains receding before the morning light. Thus Zebul gains time, and Gaal and his army become more vulnerable. The defeat of Gaal, no real friend of Shechem and Zebul, takes place outside the walls of Shechem. The city still stands in opposition to Abimelech.

Judges 9:42-45. In an ambush similar to the one used by Israel at Ai (see Joshua 8:1-23), Abimelech's army attacks the Shechemites as they come out of the city in the morning to work in their fields. Abimelech leads his company to the city gates both to gain entrance to the city and to block off any escape by the citizens back into the safety of the city walls. He slays all those in the fields and all those within the city walls. Then he destroys the outer town and scatters salt over it.

Judges 9:46-49. Most ancient cities had outer walls as a first line of defense. They also had inner fortresses that could be used as a second line of defense in case the walls were captured. In Shechem, this inner fortress is also the temple of El-Berith, the god of the covenant. Archaeological research suggests that fortress temples were relatively common structures in the middle of the second millennium B.C.

Abimelech uses fire to destroy this final defensive structure. Just as slaying his brothers on one stone had sacrificial overtones, burning the people in their temple also has sacrificial implications. In addition, the burning of the temple carries out the words of Jotham's curse (see 9:15).

Excavations at Shechem show a fortress-like structure that may have doubled as a temple and that was destroyed about 1100 B.C.

Judges 9:50-57. The fulfillment of the second half of Jotham's curse—the destruction of Abimelech—takes place at nearby Thebez. Although Abimelech is not literally burned to death (see verse 20), he is struck down in the act of setting fire to the inner fortress of Thebez. The upper millstone that the woman uses to strike down Abimelech was a stone that turned above a stationary stone. Between these two, grain was ground into flour. Despite his intention, Abimelech does not escape a dishonorable death. Later, David's commander, Joab, remembers that Abimelech died by a woman's hand (see 2 Samuel 11:21).

The story of Abimelech ends with a typical Israelite affirmation that it is God who punishes evildoers for their crimes. In fulfillment of Jotham's curse, the evildoers Abimelech and Shechem destroy each other.

Judges 10:1-5. The accounts of the judges' activities take two forms. The first form, which we have seen up to this point, consists of stories describing in varying detail the activities (usually military) of those who judge or deliver Israel. In two places, here and in Judges 12:7-15, we come across the second form. This form is a short notice that tells us only the name of the person who judged Israel, along with his place of residence. Sometimes a note on descendants and property, years of service, or place of burial is also included. These persons are often called the minor judges to distinguish them from the major judges described in the rest of the book. Calling them minor judges does not evaluate the quality of their work, but rather the quantity of material we have about them. In a similar way, we give the title Minor Prophets to the twelve short prophetic books to distinguish them from Isaiah, Jeremiah, and Ezekiel, which we call the Major Prophets.

Since so little data is available about these minor judges, we cannot be certain why they are called judges. Some scholars suggest that they are persons who recite God's law at the tribal assemblies. Others say they are peacetime administrators over the tribes. We do not have enough information to decide what the minor judges do to deserve their inclusion in the Book of Judges. However, we can say that including them brings the number of Israel's deliverers in this period to a total of twelve, the same number as the tribes of Israel.

Judges 10:10-16. As the student book notes, these are the only words of confession uttered by Israel in the whole Book of Judges. However, verse 15 shows that the people do not truly repent. They are not sorry for what they have done. They are coming to the Lord only because they need God to deliver them from their oppressors. According to verses 11-14, God rejects such a self-serving confession. The Lord turns away from those who only "repent" in times of trouble. Although God tells them to go back to their other gods, the people put away the foreign gods. God does not raise up a deliverer because of what the people have done. Rather, the Lord acts on the basis of an inability to allow the people to suffer further.

Judges 10:17-18. With the Ammonite oppression we move into the territory east of the Jordan River, the area of Gilead.

Judges 11:1-3. To help the group understand how little standing Jephthah's illegitimacy gave him, read aloud Deuteronomy 23:2. According to the law, Jephthah cannot even enter the Lord's sanctuary. Yet he is the one who now delivers Israel. The thematic portrayal of the major judges as outcasts from society comes forth most clearly with Jephthah. Notice that Jephthah does what Abimelech did (Judges 9:4) and what David will do (1 Samuel 22:1-2). He gathers outcasts like himself into a private army.

Judges 11:4-11. The choosing of Jephthah as leader shows that Israel continues on her downward path of unfaithfulness. Israel has just called on God for aid, but rather than waiting for the Lord to choose Israel's deliverer, the people choose their own leader. Jephthah does not usurp his leadership role as did Abimelech. But he does accept his role from human rather than divine hands. For his presumption, Jephthah will be punished severely (see 11:34-39).

Judges 11:12-28. As we discovered in the preceding passage, Jephthah is adept at bargaining. He now tries to settle Ammon's dispute with Israel through diplomatic negotiation.

Judges 11:29. The Spirit of the Lord comes upon Jephthah only after he finally places the Ammonite dispute before the Lord, the rightful Judge. Jephthah fails when he depends on himself. When he gives the problem over to God, he receives the power to deal with the issue.

Judges 11:30-40. Israelite law does not require the Lord's worshipers to make vows. But if a person does make a vow, he or she must carry it out. You might read Numbers 30:2 and Deuteronomy 23:21-23 to the class members so they understand the biblical attitude toward vows. This total necessity to carry out a promise made in the name of the Lord is the real reason God commands Israel, "You shall not misuse the name of the LORD your God, for the LORD will not hold anyone guiltless who misuses his name" (Deuteronomy 5:11).

By leaving indefinite who or what will be sacrificed (the Hebrew of verse 31 literally reads, "the coming out one that comes out"), Jephthah allows the Lord to decide what will come out to Jephthah. He probably assumes that the first one to come out of the house on his return will be an animal, since houses served as residences for both people and animals. While the family lived on a raised platform within the house, the animals had access to the floor area.

Normally, when a family heard a returning warrior, they had to shoo some animals out of the house before they could come out. However, when Jephthah comes home, his daughter is the first to come out.

Although human sacrifice is prohibited by Israelite law (see Leviticus 20:1-5), the sacredness of a vow made in the Lord's name takes precedence over that law. Also, since Jephthah left to the Lord the choice of the one to be sacrificed, the coming forth of his only child indicates that she is the one God wants. The harshness of this story cannot be softened. Jephthah's constant attempt to control events through bargaining has rebounded on him. He finds in his attempt to bargain with God that the Lord accepts only Jephthah's best.

You might want to compare the story of Jephthah's vow with the story of the sacrifice of Isaac in Genesis 22:1-14. One main difference is that in the Genesis account, God intervenes to save the child and substitutes a ram. Have the class members discuss other differences and similarities between the two stories.

Judges 12:1-6. Gideon had been able to placate Ephraim's anger about being left out of the battle (see 8:1-3). Still, Gideon destroyed two Israelite towns that opposed his purposes (see 8:13-17). His son, Abimelech, also destroyed towns within Israel (9:45, 50). That Israel still continues on a downward spiral away from God is shown now by the outbreak of intertribal warfare. The Ephraimites oppose the one whom God has chosen and suffer defeat for their presumption. To explain the testing of the Ephraimites, perhaps some class members who have traveled can share their experiences of different dialects in our country. What are some words they have spoken elsewhere that people did not understand?

DIMENSION THREE:
WHAT DOES THE BIBLE MEAN TO ME?

Judges 9:7-15—Can Thorns Give Shade?

When asked whether or not the Jews should pay taxes, Jesus said "Give to Caesar what is Caesar's and to God what is God's" (Mark 12:17). However, Christians have not always agreed about how this statement applies to our relationship to the state. Does your denomination or local church have a written position statement on its relationship to the political community? If so, read or highlight its contents to the group. Does it say anything about civil obedience and civil disobedience? Does it say anything about your members holding elective office in the community, state, or federal government? If your local church has members who hold elective office, you might invite them to join your discussion. How do these modern issues relate to the issues raised in Jotham's fable? Emphasize specific rather than theoretical ways that we can bring our faith to bear on our political decisions.

In Matthew 6:1-18, Jesus discusses the issues raised in Judges 10. Basically, Jesus says that if we are being religious to receive a reward, we won't. God rewards only those who are righteous without the ulterior motive of receiving a reward for what they have done.

The question of repentance is also dealt with in the opening two chapters of Job. Satan tells the Lord that the only reason Job is righteous is that God has made it worth Job's while. If God withdraws Job's wealth, Satan wagers, Job will curse God. (See Job 1:9-11.) Fully trusting in the depth of Job's faith, the Lord agrees that Satan may take back all that has been given Job (Job 1:12). Job does not curse God, but affirms the Lord's right to give and take away (Job 1:21). Even upon the ash heap of a destroyed life, Job reveals that his relationship to God is based not on what God gives him, but on who God is (Job 42:2-6).

Jesus tells us many times what God requires of us. He says we must love God with our whole lives and hearts: "Love the Lord your God with all your heart and with all your soul and with all your mind and with all your strength" (Mark 12:30; compare Deuteronomy 6:5).

Jesus also uses vivid terms to describe what we may be called upon to do or give up (see Mark 8:34-38). You might share this passage with the class members to aid their discussion.

Close the session by asking the class members to share insights they have gained in their study of today's lesson. Then list these insights on chalkboard or a sheet of paper.

Having put him to sleep on her lap, she called a man to shave off the seven braids of his hair, and so began to subdue him (16:19).

11

Samson the Nazirite

Judges 13–16

DIMENSION ONE:
WHAT DOES THE BIBLE SAY?

Answer these questions by reading Judges 13

1. What does the angel of the Lord say to the wife of Manoah? (Judges 13:3)

   The angel of the Lord tells her she shall conceive and have a son.

2. What must never happen to the woman's child? (Judges 13:5)

   Since the child will be a Nazirite, a razor must never touch his head.

3. What limitations does the angel place upon the woman? (Judges 13:13-14)

   She must not eat anything that comes from the grapevine or is unclean. She also cannot drink wine or other fermented drink.

4. What does the angel say when Manoah asks his name? (Judges 13:18)

   The angel asks why Manoah wants to know his name and says that it is beyond understanding.

5. What happens when Manoah makes his offering? (Judges 13:20)

   The angel of the Lord ascends in the flame of the offering.

6. Why does Manoah's wife conclude they will not die? (Judges 13:23)

   She concludes that the Lord would not have accepted their offerings and announced these things if God had meant to kill them.

Answer these questions by reading Judges 14

7. What does Samson demand from his parents after his trip to Timnah? (Judges 14:2)

   Samson demands that his father and mother get the Philistine woman he saw in Timnah to be his wife.

8. Why is Samson attracted to the Philistine woman? (Judges 14:4)

   Samson's attraction to the woman comes from the Lord, who is seeking a confrontation with the Philistines.

9. What happens in the vineyards of Timnah? (Judges 14:5-6)

   Samson meets a lion, and, by the Spirit of the Lord, tears it apart.

10. What does Samson find when he turns aside on a later journey to Timnah? (Judges 14:8)

   Samson finds a swarm of bees making honey in the lion's carcass.

11. How do the Philistines extort the answer to Samson's riddle from his wife? (Judges 14:15)

   They threaten to burn her and her father's household to death.

12. How does Samson pay off his debt to the thirty men? (Judges 14:19)

   He kills thirty men of Ashkelon and gives their garments to those who answered his riddle.

Answer these questions by reading Judges 15

13. What does Samson do to the Philistine fields when he finds his wife has been given to another man? (Judges 15:4-5)

   Samson ties torches to the tails of 300 foxes and releases them in the Philistine fields.

14. How to the Philistines avenge what Samson has done to their fields? (Judges 15:6)

They burn Samson's wife and father-in-law.

15. Why do the three thousand men of Judah come to Samson's place of refuge at the rock of Etam? (Judges 15:12)

They come to bind Samson and hand him over to the Philistines.

16. What happens when the men of Judah deliver Samson to the Philistines? (Judges 15:14-15)

Samson's bonds fall off. Then he slays a thousand men with a fresh jawbone of a donkey.

Answer these questions by reading Judges 16

17. What does Samson do to the gates of Gaza? (Judges 16:3)

He tears them loose and carries them on his shoulders to the top of a hill near Hebron.

18. With whom does Samson fall in love? (Judges 16:4)

Samson falls in love with Delilah.

19. What do the rulers of the Philistines offer Samson's beloved to deliver him into their power? (Judges 16:5)

Each ruler promises to pay Delilah 1,100 shekels (pieces) of silver.

20. How does Delilah strip Samson of his strength? (Judges 16:19)

While Samson sleeps on her lap, she calls a man to shave off Samson's seven braids of hair.

21. How do the Philistines treat Samson once they capture him? (Judges 16:21)

They gouge out his eyes, put him in shackles, and set him to grinding in the prison.

22. Why do the Philistines call Samson into the house of their god Dagon? (Judges 16:25)

They call for him so that he can entertain them.

23. How does Samson kill himself and all the people in the house? (Judges 16:29-30)

Grasping the two middle pillars upon which the house rests, Samson pushes with all his might. The house falls on all those within it.

DIMENSION TWO:
WHAT DOES THE BIBLE MEAN?

Judges 13:1. Since God earlier rejected their false words of repentance (Judges 10:10-16), the Israelites do not even bother now to cry out to the Lord when God gives them into the hands of the Philistines. See Lesson 5 in this teacher book, on Joshua 13:1-6, page 211.

Judges 13:2-7. Thus far in the Book of Judges, God has designated many different types of people to deliver Israel. However, none of them has successfully returned Israel to the Lord. Since choosing a person already available has not accomplished the purpose, God now intervenes directly to save the Israelites. God sends a messenger to a sterile woman to announce the imminent birth of a son who will begin to deliver Israel. God tries to ensure the purity of this future judge. The Lord declares that the child will be a Nazirite from birth.

You might review with the group the laws concerning Nazirites (see Numbers 6:1-21). The purpose of the Nazirite vow is to separate a person from the everyday world for a time so that he or she would be especially sanctified for God's service. The main elements of the vow are the prohibitions against drinking alcohol, coming near any dead body, and cutting one's hair.

Since wine and strong drink were closely linked to Canaanite religion, drinking them during a period of dedication to the Lord was inappropriate. Death, since it opposes God (compare 1 Corinthians 15:26; Revelation 21:4), was also not to be confronted at this time. Hair symbolized a person's strength and power (see 2 Samuel 14:26). So it remained uncut until the time the vow was completed. Then it was shaven and given in sacrifice to God, signifying the dedication of one's strength and power to the Lord.

To further guarantee the purity of this future judge, God also commands the mother to follow the Nazirite rules until the birth of the child. As we will see, God's intention to guarantee the savior's purity is not the actual result. Samson breaks the vows against drinking wine and avoiding corpses. Finally, he betrays his last vow by divulging to Delilah the power of his uncut hair. Jephthah, the outcast, illegitimate son, fulfills his vows to God more faithfully than does the one whom the Lord personally selects to be Israel's savior! By breaking vows in a culture where vows are sacred, Samson makes himself an outcast from his society. Still, God uses him to deliver Israel.

Samson's birth announcement shares similarities with other biblical reports of miraculous births. The narrative of Samuel's birth follows a similar outline (see 1 Samuel 1:3-20). The angelic announcements to Zechariah (Luke 1:5-25) and Mary (Luke 1:26-56) follow this same basic pattern. You might want to have the group compare these announcements with the passage about Samson's birth. The announcement of John's birth is virtually identical to that of Samson's birth. However, with Jesus' birth, God acts in a new way. Instead of following the typical pattern of making a barren woman fertile, God implants the Holy Spirit directly into the womb of a virgin. Whereas Samson fails to live up to God's selection of him as a savior, Jesus fulfills the function of this divinely appointed office.

Judges 13:8-14. God has sent his messenger. But Manoah is not satisfied by hearing God's word through his wife. He wants to hear God's word directly. Apparently, Manoah does not completely trust his wife and we, the readers, know he has good reason not to trust her. After all, she does not transmit to her husband the angel's complete message. She deletes the part about no razor ever touching the child's head and the part that says he will begin Israel's deliverance. However, upon meeting the angel directly Manoah learns even less than he knew before. The angel says nothing about the child, only what the mother must do.

Judges 13:15-23. Manoah offers hospitality to his guest. The angelic visitor refuses food, but calls for a sacrifice. Manoah's experience with the divine messenger closely parallels that of Gideon. (See Judges 6:11-24.)

Judges 13:25. The Lord's Spirit will come upon Samson more than it has come upon any other judge. (See Judges 14:6, 19; 15:14.)

Judges 14:1-4. This passage shows that the Israelites and Philistines lived next to each other in fragile harmony. Open warfare between these two peoples does not break out until the time of Samuel (see 1 Samuel 4:1-2). Israel and all the nations around her performed the act of circumcision, except the Philistines. The term *uncircumcised* became a derogatory ethnic slur by Israel against the Philistines.

In Israel, parents arranged the marriages of their children. Thus Samson is contemptuous of custom not only by marrying a non-Israelite but also by choosing his own wife. Samson's demands verge on breaking the commandment to honor one's father and mother. We quickly learn that young Samson is not a very faithful Israelite, even though he is a Nazirite. Strangely enough, verse 4 tells us that the Lord causes this disobedience in order to begin the deliverance of Israel from Philistine domination.

Judges 14:5-9. Hercules, the legendary Greek hero, also slew a lion with his bare hands. Enkidu, a less famous hero from Mesopotamia, accomplished the same feat.

For the first time, the Spirit of the Lord empowers Samson to accomplish a specific act. Samson acts under the Spirit's power, but then he violates his oath not to approach a dead body when he goes to the lion carcass. This alternation between the coming of God's Spirit and Samson's disobedience of God's will continues throughout these chapters.

Judges 14:10-18. Samson continues to violate his Nazirite office by hosting a drinking session. Although he is disobedient, we learn in this passage that Samson is not dumb. He proposes a riddle contest—an ancient intellectual test.

Most of the riddles we hear today are designed for children. You might ask the class members to share any childhood riddles they remember. Then emphasize that the ancient Israelites saw riddles in very different terms.

Ancient peoples were fascinated with how often different things had common characteristics. They used riddles to explore the interrelationships between objects and events in the world. The riddle was not just a game to make people laugh. Riddles were serious attempts to discover common patterns in God's creation.

As an example of the serious purpose behind riddles, you might read to your class some of the riddles and answers in Proverbs 30:15-31. Originally, as riddles, these passages listed the various items and asked what they had in common. Now, the answer is given in the first verse of each unit. In the ancient world, then, a riddle was a thoroughly intellectual quest for understanding the world. Answering riddles required the ability to see beyond mere surface differences to the deeper interrelationships among the elements in God's creation.

This passage in Judges exhibits another serious use of the riddle in the ancient world. Sometimes riddles were used in order to destroy others. A person used a riddle with the understanding that, if the other person could not answer it, he or she would die. Scholars call these *neck riddles*, because a person's neck was literally on the line in attempting to answer them.

Perhaps the most famous neck riddle is the riddle of the sphinx. In Greek mythology, the sphinx is a creature who controls the entrance to a town. To each person who wants to pass, she asks, "What goes on four legs in the morning, two legs at noon, and three legs in the evening?" Any person who cannot answer is killed by the sphinx. Oedipus finally frees the city when he discovers that the answer to the riddle is a human being. Human beings crawl on all fours as children, walk on two legs as adults, and walk with canes as older adults.

Since the purpose of neck riddles is to destroy, they seldom give the opponent a fair chance. Only Samson has seen honey bees in the lion's carcass. Since bees normally have nothing to do with decomposing corpses, Samson puts the Philistines at a total disadvantage.

The Philistines realize that Samson has posed a neck riddle meant to destroy them (see verse 15). Samson has used his own wedding to a Philistine woman as an attack on the Philistines! So the Philistines attempt to turn the tables on Samson by using his wife to learn the answer. They discover the answer and, on the last day of the wedding, they attack Samson with a riddle whose most logical answer is *love*. Obviously the love between Samson and his wife is neither sweeter than honey nor stronger than a lion. Samson quickly recognizes her betrayal.

Samson used his marriage to a Philistine to attack the Philistines; they countered by using his Philistine wife to save themselves and attack Samson. Thus Samson's wife is a weapon used by both sides in their war against each other.

Judges 15:1-8. Samson returns to visit his wife, bringing the customary gift. His father-in-law explains that he has given his daughter to another man. By offering his younger daughter instead, the father admits he has wronged Samson. Thus Samson can say he is now blameless in what he does to the Philistines. He is merely seeking his just vengeance for what has been done to him.

We see here the beginning of a major theme in the Samson story: the search for vengeance. The rest of the story shows how the search for vengeance never ends, but rather continues to grow. First Samson seeks vengeance (15:3), then the Philistines do likewise (15:6), then Samson counterattacks (15:7-8), and so on. Samson says he will quit after he has avenged his wife's death. But as we will see, he cannot stop the spiraling cycle of vengeance until he eventually destroys himself.

You might want to review the material on Israel's attitude toward blood vengeance. See the notes on Joshua 20:1-6 in Lesson 6 of this teacher book, page 216.

Judges 15:9-13. This section emphasizes again the Deuteronomic history's theme that, the longer the period of the judges continues, the more intertribal unity deteriorates. Last week we saw two tribes at war with each other (Judges 12:1-6). Here in these verses we see the sad spectacle of the tribe designated by God to lead Israel (see Judges 1:1-2) giving an Israelite into the hands of an enemy.

Judges 15:14-17. Samson's strength does not reside in himself or in his own abilities. His power depends on the coming of the Lord's Spirit. However, in verse 16 Samson tries to take full credit for the victory.

Read these verses in the New Revised Standard Version. Samson's poem contains a pun, or a play on words. The Hebrew words for *donkey* and for *heap* are the same.

Judges 15:18-19. Samson's boasted self-reliance melts in the face of his very mortal thirst. He now calls on God to deliver him. In this prayer, Samson calls himself the Lord's servant. No one has received this title since Joshua. The Lord answers Samson's call and the Spirit returns, reviving Samson.

Judges 16:1-3. This section clearly shows that Israel's moral system in this period was different from our own. There is no law against an Israelite male going to a prostitute. However, there is a strict rule against an Israelite woman becoming a prostitute (Leviticus 19:29). Later, Israel frowns on frequenting prostitutes (see Proverbs 5), but the practice is never outlawed.

Samson's act of carrying Gaza's gates into the heart of Judah may involve a kind of practical joke. As we have seen, the capture of the city gates is critical to the capture of the city itself. (See Judges 9:44-45.) Now the tribe of Judah, which is so afraid of the Philistines, possesses the city gates of one of their major cities! But they do nothing about it.

Judges 16:4-22. All the other women in Samson's life have been nameless: his mother, his Philistine wife, the Gaza prostitute. Nowhere have we been told that he loved any of them. Now we meet the woman Samson loves, and we learn her name. This story is almost a commentary on the riddle of the Philistines. Love should be sweeter than honey and stronger than a lion. Here Delilah betrays Samson's love for a large amount of money. Thus we see that Samson—who betrayed his three Nazirite vows (14:8, 10; 16:17)—is in the end betrayed three times. With the breaking of his last vow, his special dedication to the Lord ends and God leaves him.

But this section ends on a hopeful note. Samson's hair begins to grow again. The vow-breaker may still accomplish the Lord's will.

Judges 16:23-31. The Philistines celebrate their victory over Samson by worshiping their god. Dagon is an ancient Canaanite deity. According to some sources, he is the father of Baal. Apparently, when the Philistines entered Palestine, they adopted the gods of that country. As we have seen, some of the Israelites did the same thing (Judges 2:11-13).

As part of the festivities, Samson is brought in to entertain the Philistines. He asks the servant who leads him to allow him to feel the pillars "so that I may lean against them." Samson calls upon the Lord once more. His words reveal that he seeks massive vengeance. However, Samson appears to realize that the only way he will be able to stop the cycle of vengeance with the Philistines is by bringing about his own death. The final irony is that Samson kills more Philistines in his death than he had in his life.

DIMENSION THREE: WHAT DOES THE BIBLE MEAN TO ME?

Judges 13:15-20—Desire to Detain the Holy

Ask the class members to share times when they have felt especially close to God. Stress the need to hang onto these moments and what they mean for us. You might want to look at the account of the appearance of the resurrected Jesus to Mary Magdalene in John 20:11-18. Jesus' words to Mary are instructive: "Do not hold on to me" (verse 17). Mary has seen the resurrected Lord. He tells her not to try to possess this experience. Mary then goes to tell the disciples what she has seen. Her action suggests that a religious experience is not something to possess, but is something to share and witness to others. (See also Acts 22:6-16.)

Judges 15:14-20
Putting Our Deeds in Perspective

Human beings tend to glorify their place in creation and to assume that what they desire is what God desires. But much of the Bible reminds us that God's thoughts are not human thoughts, and God's ways are not human ways. (See, for example, Isaiah 55:8-9.) God works in a totally opposite way from human expectations and desires. According to Jesus, accepting a relationship with God involves realizing the difference between God's nature and our own, seeing the world from God's perspective, and acting accordingly. (See Matthew 5:43-48.)

Judges 16:28-31—Vengeance Destroys the Avenger

A good place to begin this discussion is with Jesus' own words directly countering the rule of "an eye for an eye" (see Matthew 5:38-41). Jesus' answer to Peter on how many times we should forgive a brother who has wronged us also speaks to this issue (see Matthew 18:21-22). Vengeance must ultimately be left to God, not to humankind.

You might want to mention the contrast between the deaths of Samson and Jesus. Samson dies in a final attempt to exact vengeance from his enemies. He kills himself and many others. Samson's story ends with his burial in the tomb of his father (see Judges 16:31). Jesus dies trying to reconcile the world to God.

Rather than seeking vengeance for what others have done to him, Jesus asks for their forgiveness (Luke 23:34). Jesus is buried in a borrowed grave, but his story does not end there! With Jesus, God finds the true deliverer.

Close today's session by asking group members to share new insights they have gained from their study of Judges 13–16. If time allows, list these insights on chalkboard or a sheet of paper.

12

Micah and the Danites

Judges 17–21

DIMENSION ONE:
WHAT DOES THE BIBLE SAY?

Answer these questions by reading Judges 17

1. How much money had Micah stolen from his mother? (Judges 17:2)

   Micah had stolen 1,100 shekels (pieces) of silver from his mother.

2. What does Micah's mother do with the returned money? (Judges 17:4)

   She takes part of it and has it made into an image and an idol.

3. What is the political situation in Israel at this time? (Judges 17:6)

   There is no king in Israel, and everyone does as he sees fit.

4. What does Micah offer the young Levite? (Judges 17:10)

   Micah offers the Levite ten shekels (pieces) of silver a year, clothing, and food if he will be his priest.

Answer these questions by reading Judges 18

5. Why do the Danites send five men to spy out the land? (Judges 18:1-2)

   Since the Danites have not possessed their inheritance, they send out the spies to find land.

6. How does the priest respond to the Danites' question about their journey? (Judges 18:6)

   The priest tells them to go in peace, for their journey has God's approval.

7. What kind of people do the five spies find in Laish? (Judges 18:7)

   The spies find a quiet, unsuspecting, and prosperous people living in security.

8. When the Danites return to Micah's house, what do they do? (Judges 18:17-18)

   The Danites steal Micah's carved image, ephod, household gods, and cast idol.

9. How do the Danites convince the priest to go with them? (Judges 18:19)

   The Danites ask the priest whether it is better for him to be a priest to one man's house or to a whole tribe.

10. What do the Danites do to the city of Laish? (Judges 18:27)

    The Danites kill the people and burn the city.

Answer these questions by reading Judges 19

11. Why does the Levite from Ephraim go to Bethlehem in Judah? (Judges 19:2-3)

    The Levite goes to Bethlehem to make peace with his concubine, who had returned to her father's house.

12. Why does the Levite refuse to turn aside at Jebus on his return home? (Judges 19:11-12)

    He will not turn aside into a city of aliens who do not belong to the people of Israel.

13. Who finally offers the Levite a place to stay in Gibeah? (Judges 19:16, 20)

    An old man from the hill country of Ephraim who is living in Gibeah offers the Levite a place to stay.

14. What do the wicked men of Gibeah demand concerning the visitor? (Judges 19:22)

They demand that the old man bring out his visitor so that they can have sex with him.

15. Who does the Levite's host offer to give the men? (Judges 19:24)

The host offers to give the men his virgin daughter and the Levite's concubine.

16. What does the Levite find in the morning when he opens the door of the house? (Judges 19:27)

He finds his concubine lying at the door of the house with her hands on the threshold.

17. Upon arriving home, what does the Levite do to his concubine? (Judges 19:29)

He cuts his concubine into twelve pieces and sends them through all of Israel.

Answer these questions by reading Judges 20

18. What accusation does the Levite make against the men of Gibeah in Benjamin? (Judges 20:5)

The Levite accuses them of raping his concubine and of intending to kill him.

19. How does the tribe of Benjamin respond to Israel's demand to turn over the offenders for execution? (Judges 20:13-14)

The Benjamites refuse the demand of the people of Israel. They come out to battle the rest of Israel.

20. How many Israelites fall before the Benjamite army in the first two battles? (Judges 20:21, 25)

In the first battle Israel loses 22,000 men to Benjamin; in the second battle Israel loses 18,000 men.

21. How does Israel finally defeat Benjamin? (Judges 20:36-37, 40-43)

The men of Israel set an ambush. Then they fall back before Benjamin until those in ambush capture the city. Next Israel turns about, trapping and killing the Benjamites.

22. How many Benjamite males survive the battle? (Judges 20:47)

Only six hundred Benjamite men survive by fleeing into the desert.

Answer these questions by reading Judges 21

23. What had the men of Israel sworn at Mizpah? (Judges 21:1)

The men of Israel had sworn not to give their daughters in marriage to any Benjamite.

24. Why do the people weep at Bethel? (Judges 21:2-3)

The people weep because one tribe has been lost.

25. Why does Israel slaughter everyone but the virgins in Jabesh Gilead? (Judges 21:8-14)

Jabesh Gilead had not answered the call to the tribal assembly. Since Benjamin needs wives, the virgins are turned over to them.

26. What do the elders of the congregation tell the Benjamites to do in order to get the wives they need? (Judges 21:20-21)

They tell the Benjamites to hide and watch in the vineyards during the feast at Shiloh, seize the women who come out to dance, and make them their wives.

27. How does this plan by the elders keep Israel from violating her oath? (Judges 21:22)

Since the Benjamites take the women, Israel is not guilty of giving her daughters to them.

DIMENSION TWO: WHAT DOES THE BIBLE MEAN?

In the last chapters of Judges, we see how far Israel has turned away from the Lord, how much she is at odds with herself, and how much she still needs God's salvation. No divinely appointed judge appears to deliver Israel now. Idolatry, theft, threat, inhospitality, and arbitrary violence against others and among the tribes swirl through these stories. The situation has deteriorated so much that Israel no longer needs an outside oppressor to punish her for her sins. Israelite now oppresses Israelite! These stories vividly portray Israel at her worst.

The Deuteronomic history has a purpose for including these violent stories. This purpose is revealed in the recurring statement, "In those days Israel had no king; everyone did as he saw fit" (see 17:6; 21:25). In these stories, the downward spiral of Israel's history strikes bottom. Temporary deliverers have not restored the people to the Lord. If Israel is to be saved from the depths of sin to which she has descended, God will have to try something else.

Salvation occurs when God, in answer to the people's request, raises up a king over Israel. God's new attempt to bring the people back will be narrated in the next two volumes of the Deuteronomic history, First and Second Samuel.

These last chapters of Judges, then, depict the darkness before the dawn of kingship. The Deuteronomic history intentionally highlights Israel's depravity in order to show the necessity for the rise of kingship.

Judges 17:1-6. Micah has broken two of the Ten Commandments: "Honor your father and your mother" and "You shall not steal" (Exodus 20:12, 15). Apparently, he does not fear the consequences of his violations of God's law. However, he does become alarmed when his mother curses the thief. Since curses have the independent power to carry out the destruction of the person upon whom they are placed, Micah tries to counter the curse by returning the money.

Micah's mother, probably aghast at her unknowing condemnation of her own son, also tries to block the curse by uttering a blessing. Curses and blessings, since they both use the Lord's name, cannot be misused (Exodus 20:7). Once delivered, they cannot be taken back. The interaction of the curse on the thief and the blessing on the son is the background for the rest of Micah's story.

With a portion of the money dedicated to the Lord, Micah makes an image of God, thus breaking still another commandment (see Exodus 20:4). Micah, whose name proclaims "the Lord's greatness," is contemptuous of the Lord's commandments.

Judges 17:7-13. Micah continues to work against the power of the curse by enlisting a young Levite as priest for his shrine. Since they were without any land of their own in an almost totally agricultural society, Levites had to go wherever they could find work. Since they could not always find cultic positions to fill at local or private sanctuaries, they often had to depend on charity to survive. (See Deuteronomy 14:28-29.) The presence of an authorized priest in his home assures Micah that the curse has been overcome and that the prosperity of the blessing has begun. However, the Levite will shortly be the cause of Micah's undoing.

Judges 18:1-10. You might want to read to the group the other accounts of Dan's inability to control its original allotment and its resulting need to migrate. (See Joshua 19:40-48.)

Although no individual judge appears in this story, Dan serves as the agent of Micah's punishment. The name *Dan* means "judge" or "judgment." In other words, a whole tribe—an outcast tribe that cannot secure its own land—unknowingly acts as judge.

Like other judges we have met in this book, Dan is not totally faithful to the Lord. The tribe sends out spies without first consulting the Lord. The spies ask whether they are doing the right thing only as an afterthought when they happen to meet a Levite. They see in the Levite's ambiguous oracle God's favorable judgment upon their search. (The literal translation of verse 6 is "under the eye of the Lord." It means only that God is watching what they are doing, not necessarily that God approves.) When the spies report, they say God has given Laish into Dan's hands, although the Lord has said no such thing. The Danites assume that what they want to do is what God wants them to do.

Judges 18:11-20. The five spies tell the Danite war party about Micah's house, where they received what they thought was a favorable oracle from the young Levite (verse 6). The Danites decide to take the carved image, the ephod, the household gods, and the cast idol with them, since these items appear to be sources of blessing. When the priest/Levite protests this theft, they silence him and tell him to come with them. Earlier they had asked him to speak (see 18:5). Now they command him to keep quiet.

This story clearly reveals why the Lord commands worshipers to make no idols (see Exodus 20:4-6). Persons begin to believe that they can control God's blessing just because they possess a physical representation of what they think is God. With images and a Levite to serve the images, Micah assumes he will prosper. The Danites assume the same thing to the point of stealing both the idols and the priest to secure blessing for themselves. Rather than understanding God as the one who controls them and who calls for righteous behavior, Micah and the Danites believe that mere possession of idols guarantees their security.

Judges 18:21-26. Micah loses the God he thought he possessed. He sought to control both the curse and the blessing, but the Danites ruin his plan by stealing his idols and his priest. Micah still has his life, but he has lost everything he has valued.

Judges 18:27-31. The Danites invoke the ban against Laish (see Lesson 2 in this teacher book on Joshua 6:17-25, page 198). Although they set up the idols and install the Levite, the Danites can control the Lord's blessing no more than Micah could. The passage notes that possession of the idols did not keep Dan from going into captivity. The Lord's will prevails. Humans cannot control or possess God.

Judges 19:1-9. The Levite's father-in-law lavishly entertains his guest. Here we see the rules of hospitality followed in detail. The host tries to prolong his guest's stay as long as possible.

Judges 19:10-15. The Levite rejects his servant's suggestion that they spend the night in non-Israelite Jerusalem. He would rather go a few extra miles to stay safely—or so he assumes—in a city of fellow Israelites.

Judges 19:16-26. This account of the Levite's experience in Gibeah has many parallels to the experience of Lot's angelic visitors in Genesis 19:1-11. You might want to have the group compare these two stories. The Deuteronomic history is saying that Israel has become as evil as ancient Sodom, the city the Lord destroyed because of its great wickedness.

Earlier we sympathized with the Levite because he takes the first step in reconciling himself with his concubine by going to Bethlehem. Now his callous sacrifice of her to the townsmen turns our sympathy against him. After a night of abuse, she is barely able to reach the door of the house.

Judges 19:27-30. The Levite's insensitivity is revealed even more clearly in the morning. Finding his concubine lying at the threshold, he commands her to get up. When he receives no answer, he places her upon a donkey and returns to his home. We do not know whether his concubine is dead or just unconscious!

Once home, the Levite dissects his concubine in the same way he, as a priest would ritually cut up a sacrificial animal. Then he sends the twelve pieces around to the tribes, one piece to each tribe. The silence of the passage as to whether she is alive or dead raises the horrifying possibility that she was not yet dead when he began to cut her up. Since the Deuteronomic history wants to portray how evil Israel has become, perhaps the passage intends to imply that the Levite dissected his still-living concubine.

In verse 30, the tribes declare that such a thing has never happened before in Israel. The phrase "such a thing" refers to what the Levite has done to his concubine, not to what has happened at Gibeah.

Judges 20:1-7. The man who has assumed the role of judge and has summoned the tribes now explains why. If you compare his version of the events with what happened in 19:22-26, you will see that he goes beyond the facts of the case. He says the men of Gibeah meant to kill him, while they had meant only to rape him (19:22-24). He implies that the men killed his concubine, although he does not directly accuse them of murder. He just carefully notes that she is dead.

The Levite's silence about the cause of her death suggests that the men of Gibeah are not guilty of killing her. Perhaps the murder is the Levite's own crime, which he has committed in order to arouse all Israel against the Gibeahites who insulted him. This Levite, who makes himself judge in order to achieve personal vengeance, is at least a liar if not a murderer. Indeed, Israel has not seen such a thing before. The Levite's actions and words have horrifying consequences.

Judges 20:8-48. When the Benjamites refuse to turn over the criminals, the rest of Israel goes to war against them. On the testimony of a single witness—one we know has given false testimony—Israel enters into a holy war against herself. According to Deuteronomy 17:6, at least two witnesses are required by the law for capital crimes.

The Book of Judges has now come full circle. At the beginning, the Lord appoints Judah to lead the tribes (see 1:1-2). In Judges 20, Judah is again designated as the one who shall go first (verse 18). However, a big difference exists between the first and last appointments of Judah to leadership. In the first chapter, Judah was to lead Israel against the Canaanites. Now Judah leads Israel against a portion of Israel. Rather than destroying her enemies, Israel has fallen so far that she seeks to destroy herself.

You might want to have the group compare this account of the battle at Gibeah with the ambush at Ai (see Joshua 8:3-23). Have the class members suggest similarities and differences between the two stories, and list those suggestions on a chalkboard or paper.

Judges 21:1-7. In Judges 21 we encounter another story of an attempt to circumvent an oath. Israel realizes too late that she has almost destroyed one of her own members. Israel's oath not to give any of her daughters as wives to Benjamin further guarantees that the tribe's 600 remaining males will be unable to have children. The tribe of Benjamin faces extinction.

Although the Israelites ask God why this disaster has happened, they do not wait for the Lord's answer. On their own initiative, the Israelites act to save Benjamin. As so often happens, pain and agony result when the people try to save themselves instead of waiting for God's redemption.

Judges 21:8-15. To save her own, Israel attacks her own! Throughout Israel's history, a close relationship has often existed between Benjamin and Jabesh Gilead. (See 1 Samuel 11:1-11.) Thus, this town east of the Jordan refuses to participate in the attack on Benjamin. In order to punish Jabesh Gilead for not coming when called, and also to find for Benjamin young Israelite women whose fathers have not participated in the oath, Israel destroys one of her own cities. Compassion for Benjamin and fear about breaking an oath are reasons for Israel to continue to harm herself.

Judges 21:16-25. To complete the number of women needed by Benjamin, the elders of Israel now conspire with the remaining men of this tribe to steal wives during the festival at Shiloh.

During harvest times and "annual festival[s] of the LORD," Israel's rigid sexual code is relaxed. Apparently, these festivals serve as a kind of safety valve for letting off pressure in a society governed by the constant demand to be righteous.

Although the elders give the Benjamites an excuse to use in case the men of Shiloh come after them, they never have to use this excuse. Perhaps wife-stealing at such festivals is not a totally unexpected event. Israel apparently believes that her end of restoring Benjamin justifies her brutal means. Thus while seeking unity, Israel dismembers herself.

DIMENSION THREE: WHAT DOES THE BIBLE MEAN TO ME?

Judges 18:14-20—Why Should Ministers Move?

The Levite's mercenary view of his priesthood is a good context in which to discuss when and why ministers should move. Jesus and Paul comment on these issues in Luke 10:1-16 and Romans 1:9-15.

Discuss with the group your denomination's policy and process for moving clergy from one local church to another. What are the reasons a congregation may want a clergy change? What are some reasons clergy may wish a move? What are some of the joys and sorrows accompanying a clergy move?

Judges 19:10-30—The Visitor in Our Midst

On our responsibility as Christians to love each other, see 1 John 4:7-12. John emphasizes that love between Christians is the sign that we are truly disciples of Christ. The command by the resurrected Lord to "Go and make disciples . . . teaching them to obey everything I have commanded you" (Matthew 28:19) also enjoins us to reach out and welcome all newcomers into our fellowship. Have the group develop specific ways your church can make new persons feel welcome.

Judges 21:16-24—Destroying Our Own

The Bible often deals with the issues raised in this section. The story of Cain and Abel is perhaps the best-known biblical account of family conflict (see Genesis 4:1-16). But we also read about the feuds between Jacob and Esau (Genesis 25–27) and Absalom and Ammon (see 2 Samuel 13). Jesus, too, had conflicts with his friends and family. His friends think he is insane (Mark 3:21), and apparently his family opposes his ministry (Mark 3:31-35; Matthew 10:34-39).

On how we can avoid family conflicts, see the duties of each family member toward each other (Ephesians 5:21–6:4). You might want to share this passage with the group to begin the discussion. Many persons argue that this Ephesians passage proclaims male dominance. However, if you read the passage carefully you will see that it emphasizes the mutual interdependence of family members. Wives depend on husbands; husbands love their wives as they love themselves. Children are to obey their parents; parents are not to provoke their children to anger. This passage says that the way to avoid destroying those we love is by trying to care for their good more than our own. Family members should not insist on their rights, but should do what best expresses their love for others.

Close this session on Judges 17–21 by asking the class members to share insights they have gained about this Scripture. If time allows, list these insights on a chalkboard or a sheet of paper.

13

The Story of Ruth

Ruth 1–4

DIMENSION ONE:
WHAT DOES THE BIBLE SAY?

Answer these questions by reading Ruth 1

1. Why does the family of Elimelech move from Judah to Moab? (Ruth 1:1-2)

   There was a famine in the land.

2. What were the names of Mahlon's and Kilion's wives? (Ruth 1:3-5)

   The name of one was Ruth and the name of the other Orpah.

3. How does Naomi respond when her daughters-in-law first refuse to leave her? (Ruth 1:11-13)

   Naomi tells her daughters-in-law to return home.

4. How does Ruth respond to Naomi's request that she return to her "mother's home"? (Ruth 1:16-17)

   Ruth begs Naomi not to make her leave. She says she will go and stay wherever Naomi goes and stays and die and be buried wherever Naomi dies and is buried.

5. What name does Naomi give herself? Why? (Ruth 1:20-21)

   She asks to be called not Naomi, but Mara, for the Almighty has made her life very bitter.

6. What important agricultural event is occurring when Ruth and Naomi return to Bethlehem? (Ruth 1:22)

   They come to Bethlehem at the beginning of the barley harvest.

Answer these questions by reading Ruth 2

7. Who is Boaz? (Ruth 2:1)

   Boaz is a man of standing who is related to Naomi's husband.

8. Why does Ruth come to the part of the field belonging to Boaz? (Ruth 2:3)

   She comes there to glean after the harvesters.

9. What does Boaz say to Ruth at their first meeting? (Ruth 2:8-9)

   Boaz tells Ruth to stay and glean in his field. When she is thirsty, she may drink from the water jars the men have filled.

10. Why has Ruth found favor in Boaz's eyes? (Ruth 2:11)

    He has heard all Ruth has done for her mother-in-law.

11. What recompense for Ruth does Boaz ask from the Lord? (Ruth 2:12)

    Boaz asks that the Lord give Ruth rich reward for all she has done.

12. What happens at mealtime? (Ruth 2:14)

    Boaz invites Ruth to eat bread dipped in wine vinegar.

13. How does Naomi react when she finds out Ruth has worked in Boaz's field? (Ruth 2:20)

    She asks the Lord to bless Boaz. She also tells Ruth he is one of their "kinsman-redeemers."

Answer these questions by reading Ruth 3

14. What does Naomi tell Ruth to do on the night Boaz is winnowing barley? (Ruth 3:3-4)

    She tells Ruth to wash, go down to the threshing floor, uncover the feet of Boaz, and lie down.

15. What does Ruth tell Boaz to do when he discovers her beside him? (Ruth 3:9)

    She tells Boaz to spread his garment over her.

16. How does Boaz reply to Ruth's request? (Ruth 3:10-11)

He asks the Lord to bless her and promises to do all that she asks because she is a woman of noble character.

17. What problem stands in the way of Boaz fulfilling Ruth's request? (Ruth 3:12-13)

There is a kinsman-redeemer nearer to Ruth than Boaz.

Answer these questions by reading Ruth 4

18. What does Boaz first say to the kinsman-redeemer at the city gate? (Ruth 4:3-4)

He says that Naomi is selling the piece of land that belonged to Elimelech.

19. How does the kinsman-redeemer react when he finds he must take Ruth when he buys Elimelech's land? (Ruth 4:5-6)

He cannot redeem it, lest it endanger his own estate.

20. After the first kinsman-redeemer refuses to redeem the land and Ruth, what does Boaz do? (Ruth 4:9-10)

He buys all that belonged to Elimelech, Kilion, and Mahlon, and takes Ruth as his wife.

21. What blessing do the people and the elders pronounce after they have witnessed Boaz's statement? (Ruth 4:11-12)

They hope Ruth will be like Rachel and Leah, that Boaz will prosper in his home region, and that their house will be like the house of Perez.

22. What name do the women give to Ruth and Boaz's child? (Ruth 4:17)

They name him Obed.

23. What important Old Testament person descended from Ruth? (Ruth 4:17)

David descended from Ruth.

DIMENSION TWO:
WHAT DOES THE BIBLE MEAN?

Begin this lesson by helping the group compare life as described in the Book of Judges and in the Book of Ruth.

Note that Judges portrays the time as one of constant military struggles. In contrast, Ruth speaks of no battles or wars. This book concentrates on normal, everyday experiences of hardworking farming people. Judges emphasizes the out-of-the-ordinary experiences of spirit-driven leaders.

Ruth 1:1-5. Using a map of Palestine, point out where Bethlehem and Moab are in relation to each other. The normal route between the two places would be around the north end of the Dead Sea.

Palestine has no great rivers as do Egypt and Mesopotamia, so it depends entirely on rainfall for its source of water. When rainfall is insufficient to raise adequate crops, famine results. Migration out of Palestine in the face of famine occurs frequently in the Bible. During famines Abraham went to Egypt (Genesis 12:10), Isaac moved to Philistia (Genesis 26:1), and Jacob and his sons journeyed to Egypt (Genesis 45:9-11).

Even though they were closely related, Israel and Moab were seldom on good terms with each other. We witness Israelite feelings both of closeness and antagonism toward the Moabites in Genesis 19:30-37. Here the Bible says that Moab descended from the incestuous relationship between Lot (Abraham's nephew) and one of Lot's daughters. According to Deuteronomy 23:3, Moabites and their descendants could not enter the assembly of the Lord.

Moabites returned Israelite hostility in kind. The Moabite Stone, a monument from about 830 B.C., commemorates the victory of King Mesha over Israel. Mesha celebrates his total destruction of several Israelite cities. Thus, for an Israelite to portray a Moabitess as a heroine is about as strange as Jesus describing a "good" Samaritan.

We can see the pitiful situation that widows faced in the ancient world in passages like 1 Kings 17:8-16 and 2 Kings 4:1-7. With the heavy physical labor necessary in the largely agricultural society of Israel, a lone woman could barely raise enough food to survive. For this reason, widows along with their children were placed under divine protection. (See Exodus 22:22-24; Deuteronomy 10:18.) People were to show charity to widows. The custom of gleaning, which we encounter later in Ruth, was one means for this charity. Widows also were to be given part of the ten percent of the produce an Israelite gave to God (Deuteronomy 26:12). Apparently such charity was not always given and a widow might be reduced to the unacceptable practice of prostitution in order to live. (See Genesis 38:24.)

Ruth 1:6-18. The levirate custom, in which the nearest male relative had intercourse with the widow of a childless man until she gave birth to a son, appears strange to us. The early Israelites did not believe in immortality. They believed that a man's personality and nature were somehow carried on in his sons. Without a son, death ended a man's continued tie to life. Consequently, the levirate marriage provided a legal heir for the dead man. This heir carried on the dead man's name, inherited his property, and took over the care of his widow when he came of age. Much of Naomi's bitterness results from the fact that she had no sons left to give to Ruth and Orpah. With no sons, Elimelech, Mahlon, and Kilion are cut off from any future life.

The story makes no negative judgment on Orpah for returning home. She had already gone beyond her duty by wanting to stay with her mother-in-law. She now follows Naomi's command to return home. However, Orpah's obedience stands in stark contrast with Ruth, who insists on doing much more than could normally be expected of her.

Ruth disobeys Naomi's command in order to maintain their relationship. For Ruth, her relationship with her mother-in-law supersedes the commandment to honor mother and father. Here she stands in the tradition that Jesus shares—the belief that relationships are more important than commandments. For Jesus, the demands of love take precedence over the divine commandments, such as the sabbath law, the laws of impurity, and the command to honor father and mother.

Ruth 1:19-22. Israel believed that a name revealed a person's nature. So a name change like Naomi's means that her essential character is changed. Rather than pleasant she is now bitter, and thus she should be called. As the story of Ruth continues, Naomi's pleasant nature is gradually restored.

The Book of Ruth centers on the themes of emptiness and fullness. The first chapter concentrates on emptiness, with the emptying from the land, the emptying of the family, and the emptying of the individual, Naomi.

The restoration to fullness begins in Ruth 1:22. Ask the group to find other places that point to the fullness theme. Examples are: Boaz asks that the Lord give Ruth her "rich reward" (2:12); Ruth eats until she is satisfied, and has some left over (2:14); Ruth shows Naomi what she has gleaned and also gives her the food "she had left over after she had eaten enough" (2:18); Boaz sends six measures of barley to Naomi so that Ruth does not go back empty-handed (3:17); and Ruth and Boaz have a son who will be to Naomi a renewer of life and a sustainer in old age (4:15).

Ruth 2:1-16. To explain this section on gleaning, you might want to read to the group the laws concerning gleaning found in Leviticus 19:9-10; 23:22 and Deuteronomy 24:19-22. Although gleaning allowed the widow some food, in those days of hand cutting and gathering much less was missed or lost in harvesting than with today's machines. Normally a person could glean very little from a field. This is why Boaz tells his workers to leave extra sheaves for Ruth on purpose.

As a widow and an alien, by right Ruth could glean in any field. But still she asks for permission (2:7). This request reveals part of her character. You might want to have the group discuss Ruth by listing some of her character traits on a chalkboard or a sheet of paper. Other hints of the type of person she is are found in 1:16-17 (loyal); 2:2 (purposeful); 2:10, 13 (thankful); 2:7, 23 (hard working); 2:18 (generous); and 3:9 (aggressive).

Despite Ruth's loyalty to her mother-in-law, she is not totally obedient to Naomi. She goes against Naomi's command to return to her homeland. At the threshing floor she disobeys again (see 3:9). Naomi had told her a course of action to follow, which she is to conclude by waiting for Boaz to tell her what to do. However, Ruth does not wait for Boaz to speak. She tells him what to do.

Ruth 2:17-23. Leviticus 25:25, 47-49 contains the laws concerning the nearest of kin's duty to redeem members or land of his family. The kinsman-redeemer was not usually the same one who performed the levirate (brother-in-law) obligation. As the Book of Ruth attests, these two roles could converge in situations where no immediate male relative was available to perform the marriage duty.

Ruth 3:1-10. This chapter can be difficult to teach because it deals explicitly with Israelite sexual customs. We are not always comfortable with the subject of sex—especially in the Bible. Some persons believe this is an explicit seduction scene. Others think it is only a ritual invitation to marriage. The decision on how to read the sexual overtones of this chapter involves how we understand the phrase she "approached quietly, uncovered his feet and lay down." Do we read the word *feet* literally, or as the common biblical euphemism for sexual organs? Ruth gets washed, perfumed, and dressed in her best clothes. Then she waits until he had "finished eating and drinking and was in good spirits" (3:7). Combine all these preparations with our knowledge that at harvest time, more sexual license was allowed in Israel than normally permitted. (See Judges 21:20-23.) We must probably conclude that Ruth goes to the threshing floor with the intention of seducing Boaz. In Israel, intercourse itself could constitute marriage. (See Exodus 22:16; Deuteronomy 22:28-29.) Ruth calls upon Boaz, using his own words, to fulfill the words of his earlier blessing.

Ruth's motive for attempting this seduction is totally honorable. She seeks a son so that the life of her husband and father-in-law will continue in a legal heir. That her motive is loyalty to the dead and not personal sexual pleasure is evident in the blessing of Boaz. She has come to him, an older man, rather than going after young men (3:10).

Ruth 3:11-18. Although sexual language appears throughout this chapter, intercourse between Ruth and Boaz probably does not occur. Boaz informs Ruth that the duties of the next of kin fall to one still closer. As an honorable man, Boaz refuses to infringe on the rights of this kinsman. He promises Ruth he will do as she asks if the other declines. Boaz does two things by asking Ruth to spend the night lying beside him. First, he protects her from being molested (see 2:9, 22). Second, he signals his own affection for her.

Ruth 4:1-12. We can see the importance of judicial work carried on by the elders at the city gate in passages like Deuteronomy 21:19 and 22:15. In Ruth the elders are called to witness a possible legal transfer, rather than to make a judgment.

The mention of land owned by Naomi appears suddenly in the story. Perhaps squatters had moved onto Naomi's land during the long absence of Elimelech's family, and the widow was not strong enough to evict them. Or perhaps this is land that Naomi did not know her husband owned.

The maneuver of Boaz reveals to the reader the character of the unnamed kinsman. He quite willingly accepts his duty to redeem the land in order to increase his property. However, he decides to pass on his responsibility when he discovers that fulfilling it will probably cost him more than he will gain. He will be responsible for Ruth as well. As in the case of Orpah, the story passes no judgment on this man. Both are willing to do their duty to a point. But when it becomes evident that they are called to do more than duty, they turn away.

How could anyone be expected to begin a life as a widow in a strange land or to accept the burden of taking care of another man's wife, daughter-in-law, and at least one child (to be born in the future)? By human standards, no one should have to do such things. However, the purpose of the Book of Ruth is to show that we must do more than can normally be expected of us.

We do not totally understand what lies behind the custom of taking off the sandal and giving it to the other. We read about this practice in another context in the Book of Deuteronomy. Deuteronomy 25:9 says that when a man refuses to marry his brother's wife, the widow should take off his sandal and spit in his face.

In reality, only the land's owner had the right to walk upon it. Perhaps in this context, giving the sandal shows symbolically that now another has the right to the land. Whatever the basis of this action, it clearly completes the transfer of the redeemer's rights and duty to Boaz. The elders and people witness his acceptance of responsibility for the land and for Ruth.

Ruth 4:13-17. Here we read about the marital union between Ruth and Boaz. The final legal problem that separated them, which Boaz revealed to Ruth the night before, has been overcome. Now the honorable Boaz can take Ruth rightfully as his wife.

Israel always saw God as the ultimate agent of conception (see Genesis 4:1). The blessing spoken by Bethlehem's women nicely counters the bitter words Naomi uttered to them in 1:20-21. Here the women call her *Naomi* ("pleasant"), and not *Mara* ("bitter"). By the levirate custom, the child belongs legally to Naomi and her deceased husband, Elimelech.

The story concludes with an intriguing revelation. David, Israel's greatest king, was the great-grandson of a Moabitess. Remember Deuteronomy's stipulation that no Moabite or any of his descendants can enter the worshiping assembly of the Lord (Deuteronomy 23:3). Because Ruth is such a clear exception to Deuteronomy's radical exclusion, some scholars feel the book was written in part against Jews who wanted to exclude all non-Jews from the worship of God.

Ruth 4:18-22. This genealogy that ends the Book of Ruth does not include Ruth's name. So it is interesting that Matthew includes Ruth (one of relatively few women) in his genealogy of Jesus Christ (see Matthew 1:5).

DIMENSION THREE: WHAT DOES THE BIBLE MEAN TO ME?

Ruth 1:1-21—Questioning God's Faithfulness

To prepare for this section, ask yourself the questions found in the student book. For a better understanding of the biblical complaints against God, you might look at passages like Job 3:1-26 and Jeremiah 20:7-18. In the Old Testament, people argue against and complain to God without interrupting their relationship with God.

Laments play an important role in the Book of Psalms. Prayers such as Psalms 10, 13, and 22 reveal the questions Israel often addresses to God along with the assurance that God will ultimately help. Mark and Matthew portray Jesus crying out in anguish to God on the cross with the opening words from Psalm 22. (See Matthew 27:46; Mark 15:34.)

The Bible understands that a true relationship with God can stand up to—and may even become stronger with—anger and complaint. Just as a friendship may be deeper after the settlement of an argument, the Bible affirms that God understands and may even commend us for those times we complain. (See Job 42:7.)

Ruth 1:22-2:7—God's Providence

Ask the class members to reflect on the times in their lives when they recognized that God was at work. Then compare the number of ordinary and extraordinary events, and ask them what these numbers mean. Consider Jesus' words in Matthew 16:1-4. Here Jesus alludes to the importance of everyday signs, while rebuking those who seek for miraculous signs. In John 20:29, the resurrected Lord blesses those who believe without seeing signs.

Ruth 4:1-22—Restored to Fullness

Ask the class members how often they have experienced positive results from negative situations. Ask them to share examples with the rest of the group. When have we become better persons because we have suffered a period of trial? The Bible does not place a premium on suffering. It states that ultimately God does not intend that we suffer. (See Revelation 21:4.) But the Bible also witnesses to the experience that God has often been found in persons' personal darkness, rather than in their light. Think of Job, coming out of his horrible experience, saying, "My ears had heard of you / but now my eyes have seen you" (Job 42:5).

For the Christian, the cross and the Resurrection reveal most clearly that fullness comes only after emptying. Jesus came that we "may have life, and have it to the full" (John 10:10). The cross was the way to that "full."

Close today's session by listing, on a chalkboard or a sheet of paper, any new insights the class members have gained in their study of Ruth.

If time allows, you might want to review with the group the highlights of each lesson on Joshua, Judges, and Ruth.

1 AND 2 SAMUEL
Table of Contents

About the Writer

The writer of these lessons is Dr. Frank Johnson. Dr. Johnson is a professor in the Department of Religion and Philosophy at Florida Southern College, Lakeland, Florida. He is also an ordained United Methodist minister.

—1—

Samuel, a Prophet of the Lord

1 Samuel 1–3

DIMENSION ONE:
WHAT DOES THE BIBLE SAY?

Answer these questions by reading 1 Samuel 1

1. Which of Elkanah's wives has no children? (1:1-2)

   Hannah has no children.

2. Where does Elkanah go to sacrifice, and who is the priest there? (1:3-5)

   He goes to Shiloh. Eli is the priest there.

3. Why does Hannah's rival provoke her? (1:6)

   Hannah's rival provokes her because Hannah has no children.

4. What vow does Hannah make to the Lord? (1:11)

   She promises that if the Lord will give her a son, she will give him to God's service.

5. How does Eli react to Hannah's praying in the Temple? (1:12-17)

   First he thinks that she is drunk, but then he tells her to go in peace.

6. How does God answer Hannah's prayer? (1:19-20)

   God gives Hannah a son.

Answer these questions by reading 1 Samuel 2

7. How does Hannah describe God in her song? (2:1-10)

   God is holy. God has knowledge. God brings death and life, poverty and wealth. God is just, judging, and powerful.

8. What sins do Hophni and Phinehas, the sons of Eli, commit? (2:17, 22)

   They treat the Lord's offering with contempt, and they sleep with the women who served at the entrance to the Tent of Meeting.

9. What is the Lord's attitude toward Samuel? (2:26)

   God favors Samuel.

10. As a consequence of the sins of Eli's sons, what will happen to them? (2:34)

    They will both die on the same day.

Answer these questions by reading 1 Samuel 3

11. Where is Samuel when the Lord first speaks to him? (3:3)

    Samuel is inside the Temple of the Lord.

12. Why does Samuel fail to recognize the Lord when God speaks to him? (3:7)

    Samuel does not yet know the Lord.

13. How does Eli advise Samuel to respond to God's voice? (3:9)

    "Speak, LORD, for your servant is listening."

14. What will God do to the house of Eli? (3:13-14)

    God will forever punish Eli's house because of the sins of his sons.

15. How does Eli react to Samuel's message from the Lord? (3:17-18)

    He accepts it as God's will.

16. What does Israel know about Samuel? (3:20)

Israel knows that Samuel is a prophet of the Lord.

DIMENSION TWO: WHAT DOES THE BIBLE MEAN?

Background Information on First and Second Samuel

The authorship of First and Second Samuel continues to perplex scholars. Most scholars agree that these books are collected arrangements of different stories and sacred traditions. That traditions from different perspectives have been assembled here is clear even to the untrained eye. In 1 Samuel 8, the idea of kingship is unacceptable to both God and Samuel. In Chapters 9 and 10, Samuel consecrates Saul as king with God's blessing. In 1 Samuel 16, David comes to Saul as a musician. But in Chapter 17, Saul seems to have no knowledge of David—the warrior who kills Goliath.

Some parts of these books interrupt the story line. Examples are the ark narrative (1 Samuel 4–6), Eli's sinful sons (1 Samuel 2:27-36), and the song of Hannah (1 Samuel 2:1-10). Parts of these books portray the institution of kingship as essential to Israel's political well-being, in view of the Philistine menace. Other parts consider the monarchy a potential violation of the first commandment, since most other nations at this time consider their kings to be divine.

A twentieth-century German scholar, Martin Noth, has developed the theory that during the Exile (587–538 B.C.), different traditions and stories were brought together. These parts were arranged in chronological order by an anonymous editor known as the Deuteronomistic historian. The purpose of this massive historical work was to describe the sins of apostasy by the kings of Israel and Judah. These sins of disloyalty to the Lord, forewarned in Deuteronomy 30:15-20, led to the destruction of both kingdoms.

In order to understand Samuel's role in early Israelite history, we need to know something about his time. Most scholars date Samuel to the last quarter of the eleventh century B.C. (about 1025). The Hebrew tribes had no centralized government and no formal state at that time. They were a loosely joined group of tribes who lived in the rural and semi-rural areas of Canaan. Most members of these tribes worshiped God at major religious centers such as Shiloh and Bethel.

In situations of crisis, usually arising from a threat by the neighboring Philistines, these tribes united around a single individual for military protection. These individuals were known as *judges*. When the crisis was resolved, the judges returned to their previous occupations. This eventful and exciting period is portrayed in the Old Testament Book of Judges.

In addition to political uncertainties, the Hebrew tribes also faced the religious temptation to worship the Canaanite god Baal instead of the Lord. More than once in the days of the judges, Israel was unfaithful to her covenant with God. As a result, God punished her with attacks from the Philistines. Two quotations from the Old Testament provide summaries of the political and religious chaos in Canaan during the eleventh century.

In those days Israel had no king; everyone did as he saw fit. (Judges 21:25)

In those days, the word of the LORD was rare; there were not many visions. (1 Samuel 3:1)

1 Samuel 1. The exact location of Samuel's birthplace is uncertain. First Samuel 1:1 says that his parents lived in Ramathaim (in Ephraim). However, in 2:11 and elsewhere, Ramah (in Benjamin) is mentioned as his ancestral home. Most commentators and historians prefer the Ramah site in Benjamin as Samuel's authentic home.

The word *ramah* means "high place", and refers to a number of different sites in early Israel. So the confusion about Samuel's birthplace is understandable. The Old Testament also associates Samuel with Shiloh, the site of the ancient sanctuary housing the ark of the covenant.

As the student book states, Shiloh is an important religious center in early Israelite worship. In fact, Shiloh is even designated as a temple, which indicates its prominence as the site of the famous ark.

The ark is a sacred box that contained objects of importance to Israel's early religion. Among the tribes, the ark is the visible symbol of God's earthly presence. Where the ark resides, God can be found.

Shiloh is also important among the early Israelite sanctuaries because an annual feast occurs there (Judges 21:19). Other early religious sanctuaries are Bethel (1 Samuel 10:3), Gilgal (1 Samuel 7:16), Mizpah (1 Samuel 7:5-6), and Beersheba (1 Samuel 8:1). All these cultic sites were closed later by King Josiah, who wanted to restrict the worship of God to Jerusalem.

Eli and his sons conduct worship at Shiloh. Their duties include offering sacrifices; instructing in cultic, ethical, and legal matters; and delivering oracles from God. As part of their salary the priests claim selected portions of the sacrificial meal after the Lord's requirements have been satisfied. The sacrificial meal and its accompanying offerings are primarily intended for the nourishment and appeasement of God.

The concepts of sacrifice and appeasement are foreign to modern ideas about God's nature. However, we must remember that the Bible reflects very ancient religious practices. Sacrifice and pilgrimage were legitimate and meaningful cultic practices in the early days of Israel. How we honor and serve God changes with history and with revelation. We must resist the notion that our worship practices are superior to those of ancient Israel.

The expression *Lord Almighty* in 1:11 occurs here for the first time in the Old Testament. The word *Lord* (Hebrew: *Yahweh* or *YHWH*), is the personal name for Israel's God. The name is initially revealed to Moses atop the holy mountain (Exodus 3).

In all likelihood, the word *Yahweh* was already a proper name for a deity when it entered Israel's vocabulary. The similarity of *YHWH* to the Hebrew word for "to be" may signify a living, active, dynamic God in contrast to the Canaanite idols.

The term *almighty* reflects the belief that God, in the form of the ark, stands at the head of the armies of Israel.

1 Samuel 2:1-10. The account of Samuel's life is interrupted by Hannah's hymn of praise and thanksgiving. Verse 11 of Chapter 2 continues the story of Elkanah's annual visit to Shiloh (1:28). Hannah's hymn is theologically and historically appropriate to this situation. Its appropriateness is especially clear in verse 5: "She who was barren has borne seven children." God has wrought a birth miracle through this otherwise childless woman.

Apart from this reference in 2:5, the description of God's many blessings cited within the hymn could have occurred at any time to anyone. The faith this song exhibits is a remarkable testimony to God's timely intervention on behalf of Israel. YHWH, the God of Israel, is active in history. This faith in God furnishes confidence and certainty.

The singer celebrates the Lord's victory over the enemies of God's people, and dramatizes the Lord's raising up of the lowly and suppressing of the powerful. As in other hymns, the adversaries are unnamed. But the contrast between the powerful but faithless and the powerless but faithful is vivid.

The term *anointed* in verse 10 designates a person whom the Lord chooses to rule the people. A person anointed is empowered with strength and knowledge.

1 Samuel 2:12-26. The narrative of Samuel's early life as a young priest at Shiloh continues now with a contrasting account of the wickedness of Hophni and Phinehas. The student book describes the cultic nature of their sins. They demand the Lord's portion of sacred meat and sexually abuse the women who work at the Temple. The clear evaluation of their actions leaves nothing to the reader's imagination: "This sin of the young men was very great in the Lord's sight" (verse 17). Contrast this evaluation with that of Samuel in verse 26: "The boy Samuel continued to grow both in stature and in favor with the Lord and with men."

The statement in verse 25 that "it was the Lord's will to put them to death" may strike a discordant note in the ears of modern readers. Many of us place a high value on individual freedom and self-determination. Phrases such as "It's never too late!" and "There's always hope" appeal to most of us and serve as incentives to continue what otherwise might be hopeless struggles. Also, we often react negatively to any notion that God's will is coercive and unforgiving.

However, we must accept the Old Testament conception of God as an unchangeable God. Compare God's attitude toward the Egyptian pharaoh (Exodus 14), or God's attitude toward sinful Israel in Isaiah 6:10 or Amos 9:1-3. In these passages, God judges persons for evil and cannot be dissuaded.

But verse 25 says more about the nature and magnitude of the lads' sins than about God's unalterable will. Their sins are a direct insult to God and a violation of God's word.

The linen ephod mentioned in verse 18 is to be distinguished from the ephod used by the priest to determine God's will (Exodus 28:5-14). The apparel is one more sign of Samuel's priestly role. He is now totally immersed in the religious traditions of his day, and persons associate him with the cultic sanctuary at Shiloh.

1 Samuel 2:27-36. For a second time in Chapter 2, the story of Samuel's early life is interrupted. This time God's messenger announces judgment against Eli and his house. It is not accidental that this announcement occurs just after the description of Hophni and Phinehas's sins and Eli's inability to restrain them. The seriousness of their sins (2:17) and the Lord's wrathful displeasure (2:25) are now reconfirmed through the announcement of judgment delivered by an anonymous man of God.

These words of the holy man create history. Hophni and Phinahas are scheduled for an appointment with destiny, and Eli's priestly line will end. Once the prophet announces God's word, history is created. The eventual result is the fulfillment of what has been announced. No predictions here! Following in the traditions of the great Old Testament prophets, the Deuteronomistic historian forcefully explains the collapse of Eli's house and the fall of Shiloh.

The identity of the faithful priest in verse 35 is a mystery. In the context of this narrative, it must refer to Samuel. However, in view of David and his rise to God's favor as the "anointed one," the passage probably points forward to the days of the monarchy. Thus the editor or editors anticipate forthcoming events by adding to previously existing narrative. As we continue to examine First and Second Samuel, we will discover more examples of this artistic and literary process.

1 Samuel 3. Returning to the story of Samuel's early life, we encounter a vivid and dramatic account of Samuel's call to prophetic service. Although the passage does not tell us Samuel's age at this time, Jewish tradition maintains that he is about twelve years old. Also at this age, Jesus encountered the learned scribes in the Jerusalem Temple. Even today, the age of twelve is a turning point in the lives of Jewish children.

Similar calls occur in many Old Testament prophetic books: for example Amos (7:10-15), Jeremiah (1:4-10), Ezekiel (1:4-28), and Isaiah (6:1-13). Each of these reports confirms the recipient as God's authorized spokesman. Each one establishes the prophet as God's messenger. As bearers of God's potent word that creates history and affects the lives of their people, these prophets are to be revered.

As the speeches of the great prophets were collected and arranged into written form, they were often accompanied by reports of prophetic calls. Here in First Samuel, God's call places Samuel within a tradition of prophets who, by virtue of their authoritative words, transformed the history of Israel.

DIMENSION THREE: WHAT DOES THE BIBLE MEAN TO ME?

1 Samuel 1:1-28; 2:26—God in History

One of the central theological affirmations of the Bible is that human existence is purposeful and meaningful. Unlike some modern religious cults that deny the worth or importance of human existence, the Bible affirms that our present life is meaningful and precious because of God and God's sovereign rule.

Deuteronomy 26:5-9 is a small creedal affirmation that God has been active in the life of the earliest Hebrews. The creed also says that this providential leadership long ago will furnish their lives with a sense of direction later. In times of national emergency, God intervenes on Israel's behalf and raises up leaders such as the judges or Samuel or David to provide guidance for the people. This intervention may not have always been understood clearly nor obeyed willingly, but God remains near.

How many Christians today sincerely believe that God is active in history? The student book lists some of the major problems of today: urban and rural crime, hunger, and depletion of world resources. If God is truly in control of the world, how can we understand these human tragedies?

On the other side, many Christians affirm divine activity in history, even to the point of absolute determinism. These persons might explain the tragic death of a young child as "the will of God." While the Bible teaches us that God is truly involved in the world and receptive to our concerns, nowhere does it say that a loving God maliciously destroys innocent lives. Such a thought is incompatible with either the Old Testament or the New Testament.

Natural disasters do occur from time to time, but these are byproducts of the way God created the natural order. Many of the other types of apparent divine evil are caused by our willful misuse of our freedom. God is indeed active in the affairs of the world. Perhaps our problem is that we are uncertain where to look or how to understand this revelation when we see it.

Part of the prophetic role is helping persons see and understand God's revelation. Who are the Samuels of today, and what are they saying to us?

1 Samuel 2:1-10—Celebrating God's Reign

This hymn of thanksgiving continues the basic theme introduced in the previous section—namely, the purposeful activity of God in history. The hymn celebrates God's deliverance of Hannah from barrenness. It is an affirmation of faith. Throughout the Bible, God appears on the side of the powerless, the oppressed, and the hopeless. Rarely does God help those who help themselves. Exactly the opposite is true. God helps those who cannot help themselves.

God did not choose Israel because of her might or her prominence among the nations but out of God's free grace (Deuteronomy 7:6-8). God does not choose Hannah because of her qualities of "motherhood," but because of God's loving desire to deliver persons from their distress. This theme of grace is basic to biblical theology and finds ultimate expression in the Incarnation (John 3:16).

A second theological issue raised by Hannah's hymn is that all theology is a response to what God has done, is doing, or is about to do. The Old Testament contains many hymns, particularly in the Psalms, praising the mighty acts of God. For most Christians today, response to God takes the form of worship. Worship, therefore, is an important dimension of the religious experience. It is a chance to express—inwardly and outwardly—our faith in the purposeful activities of God.

Many of the hymns we use in the church today reflect this similar theme. "A Mighty Fortress Is Our God" is a good example. The verses of these grand hymns touch a dimension of our being that we often neglect. Worship and celebration may not be serving the immediate needs of the poor. But they are preparing us for such service, and so are important in the total framework of our religious experience.

1 Samuel 2:12-17, 22-26—The Nature of Sin

When most persons today think of sin, they think of illicit sexual activity, drug abuse, crime, lying, alcoholism, not attending church, and a host of other sins. Yet, many of us fail to concern ourselves with social problems such as racism, pollution, immoral business practices, and the like.

Begin this section by having the class define the word *sin*. You might want to look up *sin* in a Bible dictionary, or have a class member look it up. Is sin an action that persons commit? Or is sin a disorder of the soul?

Certainly the biblical view of sin is a variegated picture. Sin is both corporate and individual. It involves apostasy, social abuse, religious apathy, and many more actions. But at base, the Old and New Testaments view sin as willful disobedience to the will of God. Whether it is Eve's eating the forbidden fruit, Hophni and Phinehas's disregard for cultic law, or the proud Pharisee in the Temple, the breaking of God's word is sin.

We are all guilty! But here grace and repentance come in. In our story, Samuel's birth is an act of grace. The remaining chapters in First and Second Samuel describe Israel's response. How is God's grace available to us today? How can we respond to and acknowledge this grace?

Close today's session by asking the class members to share any new insights they have gained from their study of 1 Samuel 1–3. If time allows, list these insights on a chalkboard or a large piece of paper. At the end of your study of First and Second Samuel you will have a handy catalog of what the class has learned.

2

The Ark of the Covenant

1 Samuel 4–6

DIMENSION ONE: WHAT DOES THE BIBLE SAY?

Answer these questions by reading 1 Samuel 4

1. Who are the major military opponents of Israel during the days of Samuel? (4:1)

   Israel's major military opponents are the Philistines.

2. What symbol of God's presence encourages the Hebrews in battle? (4:3)

   The ark of the covenant encourages the Hebrews.

3. Where is the ark kept? (4:3-4)

   The ark is kept at Shiloh.

4. Why are the Philistines frightened upon learning that the ark is in the Israelite camp? (4:7-8)

   They recognize that the God of Israel is the same God who caused plagues in Egypt.

5. What is the outcome of the battle? (4:10-11)

   The Philistines defeat Israel and capture the ark. Hophni and Phinehas die.

6. How does Eli learn of the outcome of the battle, and what happens to him after hearing this news? (4:12-18)

   Eli is told by a Benjamite that the battle is lost. After learning the outcome, he dies.

7. What does the name *Ichabod* mean? (4:21)

   The name Ichabod *means "the glory has departed from Israel."*

Answer these questions by reading 1 Samuel 5

8. Where do the Philistines take the ark? (5:1, 8, 10)

   The Philistines first take the ark to Ashdod, then to Gath, then to Ekron.

9. What happens in these cities because of the ark's presence? (5:1-12)

   In Ashdod, the statue of Dagon falls over and is dismembered before the ark. In Ashdod, Gath, and Ekron tumors infect the citizens.

10. Who is the main god of the Philistines? (5:1-2)

    Dagon is the main god of the Philistines.

11. What do the Philistines want to do with the ark? (5:11-12)

    They want to send it back to the Israelites because they are afraid it will kill them all.

Answer these questions by reading 1 Samuel 6

12. How long do the Philistines have the ark? (6:1)

    The ark is with the Philistines seven months.

13. When the Philistines return the ark, what do they send along with it? Why? (6:1-6)

    When they return the ark, they also send the images of five golden tumors and five golden rats to appease the angry God of Israel.

14. Where do they first send the ark? (6:14)

    The ark first comes into a field belonging to a certain Joshua of Beth Shemesh.

THE ARK OF THE COVENANT

15. Why do some of the men of Beth Shemesh die? (6:19)

Seventy men of Beth Shemesh die because they look into the holy ark.

16. Where is the ark taken next? (6:21)

The ark is carried to Kiriath Jearim.

DIMENSION TWO: WHAT DOES THE BIBLE MEAN?

Background Information on 1 Samuel 4–6

First Samuel 4–6 may be divided into four major sections: (1) the loss of the ark (4:1-11); (2) reactions to the loss of the ark (4:12-22); (3) divine judgment against the Philistines (5:1-12); and (4) the return of the ark to Israel (6:1-21). The focus of these chapters shifts from Samuel and his activities as a servant of God to the ark and its role in early Israelite history. In fact, Samuel is not mentioned at all in Chapters 4–6. The connecting points between these three chapters and 1 Samuel 1–3 are the idea of the ark residing at Shiloh and Eli, Hophni, and Phinehas as guardians of the ark. No mention is made of the wickedness of Hophni and Phinehas, which is so prominent in the preceding chapters. Also, nothing is said of God's intention to remove the priesthood from Eli's family. These omissions suggest that Chapters 4–6 were written by a different author than the one who composed Chapters 1–3.

1 Samuel 4:1-11. The Philistines are the major adversaries of the Israelites during the twelfth and eleventh centuries B.C., during the times of the judges and during the early days of the monarchy. The Old Testament reports that the Philistines come from Caphtor (Amos 9:7; Jeremiah 47:4-5; Deuteronomy 2:23), which may refer to the island of Crete. They may have entered Palestine sometime in the late thirteenth or early twelfth century B.C. The name *Palestine* comes from the word *Philistine.* Following their immigration, they organized into five city-states in the southern coastal area, ruled by lords. These cities are Gaza, Ashkelon, Gath, Ashdod, and Ekron. From these cities, they began to push inland toward the hill country that had been settled by the tribes of Israel. The Philistines were a threat until they were defeated by King David around 1000 B.C.

The battle described in 1 Samuel 4 takes place between Aphek and Ebenezer. The location of Ebenezer is unknown but is apparently close to Aphek, a city located between the coastal plain and highland area in central Palestine. Control of this small area is important for commercial and military reasons. The number of Israelites killed in the initial encounter is probably exaggerated to indicate the importance of this particular battle.

The Philistines are more adept at open-plain battles. Warfare in the open plain is not particularly advantageous for the early Israelites. They are much more accustomed to raids (Judges 7–8; 18:11-26) or early morning surprise attacks (Joshua 8; Judges 9:36-45). Saul is killed in such an open-plain battle at the foot of Mount Gilboa (1 Samuel 28:4). There, the defeated troops of Israel flee in disarray. On the other hand, the Philistines seem to be much more adept at open-plain battles. Some scholars suggest they prefer the open plain because they use chariots and have greater mobility. Certainly, at the battles in question, the Philistines demonstrate superiority over the Hebrews.

The major weapons used in warfare are bows and arrows, spears (or javelins), knives, and swords and shields. The opponents line up opposite one another at an appointed time, and, when a battle shout is sounded, the battle begins. Usually, a line of soldiers carrying shields leads, followed by swordsmen and archers. As the two lines converge, hand-to-hand combat ensues. Finally, a victory horn is sounded, or a horn is blown for retreat. The troops retire to prepare for another battle, either later that same day or the next day.

The armies of Israel really did not excel in warfare until the leadership of King David. Then, Israel defeated the Edomites, Moabites, Ammonites, and Philistines. They also managed to gain control of Jerusalem from a group of people known as the Jebusites.

The ark of the covenant and the Tent of Meeting are the sacred memorabilia of Israel's early days in the desert (Exodus 16–19). Once the Israelites settle in Canaan, the ark is stationed at Shiloh, at least until the events described in this section. The ark is described in Exodus 25:10-22 and Exodus 37:19. Following its capture and hasty return by the Philistines, the ark remains at Kiriath Jearim until David takes it to Jerusalem. When Solomon completes the Temple in Jerusalem, the ark is placed within the inner sanctuary (1 Kings 8:6-13).

1 Samuel 4:12-22. Two brief but graphic reactions illustrate the sense of national panic and depression that besets the Israelites when they learn of the defeat of their army and the loss of the ark. Eli, the old priest, falls over dead instantly, and Phinehas's wife bears a son prematurely. The child is named *Ichabod*, meaning something like "the glory has departed from Israel" or "no glory." His mother dies in childbirth.

The problem of Eli's watchful station mentioned in the student book is due to a defective Hebrew manuscript. We will never know exactly where he was sitting, nor can we explain how he missed the messenger running into the city. Although details such as these may bother our modern need for precise information, they would have been of little concern to the biblical writer. The overall impression of the mood or atmosphere prevalent in the city is more important. Modern readers cannot expect the writers of the Bible to speak as modern historians would speak.

Imposing twentieth-century standards of journalism on the Scripture is not appropriate.

The reaction of these selected persons is very clear: fear permeates them because the symbol of God's powerful presence is gone.

The practice of giving children symbolic names is widespread in the days of the Old Testament. Hosea and Gomer (Hosea 1:2-9) prophetically announce judgment against Israel through the names they give their children. Isaiah announces the fall of Damascus and Samaria by the names of his son.

Names were of great significance in the ancient Near East. They conveyed the essence or ultimate nature of a person or a thing. To understand another person's name gave power or dominance over the person (Genesis 32:22-32). Adam's naming the animals in Genesis 2 signifies his power to subdue the creatures of the earth.

The wife of Phinehas is following a long-standing tradition by describing Israel's vulnerability at the moment. When this story is placed alongside the death of Eli, it shows that the people of Israel are gripped by a sense of dread and despair over the loss of their ark. To fail to empathize with their feelings at this time is to miss a major intention of the biblical narrative.

1 Samuel 5. The focus of the narrative now shifts away from Israel's despondency over the loss of the ark. The captured ark is in the camp of the enemy. The ultimate symbol of national supremacy in the ancient Near East is the capture of an enemy's national god. To the Philistines, their ascendancy over Israel is now secured. Israel's army is in retreat and her God is in their hands. So with great pride, the Philistines deposit the ark of Israel in the temple of Dagon, their god. Another trophy is added to their shelf. They must have felt proud and boastful.

But suddenly, on the morning after they put the ark in Dagon's temple, the Philistines find their statue of Dagon lying face down before the ark in a subservient position. The very next morning, they receive a second jolt: Dagon has been dismembered. Then a plague breaks out among the people, followed by an invasion of rats. Clearly, what began as a victory over an alien god has turned into a national catastrophe. These events cannot be mere accident or chance. They are the judgment of an angry and offended God.

The Hebrew text of Chapter 5 is filled with literary problems, such as words that are incorrectly spelled, missing words, and misplaced phrases. As a result, the specific details of the judgment episodes are difficult to reconstruct. To aid in the resolution of these problems, scholars have turned to the Greek Old Testament (Septuagint). The Greek text adds a phrase in 5:6 describing an invasion of rats as an additional disaster befalling the Philistines. (See *The New English Bible.*) Such an addition makes sense in view of the sacrificial offering the Philistines send with the ark they return to Israel (1 Samuel 6:5). Problems such as these need not detract from the authority of the Bible, but should be understood as the unfortunate results of hundreds of years of both oral and written transmission.

Dagon is an early Canaanite agricultural deity. The Philistines adopted this god when they settled in the area. Israel, on the other hand, remains loyal to the Lord despite competition from Baal, Dagon, and other native Canaanite gods. Many of the stories in the Old Testament are told and retold to illustrate the power and authority of Israel's God over rival gods (1 Kings 18:20-40 and Exodus 14). Dagon is clearly overwhelmed by the Lord of Israel, and falls prostrate before God.

1 Samuel 6. Following the outbreak of disease and the infestation of rats, the Philistine lords consult their holy men about how to return the ark and rid the country of pestilence. They decide to send back the ark along with appropriate offerings. The ark arrives at Beth Shemesh and everyone rejoices. The cart conveying the ark, along with the milking cows who pulled it, are sacrificed on an altar. As a result of a breach of religious tradition some of the men die. The ark is then transported to Kiriath Jearim where it remains until David moves it to Jerusalem. The outward plot of this chapter is clear and easy to follow. God's holy ark is once again back among the people, and calm prevails.

The diviners and priests indicate that images of both tumors and rats must accompany the ark. Thus, it seems likely that the two types of calamities ravaged the land—plague and rats. No connection is made between the two events. Whether the rats are carriers of plague germs is unanswered. The Philistines believed that Israel's mighty God stood behind these disasters. Therefore, this God must quickly be appeased lest some other disaster occur.

The number five represents the five major cities of the Philistine state. Ancient religions held a belief of sympathetic magic. By physically depicting the tumors and mice and sending them out of the land, the country can be cleansed and purified.

For a second time in this section, the Philistines refer to activities of Israel's God against the Egyptians. Earlier in 4:8 they express fear at the God who infected the Egyptians with all kinds of plagues in the desert. To be sure this reference does not correspond with the account of God's punishment of Pharoah. The source of the error may have been attributed by early Hebrew writers to Philistine ignorance. Although their knowledge of the specific details may be incorrect, the Philistine perception of the power of the Lord is accurate.

Pharoah's obstinacy brought terrible plagues upon the land. Why should the Philistines likewise be so stupid? Comply with Israel's God and peace will return to the land. The national and even international fame of the Lord, God of Israel, is spreading. Now foreign nations are being forced to submit to God. Just as Israel's God was victor over the stubborn Egyptians, so now has God triumphed over the Philistines.

In verse 19, another serious textual problem makes understanding difficult. The Hebrew text explains the death of the seventy men of Beth Shemesh as a consequence of violation of a sacred law: namely, nonpriestly contact with the ark. The Septuagint has a different account, saying, "The sons of Jeconiah did not share in the joy of the men of Beth Shemesh when they looked upon the ark of the Lord, so he slew. . . ."

Commentators are divided in their preference between the two texts. Here again a difficult Hebrew text makes it impossible to explain why seventy men died. They may have died because there were no priests at Beth Shemesh to handle the holy object. Or, they may have died as a result of apathy toward the ark. Clearly, either reason causes even God's chosen people to stand in awe of the ark. God is holy and the ark must be approached properly and with care. God's symbolic presence in the ark must caution persons to behave properly.

The section concludes with the ark being transported to Kiriath Jearim, a short distance away. The crisis begun in Chapter 4 with the capture of the ark is now resolved. God's holy object is back in the hands of the chosen people. Once again, God's power has been demonstrated to a foreign adversary, and once again the Lord met the challenge.

DIMENSION THREE: WHAT DOES THE BIBLE MEAN TO ME?

1 Samuel 4:1-11—God's Holy Purposes

How can we discern God's purposes in events that seem tragic to us? After losing the initial battle, the elders of Israel ask, "Why did the LORD bring defeat upon us today before the Philistines?" How could God permit a pagan power to defeat the chosen people? The question is intensified with the loss of the ark, as the reactions of Eli and Phinehas's wife indicate.

No one seems to be able to answer this perplexing question. They are uncertain. But, as events proceed and history develops, the original question is clearly answered. The defeat of the Israelites and the capture of the ark allow God to prove to the Philistines that Dagon has no real power. At the end of the narrative, even Dagon's own people believe in God's universal sovereignty.

Many persons today still ask, Why does God allow certain things to happen? Few of us remain untouched by tragedies. Accidental drownings, automobile accidents involving young people, racist and sexist discrimination, and other such events challenge our faith. They may seem incompatible with our belief in an all-loving God. This theme is raised many places in the Bible, and receives many treatments. As we move through our study of the Bible, we will doubtless encounter it many times. No single, universally satisfying answer is given to the question of suffering.

For the moment, let us examine the answer offered in this passage.

The meaning of certain events cannot be understood until God's work is completed. The Israelites could not understand the capture of their ark until God caused havoc among the Philistines. Perspective and point of view are the two essential elements here. Not until God has finished working will we understand some events. The early events must be interpreted in light of later events. The capture of the ark is understood in the light of the calamities God brought against the Philistines. The temporary despair in Israel is justified and explained by God's proof of superiority over Dagon.

For Christians today, these lessons on the ark counsel patience and trust in God's sovereignty. The seeming injustices that occur in our lives await fuller explanations at later times. In the face of disaster, we must believe that God is not finished. The Lord's work is not yet complete. We must await its fulfillment.

Such a view of tragedy offers little solace at the moment. In fact, there may be little to ease our present hurt, grief, or pain. But for the Christian, the knowledge that God is still present and still in control can bring gradual acceptance. God does not cause hurt or will the suffering of innocent persons. But, when these events occur they must be understood within the larger framework of our lives. God can turn sorrow into joy, defeat into victory, and death into life. Faith in God involves patience, trust, and confidence that God will prevail. This is the message Israel learned when the Philistines captured the ark.

1 Samuel 5—God's Awesome Power

As students work their way through the Bible in the Genesis to Revelation series, they will quickly learn of the many and diverse ways God is disclosed. Some of these moments of revelation in the Old Testament will be familiar, such as Moses' experience at the burning bush and Elijah's audience with the still small voice of God. In the New Testament, one may recall Jesus' experience at the Jordan River where he was baptized by John, Paul's experience on the Damascus road, or the experience of the thieves on the cross.

In addition to these well-known instances of divine revelation, we also encounter forms of God's disclosure that are new and surprising to us. In fact, many of these moments of God's presence are terrifying and awesome. They may seem very alien or even incompatible with the loving and merciful conception of God taught by Jesus. God's frightening display of power against the Philistines in 1 Samuel 5 is just such a moment. The slaughter of the men of Beth Shemesh is even more surprising.

How do we reconcile the awesome destructiveness of God's holy power with the compassionate but firm image of God evident in the New Testament? In terms of the broader theological issue, how are Christians to understand the relationship between the Old and New Testaments?

Certainly, the belief that there is only one God is fundamental. The God of Jesus and Paul is also the God of Abraham, Moses, and Samuel. Also, we need to remember that there is a broad historical gap between much of the Old Testament and the New Testament. In some cases the gap is as much as a thousand years or more. Many of the accounts of God's encounters with persons in the Old Testament reflect the values of very ancient cultures.

From the perspective of Jesus and Paul, the values of Samuel and David must have seemed strange and primitive indeed. History marches on. God does new things in new ways as situations change. But, God's nature as the creator of the world and the redeemer of humanity does not change. The particular way that God confronts humanity and the ways that we express our experiences of God do change. We neither speak nor think as people of the first century A.D. did, or people of the eleventh century B.C. In fact, these expressions must change if our confession of God's leadership is to have any meaning at all.

The writers of the Bible were selective in which narratives they chose to pass on to future generations of believers. How they selected these stories is not always clear to us as readers, nor do the stories give us all the detail that we might like. But, we may be certain that their inclusion in the Scripture is not without careful thought and divine inspiration. We must probe beneath the surface to determine what this or that narrative means.

In the case of the terrifying display of God's awesome power among the Philistines, the emphasis is on God's universal sovereignty. This passage reveals a contest between national gods: the Lord, God of Israel is pitted against Dagon, god of Philistia. The narrative shows who is the real God and inspires trust and belief in this God.

To ancient Hebrew folk, proof of God's supremacy took the form of a fearsome pestilence bringing chaos and devastation to a boastful and overconfident enemy. By retelling this story of God's mighty acts among the Philistines, Israel inspires faith in her God. To focus on the specific detail of what God did or how God did it is to ask unimportant questions of the biblical narrative. The awesome and sometimes frightening nature of God's revelation in many Old Testament narratives is ancient confession of faith.

Studying the narratives intended to prove God's authority makes us more sensitive to an ever-widening range of experiences today through which God may address us. God may not send tumors or rats among our enemies, but the Lord is still very much at work in our world. What kind of stories do we tell today to inspire faith in God?

Close today's session by listing on chalkboard or a large sheet of paper any new insights class members have from their study of 1 Samuel 4–6.

Appoint a king to lead us, such as all the other nations have (8:5).

3

The People Ask for a King

1 Samuel 7–10

DIMENSION ONE:
WHAT DOES THE BIBLE SAY?

Answer these questions by reading 1 Samuel 7

1. What does Samuel tell the Israelites they must do to return to the Lord? (7:3-4)

   They must put away the foreign gods, the Baals and the Ashtoreths, and serve only the Lord.

2. How is the Philistine army defeated at Mizpah? (7:10)

   The Lord causes thunder, and the Philistines flee in panic.

3. What is Samuel's occupation? (7:15-17)

   Samuel is an itinerant judge.

Answer these questions by reading 1 Samuel 8

4. Who are Joel and Abijah? (8:2)

   They are the sons of Samuel.

5. When Samuel's sons are judges, what do they do? (8:3)

   Joel and Abijah accept bribes and pervert justice.

6. Why do the elders want a king? (8:5)

   They want one because Samuel is old and his sons are corrupt.

7. How does Samuel feel about their request for a king? (8:6)

   Samuel is displeased and prays to the Lord.

8. What does the Lord tell Samuel to do? (8:7-9)

   The Lord instructs Samuel to listen and follow the wishes of the people.

9. What does Samuel say a king might do? (8:10-17)

   The king can require mandatory service in his royal army and on his farms, and he can seize private property.

10. Do the people change their minds? (8:19-20)

    No. They still insist that Samuel appoint a king.

Answer these questions by reading 1 Samuel 9

11. Who is Kish? (9:1-2)

    A Benjamite, Kish is the father of Saul.

12. How does Saul happen to meet Samuel? (9:3-14)

    Saul and a servant are searching for his father's lost donkeys and consult a prophet.

13. Why does Samuel recognize Saul? (9:15-16)

    The Lord had revealed that such a man would appear the next day.

Answer these questions by reading 1 Samuel 10

14. What does Samuel tell Saul? (10:1)

    Samuel tells Saul that the Lord wants him to be leader over the people of Israel.

15. What happens to Saul when the spirit of God enters him? (10:6, 9-11)

    Saul's heart is changed and he begins to prophesy.

16. How does Samuel choose Saul as king? (10:20-24)

    Each tribe and family comes before him until Saul is chosen.

17. Where is Saul? (10:22)

He is hiding among the baggage.

18. Where is Saul's home? (10:26)

Saul's home is Gibeah.

DIMENSION TWO:
WHAT DOES THE BIBLE MEAN?

---

1 Samuel 7. Verses 1 and 2 of this chapter complete the narrative of the return of the ark (Lesson 2). Following its return to Beth Shemesh, the ark is transported to Kiriath Jearim. There, Eleazar is consecrated as a priest to care for the holy object. The ark remains there until David brings it into his new capital, Jerusalem.

The word *mourned* (verse 2) is difficult to understand. Why would Israel mourn? The ark has been returned and the Philistine menace has been stilled. The Greek Old Testament has changed "mourned" and now reads "turned," suggesting a positive move back toward the Lord. As indicated in Lesson 2, the Hebrew text of Samuel is often difficult to translate and to interpret.

With verse 3, the narrator returns to Samuel as the principal figure in Israel's early history. In Lesson 1 we read that Samuel received God's word and was generally recognized throughout Israel as a prophet of the Lord. However, here his role shifts to that of a judge. In the person of Samuel, two leadership roles merge—prophet and judge.

Samuel's leadership among the early tribes of Israel is both timely and distinguished. Perhaps more than any other figure during this exciting period in Israel's history, Samuel appears as the stabilizing force. As God's spokesman, he wields power and commands the utmost respect from all Israel.

The plot of this chapter is simple, concise, and clear. In the midst of a national celebration for atonement of sin, the Israelites at Mizpah are suddenly threatened by attack from the Philistines. Samuel offers a special sacrifice on their behalf. The Lord responds by causing thunder, and the Philistines flee in total panic. The Israelites pursue them to the outermost fringes of their territory.

A final note is added about Samuel's activity as a circuit judge among the cities of Bethel, Gilgal, Mizpah, and Ramah. This narrative is reminiscent of the feats of other judges such as Samson and Gideon. There too, the Lord intercedes miraculously on behalf of the people against an adversary. Israel's faith in the Lord is vindicated time and again in these narratives about Israel's early leaders.

Verse 4 mentions important Canaanite deities—Baal and the Ashtoreth. Archaeological discoveries at major Canaanite cities such as Ras Shamra and Byblos (both north of Israel on the Mediterranean Sea) have given us a clear picture of their religion. The Baals and their female companions, the Ashtoreths, are the general names for several local fertility gods and goddesses in Canaan. They were closely associated with early agricultural communities, and were thought to possess powers of control over the fertility of the soil. Many early religious centers and sanctuaries were dedicated to these deities.

When the Israelites entered the land of Palestine, Canaanite agricultural techniques were vastly superior to their own. Thus the Israelites began to adopt Canaanite ways of farming, including worship of the Baals and the Ashtoreths. The early Israelites must have connected Canaanite agricultural success with Canaanite religion. Such worship of foreign gods was a strict violation of the Mosaic law, and was known as apostasy.

The city of Mizpah was a famous religious site during the days of Samuel. Unfortunately, the exact location of the holy place is disputed among archaeologists. Two sites, each about five miles north of Jerusalem, are the leading candidates. Without written record, identification of many of these biblical cities is difficult.

Verse 6 refers to the ritual of pouring out water before the Lord. The use of water as part of a religious celebration is somewhat unusual in biblical times. Since water is scarce at certain times and in certain places in Palestine, its use here as a precious substance is understandable. By means of such offerings, the community could be purified before the Lord.

The chapter concludes with a description of Samuel's role in the history of Israel. For as long as he lived, peace existed between Israel and the Philistines. This time of peace was due to Samuel's special place before God. Whether or not Samuel is a great warrior is not the major issue. Samuel is the faithful, anointed servant of God, and God listens to Samuel's prayers (7:9). The people's confidence in Samuel is well founded.

Samuel's role as judge is described in verses 15-17. Here, he is depicted as an itinerant judge who resolves disputes in four towns. He visits each place periodically and serves as a magistrate. We can see from this passage that there was no separation between church and state in early Israel. Samuel is both a civil and a religious leader whose fame has spread throughout all Israel.

1 Samuel 8. In this very important chapter we witness the beginning of a major transition in the history of Israel. We have reached the end of the era when Israel has been ruled by judges, and we enter the period of the monarch. This transition is decisive for Israel! No longer will she be a loosely organized association of tribes. Israel is rapidly becoming a modern state.

This transition is not without critics. Samuel harshly criticizes the people's request for a king. Samuel sees Israel as a unique community, ruled by the Lord and the judges. Israel's king is the Lord. Any threat to God's lordship is a breach of faith.

The request of the elders of Israel for a king is clear and historically well founded. In verse 4, they point to Samuel's old age and to the corruption of his sons. Moreover, in verse 5 and 20, they ask to be governed like other nations. This request is a plea for stronger leadership and better organization. The time has passed when temporary leadership sufficed. Perhaps if all leaders could be of the caliber of Samuel, their demand for a king would be unnecessary. But the elders knew better.

Although we have the impression from 17:13-14 that Israel is at peace, the turbulent days of Philistine threats remain vivid in their memories. The Israelites have feared that their present state of calm would be short-lived. From their perspective, a more formal institution is needed to insure peace.

However, Samuel is reluctant to grant their wishes. From his perspective, their desire to formalize leadership and be like other nations is a betrayal of their covenant faith and a denial of God's leadership. Israel's God rules by means of special appointments, as through judges such as Gideon and Samuel. From Samuel's point of view, Israel is a sacred community, specially chosen and nurtured by the Lord. She is not like other nations. Samuel consults God who, surprisingly, instructs him to appoint a king. But first, Samuel is to warn the people of the dangers of monarchy.

Samuel's description of the powers and privileges of kingship is vivid and unflattering. The king can conscript young men for service in the army, for work on royal lands, or for assistance in the palace. He can levy taxes and impound private property. In general, the king can rule as he sees fit. Even worse, once the office is filled, there is no turning back. Kingship will always be a part of Israel's life. But the people disregard Samuel's warning and continue to cry for a king.

Samuel's understanding of kingship was informed by his cultural surroundings. In larger countries such as Egypt, Babylon, and Assyria, as well as Israel's smaller immediate neighbors (Edom, Moab, and Ammon), kingship was the traditional form of government. With few exceptions, the king was considered to be divine. His word was understood as the authoritative pronouncement from the gods. His will conveys the will of the gods. His power is absolute and beyond question. Thus, it is with good reason that Samuel warns the eager Israelites about the dangers of monarchy. Kingship is incompatible with Israel's special sense of destiny as God's chosen people. Precisely because Israel is not like other nations is kingship undesirable.

The chapter concludes with the Lord granting permission for a king. Samuel then dismisses the elders in order to ponder the matter further. Despite the Lord's instruction to name a king, Samuel is still reluctant. His leadership role in this moment of transition must have been truly burdensome. And he must have struggled to understand God's surprising demand to name a king.

1 Samuel 9:1–10:16. The scene suddenly shifts from Samuel's deliberations about monarchy to a new character—Saul. This section reveals a different attitude toward kingship. Here, Samuel willingly and quickly names Saul as king.

The plot of this section is very simple. As if by chance, the donkeys of Kish are lost and are sought by Saul and an anonymous companion. During the search, they find themselves near a city where there is a famous holy man. Thinking that this holy man can assist them in locating the wayward beasts, they seek him out. Much to his surprise, Saul learns that not only are the animals no longer lost, but that he is to rule over Israel as God's anointed prince. Everyone except Samuel is surprised by this turn of events.

The providential hand of the Lord is once more operating behind the scenes. God is carefully setting the stage for a new chapter in the history of Israel. Old ways of leadership must now give way to newer forms. Israel will have a king. As the biblical narrative unfolds, we realize that the Lord has chosen Saul as king. The accidental character of history is replaced by the providential hand of God directing the affairs of humankind.

Whereas in the preceding section (8:1-22) the Lord views monarchy as apostasy, here God supports kingship as necessary for military leadership. The person who rules God's people is chosen not by popular vote or by military powers, but by the Lord. Through the prophets, the Lord appoints the ruler, endows him with divine spirit (10:6), and empowers him with special abilities. It is not until later, following a great military victory (1 Samuel 11), that Saul is publicly proclaimed king.

Verse 9 makes an important distinction between two types of religious persons—the seer and the prophet. The seer is more common among the seminomadic tribes, and generally moves around with the tribes. The seer is a type of diviner who envisions future events. His medium of revelation is the dream.

The prophet, on the other hand, is usually found among the more settled, agricultural regions. The term *prophet* refers to several different types of religious figures: ecstatic groups, classical prophets such as Isaiah, cultic prophets, and royal prophets.

The practice of anointing the one to be king was a sacred act in Israel. Anointing was a solemn initiation into a special office that marks the new leader as God's agent. The use of oil is less important than the person who actually places hands upon the head. Here Samuel, as God's favored spokesman, transfers God's blessing to Saul. Public celebrations bestow the title of king upon him only after God has "anointed" him. The word *anointed* appears in Hebrew as *messiah*. The term does not refer to a divine being, but to a person God has selected and empowered to rule over the chosen people.

In 10:6, we read that the Spirit (literally, *breath*) of God comes into Saul and transforms him into another person. This gift of divine Spirit is usually referred to as charismatic endowment. The indwelling of God's Spirit animated human beings in the Creation story. It gave Samson, Gideon, and other judges superior insight and leadership ability. It is bestowed on Jesus as he is baptized by John in the Jordan River (Mark 1:10; John 1:32-34).

The Spirit also comes to the disciples following the resurrection of Jesus (Acts 2:1-4). Among the disciples and some of the Corinthian Christians, the outward effect of the indwelling of God's Spirit is *glossolalia*, or speaking in tongues. These utterances are incomprehensible to the human mind, but are interpreted by God back to the person.

After receiving God's Spirit, Saul begins to prophesy. Since Saul does not ordinarily prophesy, this behavior is strange and surprising to his acquaintances. Saul may look like the former person, but his behavior is quite different. This episode produced ancient Israel's proverb about unusual behavior—"Is Saul also among the prophets?"

This divine Spirit is precisely what enables Saul to lead Israel so effectively. It is also what strengthens and illumines all recipients. The charismatic endowment is a source of unusual strength and insight for prophet, priest, or king. But when Saul disobeys God and the divine Spirit is withdrawn, Saul deteriorates rapidly both personally and professionally, as we will see in future lessons.

1 Samuel 10:17-27. We now learn of a ceremony whereby Saul is chosen king. This narrative resumes the story following Samuel's dismissal of the people in 8:22. They reassemble at Mizpah, the important religious center mentioned in 7:5. The people march by Samuel, tribe by tribe, clan by clan, family by family, man by man. The various tribes, clans, and families are eliminated, until finally Saul is selected king. The reluctant king is found hiding among the supplies, and is immediately brought forth and proclaimed king. Samuel then reads him the duties of his new office, and the assembly dismisses with almost complete support of Saul.

Samuel's address to the Mizpah assembly follows the standard form for a prophetic announcement of judgment. It begins with the words "This is what the LORD, the God of Israel, says." Next Samuel gives reasons why judgment is coming. He recites God's previous acts of love for Israel (the Exodus), and contrasts God's help with Israel's unfaithfulness in her request for a king. Next, we are told about the process by which the king is selected. It almost appears that kingship is a form of judgment against Israel. It will not be a blessing but a punishment.

The selection is a means of inquiry used several places in the Old Testament. Joshua uses this method to identify Achan as a violator of the rules of religious war (Joshua 7:16-18). In 1 Samuel 14:38-42, Saul uses the method to identify Jonathan as the one who broke his oath. The process of selection proceeds from the larger units (tribes) to the smaller units (families). Then the people march by until the Lord makes known the divine choice. Just as in the procedures for choosing a prince, here too the Lord's hand is decisive. God is the power behind the choosing!

We are not certain why Saul hid among the baggage. He may have been too timid to accept God's will. Perhaps his traditional sense of modesty made him less than aggressive

to accept the kingship. Either possibility is less than flattering to Saul.

The Mizpah assembly concludes with the instructions Samuel delivers to Saul. To write them on a scroll suggests the formality and the authority of these duties. Unfortunately, we never hear of this scroll again.

The mention of the few persons in Israel who were not in accord with Saul's choice (10:27) is rather surprising. By now, even Samuel seems to be in agreement. All Israel has exclaimed, "Long live the king!"

Chapter 10 contains two different accounts of Saul's rise to kingship. These two accounts were probably written by two different persons. However, the biblical writer who finally joined these two accounts side by side saw a basic agreement between them. This agreement is in the ultimate divine cause in the selection of Saul. In both versions, God plays a decisive role in the selection of Saul as a ruler over the people.

The writers of the Bible are much more interested in theological matters than in historical detail. Differences in historical detail do not detract from the writers' belief that God is always at work in one way or another. For modern readers to dwell on discrepancies in detail is to engage in faulty biblical interpretation. The two accounts of Saul's selection teach us to look deeper at the theological issues. After all, the writers of both accounts stress God's clear and decisive role. It is actually enriching to our faith that dual accounts witness to the active and invigorating power of God.

DIMENSION THREE: WHAT DOES THE BIBLE MEAN TO ME?

1 Samuel 8:10-22—Church and State

The relationship between church and state is an important issue in the American mind. The framers of our Constitution included in the First Amendment strict separation of these two realms of authority.

The history of western civilization has not always known the distinction between the civil and the religious. Separation of authority is a relatively modern concept, designed to protect religious freedom and insure the right of individuals to worship as they choose. History is filled with tragedies resulting from abuses of power from both church and state.

In this section from First Samuel, the problem is whether a king is compatible with Israel's faith in the sovereignty of God. Since the king is divine or semidivine in most other nations of the ancient Near East, would a king in Israel be worshiped in a similar way? In one version of Saul's rise to power (8:1-22; 10:17-27), both Samuel and the Lord fear this possibility. In 8:7-8, the Lord clearly views Israel's request for a king as an act of faithlessness.

However, the Lord is still active in the selection of a leader. And Israel's king rules with the empowerment of

God's Spirit. Thus, even though Israel now has a king, there is still a union of church and state because the king rules (or fails) by the power of God's Spirit. When the people ignore God, and commit apostasy, things begin to break up. The downfall of the Israelite monarchy comes at the hands of the kings who do not follow God's commandments.

Few Christians today would endorse state control over religious belief or over the practice of religion. The First Amendment guarantees all citizens the right of freedom of conviction.

But on the other side of the issue, to what extent can or should Christians, individually or collectively, try to influence federal or state legislation? Can sincere Christians fail to protest violations of human rights? Is it theologically or morally improper for the church to take a stand on the abortion issue or on American foreign policy? These are delicate but important issues confronting our churches today.

Although Christians will differ on the particular resolutions, perhaps they can agree on the fact that our faith must express itself politically. The precarious balance between church and state can only be maintained by obedience to God's word as it is addressed to us, individually and collectively, in all spheres of human activity.

1 Samuel 10:9-13—The Gift of God's Spirit

Clearly, God's Spirit animates persons and empowers them to great feats of valor. This same theological statement of the impact of God's presence is seen in the two accounts of Creation, in the lives of famous Old Testament persons, in the moral order of the universe, and elsewhere. In the Gospel of John, the Spirit is promised as God's abiding presence to nurture and sustain the church. In Acts, the Spirit enables the disillusioned disciples to go forth to face an unbelieving world. There is no question as to the importance of the work of the Spirit. The real problem arises in recognizing the diversity of the Spirit's work.

Many Christians profess the activity of God's Spirit in their lives. Most of us understand that this deep and abiding presence of God is often inexpressible and even incomprehensible. Many claim that one fruit of this Spirit is the ability to speak in tongues. But a real problem arises when some Christians claim that the gift of tongues is the sole mark of God's spiritual presence.

God's Spirit is manifested in many forms throughout the Bible (as Paul says in 1 Corinthians 12–14), and also today. There are many fruits of God's Spirit, and those that are genuine are of equal value. Let all Christians rejoice in the many diverse activities of the Spirit. Let us embrace one another in love and join together around our common devotion to God. There is more to bind us together than there is to draw us apart.

Close the session by asking class members to share their new insights on 1 Samuel 7–10. If time allows, list these new insights on chalkboard or a large sheet of paper.

— 4 —

The Kingship of Saul

1 Samuel 11–15

DIMENSION ONE:
WHAT DOES THE BIBLE SAY?

Answer these questions by reading 1 Samuel 11

1. Which Israelite town does Nahash the Ammonite threaten? (11:1)

   Nahash threatens Jabesh Gilead.

2. What terms does Nahash offer the men of Jabesh Gilead? (11:2)

   Nahash says he will make a treaty but gouge out the right eye of everyone to put disgrace on Israel.

3. How does Saul respond to this crisis? (11:11)

   Saul assembles an army and slaughters the troops of Nahash in an early morning attack.

4. What does Samuel do after Saul's victory at Jabesh? (11:14-15)

   Samuel convenes an assembly at Gilgal and publicly announces that Saul is king.

Answer these questions by reading 1 Samuel 12

5. What do the people say to Samuel? (12:4)

   Samuel has neither cheated nor oppressed nor stolen anything during his service to the Lord.

6. What does Samuel remind the people that the Lord has done? (12:7-8)

   Samuel mentions the deliverance from Egypt and the settlement in Canaan.

7. What was Israel's sin during this period, and how did the Lord respond? (12:9-12)

   Israel forgot the Lord, who then gave her into the hands of her enemies.

8. What conditions does God give for Israel to obtain continued blessing? (12:14)

   Israel must (1) fear the Lord, (2) serve the Lord, (3) not rebel against the Lord's commands, and (4) follow the Lord.

9. What will happen if Israel and her king do not abide by these terms? (12:25)

   If Israel and her king disobey them, they will be swept away.

Answer these questions by reading 1 Samuel 13

10. Who are the opponents of Saul and the Israelites during this period? (13:4)

    Their opponents are the Philistines.

11. Why does Saul proceed with the sacrificial offerings at Gilgal? (13:11-12)

    Samuel has not arrived, and the Philistines are threatening attack.

12. How does Samuel react to Saul's deeds at Gilgal? (13:13)

    Samuel is angry with Saul, saying that he has not kept God's command.

13. Why do the Hebrews have so few metal weapons to use in their wars against the Philistines? (13:19)

    The Hebrews lack weapons because the Philistines will not permit blacksmiths to work in Israel.

Answer these questions by reading 1 Samuel 14

14. How is Jonathan related to Saul? (14:1)

    Jonathan is the son of Saul.

15. How does Jonathan characterize the non-Semitic Philistines? (14:6)

Jonathan calls them uncircumcised fellows.

16. Who is Ahijah and what role does he play in the Saul stories? (14:3, 18)

Ahijah is a descendant of Eli. He tends to the ark of God.

17. What is Saul's oath during this period of warfare? (14:24)

Saul proclaims he will fast until he has avenged himself on his enemies.

18. Which Israelite does not follow Saul's oath? (14:27)

Jonathan does not follow Saul's oath.

19. How does Saul learn that Jonathan has violated the oath? (14:41-42)

Saul invokes the second lots and the lot falls to Jonathan.

20. How does Jonathan escape death for his sin? (14:45)

The people rescue Jonathan.

21. Who are Saul's family members? (14:49-51)

Saul's wife is Ahinoam. His sons are Jonathan, Ishvi, and Malchi-Shua, and his daughters are Merab and Michal.

Answer these questions by reading 1 Samuel 15

22. What does Saul spare in the battle with the Amalekites? (15:9)

Saul spares Agag, their king, as well as their choicest animals.

23. What excuse does Saul offer Samuel for this act of disobedience? (15:21)

Saul says that he spared Agag and the choice animals so that they could be offered to God as a sacrifice.

24. How does the Lord react to Saul's sin? (15:35)

The Lord regrets having named Saul king over Israel.

DIMENSION TWO:
WHAT DOES THE BIBLE MEAN?

The arrangement of the biblical material in Dimension Two does not follow the chapters consecutively. As discussed in Lesson 3, the writer of First Samuel is blending two or more sources together that do not always agree on the historical details. The divisions reflect the order of the sources. These accounts must be unraveled in order to understand the proper sequence of events.

Once each treatment of Saul's kingship has been reviewed, then we can comprehend the relationship between them and the intentions of the biblical writer who finally joined them together. It would be a mistake either to ignore the differences in the two stories, or to fail to reassemble them and view them from the point of view of the biblical writer who put them together. Both steps are necessary in order to understand the richness and the depth of what this section of the Bible means.

In this lesson, we cover the early days of the Israelite monarchy. While it is true that Saul is named king, he does not rule over a united, centralized state. Instead, his rule is reminiscent of the period of the judges. Each Israelite tribe is still essentially independent. There is no formal system of taxation. Armies must be gathered from each tribe, at least at the beginning of Saul's reign.

Saul marks the beginning of kingship in Israel, and he paves the way for David, his successor. This period is characterized by almost constant warfare and uneasy truce from time to time. It is a period when the rights and responsibilities of monarchy are hazy and unclear. And finally, it is a time of transition in Israel, from the tribal association of the judges to the nation under the leadership of David and Solomon. From any angle, the kingship of Saul, with all its successes and failures, stands as one of the truly important periods in the history of ancient Israel.

1 Samuel 11. In Lesson 3, we discussed two accounts of Saul's rise to power: (1) 9:1–10:16—he is anointed prince in a private ceremony by Samuel, confirming God's own choice; (2) 10:17-27—he is selected king by elimination. In the present passage, Saul is proclaimed king of Israel in a public celebration at Gilgal, following his defeat of the Ammonites. God's choice of Saul is vindicated fully. Saul proves himself a worthy recipient of the Lord's trust. His actions here more than answer the question of his doubters, "How can this fellow save us?" (10:27). His expert leadership in crisis confirms God's confidence in Saul.

Ammon is a small country lying east of the Jordan River. Its territory overlaps with areas also claimed by Israelite tribes such as Reuben and Gad. At times, peace prevailed between Israel and Ammon. At other times they went to war over disputed territories. Like the Israelites, the Ammonites are Semitic-speaking people whose ancestry dates far back into ancient Near Eastern history.

In the incident reported in 1 Samuel 11, Nahash, an Ammonite, besieges Jabesh Gilead, an Israelite city in the northern part of the Trans-Jordan. Later, in 2 Samuel 10:1-2, David sends a delegation to the funeral of Nahash, and they receive bad treatment from Hanun, Nahash's son. The relationship between the two kingdoms often changes, depending upon the rulers and their relative strength.

Upon learning about the plight of the men of Jabesh, Saul receives an infusion of God's Spirit. He quickly assembles an army, conducts a morning raid against the Ammonites, and frees the city. It is important for us to understand the significance of Saul's charismatic endowment. His office as king was filled by divine appointment and empowered by the gift of God's Spirit. Saul rules with God's approval and support as long as he obeys the divine commands. When Saul's obedience ceases, God withdraws support and Saul's reign collapses.

1 Samuel 12. Few chapters in the Old Testament equal 1 Samuel 12 in its capacity to summarize Israel's history and preview events that are about to happen. In the twenty-five short verses of this chapter, Samuel swears an oath of moral purity, reviews Israel's holy history, and affirms his continued support on behalf of God's people.

Samuel begins the chapter with an oath of innocence. His purpose in taking this oath is to establish the moral virtues of his reign. He has been a fair administrator of the law, as well as a faithful and obedient servant of the Lord. Oaths have great religious significance, and the penalties are grave if untrue statements are made. Both the Lord and the people are witnesses. Samuel has told the truth.

Next, Samuel reviews the history of Israel since the days of Moses and the Exodus. Samuel is tracing this sequence of events to show how successfully God has ruled.

According to Samuel, the apostasy Israel has committed previously is of small account when compared to Israel's current act of unfaithfulness in requesting a king. The demand for a king is a direct affront to the Lord's leadership. As confirmation of the people's sin and Samuel's special place before God, Samuel prays. The Lord responds with an unseasonal thunderstorm. All Israel trembles before this display of power and begs Samuel to intercede. Samuel agrees to continue his service among them.

The heart of the Mosaic faith, believed and preached by Samuel and the later prophets of the Old Testament, is that the Lord is one God. Israel is to worship none but the Lord. At crucial points in her history, famous leaders remind Israel of her responsibility to honor this divine commandment in new and changing situations. Thus, as Israel moves from the era of the judges to the era of kingship, Samuel reminds her of this duty.

Despite his own dissatisfaction with Israel's request for a king, and the Lord's surprising response, Samuel promises to continue his work among the people. His own description of his role is twofold: (1) to continue as intercessor, and (2) to serve as a moral and religious guide. These functions are significant for future generations of prophets in the Old Testament. Each prophet, in his own way, fulfills these same functions. Thus, Samuel is a prototype of the prophetic office.

1 Samuel 13–14. This section recounts Israel's extended warfare with the Philistines. To meet this crisis, Israel requests a king. The Philistines consume much of Saul's attention during his reign. And the Philistine defeat of Saul's army is the reason for his suicide (1 Samuel 31).

The historical background of these two chapters is a strong Philistine dominance over Israel, at least in the central hill country where Saul lives. In part, the Philistine control of Israel rests on their control of the metal industry. Also, the Philistine armies use chariots, although they are less effective here in the rugged terrain around Micmash than they would be in the open plains.

The relative ease with which the Philistines occupy Micmash and the taunt they level against Jonathan and his armor-bearer (14:11) suggest that they are confident Israel poses no serious threat. But once again, as in the ark episode (1 Samuel 4–6), they fail to take due account of the power of Israel's Lord. Then, as now, this oversight is disastrous.

Following a stunning and rather surprising defeat of the Philistine troops stationed at Geba, the Philistines quickly move into battle positions in Micmash. The men of Israel, once brave, now retreat to hide in caves or flee to safe territory across the Jordan.

For awhile the Philistines control the territory by sporadic raids and by disarming the Israelites of metal weapons. Then, in a daring act of bravery by Jonathan, the Philistine watch is attacked. Almost immediately the Philistines panic at the sheer boldness of this act. Saul hastens quickly to aid Jonathan, and the rout of the Philistines has begun. Micmash is freed and Israel is in hot pursuit of the enemy.

As is true in other events in Israel's early history, the resolution of this crisis cannot be explained by Hebrew military superiority or by the natural leadership of Samuel, Saul, or Jonathan. The Bible is very clear about the ultimate explanation for victory: "So the Lord rescued Israel that day" (1 Samuel 14:23).

Saul's oath in 14:24 prohibits any Israelite soldier from eating during the day of battle. Presumably, this fast is intended to please the Lord and to enlist God's support against the Philistines. But, as events turn out, the oath reveals Saul's poor judgment. Saul's demise has begun. By sheer accident, or so it would seem, Jonathan is not told of the oath until he has eaten the honey. Even then Saul remains unaware that his oath has been violated until the voice of God is silent when approached about renewing the battle.

A curiously tragic tone dominates this episode. Saul and his family are doomed. Future events will complete Saul's headlong plunge into disaster. The reader is left with mixed emotions toward Saul. His intentions seem honorable, but his actions never quite turn out as they should. We cannot help but feel a tinge of pity for Saul.

Chapter 14 concludes with an evaluation of Saul's kingship from a political and military standpoint. He is able to subdue Israel's aggressive neighbors and establish at least some measure of freedom and stability in the country. Saul's accomplishments are stated clearly, succinctly, and appreciatively.

1 Samuel 13:7-15; 15:1-35. In these sections, we find two versions of Saul's disobedience. The theme of both narratives is identical but the details are different. They are probably parallel accounts by different writers. Each version arose from a different site in early Israel, and was later incorporated into a larger narrative about Saul and Samuel. Despite differences in detail, both accounts point to the same conclusion. Saul has disobeyed the Lord and now his kingship will be short-lived. Israel will soon have a new king.

The first account in this section interrupts a narrative about Israel's long struggle with the Philistines. The first half of verse 7 is continued at the second half of verse 15. Saul follows Samuel's instruction to proceed to Gilgal, but at the end of the designated period Samuel has not arrived. The Philistine threat is mounting and his own Israelite army is beginning to disband in fear. To complicate matters further, Saul does not wish to do battle without securing the Lord's blessing. So he takes matters in hand and offers the sacrifices himself. When Samuel arrives later, he is outraged at Saul's behavior. Samuel reprimands Saul, declaring that Saul's kingship is to be terminated. The Lord is displeased with Saul.

In the second account of Saul's disobedience (15:1-34), Saul's offense is different. Here Samuel instructs Saul to initiate a holy war against the Amalekites. He is to annihilate everything the enemy owns: men, women, children, and animals. Saul complies, and the Amalekites are destroyed. But he does not kill King Agag or their choicest animals.

Samuel condemns Saul for this willful act of disobedience. He indicates that the Lord's pleasure is in obedience rather than sacrifice (a theme found later in Amos 5:21-24). Samuel issues the ultimate judgment: Saul will lose the kingship to another person.

The symbolism in verse 27 of tearing Saul's robe is graphic. Just as Samuel has torn Saul's garment, so is the Lord tearing the kingdom from Saul. No future acts of appeasement on Saul's behalf make any difference. The Lord has decided. Saul has to go! From this point forward, Saul and Samuel both recede into the background as David begins to move to center stage. The next lesson completes David's rise to power.

DIMENSION THREE: WHAT DOES THE BIBLE MEAN TO ME?

1 Samuel 12:6-18—Divine Retribution

Retribution refers to the belief that God rewards the righteous person and punishes the wicked person. This belief is held by many religions, including Hinduism, Buddhism, Islam, Judaism, and Christianity. The particular way in which persons are rewarded or punished differs greatly, depending on the religion. Nevertheless, some form of accountability is always present. Ignoring the will of God is dangerous.

In Chapter 12, Samuel points out the obligations Israel has before the Lord. The people are to fear the Lord, serve and obey the Lord, and not rebel against his commands. These words of Samuel summarize Israel's ethical and religious responsibilities. They remind us of Moses' words in Deuteronomy 30:15-20 or the words of Joshua in Joshua 24:14-15. Israel's subjugation by her enemies, from the days of the judges to the Babylonian Exile, results from Israel's failure to keep God's commandments.

Samuel looks both backward and foward in his directives. He lays the matter of faithfulness at the center of Israel's faith and practice. Both king and people must share this responsibility. As the great prophets Amos, Hosea, and Isaiah point out, apostasy leads to punishment. Divine retribution is real!

Accountability for human behavior is still part of Christian faith. We still have to choose between obedience and disobedience. Regardless of how persons understand Christian ethical obligation, we are still responsible for what we do and think, and for who we are.

We may be devout followers of the Beatitudes, and try to follow the moral regulations of the New Testament. Others of us may interpret the requirements of the Christian faith more broadly, and fill in the specifics of love as the situation demands. For both groups, the failure to honor obligations results in some type of judgment. It may be a shattering breach of the natural order, or it may be a kind of personal uneasiness and guilt. But it is still God's retribution.

Many of us have heard of, or perhaps have even experienced, tragedies that have been perceived as judgment for sin. How individual Christians understand these experiences is a highly personal matter. But a word of caution here is in order. In the Old Testament, retribution falls upon the guilty party, not the innocent victim. And if we sin, God holds us responsible.

1 Samuel 13:8-15—Obedience to God

The idea of obedience is closely connected to retribution. In fact, obedience is the precondition for a person's accountability. Because God sets certain standards for our conduct, God can reward or punish us. From Genesis to Revelation, God's expectation is obedience. Will persons follow the express commands of the Lord? Samuel outlines this theme very clearly to Israel as she is gathered about her new king. Samuel condemns Saul for disregarding the Lord's commands. Disobedience is sin.

Few Christians today would dispute the obligation to obey God's will. But the problem lies in understanding what is God's will. How can we be certain that what we feel or think or even hear proclaimed in church is truly from God? Is our conscience the same as the will of God? Must we obey the teachings of Jesus, even down to the letter?

These questions are all important to Christians. Thoughtful and sincere Christians do not always agree on answers. One of the great legacies of our Reformation faith is the notion of the priesthood of all believers. You and I can come before God without a priest to assist us. We can read the Scriptures and learn for ourselves what God said and did. We come before God confident that God acknowledges each of us. There are no infallible authorities to tell us God's particular will for us.

Through careful study of the Bible, through prayer, and through active participation in the Christian community, individuals can answer the preceding questions. Christian faith means believing that God's will is revealed to those who truly seek it. Christian ethics is obedience to what we understand God to be expecting of us. None of us can afford the fate of Saul's disobedience.

Close today's session by asking class members to share any new insights they have gained from their study of 1 Samuel 11–15. If time allows, list the insights on chalkboard or a large sheet of paper.

David came to Saul and entered his service (16:21).

5

David's Early Years

1 Samuel 16–20

**DIMENSION ONE:
WHAT DOES THE BIBLE SAY?**

Answer these questions by reading 1 Samuel 16

1. Why does Samuel visit Jesse the Bethlehemite? (16:1)

   The Lord has chosen the next king from among Jesse's sons.

2. What does Samuel tell the elders of Bethlehem? (16:5)

   Samuel tells the elders that he comes in peace to offer a sacrifice to the Lord.

3. How does the Lord know which person is to be king? (16:7)

   The Lord looks into persons' hearts.

4. Who does Samuel anoint as king? (16:13)

   Samuel anoints David as king.

5. How does David receive God's power? (16:13)

   The Spirit of the Lord comes upon David.

6. What happens to Saul when the Spirit of the Lord leaves him? (16:14)

   An evil spirit from the Lord torments him.

7. How do Saul's attendants treat his illness? (16:18-23)

   They bring David who plays his harp, and Saul feels relief.

Answer these questions by reading 1 Samuel 17

8. Who comes from the Philistine army to challenge the Israelite army? (17:4)

   The Philistine champion is Goliath of Gath.

9. Who are David's three eldest brothers and what do they do? (17:13)

   David's brothers are Eliab, Abinadab, and Shammah. They are soldiers fighting the Philistines.

10. Why does Jesse send David to his brothers? (17:17-18)

    Jesse sends David to carry food and to bring back news of their welfare.

11. What rewards does Saul offer anyone who kills Goliath? (17:25)

    Saul promises to give the person great wealth, his daughter in marriage, and exempt his family from paying taxes.

12. Why doesn't Saul want David to fight Goliath? (17:33)

    Saul says David is too young and inexperienced.

13. How does David refute Saul's objections? (17:36-37)

    David says he has fought lions and bears and that he has the help of the Lord.

14. What does David carry with him to meet Goliath? (17:40)

    David carries his staff, his sling, and five stones.

15. What does David say his victory over Goliath will prove? (17:47)

    David says a victory will prove that the Lord saves not with the sword or with the spear, but by divine power.

16. What does David do to the fallen Philistine? (17:51)

    David takes Goliath's sword and cuts off his head.

17. Who is Abner? (17:55)

Abner is the commander of Saul's army.

Answer these questions by reading 1 Samuel 18

18. What is Jonathan's attitude toward David? (18:1)

Jonathan loves David as himself.

19. Why does Saul's initial affection for David change? (18:8-9)

Saul becomes jealous of David's popularity and his military successes.

20. Why does Saul present David with Michal, his daughter? (18:20-25)

Saul thinks Michal might be a snare to David with the Philistines and that David might die in battle.

Answer these questions by reading 1 Samuel 19

21. Apart from jealousy, for what other reason does Saul attempt to kill David? (19:9)

An evil spirit from the Lord comes upon Saul.

22. How does Michal help David escape? (19:13-14)

She disguises an image with goats' hair and clothing.

23. Who does David join at Ramah? (19:18)

David joins Samuel.

24. What happens to Saul as he enters Naioth? (19:23-24)

The Spirit of God enters Saul and he removes his clothing and begins prophesying.

Answer these questions by reading 1 Samuel 20

25. What does Jonathan learn that Saul intends to do? (20:33)

Saul intends to kill David.

26. What does Jonathan tell David to do? (20:42)

Jonathan tells David to go in peace.

DIMENSION TWO: WHAT DOES THE BIBLE MEAN?

1 Samuel 16:1-13. In Chapter 16, we have two accounts of David's introduction into Israel's history. In one, David is anointed by Samuel, and in the other, David joins Saul's court. Perhaps from different sources, these two stories about young David compliment each other. In the anointing narrative, the reader is prepared for David's eventual rise to kingship. In the other narrative, David enters the court of the present king. From this moment David lives under God's watchful eye. Everything he does is successful. Both stories bring David one step nearer to the throne and Saul one step farther away.

The narrative in 16:1-13 is a continuation of the Chapter 15 story of Saul's disobedience. Saul and Samuel have parted, and Samuel continues to worry over Saul's kingship. The Lord sends Samuel to select a new ruler for God's people. Fearing Saul's angry reprisals, Samuel hesitates to go. The Lord suggests that Samuel go to Bethlehem to offer a sacrifice and invite Jesse to attend the ceremony. Samuel complies and soon finds himself screening candidates for the anointing. After rejecting seven of Jesse's sons, he inquires if there are any others. David, the youngest, is then brought in, and the Lord tells Samuel to anoint him. God then empowers David with the Spirit of the Lord.

A critical reader will find many details missing in this brief but important narrative. For example, no rationale is offered for the selection of Jesse, the Bethlehemite, as the honored house. And how is David's anointing kept from Saul or his staff, since they obviously have no such knowledge in the next story?

The biblical writer is interested in the theological issues rather than historical ones. God has not abandoned monarchy as the proper style of leadership for the Israelites. Instead, God carefully selects the king who is to follow Saul. God stands in the center of Israel's history. The charismatic endowment of David, and its withdrawal from Saul, clearly indicate that Israel's history moves by means of divine power. God shapes history by influencing the lives of persons such as David.

1 Samuel 16:14-23. The second story brings Saul and David together. David, a young man recognized for his military valor as well as his musicianship, is brought to soothe Saul's anxiety when an evil spirit from the Lord invades him. Almost instantly, David ingratiates himself to Saul, and they develop a close personal attachment.

Although David is far from perfect, the biblical writers hold him in highest esteem. He is described by Saul's attendants in superlative terms—He "knows how to play the harp. He is a brave man and a warrior. He speaks well and is a fine looking man." But most important of all, we learn, as does Saul, that "the LORD is with him." Such a glowing appraisal is accorded few persons in the Old Testament. David is clearly destined for greatness.

1 Samuel 17. David's victory over Goliath, the Philistine champion, is one of the celebrated heroic tales of the Old Testament. The young shepherd comes to his brothers to bring them food and offer encouragement. He offers his services, but is told that he lacks the experience necessary to confront a man of war such as Goliath. But David insists, citing his defense of his flocks as training, and adds that the Lord will be with him.

David bravely marches forth armed with only a sling and five small pebbles. One swing from his arm and the Philistine giant topples over with a single blow. David completes the job by beheading Goliath. The story is told with great pride and joy—it is a story of assurance in the might of Israel's God.

The outward plot of the story is simple, but closer reading reveals several problems. First, it conflicts with Chapter 16 where David is a trusted servant of Saul. Yet in 17:56, Saul inquires who David is. In 16:18, David is described as a warrior. But in 17:15, David is a young shepherd who delivers food to his brothers. How can we explain these problems? Two separate traditions must have existed in early Israel about David's introduction to Saul. They were later combined as we now have them in First Samuel.

The difficulties in reconciling these contradictions are unimportant when we consider the theological message. This theme is clear: The Lord overcomes the mighty, the proud, and the strong through the weak and seemingly defenseless. Against all odds, the Lord empowers the inexperienced shepherd to slay the trained warrior. David says it best, "All those gathered here will know that it is not by sword or spear that the LORD saves; for the battle is the LORD's, and he will give all of you into our hands."

David's victory over Goliath clearly establishes him as the rightful successor to Saul as the ruler of Israel. Here is a man strengthened by the Lord. David is effective as a military leader because of charismatic endowment. He is following a line of such leaders, all of whom are authorized by the Lord. Israel's leadership once again promises to be in safe hands. But before David becomes king, the reign of Saul must conclude.

1 Samuel 18. Verses 1–5 of Chapter 18 continue the Goliath narrative. The popularity of the young shepherd is universal. Jonathan, Saul's son, is attracted to David. Saul promotes David to a high rank in the army. All of Saul's court officials are impressed with David, and all of the people react positively to him. In fact, the entire chapter celebrates David's success in all that he does.

In contrast, Saul becomes a man driven by rages of jealousy and victimized by ill fortune. His desperation drives him to plot continually to kill David. Even his attempt to get David killed while acquiring a marriage dowery of 100 Philistine foreskins meets with ironic failure. The chapter concludes with a flattering summary of David's remarkable accomplishments.

In 18:1 and 3, the expression Jonathan "loved him as himself" appears to have double meaning. It does, of course, refer to a deep bond of friendship between the two men, a covenant of loyalty. But many commentators suggest that Jonathan is acknowledging David's right to succeed Saul as the leader of Israel. Saul's son makes this acknowledgement willingly and approvingly. Both men

maintain this bond—despite Saul's plots to kill David—until the death of Jonathan.

Saul's jealousy increases with David's success. The song of the women (18:7) and David's popularity in Israel and Judah (18:16) fuel Saul's sense of panic. His plots to kill David fail and only serve to demonstrate David's invincibility. We do not know if Saul realizes that events are beyond his control. Saul's rapid deterioration is the result of his loss of God's Spirit. He and his reign are doomed.

David's star rises as fast as Saul's star declines. Not even the large marriage dowery stops him. All of Saul's evil plan turns to David's advantage. David's friendship with Jonathan, his military success, and his marriage to Michal solidly entrench him as Saul's legitimate successor. To this end, the Lord has anointed him.

1 Samuel 19. Saul's jealousy of David becomes public. He personally speaks with his servants about killing David (19:1). He makes three unsuccessful attempts on David's life. But just as Saul's previous plans failed, he also is unsuccessful here. To make matters worse, David is aided by Jonathan and Michal. The common thread knitting these three stories together is David's success at escaping Saul. The split between king and servant is now irreconcilable. Persons must choose with whom they will side.

The events in 19:1-7 are difficult to follow. In verse 2 Jonathan tells David to hide in a secret place so he can find out his father's intentions and report back to David. Yet, in verse 3 he speaks of standing beside Saul in the field where David is. Verse 3 probably assumes that David can overhear the conversation and draw the appropriate conclusions for himself. In spite of these differences, Jonathan's kind words on David's behalf convince Saul to delay his efforts to kill David. The covenant of friendship between Jonathan and David proves its value.

But David's reprieve is short-lived. The evil spirit reenters Saul, and again he throws a spear at David. Again, he misses.

Later Michal, David's wife, helps him escape from Saul's watchmen. The house is probably attached to the city wall, so David can escape down the outside wall without detection. Then, Michal places a family god (a small statue) in the bed to fool Saul's servants. Saul is furious with Michal after he discovers David has escaped once again. She manages to save herself by lying (telling Saul that David threatened to kill her).

David then flees to Ramah to join Samuel. Saul learns of David's whereabouts and sends soldiers to bring him back. But before the soldiers can capture David they are thrown into a state of prophetic ecstasy. David's assailants are thrown into confusion three times. The third time involves Saul himself. In fact, Saul's behavior is so erratic and unusual that it gives rise to a popular saying in Israel, "Is Saul also among the prophets?" This is the second account of the origin of this proverb (1 Samuel 10:11).

1 Samuel 20. The outward plot of this chapter is simple. Once again, David seeks Jonathan's help in determining Saul's intentions. Unconvinced of Saul's malice, Jonathan nevertheless agrees to aid David. Jonathan is to relay the news to David by means of an arrow. The news is bad. David's life is in jeopardy. The two friends part company, but not before swearing allegiance.

The chapter raises two major issues: (1) David is now removed from Saul's court, and (2) Jonathan willingly accepts that David will become king.

David's departure from Saul's court appears to make it more difficult to move into Saul's position. But David is in truth protecting himself until Saul is no longer a threat. The Lord will control history, and David's faith sees him through even the most difficult days.

Jonathan also seems to know, understand, and accept David's destiny. Dating from the Goliath incident, Jonathan's covenant with David is an acknowledgement of David's future. Jonathan's pledge in 20:13 that the Lord be with David, just as with Saul, confirms his loyalty. Jonathan seems content to allow David to pursue his appointed destiny. Even when Saul points out that his friendship with David is costing him the throne, Jonathan still refuses to break faith with David. David and Jonathan part ways, never to be together again.

DIMENSION THREE:
WHAT DOES THE BIBLE MEAN TO ME?

1 Samuel 17:31-54—The Weak Humble the Strong

The first major theological theme emerging from this lesson is the Lord's intercession on behalf of the weak. In the Goliath story, the hero appears as a young shepherd whose main battles have been with the lions and bears that attacked his flocks. He has no armor. He is small, untrained, and untested. Goliath, on the other hand, is described as an enormous warrior who has fought since his youth. His armor is forbidding. His taunts are intimidating. The contrast makes David's victory all the more impressive. But, David also is a boy of great faith and he trusts that the Lord will prevail. And so David wins. The Lord has delivered the mighty into the hands of the weak.

A popular proverb today says, "The Lord helps those who help themselves." Where is this verse found in the Bible? Nowhere! In fact, such a saying is generally the opposite of what the Bible teaches. As I read and study the Scriptures, I find that the Lord helps those who cannot help themselves. Time and again in the Old and New Testaments, the Lord responds to aid the weak, the defenseless, the outcast. This point is well illustrated in the Goliath story.

The great prophets, too, demand justice for the poor, not sacrifice. Israel, herself, was among the smallest and the weakest nations in the ancient Near East. The Lord did not choose Assyria or Babylon or Egypt. The Lord chose Israel and elevated her as the chosen people. The Lord helps those who cannot help themselves.

Certainly, this idea does not suggest that we all go immediately and divest ourselves of our wealth or our power. Nor is it a call to passivity or to idleness. On the contrary, the Lord demands obedience and trust. The Lord is interested in who we are, not in what we have. God looks on the heart, not on the outward appearance (1 Samuel 16:7). When we rely on our egos, our strength, our intelligence, to the exclusion of God, we exhibit undue pride. These dimensions of ourselves are important, but they must be placed into perspective by our faith. God aids those who trust in God, not in themselves.

For many of us, this trust and reliance on the Lord does not come easily. We are used to taking care of ourselves. The balance between responsible stewardship of our personal resources and obedient faith in the Lord is precarious and delicate. Yet, Christians are challenged to find and maintain this balance.

1 Samuel 19:8-24—Evil Spirits

The second theological issue arising from these chapters is God's use of evil spirits to attack Saul. For most Christians today, the nature of God's goodness excludes the possibility of God using evil. Moreover, the belief in spirits as representatives of God, causing events to occur on earth, goes against our scientific view of the world. A contemporary psychologist might explain Saul's periodic depression as a type of psychosis or neurosis. He is paranoid about David, and his jealousy is merely a manifestation of his latent insecurity. How are we to reconcile the difference between these perspectives? What does this issue suggest about our conception of God?

First, the conflict between science and religion can be reduced in stature if we realize that each perspective approaches its subject matter differently. The scientist collects and observes the data, then suggests a hypothesis to explain why things occur as they do.

The theologian, on the other hand, begins with a confession of faith in a reality that transcends nature and is the ultimate explanation of all that exists. The theologian would argue that proper understanding requires more than observation of the natural order.

To the scientist, Saul's moments of depression and anxiety could be understood as a psychosis. But to the theologian, especially an ancient theologian in a prescientific culture, Saul's rages of torment mean that he is under attack from an evil spirit. The biblical writer uses different language, has different beliefs about the world, and operates under a different system of logic than the person of today. We must respect this difference by refraining from imposing our value judgments on the biblical writers.

Since ancient Israelites believed in only one supreme power, God must be the source of both good and evil. So God could send an evil spirit to torment Saul. The activities of these evil spirits are easier to understand when we recall that Saul lost the Spirit of God and would shortly lose his kingdom. The meaning of Saul's depressions is clear. He is a man without God, vulnerable and frightened.

1 Samuel 20:35-42—The Quality of Relationships

The covenant of loyalty between Jonathan and David, and the jealousy Saul has toward David are important. The former relationship is strong, helpful to both men, and a source of support. Saul's envy of David has dire consequences. These relationships are instructive for persons today.

The Bible acknowledges that all persons are social in nature. Persons were meant to live in relationships with each other. Our personhood develops best in strong, nurturing social contexts. Love, trust, fidelity, and honor are the bases for human relationships. Weak, improper, and unhealthy relationships are detrimental to our well-being as persons.

A friend of mine, a clinical psychologist, tells me that most of his patients are persons who, in one way or another, lack proper social relationships—spouses not relating to spouses, children not relating to their parents, employees not relating to employers. Practically everywhere we turn, we observe human relationships disintegrating. Many popular self-help books stem from this loneliness and isolation that pervades our society.

The covenant between David and Jonathan serves as a model for us today. The covenant is a bond of mutual respect and admiration. One person truly cares about the well-being of the other. These two persons trust each other without selfishness or greed, and they honor this trust no matter how trying the circumstances. The result is a sense of wholeness in both persons. Genuine human relationships enhance our personal growth, unlike Saul's feelings of jealousy, envy, hatred, and malice.

Close the session by listing on chalkboard or a large sheet of paper any new insights class members have gained from today's lesson.

Day after day Saul searched for him, but God did not give David into his hands (23:14).

6

David and Saul

1 Samuel 21–26

DIMENSION ONE:
WHAT DOES THE BIBLE SAY?

Answer these questions by reading 1 Samuel 21

1. Who is the priest at Nob? (21:1)

   The priest at Nob is Ahimelech.

2. What request does David make of Ahimelech? (21:3)

   David asks Ahimelech for five loaves of bread.

3. How does Ahimelech respond to this request? (21:4-6)

   Ahimelech says he has no ordinary bread, only consecrated bread. David takes the consecrated bread.

4. Who else observes the exchange between David and Ahimelech? (21:7)

   Doeg, Saul's head shepherd, observes the exchange.

5. What additional item does Ahimelech give to David? (21:8-9)

   Ahimelech gives David the sword of Goliath the Philistine.

6. How does Achish, king of Gath, react to David's visit and his strange behavior? (21:14-15)

   Achish thinks David is mad and refuses to accept David into his house.

Answer these questions by reading 1 Samuel 22

7. Who joins David while he is hiding in the cave of Adullam? (22:1-2)

   David is joined by his family and those who are distressed, in debt, and discontented.

8. Why does David visit the king of Moab? (22:3)

   David wants to leave his parents in Moab so they will be safe.

9. What information does Doeg furnish King Saul? (22:9-10)

   Doeg says he saw David at Nob and that Ahimelech, the priest, prayed to God for David and also furnished him with food and with the sword of Goliath.

10. As a result of his aid to David, what happens to Ahimelech and his priestly family? (22:18-20)

    Doeg kills all of Ahimelech's family except Abiathar, who seeks safety with David.

Answer these questions by reading 1 Samuel 23

11. What threat prompts David's intervention at Keilah? (23:1)

    The Philistines are raiding the city and robbing the threshing floors.

12. How does David learn what the citizens of Keilah will do if he remains there? (23:9-12)

    He consults the ephod kept by Abiathar.

13. Who meets David at Horesh to offer him encouragement and support? (23:16)

    Jonathan meets David at Horesh.

14. What prevents Saul from capturing David in the Desert of Maon? (23:26-27)

    Saul has to halt his pursuit of David in order to fight the Philistines.

Answer these questions by reading 1 Samuel 24

15. Why is David unable to kill Saul when he has an opportunity? (24:6)

    David is unable to kill Saul because the king is still the Lord's anointed ruler.

16. What evidence does David offer Saul of his innocence of treason or wrongdoing? (24:11)

    David says the fact that he cut Saul's robe instead of killing him is proof of his good faith.

17. How does Saul react to David's words? (24:16-17)

    Saul weeps and declares David more righteous than he.

Answer these questions by reading 1 Samuel 25

18. What famous leader dies, and where is he buried? (25:1)

    Samuel dies and is buried at Ramah.

19. Why does David feel justified in requesting provisions from Nabal? (25:7)

    David has protected Nabal's shepherds and they have lost nothing during his watch.

20. How does Nabal respond to David's request? (25:10-11)

    He denies knowing David, and refuses to honor his request.

21. How does Abigail resolve this dispute? (25:25-27)

    Abigail apologizes for Nabal's ill temper, flatters David, and offers him and his troops provisions.

22. As a consequence of her kindness to David, what happens to Abigail? (25:40-42)

    When Nabal dies suddenly, David brings her to his home and makes her his wife.

Answer these questions by reading 1 Samuel 26

23. How does Saul learn where David is hiding? (26:1)

    The Ziphites tell Saul where David is hiding.

24. What do David and Abishai do to Saul? (26:12)

    David and Abishai remove Saul's spear and a water jug.

25. How does David use Saul's spear and his water jug? (26:15-16)

    He uses them to demonstrate Abner's failure to watch Saul properly.

26. What does Saul say to David after hearing his declaration of innocence? (26:21)

    Saul admits that he has erred and promises not to harm David.

DIMENSION TWO: WHAT DOES THE BIBLE MEAN?

Background Information on 1 Samuel 21–26

As in previous lessons, we find in these chapters an interlacing of different sources. There are parallel accounts of David sparing Saul's life (24:6 and 26:11). There are discrepancies between Doeg's report to Saul about Ahimelech and David, and the earlier version of the incident in Chapter 21. The richness of the variety of the biblical narrative begins to unfold as one unlocks the history of its literary development.

We cannot say precisely when these stories became Scripture. But the combining of traditions into Scripture is sufficient testimony to divine inspiration. The theological themes in these ancient narratives transcend the historical situations that gave rise to them. These stories have the power to make statements about God and about our human condition. The historical situation has changed, but God's will for our obedience has not changed.

1 Samuel 21. The two scenes in this chapter depict David as a man adept at survival. His deception of Ahimelech, the priest, secures food for his troops, plus a weapon of great renown. Similarly, his award-winning performance before Achish clearly saves his life.

Ahimelech's concern about David's request arises from the fact he has only consecrated bread remaining. As the student book mentions, this holy bread, replaced weekly on the sabbath, is ordinarily taken by the priest. Cultic laws are very strict about such matters. David's assurance that his men are holy refers to the custom of sexual abstinence during holy wars. Ahimelech's concern is appropriate in view of religious regulations of the day.

According to 21:6, Ahimelech provides David with the sacred bread and also with Goliath's sword. There is no mention of any other service. Yet in 22:10, Doeg accuses Ahimelech of giving David provisions. And in 22:15, Ahimelech himself admits inquiring of the Lord for David. The term *provision* may be simply a substitution for the word *bread*.

However, to consult the Lord on an enemy's behalf is a serious matter. Ahimelech's consultation with the Lord is characteristic of David's method of operation. He usually seeks the will of the Lord prior to battle. To Saul, however, Ahimelech is guilty of aiding and abetting the enemy. This deed amounts to treason and is a capital offense.

This section on David and Ahimelech serves two purposes. First, we understand Saul's wrath against the priest and his orders for a wholesale massacre at Nob. Such a drastic act on his part further alienates Saul from the Lord and drives the single remaining priest into David's camp. Second, the passage shows David's continued involvement with authorized representatives of God. Even as a fugitive, David comes under divine protection.

The brief encounter with Achish (verses 10-15) relates a humorous story that must have brought laughter to the lips of the early Israelites. The nimble-witted young warrior tricked a mighty king! The phrase *king of Gath* is a term of respect, not an official designation. The Philistines know full well that Saul is king, but they also know David is an able and popular hero.

1 Samuel 22. Before describing the bloody slaughter of the priests at Nob, the Bible presents two brief episodes in David's career as a fugitive: his move to the stronghold at Adullam and the relocation of his parents in Moab. Adullam is located in the hill country of southwestern Judah, close to Philistine territory. Adullam offers David safety from Saul and a defensible base of operations.

Moab is an appropriate choice as a temporary refuge for David's parents because of ancient ties of kinship with the people in this region. The Book of Ruth also describes Moab as a resting place for fugitives from Bethlehem. David's parents likely remain in Moab until David is well established as king in the south.

Gad, the prophet, appears again in 2 Samuel 24:13. In addition to his regular army, David has begun to acquire a retinue of holy men, including prophets and priests, to see that his channels of communication with the Lord remain open. Abiathar, the sole remaining priest, joins the group shortly.

Saul's council beneath the tamarisk tree conveys a well-known image of government in the ancient Near East. The king seats himself in the center and surrounds himself with his counselors. The tamarisk tree is a tree of distinction in Israel. Here at Gibeah, it marks a holy place.

Saul's attempt to gather information about David provides Doeg with a good opportunity to tell what he saw earlier (21:7). Saul quickly sends for Ahimelech and the other priests, and the interrogation begins. Ahimelech's defense is reasonable: (1) he cites David's exalted place in Saul's army, (2) he has inquired of the Lord for David on previous occasions, and (3) he was ignorant of the problems between Saul and David.

But Saul is not a rational man. He is tormented by evil spirits and is hopelessly paranoid about David. He immediately orders the execution of Ahimelech and the other priests and extends the carnage to their city, Nob. The refusal of Saul's own men to comply with his order indicates the sacredness of priests. Doeg, a foreigner, does not share their fears of divine reprisal. He performs the despicable act with gusto, with only Abiathar escaping the sword.

The significance of this passage is the preservation of the Lord's priesthood by David. Henceforth, Saul is unable to communicate with the Lord, and tries unsuccessfully to thwart David's triumphs. On the other hand, David continues to prosper, now aided by the presence of an authorized priest.

1 Samuel 23:1-13. Illustrating the advantage of a priest, the Bible tells now of how David rescues the city of Keilah and avoids capture by Saul by means of divine counsel.

Keilah is a city located in the Judean hills. By virtue of its close proximity to Philistine territory, Keilah would have been prone to frequent attacks from these aggressive warriors. From their willingness to hand David over to Saul, we may presume that the citizens of Keilah were not from the tribe of Judah. David's principal interest in the city would therefore be for reasons of military strategy, not for protection of family interests.

The mention of bringing away the Philistine livestock (verse 5) is odd. Why would the Philistines have made a military raid on a neighboring city accompanied by slow-moving livestock? Perhaps they brought the livestock to finish eating the grain left on the threshing floors (verse 1).

The ephod accompanying Abiathar is the small box containing the sacred lots, Urim and Thummim. Used by the priest, the lots could yield a yes or no answer to questions. The lack of this means of divine communication certainly handicaps Saul. Saul's power and influence are still insufficient to offset the Lord's protection of David.

1 Samuel 23:14–24:22. David leaves Keilah (verse 13) and flees further south to the desert regions around Ziph. Now he is even deeper into the territory of Judah. But not even this remote region provides more than a temporary resting place for David, for soon he must move on.

Jonathan's visit to David reaffirms their covenant of friendship, but adds a new note: the inevitability of David's kingship. Regardless of the present circumstances, God still intends to see that David rules the people.

David's miraculous escape from Saul at the Sela Hammahlekoth, "Rock of Parting" (23:24-29), further illustrates the Lord's protection of David. The Lord's favor shows itself more powerful than Saul's excellent military tactics.

En Gedi, David's next stopping place, was a popular and important watering site close to the southern shores of the Dead Sea. Nestled amid the rocky cliffs of the Judean desert, En Gedi has offered water and shelter to more than one generation of Israelites.

David's refusal to kill Saul or to permit his men to slay the king is not to be understood as the mere generosity of a gracious man. David understands full well that Saul is holy. Despite all his personal failures, Saul is still the anointed king of Israel and thus the bearer of God's special mark. What the men of David perceive to be a golden opportunity to end Saul's pursuit permanently, David views as an occasion to protect the Lord's anointed servant and show good faith to Saul and to God. The temptation to kill Saul must have been great, but David's better judgment prevails. The symbolism of cutting off Saul's robe points to David's honor and strength. He could have cut off more than the skirt!

Verse 15 of Chapter 24 is a final oath of innocence, placed before the Lord for judgment. David has argued his case and now leaves it for God to assess. Saul acknowledges two points: (1) David is innocent of treason, and undeserving of punishment; and (2) David is destined to become king and establish a dynasty. The only explanation as to why Saul continues his frantic pursuit of David is that Saul is not fully rational and not in total command of himself.

1 Samuel 25. The mention of Samuel's death and burial (25:1) seems rather brief for a man of his stature in Israel. The phrase *at his home* is difficult to interpret due to an ambiguous preposition. The same preposition in Hebrew can mean *at, beside, near,* or even *in.*

This narrative about David and Abigail is an interlude in the stories about David and Saul. As before, David avoids bloodguilt from taking the life of an opponent (24:7). In the preceding narrative, David's own self-restraint halted him from slaying Saul. Here, the convincing argument of Abigail prevents him from taking reprisals against Nabal.

Abigail's argument sets David's threatened action within the context of his future kingship (verse 31). No bloodguilt should be attached to the Lord's future king. As we have seen in earlier narratives, and as we will see later in the matters of Saul and Ishbosheth, David remains free from bloodguilt and innocent of wrongdoing. He effectively submits himself to divine guidance and does not display greed, malice, or revenge.

The Carmel mentioned in this story is a city located in southern Judah, between Maon and Ziph. The city must not be confused with the famous Mount Carmel on the northern coast of Israel.

In Israel, sheep-shearing time was marked by feasting and celebrating. Since David had, in effect, performed a valuable service for Nabal (verse 7), his self-invitation to the feast is appropriate. In fact, such protective measures were common practice to ward off Bedouin raiders. To refuse the request of a strong champion is foolish, as Nabal's name indicates.

1 Samuel 26. This episode and the earlier account of David sparing Saul's life (Chapter 24) are similar. Both times, David is betrayed by the Ziphites. In both accounts, David restrains his men (or man) from taking Saul's life. And both narratives conclude with Saul proclaiming David's innocence.

The two stories also differ in several ways: (1) setting, (2) David's companion, and (3) the circumstances of David's encounter with Saul. You might want to have the class compare these two accounts in detail. Have the group members, individually or in teams, list similarities and differences. Then have someone write the lists on chalkboard or a large sheet of paper.

The literary relationship between these two chapters is uncertain. Fortunately, we can understand the message of the two chapters without knowing their literary history. David continues to elude Saul by the power of divine intervention rather than by his own strength. At the same time, he remains free from religious, moral, or legal violations by resisting the temptation to kill Saul or punish Nabal.

Abishai (verse 6) is David's nephew. He and his brother Joab play important roles later in David's reign over Israel. Ahimelech the Hittite is one of several foreign soldiers serving in David's army.

Unlike the Chapter 24 version, the involvement of the Lord in this affair is stated clearly. God causes Saul's army to fall into a deep sleep (verse 12). In restraining the enthusiastic Abishai, David refers to the severe punishment for anyone doing harm to the Lord's anointed. David allows the Lord to decide Saul's fate (verse 10).

DIMENSION THREE: WHAT DOES THE BIBLE MEAN TO ME?

1 Samuel 21:1-6—Human Needs Versus Institutions

The student book contains a discussion of David's bold assertion of human need over institutional regulations. He took the consecrated bread usually reserved for the priest and used it to feed his soldiers. Similarly, Jesus performed work on the sabbath by picking grain and healing the sick. Both these actions violated religious requirements, and doubtlessly shocked many persons. David and Jesus placed basic human needs over religious laws. They stood in opposition to organized religion and refused to be tied to conventions of the day.

Many persons are bothered by actions that break with established practice. They are threatened by others who elevate human needs to a position above church law. However, the actions of David and Jesus provide a precedent for us today. We must learn to step outside the perimeters of church work and attend to basic needs of God's people. Both individually and collectively, we are obliged to love our neighbors in need, even to the point of placing these needs over our responsibility to the church.

As you teach this lesson, some persons will have difficulty identifying what needs should have priority and how they should be met. Unfortunately, the Bible does not provide us with formulas or prescriptions to answer these questions. Some persons may object that we are not David or Jesus, and we lack the trust God placed in them.

The Easter experience means that God's trust is available to all persons. So we can read the Scripture and decide for ourselves what God expects of us. The accumulated traditions of the church and the ever-present Spirit of God will also illuminate our decisions. But even so, we must decide for ourselves what God expects of us! When we reach this decision after sincere thought and prayer, we must act—even if it cuts across the grain of convention. We must be courageous enough to act out our faith, and, when necessary, to place the satisfaction of basic human needs over institutional regulations.

1 Samuel 25:23-35—Divine Leadership

The second issue in these chapters is submitting our lives to God's leadership. David's close association with prophets and priests provided him with ready access to the Lord. He consulted the Lord before many of his battles. He turned to the Lord at Keilah when threatened by Saul. He listened to Abigail and spared Nabal, just as he was about to punish the ungrateful fool. David's success can be attributed to the providential guidance of the Lord, and his willingness to follow this guidance.

In an age of independence, when most of us subscribe to the notion of self-reliance, we are not certain what it means to submit our lives to God's guidance. And even when we understand the Lord's will, we may lack the courage to comply. In the minds of many persons, dependence has become an indication of weakness.

However, dependency on the Lord is not the same as dependency on other persons. While both forms of dependency acknowledge human limitations, submission to God's will is a positive experience. We are incomplete without a relationship with God and out of step with ourselves. This incompleteness results in frustration, unhappiness, and a sense of unfulfillment. The peace that comes from submission to God leads to inner unity and harmony.

The particular ways individual persons submit to the Lord's guidance vary greatly. None are easy in the ordinary sense of that word. And few are instantaneous. Spiritual growth to dependency is a slow process. We often find it difficult to admit that our powers of human reason have limitations. But part of submission to God's will means acknowledging that faith and reason work together. Submission to God's will is both an act of the mind and an act of the soul.

At the close of the session, ask class members to share any new insights they have gained while studying 1 Samuel 21–26. List those insights on chalkboard or a large sheet of paper.

7

Saul's Last Days

1 Samuel 27–31

DIMENSION ONE:
WHAT DOES THE BIBLE SAY?

Answer these questions by reading 1 Samuel 27

1. To what city does David flee? Who is king? (27:2)

    David flees to the Philistine city of Gath, whose king is Achish.

2. What does Saul do when he hears of David's defection to the Philistines? (27:4)

    When Saul learns David has fled to Gath, he stops his pursuit.

3. How long does David stay with the Philistines? (27:7)

    David stays with the Philistines for one year and four months.

4. How does David gain the confidence of Achish? (27:8-12)

    David tells Achish that he raided tribes in Judah, such as the Jerahmeelites and the Kenites.

Answer these questions by reading 1 Samuel 28

5. What position in his army does Achish give David? (28:2)

    Achish appoints David as his bodyguard for life.

6. Who does Saul expel from Israel? (28:3)

    Saul expels the mediums and spiritists.

7. Who does Saul visit for help? (28:7-8)

    Saul makes a night visit to a medium at Endor.

8. With whom does Saul wish to speak? (28:11)

    Saul wishes to speak with Samuel.

9. What does Samuel tell Saul? (28:16-19)

    Samuel tells Saul that the Lord is punishing him for his disobedience, and that Saul and his sons are to die in battle the following day.

10. What else does the medium do? (28:24-25)

    She prepares food for Saul and feeds him.

Answer these questions by reading 1 Samuel 29

11. Why don't the Philistines want David to fight with them? (29:4)

    They fear David might turn against them in battle.

12. What is Achish's response to their objections? (29:9-10)

    Achish must honor the request of his Philistine colleagues. He sends David back home.

Answer these questions by reading 1 Samuel 30

13. What do David and his men discover when they return to Ziklag? (30:3)

    They find that the Amalekites have raided Ziklag and taken captive their families.

14. What does David do? (30:6-9)

    David sends for Abiathar, the priest, and they consult the Lord. The Lord tells David to pursue the offenders and rescue the captives.

15. How does David find the Amalekites? (30:13-15)

    An Egyptian mercenary, who had been abandoned as ill by the Amalekites, shows David their camp.

16. How does David distribute the booty taken from the Amalekites? (30:21-31)

Although some troops did not participate in the battle, they receive their fair share of the booty. David also distributes booty among some of the major tribes of Judah.

Answer these questions by reading 1 Samuel 31

17. How does Saul die? (31:4)

After being wounded by the Philistines, Saul takes his own sword and kills himself.

18. Who else dies in battle that day? (31:2)

Saul's sons, including Jonathan, are killed.

19. What do the Philistines do when they discover Saul's body? (31:9-10)

They decapitate Saul, strip off his armor, and hang his body on a wall at Beth Shan.

20. Who removes Saul's body and gives it a proper burial? (31:11-13)

The men of Jabesh Gilead remove his body, cremate it, and bury the remains.

DIMENSION TWO: WHAT DOES THE BIBLE MEAN?

Background Information on 1 Samuel 27–31

With this lesson, Saul's reign comes to an end. But before his death, several interesting incidents occur. David serves as a Philistine mercenary soldier; Samuel prophesies doom for Saul; David's troops almost revolt when they learn of the Amalekite raid on Ziklag; and Jonathan, David's beloved friend, is killed by the Philistines.

Events move swiftly and surely as the first chapter in the Israelite monarchy concludes. One has mixed feelings toward Saul—a sense of relief, yet sadness that he came to such an inglorious end.

Saul's accomplishments included establishing an army, bringing organization to the Northern Kingdom, and keeping the Philistines from entirely overrunning the country. However, he also usurped the place of the Lord, and the Lord's prophet, Samuel. Consequently, God's Spirit left Saul and he was condemned to failure and ill fortune.

The chronology of Saul's reign is not easy to determine, but he reigned from approximately 1020 B.C. to 1000 B.C. Archaeological finds have not given us a precise date for Saul. Also, the sequence of events, as they have been recorded in First Samuel, may be out of order. The biblical writer inserted other stories, such as the story of Abigail (1 Samuel 25) that interrupt the story of Saul's pursuit of David. The "two years" mentioned as the length of Saul's reign in the original Hebrew text of 1 Samuel 13:1 is generally disregarded by most commentaries as a textual error. The NIV suggests that forty-two years is possible. When we first encounter Saul, he is a young man, still a member of his father's household. In Chapters 28–31, he is an elder statesman and has three grown sons.

Saul's fortress at Gibeah reflects the predominantly military character of Saul's reign as king. Leading archaeologists claim that the remains at Gibeah have few of the signs of a fully developed governmental bureaucracy, as was found under Solomon. Saul's rule arose in response to a military crisis.

Saul's influence is centered in Ephraim and Benjamin, with some control extending northward toward Jezreel and eastward toward Gilead. Saul also had supporters from the south, such as the Ziphites and the men of Keilah. The precise nature of Saul's administration is unclear. Saul probably did not organize his kingdom for purposes of taxation, but occasionally levied taxes and drafted men for the military. His primary concern was defending his areas of control from the Philistines.

1 Samuel 27:1–28:2. Following Saul's words vindicating David in 26:21-25, it seems inappropriate now that David must again flee from Saul. Why is David seeking refuge with a foreign king if Saul promised to abandon his pursuit? Actually, David's words and actions more appropriately follow the near miss at the Rock of Parting in 23:24-29. As indicated earlier, the narratives in this section are not necessarily in chronological sequence. Also, we must remember the possibility that not all the episodes involving David and Saul have been included in the Bible. Perhaps several incidents occurred between the times reported in 26:25 and 27:1 that led David to distrust Saul again.

The words "David thought to himself" is just one of the occasions in these narratives where the Bible allows the reader access to the inner thoughts and motives of the characters.

The king, Achish, is presumably the same king of Gath mentioned earlier in 21:10. Here Achish reacts differently to David than he previously did. Perhaps now that David has acquired a capable army, Achish plans to take advantage of the positive benefits of an alliance with him. Earlier, David was only a fugitive, accompanied by a small group of men. Now the fact that David and his men bring their wives suggests that the move is permanent.

David's move from Gath to Ziklag is important for two reasons. First, he and his troops will no longer be under the watchful eye of Achish. Second, he will be able to show his fellow Judahites that his defection to the enemy is merely a temporary ploy to avoid Saul. Now, he can conduct raids against enemies of Judah, deep in the south, and assure Achish of loyalty. This arrangement also enables

David to retaliate against the much-hated Amalekites. David's plan is brilliant. To ensure that Achish does not find out, David makes certain that the cities he attacks have no survivors.

David's plan works to perfection. He retains the loyalty of his older friends in Judah and perhaps even wins new support. At the same time, he avoids Saul. Achish is completely fooled since he makes David his permanent bodyguard. Achish believes David has become a true enemy to his people and loyal to Achish.

1 Samuel 28:3-25. As with the preceding chapter, Chapter 28 is out of chronological sequence. Since Saul's night visit to the medium occurs after he sees the sizable Philistine army, this scene belongs after Chapter 30. In verse 28:4, they are at Shunem ready for battle. But in verse 29:1, they have just assembled at Aphek, far to the south of Shunem. Also, the selection of David as Achish's personal bodyguard should be followed by Chapter 29 where this selection is questioned by other Philistine lords. Finally, the mention of Samuel's death again is necessary to the Endor scene, but it interrupts the stories of David and the Philistines.

The mediums and the spiritists Saul expelled were persons who communicated with the dead in Sheol, the realm of the dead. (Sheol is a cheerless place where the dead sleep.) Israelite law (Leviticus 19:31) clearly prohibits association with these spiritualists, and Saul evidently enforced that law. That Saul's men located a medium so promptly indicates that they had not left Israel altogether, but had merely gone underground. Even those closest to the king knew who to contact when they needed a medium.

The woman's initial suspicions of Saul's request indicate her fear of entrapment. Saul must have dealt severely with those who broke this law. Only his personal oath can assure her of safety. Explaining why she recognizes Saul at the moment she sees Samuel's apparition rising from the ground is difficult. Some scholars suggest replacing *Samuel* with *Saul,* in verse 28:12, and interpreting *saw* to mean that she looked more closely at the man making the request. Thus, her recognition of Saul occurred when she got a better look at him. Although this suggestion clarifies the incidents, it lacks support from the text.

The Hebrew word *elohim* is generally translated *god.* The NIV gives a more probable translation of *spirit.* Samuel's robe indicates his prominence as a man of great honor, even among the dead. Even though they have left this world, the inhabitants of Sheol are thought to have knowledge of the fates or divine will—all the more reason they were placed off limits in Hebrew law. Saul evidently hopes that Samuel will help him.

Samuel's words recall his earlier prophecy that the Lord would take the kingdom from Saul's hand (1 Samuel 13:14). The Amalekite debacle is also noted (1 Samuel 15:28). Saul will be punished soon. Furthermore, Saul's ravage at Nob now returns to haunt him. Having killed the priests, he is forced to resort to illicit means for gaining information. The fulfillment of God's word—although spoken by an inhabitant of Sheol—is a sure and certain reality. Not even the forbidden and sinister way that Saul learns of the impending tragedy detracts from this message. Saul is guilty of disobedience and he must suffer the consequences.

1 Samuel 29. This chapter could go before Chapter 28, because there they are already encamped at Shunem. Yet, clearly, Chapter 29 belongs immediately prior to Chapter 30. So a better order might be 29, 30, 28, and 31. The problem in arranging this material begins to become clearer when one realizes that 28:4 provides the proper background for the Endor story. Probably, some of these events occurred simultaneously. That more than a single tradition appears is also a possibility. The present arrangement of chapters follows a theological rationale rather than a chronological sequence.

The Philistine cities were ruled by a civil official called a *lord.* Yet here the *commanders* seem to be the ones in power since they review the military parade. The Philistine commanders seem to have power or authority over Achish. This arrangement, with the military leaders exercising authority over civil officials, is strange.

The Philistine commanders' suspicions about David are probably correct. Only Achish is fooled. Even David's ambiguous statement in 29:8 about fighting "against the enemies of my lord the king" lends credence to the notion that David would have turned against the Philistines. The Hebrew word *satan* is translated in 29:4 as "someone who will turn against" or an enemy. David would turn against them. This same word appears in Job 1–3. It is doubtful that in either place it refers to the New Testament notion of the Devil as God's rival. *Satan* is a commonly used Hebrew word for "enemy." Only much later does the word *satan* acquire connotations of evil.

Achish, king of Gath, invoking the name of the Lord—David's God—is something of a surprise. Surely, we are not to believe Achish had become a devotee of David's God. Possibly he was merely trying to avoid further insulting his friend, David. Perhaps the biblical writer made a slip in describing Achish's vow.

David's early morning return to Ziklag, while the Philistines march northward to meet Saul, concludes this chapter. Chance did not spare David from betraying Achish or fighting against his own people. Divine providence protects David.

1 Samuel 30. Throughout the Old Testament, the Amalekites are enemies of the Israelites. They resisted the Israelites when they escaped the Egyptian army during the Exodus. Saul goes to war against them (1 Samuel 15). The Amalekites lived south of Judah on a plain between Egypt and Canaan. They made frequent raids against the cities in Judah and may have been active in some type of slave trade. The presence of an Egyptian slave in their entourage, plus their abduction of everyone from Ziklag, may indicate such an interest. Part of David's military activity while he was at Ziklag was directed against them. No wonder. The moment his city is left unguarded, the Amalekites attack.

"But David found strength in the LORD his God" means that he turned to the Lord in order to face this crisis. David consults the Lord through Abiathar, the priest who escaped from Nob, and the ephod. He resists the temptation to retaliate without first securing divine blessing.

Some of David's men stopped at Besor, unable to complete the march against the Amalekites. They had just marched between fifty and sixty miles, from Aphek to Ziklag, in two days. To move out again was more than many of them could endure.

The Kerethites (30:14) are tribes south of Judah. Some scholars connect these Kerethites with Cretans, making them ethnically related to the Philistines. Later, these able warriors will serve David as mercenaries. The Negev of Caleb is located around Hebron.

David's decision to divide the spoils of war with the men who remained at Besor and with some of the major cities of Judah, is both politically and legally significant. David is reaffirming his loyalty to his fellow Judahites and preparing for his eventual succession as their king. This action dispels any possible notion that he has become a traitor. Legally, David establishes a precedent for the distribution of the spoils of war. This act clearly indicates that the victory belongs to the Lord, and not to any one group or individual. The Lord fights on behalf of all the people, and the spoils should be divided among everyone.

1 Samuel 31. The battle atop Mount Gilboa almost immediately follows Saul's night visit to the medium at Endor. David is probably fighting the Amalekites about the same time as this battle. In 2 Samuel 1:2, David is in Ziklag only two days before he hears about Saul's death. Ziklag is easily two days journey from Mount Gilboa; so, as indicated earlier, some of these events occur simultaneously.

Mount Gilboa is in the northern part of Israel, along the edges of the famous Valley of Jezreel. This fertile valley is an important caravan route and has agricultural and military significance. The valley is bracketed by the cities of Beth Shan on the east and Megiddo on the west. After their victory here, the Philistines move quickly to possess the cities in this region. It then takes David several years to rout them from their foothold on the region.

The armor-bearer refuses to kill Saul to spare him humiliation if he should be discovered alive by the Philistines. The armor-bearer knows that the wounded king is still sacrosanct. One does not kill the Lord's anointed.

The Israelites suffer a tremendous loss at this battle. In addition to thousands of troops, they also lose their king and three of his sons. Major Israelite cities are lost. Saul's army scatters far and wide. Later Abner, Saul's major general, restores order to some extent. But even then, the incompetent rule of Saul's only surviving son Ish-Bosheth prolongs Israel's plight. Not until David assumes the rule of the north, along with the south, do things return to calm.

The Philistines revel in their victory by publicly displaying the fallen king and his sons. In the ancient world, improper burials were a disgrace and brought everlasting shame. One's life in Sheol could be severely disrupted. Also, the unburied dead were the subject of many early religious superstitions. So with good reason, the men of Jabesh slip into Beth Shan, remove the corpses, and properly bury them, as a matter of justice and religious custom.

DIMENSION THREE: WHAT DOES THE BIBLE MEAN TO ME?

1 Samuel 28:3-25—The Nature of Revelation

In 1 Samuel 28:6 Saul mentions three traditional means of revelation in the Old Testament: dreams, the Urim, and prophets. One does not need to look far in the Old Testament to discover that dreams are an important means of divine revelation.

Jacob, fleeing from Esau, stops at Bethel for the night (Genesis 28:10-17). He dreams of a ladder extending into heaven with angels moving up and down it. In the midst of the dream, the Lord reconfirms the covenant made earlier with Abraham. Joseph (Genesis 37:5-11) dreams about his future sovereignty over his brothers. Job's comforter, Eliphaz (Job 4:13-14), reports that God addresses him in a dream about the inherent impurity of persons.

The early religion of Israel accepted dreams as a legitimate and important form of revelation. Many of Israel's neighbors in the ancient Near East compiled books of dreams to aid them in discerning the will of God. Dreams are also important in the New Testament (Matthew 1:20; 2:13).

Few persons today interpret their dreams as revelations. Most psychologists tell us that dreams reflect our subconscious desires or fears and arise from the innermost recesses of our minds, not from God.

The Urim and Thummim are small metal or stone objects similar to dice that are kept in the ephod (box) worn by priests. When persons needed advice, they went to a priest who in turn consulted the Urim and Thummim. From a throw of these sacred lots, God's will was expressed, usually in the form of a yes or no answer.

David consults the sacred lots on several occasions during his days as a fugitive from Saul. Saul discovers Jonathan's guilt (1 Samuel 14:41-42) by use of the sacred objects.

In many places, the term *ephod* is used synonymously for Urim and Thummim (1 Samuel 23:9; 30:7). But actually, the ephod was the container for the sacred dice. Two conditions existed for their use: (1) they must be used under the direction of a priest, and (2) the questions must be yes or no questions. Always, the person initiates the contact with God, as opposed to dreams that are initiated by God.

Prophets are the third form of revelation mentioned in this section. Samuel is among the first in a long line of prominent figures in the Old Testament known as prophets. These persons receive messages from the Lord, and are responsible for delivering God's word to the people.

Often these messages are unpleasant, for they are words of judgment (Amos 1–3). Jeremiah is angry at being chosen as the bearer of God's message of judgment (Jeremiah 20:7-18). Isaiah questions God, "For how long, O Lord?" (Isaiah 6:11). Other prophets, such as Second Isaiah (Isaiah 40–55) herald the joy of Israel's release from Babylonian captivity and her return to Jerusalem.

Many of these prophets are called or commanded by God to be prophets (Isaiah 6; Ezekiel 1–3; Jeremiah 1:4-19). These people are announcers of God's word. And since it is God's word, it necessarily causes things to happen. The true prophet utters words that come true, whereas the announcements of false prophets never occur (Deuteronomy 18:21-22).

These three forms of revelation—the dream, the Urim and Thummim, and the prophet—constitute a pathway between God and persons. As long as we are in an acceptable stance before God, we can discover the will of the Lord. But woe to the person the Lord deserts, as Saul discovered. Through these channels, God imparts salvation to the people. But through them God also imparts judgment.

Close today's session by asking class members to share new insights they have gained from their study of 1 Samuel 27–31. List these insights on chalkboard or a large sheet of paper if time allows.

8

David the King

2 Samuel 1–4

DIMENSION ONE:
WHAT DOES THE BIBLE SAY?

Answer these questions by reading 2 Samuel 1

1. What news does the man from Saul's camp bring David at Ziklag? (1:4)

   He says that Saul and Jonathan have died in battle.

2. What proof does this man have that Saul is dead? (1:10)

   The man says that he himself slew Saul.

3. How do David and his men react to the news of Saul's death? (1:11-12)

   They mourn, weep, and fast all during the day.

4. Why does David punish the man who brought him the news? (1:16)

   The man killed the Lord's anointed.

5. Where is David's lament over Saul and Jonathan recorded? (1:18)

   It is recorded in the Book of Jashar.

Answer these questions by reading 2 Samuel 2

6. Following Saul's death, where does the Lord tell David to go? (2:1)

   The Lord tells David to go to Hebron.

7. Which office do the men of Judah award David when he arrives at Hebron? (2:4)

   They anoint David king of Judah

8. Who is named king of Israel to succeed Saul? (2:8-9)

   Ish-Bosheth, Saul's son, is named king of Israel.

9. How long does David reign as king of Judah at Hebron? (2:11)

   David reigns at Hebron for seven years and six months.

10. Who are the two leaders of the conflict between Ish-Bosheth and David? (2:12-13)

    The leaders are Abner and Joab.

11. Who wins the initial battle? (2:17)

    Joab and the men of David defeat Abner and the men of Ish-Bosheth.

12. Which relative of Joab does Abner slay? (2:23)

    Abner kills Asahel, the brother of Joab.

Answer these questions by reading 2 Samuel 3

13. Which sons of David were born at Hebron? (3:2-5)

    Amnon, Kileab, Absalom, Adonijah, Shephatiah, and Ithream were born at Hebron.

14. How does Ish-Bosheth make Abner angry? (3:7-8)

    Ish-Bosheth accuses Abner of violating his father's concubines.

15. What offer does Abner make to David? (3:21)

    Abner offers to bring all Israel under David's leadership.

16. What does Joab do to Abner? (3:27)

    Joab kills Abner.

17. What is David's response to the killing of Abner? (3:28-29)

He places a curse on Joab's house.

Answer these questions by reading 2 Samuel 4

18. What is the relationship between Jonathan and Mephibosheth? (4:4)

Mephibosheth is the son of Jonathan.

19. What do the sons of Rimmon, Rechab and Baanah, do to Ish-Bosheth? (4:7-8)

They kill Ish-Bosheth and bring his head to David.

20. How does David respond to their deed? (4:12)

He has them killed, has their hands and feet cut off, and hangs them at Hebron.

DIMENSION TWO:
WHAT DOES THE BIBLE MEAN?

Background Information on 2 Samuel 1–4

Saul's death does not bring instant enthronement of David as king of Israel. Other matters must be resolved first. David's road to the throne is winding and marked by numerous detours. Yet, behind this gradual movement toward fulfillment of Samuel's anointing (1 Samuel 16:13), we can see the firm and steady hand of the Lord. David will become king and rule over the people of God. There is little doubt in anyone's mind, even Abner and Ish-Bosheth's, that David is destined to receive Saul's throne.

The literary problems in First Samuel diminish considerably as we move into Second Samuel. There are fewer places with parallel versions of the same story. For the most part, Second Samuel is the product of a single editor who carefully composed the material or else left the sources intact with little or no editorial work. There are few contradictions or repetitions in Second Samuel. Unfortunately, the quality of the Hebrew text does not improve, and the English translations frequently gloss over serious problems.

Saul's defeat at Mount Gilboa leaves a vacancy on the throne of Israel. This catastrophe also allows the Philistines to occupy several towns or villages in the north. Abner, Saul's commander, hastily forms a new government and relocates its capital in Mahanaim, to the east of the Jordan River. Ish-Bosheth, Saul's only surviving son, becomes king, but he is only a puppet. Abner exercises real control over what remains of Saul's kingdom.

Meanwhile in the south, David brings a new measure of unity to the tribes of Judah. Undoubtedly, David's rule in Hebron has the knowledge and approval of the Philistines. They probably still consider him a Philistine vassal loyal to them. There is no evidence that they consider him a threat. The tribes in Judah now begin to assume a prominence and cohesiveness earlier reserved for the tribes of Israel and the Philistine cities. The elders of these tribes see David as a loyal and competent leader who can offer them needed protection and stability. No one is unhappy with David's rule in Hebron, except Abner and Ish-Bosheth.

2 Samuel 1. This chapter consists of two related events: 1:1-16—David learns of the deaths of Saul and Jonathan, and 1:17-27—David laments over Saul and Jonathan. David receives word of the ill-fated battle at Gilboa shortly after he has returned from his successful retaliation against the Amalekites for their attack on Ziklag. An Amalekite sojourner brings David the tragic news.

An alien is a foreigner who has taken up residence in another country. In Israel, aliens came under the protection of the law and were extended some of the rights of native citizens. But just as they were extended partial rights by law, they were also accountable and responsible to Israelite law. Thus, when the Amalekite confesses proudly to the killing of Saul, he condemns himself on religious as well as criminal grounds.

David's interrogation carefully leads the Amalekite to self-condemnation. "Why were you were not afraid to lift your hand to destroy the LORD's anointed?" Surely, David reasons, an alien would have known about the penalty for murdering a king! This man was after a reward, David thinks. But David wants no part of Saul's death! And, although he does not stand to profit from the now vacant throne, David does not rejoice in the death of Saul. To remove any possible thought as to his personal involvement in the matter, David has the overly ambitious Amalekite killed. Now he expresses his own sense of loss and sadness for Jonathan.

The lament chanted by David is one of the most beautiful laments in the Old Testament. The rhythmic lyrics and the poignant imagery touch the depths of our souls even today. One can almost feel David's sorrow and sense his deep loss over the deaths of Jonathan and Saul.

One main characteristic of Hebrew poetry is its parallelism, or balance between each pair of stanzas or lines. For instance, in verse 20, the phrase "Tell it not" is parallel to "proclaim it not." This is *synonymous parallelism*, in which both stanzas contain essentially the same idea. Synonymous parallelism also characterizes the next two stanzas.

Another type of parallelism is *synthetical*, where the second line develops the idea of the first line. Verse 1:25 is synthetical parallelism. By understanding the structure of Hebrew poetry, we can grasp better the thoughts of the ancient writers. Parallelism is one of their literary techniques for emphasis and reinforcement of ideas.

The imagery of this lament is vivid and striking. Gilboa, a former holy place on top of a mountain, is condemned to drought. Saul and Jonathan are praised for their valiant deeds, as well as their close personal relationship. They are compared to the eagle renowned for speed and the lion famed for strength. The words of love and affection for Jonathan remind us of the strong bond of friendship between these two men. Lavish in praise, lofty in imagery, and penetrating in pathos, David's lament over Jonathan and Saul is truly a fine piece of literature.

2 Samuel 2:1-11. David appropriately consults the Lord before moving to Judah and assuming power. Part of David's favored position before the Lord comes from his obedience to the Lord's will. On numerous occasions, David consults the Lord before making a crucial decision. Usually, he makes use of the sacred lots, the Urim and Thummim. Here, we are not told how David obtains the Lord's word, but possibly he used the lots once again.

Hebron is an important city located about twenty miles south of Jerusalem. It is the traditional burial site of Abraham and Sarah. It is also an important gathering place for major tribes of the south. Hebron is thus a strategic choice as David's capital for political as well as religious reasons. When the men of Judah come and anoint David as king, David reaches an important milestone in his quest for kingship of the people of God. He now has half his kingdom.

David's kind words for the men of Jabesh (verses 5-7) conceal mixed motives. Certainly he did appreciate proper burial for the slain king and his sons. Improper burials seriously affected a person's sojourn in Sheol following death. In fact, persons regarded an improper burial as divine judgment. On the other hand, by reminding the men of Jabesh that Saul is dead, and that now he (David) reigns over Judah, he is clearly suggesting that he would welcome them into his fold. He presents himself as a deserving candidate for their loyalty and support.

Abner, Saul's uncle, hastily sets up a provisional government across the Jordan River in a city called Mahanaim. Saul's son Ish-Bosheth is named king, although the real power lies with Abner. Ish-Bosheth (formerly called Ishbaal) must have been a weak, ineffective king, haunted by suspicions of Abner's disloyalty.

If the territory ascribed to Ish-Bosheth's government is trustworthy (verse 9), then Saul's kingdom remains partially intact following the slaughter at Mount Gilboa. Most commentators feel that Ish-Bosheth and Abner exercised minimal control over the central hill country of Ephraim, Benjamin, and Galilee. But this puppet regime does not last long. When Abner dies, Ish-Bosheth is murdered shortly thereafter. The claim that Ish-Bosheth was forty years old and reigned two years does not match the story and cannot be right. His reign at Mahanaim coincides in length with that of David, a period of seven and one-half years. The scene is now set for a long civil war between Judah and Israel.

2 Samuel 2:12-3:39. This section describes the diplomatic relations between Judah and Israel. The time frame encompassed by these events may be as much as seven years. The biblical writer has carefully selected traditions that illustrate David's increasing power and the fulfillment of the Lord's will to make him ruler over Israel and Judah.

In the first event (2:12-32), Joab and Abner match some of their men in a contest. The exact details of this contest are unclear, but possibly each contestant fights by thrusting a sword or dagger at his opponent, while holding onto the hair. The contest was originally intended as play. Evidently, the participants become too involved, one thing leads to another, and a full-fledged battle erupts. There are numerous casualties, particularly among Abner's troops.

Abner's speedy retreat is matched by the fleet-footed Asahel, brother of Joab. When Asahel refuses to abandon his pursuit, Abner kills him. This murder establishes a blood feud between Joab and Abner. It is doubtful that this skirmish alone provoked a major war between Israel and Judah. But this brief episode serves two purposes: (1) it explains the blood feud between Joab and Abner, and (2) it shows the superiority of David's veteran troops over the raw recruits of Abner.

The struggle between Judah and Israel reaches a climax when Abner attempts to negotiate a transfer of power to David (3:12-21). Unfortunately, he does not live to see the move take effect because Joab avenges his brother's death by killing Abner. Abner's move toward reconciliation with David occurs because Ish-Bosheth accuses Abner of having sexual relations with Rizpah, one of Saul's concubines. Traditionally, a king's wives and his concubines were passed along to his successor.

If Ish-Bosheth's charges are true, then perhaps Abner is making a move toward claiming the throne for himself. But we do not know whether Abner is guilty or innocent. He reacts strongly to the allegations and responds with a surprisingly strong threat to abandon Ish-Bosheth and join David. Could his overreaction be deliberate? Perhaps he needs an excuse to switch loyalties and join the winning team.

David's request for the return of Michal, his first wife, is politically important. It will legitimate his claim to Saul's throne. Judging from her actions of anger later (2 Samuel 6:20-23), she never forgave David for his insensitivity to her personal affections for her second husband. And Ish-Bosheth is too weak to refuse David's request.

By now, Abner has lined up considerable support for David, including the oldest and most important men in Israel. This union of Israel and Judah would complete David's rule over both the north and south. Abner's motives are unclear. Perhaps he was seeking an important post in David's army.

David's outrage at Joab's murder of Abner (see 3:28-39) appears to be sincere and severe. The curse he places on Joab's house is strong. Had the offender been someone with less power, David would certainly have sentenced him to instant death. But Joab is too important to David and perhaps too strong. David's lament and his public mourning allay all suspicions of his personal involvement. Otherwise, the Israelites and Benjaminites might have second thoughts about uniting with David.

This section concludes with David turning the responsibility for revenge on Joab over to the Lord. David has now moved even closer to fulfilling his divinely ordained destiny. Only Ish-Bosheth remains in his path, but not for long.

2 Samuel 4. With the death of Abner, Ish-Bosheth and his fragile government begin to disintegrate almost instantly. Ish-Bosheth realizes that Abner has been the real power behind his rule. Abner's death signals the loss of any hope that Saul's kingdom might remain in his hands. This feeling of desperation grips the men of Israel, also. Negotiations with Abner to transfer their loyalties to David certainly must be resumed before they lose all bargaining power.

The remark about the two sons of Rimmon explains why Beeroth, a Gibeonite city, is included among the cities of the Benjaminites. The original inhabitants of Beeroth fled earlier to Gittaim, another Benjaminite city, to avoid persecution or destruction by Saul. Beeroth was then probably occupied by families from Benjamin, one of whom was Rimmon.

Why fellow Benjaminites would seek the death of Saul's own son is not clear. Some commentators resolve the problem by assuming that Rimmon and his sons were not actually Benjaminites, but only resided there. They may have been descendants of the earlier Canaanite group persecuted by Saul. If so, revenge would have been their motive.

The description of Ish-Bosheth's assassination (verses 5-8) leaves much to be desired. The English translation glosses over severe difficulties. Other early translations, such as the Greek Septuagint, provide little help. Somehow the two officers are successful in their plan to kill Ish-Bosheth, and they hurry to tell David of their deed. Privately, David's reactions are probably mixed, since now the way is open for including the northern tribes under his rule. But publicly he must mourn and lament the death of Ish-Bosheth to dispel any notion of his personal involvement.

David has the assassins killed and their bodies mutilated. Even worse, their bodies are not provided with proper burial. Ish-Bosheth, on the other hand, receives an honorable burial.

DIMENSION THREE:
WHAT DOES THE BIBLE MEAN TO ME?

2 Samuel 3:26-30—Motives for Punishment

When Joab and Abishai ruthlessly slay Abner (3:30), they fulfill traditional expectations of blood feuds in early Israel. Abner killed Asahel, their brother; now, they must avenge his death. Their motive is clearly one of punish-

ment. In this case, the circumstances surrounding Asahel's death are of little importance. At worst, Abner's action was done in self-defense. Certainly he does not plot against Asahel, nor maliciously conspire to take his life. Asahel pursues Abner and despite Abner's warning, he continues the chase until Abner strikes him in the stomach with his spear. Abner's plea to Joab to call a truce (2:26-27) suggests that he had no intentions of starting a blood feud. Nevertheless, Joab and Abishai remember Abner's deed and await an opportune moment to get their revenge.

This situation prompts some thought as to the primary purpose of any system of justice. What motives lie beneath punishment? Why do we wish to see the offender punished? Because the law has been broken? Because someone has been injured? Or, do we wish to see the offender rehabilitated? Or, is the primary purpose of a justice system to discourage certain socially unacceptable acts? Here, the thought is that a potential offender will be discouraged after discovering what the punishment would be.

Ask the class members to share their feelings about this matter. What should our purposes be in a system of criminal justice? How well do our present laws achieve their purposes? How do we reconcile the revenge theory with Jesus' teaching about turning the other cheek? How can we love the person who breaks the law?

2 Samuel 3:31-39—The Limitations of Leadership

Joab's part in the death of Abner prompts an outcry from David that is interesting: "And today, though I am the anointed king, I am weak, and these sons of Zeruiah are too strong for me. May the LORD repay the evildoer according to his evil deeds!" (See 2 Samuel 3:39.) Here David confesses that there are limits even to the power of the Lord's anointed servant. He simply cannot control the behavior of his subordinates. In some instances, David himself punishes the guilty parties, as with the opportunistic Amalekite or the sons of Rimmon. But here, Joab is beyond David's ability to discipline. Only the Lord can and should give Joab his due.

A sign of real wisdom is knowledge and acceptance of limits to one's authority. Had David attempted to punish Joab and Abishai for their reprisals against Abner, he would have violated a very powerful tradition in early Israel. Even kings must move carefully and judiciously when they abandon long-standing customs. And the practice of blood feud goes far back into Israel's heritage. David also failed to discipline Joab and Abishai out of respect (or fear) for their high standing in the army. And, the two avengers were relatives of David—his nephews (1 Chronicles 2:13-16). These restrictions temper David's capacity to punish Joab and Abishai.

In leaving the punishment ultimately in God's hands, David clearly made a proper decision. Final justice must be reserved for God. We are called upon to carry out God's will as fully as possible, but there are limits to our authority and to what God expects of us. Christians are commanded to carry the good news of God's love to all persons. We are responsible for caring for the children of God, and for addressing the needs of the oppressed of this world. We are to proclaim God's redemption and grace. But we are not called upon to take the place of God. As leaders among the people of God, we have limits to our responsibility. "May the LORD repay the evildoer according to his evil deeds!"

Close today's session by listing on chalkboard or a large sheet of paper any new insight class members have on 2 Samuel 1–4.

9

The Empire of David

2 Samuel 5–8

DIMENSION ONE:
WHAT DOES THE BIBLE SAY?

Answer these questions by reading 2 Samuel 5

1. What responsibility do the elders of Israel bestow upon David? (5:3)

   They anoint him their king.

2. How long does David rule over Israel and Judah together? (5:5)

   He rules over Judah and Israel for thirty-three years.

3. Who occupies Jerusalem at David's inauguration? (5:6)

   The Jebusites dwell in Jerusalem.

4. How does David infiltrate Jerusalem and overcome the Jebusites? (5:8)

   His men enter through the water shaft and defeat the Jebusites.

5. Which neighboring king sends men and materials to David for the construction of a royal palace? (5:11)

   Hiram king of Tyre sends messengers, craftsmen, and supplies.

6. What traditional enemy attacks Israel after David becomes king? (5:17)

   The Philistines attack Israel.

Answer these questions by reading 2 Samuel 6

7. What sacred object does David wish to bring into Jerusalem? (6:2)

   David wants to bring the ark of God [the covenant] to Jerusalem.

8. Why does Uzzah die during the march to Jerusalem? (6:6-7)

   Uzzah dies because he puts forth his hand and touches the sacred ark to prevent it from falling off the cart.

9. How does David react to Uzzah's death? (6:8-10)

   He is both angry with and afraid of the Lord. He carries the ark no further, leaving it at the home of Obed-Edom.

10. What does David do as the ark enters Jerusalem? (6:14)

    David dances before the Lord with all his might.

11. How does Michal, David's wife, react to David's behavior? (6:16)

    She despises David in her heart.

Answer these questions by reading 2 Samuel 7

12. Who is Nathan? (7:2)

    Nathan is a prophet.

13. What does David say to Nathan? (7:2)

    David tells Nathan that he is concerned that the Lord lives only in a tent, while he lives in a house of cedar.

14. What does the Lord promise David? (7:10)

    The Lord promises to provide a place for Israel to dwell.

15. Who does the Lord say will build God's house? (7:12-13)

    The Lord says that David's offspring will build the house.

16. Who does David conquer during his reign over Israel and Judah? (8:11-12)

David conquers Edom, Moab, the Ammonites, the Philistines, Amalek, and Hadadezer.

17. Who is the recorder during David's tenure as king? (8:16)

The recorder's name is Jehoshaphat.

18. Who are David's priests? (8:17)

His priests are Zadok and Ahimelech.

19. Who is the royal secretary? (8:17)

The royal secretary is Seraiah.

DIMENSION TWO: WHAT DOES THE BIBLE MEAN?

Background Information on 2 Samuel 5–8

This period in Israel's history is known as the United Monarchy. David probably became king around 1000 B.C. Israel remains a unified nation until shortly after Solomon's death in 922 B.C. During this period, the name *Israel* refers to an organized political state, rather than to a loosely knit tribal confederation, as during the days of Saul.

David establishes Israel as one of the most powerful nations in the Near East. The United Monarchy, including Solomon's reign, marks the political heyday of Israel's national existence. The days of David and Solomon are glorious. In this lesson, we stand on the foreground of this period.

With David as king, the condition of the people of God improves dramatically. Instead of a loosely knit political organization, as during the days of the judges, we have the beginnings of a modern state. Israel is now governed by one ruler and has an increasing governmental bureaucracy, a standing army, and a national religion. David's control extends over a large territory and many foreign leaders seek to befriend the new king.

Yet, for all these historic changes, David's empire remains a fragile union, bound together by a single person. Israel is made up of many different tribes and is unaccustomed to centralized authority. She is reticent to relinquish political autonomy, except in emergencies. Several times during David's reign the tribes rebel, but David manages to control them. Shortly after Solomon's death, this uneasy union ends in a split between North and South.

David did much to heal the factionalism that divided his realm. Bringing the ark into Jerusalem was one of the most important moves he made. This linked past with present and church with state. Certainly, this move must have impressed many of the king's detractors. Also, his selection of the neutral site of Jerusalem as his capital appeased many critics. His small but well-trained army brought security to a land that had been ravaged by wars for centuries. These accomplishments fostered a new sense of unity in Israel.

2 Samuel 5. Verses 1-5 of this chapter give the account of David's being anointed as king over Israel. The murders of Abner and Ish-Bosheth have left the elders of the North without a leader. The anointing ceremony was probably an elaborate process, in spite of the brief account. In verse 1, "all the tribes of Israel" come to David, but David is anointed by only the elders in verse 3. Either verse 1 is a summary of verse 3, or perhaps there were two separate ceremonies. On the first occasion, numerous representatives from the ten northern tribes meet with David and ask him to become their king. This meeting is followed shortly by a formal coronation ceremony. Only the elders anoint David as king and form a covenant with him. The United Monarchy has begun.

The directive of the Lord referred to in verse 2, does not appear in any of the biblical stories. Yet, from 1 Samuel 16 on, that David was chosen by the Lord is clear to everyone, including Saul. The pastoral image of "shepherd [of] my people" is an appropriate one for David, given his particular background. Kings are called shepherds often in the Book of Psalms.

The terms of the covenant are unstated, but David certainly received pledges of loyalty and support in return for his leadership. The covenant probably also grants the northern tribes and the southern tribes the same guarantees of protection. The ceremony itself takes place "before the LORD" at Hebron, a holy city in Judah. This location suggests that kingship functions with religious as well as civil and military sanctions.

The exact method David uses to capture Jerusalem is difficult to determine. The Hebrew text is almost unreadable in places. Words are used that are unknown to us (for example, the *Millo*, the water shaft), and obscure idiomatic phrases conceal the manner of capture.

Jerusalem is an ancient city, mentioned in Egyptian documents as early as 1400 B.C. Joshua and the invading Israelites are unable to drive the original inhabitants, the Jebusites, out of Jerusalem (Joshua 15:63; Judges 1:21). Thus from the Exodus (1250 B.C.) to the present time (1015 B.C.), Jerusalem remained in Jebusite hands.

The reference to the "blind and lame" (verse 8) may refer to Jewish demands for cultic purity in the Temple. Since blind and lame persons were thought to be unclean, they were considered unfit to enter the sacred "palace." The earlier reference to the "blind and lame" (verse 6) is probably a taunt against David indicating that almost anyone could keep the Israelites out of the city. (For another account of the assault on Jerusalem, see 1 Chronicles 11:4-9.)

The reference to Hiram's aid to David seems premature, since Hiram probably would have waited to see how David fared against the Philistines before offering him aid. The genealogy in 5:13-16 continues the list of David's family begun in 3:2-5. The number of David's wives and heirs to his throne will eventually lead to jealousy and intrigue in the royal court.

Old Testament scholars are unsure about the proper sequence of events here. Some believe that the capture of Jerusalem occurred after David subdued the Philistines. Others contend that Jerusalem was captured between the two battles with the Philistines. Still others view the capture of Jerusalem as the catalyst provoking Philistine warfare. The third alternative is the most likely one. David moved to incorporate Jerusalem into his kingdom immediately after being named king at Hebron. While David was the king of Judah only, and Ish-Bosheth and Abner were alive, the Philistines saw no real threat. Now that David controls the North, the South, and Jerusalem, the Philistines move quickly to challenge his power.

The "stronghold" in verse 17 cannot be identified for certain, nor can Baal Perazim or the site of the Valley of Rephaim. In two separate but consecutive battles, David defeats the Philistines. The details of these battles leave many unanswered questions—location, tactics, size of armies, and duration of the battles are all very obscure. Nevertheless, David successfully pushes the Philistines back along the southwestern coast and contains them there permanently. Israel's major rival for control of Palestine has been conquered.

2 Samuel 6. David now moves decisively to gain widespread popular support. First, he adds theological legitimacy to his reign by bringing the holy ark into his new capital, Jerusalem. Unfortunately, the Bible leaves several questions of detail unanswered. We have only a general idea of how the ark is moved. But, there is no question about the immense significance of this action. Jerusalem becomes the religious and political center in Israel.

The move to Jerusalem is interrupted by the outbreak of God's wrath after Uzzah touches the ark to keep it from falling. In 2 Samuel 6:2, the ark is at Baalah of Judah. In 1 Chronicles 13:6, another version of the same story, the ark rests at Kiriath Jearim, also called Baalah. Whether these three names refer to the same site cannot be determined. In 1 Samuel 7:2, the last mention of the ark, it had come to rest at Kiriath Jearim, a site seven miles west of Jerusalem. No other stories tell of the ark being moved. Given Saul's hostility to the descendants of the Shiloh priesthood, where the ark formerly rested, and Samuel's opposition to Saul, it is little wonder that the ark plays no role in the Saul stories. The ark traditions and the Saul traditions have few points in common. So, the exact site where the ark rested at the time of David is unknown.

David chooses an unusually large number of soldiers to accompany him on this expedition. The number could be high to emphasize the importance of the occasion, or perhaps David anticipated resistance from the Philistines. (Compare 8:1 with 5:25.)

The procession out of Kiriath Jearim has all the elements of a great festival—music, dance, religious activity, military presence, and the new king. Even a new cart denoting purity is built to carry the ark. Two brothers, Uzzah and Ahio, drive the cart. We do not know why these particular men are chosen for this task. Perhaps there is some genealogical link between them and the Eleazar in 1 Samuel 7:1 who is placed in charge of the ark.

Suddenly, disaster strikes this grand procession. Translation difficulties deny us clarity about the actual events. For some reason Uzzah touches the ark to steady it. He dies instantly, as the victim of an angry God. The oxen may have stumbled, Uzzah himself may have stumbled, or the cart may have tilted. Whatever happens results in Uzzah's being struck dead.

This tragedy frightens David so much that he abandons his mission. The ark is left at the home of Obed-Edom, a Gittite from Gath, until the Lord's anger abates. Obed-Edom is a resident alien, not an Israelite. Gittites are former residents of the Philistine city of Gath who now live in Israel. For three months, the ark stays with the Gittite. Then the Lord's anger subsides and the journey to Jerusalem continues.

David enters Jerusalem with much pomp and celebration. David's particular dress for the occasion, his participation in the cultic ceremony, and his distribution of the sacrificial meal all underscore the king's priestly or religious role. A direct connection now exists between the early Israelite religious symbol, the ark, and Samuel, David, and Jerusalem. This connection gives new legitimacy to David's kingship and to his royal city.

The story of Michal's rebuke of David and his alienation from her indicates David's sense of security in his new position. He no longer needs a link to the house of Saul to confirm his authority over the tribes of the North. Neither does he need a son from her to unite the country. Whatever he feels for Michal, he is hurt by her insulting remarks. He replies that she is offending not only the king, but also the Lord, who chose him over her father Saul. Even the slave girls stand in reverence before the Lord's anointed prince. David permanently rejects Michal, and the Lord uses her barrenness to punish her.

2 Samuel 7. Nathan, the official court prophet, is the instrument of God's word to David. Nathan appears again in Chapter 12 in the Bathsheba affair, and in 1 Kings 1, in Solomon's accession. The court prophet serves as a religious advisor to the king along with the priests, Abiathar and Zadok. Gad, another prophet (or seer), also is mentioned in the David stories (1 Samuel 22:5; 2 Samuel 24:11-14).

Two other reasons are given in the Old Testament for why David did not build the Temple: (1) 1 Kings 5:3 says he was too busy, and (2) 1 Chronicles 22:8 says it is because of David's personal involvement in war.

In 2 Samuel 7, the rejection of David's offer to construct a permanent home for the ark represents an anti-temple tradition in the Old Testament. This tradition celebrates God's periodic visits to the people in the tent. Wherever the people go, the tent goes also. This way God is not limited to a particular location, much less to a special building. A permanent temple would localize God in a single place, and diminish God's presence among the tribes of Israel. So, the notion of a temple cuts deeply across the early traditions of a movable, dynamic God. How could God be restricted to a single place?

Instead of David building God a "house," the Lord will build David a "house." The play on the word *house* is impressive. David's line (or "house") will be established forever. The Lord's support and guidance of David made him king over Israel. All the events leading up to this moment have been orchestrated by God. The Davidic dynasty is now at hand, and God intends to see that this special relationship continues (verses 14-15).

Biblical theologians, including prophets like Isaiah, look back to this period as a pristine period of godly rule. The age of King David is seen as the great day in Israel's national life. This time also serves as the model for the messianic age to come (Isaiah 11). Future generations of Jews will stand and wait in expectation of the Davidic figure who can restore their historic place among the peoples of the world. The combining of the themes of temple and dynasty, clearly links the history of Israel to the history of David.

David's final prayer is a model of piety and faith. The king clearly understands that his rule is a consequence of divine guidance. The prayer reiterates the promise of Nathan that the Lord will continue to bless David through his dynasty that is to follow.

2 Samuel 8. Following the promise of Nathan (7:11) that God will give David rest from his enemies, the king extends the boundaries of his empire and solidifies his control over rival nations. This chapter appears to be a summary of a more extensive set of documents, possibly official court records. David is shown as a man skillful at war, as well as a man of great faith. To transform divergent tribes of questionable power into a large and prospering nation is no small accomplishment. "The LORD gave David victory wherever he went" (verse 14), clarifies that God is behind David's success.

The Philistines, according to 5:25, have already been limited to the southern coastal region. More complete accounts of the earlier prolonged warfare with the Philistines occur in 2 Samuel 21:15-22 and 23:8-39. The summary here offers only a general reminder of his previous success. If Metheg Ammah (verse 1) is a site, then it has not been located to date. It could be the name of a Philistine god or perhaps a king.

Moab, a small nation east of the Dead Sea, receives particularly harsh treatment from David. This action is surprising in view of Moab's willingness to provide sanctuary for David's parents when Saul threatened them (1 Samuel 22:3-4). Perhaps the locations are confused in the earlier episode, or else, possibly, hostility broke out between Moab and David later. For whatever reason, the Moabites become the servants of Israel for the next century.

Further north, David moves against the Syrians and the small kingdom of Zobah, north of Syria. Biblical writers often exaggerate numbers in the Old Testament, and 8:4 is no exception. Exactly how far north David's control extended is unclear. He controlled the lucrative trade routes through Damascus for a time. How long Israel held control over the Aramean kingdom is also unknown. Many of the countries that David did not conquer established friendly diplomatic relations with Israel. Hamath was such a country.

Whether or not David administered justice is open to question (verse 15). David's lack of a judicial system is the reason Absalom is critical of his father (15:4).

The list of officials in David's court is found again in 2 Samuel 20:23-26, with slight variations. Joab's command extends over the hosts of Israel, the national army drafted for special campaigns. The precise functions of the recorder are unknown. He may have been a personal secretary who reminded the king of his duties and obligations. Zadok, a priest, appears here for the first time. No mention is made here of his ancestry. Later, in 1 Chronicles, Zadok is listed as a direct descendant of Aaron (1 Chronicles 6:3-8). David's sons are not mentioned as royal advisors anywhere else. In fact, their names are omitted from the later list.

DIMENSION THREE:
WHAT DOES THE BIBLE MEAN TO ME?

2 Samuel 6:1-15—Institutionalized Religion

When King David offers to build a house for the Lord (2 Samuel 7:1), it is impossible for us to detect his motives. Perhaps he feels guilty living in a splendid mansion of cedar while the Lord's ark sits in a tent. Perhaps he wants to make certain Jerusalem remains the religious center of his fledgling nation. Or, perhaps he has a genuine desire to honor God in a tangible way.

Regardless of the king's motives, the construction of a temple would have affected the religious life of ancient Israel, as it clearly does later during the days of Solomon. The formal link of church to state in a single city gives Israel's kings tremendous power and authority. As long as the kings are responsive to divine guidance, this arrangement works well. But all too quickly, corruption sets in and Israel's kings become agents of their own greedy desires. First and Second Kings record all too vividly a history of this perversion.

The Lord's caution to David about building a house signals the danger implicit in institutionalizing religion. To associate the worship of the Lord with a single structure, in a single city, under the watchful eye of an all-powerful sovereign would threaten any religion. Symbolized by the ark, the Lord went about in the midst of the people. God was with them in their wilderness experience (Exodus 1–18). God was with them as they fought to secure a foothold in Canaan (Joshua 1–12). God was with them as they struggled against the powerful Philistines.

First at Shiloh, then at Kiriath Jearim, the ark always remains close to the people of God. When they move, the Lord moves with them. Through priests and prophets, the Lord speaks to the people and provides guidance. Since holy sites were plentiful in early Israel, people had little difficulty communicating with the Lord. The possibility of housing the ark in a permanent structure threatens this active, personal contact between God and the people. The Lord therefore opposes a temple, at least for the moment.

Religion in America suffers from excessive institutionalizing. Huge sums of money are often invested in sanctuaries and other facilities. A priestly hierarchy dogmatically prescribes forms of worship. Creeds are mumbled on days of worship as a matter of custom, with little thought given to their meaning. For many of us, religion is an exercise we perform weekly, often to ease our consciences or to gain material blessings. Ask the class members whether they agree with this assessment of religious life in America. Why or why not? Ask for suggestions about how we might invigorate our religious exercises. List these suggestions on chalkboard or a large sheet of paper. How might we let the institution become servant (or means) rather than master (or the end)?

2 Samuel 7:18-29—David, Model of Faith

King David stands out as one of the principal figures in the Old Testament. His successful blending of religious, political, and military power results in a character of tremendous influence on his nation. The story of his humble beginnings, his rapid ascent to the thrones of Israel and Judah, and his transformation of his small kingdom into a mighty nation are witnesses to the active and providential hand of the Lord.

But David also furnishes us with yet another model. David is a model of faith. He has confidence in the Lord, and submits to the Lord's will. He has the courage to carry out the work of the Lord. David's confidence is manifested in his willingness to place human need over priestly prescription, as in taking of the consecrated bread during a famine (2 Samuel 21). David's response to Michal's complaints about his behavior also indicates confidence in God's special appointment (2 Samuel 6:20). That David almost always consults the Lord before embarking on a military engagement suggests his submissiveness to the will of the Lord.

David's bravery in confronting Goliath, his daring exploits as a fugitive from Saul, and his transformation of Jerusalem into a holy city cradling the ark are all evidence of his courage to act on his understanding of God's will. These three elements form a useful model of faith. From this model, we learn that faith is more than blind trust or superstition. Faith is confidence, submission, and courage.

David's model of faith provides a pattern for us to follow. We must adapt his pattern to our lives today and try to embody the three principles his faith reflects: confidence, submission, and courage. Ask the class members to think about these characteristics of faith and how they are reflected in our lives today.

Close the class session by having the group reflect on new insights from today's study of 2 Samuel 5–8. Have group members share these insights, and list them on chalkboard or a large sheet of paper if time allows.

— 10 —

David, Bathsheba, and Solomon

2 Samuel 9–12

DIMENSION ONE:
WHAT DOES THE BIBLE SAY?

Answer these questions by reading 2 Samuel 9

1. Who is the servant of Saul that David locates? (9:2)

   His name is Ziba.

2. How does Ziba help David? (9:3)

   Ziba identifies Mephibosheth as the only living relative of Saul.

3. What does David do for Mephibosheth? (9:7)

   David restores to Mephibosheth all of Saul's lands, and gives him a place at the royal table.

4. Who is Mica? (9:12)

   Mica is the son of Mephibosheth.

Answer these questions by reading 2 Samuel 10

5. Why does David send his servants to Hanun, king of the Ammonites? (10:1-2)

   David sends his servants to pay condolences to Hanun upon the death of his father.

6. How does Hanun treat David's servants? (10:4)

   Hanun shaves off half their beards and cuts off their garments in the middle at their buttocks.

7. What do the Ammonites do next? (10:6)

   The Ammonites hire Aramean soldiers to help them fight against Israel.

8. What is the outcome of the battle? (10:13-14)

   Israel defeats both the Arameans and the Ammonites.

9. What does Hadadezer do after the first battle? (10:16)

   Hadadezer regroups the Aramean troops and fights a second battle against Israel.

Answer these questions by reading 2 Samuel 11

10. Who is Israel fighting at this time? (11:1)

    Israel is fighting the Ammonites.

11. Who is Bathsheba? (11:3-4)

    She is the wife of Uriah the Hittite.

12. Why does David's plan to conceal his affair fail? (11:9)

    Uriah refuses to spend the night at his house, thereby eliminating himself as the possible father of Bathsheba's child.

13. How does David arrange for Uriah to die? (11:15)

    David has Uriah placed on the front line of battle.

14. Following Uriah's death, what arrangements does David make for Bathsheba? (11:27)

    David makes Bathsheba his wife and brings her to his court.

15. What is the Lord's attitude toward the matter? (11:27)

    The Lord is displeased with the matter.

Answer these questions by reading 2 Samuel 12

16. Who delivers the Lord's message to David? (12:1)

    Nathan delivers the Lord's message.

17. How does Nathan illustrate David's sin? (12:1-5)

He tells a story about a rich man who stole the beloved lamb of a poor man in order to feed a dinner guest.

18. How does the Lord punish David? (12:7-18)

The Lord tells David that his house shall be troubled forever and that his wives shall be given to one close to him.

19. What do David and Bathsheba name their second son? (12:24)

They name him Solomon.

20. How does David treat the conquered Ammonites? (12:31)

He puts them to work with saws, axes, and picks. He also makes them labor at his brick kilns.

DIMENSION TWO:
WHAT DOES THE BIBLE MEAN?

Background Information on 2 Samuel 9–12

With 2 Samuel 9 we encounter one of the truly sublime prose narratives in all of the Old Testament. This narrative continues all the way through 1 Kings 2. The author of this material was someone very close to David's court, who knew the intimacies and intrigues of the personal lives of the royal household. Quite possibly this narrative is an eyewitness source.

Most scholars consider this section to be historically reliable and accurate. The details have not been altered for political or theological reasons. This is quite a contrast with the earlier narratives about Samuel and Saul that we have studied previously. Any serious student of the Bible cannot help but recognize and appreciate the literary diversity of the historical books. But there is also a commonality in the providential guidance of the Lord.

The divine inspiration of this material lies not in its historical or factual reliability, but in its capacity to capture and portray the profound theological dimension of existence. In its final form, the Bible was written from the standpoint of faith, and must be interpreted also from the standpoint of faith.

When the Bible presents an accurate reconstruction of events, we receive a bonus in our quest for understanding. The narratives about David's associates and the intimate details of their personal lives give us a close look at one of the most exciting periods of Israel's history. David's reign in Jerusalem is filled with ups and downs. Through the careful work of an early Israelite history writer, we can relive these days.

This large block of material (2 Samuel 9–1 Kings 2) is called by scholars the Court History of David, or the Throne-Succession Narrative. The latter name focuses on the major theme of these chapters, that of determining David's successor.

The brief family histories in 2 Samuel 3:2-5 and 5:13-16 indicate the substantial list of claimants to David's throne. Amnon and Absalom are the two leading candidates, with Solomon far down on the list. The sordid events precipitated by these first two sons, along with others close to the throne, are an embarrassment to generations of Israelites. Only a person very close to the royal household could have known of such activities within the royal family. David was a military success. But as a father, he left much to be desired.

The throne-succession narrative is one of the literary masterpieces in the Old Testament. Its portrayal of characters, their motivations, and their illicit behavior is almost matchless in the Bible. The real purpose of the narratives is to justify Solomon's accession to the throne. But in the meantime, it provides us with a reliable witness to the times of King David.

2 Samuel 9. The terse, but polite dialogue between David and Ziba is typical of ancient Near Eastern etiquette. Commoners utter few words in the presence of the king. Also, Ziba is probably uncertain as to David's real motives. That Ziba is identified as a servant is not a commentary on his economic condition. Verse 10 indicates that Ziba himself has twenty servants.

David's restoration of family lands to Mephibosheth carries him far beyond his ordinary covenant obligations. David honors a potential threat who, although he is lame in both feet, has sired a son that might one day lay claim to the throne of his great-grandfather. Of course, by restoring this lad to a favored position, David can keep a watchful eye on him and his son. David's loyalty to Jonathan, his friend, blends well with political realism.

2 Samuel 10:1–11:1; 12:26-31. As indicated in the student book, the Ammonite and Aramean wars are the setting for the story of David and Bathsheba in Chapters 11 and 12. Therefore, the events are narrated in a brief fashion.

The victories described enable David to double or even triple his sphere of influence. With the defeat of Zobah, David's control extends almost to the Euphrates River. While he may not have actually claimed the throne of Zobah, he did force them to make favorable treaties with him and provide him with some form of tribute.

Also, David now controls most of the inhabited areas east of the Jordan, including Moab and Edom (8:12). For Israel to develop from a loose assortment of tribes and a small volunteer army during the days of the judges into a large state with a competent and well-trained army is no small accomplishment. Much of this success comes under King David and his son, Solomon.

David's army consisted of three components. The largest fighting force was known as the host of Israel, under the command of Joab. This group was a general army that included men from all the tribes under David's rule. The second group was a type of highly trained militia, known as "the mighty men." This small but effective contingent was under the command of Abishai, Joab's brother. Finally there was David's personal army under the command of Benaiah.

Understanding his opposition, David calls out only the mighty men. When Joab finds himself overcome by the Ammonites and Arameans, he divides his small army. Although grossly outnumbered by the opposition, Joab and Abishai win a great victory and the Arameans flee. Much of David's success can be attributed to his highly skilled army and effective military leadership.

David's defeat of the Ammonites (12:26-31) greatly enriched his treasury. The brick industry provided considerable revenue for the royal treasury. Also, the additional labor David acquired doubtless contributed to the massive building program David began. Further to the north, on Zobah, David's conquests netted him copper ore and other metals of value. Thus in addition to the political and military advantages resulting from these wars, David profited financially and Israel began to acquire more wealth than she had ever imagined. Under Solomon, David's son, this wealth became legendary.

2 Samuel 11:2–12:25. In assessing the significance of this story in the traditions of early Israel, it is important to note that the author of Chronicles omits the Bathsheba affair. Most of the other events of David's life are included in the Chronicles version. But because of the embarrassing picture it conveys of a morally weak king, the Chronicler chose not to include it. To the author of Chronicles such a story detracted from the lofty image of David as a national hero. David's sins were not a source of national pride. But for the writer of Second Samuel, God's kingdom does not rise or fall on the moral or immoral behavior of a single individual. That is why our present narrative includes the story of David and Bathsheba.

The introduction to the story contains several pertinent details. Eliam, mentioned in 11:3, appears again in 23:34 as the son of Ahithophel. If this is the same Ahithophel who joins Absalom in a conspiracy against David (15:12), he would have had good reason for his hatred of David. After all, the king brought shame and disgrace to his house through his granddaughter. Also, it is not unusual for David to remain at home and allow Joab and the troops to conduct warfare. The setting is perfectly told and makes the events occur within the bounds of normal activity.

To find Uriah, who is of Hittite ancestry, serving in David's army is not surprising. What is important is the moral and religious character of Uriah, surpassing that of King David. The contrast between David and Uriah is intentional! Uriah refuses to go home to relax both out of obligation to his colleagues and allegiance to holy war bans. There are no indications that he suspected David and Bathsheba were having an affair. It is precisely Uriah's unimpeachable character that makes David's immoral conduct so offensive.

David's conspiracy to have Uriah killed compounds the sin of adultery with the crime of murder. The narration of Uriah's death indicates none of the inner feelings of the participants. Bathsheba mourns the death of Uriah, possibly for public appearances. But none of the characters involved acknowledge their guilt.

The reference to Abimelech (verse 21) points to an incident reported in Judges 9:53-54. As here, Abimelech gets too close to a wall and is killed. Uriah's precarious position directly leads to his death. And David, not Joab, is to blame.

Nathan's famous parable of the poor man's lamb has become a classic for condemning injustice. The advantage of a parable over other forms of discourse lies in its ability to involve the hearers in a moral situation. To their embarrassment or delight, persons hearing parables find themselves in the story, or empathize with the situation.

In the present situation, David's own deep involvement in the parable elicits a response of moral outrage—the man deserves to die. David has been touched at a primal level of human decency, just as we who read the parable are affected by its message. The cruel and insensitive theft of personal property is an offense of the highest magnitude. It cannot go unchecked.

David's sins affect both God and other persons. He has despised the word of the Lord, slain Uriah, and taken his wife. By law, premeditated murder demands expiation by blood, and in this case is ultimately satisfied by the death of the child. David's repentance (12:13) gains a reprieve for his own life. But the promise of violence and crime in his own family remains. Thus while God forgives the repentant sinner and spares his life, the social effects of his sin remain.

With the death of the child, David's sins are set aside before God. It seems tragic that a young life is taken to atone for the sins of the parents. However, we are not asked to judge the fairness of such a belief. The death of the child indicates the seriousness of David's sin. To dwell on the sad and tragic results is to miss the real point of the biblical narrative. David's deed was a capital offense. God's verdict is irrevocable.

DIMENSION THREE: WHAT DOES THE BIBLE MEAN TO ME?

2 Samuel 11:1-13—Sin and Punishment

Chapters 11 and 12 abound with important theological issues, most of which relate to the broader issues of human sin and divine punishment. The situation is dramatized more highly because the chief agent of sin and its consequences is King David, the Lord's anointed leader. Not that David's sin is greater than the sins of others, but precisely that it is not less, is one of the prime messages of this unit. Accordingly, David must face divine judgment for his behavior, just as any other person would.

The God of the Old Testament expects moral obedience from all persons, regardless of their status. Adultery is wrong, no matter who is involved. Hebrew law is quite clear about adultery, for both the man and the woman. If they are guilty, then they shall both be put to death (Leviticus 20:10). This law applied to king as well as to ordinary citizen.

David and Bathsheba are guilty of a breach of divine law, and the result of their sinfulness is judgment. We must also remember that their sin touched the lives of many other persons. Human sin is rarely a private matter.

There is something painfully true in the idea of a double standard of morality. As parents, we are guilty of this unfairness when we impose regulations on our children for the sake of health and yet abuse our own bodies through excessive use of alcohol and tobacco. Congressional leaders are guilty of a double standard when they publicly oppose increases in taxes yet continually raise their own salaries or pad their expenditures. Ministers are guilty when they condemn social injustice from their pulpits and fail to provide leadership that promotes social change. But the most blatant and debilitating double standards exist in society's laws and customs regarding opportunity for black and white, male and female, poor and wealthy.

In truth, most of us are guilty of using some type of double standard. Ask class members to suggest instances of double standards they have experienced. How can concerned Christians begin to rectify these injustices?

2 Samuel 11:26-27—God and Human Weakness

The second theological issue arising from these chapters concerns God as the primary motivator of history. In the earlier stories of Samuel, Saul, and David, we saw how God worked through the lives of men and women to bring about the divine will for the people. Through Samuel and Saul, God began to move from divine leadership under the judges to leadership by means of kings. Nathan, a prophet, now becomes a spokesman for God, giving added prominence to the prophet as an authorized messenger of God. And David is God's own choice as the founder of a dynasty to rule over the people of God.

In all these episodes, we see the active hand of the Lord directing the affairs of history. And God uses ordinary human beings to carry out the divine will. Ordinary human beings occasionally exhibit sin. Characters such as Noah, Abraham, Jacob, Moses, and even David are all subject to temptations of disobedience. And from time to time they falter. But God's kingdom moves forward in spite of human weakness.

That God has ultimate responsibility for directing history means that we live under divine grace, not under law. David committed a serious sin against God and received judgment despite his favored position before God. But he was also a repentant sinner who, in addition to judgment, also received God's forgiveness.

Faith demands obedience to God's will as it comes through Scripture, tradition, and experience. God's Spirit helps determine our obligations toward God and others. God's Spirit strengthens our ability to fulfill these obligations and to love as Christ loved. But we are still fallible human beings. We stand accountable before God to receive judgment.

We do not have to be morally perfect to be acceptable before God. God loves us just as we are. Like David, you and I are prone to instances of disobedience. Also like David, we must accept judgment. And just as David did, we know that when we truly acknowledge our sins, we find forgiveness in the grace of God. The atonement of Christ means that God no longer requires innocent blood as expiation for sin.

Jesus' suffering, death, and resurrection change the way of obtaining forgiveness. Our own sincere repentance and faith in Christ are sufficient. This difference between Old and New Testaments becomes clear as we reflect on the deeper theological implications of this story. David, too, lived under grace and received divine forgiveness, but the innocent child had to atone for his sin. In Christ, our atonement is already made.

At the close of today's session, ask the class members to share any new insights on 2 Samuel 9–12. Then list these insights on chalkboard or a large sheet of paper.

—— 11 ——

Absalom's Rebellion

2 Samuel 13–16

DIMENSION ONE: WHAT DOES THE BIBLE SAY?

Answer these questions by reading 2 Samuel 13

1. How is Tamar related to Absalom? (13:1)

   Tamar is Absalom's sister.

2. How does Amnon feel about Tamar? (13:1-2)

   Amnon loves Tamar very much.

3. What does Amnon do to Tamar? (13:14-18)

   Amnon rapes Tamar and sends her away.

4. How does Absalom respond to Amnon's abuse of Tamar? (13:23, 28)

   Two years later, at a sheep-shearing festival, Absalom instructs his men to kill Amnon.

5. Where does Absalom seek refuge? (13:37)

   Absalom flees to Talmai, king of Geshur.

Answer these questions by reading 2 Samuel 14

6. Who wants David to bring Absalom back to Jerusalem? (14:1-2)

   Joab wants to bring Absalom back.

7. How does Joab convince David to bring Absalom back? (14:1-20)

   Joab sends a wise woman to remind David of the dangers of being without an heir to his throne.

8. How does David treat Absalom when he returns to Jerusalem? (14:24, 28)

   David will not see Absalom and makes him live in his own house.

9. Why does Absalom set fire to Joab's barley field? (14:29-30)

   Absalom sets the field ablaze because Joab has ignored his repeated summons.

Answer these questions by reading 2 Samuel 15

10. How does Absalom gain popularity among the men of Israel? (15:1-6)

    Absalom stands beside the city gate and judges disputes between citizens.

11. How does Absalom plot to gain the throne? (15:7-10)

    Under the pretext of going to worship the Lord at Hebron, Absalom really intends to revolt against David.

12. What does David do after hearing about Absalom's conspiracy? (15:14)

    David and his troops flee from Jerusalem.

13. How does Ittai, the Gittite, show loyalty toward David? (15:21)

    Ittai chooses to accompany the king wherever he goes.

14. What sacred object does David leave behind? (15:25)

    The ark of God [the covenant] is left behind.

15. Who does David ask to become a spy? (15:32-34)

    He asks Hushai the Arkite to spy on Absalom.

Answer these questions by reading 2 Samuel 16

16. What charge does Ziba bring against Mephibosheth? (16:3)

    He says that Mephibosheth is staying in Jerusalem so that he can regain his father's kingdom.

17. What does David do? (16:4)

   David gives all of Mephibosheth's possessions to Ziba.

18. Why does Shimei curse the fleeing king? (16:7-8)

   Shimei curses David to condemn him for taking the monarchy from the house of Saul.

19. What is David's reaction to Shimei's cursing? (16:10-11)

   David refuses to allow harm to Shimei, thinking that this may be part of the Lord's punishment.

20. What advice does Ahithophel give Absalom? (16:21)

   Ahithophel advises Absalom to have sexual relations with David's concubines.

DIMENSION TWO: WHAT DOES THE BIBLE MEAN?

Background Information on 2 Samuel 13–16

Since King David has several wives, determining who will succeed him as king presents a problem. If the matter is settled by chronological age, then Amnon, the eldest, is first in line. Chileab is next, then Absalom, and so on. Solomon is far down the line. But succession is not guaranteed by birthright. The leader must have the blessings of God and popular support, as had David, Samuel, and Saul in his early days. The following chapters tell of a power struggle that eventually climaxes in 1 Kings 2, with the accession of Solomon.

The days preceding Solomon's kingship are filled with intrigue, mystery, and even murder. David is a better military man than he is a politician. As a result his rule is marked by treason, rebellion, and civil strife. Yet he prevails as God's anointed servant, and his dynasty continues.

Comparing the space allocated to the internal problems of David's palace with the space devoted to David's military conquests gives us an idea of the importance of David's problems. Almost three chapters (2 Samuel 5, 8, and 10) are devoted to David's military conquests. But, it requires Chapters 13–19 to describe David's domestic problems with his sons, as prophesied by the Lord (2 Samuel 12:11). The Bible is more concerned with God's relationship to David and to his son Absalom, than with David's success as a general. In Amnon's rape of Tamar, Absalom's murder of Amnon, and Absalom's rebellion, God calls David to account for his sins with Bathsheba and against Uriah.

The stories of David's problems with Absalom help explain how Solomon eventually succeeded David as king over Israel. The linkage of retribution within David's own family to Solomon's accession as king is brought about by the Lord's direction of history. These two themes compliment each other, and provide ample theological reason for Solomon's eventual rule as king.

2 Samuel 13. The parallel between David's adultery with Bathsheba and Amnon's rape of Tamar can hardly be coincidental—both actions violate sexual laws and customs. Also, David's responsibility for Uriah's death and Absalom's responsibility in Amnon's death form intentional parallels. This intertwining of motifs dramatizes the fulfilling of Nathan's prophecies against David (12:10-11). The real meaning of these episodes within David's family is larger than the personal actions of the principal characters, and in order to understand the meaning of these events we must look at them from a theological viewpoint. Amnon's rape of Tamar and Absalom's revenge must be interpreted not as personal acts of immorality, but as fulfillment of the Lord's judgment against David.

Most of David's sons, along with their mothers and sisters, probably live outside the royal palace in their own private homes. Some sons, such as Amnon, may have even lived alone (13:7).

In Hebrew the word *crafty* basically means "wise." The particular meaning in 13:3 derives from Jonadab's involvement in an immoral plan. He uses his wisdom for morally questionable purposes. Later, when David believes all of his sons are dead after the sheepshearing incident, Jonadab is the one who corrects the rumors and explains Absalom's motives. His wisdom is his ability to make the most of every opportunity.

Amnon's love for Tamar is exclusively physical in nature. As soon as his physical needs are met, his affection turns to contempt. Such shallow love contrasts greatly with genuine concern for the well-being of another person.

A great deal of emphasis is placed on the fact that Tamar is a virgin. Ordinarily, virgins are given special protection, since they are of immense political value. Amnon's initial torment is caused partially by Tamar's invulnerability—"it seemed impossible for him [Amnon] to do anything to her." Only by using cunning is he able to be alone with her. Tamar's rape is a traumatic and inhumane violation of her personal dignity. It also lessens her usefulness in a political marriage. She now must spend the rest of her life in shame and disgrace.

Tamar pleads with Amnon, appealing to his sense of social practice ("such a thing should not be done in Israel") and his dignity ("you would be like one of the wicked fools in Israel"). However, her logic falls on deaf ears. Not even the suggestion of marriage tempers Amnon's passion. But to make matters even worse, Amnon sends her away. He is totally devoid of moral conscience or sensitivity. Yet David, his father, does not punish him.

Absalom's revenge against Amnon serves two purposes. First, it satisfied family obligations for the crime committed against his sister. He attempts to restore his sister's honor and gain revenge. Since David does not punish Amnon, Absalom takes matters into his own hands and executes judgment ruthlessly. Second, by Amnon's death, Absalom is closer in succession to David's throne. The Bible does not mention Kileab, the son between Amnon and Absalom in age. Following Amnon's death, Kileab should have become heir apparent. Judging from the appeal made in Chapter 14 for Absalom's return, Absalom, not Kileab, was next in line. In fact, after 2 Samuel 3:3, Kileab is never mentioned again.

2 Samuel 14. Joab understands that proper provisions for succession to the royal throne are important in any kingdom, especially a new one like Israel. As we have already observed, Saul's kingdom collapsed following his death and the weak, ineffective leadership of Ish-Bosheth. A recognized successor to David is important now. Absalom must return to Jerusalem.

Joab's plan, however, is out of character, for he is usually direct and blunt with the king. Here, he devises an indirect plan, similar to Nathan's parable of the lamb. The fictitious story by the wise woman from Tekoa involves David in a difficult legal case that places governmental law against custom and tradition. Clearly the seriousness of the legal issues involved explain why David himself handles the case. Next to God, the king is the final authority and he hears the most difficult cases. Here the matter of bloodguilt, as sanctioned by custom, stands in the way of the preservation of a family name. Will the legal structures allow bloodguilt to permanently end the name of this family?

David's response that the name must be preserved commits him to see that Absalom is returned. His intense, personal involvement in the case exposes his own family and national dilemma—who will succeed David if Absalom dies in a foreign land? Joab knows the people of Israel fear the loss of leadership. David must bring Absalom back home.

David's delay in reconciling with Absalom (two years) shows poor judgment. If leniency was David's fault with Amnon, severity is now his problem with Absalom. If David had a better relationship with his son, the later revolt could possibly have been avoided. No doubt, Absalom grew resentful during this two-year period of separation and may have devised a scheme to get even with his father. The belated reconciliation (verse 33) is insufficient to assuage Absalom's hatred of his father.

In the Bible Absalom is pictured as a true son of David. He is handsome and a man of good presence. He is immensely popular with the people and has a large following when he starts his rebellion. Absalom defends the honor of his family and judges legal complaints fairly. But, also like David, he is a man of passion, emotion, and impatience. He is not above taking the law into his own hands. Such similarities in character are not accidental.

2 Samuel 15:1-12. Impatient to begin his rule and uncertain that David will name him successor, Absalom boldly sows the seeds for a full-scale rebellion to insure his enthronement. Heredity is not yet an established pattern of succession, as evidenced by the elders of Israel naming David king. Absalom takes matters into his own hands and begins by undermining David's popular support.

Absalom sets himself up as a staunch defender of human rights. As the men of the northern tribes of Israel pass in and out of Jerusalem, Absalom listens sympathetically to their cases. His natural attractiveness, combined with his royal entourage, must have impressed everyone. Also, some people in Israel probably believe David's hands are still bloody from the death of Saul's family.

Absalom's popularity grows, until at last, he goes to Hebron to begin the revolt. Political rhetoric once again sways public sentiment. The expression, "he [Absalom] stole the hearts of the men of Israel," means the people shifted their allegiance to Absalom because they thought he would give them a better deal than David. Persons who are frustrated with an existing judicial system will follow someone who takes their side. Absalom does not attract the deep loyalty and intense devotion from these citizens that his father had attracted. But, Absalom is the hero of the hour.

Since the Lord can be worshiped at Hebron, David is not suspicious when Absalom goes there. Absalom, David likely reasons, is merely returning to his birthplace to worship. Hebron is an excellent site from which to launch a rebellion. The people of Hebron possibly are still angry that David relocated his capital in Jerusalem. And Hebron is an important tribal center in Judah, where leaders from the South assemble and discuss important matters. Absalom can pick up important support from these leaders. The great sacrificial feast Absalom holds gives religious substance to his cause.

The two hundred persons who accompany Absalom to Hebron seem to know nothing of Absalom's plans. Although their identity is not stated, they are probably civic, business, and government leaders whose expertise would be valuable to Absalom once he usurps the royal throne. In truth, these two hundred persons are innocent participants in a precarious position. If they stay with the prince, David will view them as traitors. But if they attempt to escape and return to Jerusalem, Absalom will have them killed. Ahithophel probably wishes to see David humiliated and deposed because of his affair with Bathsheba, his granddaughter.

The cry "Absalom is king in Hebron" has been preceded by four years of careful preparation. Absalom has used every possible means to capitalize on weaknesses in David's judicial system and to muster widespread public sympathy in both the North and the South. His plan is to overwhelm David by massive popular support. Absalom thinks his large army will be able to defeat the small contingent of troops left to David. Surprise and numbers are Absalom's allies.

2 Samuel 15:13–16:14. The scene of David leaving Jerusalem conveys the atmosphere of a ritual ceremony rather than a military operation. The public mourning (verse 23) when David leaves is an expression of public lament. Weeping, being barefoot, and covering his head as David goes up the

Mount of Olives suggests rituals of grief. Being driven from Jerusalem and insulted by Shimei are punitive actions against the king for his sins. The entire community and its leaders are purged by means of ritual humiliation as David flees Jerusalem. The religious overtones of this procession out of Jerusalem are difficult to overlook. David is suffering for his sins, but at the same time, he is being purged and forgiven by God.

No clear explanation is given for David's hasty decision to leave his fortress at Jerusalem. Certainly, he fears Absalom (verse 14) and is concerned about the city. But is his defense system really so weak as to be seriously threatened by Absalom's rebellion? Perhaps he fears internal conspiracy and desires to spare the city possible destruction.

David still has total control of his personal bodyguard and the "mighty men" (23:8). His support within the city is still strong and extensive. Perhaps if we knew who the two hundred men from Jerusalem were that accompanied Absalom to Hebron (15:11), we could assess David's internal strength. Also, the city's fortifications are strong enough to defend the city against Absalom's inexperienced army. On other occasions, Jerusalem defended itself against stronger armies. Other factors, unknown to us, must have prompted David to seek safer territory east of the Jordan.

The claim (verse 13) that "the hearts of the men of Israel are with Absalom" is probably exaggerated. The extent of Absalom's support in either Israel or Judah is impossible to know. A major shift in loyalties on the part of many people has occurred, but David retains the loyalty of many others. Quite possibly the number of defectors to Absalom has been enlarged to deepen David's personal humiliation. The greater Absalom's rebellion appears, the more profound is David's suffering and shame.

David is accompanied by his royal household. Ten concubines are left to care for the palace. His many wives, children, and servants all join in the march. Next come his personal bodyguards and then the foreign mercenaries. The evacuation route is marked by designated stops for the purpose of review and public display. Again, we see the ritual elements of a mourning procession.

Loyalty to David is another important theme underlying these incidents. Ittai, a resident alien from Gath, chooses to follow David rather than wait and join Absalom. The Kerethites and Pelethites also stay with David. The priests carrying the ark, Abiathar and Zadok, attempt to join the group, but return to Jerusalem to be spies for David. Hushai, David's friend, is also sent back to Jerusalem. He is needed to implement a counter-intelligence plan. An opportunistic Ziba even shows up with provisions and drink for the weary travelers. The citizens-at-large remain loyal in David's time of need.

Finally, as the procession nears Bahurim, eight or nine miles northeast of Jerusalem, Shimei comes out to curse the king and throw stones at him. David thinks this is part of his punishment. David's understanding of these actions to be more than the insults of an angry Benjaminite reflects insight on his part. His confidence in the Lord has not wavered. His present humiliation is clearly God's doing. Shimei is thus playing a role in God's plans.

2 Samuel 16:15-23. By gaining Absalom's confidence, Hushai puts himself in a position to challenge Ahithophel's counsel. Also, when Absalom publicly possesses David's concubines, he destroys any possibilities for reconciliation with his father. Absalom has begun a process from which there is no return.

The office of the king's friend must have carried with it special privileges. Hushai seems to have ready access to the kings, both David and Absalom. His counsel is weighed comparably to that of Ahithophel, and Absalom takes his advice. In a list of royal personnel in 1 Kings 4:5, the position of king's friend is cited, but the functions are not described. Absalom's surprise that Hushai would desert his former master so quickly is adequate testimony to the importance of the position. Hushai's strategy in winning over Absalom is not particularly original, but highly effective—he flatters Absalom. Note also that Hushai appeals to both divine benediction and popular acclaim as sources for authorizing kingship. By such means, Hushai distinguishes himself to a dubious Absalom.

David's ultimate humiliation comes when Absalom publicly has sexual relations with the remaining concubines. By this act, the old king is officially dethroned, as the custom goes. Taking David's concubines, Absalom claims all the rights and privileges of a royal throne. Recall how upset Ish-Bosheth became when he thought Abner had taken Rizpah, Saul's concubine. Such an act was a direct challenge to the deposed king.

Verse 23 explains how highly both David and Absalom regard Ahithophel's advice. To compare his counsel with that issued by God is indeed a compliment. Judgments from Ahithophel must be taken seriously. Absalom shows incredible stupidity when he ignores Ahithophel's advice at a crucial moment. He pays for this folly with his life.

DIMENSION THREE: WHAT DOES THE BIBLE MEAN TO ME?

2 Samuel 15:24-29—David's Trust in the Lord

When David sends the ark of the covenant back to Jerusalem, along with its attending priests, he displays a trust in God that is seldom found among persons in the Old Testament. The presence of the ark has historically symbolized the closeness of God to the people. The Israelites carried the ark on their trek in the desert. It accompanied them in their fights for control of Palestine. Its presence in Jerusalem adds a note of religious legitimacy to David's new capital. For David to bring the ark along as he flees from Absalom would indeed have been a kind of insurance policy. It would have been both natural and appropriate. And yet, he sends it back to Jerusalem. Why?

Sending the ark back shows that David trusts the Lord to deal with Absalom's rebellion. In a sense, David releases his physical hold on the power symbol of God's presence. God is now free to act. God can confirm Absalom or reconfirm David. David opens himself to either possibility, trusting that God will do what is right. And David is prepared to accept the consequences of God's choice.

One additional point must be added. David uses any opportunities available to protect himself. He uses the sons of the priest as spies, and he assigns Hushai the responsibility of discrediting the counsel of the famed Ahithophel. He carries the matter as far as he can, then he trusts the Lord. David does not have a passive trust or mindless faith. He uses his own resources to whatever extent possible, then leaves the rest up to God.

Such a model of faith is a goal for us today. We ought to be challenged to do what we can, then back off, and leave the rest up to God. Like David, we must learn to recognize and accept the limitations of our abilities. God's will must become our will, and this means trusting enough to let God lead. This is the power of active submission.

2 Samuel 16:15-23—
Absalom's Trust in Human Counsel

Absalom's impassioned revolt, on the other hand, is a lesson in the folly of relying solely on human wisdom. Impulsively, Absalom always takes matters into his own hands. He never invokes the Lord's blessing, or consults the Lord before initiating a move. His trust is either in himself or in the counsel of others, Ahithophel and Hushai for instance. Absalom neither solicits nor desires the counsel of God's priests. As a result, his actions are frequently disastrous and eventually lead him to a tragic death (2 Samuel 18:15).

Self-reliance and personal initiative are two important qualities. Certainly no one succeeds without them. They represent responsible stewardship of our personal resources, a part of our divine endowment. David certainly makes good use of both of them. But he uses them in conjunction with his faith in God, and trust in divine leadership. He puts his resources at God's disposal and actively seeks divine guidance. In summary, David uses the resources and avenues available to him, and trusts God to complete the matter.

Lead the class in a discussion that compares David's methods with those of Absalom. Then have group members discuss some or all of the questions in Dimension Three of the student book.

Close the session by asking class members to share new insights on 2 Samuel 13–16 and list these insights on chalkboard or a large sheet of paper if time allows.

—12—
David Regains His Throne

2 Samuel 17–20

DIMENSION ONE:
WHAT DOES THE BIBLE SAY?

Answer these questions by reading 2 Samuel 17

1. How does Ahithophel tell Absalom to conquer David? (17:1-2)

   Ahithophel wants to pursue David immediately and attack while David is weary and weak.

2. Who else does Absalom consult? (17:5)

   He consults Hushai the Arkite.

3. How does Hushai's advice differ from Ahithophel's? (17:11)

   Hushai thinks Absalom should wait until he can lead a large army in person.

4. How does Hushai warn David? (17:17)

   Hushai sends word by a servant girl to Jonathan and Ahimaaz who warn David.

5. What does Ahithophel do when he learns that Absalom has disregarded his advice? (17:23)

   Ahithophel commits suicide by hanging himself.

6. Who does Absalom choose to replace Joab as head of his army? (17:25)

   Absalom chooses Amasa as his chief military leader.

7. Who befriends David during his stay at Mahanaim? (17:27)

   Shobi, the Ammonite; Makir from Lo Debar; and Barzillai, the Gileadite aid David.

Answer these questions by reading 2 Samuel 18

8. What does David tell Joab, Abishai, and Ittai as they go out to fight Absalom? (18:5)

   He tells them to deal gently with Absalom.

9. What do Joab and his men do with Absalom when they find him in a tree? (18:14-15)

   Joab hurls three javelins into Absalom's heart, and his men kill Absalom with their swords.

10. How do they bury Absalom? (18:17)

    Absalom is thrown into a pit and covered with rocks.

11. Who tells David of Absalom's death? (18:32)

    An anonymous Cushite servant tells David indirectly that his son is dead.

Answer these questions by reading 2 Samuel 19

12. What does Joab tell David? (19:7-8)

    Joab tells David that he should publicly thank his loyal supporters instead of grieving over a rebellious son.

13. Who does David appoint as commander of his army? (19:13)

    He appoints Amasa, a relative.

14. How does King David treat Shimei? (19:23)

    David pardons Shimei.

15. What does David do after Mephibosheth explains why he did not flee with the king? (19:29)

    David divides Saul's estate equally between Mephibosheth and Ziba.

16. Who does the aged Barzillai send to go with the king? (19:37)

He sends Kimham.

Answer these questions by reading 2 Samuel 20

17. Who leads a minor revolt against David? (20:2)

Sheba son of Bicri leads a revolt.

18. Who kills Amasa? (20:10)

Joab kills Amasa.

19. How does Joab stop the revolt of Sheba without destroying Abel Beth Maacah where Sheba is staying? (20:16-22)

A woman from the city suggests a plan to assassinate Sheba within the city and toss his head over the wall.

20. Who are the officials in David's government at this time? (20:23-26)

Joab commands the army; Benaiah is over the Kerethites and Pelethites; Adoniram is in charge of the forced labor; Jehoshaphat is the recorder; Sheva is secretary; and Zadok, Abiathari, and Ira are priests.

DIMENSION TWO: WHAT DOES THE BIBLE MEAN?

Background Information on 2 Samuel 17–20

Events happen quickly in these chapters. David leaves Mahanaim to return triumphantly to his beloved Jerusalem. But the days are a mixture of deep sadness and great joy for King David. Absalom, his son, is killed as he dangles from a tree where his head has been wedged while he was riding underneath. Amasa, a relative of David, is killed by Joab. But despite these casualties of war, David regains his throne and reunites the tribes of Israel and Judah, at least for the moment.

The substantial amount of detail in these narratives suggests the original writer may have personally witnessed the events. The intimate moods of the king, the effective reprimands of Joab, and the plot of the wise woman from Abel Beth Maacah are the types of information available only to an eyewitness or someone close to the events. Most scholars consider these chapters to be authentic and reliable Old Testament history.

While the main purpose of these narratives is to describe the internal struggle in determining a successor to David, the events retold in 2 Samuel 9–20 also reveal a surprising amount of political unrest. Absalom's rebellion provides the focal point for much of this uneasiness. There appears

to be much dissatisfaction in Israel over David's judicial system. The tribes of Judah are unhappy that the capital was moved from Hebron to Jerusalem. The Benjaminites still believe that David is guilty for the deaths of Saul and his children. The family of Ahithophel, Bathsheba's grandfather, still lives under the scandal of Bathsheba's affair.

The revolts of Absalom and Sheba (2 Samuel 20) seem to be only part of the political restlessness. The peace and prosperity David brought to Israel and Judah are fragile, at best, and conceal deep and abiding conflicts of loyalty. The United Monarchy manages to survive through Solomon's reign, but then it will fall apart. The military power and personal magnetism of David and Solomon form the glue that holds the empire together. And even then, as this lesson shows, the bond weakens at crucial points.

2 Samuel 17. Ahithophel had urged Absalom to claim the ten royal concubines. Here he counsels Absalom for the second time. The advice on military strategy is sound, too. Ahithophel suggests that Absalom allow him to gather an army and pursue David immediately. Such an attack will have the important element of surprise. Traveling slowly because of the presence of women and children, David will be tired and disorganized. The fugitive king has had no opportunity to plan an attack against Absalom. Once David's weary soldiers begin to fall, he can be captured and everyone will run to Absalom as king. The plan would accomplish several desirable goals with minimum destruction and loss of life. David can be captured, his supporters can switch loyalties, and Absalom would be king.

Hushai's plan, on the other hand, sounds impressive but lacks the surprise and speed of Ahithophel's plan. Instead, Hushai advises Absalom to wait and amass a large army and then overwhelm David with numbers. Besides, he argues, David is a great warrior with veteran troops and they are not, as Ahithophel assumes, just waiting around to be attacked. They are hiding in caves and can easily repel a hasty and ill-conceived attack. Rumors will spread about David's slaughter of Absalom's troops and then the entire rebellion would be jeopardized.

Flattery to the new king and notions of a glorious victory sway the hearts of Absalom and his other advisors. Hushai has won. Or perhaps we should say that the Lord won, because it was the Lord who saw that Ahithophel's plan would be rejected. By the Lord's design, Absalom turns to Hushai and follows his advice to reject Ahithophel's plan.

While the final decision is being made, Hushai uses David's counter-intelligence operations. The two sons of Zadok and Abiathar are camping outside the city to avoid incriminating their fathers. A servant girl acts as a courier, since her frequent trips in and out of the city would not arouse suspicion. She makes only one trip to the spies, since Absalom's deliberations follow shortly after his arrival in Jerusalem. David has not yet crossed the Jordan. Following a short delay when they hide to avoid discovery, Jonathan and Ahimaaz warn David, and he escapes over the Jordan to Mahanaim.

DAVID REGAINS HIS THRONE

Suicides are rare in the Old Testament. Saul and his armor-bearer take their own lives (1 Samuel 31:4). Zimri, king of Israel, burns his house with himself inside (1 Kings 16:18). While there are laws prohibiting murder, suicide is not actually condemned in the Old Testament. But neither is it condoned. Since there are so few suicides in the Old Testament, we may conclude that it carried extremely negative connotations.

Amasa's genealogy is confusing. While some commentators feel that Nahash of verse 25 is the same Nahash of Ammon (10:2), this is by no means certain. Also, the relationship of Zuriah, Joab's mother, to Ithra is unclear. Regardless of the actual relationships, the biblical writer explains that Joab and Amasa are related. This kinship later will become an important issue in David's new army when he returns from his exile. Amasa temporarily replaces Joab as commander of the army.

The section concludes with a list of notable persons who befriend David in his time of need. These wealthy and powerful persons exhibit courageous loyalty to their friend, demonstrating once again the theme of loyalty mentioned in the preceding lesson. In passing, note the nutritional value of the foods supplied to David and his contingents; high in protein, vitamins and minerals, and fiber! Modern people are not the only ones who understand the importance of a proper diet.

2 Samuel 18. As an experienced general, David divides his well-trained troops into three divisions. The large numbers (verse 1) probably indicate the relative ranks of the leaders, rather than precise head counts. We cannot be sure of the size of David's army, but certainly it is smaller than Absalom's army. The deployment into three divisions is typical of battle strategies at that time as it permits flanking and pincer operations with a minimum of manpower. David also keeps a few troops in Mahanaim in case things go badly. Joab, Abishai, and Ittai lead the three divisions.

The hilly, rough terrain definitely favors David's small, but skilled and disciplined army. It works against Absalom's large, untrained fighters. The outcome might have been different had the battle taken place in an open field. But the quick-moving, hard-hitting troops of David quickly defeat Absalom's large army. Hushai's delay gave David time to prepare, and almost as quickly as it began, Absalom's revolt ends.

King David wants to lead his army against Absalom, but he is advised against it. Neither the flight of his army, nor the loss of half the men make the difference he makes. "You are worth ten thousand of us," they say (18:3). This concern for David appears again in 2 Samuel 21:17 where he is described as "the lamp of Israel." In a very real sense, the well-being of the nation rests with the king. He is more than a military or political leader. He embodies the national spirit and supplies the national conscience. Through him, the nation realizes its destiny and leaves its mark on the world.

People of the ancient Near East believed that when the gods bless the king, the entire nation receives a blessing. But when the king falters, the well-being of the nation is threatened. So it is understandable that David's men would prefer that he remain at home.

The account of Absalom's death reveals Joab's insight and his boldness. His dialogue with the man who discovers Absalom hanging from the tree is terse and impatient. He completely disregards David's instructions, as well as the king's attachment to his son. Not even the promise of money can tempt the man to kill Absalom.

Joab abruptly ends the conversation and first draws blood from the defenseless Absalom. Joab's ten armor-bearers then kill Absalom. In all likelihood Joab does not do this out of meanness, for remember that Joab secured Absalom's return from exile. Joab considers the security of David's reign and national interest more important than David's feeling for Absalom. He acts for what we might call the good of the nation. Absalom's continued divisiveness could mean nothing but trouble for David's kingdom.

David receives word of the approaching messenger as he sits between the two gates (inside and outside) of the city wall. He hopes the news of the approaching runners is good news. A messenger bearing bad news would probably not run so fast. Since the speedy Ahimaaz outran the Cushite that Joab sent first, he gets to the king first. But his courage fails him at the crucial moment, and he is afraid to tell David that Absalom is dead. The indirect pronouncement of the Cushite (18:31) is hardly better, but at least is sufficient for David to guess the truth. Ordinarily, a victorious king rejoices, but instead David mourns for his son, Absalom. A father's compassion reaches out for the very son who sought to take his crown and kill him. "My son, my son Absalom! If only I had died instead of you!"

2 Samuel 19. David is grief-stricken and mourns in public. Upon learning of Absalom's death, he retires to a chamber just above the city gate and cries loudly. The Bible is sympathetic to David, but there is potential danger in such behavior. Joab, who can sense the mood of the people, confronts David face-to-face with the real dangers of his present conduct. Joab urges him to meet the demands of his royal office. He even threatens the king with mass defection and further rebellions.

Despite all Joab's weaknesses, he is faithful to the king and knows what needs to be done at the moment. Such boldness does not endear him to David because he soon replaces Joab as the commander of the army. But it does spare David further mistakes and enables the Lord's anointed servant to see his duty more clearly. Just as the king blessed his small army when they left the city to fight for him, he now welcomes them back as conquering heroes. He puts aside his grief and does his royal duty.

The remaining sections of the chapter deal with the mounting tension between the tribes of the North and the tribes of the South. Fearing reprisals from David for their role in the rebellion, the men of Judah hesitate to approach David until he makes the first move (19:11-15). The men of Israel, on the other hand, recognize quickly that David is still their best and possibly their only alternative (19:9-10).

Soon after David begins his journey back to Jerusalem, quarreling breaks out between Israel and Judah as to which is closer to the king. While the northern tribes of Israel are hesitant to give up their ancient tribal autonomies, they quickly acknowledge the necessity of David's protective leadership. The South claims blood kin to David. Thus, the fragile union is restored for the moment. Kingship means something different in the North from what it means in the South. The men of Israel find protection and leadership in monarchy, while the South finds divine approval and a dynasty in King David.

On his return trip to Jerusalem, David meets some of the same persons he met when he was leaving. They have all changed their attitude toward David. Shimei now begs forgiveness, claiming that he is the first among the Benjaminites to greet the returning king. Mephibosheth looks bedraggled and pleads that he has been the victim of Ziba's malicious lies. How power elicits renewed loyalty! Individuals and nations flock to regain the favor of the king. Of this number, only the genuine affection of the aged Barzillai has credibility. Serving David while in Mahanaim, presenting the servant Kimham, and accompanying David to the Jordan all signal Barzillai's sincerity.

2 Samuel 20. The unrest among the northern tribes continues when a minor revolt is led by Sheba, the son of Bicri. The Benjaminites are members of Saul's tribe, and the revolt is limited to that tribe. While verse 2 indicates that "all the men of Israel" withdrew at Sheba's command, verse 14 suggests that by the time Sheba reached Abel Beth Maacah, his support had dwindled to only those men of his tribe, the Bicrites. Nevertheless, David does not underestimate the potential threat of further strife. He moves quickly to quell the rebellion, in an attempt to ease the tensions between the North and South.

In 20:1, Sheba is called "troublemaker" because of the trouble he causes with his rebellion. His denial of any form of relationship to David may be caused by latent hostilities surfacing from Saul's tribes. They also may be jealous of David's kinship with families in the South. This same saying is also present in 1 Kings 12:16 when the North splits with the South. In contrast to the dissatisfaction in Israel, "the men of Judah stayed by their king all the way from the Jordan to Jerusalem" (20:2).

The ten concubines (20:3), left behind by David but raped publicly by Absalom, are treated with appropriate care. But since they have been sexually defiled, they are removed from the palace and placed in another house. They are cared for, but David never goes in to them again. In matters of state, individual lives are manipulated at will, regardless of the consequences. The concubines are innocent victims of a political struggle. Like Tamar earlier, they deserve a better fate.

To reward the southern tribes of Judah for their loyal support David names Amasa, a Judahite, as the new commander of the army. Joab disobeyed David once too often and stung the king's conscience one time too many. When Amasa fails to produce the army at the designated time, David turns to Abishai, Joab's brother, to stop Sheba's revolt. Perhaps the king is too proud to reappoint Joab as commander. Also, David knows that it will not be long before Joab assumes control of the army, regardless of his present position. When Amasa learns that the mighty men have left Jerusalem in pursuit of Sheba, he follows them and catches up at Gibeon.

In one of the most brutal and ruthless murders in the Bible, Joab kills Amasa. The corpse is tossed thoughtlessly into a nearby field after too many people stop to stare. No mention is made that Amasa receives proper burial. The troops now are compelled to choose who they will follow and they only have one choice, Joab! This treacherous side to Joab's personality is foreboding and frightening. Even David cannot deal with him (3:39). Fortunately, Joab is loyal to King David.

Sheba's revolt is ended quickly. Accompanied only by a few persons from his own tribe, the Bicrites, Sheba flees to Abel Beth Maacah. This important city in northern Israel is identified as "a mother in Israel" (20:19). Exactly what this expression implies is not altogether clear. It could mean that the city has several smaller villages under its jurisdiction (like a county seat). Or, it may indicate that the city provides order and structure amid the people of God. Certainly the woman who tries to save the city and avoid destruction acts wisely. Joab's elaborate fortifications indicate the seriousness with which he began his assault on the city. No stone would be left standing. Only by her wisdom does the woman avert disaster—at the expense of the rebel, Sheba. The citizens within the city listen to her arguments and agree with her. Sheba must die so their city will be spared.

The list at the end of this chapter in Second Samuel contains David's government officials. During David's reign, persons were obliged to spend a certain amount of time in government work crews. This is called forced labor. Undoubtedly, this practice was unpopular and is one of the principal causes of the final split between Israel and Judah.

DIMENSION THREE: WHAT DOES THE BIBLE MEAN TO ME?

2 Samuel 17:1-23—Confidence in God

Second Samuel 17:14 makes clear that Absalom's rejection of Ahithophel's counsel was no mere accident. "The LORD had determined to frustrate the good advice of Ahithophel in order to bring disaster on Absalom." To understand this verse properly, we must recall David's earlier prayer in 15:31 where he asks God to turn Ahithophel's counsel into foolishness. God answers David's prayer affirmatively. This positive affirmation of David's prayer leaves little doubt as to God's sovereign control over history. The prayers of a sincere individual do not fall upon deaf ears.

Many of us may question from time to time, Does God really hear our prayers? And if God does, Why are we sometimes unaware of the response? Or, How do we know that our prayers are in harmony with God's will? These questions are important because they stand at the heart of Christian faith. History attests to a variety of answers. Each generation must explore these issues anew and discover God's fresh word.

We may lack the insight to understand the nature of prayers properly and we may not particularly like the responses we get. But we may be certain that our prayers do not go unheard. The witness of Scripture is constant, clear, and convincing: God answers prayers.

2 Samuel 18:24-33—Paternal Love

David's famous exclamation has become a byword for a father's anguish, "My son, my son Absalom! If only I had died instead of you." Absalom seems to have been a moral failure as a person. In bloodthirsty revenge, he orders the assassination of his brother, Amnon. He publicly criticizes his father's inept administration of justice, and touts his own case. He "stole the hearts of the people." He stages a major rebellion against his father and even sets out to kill him.

Absalom is completely devoid of filial devotion. His arrogance and impatience push him to destruction. His inglorious death, dangling from a tree, is matched only by the indignity of his nameless burial site. Yet, David grieves over Absalom almost to the point of losing his army because of his lack of gratitude. Perhaps guilt may explain part of David's reaction. However, such a profound confession could not have been caused by guilt alone. Rather, David's anguish was probably the genuine consequence of a father's love for his lost son. Regardless of his behavior, Absalom was still David's own flesh and blood, and his love was not conditional on the boy's conduct. This type of fatherly love does not keep score nor does it hold a grudge. David probably would have indeed exchanged his life for that of his son.

David's love for Absalom is similar to God's love for each of us. No better statement of this truly selfless divine love is to be found anywhere in the Bible than in John 3:16, "For God so loved the world that he gave his one and only Son, that whoever believes in him shall not perish but have eternal life."

When Karl Barth, a famous Swiss theologian of the mid-twentieth century, visited America, a reporter asked him to summarize his theological position in one or two sentences. Barth replied with profound simplicity, "Jesus loves me, this I know, for the Bible tells me so." This love is the good news of the Scripture, Old Testament and New. God loves us just as we are. God allows us the freedom to err and chastens us when we sin. Even so, God still loves us.

Close this session by listing on chalkboard or a large sheet of paper any new insights class members have after studying 2 Samuel 17–20.

The Spirit of the LORD spoke through me (23:2).

— 13 —

The Last Words of David

2 Samuel 21–24

DIMENSION ONE:
WHAT DOES THE BIBLE SAY?

Answer these questions by reading 2 Samuel 21

1. Why is there a famine for three years during the reign of King David? (21:1)

   The Lord is avenging the bloodguilt on Saul for killing the Gibeonites.

2. How does David resolve the claim of the Gibeonites? (21:8-9)

   David takes the remaining sons of Saul and five grandsons and delivers them to the Gibeonites.

3. Who mourns the death of her kinsmen and protects their bodies? (21:10)

   Rizpah, the concubine of Saul, mourns for her sons.

4. What response does her mourning evoke from King David? (21:14)

   David buries Saul and Jonathan in the land of Benjamin.

5. With whom does Israel go to war? (21:15)

   Israel fights against the Philistines.

6. Why is David restrained from participating in further battles? (21:16-17)

   His men do not want to see David, the lamp of Israel, harmed.

7. How are the four Philistine soldiers killed by David and his servants described? (21:22)

   They are descendants of Rapha, the giant of Gath.

Answer these questions by reading 2 Samuel 22

8. How does David describe God in the first part of his hymn? (22:2-4)

   God is described as his rock, his fortress, his deliverer, his shield, the horn of his salvation, his stronghold, his refuge, and his savior.

9. What is about to happen to David before the Lord intercedes? (22:5-6)

   He is on the verge of death.

10. Why is David on the verge of death? (22:18-19)

    His foes are too strong for him.

11. Why does David feel the Lord has rewarded him? (22:24-25)

    David has remained blameless before God.

12. How does the Lord treat the crooked and the haughty? (22:27-28)

    The Lord is shrewd with the crooked and brings low the haughty.

13. Who is this God who helps David? (22:32)

    This God is the Lord.

Answer these questions by reading 2 Samuel 23

14. How does God appear to the just ruler? (23:4)

    He is like the light of the sunrise on a cloudless morning, like the brightness after rain that causes the grass to grow.

15. What has God done for David's house? (23:5)

    God has made an everlasting covenant with David's house.

THE LAST WORDS OF DAVID

16. What are the names of David's mighty men? (23:8-12)

Their names are Josheb-Basshebeth, Eleazar, and Shammah.

17. Who is the leader of the thirty mighty men? (23:18-19)

Abishai is chief.

18. Who is the commander of the bodyguards? (23:22-23)

Benaiah is in charge of the bodyguards.

Answer these questions by reading 2 Samuel 24

19. How does the Lord ask David to punish Israel for her sins? (24:1)

The Lord tells David to take a census of Israel and Judah.

20. How does the Lord punish David for his sin in taking the census? (24:15)

The Lord sends a plague on Israel.

21. What does David do to appease the anger of the Lord? (24:24-25)

David buys the threshing floor of Araunah, erects an altar there, and makes offerings.

DIMENSION TWO: WHAT DOES THE BIBLE MEAN?

Background Information on 2 Samuel 21–24

These chapters conclude the career of King David. They consist of an interesting mixture of hymns, poems, lists of army personnel, census records, war narratives, and other narratives dealing with a variety of subjects. The chronological sequence of some of the narratives is confusing; for example, Chapter 21 should be before Chapter 9. The events they recount belong at earlier periods in David's career.

At first glance, there are some inconsistencies in the narratives. In 24:1, the Lord tells David to take a census, but in 24:10, David begs for God's mercy because he sinned by taking the census. These chapters lack the unity of style and continuity of action characteristic of the earlier chapters in Second Samuel. Even so, they contain important historical information as well as one of the most elegant and inspirational songs in the Old Testament.

Chapters 21 through 24 also change the essential focus of the narrative from the question of succession to a variety of other themes. Since David's reign is coming to a close, the biblical writer has several brief episodes and components and no appropriate place to include them in the narrative. Probably these incidents were not a part of the court history, but needed to be included to lay the foundation for future actions or to explain a problem in the past. So the biblical writer placed them at the end of David's reign as a kind of appendix.

As this section closes, a few brief remarks about David's contributions to Israel's history are in order. David transforms a dozen separate tribes into a united country. While some tribes are reluctant to relinquish their autonomy, David's government is able to withstand rebellion. David's administration is well organized and functions effectively for a young nation. It contains the bureaucracy necessary for a nation to sustain itself. David is an exceptional military leader. He frees Israel permanently from the Philistine threat and extends the limits of his control from northern Syria to the deserts of the Negeb in the south. His army is the best equipped and best trained of the day.

Economically, David brings wealth into an otherwise impoverished country. His conquests of foreign nations increase the national treasury. Finally, David elevates Israelite tribal religion into the official state religion by installing the ark in his new capital, Jerusalem. This close identification of church and state helps pacify political unrest, but it fails to resolve the tensions completely.

But David was not as successful in all areas. He cannot dissolve the deep-seated tensions between the tribes of the North and the tribes of the South. His reign is marred by sporadic revolts. Neither did he come up with a universally acceptable plan for choosing a royal successor. The South clings to the dynastic principle of the proper Davidic heir, but the North prefers charismatic endowment for selecting their kings. Finally, David fails to establish a comprehensive and fair judiciary system. Despite these shortcomings, David is without equal in Israel's history. Many orthodox Jews still await the return of a Davidic-like messiah!

2 Samuel 21:1-14. This narrative has two themes, one theological and the other historical. The theological theme explains the close connection between human conduct, especially on the part of a king, and national well-being. Human sin is met with divine punishment. And this punishment can take the form of natural disasters, such as drought that brings famine. Saul's massacre of the Gibeonites cries for revenge. Proper atonement must be made before God will end the famine. The famine is judgment.

Historically, the narrative explains why David is searching for Saul's relatives in 2 Samuel 9. He cannot find any because he had most of them killed (21:7-9). Despite their obvious dislocation, these verses contribute significantly to our understanding of David and his position before the Lord. He appears as an expiator of guilt rather than an avenger of blood.

The Gibeonites trick Joshua (Joshua 9) into sparing them from destruction during his conquest of Canaan by disguising themselves as travelers from a distant land. They appeal to Joshua for mercy and urge him to make a covenant of peace with them. Since Israel could make peace with foreigners but not with natives, who must be killed, Joshua makes a covenant with the Gibeonites. When he discovers that he has been tricked, he forces the Gibeonites to do manual labor around holy places. They are "wood-cutters and water carriers" (Joshua 9:27). They remain associated with these holy places well into the times of David and Solomon. Evidently Saul conducted a raid against the Gibeonites that is not reported in the Old Testament. Perhaps when Saul killed the priests at Nob for unwittingly helping David, he killed the Gibeonites there, too. Otherwise, his destruction of Gibeonite citizens, whenever it occurred, is an example of Saul's intolerance of non-Israelites. Saul's zealousness for ethnic and religious purity may have gotten out of hand with the Gibeonites as with other non-Israelites (1 Samuel 13, 14, 15; 28:3).

When the Gibeonites insist on revenge rather than money, they draw upon the ancient principle of retaliation in Near Eastern law, *lex talionis* (Exodus 21:23-25; Leviticus 24:19-21). In verse 6, the Gibeonites insist that seven of Saul's sons be sacrificed to wipe away the sin. (In later Hebrew law, money can be received as expiation for sin, as well as offerings.) David turns over two sons and five grandsons of Saul to the Gibeonites. Their bodies are left hanging for several months. Rizpah, Saul's concubine and the mother of two of his sons, protects the bodies until David has them buried properly.

The biblical writer offers a note on divine forgiveness, "After that, God answered prayers in behalf of the land," at the conclusion of the story. David gathers the bones of the sacrificed sons, along with those of Saul and Jonathan, and furnishes a proper burial for everyone. Saul's sins are fully expiated, and proper burial procedures are observed so that the Lord is now satisfied. God ends the drought. A condition of *shalom* (wholeness) has been restored to the community by David's righteousness and honor.

2 Samuel 21:15-22. These stories about David's war against the Philistines center on the giants. The stories are not in historical sequence. Their dislocation in the total history of David stands out sharply. This section should be read in conjunction with 2 Samuel 5:17-25 and 23:8-29. David's ability to send his army north and east to conquer surrounding nations assumes a stable political situation at home. Thus his control of the Philistines must come at the beginning of his reign as king of Israel and Judah rather than at the end. These stories illustrate that the Lord's choice of David gave him the ability to defeat enemies of enormous size and superior strength.

The first episode, in which Abishai saves David's life, makes a case for the unequaled importance of the king in the life of a nation. We are reminded here of an earlier episode, when David is restrained from active participation in quelling Absalom's revolt, "But you are worth ten thousand of us" (18:3). In this passage, David is identified as the "lamp of Israel" (verse 17). In a very real sense, David is the single unifying force in the country. People honor and serve David, not the country he has established. Moreover, the king represents God's new means of guiding the people. So, Abishai and the men insist with good reason that David no longer accompany his troops into battle.

The three stories involving the giants came from folk legends about David's exploits. A legendary race of early Canaanite giants, the descendants of Raphah, appears at various places in the Old Testament. (See Deuteronomy 3:11.) These rather sizable adversaries are almost always overcome by the servants of the Lord. Also, in this section there is a variation of the Goliath story; here, Elhanan slays him. This conflict is resolved in 1 Chronicles 20:5, where it states that Elhanan killed Goliath's brother Lahmi.

All the giants seem to come from the Philistine city of Gath. In 1 Samuel 27:3, David allies himself as a vassal to Achish, king of Gath. David's devoted servant, Ittai, brings mercenary soldiers from Gath to accompany the king as he flees Jerusalem during Absalom's revolt. Gath is even familiar with the popular proverb about David killing "his ten thousands" (1 Samuel 21:11). David's career is thus closely associated with this important Philistine city in more than a casual way.

2 Samuel 22. This elegant and moving hymn of thanksgiving appears also in Psalm 18 with only minor changes. Before its incorporation into Second Samuel, it was probably used in the Temple or in sanctuaries around Israel as part of a liturgy. It may have been used in a national festival or sung on holy days such as the New Year.

Scholars are uncertain whether David actually composed this particular song or whether it was written for him or in honor of him. Evidence within the Old Testament shows that David composed many songs. The tradition is too strong for it to be otherwise. But, not every hymn that bears David's name was written by him.

Regardless of authorship, 2 Samuel 22:2-51 ranks among the superb hymns of the entire Old Testament. It celebrates David's movement from humiliation, almost at the brink of death, to exaltation and triumph by the mighty hand of God. Out of David's own life comes ample testimony to the power and grace of God—just reasons for thanksgiving.

The introduction (verses 1-6), typical of psalms of this type, begins by proclaiming God's act of salvation in delivering David from his enemies. The opening images are appropriate to David's early life as a warrior: "The LORD is my rock, my fortress and my deliverer; / my God is my rock in whom I take refuge, / my shield and the horn of my salvation. / He is my stronghold, my refuge and my savior." Using the graphic imagery of threatening waters, David describes his nearness to death. The enemies remain unnamed, but no less menacing. Confident in God's past action, David confronts his persecutors and prays for divine deliverance.

Responding to David's plea, God moves to the rescue amid a theophany, or manifestation of God (verses 7-16). All of nature trembles at the awesome approach of an angry

God. Fire blazes from God's nostrils and the earth shakes. God quickly responds to the plaintive cry of the faithful servant. Images such as these cause fear and throw the evildoer into instant panic.

The third section of this song describes God's faithful deliverance of David. As we have stressed throughout these lessons, David's history must be understood as a history of God's providential guidance. David became the great leader he is because of God's trust and support in him. David's own life is a curious mixture of humiliation and exaltation, of reward and punishment, of sin and forgiveness. In the images and language of religious worship, this song tells about God's deliverance of David. The references are difficult to relate to specific events in David's life. Yet the generality of the evil and God's subsequent deliverance is precisely what made them meaningful to future generations. David's cry for help is met by God's attentive word of grace.

The hymn concludes with resounding affirmations of God's deliverance. This confidence and assurance are based on David's own experience, and give cause for others to trust God also, for as God delivered David, so too will God deliver others. In the larger scheme of things, God's victory over the forces of evil is also our victory; David's thanksgiving song can become our own song of thanksgiving.

2 Samuel 23:1-7. This beautiful and moving poem offers us an incomparable theological estimate of King David and his reign. In Hebrew, the carefully composed metrical structure is perfectly balanced and harmonious. Unfortunately, a poorly preserved Hebrew text renders many words unclear, but the meter is still clear. Most scholars believe that David himself wrote the poem.

Following the forthright and flattering self-introduction in verse 1, David describes himself as living under the influence of the Spirit of the Lord, that is, charismatic endowment. As in the preceding psalm of thanksgiving, David faithfully attributes his successes to the Lord's guidance. This charismatic gift links David with the great Israelite leaders of the past: Moses, Joshua, the judges, and Samuel. The three similies from nature are powerful images. The association of the sun and the justly rule of kings in the ancient Near East is well known. Both sun and water are essential to life and the king is essential to the well-being of the nation. He is the "lamp of Israel."

The blessings are extended also to the house of David. Here, the reference is to the Davidic covenant (2 Samuel 7:4-17). God will honor the promises to David of fame, peace and rest for Israel, and a dynasty. The godly rule is to continue through David's children for generations to come. Everything is "arranged" (verse 5) just as God established order at Creation and it will continue through the rule of David and his sons.

2 Samuel 23:8-39. Within David's personal militia the highest recognition went to a small, select group known as *the Three.* This special threesome were Josheb-Basshebeth, Eleazar, and Shammah. Their deeds were not merely brave or even exceptionally striking, but their heroic actions furthered the Lord's cause during a religious war. Membership in the Three highlights their special service to the Lord as well as military bravery. Acts of faith, then, are also acknowledged by inclusion among the Three.

The incident at Adullam enriches the earlier narratives in 5:18 and 21:16. David has not yet rid the land of the Philistines. His comment about wishing for water from a well near his native Bethlehem should not be taken as a statement of need, but as a casual observation. His men, possibly "the three" mentioned above, however, take him seriously. They fetch David the special water at great personal risk. But David is unable to refresh himself at such a risk to his men. Graciously, he pours out the water as a religious ritual. His concern for the well-being of his men attracts loyalty and devotion that lasts even through his later humiliations at the hand of Absalom.

The "mighty men" consisted of thirty men, at any given time, including Joab, Abishai, Asahel, Benaiah, and others. An expanded version of this list appears in 1 Chronicles 11:10-41. These men came from Judah and Israel and a few, like Uriah the Hittite, are resident aliens.

2 Samuel 24. In order to understand the connections among three incidents (a census, a plague, and the construction of an altar), one must look to the end of the narrative pointing forward to the eventual construction of the Temple. The entire sequence of events is related. David's census, albeit demanded by God, causes divine anger and leads to a great plague. Just as the angel threatens Jerusalem with death, God's anger abates and the plague stops. At the place David experiences the angel, he purchases land and constructs an altar. This site is used by King Solomon for the Temple. Theologically, we move from judgment (the plague) to blessing (the Temple). The emphasis is on God's guidance in choosing a location for the Temple.

It is difficult to determine why the census is so unpopular. Perhaps it is perceived as an infringement on ancient tribal freedoms. Verse 9 indicates a military purpose for the census, possibly for a future military draft. Joab's objections fall on deaf ears; so he begins the census at the southeastern portion, and goes in a circular pattern ending in Beersheba. The almost unbelievably high number (1,300,000 fighting men) indicates both the enormous task at hand as well as the tremendous size of David's empire. Most scholars question these numbers as being too large for that area at that time.

The appearance of Gad the prophet (see also 1 Samuel 22:5) signifies the seriousness of David's sin and God's displeasure. Gad seems to be an official advisor on religious matters similar to Nathan. David never lacks for a means of communication to the Lord. The options for punishment the Lord offers David range in duration by lengths of three—three years, three months, and three days. The king wisely rejects judgment by peer and leaves it up to the Lord to decide between famine and plague. God sends an angel to bring plague, and for three days he brings death to Israel. Only the mercy of God spares Jerusalem.

David experiences a true theophany on the site where the angel stops. This spot, henceforth, is holy. David purchases it from Araunah and constructs an altar. The sacrifice David then offers God serves as an expiation for the plague. What began as sin—the census—now ends in blessing.

DIMENSION THREE: WHAT DOES THE BIBLE MEAN TO ME?

2 Samuel 21:1-6; 24:1-17—God and Nature

Two principal disasters occur in these chapters, a famine and a plague. According to the Bible, the famine is the result of Saul's bloodguilt against the Gibeonites. When appropriate expiation is made in the form of the death of seven members of Saul's house, the drought ends and the rains come. A plague besets Israel because of David's sin regarding the census. When the Lord intervenes, the messenger of death ceases. For different reasons, God is angry and directs the punishment through the natural order. God caused the famine and the plague.

We have difficulty appropriating the belief that God directly causes events in nature. Such a difficulty obviously arises from our commitment to a scientific view of the world where all events have natural causes. And these causes can eventually be known and understood. Few persons today believe God orders hurricanes or tornadoes to happen. Diseases afflict persons because of germs. We even hope soon to eliminate disease and natural catastrophes, or at least temper their devastation and ruin.

This conflict in world views has led to much controversy in the church, in public education, and elsewhere. Excessive and erroneous claims have been made on both sides. The bottom line is that there is a difference in assumptions. The scientist works with observable and measurable data and hypotheses that carry high probability. The theologian works in the area of meaning and value, and with the belief that nature does not exhaust reality.

The positive results of science and technology make our lives easier, healthier, and happier. But at base, humankind is a religious creature, born of and for fellowship with God. To view natural events from a theological perspective is to step outside the capability of the scientist. It is to make a confession of faith. And this faith is precisely the perspective of the Bible.

2 Samuel 21:15-22—Politics and Faith

In the study of David and his kingship, it is impossible to divorce politics and religion. David constantly seeks divine guidance before undertaking a military venture. He brings the ark into his royal city. He acknowledges his sins on several occasions, and pleads for God's mercy. As we pointed out in Lesson 11, David, in his confidence of divine election, serves as an excellent model of faith. In his magnificent poem (23:1-7), he points out the positive results of a king who rules by the faith of God. Such a king brings light out of the darkness, hope out of despair, and nurture for his people. David's rule embodies these qualities. Although David committed many sins, he nevertheless acknowledges his guilt and tries harder to be an obedient servant. There is a unity here between a ruler's faith and his leadership.

Honorable, competent, and credible political leadership is just as important today as it was then. The general citizenry is still dependent on government officials to sponsor and implement proper laws. A crisis in a country's leadership is felt by everyone. Injustice, oppression, and discrimination gnaw away at the fabric of society if not checked by sensitive and value-conscious politicians. The church can no longer afford to remain silent in the American process for choosing political leadership. We must aid and support officials whose values arise from a deep and abiding faith in God. They must be well trained and expert in politics, but they must also rule "in the fear of God." For leaders to have values and beliefs shaped by the Christian faith is no abridgement of separation of church and state.

Close today's session by listing on chalkboard or a large sheet of paper any new insights class members have on 2 Samuel 27–31. You may want to set aside time at a later date for a general review of First and Second Samuel.

1 AND 2 KINGS
1 AND 2 CHRONICLES
Table of Contents

About the Writer

Charles R. Britt wrote these lessons on First and Second Kings and First and Second Chronicles. At the time of writing, he was assistant professor of family and child development at Auburn University, Auburn, Alabama. He is ordained as a United Methodist minister in the Alabama-West Florida Conference and is now retired.

INTRODUCTION TO
FIRST AND SECOND KINGS

by Linda B. Hinton*

First and Second Kings are part of a great history. Joshua, Judges, Ruth, First and Second Samuel, and First and Second Kings (grouped as the Former Prophets in the Hebrew Bible) are chapters in the saga of the Hebrew people in the Promised Land. They tell the story of the settlement of the land, the rise of the nation as a political unit, its division into two kingdoms, and its absorption by Assyria and Babylon.

Samuel and Kings were once one book, divided into four parts when scrolls were still used. The Septuagint (the oldest Greek translation of the Old Testament) named First and Second Samuel as the first and second books of the "Kingdoms" and First and Second Kings as the third and fourth books of the "Kingdoms." Our English title *Kings* is a translation of the original Hebrew title.

Content in the Books of Kings

The content of Kings may be divided into three parts: (1) David's death and Solomon's reign (1 Kings 1–11), (2) the history of the Divided Kingdom (1 Kings 12–2 Kings 17), and (3) the history of Judah to the Babylonian Exile (2 Kings 18–25). (Note: The word *Israel* is used in three senses in Kings. At times, it is used as a religious term referring to the covenant community, the original twelve tribes. At other times, such as during the reigns of David and Solomon, Israel or all Israel refers to the nation as a political unit. After the division of the kingdom, Israel refers to the Northern Kingdom and Judah to the Southern Kingdom.)

All the reports on the kings of Judah and Israel are written in a similar style. Though the reports are not complete in every instance, certain words and phrases are common. "Rehoboam son of Solomon **was king in Judah**. He **was** forty-one **years old when he became king, and he reigned seventeen years in Jerusalem**. . . . **His mother's name was** Naamah; she was an Ammonitess" (1 Kings 14:21). "**As for the other events of** Rehoboam's reign, **and all he did, are they not written in the book of the annals of the kings of Judah? And** Rehoboam **rested with his fathers and was buried with them in the city of David**. . . . **And** Abijam **his son succeeded him as king**" (1 Kings 14:29, 31).

Some reports on the kings of Israel do not include the kings' ages, nor are their mothers' names included. (See 1 Kings 15:25-32, for example.) The introduction or conclusion or both are missing in some cases (for example, 2 Kings 9:22-28).

The Books of Kings are organized according to the rise and fall of Judean and Israelite kings, all of whom are evaluated by the same standards. Those standards are the purity of worship and whether that worship centers in Jerusalem. Most of the kings are condemned because they tolerated the worship of foreign gods within their lands. (See, for example, 1 Kings 14:22-24.) Such condemnation agrees with the attitude about the worship of foreign gods expressed in Deuteronomy. (See 12:1-3.) The destruction of pagan idols and places of worship was necessary to safeguard the purity of Israelite worship as required by the covenant.

The Writers of First and Second Kings

Some scholars call the writer of Kings a Deuteronomic historian because the structure and general outlook of Kings is strongly Deuteronomic. The writer emphasizes the covenant relationship; God as the one true God; and the necessity for one central place of worship, Jerusalem. All these emphases are also found in Deuteronomy.

The Books of Kings probably had more than one writer. The writer of 2 Kings 22:20 does not know of Josiah's death on the battlefield of Megiddo (23:29-30). The destruction of the Temple in Jerusalem (1 Kings 9:6-9) is not known about in 1 Kings 8:8. Perhaps part of Kings was written before Josiah's death in 609 B.C. References to the destruction of the Temple (1 Kings 9:6-9) and to the exile of Judah in Babylon (1 Kings 8:46-53; 2 Kings 21:11-15), as well as the other part, were probably written by a later writer, around 550 B.C. First and Second Kings developed in two stages, with the later writer adding material within the earlier structure and perspective.

The Chronology of First and Second Kings

The chronology used in Kings is complicated because the dates of kings are synchronized—the date of one king is used to establish the date of another. This system is not always reliable. Differences often exist between the synchronized years of a king and the number of years allotted to him. Differences also appear when we compare these years to dates from Babylonian and Assyrian history. For example, from the revolution of Jehu to the fall of Samaria is 170 years by the synchronized system, 165 years by the dates for Judean kings, 143 years and 7 months by the dates for Israelite kings, and 121 years according to Assyrian documents. Most scholars accept the essential accuracy of the synchronized system but also allow for inaccuracies.

Sources for the Books of Kings

Three books are mentioned by name in Kings: The Book of the Acts of Solomon, The Book of the Chronicles of the Kings of Israel, and The Book of the Chronicles of the Kings of Judah. The Acts of Solomon was a collection of stories about Solomon's wisdom and of information from palace and Temple archives. The Chronicles of the Kings of Israel and of Judah were official records from the royal archives. Other unnamed records used in Kings may have contained the narratives about David's court, Elijah, Elisha, Ahab, and Isaiah.

Special Emphases

The Books of Kings forcefully emphasize God's guidance in the course of human history. The books have been likened to a sermon using the history of Judah and Israel as illustrations. The stories of falling away and of the consequences serve to remind, to teach, and to call the people to renewed commitment to God. This commitment was to be expressed in the purity of worship in the Lord's chosen temple in Jerusalem and in every aspect of daily life. The actions of the kings of Judah and Israel were the key to the fortunes of the people. Fulfilling the demands of the covenant was a requirement which, according to these books, most kings failed to meet.

The writers of Kings offered the chosen people their past. They organized and evaluated the past in order to reshape the future. They wanted their people to remember that the past, the future, and they themselves belonged to God.

*The writer of this Introduction and the Introduction to First and Second Chronicles is Ms. Linda B. Hinton. Ms. Hinton received the Master of Theological Studies from the Candler School of Theology, Emory University. Ms. Hinton is also the author of *Ezekiel and Daniel* in this series.

1

Solomon's Accomplishments

1 Kings 1–9

DIMENSION ONE:
WHAT DOES THE BIBLE SAY?

Answer these questions by reading 1 Kings 1

1. What does Bathsheba want for Solomon? (1:13)

   She wants him to succeed David as king.

2. Who challenges this ambition? (1:5)

   Adonijah, son of Haggith, wants to be king.

3. What things may have spoiled Adonijah? (1:6)

   King David never questioned his behavior, and he "was born next after Absalom."

4. How does David ensure Solomon's right to the throne? (1:32-40)

   He has Solomon anointed and proclaimed king at Gihon by Zadok and Nathan.

5. Why does Adonijah hold onto the horns of the altar? (1:50-51)

   He fears Solomon, and the altar provides a place of refuge.

Answer these questions by reading 1 Kings 2

6. How does David feel about dying? (2:2)

   He accepts death calmly as a natural thing.

7. What does David tell Solomon to do? (2:5-9)

   Solomon must kill Joab and Shimei and deal generously with David's supporters.

8. How many years does David reign as king? (2:11)

   David reigns forty years.

Answer these questions by reading 1 Kings 3

9. What two things does Solomon do that David did not do? (3:3)

   He continues to sacrifice and burn incense at the high places.

10. What gift does Solomon ask from God? (3:9)

    Solomon asks for "a discerning heart" to govern God's people and to be able "to distinguish between right and wrong."

11. How does God respond to Solomon's request? (3:10)

    It pleases the Lord that Solomon has asked this.

12. How does Solomon show his wisdom? (3:16-28)

    He identifies the real mother of a child who is being claimed by two women.

Answer these questions by reading 1 Kings 6–7

13. What materials are used in building the Temple? (6:31-36)

    Olive wood, gold, pine, stone, and cedar are used.

14. How many years are spent in building the Temple? (6:38)

    Seven years are spent in building the Temple.

15. How long does Solomon work on his palace? (7:1)

    Solomon worked on his palace for thirteen years.

16. What does Huram do for King Solomon? (7:13-14)

Huram does all the bronze work for the Temple and palace.

Answer these questions by reading 1 Kings 8

17. Where is the ark of the covenant placed in the Temple? (8:6)

The ark is placed in the inner sanctuary, in the Most Holy Place.

18. What objects are in the ark? (8:9)

The ark contains the two stone tablets that Moses put there at Horeb.

19. How do the priests know God is in the Temple? (8:10-11)

A cloud and the glory of the Lord fill the Temple.

20. What does Solomon ask God to do when the people pray? (8:30)

He asks God to hear and forgive the people.

21. Does Solomon believe that all people sin? (8:46)

Yes. There is no one who does not sin.

Answer these questions by reading 1 Kings 9

22. What does God want Solomon to do? (9:4)

Solomon must walk before God with integrity of heart and uprightness, follow all God's commands, and observe God's decrees and laws.

23. Where does Solomon keep his fleet of ships? (9:26)

Solomon keeps his ships at Ezion Geber.

DIMENSION TWO:
WHAT DOES THE BIBLE MEAN?

Background Information on 1 Kings 1–9

This lesson can be divided into two important historical sections. The first section is an accounting of the closing days of the forty-year reign of David. For seven years he was king over Judah; and for thirty-three years he ruled over Judah and Israel, the United Kingdom.

The second section is a summary of the events leading to Solomon's succession to his father's throne. This summary is then followed by a description of Solomon's greatest accomplishments, building the Temple and constructing his palace.

The writer of First Kings believes that God has chosen David and his descendants to rule over the Hebrew people. The United Kingdom is to be, in essence, a theocracy, a nation ruled by God. David and his descendants, as long as they remain faithful to God, are the Lord's deputies for the governing of Israel.

Wisdom, the writer feels, is the greatest quality desired in the deputies of God. (See 1 Kings 3:9-10.) This wisdom, when accompanied by love for God (See 1 Kings 3:3.) and by obedience to God's requirements (See 1 Kings 3:14.), endows a ruler with qualities needed to establish his people in peace and prosperity. (See 1 Kings 4:20, 25.)

The writer regards Jerusalem as the central focus of Hebrew loyalty. The Temple symbolizes this focus of Israel's life around Jerusalem. Worship is to be conducted in the manner known to be especially pleasing to God. The minds and hearts of God's faithful people are to turn repeatedly to the Temple. (See Luke 2:41-47.)

1 Kings 1:1-4. Our study opens with a description of David's failed sexual vigor. These verses modestly hide the fact of David's impotence behind some evasive phrases brought into the Scripture by translation. David's inability to have sexual intercourse with Abishag is central to Adonijah's rebellion. This rebellion, of course, necessitates Bathsheba's struggle to retain the throne for her son Solomon.

We have here an instance in which the Hebrews shared the mentality of the peoples around them. The belief that the fertility of the soil and the prosperity of the people were linked to the fertility of the king was a common belief in the ancient Near East. When the king became impotent, the life of the nation was threatened.

This primitive idea seems strange to us. However, if we make no attempt to understand ideas such as this, we miss the point of this and other incidents in the Bible.

The time of the kings was a pre-Christian time. We cannot always expect to find these spiritual ancestors of ours thinking in Christian terms. The time of the kings was a pre-scientific time as well, and we cannot expect the Hebrews to be different from the people around them.

The Hebrews also believed that God could only be worshiped on Israel's soil. (See 1 Samuel 26:19.) We are privileged to know that the day will come when the Temple at Jerusalem will itself be replaced with a temple not made with hands. (See Mark 13:1-2; 14:58.) This will be a temple of the spirit of God and the spirit of humankind. True seekers after God will be able to worship without any ritual or building or priest. This will be a temple that a man or woman can enter into wherever or whenever the heart turns to God. (See John 4:20-24.)

So the immediate reign of David ended with a statement on his sexual impotence and an event we may find strange and perhaps distasteful. However, his influence continues as a vital part of Jewish and Christian thought to the present time.

With the passing centuries David's personal failures were forgotten, though the sin with Bathsheba was remembered. (See 1 Kings 15:5.) Increasingly, the virtues of David were celebrated. He was remembered as the king who was faithful to God. He was remembered as the ruler for whom God had a special love. David's relationship with God was thought to be one that had often saved the Hebrews from great danger. (See 1 Kings 15:4; Isaiah 37:33-35; 55:3.)

Centuries later, Jesus was to be identified as "the son of David." (See Matthew 1:1; 9:27; Mark 10:48.) His triumphal entry into Jerusalem was greeted as a signal of the return of the kingdom of David. (See Mark 11:10; Matthew 21:9-10.) So David became the pattern of the Messiah, and for years after his death the Hebrew people were looking forward to his return or the rule of his descendants.

Today Christian worship is filled with phrases from psalms associated with David. Most hymnals and worship books contain dozens of psalms from David in the rituals, and many of these psalms are a basis for some of our most popular hymns.

1 Kings 1:50-53. The horns of the altar are carved representations of the horns of a great bull. One horn is found at each of the four corners of the altar. (However, no one is sure exactly what they looked like.) Having horns on the altar is another of the ways that the Hebrew worshipers were like their counterparts in the varied cultures around them. The altars of Israel were similar to the altars of the surrounding peoples. Bronze horns were part of the altars at Babylon and Nineveh. They were horns like those of great bulls and symbolized the strength of the deity worshiped at those particular altars.

These horns were, the Hebrews believed, special points of contact with God. They became the points where trembling, fearful refugees could catch hold of the strength and grace of God. The horns were, for a time at least, a place that was safe from the bitter wrath of those who pursued the refugees. Persons could take refuge here as they once had been able to do in the cities of refuge. (See Numbers 35:6, 11.)

We must remember that in Israel, God was known for the qualities of mercy and protection. If indeed God chose to meet the people at the altar (See Exodus 30:2, 6.), it was natural that Adonijah would seek safety by fleeing to the horns of the altar. He had failed in his unwise and irreligious attempt to seize the throne. But he did find safety at the altar. (See 1 Kings 1:53.) Adonijah remained secure until his request to marry Abishag was interpreted as a new attempt to overthrow Solomon. (See 1 Kings 2:13-25.)

1 Kings 3:3. This is one of many places in the Old Testament where "the high places" are spoken of with great disapproval. We shall note this repeatedly in our current study of Kings and Chronicles.

Here, as in many of the other places we shall note, continued worship at the high places is interpreted as evidence of an imperfection or unworthiness in the allegiance of an individual to God. Worship at the high places is also interpreted as a sign of unfaithfulness on the part of the nation.

These high places were hilltop shrines formerly used by the Canaanites in the worship of their fertility gods. As the Jews took over the land, it became natural and easy for them to use the same spots for the worship of the living God. Even today in Europe certain great Christian cathedrals stand upon spots that were originally places of pagan worship.

The struggle of the Hebrew people to become a moral people worshiping only one God who is utterly ethical and moral required that all traces of former paganism be eliminated. All local shrines were to be rejected, and the true worship of God was to be concentrated at Jerusalem. This emphasis comes to its climax in the reforms of Josiah as described in 2 Chronicles 34. But already, as in the passage under consideration, the movement to reject these high places is underway.

Later, the reforming zeal that is inherent in much of Old Testament religion will view Solomon's marriages to non-Jewish women as the cause of Solomon's infidelity to God and, as a result, of all Israel's unfaithfulness to the Lord. Solomon's marriages to women from outside the chosen people caused him to worship other gods. (See 1 Kings 11.)

Why did Solomon enter into these marriages? They probably were politically motivated. Solomon probably wanted political and military alliances with the powers around Israel. These alliances were available to him through these marriages. Political marriages were a common custom of the day.

The king's continued practice of worship at the high places functioned as a political gesture of goodwill toward the pagan nations with whom he was allied by marriage. (See 1 Kings 11.) But in the mind of the writer of First Kings, these marriages and the pagan worship they led to were abominable. These marriages were the cause of some of the great trouble that later came upon the nation, as we will see in the next lesson.

1 Kings 5–7. These chapters contain a detailed, elaborate, and fascinating description of Solomon's building program. As noted in the student book, this construction program included houses for Solomon and for Pharaoh's daughter (his wife), a complex of buildings for governmental functions, and the Temple. This building program required great administrative skill on the part of Solomon. First Kings 4:7-19 and 5:1-18 record some of the details of Solomon's skill at this point. These passages also point to the heavy human cost for construction of these magnificent buildings. (See 5:13 and 9:15-21.)

The Temple is the primary focus of attention in these chapters. The spot chosen for the Temple was Mount

Moriah. The Temple stood at its peak. The Temple was about ninety feet in length, about thirty feet wide, and about forty-five feet in height. (See 1 Kings 6:2.) That size seems modest to us, but anyone who has visited Saint Chapelle in Paris knows how absolutely exquisite and deeply moving even a comparatively small place of worship can be when it is as richly decorated and carved as Solomon's Temple was. Of course, the great significance of this Temple was not its size but what it contained.

The Temple contained two extremely valuable treasures for the Hebrew people and their religion. One treasure was the ark of the Lord with the Ten Commandments on the stone tablets. The other treasure was the very presence of God. (See 1 Kings 8:6-10.)

Here and elsewhere in the Old Testament, God's presence is discovered in the cloud. This time the cloud fills the Temple, the house of the Lord. The student book refers to previous identifications of God's presence in this manner. Some specific places are Exodus 13:21-22; 19:9; 34:5-8. Read also Leviticus 16:2 and Numbers 9:15.

When we examine these passages, we discover that the cloud is always associated with God's purposeful presence with the people. God is there for a reason. God is with them to guide them. Exodus 34:5-8 has a moving description of God's character. God is merciful, gracious, slow to anger, and abounding in steadfast love and faithfulness.

It is this God who chooses on this day of the great Temple's dedication to say, "My Name shall be there." (See 1 Kings 8:29.)

Our Hebrew predecessors always associated the name of a god with that deity's essence and character. Thus when we read that God's name is in the Temple, we are hearing faith confessed. The Hebrews are hoping that God's character will be celebrated in this place. The Temple is where God will be known by those who faithfully seek the Lord.

1 Kings 8:14-53. This section contains one of the greatest intercessory prayers in the Bible. We are reminded of Abraham interceding with God for Sodom and Gomorrah (Genesis 18:16-33) and of Moses' praying for the unfaithful Hebrews (Exodus 32:31-32). As Christians we remember the great intercession of Jesus. (See John 17.) We are stirred when we read Paul's meditations upon the intercessory life of Jesus. (See Philippians 2:1-8; Romans 5:6-11.) We do not forget Paul's' own deep desire for the salvation of his people. (See Romans 9:1-5; 10:1.)

Let us read the prayer of Solomon with great care. The prayer has a refrain, "hear from heaven." (See verses 30, 32, 34, 36, 39, 43, 45, and 49.) The Hebrews knew that God was greater than the Temple. God was beyond that Temple, though choosing to meet the people there.

In his prayer, Solomon asks for a wide variety of moral and spiritual needs to be met. His prayer deals with the common human need for forgiveness (verse 30); vindication of the righteous (verse 32); restoration in times of national defeat (verse 34); relief in time of drought (verse 36); and rescue in time of crop failure, famine, and plague

(verse 37). Solomon also mentions the need for including foreigners in the community of God's people (verse 43) and fulfilling a national destiny (verse 53).

Solomon offers his prayer in full awareness that all will not be well with the Hebrews through the coming years. But for each possible ill the king prays, "Then from heaven, your dwelling place, hear their prayer and their plea, and uphold their cause" (verse 49).

1 Kings 8:54-61. That God is gracious, compassionate, loving, and merciful is good. That God can be asked and expected to intervene in the life of the nation is good. But something else is needed.

That something else is the proper response of the people to God. The people are to be obedient, and their obedience is to be a testimony to the peoples of the world (verse 60). The heart of the nation—its deepest emotion, its highest loyalty—is to be directed toward the God who takes part in the people's history.

DIMENSION THREE:
WHAT DOES THE BIBLE MEAN TO ME?

The Bible means to us what we allow it to mean. These historical sections of the Bible can be read as nothing more than the mere recital of ancient historical facts. But when we read it in that way, we are only wandering in a Bible land's museum, not reading the vital Word of God.

Perhaps we should read these sections of the Bible as faith history. A better term might be *salvation history*. We should try to look within and beyond the bare facts of history for these two meanings: (1) What does the Bible affirm here about the nature of God? (2) What does the Bible declare to be God's relationship to the people? That is, is God near or far? Is God faithful or arbitrary? Is God to be thought of primarily in terms of power or primarily for ethical holiness? What does God expect of us today?

When we read the Bible as a salvation history, the sometimes dry historical sections begin to blaze with truth and power. They are alive with hope for our lives as Christian disciples in the years ahead.

1 Kings 1–3—God's Involvement in History

God uses imperfect persons, otherwise there would be none of us to do the divine will. David and Solomon were not perfect persons. Solomon's assertion that everyone sins is repeated by Paul. (See Romans 3:23; 5:12.) Our sin is often the same sin as that of David and Solomon. The sin was termed *accidie* by ancient theologians and is the sin of not being the best it is possible to be.

We find much then in the lives of David and Solomon that was reprehensible in terms of their own standards. For example, David's adultery with Bathsheba and the subsequent arrangement of Uriah's death were evil acts even by David's own pre-Christian standards.

How, in the light of our world's political terrorism and continued exploitation of many sections of our population, can we judge David for his deathbed instructions to Solomon? How severe can we be in our judgment of Solomon for his final decision to kill his half-brother Adonijah?

If we judge by perfect Christian standards, we know these deeds were wrong. However, if we look around at events in our own time, when we have the advantage of the great Hebrew tradition and nearly two thousand years of Christian teaching, what are we to say?

We are perhaps more in tune with the mind of one "greater than Solomon" (Luke 11:31) when we rightly demand the highest possible standards for ourselves. But are we not to accept all other persons because God accepts them? Are we not to forgive them because God forgives them?

1 Kings 5–7—The Value of Our Labor

These chapters contain a great deal of material concerning the construction and furnishing of Solomon's Temple and palace. A variety of costly materials were included in the buildings. The general impression is one of wealth and power.

What was the purpose of all this expenditure? It would seem that for Solomon the purpose was twofold: (1) to build "a house for the Name of the LORD" (see 1 Kings 5:3; 6:37; 8:18-19) and (2) to build a center where he could govern the people of God. Solomon's palace was to be a place where he and those who labored with him could discern between good and evil as they governed Israel. (See 1 Kings 3:9.)

The Temple was built in a spirit of reverence. We may envision the workmen going about quietly, in an attitude of homage and worship. Perhaps already they had sensed what Habakkuk was to say: "But the LORD is in his holy temple; / let all the earth be silent before him" (Habakkuk 2:20).

In the Christian tradition we know that our lives are temples of the Holy Spirit. (See 1 Corinthians 3:16-17.) Does this not mean we must treat our bodies, and the bodies of all persons, with reverence? Are we not to consider how holy is the mind of the human creature? We are called upon to deal reverently with the minds of our children, our class members, our fellow worshipers, our next-door neighbors.

First Kings 7:22 tells us the shape of lilies was upon the top of the columns. Jeremiah 52:22-23 suggests this form was a bronze pomegranate, high above the heads of the people, open in splendor only to the view of God.

The builders of the Temple created beauty where no other human would see it. No one could have cause for praise and blame. Only God would see the lily, and only

God would judge it. So it is with the inner core of our lives, down where no one knows who we are. But we know ourselves. And God knows.

In this symbolic sense then, our lives—the public aspects and the most private aspects—are important in the sight of God. Look particularly at 1 Kings 7:45-51. The gold is not what we should stress here. It is the variety of implements—pots, shovels, and sprinkling bowls. We do not know just what these were used for; but we know they were noted and remembered, for they were significant in the sight of God. Is it too much to suggest that it is the same with our lives? We do not reduce ourselves, our lives, to the status of puppets, thinking everything that happens results from the direct action of God. Yet we can believe that we do count. Our daily lives count in the sight of God. This is the thought behind the statement of Jesus in Matthew 10:29-31. This is why Jesus permits us, encourages us, to pray for daily bread. (See Matthew 6:11 and Luke 11:3.)

1 Kings 8—A Special Meeting Place

Discussion of this topic in the student book centers on the idea of a personal encounter with God at a specific place. Begin this portion of Dimension Three by having class members discuss the question, What are these places and times in your life?

In 1 Kings 8, Solomon prays that the Temple will be a special place in the life and worship of the Hebrew people. His hope was to encourage worshipers to have personal encounters with God. The goal was to learn more about the nature of God. Ask class members to reflect on what their personal encounters with God tell them about the nature of God.

Solomon's prayer is founded upon some solid convictions about the character of God. Solomon believes God is trustworthy, dependable, and consistent (8:22-24). Solomon believes God is greater than even the greatest temple we may build (8:27). God appoints times and places for direct contact with the people (8:29-30).

All our common human experiences are of concern to God. Sin, famine, drought, the presence of alien peoples, war—all these are moments when the chosen people may turn to God.

We must not assume too quickly that God is "on our side" in any particular struggle of life. That is, we must not assume God is on the side of the human race! God is forgiving (8:30). God desires that people will be faithful (8:61).

Close today's session by listing on a chalkboard or on a large piece of paper any new insights class members share about 1 Kings 1–9.

Then [Solomon] rested with his fathers. . . . And Rehoboam his son succeeded him as king (11:43).

—— 2 ——
The End of Solomon's Reign

1 Kings 10–20

DIMENSION ONE:
WHAT DOES THE BIBLE SAY?

Answer these questions by reading 1 Kings 10

1. What queen asks Solomon hard questions? (10:1)

   The queen of Sheba questions Solomon.

2. What tokens of friendship do Solomon and this queen exchange? (10:10-13)

   They exchange gold, spices, and precious stones.

3. How do Solomon's wealth and wisdom compare to those of other kings? (10:23)

   Solomon exceeds all the kings of the earth.

Answer these questions by reading 1 Kings 11

4. How do Solomon's wives influence him? (11:1-4)

   His foreign wives turn him toward other gods.

5. How is Solomon's infidelity to be punished? (11:11)

   God will tear the kingdom away from him.

6. Why does God's punishment become less severe? (11:12-13)

   God relents for the sake of David, Solomon's father.

7. What happens as a result of God's anger? (11:14, 23, 26)

   Hadad, Rezon, and Jeroboam become Solomon's adversaries.

8. To what book does the writer of First Kings refer? (11:41)

   The writer refers to the book of the annals of Solomon.

9. Who succeeds Solomon? (11:43)

   Solomon's son Rehoboam succeeds him.

Answer these questions by reading 1 Kings 12–13

10. What happens after Rehoboam becomes king? (12:16-20)

    All the tribes except Judah withdraw allegiance from the house of David.

11. How does Jeroboam try to gain the loyalty of the people? (12:25-33)

    He establishes shrines to idols at Bethel and Dan as substitutes for worship at Jerusalem.

12. What will happen to Jeroboam? (13:34)

    His family will be destroyed.

Answer these questions by reading 1 Kings 14–15

13. How do Judah and Israel get along? (14:30)

    They are at war continually.

14. Why does God continue to show favor to Solomon's descendants? (15:4)

    God continues to show favor for the sake of David.

15. What sin of David continues to be remembered? (15:5)

    God remembers David's adultery with Bathsheba and the murder of Uriah.

16. Who are the next two kings over Judah? (14:31; 15:8)

    Abijah and Asa are the next two kings over Judah.

17. What does Asa do? (15:11-14)

He discards many pagan practices, and his heart is true to the Lord.

18. Who are the kings in Israel after Jeroboam? (15:25, 33; 16:8, 15, 23, 29)

After Jeroboam come Nadab, Baasha, Elah, Zimri, Omri, and Ahab.

Answer these questions by reading 1 Kings 16–19

19. Why is Ahab punished? (16:30-33)

He married a foreign woman, worshiped Baal, and established pagan shrines.

20. What great prophet appears during the reign of Ahab? (17:1)

Elijah appears at this time.

21. What does Elijah say God is going to do? (17:1)

God is going to send a great drought.

22. Where does Elijah demonstrate God's supremacy over the prophets of Baal? (18:20)

Elijah goes to Mount Carmel.

23. Whom does God appoint to take Elijah's place? (19:16)

God appoints Elisha.

DIMENSION TWO:
WHAT DOES THE BIBLE MEAN?

Background Information on 1 Kings 10–20

Chapters 10 through 12 complete the story of Solomon. Bathsheba's son built for himself a great reputation for wisdom, wealth, and splendor. Glowing descriptions are given of Solomon's wealth, and his international trade in horses and chariots is noted. The visit of the queen of Sheba attests to his international reputation. (Sheba was a kingdom on the southwestern portion of the Arabian peninsula.)

With all this splendor, however, Solomon had one fatal flaw. He became greatly attached to his foreign wives who were from among the people God had forbidden Jews to marry. Solomon had seven hundred wives of royal rank and three hundred concubines! God became angry at Solomon because as he grew old, he allowed these foreign wives to turn him away from total loyalty to the Lord.

Solomon must pay a twofold penalty for this infidelity. First, God raises up adversaries, foreign enemies who attack Solomon's kingdom. Second, the kingdom will be taken away from Solomon's son.

Chapter 11 also tells of a revolt by Jeroboam, who is forced to flee to Egypt. He returns, however, as the first king over Israel when the nation divides following Solomon's death.

Solomon's successor, Rehoboam, is a miserable failure. Coming to the throne in 922 B.C., his lack of sensitivity to the economic plight of his people leads to a political schism. Only Judah remains loyal to the house of David.

Political division is followed by religious division as Jeroboam attempts to wean the Israelites from worship at Jerusalem. To offset the claim of that city, with its ever-present reminders of the favored position of the house of David, Jeroboam offers competing shrines at Bethel and at Dan.

Chapters 13 through 20 are more complicated in their recital of historical facts. The overall picture that emerges is of a time of repeated war between Israel and Judah, great political instability (especially in Israel), and the people being consistently misled by their rulers.

1 Kings 10–11. The wealth, fame, and wisdom of Solomon are emphasized repeatedly in Chapter 10. So wonderful was Solomon's reign in the eyes of the historian that we may be reminded of other biblical passages pointing to a golden future for the chosen people. Note especially the optimism of Isaiah 60:8-14.

The worm in the midst of this wealth and international acclaim recorded in Chapter 11 is tied up with Solomon's marriages. These marriages were to non-Hebrew women, and most of these marriages were probably more in the nature of political alliance than marriage as we know it today.

We must remember that these marriages probably represent treaties that Solomon made with the neighboring peoples. We must note also the natural tendency of these women to desire to worship their traditional gods. These women's influence with Solomon led to the establishment of various pagan shrines in the midst of a people and land dedicated to the one true God, Yahweh. We read that Solomon seems to have added the worship of these gods to his own worship of the Lord. He did not give up worshiping the God of his fathers completely. But he polluted that worship by adding to it the worship of pagan deities. These deities were fertility gods, with ritual prostitution sometimes a major element of their worship. They were gods who were understood to require child sacrifice in return for divine favor. (Compare later records such as 1 Kings 12:28-32; 16:34.)

First Kings 11:4 records the prevailing attitude toward Solomon: "His heart was not fully devoted to the LORD his God." The king who had uttered one of history's noblest prayers (1 Kings 8:22-53) has himself moved away from his own standard of loyalty to God. In doing so he has, as their ruler, led God's people astray.

First Kings 11:14-43 begins the story of Solomon's troubles and his downfall. Because of God's anger, adversaries rise against Solomon. Two of these, Hadad and Rezon, are outsiders, from among the people with whom his marriages had sealed treaties. The third, Jeroboam, is a fellow Hebrew, from the tribe of Ephraim.

Jeroboam is first given the word concerning the breakup of the United Kingdom. That division will come when Solomon dies and is succeeded by his son. (See 1 Kings 11:29-40.)

1 Kings 12:1-20. With this chapter we begin reading the history of the Divided Kingdom. The story does not conclude until 2 Kings 17.

We learn that Solomon's glory had been achieved at the cost of great dissatisfaction among his people. Use of the word *yoke* (1 Kings 12:4) in the encounter of Rehoboam with Jeroboam and the elders of Israel is of interest. In no other place in the Old Testament is this term used except in connection with the total subjugation of a foreign people by a conquering military power. The Israelites were, in effect, saying to Rehoboam, "Your father made us a conquered people in our own land. Will you treat us the same, or will you be a better king to us than that?"

Rehoboam chose to follow the young men who proposed to intensify rather than lighten Solomon's exploitation of his people. As a result, all the tribes, except Judah, revolted and made Jeroboam king of Israel. "Look after your own house, O David!" (12:16) was the parting cry. The great United Kingdom had come abruptly to an end.

Religious schism followed political division. Just as there is no longer one nation and one royal family, there will no longer be one place for the pure worship of God. Jeroboam attempted to establish shrines at Bethel and Dan that would keep his people away from Jerusalem. He feared that the focus of worship at the Holy City of Jerusalem would turn their political loyalties in that direction also. (See 1 Kings 12:25-33.) The terrible judgment upon his apostasy is recorded in 1 Kings 14:7-11.

First Kings 13 records the condemnation of the Bethel altar that was built to compete with the Temple at Jerusalem.

1 Kings 14–17. These chapters continue the account of the Divided Kingdom until the time of Elijah. The student book lists the kings who ruled in this period.

The time span is about seventy years. Elijah seems to have come upon the scene about 850 B.C., and the kingdom had divided in 922 B.C. Hebrew history during this period was marked by conflict, political instability, and refusal to return purely and simply to the religion of Yahweh. As a result, the people suffered repeated disaster.

These chapters, in common with most histories, tell only about persons who by reasons of birth or personal striving came to positions of prominence. We do not know much about the life of the common men and women. However, we can well imagine that it was a time of anxiety, economic stress, and sorrow at seeing one's sons and grandsons go off to war. Surely there must have been many a late-night, earnest discussion of the meanings of the religious division fostered by Jeroboam. The implications of such passages as 1 Kings 14:30 are awesome to contemplate.

In this section the Bible suggests that there is a close relationship between the character of a government and the quality of a nation's life. The Bible also suggests that murder, violence, and genocide, as acts of death, always carry with them the possibility of a harvest of death for those who engage in such things.

The whole sordid story of this section is relieved only by the reign of Asa in Judah, 811 B.C.–870 B.C. New life becomes a possibility because of Elijah's ministry. In him, as we shall see, the religion of Israel turns again to its earliest source, the faith of Moses.

1 Kings 17–20. These chapters cover most of the record we have of the prophet Elijah. The account of his total ministry is found in 1 Kings 17–19, 21, and in 2 Kings 1–2.

What do we know about this man? We know he had courage. He did not hesitate to pronounce God's judgment upon King Ahab. (See 1 Kings 17:1.) Elijah was a man of the desert. The description of him in 2 Kings 1:8, that "he was a man with a garment of hair and with a leather belt around his waist," reminds us of John the Baptist.

Elijah was a man for whom God was real. He did not hesitate to call upon God to show the power of the Lord before the indecisive people. His encounter with the prophets of Baal on Mount Carmel testifies with great eloquence to Elijah's faith that God could, and would, show the Israelites who the real God was. (See 1 Kings 18:1-40.)

He was passionate and merciless in rooting out what he could of the evil that he saw as a threat to the life of his people. When he called the people to renewed allegiance, following the defeat of the Baal prophets, he further ordered that the foreign prophets be slaughtered.

Yet, for all his courage and power, Elijah remains very human. He fears the wrath of Queen Jezebel. But when he flees in terror for his life, he is again privileged to encounter God. Chapter 19 is a moving account of a great moment in biblical history when God and solitary individual meet. Elijah, in the desert, caught by despair and fear, learns again that God cares.

God speaks to Elijah at Mount Horeb in such quietness that the whole conversation may well have been essentially within the heart and mind of Elijah as he was sensitive to the mind and heart of God. Was this event a foreshadowing of the new and inward covenant that Jeremiah would describe later? (See Jeremiah 31:31-34.)

Elijah learns that he is not alone in his faithfulness. (See 1 Kings 19:18.) That tremendous assurance given by God, "Yet I reserve seven thousand in Israel—all whose knees have not bowed down to Baal"—has been a beacon of hope and comfort for many a lonely, isolated, and threatened faithful believer through the centuries since Elijah's day.

DIMENSION THREE: WHAT DOES THE BIBLE MEAN TO ME?

This section of the Bible, like other historical sections, is filled with facts. Facts are important. But when we are concerned with historical facts and with moral and spiritual meaning (as in a Bible study), we must look beyond mere dates, names, and places. We need to ask some questions concerning the meaning and the relevance of these facts to our lives.

Dimension Three in the student book is divided into three sections. You may want to add or substitute a discussion of the price of Solomon's wealth based on 1 Kings 10–11.

1 Kings 10–11—The Price of Wealth

This section records Solomon's reputation for wisdom and his ostentatious display of wealth. How did Solomon become so wealthy? First Kings 9:20-21 indicates he used slave labor. First Kings 12:4 indicates a heavy tax burden was placed upon the Hebrews. First Kings 9:11-12 tells how he gave hard-earned territory to those he traded with for the costly materials of his great public buildings.

Solomon also entered into alliances with foreign nations. These alliances were confirmed through political marriages. The result of these alliances—probably not what Solomon intended—was the turning away of his own heart from faithful, unswerving loyalty to God. His own personal practice and example gave permission for his people to turn to the religions of the nations around them.

Have the class consider these questions: At what great social cost is our own nation's prestige and power sometimes secured? When you read of a single military plane costing tens of millions of dollars, do you sometimes think of the schools, hospitals, retirement homes, or medical research that might have been funded by the cost of such a plane? In our life as a nation and in our personal lives, when do we take on the non-Christian, even anti-Christian, behavior of peoples around us? Why do we take on such behavior? Are we misguided in our concern for status, recognition, or popularity?

1 Kings 12:1-20—The Effects of Leadership

What was Rehoboam's mistake? Was it that he listened to the wrong advisors? Or was it that he listened to persons who told him only what they knew he wanted to hear?

Can you imagine how Rehoboam's younger advisors reacted to the suggestion that he, son of Solomon, king of the Hebrews, should adopt a servant role in relationship to his people? We can imagine them saying, "The kingdom is

yours, not theirs! They are to be your servants, not the other way around!"

We have here a tremendous contrast with the suffering servant found in the Book of Isaiah. The servant there is not interested in building himself up but is committed to the redemption of the people. Descriptions of the servant are found in passages such as Isaiah 42:1-7 and 52:13–53:12.

The ministry suggested for the servant is to express the tenderness of God for all. He is to come as the liberator whenever men and women groan under the yoke of bondage. When hunger and thirst overtake the people, he is to guide them by springs of water (Isaiah 49:10.) He is to sustain them with words when they are weary (Isaiah 50:4).

Read again the harsh, unfeeling response of Rehoboam to the plea of his people. He is saying to them, "The pain that my father inflicted is nothing compared to the pain I am going to give to you." Could Rehoboam have taken the approach of repentance, desire for healing, and a wholehearted return to the service of God? How could he have averted the disaster that came?

Was the penalty for Solomon's unfaithfulness wholly irreversible? Would the merciful God, accepting repentance and responding to earnest prayer, have been true to Rehoboam if Rehoboam had chosen to be true to the Lord?

Have the class consider the questions in the student book. Then discuss what need we have as individuals, as local Christian congregations, and as a nation to repent. How are we at odds with the highest moral and spiritual insights we have from our Hebrew-Christian understanding of the character and purpose of God?

1 Kings 14–16—The Constancy of God

We read of a troubled era in the national life of the Hebrew people. The kingdom is divided. Only Judah remains loyal to the house of David. Judah is left alone in its commitment, while all the other tribes go with Jeroboam into rebellion and separate nationhood.

The problems encountered by the Hebrew people during this period can be attributed in part to their lack of faith in God. This lack of faith is exemplified by Solomon, whose actions show that he did not believe in the constancy of God. We know that Solomon had a deep measure of loyalty to God. We also know that there were from the beginning dark spots of infidelity. (See 1 Kings 3:3.) This early disloyalty climaxed with the seven hundred marriages, many to non-Hebrews who insisted on bringing with them their own gods.

Solomon's fascination with these women prompted him to follow them in their pagan worship. He made arrangements for that worship to be perpetuated. First Kings 11:4-13 tells this story as the Bible historian sees it. This infidelity is what causes the loss of most of the kingdom. Only for the sake of David is even one tribe left faithful.

Following Solomon's death, a rapid succession of twelve kings hold on until both nations, Israel and Judah, are near the end of their national existence.

What do these events say to us? What are the implications for the days in which we live?

The student book mentions Isaiah 51:1. Have the class read and discuss this verse. Concentrate on the question the student book raises: "In what ways is God also our rock and quarry today?" Have the class members discuss what we can learn from the mistakes of Solomon.

1 Kings 17–20—The Faith of Elijah

The student book compares the Christian faith with Elijah's faith. What was the faith of Elijah? First, Elijah's faith was a response to God. As Moses was sent down into Egypt to proclaim freedom to the enslaved Hebrews (See Exodus 3:10.), so Elijah was consecrated as the special spokesperson for God to the people of his day. In a similar manner, Isaiah and Amos were specially commissioned for their tasks. (See Isaiah 6:8 and Amos 7:14-15.) The ministry of our Lord was heralded when "the word of God came to John son of Zechariah" (Luke 3:2).

Each of these spokespersons has felt a sense of special calling and has responded to God's call. Elijah, whom we first encounter in 1 Kings 17, responded to God's call.

Second, Elijah's faith was a courageous faith. This man comes into the midst of Israel's wickedness, apostasy, and decadence. He comes with strength, courage, and a flaming vision of a holy God. Elijah does not hesitate to challenge Ahab the king, and he suffers from the wrath of Queen Jezebel. (She was the daughter of a Sidonian priest who had seized power in Tyre at the same time Omri had taken the throne in Israel.) The two usurpers had sealed their alliance by arranging the marriage of Jezebel and Ahab.

The sins of Ahab were many. He married a woman who worshiped a false god. He built an altar and worshiped that god. He erected a sacred pole, the emblem of the female goddess Asherah. Asherah, like her male counterparts in Baal worship, was a nature deity. These gods were personifications of the forces of nature, such as sexual intercourse and the resulting new life. Yahweh, on the other hand, is the God above all nature but at whose command all creation and all sources of life move.

Ahab permitted the reinstitution of the foundation sacrifices. This meant that when the cornerstone of a new house, a city gate, or a city wall was laid, some human being would be sacrificed and buried in the ground to guarantee safety and well-being.

Elijah's faith was also a determined faith. He knew that this evil could not be allowed to go unpunished. Draught, defeat of the many priests of Baal, condemnation of Ahab's policy, and condemnation of Ahab himself all follow from the hand of Elijah.

These incidents in the history of the Hebrews illustrate the judgment of God. Close today's session by praying for guidance, light, and renewal lest we too fall under God's judgment. Then have class members share new insights on 1 Kings 10–20.

— 3 —

Elijah and Elisha

1 Kings 21–2 Kings 8

DIMENSION ONE:
WHAT DOES THE BIBLE SAY?

Answer these questions by reading 1 Kings 21

1. What does Ahab do when he is denied Naboth's vineyard? (21:4)

   Ahab goes to bed, sulking and refusing to eat.

2. For what sin does Elijah rebuke King Ahab? (21:17-20)

   Ahab killed Naboth and stole his vineyard.

3. How is Ahab to be punished? (21:20-24)

   He and his family are to be destroyed.

4. Why does God delay this punishment? (21:27-29)

   Ahab humbles himself before the Lord.

Answer these questions by reading 1 Kings 22

5. Why does Ahab hate the prophet Micaiah? (22:8)

   He will not prophesy good for Ahab.

6. What happens when Ahab disregards Micaiah's message? (22:34-40)

   Ahab is killed.

7. What is the character of Jehoshaphat's reign? (22:41-46)

   He does what is right but overlooks some pagan rituals in Israel's worship.

8. What is the character of Ahaziah's reign over Israel? (22:51-53)

   He does what is evil.

Answer these questions by reading 2 Kings 1–5

9. Why does Ahaziah die? (1:1-17)

   Ahaziah dies because he does not trust the Lord, and he appeals to false gods for advice.

10. What are some of the miracles Elisha performs? (4:1-44)

    He provides a bountiful food supply, he heals, he restores from death, and he protects persons from food poisoning.

11. What kind of faith does the Shunammite woman have? (4:22-30)

    She has a persistent faith.

12. What miracles does Elisha do with food? (4:38-44)

    He saved the prophets from food poisoning. Elijah also feeds a hundred men with a small amount.

13. What disease does Naaman have? (5:1)

    He has leprosy.

14. Why do Elisha's instructions for his healing offend Naaman? (5:1-13)

    They offend Naaman because he did not want to wash in the Jordan.

15. Why does Naaman want to take Israelite soil home? (5:15-17)

    He wants to stand on holy ground when he worships the Lord.

16. How is Elisha's servant punished for his greed? (5:26-27)

    He becomes infected with leprosy.

17. When the people with leprosy discover the abandoned Aramean camp, what wrong do they feel they have done? (7:9)

They have not shared the good news and the food and riches they have found.

18. What does Elisha say Hazael will do to Israel? (8:12)

He will ravage Israel.

19. How does Hazael get the throne of Aram for himself? (8:15)

He smothers Ben-Hahad.

20. Why does God continue to show mercy to the kingdom of Judah? (8:19)

He does so for the sake of David.

21. When Jehoram fights the Edomites, what does his army do? (8:20-21)

They flee home.

22. What does it mean to walk in the ways of the kings of Israel? (8:18, 27)

It means to do what is evil.

DIMENSION TWO: WHAT DOES THE BIBLE MEAN?

1 Kings 21. In this chapter Elijah the prophet condemns Ahab's injustice to Naboth. This is an important example of the prophetic side of Hebrew religion offering a challenge to the political power.

Power corrupts, and absolute power corrupts absolutely. One of history's great lessons is summarized in that sentence. Anyone who has read a biography of Henry VIII has seen that truth tragically lived out in a life that was, in the beginning, marked with grace, beauty, and great hope for the king and for his people.

We see something of the same corruption at work in the events surrounding Ahab's desire for Naboth's vineyard. (Read also 2 Samuel 12:1-12.) The details of the event are set forward in clear order in the Bible. We have summarized them in the student book.

Several key phrases when examined may help to enlarge our understanding of this significant event. The land in question is, for Naboth, "the inheritance of [his] fathers" (1 Kings 21:3). This vineyard, then, was much more than a piece of land bought and sold in the marketplace. This land was a trust from the past (the fathers), to the present (Naboth), and for the future. In essence, Ahab was trying to take away Naboth's family identity. The issue for Naboth was something more than ownership of a piece of land. It was integrity, stewardship, family identity, and his own position in the long sweep of the history of his people.

Ahab's behavior upon Naboth's refusal is worth attention. (See 1 Kings 21:4.) His actions remind us of a child denied some desired toy. After Naboth refuses Ahab's offer, Ahab throws a temper tantrum. This is quite revealing behavior for a man seated upon a throne, presuming to see himself in some special relationship to God and to the chosen people.

Jezebel's words are also revealing. (See 1 Kings 21:7.) How reminiscent they are of Satan's words to Jesus at the time of Jesus' temptation. (See Matthew 4:3, 9.) Jezebel challenges Ahab to assert his authority. Satan insinuates to Jesus, "If you don't do this, maybe you aren't the Son of God." The queen declares to Ahab, "I'll get you the vineyard." But the vineyard was not hers to give, as indeed the "kingdoms of the world and their splendor" (Matthew 4:8) were not Satan's to give.

The phrase "two scoundrels" (1 Kings 21:10) is worth noting. In the King James Version we find the phrase translated "sons of Belial." The word *Belial* is composed of two other words that together mean "not for profit." These two men were of the sort who did not produce anything worthwhile. They were good-for-nothing. Perhaps they received a momentary gain for themselves, but the full effect of their presence was a contribution toward weakening the moral fiber of the nation.

1 Kings 22. King Jehoshaphat of Judah wishes to know God's decision on whether Judah should ally with Israel against Ben-hadad. Apparently King Ahab of Judah wanted to recapture the city of Ramoth Gilead, located east of the Jordan River.

The king of Israel assembles 400 prophets and consults with them on Jehoshaphat's behalf. All 400 prophets are unanimous: "Go, for the Lord will give it into the king's hand." But Jehoshaphat is not satisfied. He insists that Ahab consult Micaiah the son of Imlah, who has a reputation for uttering oracles unfavorable to the king. When Micaiah first speaks, he seems to be agreeing with the answer of the other 400 prophets (verse 15). But if we read further, we realize that his prophecy will not be favorable to the king. The other prophets have been seized by "a lying spirit" (22:23). In keeping with the prophecy of Micaiah, Ahab is killed in battle with the Arameans. (See verses 37-38.)

At the end of the chapter, the writer's attention turns to Jehoshaphat and his reign in Judah. Jehoshaphat is given a generally good evaluation, although we read that he was not able to remove the high places or to prevent people from sacrificing there.

Background Information on Second Kings

When you begin reading the Book of Second Kings, you are beginning a story in the middle. Since First and Second Kings were originally a single work, there is no clear division between the end of First Kings and the beginning of Second Kings. At the end of First Kings we read of the death of Jehoshaphat, king of Judah; his succession by his son Jehoram; and the beginning of the reign of Ahaziah in Israel. (See 1 Kings 22:50-53.) The Book of Second Kings continues the narrative about Ahaziah's reign.

Second Kings narrates the downfall of both Judah and Israel. Chapters 1–17 narrate the history of the Divided Kingdom until the fall of Samaria, the capital of Israel, in 721 B.C. Chapters 18–25 concentrate on the history of Judah, the Southern Kingdom, from 721 B.C. until its final downfall in 586 B.C. At the conclusion of Second Kings, the people of Judah have been taken into exile in Babylon.

The controversy between Israel's King Ahab and the prophet Elijah, narrated in First Kings, is continued in Second Kings. Here the principal characters are Ahaziah, successor to Ahab, and Elisha, successor to Elijah. Why does the prophet Elisha have a prominent place in the Book of Second Kings? Elisha was not a king; he was a prophet who stood in the shadow of Elijah, his predecessor. The Deuteronomic historian had a point to make by concentrating so much attention on the prophet Elisha. The Deuteronomic history attributes the decline and fall of both kingdoms to the actions of their kings. One major fault of these kings was that they consistently refused to heed the advice of true prophets. One of these true prophets was Elisha.

Reading 1 Kings 21 through 2 Kings 8 affords us an excellent opportunity to discover the essential nature of Old Testament prophecy. This discovery is of great importance, for we can profit from prophecy only as we understand the context in which it occurred and the central emphases of the prophetic presentation.

The political, economic, and social life of the people of God was the context of Old Testament prophecy. The original purpose of prophecy was for the person with God's message to stand in the midst of God's people and in the name of God to challenge and rebuke the evil impulses of the rulers and the people. The rulers were often evil in their relentless grab for power and material possessions. The people were often evil in their deliberate rejection of justice, honesty, fair play, and compassion. Rulers and people alike were often terribly misguided as they turned from the God who had a covenant with the Hebrews to seek advice and aid from pagan gods.

The context of Old Testament prophecy was not a pious preoccupation with the spiritual life. The context of Old Testament prophecy was the daily life of the nation.

The content of Old Testament prophecy was parallel to its context. That emphasis was not on predicting the future in the manner of a fortuneteller or soothsayer. The central function of the true Old Testament prophets was to proclaim the mind and will of God. Micaiah, for example, told Ahab the truth, whereas the 400 prophets told Ahab what he wanted to hear.

The false prophets were like some teachers of the early Christian church. We find these teachers described in 2 Timothy 4:3: "For the time will come when men will not put up with sound doctrine. Instead, to suit their own desires, they will gather around them a great number of teachers to say what their itching ears want to hear."

True prophecy, prophecy of a kind that was calculated to make a difference in the total life of the people—politically, economically, socially, and in religion and matters of the spirit—is seen in the work of persons like Elijah and Elisha.

2 Kings 1. The Book of Second Kings opens with a reference to the rebellion of Moab against Israel. Moab was a territory to the east of the Dead Sea. (See the map in in the student book.) Ahab's father, Omri, had made Moab a vassal under the authority of Israel. Second Kings 3 will tell us more about this rebellion.

Remember from the concluding words of First Kings that Ahaziah was called an evil king. First Kings 22:53 tells us that he worshiped Baal. Here in 2 Kings 1 we see proof of Ahaziah's evil ways. Whom does he consult to see whether he will recover from his illness? He consults Baal-Zebub, the local Canaanite god in Ekron. But Elijah intervenes and pronounces God's judgment of Ahaziah (verse 16).

2 Kings 2. This chapter portrays Elijah and Elisha on the road from Gilgal to Bethel, to Jericho, and finally to the Jordan River. Locate these places on the map in the student book. The passage narrates two events: the ascension of Elijah into heaven and the commissioning of Elisha as his successor.

Since he was taken up into heaven by a whirlwind, Elijah has been associated with Enoch, the only other Old Testament figure who escaped the experience of death. Tradition has also associated Elijah with Moses, since they are both credited with parting the waters of the Jordan River (verse 8).

Following Elisha's commissioning, we read about two events that are intended to prove his power and authority beyond doubt: making Jericho's water sweet and taking revenge on some youths who were ridiculing him. Many commentators have tried to gloss over the message of this latter story. (See verses 23-25.) For today's readers, such actions on the part of Elisha would in no way show his power and authority as a true prophet!

2 Kings 3. Note the many parallels between this incident involving Moab and the battle with the Arameans narrated in 1 Kings 22. You might want to have the class list these similarities in parallel columns on a chalkboard or on a large piece of paper. Apparently Israel had a literary form that was commonly used to narrate such battles.

We know of King Mesha of Moab from a nonbiblical source as well. Archaeologists discovered a memorial stone that commemorates the victories of King Mesha over Israel. The stone was discovered at Dibon in 1868.

Why did the water on the land appear to be "red—like blood" (verse 22)? The red color was probably due to the reflection of the red sand, characteristic of Edom's territory.

2 Kings 4–8. This section narrates a series of miracles performed by Elisha as well as his activities during the attack by Aram on Samaria. At the end of Chapter 8, the writer turns again to historical information about the kings of Israel and Judah.

DIMENSION THREE: WHAT DOES THE BIBLE MEAN TO ME?

1 Kings 21:17-29—God's Moral Laws

Discussion in Dimension Three of the student book centers on Elijah's challenge to Ahab in 1 Kings 21:21-24. Ask someone in the class to read this passage aloud.

As the student book notes, Elijah's confrontation with Ahab represents a conflict between the religious and political dimensions of Israel's life. The passage makes the point that no one, not even King Ahab, is above or exempt from God's moral laws. Naboth had the law on his side. But Ahab ignored that law and had to pay the price.

Likewise none of us is exempt from God's laws. To elaborate on this point, the student book focuses on two questions: (1) What is the proper use of power? (2) How can we distinguish between lawful and unlawful desires? Divide class discussion time between these two questions. Then, if time allows, have class members discuss the conflict between the religious and political realms in ancient Israel and how this conflict is reflected in our lives today.

What is the proper use of power? The student book emphasizes that each person exercises power over another at some time or another. Ask class members to think of individual examples and to share them with the group. What are the sources of power? Education? Wealth? Membership in a certain ethnic group? Membership in a certain church or denomination? Ask class members to suggest other sources of power in addition to those listed.

How can we distinguish between lawful and unlawful desires? What is the relationship between fulfillment of individual desires and the rights of other persons? The student book mentions the parable of the rich fool. Have someone in the class read the parable aloud; it is found in Luke 12:13-21. Then lead the class in a discussion of what each passage (Luke 12 and 1 Kings 21) says about the value of possessions.

The conflict between religion and politics is an old problem, as seen in this confrontation between Ahab and Elijah. This story is ultimately significant for what it says concerning the right and obligation of the spiritual leader to challenge the political leader of a people. Persons who

maintain that "religion and politics don't mix" are off base! We may not agree with either the religious left or the religious right in all details and emphases. However, no serious reader of the Bible can claim that there must be no conversation between the politician and the church—no call of the church to the political leaders to act for the genuine good of all the people of the nation.

God's provision of a ram in place of Isaac marked a great turning point in the Hebrew understanding of God's ritual requirements. In a similar way the incident of King Ahab and Naboth's vineyard and the incident of King David and Uriah's wife clearly indicate the role of the spiritual leaders as they labor with political leaders to keep the nation headed in the right direction. Elijah's rebuke of Ahab was the fulfillment of his high calling to the prophetic function. (See 1 Kings 21:17-24.)

Have the class consider what is the proper relationship between religion and politics in our society. We often hear this relationship spoken of as that between church and state. Ask the class these questions: Does the constitutional refusal to establish religion actually mean that a great chasm is to exist between church and state, between religion and politics? Or does that constitutional provision simply mean that no single form of religion is to be given a favored legal position in the life of our nation?

A century ago the Christian church challenged child labor in cotton mills and coal mines, the unbridled sale and consumption of alcoholic beverages, and the denial of voting rights to women and to minority persons. More recently the church has been involved in the issues of abusive migrant farm labor practices, abortion, and prayer in schools. Have the class consider whether the church's involvement in these issues was right or wrong. Does the church's involvement reflect an improper relationship between religion and politics? Why or why not? What social issues are worthy of the church's attention today?

I believe that the Christian leadership of a nation must address national concerns, such as budgeting and military expenditures and matters of national health and education, in terms of Christian principles. Religious persons have no greater claim to expert knowledge in how to achieve national goals than anyone else. But persons with spiritual and moral insights do wrong when they do not publicly debate these issues and bring to light the specific insights and principles of their faith! How can Christians maintain their discipleship in integrity and keep silent in the process of setting the community, state, and national agenda?

Close the session by praying the words of Saul of Tarsus, "Lord, what wilt thou have me to do?" (Acts 9:6, King James Version). Then have class members share new insights they have gained from studying 1 Kings 21–2 Kings 8.

4

The Decline of Israel

2 Kings 9–17

DIMENSION ONE:
WHAT DOES THE BIBLE SAY?

Answer these questions by reading 2 Kings 9

1. When Joram dies, what prediction comes true? (9:22-26)

   The prediction that the death of Naboth should be paid for comes true.

2. What happens to Jezebel? (9:30-37)

   She is assassinated and is eaten by dogs, as predicted.

Answer these questions by reading 2 Kings 10

3. How many sons of Ahab does Jehu have killed? (10:7)

   Jehu has seventy sons of Ahab killed.

4. Why does Jehu destroy the family of Ahab? (10:17)

   Jehu destroys the family of Ahab so that the word of the Lord might be fulfilled.

5. How does Jehu trick the Baal worshipers? (10:18-20)

   He makes them believe he is going to offer a great sacrifice to Baal.

6. How does Jehu rid Israel of Baal worship? (10:24-27)

   He kills all the Baal prophets, ministers, and priests after tricking them.

7. How does Jehu sin? (10:29)

   He allows the worship of golden calves at Bethel and Dan.

8. Does Jehu follow all the laws of God? (10:31)

   Jehu does not follow all the laws of God.

Answer these questions by reading 2 Kings 11

9. Who is queen over Judah for six years? (11:3)

   Athaliah the mother of Ahaziah is queen.

10. Who leads the revolt against that queen? (11:4-13)

    Jehoiada the priest leads the revolt.

11. What does Jehoiada do after Athaliah has been killed? (11:17)

    He establishes a covenant relationship between the Lord, the king, and the people.

12. What happens to Baal worship when Joash becomes king? (11:18)

    The temple, altars, and idols of Baal are destroyed. The priest is killed also.

Answer these questions by reading 2 Kings 12

13. What problems does Joash have with the priests? (12:6-8)

    They are taking money, but they are not using it to repair and support the Temple.

14. How does Joash respond to Hazael's threat? (12:17-18)

    He give Hazael all the treasures of Jerusalem so he will go away.

15. How does Joash die? (12:20-21)

    He is murdered by two of his officials.

Answer these questions by reading 2 Kings 13

16. Why is Israel defeated in the time of King Jehoahaz? (13:2-3)

Jehoahaz leads the Israelites into sin, so the anger of the Lord is kindled against Israel.

17. When Elisha is dying, what does he predict? (13:14-19)

He predicts Israel will completely destroy the Arameans.

18. What happens to the man being buried? (13:20-21)

When the man being buried touches Elisha's bones, he comes back to life.

Answer these questions by reading 2 Kings 14–15

19. What law of Moses does Amaziah observe? (14:5-6)

Amaziah refuses to kill the children of the men who murdered his father.

20. What illness does Azariah have? (15:5)

Azariah has leprosy.

Answer these questions by reading 2 Kings 17

21. Why are the people punished? (17:7-9)

The people are punished because they "sinned against the LORD their God."

22. When do Israel's troubles begin? (17:21-23)

They begin with the revolt of Jeroboam.

DIMENSION TWO: WHAT DOES THE BIBLE MEAN?

Background Information on 2 Kings 9–17

In 2 Kings 9–17 the Bible records a series of happenings in the life of the Hebrew people. But the writer also intends that readers of this history receive a message beyond the mere recitation of names, dates, deeds, and places.

Some biblical scholars have used a special term to describe the kind of history that we are reading in this section of the Bible. They have called it *salvation history.* That is, this rendering of history asks the reader to ponder its meaning, purpose, and direction. This salvation history asks its readers to question what the awareness of God is that is written in these pages.

The writers whose works we are reading saw events as pointing to something beyond the events themselves, something of greater significance than the events themselves. This something that was beyond and that was greater was an understanding of why the events occurred.

The following elements of the salvation history are simple but profound:

(1) God has chosen his people and entered into covenant with them.

(2) When this people, as identified with their kings and priests, are faithful to God, blessing comes their way.

(3) When the kings and priests lead this people into the customs of the surrounding nations (that is, the pagan and abhorrent practices of their neighbors), then disaster comes upon the king, the royal family, and the people as a whole. (See 2 Kings 17:7-8, 13-14, 18.)

This close identity of king and people will seem strange to many modern readers. We may find it difficult to think that one ruler's good or evil ways could determine the whole nation's relationship to God. But this was the view that was held by our writers and the way they understood historical events.

The writers of the Deuteronomic history were not the only ones who saw these events as salvation history. This view of history may be illustrated by Amos 3:2: "You only have I chosen / of all the families of the earth; / therefore I will punish you / for all your sins." A special sense of judgment is assigned to the Hebrew people because of their special relationship to God. We may also read Isaiah 6:1-13 for further help in understanding this relationship. Both Amos and Isaiah did part of their work as spokespersons for God around the time of some of the events we examine today.

Amos insists that God's special relationship to the Hebrew people calls for special judgment. Isaiah insists that the divided nations, Israel and Judah, cannot survive. Their unfaithfulness to God, as demonstrated in the events that caused the nation to divide, will bring disaster. (See 2 Kings 17:18-23.)

The prophet Hosea also spoke of this special divine/human relationship. This prophet is thought by some biblical scholars to have started his work during the reign of Jeroboam II in Israel (783 B.C.–743 B.C.) and to have lived to see the fall of Samaria in 722 B.C.

For Hosea the special relationship of God and the Hebrews is described as an experience of marriage. He declares God to be a betrayed husband who still loves his wife and will stop at nothing to restore her to a right relationship with him. That includes terrible punishment on occasion.

All these examples are important for our understanding of the salvation view of history. It is also important that we as Christians know that in the end God suffers along with the suffering people. God does not stand above and beyond the pain we must endure but is with us, within our situation. Even in disaster God labors with us to bring forth something good. (See Romans 8:28.) The description of the suffering servant that comes quite late in the Book of Isaiah sums it up: "Surely he took up our infirmities / and carried our sorrows . . . / was pierced for our transgressions, . . . / crushed for our iniquities" (Isaiah 53:4-5).

2 Kings 9:1–10:36. In this section the prophet Elisha takes the initiative to anoint Jehu as king of Israel. Omri's dynasty is so unsatisfactory that, in the manner of Samuel who secretly anointed the first two kings (Saul and David), Elisha now anoints Jehu. (See 1 Samuel 10:1.) Jehu's first act is to have Joram (king of Israel) and Ahaziah (king of Judah) killed.

In 2 Kings 9:22, Jehu uses the word *idolatry* to describe Jezebel's efforts to induce the Hebrew people to worship the fertility gods of the Baal religion. In the RSV the word is *harlotries.* In the NRSV the word is *whoredoms.* Note also that Hosea builds his entire message upon the concept of harlotry (or adultery) as descriptive of the violated covenant the Hebrews had with God. (See Hosea 1:1-2.)

Harlotry and adultery are regarded as heinous sins throughout the Bible. Certainly, the prophetic religion of the Old Testament scorns such irregular sexual liaisons. The relationship of God and the Hebrews is repeatedly described in terms of a husband-wife relationship. It is natural, then, that a description of the infidelity and unfaithfulness of the Hebrews to God would be described in terms such as harlot and harlotry.

The words are used repeatedly to describe the idolatries indigenous to Canaan, the land now occupied by the Hebrews. Other references using this description include Hosea 4:12-14; 2:2-20; Jeremiah 3:1, 6-10; 31:31-32.

The New Jerusalem Bible translates *harlotries* as *prostitutions.* Ritual prostitution of both males and females was a part of Baal worship, as was the use of phallic symbols. All these rituals were encouraged, promoted, and even made popular by Queen Jezebel. This is the evil that opponents of Baal worship sought to drive from the land. Jehu was a principal opponent of Baal worship.

Jehu laid responsibility for his blood lust at the feet of God. (See 2 Kings 9:25-26.) In the light of that understanding of God's nature that formed much of the message of Amos, Hosea, and Isaiah, we must ask if Jehu confused the goal of God (that is, the winning of the people away from Baal worship) with his own political and military ambitions. Perhaps it is possible even today to adopt methods that are ungodly in our zeal to get on with the work of God.

Jehu's reign over Israel is filled with so much bloodshed that we are tempted to accuse him of genocide. Jezebel is killed; every male member of the house of Ahab is killed; and a great slaughter of priests, prophets, and worshipers of Baal is arranged by trickery. (See 2 Kings 10:1-28.)

But Jehu's bloody zeal finds him lacking as a ruler of God's own people. (See 2 Kings 10:29-31.) He clings to the sins of Jeroboam. He allows worship of the golden calves, and he does not destroy the shrines at Bethel and at Dan.

For our writers this was religious and political heresy and treason.

The end of Israel is at hand. Second Kings 10:30-33 describes the loss of Israel's territory to Hazael, king of Aram. For our writers this means that "Yahweh began to whittle Israel down" (2 Kings 10:32; *The New Jerusalem Bible*). Later we shall see that the country is all lost.

2 Kings 11:1–17:41. These chapters cover the years 841 B.C. to 722 B.C. We move from Jehu's enthronement as king as far as the fall of the Northern Kingdom.

In the midst of this account of the decline of the nation comes the biblical insight of 2 Kings 13:22-23. With Elisha dead and Israel at the mercy of Hazael, king of Aram, their hope and comfort lie in the knowledge that the mercy of God remains with the people. God's original choice, rooted in the relationship with Abraham, Isaac, and Jacob, stands unchanged. This passage is not far from the spirit of Jesus as revealed in Matthew 9:36. Look also at Ephesians 2:4-5 and Jude 21.

We rejoice in this reality concerning the God whose people we are. But the writers of Kings will not let us forget that somehow, in some way, sin has an ultimate price tag attached to it. The perfect summary of all these events, from the special viewpoint of our Bible writers, comes in 2 Kings 17:1-23, which ends on the sad note, "So the people of Israel were taken from their homeland into exile in Assyria, and they are still there." The Deuteronomic viewpoint comes through very clearly in verse 23: "The LORD removed them [Israel] from his presence."

However, we close on a note of comfort. We come to the end of Israel, but we do not come to the end of God's love. We do not come to an end of God's own keeping of the covenant.

DIMENSION THREE:
WHAT DOES THE BIBLE MEAN TO ME?

The Bible means to me much of what it meant to its first readers. It means that God is active in human history. God enters into a covenant with people chosen to become special to God and to the world. (See Isaiah 49:5-7.)

The Bible also means that I must deal with the sternness, the moral passion, and the jealous nature of God. Affection and gratitude for a gentle and compassionate Jesus must not blind my eyes to the dimensions of God's judgment, expectations, and requirements of the chosen people. God is not a doting, indulgent grandfather!

The Bible's special dimension of meaning for Christians is found in the declaration in the Gospels that God comes, dwells among us through the Holy Spirit, and never leaves us. Ultimately, God pays the penalty of our sin and moral failure. God provided Abraham with the ram for the burnt offering. (See Genesis 22:8.) For us God provides the Lamb without blemish, slain from before the foundation of the world. (See Exodus 12:5; Revelation 5:6; 13:8.)

2 Kings 9:1–10:36—Understanding God's Purposes

The chapters that comprise today's assignment are part of the sad history of the two nations that the United Kingdom divided into after the death of Solomon. These chapters bring us to face a history in which Judah and Israel seem bent upon destroying themselves through fratricidal strife. They also face destruction from outside forces and bring terrible vengeance one upon the other—all in the name of the God of the chosen people. At the end of Chapter 17, Israel falls before the conquering power of Assyria. Judah holds on to eke out a precarious existence until Jerusalem, the City of David, is destroyed about 587 B.C.

In this section of Dimension Three, the questions in the student book focus on distinguishing between human desire and divine purpose. Review the events of 2 Kings 9–10 with the class. Ask class members to list the places in these two chapters where Jehu claims to have God's blessing for what he is doing. (See 9:6-10, 25-26; class members will be able to locate other examples as well.)

The student book emphasizes that we have an advantage over the people of Jehu's day. We have the example of Jesus' life of peace. Our criteria for determining what events reveal divine purpose are different from those of the ancient Israelites. Have the class discuss how the person and work of Christ has influenced our perception of God's purposes in the world.

2 Kings 11:1–17:40—Living in Exile

The student book suggests that these chapters ask us to deal with the thought that in the end all sin exacts a penalty. Would members of your class agree or disagree? For what reasons? In what ways does sin have to be paid for? On what grounds can the penalty be ultimately avoided or voided by the action of God in Christ? Is that cancellation of the penalty for sin something that happens in our society? Ask the class to discuss ways that our nation is in exile because we are unfaithful to God.

2 Kings 14:1-6—Responsibility for Sin

Our interest in this section is especially in 2 Kings 14:6: "Yet he did not put the sons of the assassins to death." Here we have reintroduced in the life of the Hebrew people a moral idea associated with Moses. That moral idea is the responsibility of the individual for his or her own wrong-doing.

This idea is in contrast to the other ancient Hebrew idea of human solidarity that is exemplified in the close identification of the king with the people and the people with the king.

The idea of human solidarity made possible the terrible events of Joshua 7:24-27 and 2 Kings 9:26, where whole families are wiped out because of the sin or failure of a single individual. The fact that our writers find it desirable to mention that Amaziah did not do this indicates that the murder of entire families was a common practice.

Individual responsibility before God for one's own evil and not for the evil of others is a comforting thought. Discuss with the class other ways to interpret this insight. To what extent can the person who does wrong lay the blame for his or her behavior upon society? Are we justified in thinking each time some tragic event occurs that this is a comment on the whole people? Perhaps the truth is somewhere between an attitude that would hold an individual responsible for what others have done and the opposite attitude that would allow an individual to blame failure on the social order.

You can now summarize the significance of 2 Kings 14:1-6 with these sentences:

God is involved in the national life of the chosen people. Whatever concerns them—politics, economics, social structures—is of concern to God. We should know this from the story of how God planned and worked with Moses to liberate the Israelites from Egyptian slavery. Amos believed that God had been at work in other liberation movements as well. (See Amos 9:7.)

God's ultimate intention is to bring the people salvation—a rightness of relationship with God, a fuller freedom, and a supply of daily needs.

Such affirmations are comforting. They seem easy to accept. It is more difficult to ask whether our situation is comparable to that of Amaziah in Judah and Jehoash in Israel. Can we be described as men and women who are indeed followers of the Lord, obedient to God's ways, but nevertheless have limitations? (See 2 Kings 14:3.)

Ask the class to discuss what ways we can check the quality of our living against what can be discovered of the highest and truest commandments of the Lord. (See John 17:7.)

Close today's session by listing on a chalkboard or on a large piece of paper any new insights the class members have gained from their study of 2 Kings 9–17.

5

The Kingdom of Judah

2 Kings 18–25

**DIMENSION ONE:
WHAT DOES THE BIBLE SAY?**

Answer these questions by reading 2 Kings 18

1. Why does Hezekiah break the bronze snake Moses made? (18:4)

   Hezekiah breaks the snake because the people are burning incense to it.

2. What reward does Hezekiah's devotion to God bring? (18:7)

   The Lord is always with Hezekiah, and he is successful in whatever he undertakes.

3. What happens to the Israelites when Samaria (Israel) is conquered? (18:11)

   Some of the Israelites are carried into Assyrian exile.

4. Why does this happen to Israel? (18:12)

   The Israelites are conquered because they disobeyed God.

5. How does Hezekiah respond to Sennacherib's attack? (18:13-16)

   Hezekiah submits to Sennacherib's rule and pays tribute.

Answer these questions by reading 2 Kings 19–20

6. How does Isaiah encourage Hezekiah? (19:6-7)

   He promises Sennacherib will be destroyed.

7. How does Isaiah act as Hezekiah's physician? (20:7)

   He prescribes a fig poultice for Hezekiah's boil.

8. What sign is given that God will heal Hezekiah? (20:8-11)

   The sun's shadow moves backward on the dial as a sign.

9. How does Hezekiah accept Babylon's final victory? (20:16-19)

   He is relieved it will not happen in his own time.

Answer these questions by reading 2 Kings 21–22

10. What evils does Manasseh commit? (21:1-7, 16)

    He restores Baal worship, builds an Asherah, and sacrifices his son, among other things.

11. Who follows Manasseh as king? (22:1)

    Josiah is the next king.

12. Who is Hilkiah? (22:8)

    He is the high priest.

13. What does Hilkiah find? (22:8-10)

    Hilkiah finds the lost Book of the Law.

14. How does Josiah respond to this important find? (22:11)

    Josiah tears his robes in repentance.

Answer these questions by reading 2 Kings 23

15. What sexual act of worship does Josiah banish? (23:7)

    Josiah banishes male shrine prostitution.

16. Where are child sacrifices usually made? (23:10)

    Child sacrifices are usually made at the Valley of Ben Hinnom.

17. What religious festival does Josiah renew? (23:21-22)

Josiah commands the people to keep the Passover.

18. How does the biblical writer summarize Josiah's reign? (23:25)

There was no other king like Josiah.

19. How does the Lord feel about Judah? (23:26-27)

The Lord is angry at Judah and plans to destroy it.

20. With whom is God most angry? (23:26-27)

The Lord is most angry with Judah.

21. Where are the rest of the acts of Josiah written? (23:28)

"The book of the annals of the kings of Judah" tells all that Josiah did.

22. Who kills King Josiah? (23:29-30)

Pharaoh Neco, king of Egypt, kills Josiah.

Answer these questions by reading 2 Kings 24–25

23. What foreign king exacts Judah's submission? (24:1)

Judah becomes a servant of Nebuchadnezzar, king of Babylon.

24. Who remains in the land after Nebuchadnezzar captures Jerusalem? (24:10-16)

The poorest people of the land remain.

25. What happens to Jehoiachin after thirty-seven years of exile? (25:27-30)

He is freed from prison, given an allowance, and dines at the king's table every day.

DIMENSION TWO: WHAT DOES THE BIBLE MEAN?

Background Information on 2 Kings 18–25

This section of the Bible is the history of the decline and fall of the kingdom of Judah. Second Kings 18–25 is one account of the events that occurred in Judah between the years 725 B.C. and 586 B.C. Several events that preceded the fall of Judah contributed to the decline.

The Hebrew people told Samuel that they should have a king in order to be like the other nations around them. (See 1 Samuel 8:4-22.) At that time in Hebrew history the people were ruled by judges. The judges were men and women who, by virtue of their charismatic personality or wisdom, emerged as the natural leaders of the people.

Considering what happened after Saul was anointed first king of Israel, down to the events described in today's chapters, it is very interesting to read in 1 Samuel 8:7-9 that establishment of a monarchy is viewed as a rejection of God!

With few notable exceptions—such as the years covered in today's chapters when Hezekiah and Josiah reigned—the era of the kings over both Israel and Judah was an era when it seems God was rejected as ruler over the people.

Samuel felt that appointing a king was an error, but he reluctantly anointed Saul king over Israel. (See 1 Samuel 10:1-2.) The reign of Saul was not an unqualified success. An awful summary is given in 1 Samuel 15:35: "Samuel mourned for him [Saul]. And the LORD was grieved that he had made Saul king over Israel."

David succeeds Saul but first sentences to death the man who had killed Saul. (See 2 Samuel 1:11-16.) Under David the kingdom is united and stays one nation until, as we have seen in this current series of lessons, Judah and Israel split following the death of Solomon. (See 1 Kings 12:16-20.) The royal family of David is left only with the tribe of Judah.

From that point on, to use a slang phrase, "it was downhill all the way." In today's session we come to the bottom of the hill. We reach, in our historical journey, the end of Judah, which had survived as a nation longer than Israel.

No doubt the writers of First and Second Kings were convinced that underneath the historical facts they recorded, there was something more. That "something more" was the relentless, unswerving working out of the divine demand that the Hebrew people should be a people holy to the Lord. They should do the Lord's will and walk in the Lord's commandments and statutes. (See 2 Kings 17:13.) When the people, acting primarily in harmony with the choices made by their kings, "sold themselves to do evil in the eyes of the LORD" (2 Kings 17:17), the Lord was moved to anger and sent them into exile.

2 Kings 18:1–20:21. With a sense of relief we read of the reign of one good king, one who did what was right in the eyes of the Lord. (See 2 Kings 18:3.) We find a man, Hezekiah, who apparently understood and accepted for himself the implications of the ancient covenant between God and the Hebrew people. He acts to bring Judah (the only branch of the original kingdom that we are reading about) back to the pure worship of a holy God. (See 2 Kings 18:4-6.)

In Hezekiah's own life, he is a man of faith and of prayer and worship. (See 2 Kings 19:1-4.) He is not ashamed to seek out the counsel and help of the prophet Isaiah, whom he recognizes as a man of God. Apparently Hezekiah found in Isaiah a genuine, consistent relationship with God. He found in Isaiah a man who could minister to the king's physical needs, his emotional distress, and his great concern for the welfare of his nation. Isaiah was a source of hope and encouragement to Hezekiah. (See 2 Kings 20:7-11; 19:20-34.) Hezekiah was truly one of the great kings in the history of the Hebrew people.

2 Kings 22:1–25:30. Josiah, grandson of Hezekiah, is the second of the two kings to whom our biblical writers give an unqualified stamp of approval.

The central event of Josiah's reign is finding the Book of the Law in the Temple. The book was found by Hilkiah, the high priest, and given to the king for his response. There are many important questions that can be asked about the discovery of this book. Why was it lost in the first place? What was this Book of the Law that Hilkiah found?

Most biblical scholars identify the Book of the Law found by Hilkiah with Deuteronomy 12–26, 28. The student book suggests six of the major emphases in these chapters that seem to have been integral to the reform and revival that took place under King Josiah.

The student book also suggests the scope of true religious revival. It does indeed include all the concern that we can muster for worshiping God with those attitudes and those practices that are, so far as we can discern, in keeping with the character of God. The questions of decorum in public worship, music, ritual, and setting for worship are not trivial. These questions are important because they have to do with the environment in which the human spirit may encounter the Spirit of God.

God comes to us through reading the Scripture. God comes to us on the musical notes that fall on our ears as the people sing their praises. God offers grace to us through the waters of baptism, applied to ourselves or applied to others in our presence. God is present in the bread and wine of Holy Communion. God speaks to us in the various languages we can comprehend.

The Book of Second Kings closes with the last days of the kingdom of Judah. Chapters 23–25 narrate these events in quick succession, beginning with the death of Josiah (2 Kings 23:28-30).

Jehoahaz, the son of Josiah, began to reign in Judah. The year was approximately 609 B.C. After the death of Josiah at the hands of Pharaoh Neco, Judah became a vassal of Egypt. Jehoahaz remained on the throne for three months and was replaced by Eliakim, his brother. In making this replacement, Pharaoh Neco also changed Eliakim's name to Jehoiakim (23:34). The name change signified Jehoiakim's vassalage to the king of Egypt.

Jehoiakim reigned eleven years in Jerusalem, part of that time under the subjection of Egypt. (See 23:36.) In 605 B.C., the Babylonians under King Nebuchadnezzar defeated the Egyptians. This defeat ended the vassalage of Judah to Egypt. In 2 Kings 24:1 we read that Jehoiakim became Nebuchadnezzar's vassal for three years.

At the end of this three-year period, Jehoiakim revolted against the Babylonian rule (about 602 B.C.). But the historian tells us that Jehoiakim was destined to lose this battle.

(See 2 Kings 24:3-4.) Jehoiakim was succeeded by Jehoiachin in 598 B.C. Jehoiachin reigned for three months and then surrendered to Nebuchadnezzar, who carried the king and his family into captivity in Babylon.

Nebuchadnezzar made Jehoiachin's uncle (Mattaniah) king and renamed him Zedekiah (24:17). Second Kings 25 recounts Zedekiah's ill-fated rebellion against the Babylonians and the resulting defeat of Judah. Jerusalem fell in the eleventh year of King Zedekiah (about 586 B.C.).

In 25:22-26 we read a brief account of the government of Gedaliah. Some of Gedaliah's fellow Judeans considered him to be a traitor and put him to death in the seventh month of his rule. A fuller picture of these events is given to us by the prophet Jeremiah. (See Jeremiah 40–41.)

DIMENSION THREE: WHAT DOES THE BIBLE MEAN TO ME?

2 Kings 18:1–20:21—Being a Good Person

No question is more puzzling than why one person's behavior is good while another person's behavior is evil. We are dealing in these chapters with one of Judah's few truly good kings. Why was this man's reign in such contrast with the reign of some who preceded him and some who came after him?

Perhaps Hezekiah is a good person because of the character and training of his mother, Abijah. She was the daughter of Zechariah, mentioned as a man of good repute in Isaiah 8:2. Perhaps we have here a particular family's tradition and practice of obedience to God. Ask class members to think of similar situations that exist today. Which families in your community have similar traditions of obedience to God? What does it mean to "come from a good family"? What privileges come to persons from good families?

First and Second Kings are filled with the cumulative weight and power of repeated generations of wrongdoing. Our celebration of the righteousness of Hezekiah shows us another side of our human involvements. Is there also a cumulative weight, power, and influence of righteousness and goodness? Will we who have a Christian family life and Christian community life become part of the heritage and tradition that will help men and women in future years to be faithful to God?

The student book uses the phrase "endless line of splendor" to describe a succession of men and women who, to the best of their understanding, do the will of God in their own time. Ask the class whether we can each find a place in that endless line by quietly and faithfully setting patterns of goodness in our daily lives that our children and our grandchildren may someday choose to follow. Ask the class to share stories of persons who have influenced them to be better persons.

2 Kings 22:1–25:30—Religious Revival

These chapters dealing with Josiah's reform of Judah's worship may suggest to us the role of the Bible in a revival and renewal of religion in the life of our communities and our nation.

Nearly every great turning point in the history of Christian faith has been associated with some new emphasis upon the written word of God. We may think of the conversion of the libertine, Augustine, as he heard the child's voice chanting, "Take up and read." Or we may think of Martin Luther coming upon that iridescent sentence, "The just shall live by faith," or John Wesley's personal awakening as the Epistle to the Romans was being expounded. Perhaps each of us can cite some moment when some words from the Bible came alive and made a real difference in us. Ask class members to share examples of such moments in their lives or in the lives of others.

We are called to the intensive study of the Bible. We can expect a religious revival in our churches to be very closely associated with the abolition of what has been called "our biblical illiteracy." Have class members discuss the questions in the student book and list ways that they can help begin a renewal of faith.

Then close the session by having group members share new insights on 2 Kings 18–25 that they have gained from studying today's lesson. If time allows, list these insights on a chalkboard or a large sheet of paper.

INTRODUCTION TO
FIRST AND SECOND CHRONICLES

First and Second Chronicles are a history covering the time from Adam (1 Chronicles 1:1) to Cyrus, king of Persia (2 Chronicles 36:22-23). This history parallels Genesis through Second Kings and is concluded in Ezra-Nehemiah. First and Second Chronicles and Ezra-Nehemiah were originally a single book in Hebrew. They were later divided in Greek translations because the Greek needed more space than the Hebrew, which used no vowels. Second Chronicles 36:22-23 duplicates Ezra 1:1-3, which is an ancient indication that the two are part of one book. In Hebrew, Chronicles means *things of the days*, or *events of past time*. The present English title comes from "Chronicles of the Whole Sacred History," a title suggested by Jerome, a fourth-century Italian theologian.

The Content of First and Second Chronicles

First Chronicles summarizes the period from Adam to David (Chapters 1–9) and details David's reign (Chapters 10–29). Second Chronicles deals with Solomon's reign (Chapters 1–9) and with the kings of Judah (Chapters 10–36).

We know the author only as "the Chronicler." He was probably a member of a guild (perhaps of singers or musicians) in the Temple in Jerusalem. Chronicles emphasizes the Temple, its worship, and its keepers. The books also emphasize the significance of the Jews in Jerusalem and Judah by telling the story of God's abiding relationship with them. Chronicles is written from a Judean perspective.

The Composition of Chronicles

The Chronicler was a post-exilic writer who brought Chronicles to its present form between 350 B.C. and 250 B.C. The Chronicler drew on information about the history of Judah and Israel from the Pentateuch (Genesis–Deuteronomy) and from Joshua, Samuel, and Kings. He quotes from these books verbatim (for example, 2 Samuel 7, 8, and 10 are quoted in 1 Chronicles 17–20). He also omits material from these books (such as David's adultery and Absalom's rebellion), modifies some material (Contrast 2 Samuel 24 with 1 Chronicles 21:1.), supplements with new details (for example, in the account of David bringing the ark to Jerusalem), and stresses his own views. (See 2 Kings 9:1-28; 10:11-14 as it is summarized in 2 Chronicles 22:7-9.)

The Chronicler does not mention the biblical books he used as sources. He does mention twenty-five other works and refers readers to them for further information. Some of these works are historical, and some are attributed to various prophets and seers. All these sources are now regarded as the same work, no longer in existence, that the Chronicler referred to under different titles. It was a common ancient practice to refer to a passage by name as if it were a book.

This single work referred to by the Chronicler is usually called *The Midrash of the Kings*. (Midrash is literature that investigates and elaborates upon Scripture.) We cannot know for certain whether the Midrash existed and was used by the Chronicler, the Chronicler cited a fictitious book, or composed the material himself.

Plagiarism, copyright laws, and unbiased "factual" information were not of concern to the Chronicler. Chronicles is not a history in our sense of history; it is not a disinterested account of the facts of past events. It is an interpretive recounting of the past with a particular purpose and from a particular viewpoint.

Special Emphases of the Chronicler

The Chronicler wanted to make clear to his contemporaries the significance of past events—the events of God dealing with the chosen people. The past informed the present and was also shaped by it. The Chronicler narrated past events in light of the present. The Chronicler's community (Judah) was insignificant in comparison to the empires that surrounded it. Judah was a long way from the political and economic power it enjoyed under David and Solomon. The Chronicler believed that this community was still important because its king was the one true God, whose earthly home was in the Temple in Jerusalem.

Judah was a worshiping community—people whose lives were to be spent in service to God. Anyone who worshiped the Lord alone and who followed God's laws was part of the community. This community was to center around the Temple in Jerusalem, not around the rival temples in Egypt and Samaria.

Unlike the prophets, the Chronicler emphasized the ritualistic responsibilities of the people—sacrifice, thanksgiving, praise, and prayer in worship—rather than their moral responsibilities. Faithfulness in worship was of central importance. No longer a nation in the political sense, the people of Israel were a church. The Chronicler believed that this was in keeping with their tradition, inaugurated with David and maintained by succeeding generations. The Chronicler expressed a sense of order and purpose for the community. He interpreted their heritage in a way that made sense to him in light of their present experience. This interpretation gave continuity to their tradition and direction for their future. The Chronicler interpreted the past and the present as part of and preparation for the saving work of God on behalf of the chosen people.

6

Genealogies

1 Chronicles 1–8

DIMENSION ONE:
WHAT DOES THE BIBLE SAY?

Answer these questions by reading 1 Chronicles 1

1. Who was the first man? (1:1)

   Adam was the first man.

2. Who is the Northern Kingdom named for? (1:34; 2:1)

   The Northern Kingdom is named for Israel.

Answer these questions by reading 1 Chronicles 2

3. How were Judah (the man) and Israel (the man) related? (2:1)

   Judah was the son of Israel.

4. What two men are remembered for being evil? (2:3, 7)

   Er and Achar are remembered for being evil.

5. Who are David's father, grandfather, and great-grand-father? (2:10-15)

   Jesse is David's father, Obed his grandfather, and Boaz his great-grandfather.

Answer these questions by reading 1 Chronicles 3

6. How long does David rule over the United Kingdom? (3:4)

   David rules over the United Kingdom forty years and six months.

7. From what cities does he rule? (3:4)

   David rules in Hebron and Jerusalem.

8. How many generations are there from Solomon to Josiah? (3:10-14)

   There are fifteen generations from Solomon to Josiah.

Answer these questions by reading 1 Chronicles 4

9. What man is remembered for his great honor? (4:9)

   Jabez is remembered for his honor.

10. For what two things does this man ask God? (4:10)

    Jabez asks for a larger territory and for protection.

Answer these questions by reading 1 Chronicles 5

11. Does God take sides in battle? (5:18-26)

    Yes. Sometimes God helps the Hebrews, and sometimes God helps their enemies.

12. How is Manasseh described for worshiping other gods? (5:25)

    Manasseh is described as playing the prostitute.

Answer these questions by reading 1 Chronicles 6

13. Who is Johanan? (6:10)

    Johanan is a priest in Solomon's Temple.

14. What do the men David appoints to the Temple do? (6:31)

    They are in charge of the music.

15. Who originates or founds the Temple worship ritual? (6:49)

    Moses founds the worship ritual.

16. Who is in charge of burnt offerings and incense offerings? (6:49)

Aaron and his sons are in charge of the offerings.

17. Why are these offerings made? (6:49)

These offerings make an atonement for Israel.

18. What makes the cities mentioned valuable? (6:67-81)

Their pasture lands make the cities valuable.

Answer these questions by reading 1 Chronicles 7

19. What makes these families special? (7:1-12)

The sons of these families are mighty warriors.

20. What woman do we remember for building cities? (7:24)

Sheerah built cities.

Answer these questions by reading 1 Chronicles 8

21. Where do the heads of the tribe of Benjamin reside? (8:28)

They reside in Jerusalem.

22. What important king comes from the tribe of Benjamin? (8:33)

King Saul comes from the tribe of Benjamin.

DIMENSION TWO:
WHAT DOES THE BIBLE MEAN?

As we begin our study of First and Second Chronicles, we shall find ourselves reading again the history of the Hebrew people from the days of the rule of David, through the splendor of Solomon's years, the tragedy of national division, and the bitter ending as Judah's defeat is described for us in 2 Kings 24–25.

The pattern of the history will be painfully familiar to us, since we read it first in First and Second Kings. The pattern is one of light and darkness, of obedience and disobedience, and of fidelity and infidelity on the part of the rulers of the people with whom God had entered into covenant. (See Exodus 3:1-12; 20:1-17.)

The pattern is one where we will again encounter some splendid personalities whose faithfulness and ardor for service to God cause us to think, maybe to hope, that in the end the victory will belong to righteousness and goodness. In those moments of fearful hope, we will find ourselves required to face some of the most painful and difficult questions for men and women of faith: Does evil outweigh good? Does falsehood defeat truth? Is God's purpose to raise up a holy people never to be realized and fulfilled in human experience?

First Chronicles seems to be a dull and virtually endless list of fathers and sons with occasional mention of mothers and daughters. Professional genealogists may not be quite as troubled in finding their way through these first chapters of First Chronicles as some of the rest of us. But even those whose primary interest is not genealogy can find food for thought in these long lists of ancient names and in these twisted tracings of family connections.

These first chapters of First Chronicles contain several insights. One is that the longing for land of our own and the tireless search for our own place is deeply rooted in the human spirit. But that land has not always been acquired by methods that can be judged acceptable by insights gained from the teachings of Jesus.

All of us have in our backgrounds a closeness to a pastoral-agricultural experience. How these Hebrews—our ancestors in faith and in culture—must have loved their land, their herds, and the rich pastures they found in various places!

Another insight in these chapters is that there is a vivid sense of the action and presence of God in the life of this people. God is present in their journeyings, in their transmission of life from generation to generation, and in the establishment of the nation. Part of the tragedy in the secularization of American society is that this sense of God's involvement with our lives has been lost. We have so misunderstood and misinterpreted the decision of the writers of our Constitution not to establish a religion that we have allowed much of our national life to become anti-God.

Underneath all their national and ethnic conflict and striving, these Hebrew people had a sense of their relationship to the other peoples of the earth. Though it was not always in the forefront of their thinking, there was a feeling of what theologians call universalism—a sense of God's concern and care for all peoples of the earth.

There was also a sense of continuity in the life of that nation. Kings could rise and fall, too few of them good; but the nation and the people continued to live. Enemies could arise, from within and without; but again the nation and the people continued to live.

Of course, in the end the nation ceased to exist. After the tragedy of the division following Solomon's death, there was the fall of the Northern Kingdom (Israel) and finally the humiliating fall of Judah, the Southern Kingdom.

1 Chronicles 1–2. This story of all humankind, beginning with Adam, moves swiftly to focus upon Israel and Judah. We may be reminded of Paul's statement to the people of Athens: "From one man he made every nation of men, that they should inhabit the whole earth; and he determined the times set for them and the exact places where they should live" (Acts 17:26). Luke, generally agreed to be the most universal-minded of the Gospel writers, traces the ancestry of Jesus back through Hebrew history to Adam. (See Luke 3:23-38.)

These writers are saying, in one way or another, that all humankind is more closely related than we might think. The farther back we go in our ancestry, the more likely we are to have a common ancestry with almost anyone we meet.

1 Chronicles 2–4. In our introductory questions we have dealt with three men virtually unknown to all except the most attentive Bible readers. These men are mentioned only very briefly, but to each is appended a comment or a bit of information that is worth our consideration.

Two of them, Er and Achar (also called Achan), are remembered for their wickedness. The precise nature of that evil is difficult to determine. All we know is that Er "was wicked in the LORD's sight" (2:3), and Achar "violat[ed] the ban on taking devoted things" (2:7). By reading Joshua 6 and 7, we determine that Achar (Achan) kept for his own use things from Jericho that had been labeled for destruction.

Perhaps the significance of these men for us is twofold: (1) The evil that we do may be long remembered, or we may be remembered as men and women whose influence was against the good in our community. (2) We must be as careful in the small things of life, those things that do not seem to matter, as we are careful in the major things of our commitment to the Lord. Compare the words of Jesus concerning tithing: "You should have practiced the latter, without neglecting the former" (Matthew 23:23). Jesus is not saying that the small things, the tithing of the mint, dill, and cummin are unimportant. He is saying we cannot ignore the weightier things. Jesus also said, "You have been faithful with a few things; I will put you in charge of many things" (Matthew 25:21).

Since so much of this ancient record deals with infidelity and wickedness, the mention of a man of honor comes as a refreshing note. Such a man was Jabez. (See 1 Chronicles 4:9.) Unfortunately, all that we know about this individual is contained in these verses.

1 Chronicles 6. This chapter brings us to another great concern of the Chronicler. The Chronicler was greatly appreciative of the Temple and its ritual. We will see much more of that interest in later chapters.

The worship in the Temple is affirmed to be in harmony with the leadership of Moses, since Moses helped to focus his people's life and loyalty toward God. Moses has been described as the human founder of the religion and the nation of Israel. That is, he was instrumental in establishing the covenant with God and identifying the Hebrew people as an ethnic group.

The worship in the Temple was made beautiful and meaningful by the use of music. Choral music was a very special part of the worship. First Chronicles 6:31 is one of several references outside the Book of Psalms that associate David with music and poetry.

Various kinds of sacrifices—animals, grain, incense, and others—made the worship in the Temple highly dramatic. We cannot easily imagine that a worshiper either grew bored or fell asleep. Worship was dramatic and enlivened with motion, color, sound, and even fragrance.

The purpose of the sacrifices was atonement for Israel, the expiation of Israel's sin. For these ancient people life was blood, and blood was life. (See Leviticus 17:11, 14.) They knew, however dimly, that only a poured-out life would bring persons and God into that harmony that was and is atonement.

This notion of sacrifice—the shedding of blood and the cleansing power of God—is brought together in the atoning life of Jesus Christ. We can now see the truth of Abraham's words of faith: "God himself will provide the lamb for the burnt offering" (Genesis 22:8).

DIMENSION THREE: WHAT DOES THE BIBLE MEAN TO ME?

We can easily push these long chapters of strange names away from us. We can say, "There's nothing there for me!" Or we can attempt a second and a deeper look. The student book discussion in Dimension Three centers on two issues, "Worshiping God" and "Atonement Comes From God." First Chronicles 1–8 also raises the issue of universalism, as we saw in Dimension Two. If the class decides to discuss the issue of universalism, use the information that follows to help you lead the discussion.

1 Chronicles 1–2—Universalism

The Bible is telling us that within the ultimate plan of God, no human being is meant to be a stranger or an alien to any other human being. We are placed on the earth, ultimately, not for hatred, but for love; not for war, but for peace; not for strife, but for cooperation. Recent books on anthropology have affirmed that the basic nature of the human being is social. We are made to live together. The words of Benjamin Franklin that "we must hang together or we will hang separately" are of profound implication. In the Bible's view all of humankind are ultimately one because all are descended from Adam and Eve.

In Dimension Two we have suggested that the idea of universalism is emphasized in these chapters and indeed in the rest of the writings of the Chronicler. What do we mean when we use that word *universalism?*

Universalism, as we understand it here, does not mean that all persons will ultimately be reconciled to God whether they desire it or not. We are not saying that it does not make any difference what people believe, just so they believe something. We are not saying that all religious beliefs and practices lead to the same knowledge of God. (See John 14:6.)

Universalism, as we find it here and elsewhere in the Old Testament and supremely in John 3:16, is an affirmation of the concern and care of God for the entire human race. It is an overwhelming sense of the all-inclusive love of God.

Perhaps it is accurate to insist that here we have the seed of the universalism that we shall later find in Isaiah 66:18-23. We also find that sense of the inclusive will of God reflected in the struggle over the admission of Gentiles to the church. (See Acts 11:1-18.)

Ask the class to discuss the limits and the boundaries of our acceptance of this universal love of God. If we accept God's love as being universal in its desire to save, what should the ethnic and racial makeup of our churches be? Should the local church become a meeting place and rallying point for men and women of every race, social class, occupation, and level of education?

Have the class discuss the presence (or the absence) of a sense of universalism in your local congregation. Do you, as a church of Jesus Christ, really believe that God cares for all humankind? In what ways does your congregation endeavor to share in God's love for the world? What does your church do to make visible and tangible the divine love?

1 Chronicles 6:31-48—Worshiping God

We must not forget that there is a place for legitimate concern for the quality of worship within the church. Several references in this sixth chapter of First Chronicles point to the legitimacy of this concern. First Chronicles 6:31-48 is of special importance.

The discussion of this issue in the student book centers on the contribution that music makes to the quality of our worship. We know from our own history and personal experience the value of singing the good news of God. Ask the class members to consider and discuss the role of music in the worship services of your church. What aspects of God's character are emphasized in our church music?

1 Chronicles 6:49—Atonement Comes From God

The student book mentions that the idea of atonement has different shades of meaning in different parts of the Bible. The questions for discussion concentrate on the meaning of atonement today. As background for discussing these questions, share the information in "More About Atonement" given below.

Close today's session by having class members share new insights on 1 Chronicles 1–8.

More About Atonement*

The English word *atone* is derived from the phrase *at one*. To be at one with someone is to be in harmonious personal relationship with him or her. Similarly, atonement originally meant at *onement*, or *reconciliation*. In modern usage, however, atonement has taken on the more restricted meaning of the process by which the hindrances to reconciliation are removed, rather than the end achieved by their removal. To atone for a wrong is to take some action that cancels out the ill effects it has had.

The Bible as a whole assumes the need for some atoning action, if persons are to be right with God. It is accepted as a fact beyond dispute that humankind is estranged from God and is wholly to blame for this estrangement. Our disobedience to the will of God—that is, our sin—has alienated us from God, and this alienation must first be remedied if right relationships are to be restored. The barrier raised by our past sins must be removed.

Atonement in the Old Testament

The usual Hebrew word for atone is *kaphar*. Probably its original meaning was *cover*, though some have suggested that it was *wipe off*. However, the word later came to be used in a general sense of removing the effects of sin.

One purpose of the elaborate sacrificial system of Old Testament religion was to provide such an atonement, and the word *kaphar* is frequently used in relation to sacrifice. In the ritual for the consecration of priests, for example, it is required: "Sacrifice a bull each day as a sin offering to make atonement" (Exodus 29:36). Similarly, the priests must make sacrifice for the sins of all the people that they may be forgiven (Leviticus 4:20). So also in the ritual of the Day of Atonement the first of the two goats is slain (Leviticus 16:9), but the second "shall be presented alive before the LORD to be used for making atonement" (verse 10). This live goat is driven out into the wilderness, laden with the sins of the people.

Atonement is therefore commonly associated with the death of a victim. It is not, however, exclusively so; for not only can the live scapegoat make atonement but also the offering of money for the Temple may be an offering for "making atonement for your lives" (Exodus 30:16). Incense can be effective in making atonement (Numbers 16:47), and Moses seeks to make atonement through prayer (Exodus 32:30).

Usually it is the person who must make atonement to God, by offering something that will be thought adequate to make amends for the bad effects of his or her sin. But sometimes it is God who is said to make atonement. In the NRSV this is translated as "pardon" in 2 Chronicles 30:18 and as "forgive" in Ezekiel 16:63; Deuteronomy 21:8; and Psalm 78:38.

It has often been discussed how far these means of atonement were thought of as propitiating God, or alternatively as expiating the offense. The word *propitiation* suggests that God, alienated by our sin, requires something to appease the divine anger before again showing favor to the sinner. Expiation recognizes that a hindrance to right relationship has been created by the sin and that this is removed by the means of atonement, but it does not locate the hindrance in God.

The word *propitiation*, however, is not used at all in our English versions of the Old Testament; and expiation occurs only rarely.

Atonement in the New Testament

Event though the word *atonement* does not occur in the New Testament, the meaning behind the word is constantly present. Here, however, it is no longer associated with the Temple sacrifices, still less with payments of money, or incense, or even with prayers. It is related entirely to Jesus Christ and his coming to earth, and especially with his death upon the cross. Words had to be found to declare that in Christ is that which overcomes the estrangement between humankind and God. It was inevitable that these words should largely be drawn from the familiar practice of sacrifice, partly because in this there was language all would understand, and partly because his death by crucifixion, with the actual shedding of blood, had so many unmistakable similarities to the actual practice of sacrifice.

The New Testament declares that in Christ and his death is all that persons need in order to find their sins forgiven and their lives reconciled to God; in him is that which can cancel out the ill effects of sin, release persons from the burden of their guilt, and grant them peace with God.

Conclusion

It is sin that has created the need for atonement, because sin, besides corrupting the heart and deadening the conscience and making us increasingly prone to sin again, causes us to be estranged from God, separated from God by an unseen barrier, a "dividing wall of hostility" (Ephesians 2:14). In Christ this barrier of separation from God has broken down. Christ reconciles us to God and gives us peace with God. It is one task of theologians to attempt to explain how Christ in his self-giving on the cross has achieved this end. No precise explanation, however, is offered in the New Testament, nor has the church officially sponsored any one of the theories of the atonement that have been propounded. But both church and New Testament agree in declaring with full assurance the fact of the atonement—that God has prepared the way by which we may be reconciled to the Lord and the means by which the evil consequences of past sin can be annulled. This way is Christ. This means is Christ. "He himself is our peace, . . . who has destroyed the barrier, the dividing wall of hostility . . . [that he might] . . . reconcile us . . . to God through the cross" (Ephesians 2:14-16).*

*Adapted from the article entitled "Atonement," by C.L. Mitton, from *The Interpreter's Dictionary of the Bible*, Vol. 1. Copyright © 1962 by Abingdon Press. Used by permission.

7

David, the Great King

1 Chronicles 9–14

DIMENSION ONE:
WHAT DOES THE BIBLE SAY?

Answer these questions by reading 1 Chronicles 9

1. What are the three kinds of servants for the house of the Lord? (9:10, 14, 17)

   The priests, Levites, and gatekeepers are the Temple servants.

2. Who appoints gatekeepers for the house of the Lord? (9:22-23)

   David and Samuel the seer appoint the gatekeepers.

3. Where do the Levitical Temple guards and singers live? (9:27, 33)

   They live in the Temple precincts.

Answer these questions by reading 1 Chronicles 10

4. Why does Saul kill himself? (10:4-5)

   Saul does not wish to fall into the hands of the Philistines.

5. What do the Philistines do with Saul's body? (10:8-10)

   The Philistines cut off Saul's head and nail it to the temple of Dagon, their god.

6. How does the Chronicler interpret Saul's death? (10:13-14)

   Saul dies because he is unfaithful to the Lord and does not seek the Lord's guidance.

7. To whom does the Lord give the kingdom upon Saul's death? (10:14)

   The Lord turns the kingdom over to David, the son of Jesse.

Answer these questions by reading 1 Chronicles 11

8. Where is David anointed king over Israel? (11:1-3)

   David is anointed king at Hebron.

9. What is David called? (11:2)

   David is called the shepherd and ruler of Israel.

10. By what authority do the elders make David king? (11:3)

    The elders of Israel make a compact with David by the authority of the word of God, as spoken by Samuel.

11. By what other names is Jerusalem known? (11:4-5)

    Jerusalem is called Jebus, Zion, and the City of David.

12. Who is the chief of the Three? (11:20-21)

    Abishai is the chief of the Three.

Answer these questions by reading 1 Chronicles 12

13. What military skill do the Benjaminites have? (12:2)

    The Benjaminites can use both hands to shoot arrows and sling stones.

14. Why does Amasai pledge loyalty to David? (12:18)

    The spirit of the Lord comes over Amasai, and he pledges his loyalty to David.

15. How is David's army increased? (12:19-22)

    David's army is increased by men coming to him to volunteer.

16. Why do the men of war come to Hebron? (12:38)

    The men come to Hebron to make David king over all Israel.

17. What do the people eat when they celebrate David's coronation? (12:39-40)

They eat flour, fig cakes, raisin cakes, wine, oil, cattle, and sheep.

Answer these questions by reading 1 Chronicles 13

18. What is neglected in Saul's day? (13:3)

The ark of God [the covenant] is neglected.

19. What do the people do while the ark is being taken to Jerusalem? (13:8)

David and the people sing and play instruments for joy.

20. What happens to Uzzah? (13:9-10)

Uzzah touches the ark and is killed by the Lord.

21. What does God do for Obed-Edom? (13:13-14)

God blesses all that Obed-Edom has.

Answer these questions by reading 1 Chronicles 14

22. Who helps David build his capital? (14:1)

Hiram, king of Tyre, sends David "cedar logs, stonemasons and carpenters."

23. Where is Solomon born? (14:3-4)

Solomon is born in Jerusalem.

24. What does God promise David? (14:9-10)

God promises David that he will defeat the Philistines.

25. What do the Philistines leave at Baal Perazim? (14:12)

The Philistines leave their idols (gods) at Baal Perazim.

DIMENSION TWO:
WHAT DOES THE BIBLE MEAN?

Certain themes recur in the work of the Chronicler. In this section, we will see an emphasis on the Temple and an emphasis on the family of David.

When writing about the Temple, the Chronicler records the beginnings of what we would call the clergy. For the Chronicler there were three groups of these religious professionals: priests, Levites, and gatekeepers. They shared in the worship services and kept things ready for all who came to the house of the Lord.

When reading in Chronicles about the family of David, we find long genealogical lists in the first nine chapters of First Chronicles. These tables are primarily concerned with the tribe of Judah and the descent of David. The rest of the book, Chapters 10–29, traces the history of David's reign.

The work of the Chronicler is judged by many Bible scholars to include not only First and Second Chronicles but also the books of Ezra and Nehemiah. One evidence of the Chronicler having written Ezra is the repetition at the beginning of Ezra 1 of the closing verses of 2 Chronicles 36. (Compare Ezra 1:1-3 with 2 Chronicles 36:22-23.)

The Chronicler seems bent on underscoring the Deuteronomic version of history. The Deuteronomic version of history insists that full, true life is possible for a nation only when it remains faithful to the God who has chosen it and entered into covenant with it. Remaining faithful to God involves obedience to the law of God and worshiping God in the manner, the place, and the spirit that God deems desirable.

The people's obedience to the law of God and this worthy worship of the Lord is, for the Chronicler, closely intertwined with Hebrew allegiance to David and his descendants as their royal rulers. This obedience is coupled with allegiance to Jerusalem and its Temple as the proper place for the public worship of God. The rituals of the Temple are the proper means for praise and sacrifice to the Lord.

This section of the Bible illustrates the theme that Jerusalem is the Holy City of Israel. (See 1 Chronicles 8:28; 9:34.) Arrangements are made for the worship of God in a special place, and the Temple is to be cared for. (See 1 Chronicles 9:27-32.) We use the term *special place* because there is reason to believe that, at this time, the Tabernacle for the worship of God was still at Gibeon. (See 1 Chronicles 21:29.) The emphasis now is upon a centralized place for the worship of God. Later the Chronicler will emphasize the Temple as the centralized place for worship of Israel's God.

1 Chronicles 8. This chapter identifies the family of Benjamin and its connection to Jerusalem. The importance of this connection is that Saul, Israel's first king, was from the family of Benjamin. The Chronicler seems to be saying, "From the beginning, when we asked Samuel to give us a king that we might be like the other nations, the city of Jerusalem has been at the center of our national life. It was that way in the days of Saul, our first king. It was that way with David, our second and ideal king. It must always be that way." (See 1 Samuel 8:5.)

1 Chronicles 9. Careful provisions are made for the care of the house of God. Priests, Levites, and various kinds of Temple servants are authorized. (See 1 Chronicles 9:2.) Included are gatekeepers who have a position of honor dating back to the boyhood of the prophet Samuel. (See 1 Samuel 3:15.) Others are in charge of the Temple supplies, utensils, wine, flour, spices, incense, and oil. Others are in charge of special preparation of sacred objects (1 Chronicles 9:28-32). Still others share in the valued service of providing choral music for the various public services in which God was worshiped (1 Chronicles 9:33).

1 Chronicles 10. A new element is added to the account, found earlier in 1 Samuel 31:1-13, of the death of Saul and his three sons. That new emphasis is in the interpretation of this disaster that overtook Saul. The verdict is that Saul "died because he was unfaithful" (1 Chronicles 10:13).

1 Chronicles 11–14. These three chapters are read together as an account of David, the king and founder of worship in the Temple. Again we read the familiar story of how David came to the throne of Israel. We have read this material earlier in such places as 2 Samuel 5:1-3, 6-10.

First Chronicles 11:1-3 indicates the kingship came to David because the elders recognized that, even while Saul was on the throne, David had moved into the real leadership role. David's entrance to the kingship then becomes, in part, a covenant between king and subjects. The throne comes to David, not by usurpation of position and power, but by a choice of the people.

David conquers the city of Jebus, later renamed Jerusalem, which is to occupy a good part of the world's attention from his day until ours! The city is also called "Zion" and the "City of David."

First Chronicles 11:15-19 has long fascinated readers of this biblical history. Is the passage saying to us, "Some gifts are too costly to be kept for one person alone"? Are there some gifts that must ultimately be offered not even to the greatest among us but to God who is the Lord and giver of all good gifts?

First Chronicles 12 is a record of David's first supporters and those who banded together to establish his kingship securely. The Chronicler makes it clear that David's assumption of the kingship was with the wholehearted approval of the Hebrew people. This story has no parallel in Second Samuel. Saul's relatives, and most of the tribe of Benjamin, sided with Saul's son Ishbosheth and probably would not have joined David.

1 Chronicles 13:1-14. Here we receive insight into some important emphases of the history we are examining: (1) the development of Jerusalem as the holy place for the Hebrews, (2) the nature of the celebrative worship experience of the people, and (3) an understanding of God. This latter will perhaps fall a bit strangely on Christian ears.

The Chronicler's account is paralleled in 2 Samuel 6:1-23. First Samuel 4:1–7:2 tells us how the ark came to be in Kiriath Jearim.

Now King David, bursting with exuberance, leads his people as the ark is brought to Jerusalem. It was a great moment as "all the Israelites were celebrating with all their might before God, with songs and with harps, lyres, tambourines, cymbals and trumpets" (1 Chronicles 13:8).

The account of Uzzah's death gives us an understanding of God that sees God blazing in anger at the sacrilege of the human touch. In this story, we also see an understanding of this people's sense of God's awesome majesty and the need for God's most devoted servants to be thoughtful, reverential, humble, and modest in their approach to God.

1 Chronicles 14. These seventeen verses give us a lovely picture of David's advancing years. We see him in the Holy City, enjoying building his palace, fathering a growing family, and extending the domination of the Hebrews over the Philistines. We can almost feel that the Chronicler here is suggesting, "Ah! This was a golden age!"

DIMENSION THREE: WHAT DOES THE BIBLE MEAN TO ME?

1 Chronicles 9:17-34—Worship in the Old Testament

You might want to begin the discussion of worship in the Old Testament by sharing the following general information on worship.

As class leader you have the opportunity, in today's session, to help Christian friends enrich their total biblical understanding at two crucial points:

1. We can grasp a firmer understanding of the essential nature and character of our own present-day religion.
2. We may glimpse more clearly the essential nature and character of worship as we find it recorded in the Old and New Testaments.

We find the roots of our personal and community heritage in these ancient records. Christians are not primarily men and women of the Old Testament. We are the people of the New Testament. We are men and women called to be those whose bearing towards all life rises from our relationship to Jesus Christ.

However, we may remind ourselves that some Old Testament insights into the will of God and God's expectations for us are exceeded by nothing that we find in the Christian faith. What do we have that goes beyond the themes of Amos, Hosea, and Micah? (See Amos 5:24; Hosea 6:6; Micah 6:8.) These understandings of God's most fundamental requirements stand today as firm and filled with challenge as when the prophets first voiced them.

Justice far outweighs ritual worship. This is the message of Amos.

Steadfast love of God and intimate involvement with the Lord outweighs ritual worship. This is Hosea's affirmation.

The doing of justice, the love of mercy, and a humble walk with God is what God requires. So speaks Micah.

None of these statements justifies the neglect of public worship of God. Likewise, none is to be interpreted as justification for the cheapening of the public worship experience. Far from it!

When we read our New Testament, we cannot escape the vision of the Christian congregation as the community where Christian living takes place. The Christian life is a life in fellowship. This fellowship is marked by prayer, teaching, common meals, mutual concern, and outreach to the larger community. (See Acts 1:14; 2:1, 42-47.)

The Christian's worship is a "one another" experience. (See Romans 12:5; 13:8; 1 Corinthians 16:20; Galatians 5:13; Colossians 3:13.) Likewise, the prophetic message is that ritual worship is saved from futility as it is purified and validated by the worshipers living a godly life.

Precisely what was this worship that the Old Testament people seemed so joyously to share? It was *involved* worship. The people sang, played instruments, danced, lifted their hands, and bowed in the presence of God! One did not enter the Jerusalem temple or the early Christian congregations and wonder if perhaps everyone had gone to sleep! Even the Corinthian church that carried its vitality to the point of offensiveness and division was nonetheless alive! (Compare 1 Chronicles 12:40; 13:8 and 1 Corinthians 14:23, 26-33; 11:17-21.)

Taking care of the meeting place and the quality of worship offered there is also important.

I once spent some hours in a church called Martha's Chapel. This open, country church was clean, freshly painted, well decorated, and inviting. What this congregation does with its church building is a form of testimony. It is part of their witness, their outreach to a larger community that is not always a community of faith and obedience. Ask the class members to discuss what the internal and external appearance of your church says concerning the devotion of its congregation.

On the other hand, is it possible that some of us substitute attention to the local church building for the doing of justice, the love of mercy, and the humble walk with God? Ask class members to share examples of this kind of substitution. (At Martha's Chapel there is often a most generous outpouring of concern for human needs that goes beyond the four cozy walls of the church building.) How can we establish a healthy, creative, lively, and balanced relationship between fabric and function of the church?

1 Chronicles 13—The Ark's Resting Place

We can learn what congregations think is central by the objects people's eyes focus on as they gather. In many churches we most often focus on a cross and a Communion Table. Is this just a coincidence, or does it say something of our understanding of worship and discipleship? In other churches one's eye is most likely drawn to a baptistry for the rite that is so central to these Christians.

The central object in the Jerusalem place of meeting was to be "the ark of our God" (1 Chronicles 13:3). The ark was the supreme symbol of the presence of God. It was a most powerful reminder of the covenant Israel had with God and of the law God had given for Israel's national life. If a Hebrew child asked where God was, the Hebrew parent probably answered, perhaps with various meanings, "God is there at the ark." (See 1 Samuel 4:4.)

Hebrew worship and national life revolved around God's presence and God's covenant. All else was subordinate. All else existed for the purpose of celebrating and renewing that presence and that covenant. The ark supremely identified God as one who chooses to live in the midst of the people. (See John 1:14.)

Originally, the ark seems to have been a fairly simple wooden chest. In it were placed the tablets of stone with the Ten Laws. (See Deuteronomy 10:1-5.) Later we read of an "atonement cover" (Exodus 25:17) placed on top of the ark. With it comes the promise, "There . . . between the two cherubim . . . I will meet with you" (Exodus 25:22).

Ask class members to consider what the central symbols are in your place of worship. Have them discuss the significance of each one, especially the pulpit and the Communion Table.

Close the session by listing on a chalkboard or on a large piece of paper any new insights class members have gained from their study of 1 Chronicles 9–14.

I will set him over my house and my kingdom forever; his throne will be established forever (17:14).

—8—
The Ark of the Covenant
1 Chronicles 15–21

DIMENSION ONE:
WHAT DOES THE BIBLE SAY?

Answer these questions by reading 1 Chronicles 15

1. Who carries the ark? (15:2)

   The Levites carry the ark.

2. Where is the ark? (15:25)

   The ark is at the house of Obed-Edom.

3. How are the people who carry the ark dressed? (15:27)

   They are dressed in fine linen.

4. What are the people doing as they bring up the ark? (15:28)

   The people are shouting and making music.

Answer these questions by reading 1 Chronicles 16

5. Where does the ark first rest? (16:1)

   The ark first rests in a tent David has pitched for it.

6. When David completes the offerings, what does each worshiper receive? (16:3)

   Each worshiper gets a loaf of bread, a cake of dates, and a cake of raisins.

7. What do the Levites who minister before the ark do? (16:4-6)

   The Levites make petitions, give thanks, and praise the Lord. They also make music before the ark.

8. What does Asaph sing about? (16:8, 12)

   Asaph sings about God's deeds and wonderful miracles and judgments.

9. Who gives the Hebrews their homeland? (16:14-18)

   God gives Canaan to the Hebrews as their inheritance.

10. What are the worshipers to bring as they come before the Lord? (16:29)

    Worshipers are to bring an offering to the Lord.

Answer these questions by reading 1 Chronicles 17

11. What kind of house does David live in? (17:1)

    David lives in a palace of cedar.

12. What does God tell Nathan to tell David? (17:3-5)

    God does not want a house.

13. Who will build a house for God? (17:11-12)

    One of David's sons will build God's house.

14. How does David feel about God's promises? (17:16-27)

    David feels humility, gratitude, and awe.

Answer these questions by reading 1 Chronicles 18

15. How does David reign over Israel? (18:14)

    David does what is just and right for all his people.

Answer these questions by reading 1 Chronicles 19

16. How do the Ammonites respond to David's sympathy when Nahash dies? (19:1-5)

    The Ammonites think David is spying on them, and they insult his messengers.

17. What do the Arameans and the Ammonites do at the battle? (19:14-15)

The Arameans retreat before Joab, and the Ammonites retreat before Abishai.

Answer this question by reading 1 Chronicles 20

18. In what season do kings go to war? (20:1)

Kings go to war in the spring.

Answer these questions by reading 1 Chronicles 21

19. Who originates the idea of a census of Israel? (21:1)

Satan incites David to have a census.

20. Who is in charge of the census? (21:2)

David appoints Joab to be in charge of the census.

21. How many men are reported in the census? (21:5)

1,100,000 men are counted in the census.

22. What punishment does David choose? (21:13-14)

David chooses to be punished by the Lord, who sends a plague.

23. Where is David to build an altar to God? (21:15, 18)

David is to build an altar at the threshing floor of Araunah the Jebusite.

24. Why does David refuse the threshing floor as a gift? (21:24)

David will not offer anything to God that cost him nothing.

25. What does God do when David makes his offerings on this new altar? (21:26)

God sends a fire to consume the offerings.

DIMENSION TWO: WHAT DOES THE BIBLE MEAN?

Many symbols are associated with our practice of the Christian faith. Among the most important are the cross, a dove, a fish, and an empty tomb or a butterfly to symbolize the new life. Many times in various places in our sanctuaries we see some representation of the elements of bread and wine that are used in Holy Communion.

In each instance the symbol reminds us of the reality for which it stands. A pictured cross, for example, draws its significance from our remembrance of the cross upon which Jesus died. (See Luke 23:26, 33.)

For our Hebrew ancestors, the ark was the great symbol. The ark has various names in the Old Testament. It is called the ark of the Testimony, the ark of the covenant, the ark of the Lord, the ark of God, and the ark of the God of Israel. (See Exodus 25:22; Numbers 10:33; 1 Samuel 4:6; 4:11; 5:8.)

Various descriptions of the ark are given, and various adornments or enrichments of the ark are described. Basically, the ark seems to have been a wooden chest containing the tablets of stone with the Ten Words, known to us as the Ten Commandments, written upon them. When the ark finally comes to a permanent place of rest "in the most holy place" of the Jerusalem temple, great carved cherubim stand above it and the atonement cover is on its top, beneath the cherubim wings. The atonement cover was a slab of pure gold that covered the ark, and God was thought to dwell over it. The Hebrew term translated into English as *atonement cover* is *place of propitiation*—the place where God's cleansing power is channeled to needy men and women. (See Exodus 25:17, 22.)

Chapters 15–21 deal with the ark as a central symbol of Hebrew faith. The ark is a symbol of recollection, calling to mind God's guidance of the people as they wandered in the desert. It is a symbol of the divine presence of God with the chosen people. It is a symbol of the holy law given for the ordering of the life of this chosen nation. (See Numbers 10:35-36.)

The Hebrews were not meant to worship the ark any more than we are meant to worship the cross or the Communion Table. The people were to consider the significance of the reality to which the ark witnesses.

1 Chronicles 15:1-28. When we place proper emphasis upon the symbolic nature of the ark, though it was a real object and housed the real tablets of stone that contained the basic moral law of the Hebrew people, we can then see the implication for our Christian understanding of God. We can see how some cherished phrases of hymns and gospel instruction take on meaning when we understand their origin.

The ark was associated in the Hebrew mind with the presence and the power of God. Sometimes the power of God, as associated with the ark, seems to modern Bible readers to be irrational, unpredictable, and dangerous. The power of God seems to pose a threat to those who come too near it in an inappropriate manner. First Chronicles 15:11-15 illustrates this threat.

The reference to an occasion when "the LORD our God broke out in anger against us" (verse 13) refers us to 2 Samuel 6:6-11. There we read of the blazing anger of God when the ark is improperly handled. We read also of David's anger with God and his fear of the ark. This display of the power of God so troubles David that he is afraid to take the ark into Jerusalem.

But in today's chapter, David leaves nothing to chance. The ark will be carried by the right people in the right manner. The Levites will sanctify themselves for this all-important task.

What is the meaning of this sanctification? The idea of sanctification probably held here by David, and by those to whom he spoke, was a concept of ritual holiness and purification. This sanctification required physical cleanness of the body and the avoidance of seemingly harmless experiences of common life, such as sexual intercourse, skin eruptions or irritations, or menstruation. These, and other common facets of daily life, were deemed to build a barrier between God and the men and women who experienced these things.

The sanctification that David speaks of here in 1 Chronicles 15:12-14 was probably an outward sanctification like that in Leviticus 12:1-4 and 15:16-24 rather than an inner, moral attitude like that described in Leviticus 19:11-18.

We are not suggesting that moral sanctity was alien or foreign to David and the Levites of his day. But we are saying that a fundamental characteristic of Hebrew religion was this emphasis upon certain forms of physical cleanness. We might consider cleanliness desirable, but we would not ever think not being clean had any power to keep us from the presence and the service of God.

Further, we are not to assume that this emphasis upon ritual sanctity was without practical value for the spiritual, moral, and religious life of the people. It seems to have helped the people to focus their thoughts upon God in their daily lives. This emphasis upon what we might call minor matters reminded the people about the seriousness of any act, any deed, any thought, or any event that made harmony between worshiper and God impossible.

1 Chronicles 17:1-15. We met the prophet Nathan earlier. Nathan stood before King David and chastised him for committing adultery and murder in the case of Bathsheba and Uriah. (See 2 Samuel 11.) We find Nathan now still at the court, still possessed of easy access to the presence of the king, and still involved in directing the affairs of the nation.

Nathan's first response to David's proposal for a temple is positive. Then that opinion is reversed, and we come to the strong Old Testament emphasis on a temple as David's idea but the building of a temple as Solomon's accomplishment.

The word *house* is used in this passage with a dual sense. Sometimes it means a building, as when David speaks of his palace of cedar and contrasts it with the tent in which the ark is currently resting. When God says to David, "The Lord will build a house for you" (1 Chronicles 17:10), the word is used in the sense of a dynasty or family. It is much as we might speak of the House of Windsor (British) or the House of Orange (Dutch).

Why is David's response to God's promise so profound? Perhaps because the question of a ruling family for the chosen people was a profound religious concern. If indeed these were God's people and God's purpose was to be worked out through them, it was a privilege and responsibility of great significance to be allowed to rule over them. David's words are reminiscent of Solomon's prayer a bit later. (See 1 Chronicles 17:16-18 and 2 Chronicles 1:8-10.) The promise that David's descendants would rule after his death came to David as a guarantee of a form of eternal life—the assurance that in some genuine sense he would live on through his heirs and successors. This was a promise that death itself would not blot David out of a share in the life of his chosen people.

1 Chronicles 21. Where does evil come from? If we mentally inhabit a world where there is God and anti-God, then we could credit all evil to the adversary. But the dilemma arises when we inhabit a monotheistic world—a world where only God has ultimate power. If that God is known to be a God of love, mercy, compassion, concern, and healing who wills life rather than death, we can see the dilemma. (As this paragraph is written, our newspapers carry an account of a young woman shot to death by an unknown assailant on the day before her wedding. Her fiancé is quoted as saying, "There can't be a God if this kind of thing can happen." Although we may not agree with the young man's sorrowful conclusion, we can understand the moral and spiritual anguish he is undergoing.)

Bible scholars feel that what we have here in 1 Chronicles 21:1 reflects something of that same dilemma about the origin of evil. In 2 Samuel 24 we are told, about this same census, the Lord "incited David . . . saying, 'Go and take a census of Israel and Judah' " (24:1). Both census stories indicate that great trouble came as a result of this numbering. At least seventy thousand men died of plague. Did these tragedies come indeed because of God's anger and deliberate intention to strike at Israel?

The student book refers to the Book of Job, where we again encounter the question of the origin of evil. Have someone in the class read aloud Job 1:6-12. The often-asked question of where evil comes from receives an answer in the Book of Job: "Though he slay me, yet will I trust in him" (Job 13:15, King James Version).

DIMENSION THREE:
WHAT DOES THE BIBLE MEAN TO ME?

God has a purpose for us. This purpose is expressed, at least in part, within the Bible. We must respond to the Scripture at the deep level of intention to comprehend. Even in Bible study the Christian believer is not exempt from the injunction to love God with the mind was well as with the other resources of personality. Genuine comprehension of the Bible's message produces change in the believer. We become different persons as we enter into a true "catching hold" of the biblical message.

1 Chronicles 15:1-28—The Levites Are Sanctified

As we ask what today's particular biblical passages may mean for us, we must remember certain important characteristics of Old Testament religion. Though some of the characteristics mentioned below received greater or lesser attention during the history of the Hebrew people, each of these is relevant for today's study.

The Hebrews believed there is one God over all the earth. This God is all-powerful, moral, and spiritual. They also believed that this one God is holy in the sense that God totally and utterly transcends our humanity. God is holy also in the sense that God is totally righteous. God's whole being is set in steadfast opposition to injustice, exploitation, greed, and impurity. The Hebrews also felt that the people of God are to reflect in themselves the character of the God whose possession they claim to be. (See Leviticus 11:45.)

Is there a relationship between our present-day calling, as disciples of Jesus Christ, to be Christlike women and men and the emphasis of our present chapter upon ritual sanctification of the Levites as they carry the ark? The answer to that question is yes, there is such a relationship. Both concerns, inner attitude and outward appearances, are part of the concept of sanctification.

The Hebrews may indeed have given prominence to ideas of ritual holiness and sanctity, but that was not their exclusive understanding of God's requirement. Prophets such as Nathan and Elisha called King David and King Ahab to account for their immoral acts of injustice and inhumanity. Likewise, our concept of sanctification involves not only a person's inner moral attitude. Our understanding of sanctification cannot be restricted to the realm of the moral, spiritual, and social. We also have an obligation to bring our bodies, in the best possible condition, to the service of God. Our predecessors in the Christian gospel were pointing to something important when they urged us to refrain from the use of alcohol, tobacco, and other narcotics.

Ask class members to consider and discuss the questions in the student book that pertain to our ritual cleanness reflected in how we dress for worship. Then have the class discuss whether the same is required of men and women who assume special leadership roles in the church.

1 Chronicles 15:29—Michal's Pride

The student book suggests that it was Michal's pride that prevented her from taking part in David's triumphant return to Jerusalem. Begin the discussion of this issue by reviewing the history of the relationship between David and Michal. Review especially the story of Michal's efforts to help David escape from her father, Saul, (1 Samuel 19); Michal's betrothal to Paltiel (1 Samuel 25:44); and Michal's return to David (2 Samuel 3:13-16).

The student book suggests that perhaps pride was responsible for Michal's response to David in Jerusalem. But the Chronicler does not tell us exactly why Michal despises David; we can only guess that her pride is the reason. Ask class members whether they agree with this suggestion and what other suggestions they might have.

If class members agree that Michal's pride caused her contempt of David, then ask them to look at the New Testament references that are listed in the student book. What do these passages say to us about pride? Have group members share examples of pride and its results in their lives or in the lives of others.

1 Chronicles 17:1-15—David's Good Intentions

To begin this discussion, have someone in the class read aloud 1 Chronicles 17:1-15. The student book emphasizes that God's response to David's request is a response to David's intentions rather than to David's accomplishments. That is, God does not respond positively to David, even though David has been a good and successful king. Despite David's accomplishments, God looks objectively at the request and says no. However, God responds positively to David as well. God answers David's good intentions by saying, "He [Solomon] is the one who will build a house for me, and I will establish his throne forever" (verse 12).

Have the class read and discuss the questions in the student book. Make certain group members understand the difference between intentions and accomplishments. Most persons have had experiences when intentions and accomplishments did not match or were in conflict. Encourage class members to share these experiences with one another. Close the discussion by reading aloud Romans 7:18-20.

1 Chronicles 21—David's Intercession

Here we have a display of the possible dimensions of human caring. First Chronicles 21:17 is an example of great prayer. It is both petition and intercession. It is a prayer that finds David on his knees offering himself in exchange for relief for his people. There is a similarity between David at this moment and other great moments of prayer recorded in the Bible. (See Genesis 18:22-33 for the intercessory prayer of Abraham, Exodus 32:31-32 for the prayer of Moses, and Romans 9:1-3 for the prayer of Paul.) You might want to read some or all of these passages aloud to the class.

The student book concentrates on intercessory prayer as a way to influence the future. Have the class examine the other prayers mentioned above and compare them to our present prayer in 1 Chronicles 21. Which prayers concentrate on the future? Which prayers try to influence the present?

Ask class members to think about the nature of their own intercessory prayers. What do they pray for? List their suggestions on a chalkboard or on a large piece of paper. How is this list different from the prayers mentioned above?

The student book closes with the question "What materials may we endeavor to provide for the success of those who will come after us?" Have the class discuss this question; then ask each member to share new insights gained from this study of 1 Chronicles 15–21.

— 9 —

The Temple and Its Rituals

1 Chronicles 22–29

DIMENSION ONE:
WHAT DOES THE BIBLE SAY?

Answer these questions by reading 1 Chronicles 22

1. What materials are gathered for Solomon's later use? (22:2-5)

   Stones, iron, bronze, and cedar logs are gathered.

2. Why is David forbidden to build a temple? (22:8)

   David has shed much blood and has fought many wars.

3. What will guarantee Solomon's success? (22:13)

   Solomon will be successful if he observes God's laws and has strength and courage.

Answer these questions by reading 1 Chronicles 23

4. How many adult Levites are counted? (23:3)

   Thirty-eight thousand men are counted.

5. Why do the Levites no longer need to carry the Tabernacle? (23:25-26)

   God now dwells in Jerusalem forever, so the Levites do not need to carry the Tabernacle.

6. What new duties are assigned the Levites? (23:28-32)

   The Levites are to assist in caring for the Temple, in all services, and to thank and praise God.

Answer these questions by reading 1 Chronicles 25

7. What Temple role is assigned the sons of Asaph, Heman, and Jeduthun? (25:1)

   They are to prophesy "accompanied by harps, lyres and cymbals."

8. How do Jeduthun's sons prophesy? (25:3)

   They sing songs of thanksgiving and praise accompanied by the harp.

Answer this question by reading 1 Chronicles 26

9. Why do David and others make dedicated gifts? (26:27)

   They dedicate gifts for maintenance of the Temple.

Answer these questions by reading 1 Chronicles 27

10. What kinds of property does the king have? (27:25-31)

    He has fields, vineyards, groves, herds, and flocks.

11. What does David's uncle, Jonathan, do? (27:32)

    He is a counselor and a scribe.

Answer these questions by reading 1 Chronicles 28

12. How does David describe the Temple he wants to build? (28:2)

    David describes this temple as a house of rest for the ark and a footstool for God.

13. How does David become king of Israel? (28:4)

    God chose him to be king over Israel.

14. Why is Solomon to be king after David? (28:5-6)

    God has chosen Solomon for the throne.

15. What advice does David give Solomon? (28:9)

    David advises Solomon to acknowledge God and to serve God wholeheartedly and with a willing mind.

THE TEMPLE AND ITS RITUALS

16. Who has written down the plan for the Temple? (28:19)

God wrote the plans for the Temple through David.

17. Who will help Solomon build the Temple? (28:20-21)

God, the priests, the Levites, and the people will help Solomon.

Answer these questions by reading 1 Chronicles 29

18. What do the people give to build the Temple? (29:7-8)

The people give gold, silver, bronze, iron, and precious stones.

19. How are these gifts for the Temple given? (29:9)

They are given willingly, freely, and wholeheartedly.

20. What does David say is the Lord's? (29:11)

David says all in the heavens and the earth is God's.

21. Where do the gifts the men and women offer God come from? (29:14-16)

God is the source of what the people give.

22. Who is responsible for Solomon's reputation and great splendor? (29:25)

God exalts Solomon and bestows on him royal splendor.

23. How is David's life summarized? (29:28)

David lived to a good old age and had wealth and honor.

DIMENSION TWO:
WHAT DOES THE BIBLE MEAN?

Dimension Two in the student book begins with the implied suggestion that we read the Scripture in order to discover the quality of life expected of us as followers of the way of Jesus Christ. (See Acts 9:2; 18:25-26; 19:9, 23.) We need to grow in our understanding of "the way of God," and it is for this purpose that we search the Scriptures. (Compare Acts 18:26 with Luke 24:27 and John 5:39.)

We may learn four things from the eight chapters of Chronicles that are our focus of study today. The four affirmations are as follows:

1. Christian salvation and discipleship to Jesus Christ are as much a part of this present material and social world as they are a valued facet of the world that is to come. Our calling as disciples of Jesus Christ is to serve the present age.

2. Christians are engaged in a pilgrimage of faith. The fruition of this pilgrimage lies beyond the present experience of any one of us. Thus we cannot expect that all the rich promises of God will be realized in our own time, any more than the gracious hopes held out to David by God were realized in his own day.

3. In the light of our calling to serve the present age and our hope for the future, we must help those who will come after us to be obedient to the Lord, our God.

4. We must bring the best that is within us, or whatever material blessings we may have, to the service of God.

In light of these affirmations we now examine the particular facets of our chapters assigned for today's study.

1 Chronicles 22. This chapter brings us to a new admiration for King David. We have earlier met him as a man who dreamed a great dream. At first he received encouragement to proceed in his labor for the fulfillment of his own dream in his own time. Then, quickly, that encouragement was withdrawn and he was told, in effect, that this dream would not become a reality in his generation. (See 1 Chronicles 17:1-15.)

But for David this hope deferred is no occasion for giving up his plans and resting. Rather it is a time of challenge for him, a season for action, and a time to accept his own particular place in the line of great servants of God. David can now look forward to the achievements of grandeur scheduled to appear in the days of Solomon, his son and heir.

David's action in accumulating great treasures for a future temple may be contrasted with Hezekiah's rather weak response to the prophecy of Babylon's victory over Israel. (See 2 Kings 20:16-19.) David follows his own advice to Solomon. David told Solomon to take courage. Do not be afraid. Do not give in to dismay. (See 1 Chronicles 22:13.)

In David's advice to Solomon we may discern the king's awareness that something far more valuable than gold, silver, bronze, iron, and cedar would be needed for building the great house of God. That greater treasure must exist in the character of Solomon.

Recognizing the crucial nature of Solomon's own attitude and role in building the Temple, David tells Solomon that he hopes the Lord will be with him so that he may succeed (verse 11). He also wants the Lord to grant Solomon discretion and understanding so that Solomon will keep the law of the Lord (verse 12). Next, he tells Solomon to be strong and of good courage. "Do not be afraid or discouraged" (verse 13c). Solomon must add more riches to what David has accumulated for building the Temple.

David's last piece of advice is emphatic: "Now begin the work, and the LORD be with you" (verse 16b). David's dream, his hope, and his prayer for Solomon begin and end with the priceless desire that God will be with the young king. Without God's presence and apart from wholehearted obedience to the Lord, all David's own labors and any undertakings of Solomon would be in vain. "Unless the LORD builds the house, / its builders labor in vain" (Psalm 127:1).

Perhaps we may discover real significance in a little sentence that reads almost as if tossed into the chapter carelessly: "And you may add to them" (verse 14). Perhaps David is saying, "Though I have done much, it has not all been done. Without you it will not be accomplished." Perhaps David is saying, "My work will not be complete until you have done your part."

1 Chronicles 23–26. A brief summary of the major content of each of these four chapters appears in the student book. The chapters reflect the intention of the Chronicler to affirm that the ritual of the Temple was rooted in the mind of David and in the mind of God. (See 1 Chronicles 22:1, 6; 24:19.)

The chapters further reflect a sense that in the house of God all materials and all persons must be of the finest quality, wholly dedicated, and faithful in the performance of duties.

Notice the special use of the word or concept of *prophecy* as it appears in these particular chapters. (The word is found in 1 Chronicles 25:1, 2, and 3.) This prophecy and prophesying occur in a context of music and singing. It is done by particular persons held responsible for this special assignment. Whatever else this prophesying is, it is the expression of thanksgiving and praise to the Lord.

We do not know exactly what this prophecy and this prophesying was, but it seems reasonable to assume that it involved something like a singing or chanting of some unique message from God to those who worshiped in the Temple. Perhaps it was a singing of psalms similar to those found in the Book of Psalms. There we find such unique messages from God as words of warning, invitation, instruction, encouragement, condemnation, delineation of God's purpose and call to the people, and reminders of God's historical acts on behalf of the chosen ones. These messages may have been given in the grip of ecstasy, accentuated by the musical instruments and the group singing. The prophecy had genuine meaning to those who heard, but it did not attempt to presume a speaking forth of the mind of God.

1 Chronicles 28–29. These chapters continue the themes suggested in our examination of Chapter 22. Key persons of many and varied responsibilities are assembled by David at Jerusalem for what amounts to a farewell address. (See 1 Chronicles 28:2-10.)

The story of God's choice of David and his descendants to rule over Israel is repeated. By now it sounds almost as if this story had become part of a creed for the Hebrews. The account proceeds to relate again David's desire to build a temple and God's postponement of that event.

Verse 8 is addressed to these assembled leaders of Israel. We are reminded of Exodus 20:12, the fifth commandment, "the first commandment with a promise" (Ephesians

6:2). The leaders are reminded that David and his family are not the only ones who have a stake in the land and in the future of the people. All these leaders—officials, commanders, stewards, and warriors—have their hopes and fears riding upon what is to come after David's death.

Verses 9 and 10 are addressed to Solomon. So also are verses 20 and 21. Vigorous action, faithful adherence to God, and trust in the Lord's sustaining power are urged upon the young man who is soon to ascend his father's throne.

Verses 11 and 19 have raised questions in the minds of some readers. Who devised the plan that was followed to build the Temple? Who really was the architect? Verse 19 reminds us of Exodus 25:9, where God shows Moses the plan for the Tabernacle to be carried through the wilderness. In turn, this plan becomes the foundation document for the Temple. So these verses convey the truth that the great achievement of the Temple is rooted in the mind of God. The Temple is realized from the labors of the willing mind and heart of God's faithful servant.

First Chronicles closes then with an entire chapter (Chapter 29) devoted to the theme of giving on the part of king and people for the great cause of God. At least four verses refer to free giving: verses 5, 6, 9, and 17.

David's final thoughts in prayer for his people and for his son are that this spirit of wholehearted, joyful response to the gracious giving of God will remain always with them (see verses 18-19). Our thoughts of Christian stewardship—dependence on God for our bounty and awareness that whatever our gift, it is but a returning to God of what God has given—do not go beyond verses 10-16.

DIMENSION THREE: WHAT DOES THE BIBLE MEAN TO ME?

1 Chronicles 22—Preparing to Build the Temple

Have the class members read the corresponding section in the student book. It concentrates on the importance of having a vision of the future. Ask the class to discuss the questions in the student book.

1 Chronicles 23:1-6—Administration as Service

An amazing and easy to overlook aspect of the Bible has to do with its attention to what may be called "the little things" of life. The Bible is always telling us how persons did a certain thing or how many objects were used in this or that task. The Bible seems always to be measuring and recording.

We can find evidence of this attitude in Jesus' parables related to stewardship, such as the parable of the ten virgins and the parable of the talents. (See Matthew 25:1-30.) Ask someone in the class to read these verses aloud.

We are not suggesting that the major point of the parable of the virgins is the attention (or the inattention)

of the virgins to the need of oil for their lamps. Certainly we are not suggesting that the precise use of the talents is the point of the tale of the servants. The point of both of these parables would have been missed entirely had there not been a difference in the way the characters dealt with the details!

Five of the virgins took care of their lamps, and two of the servants were astute in their handling of the talents entrusted to them. For the two servants, and we assume for the five wise virgins, the judgment is, "Well done, good and faithful servant! You have been faithful with a few things; I will put you in charge of many things. Come and share your master's happiness!" (Matthew 25:21, 23).

First Chronicles 22–26 finds David giving careful attention to "little things"—the things that have to do with the business of the Temple. In these chapters David is acting as an administrator. Obviously, each of the provisions David makes is made for some other purpose than for the sake of the detail itself. That ultimate purpose is the impact that Israel's worship of God will have on their lives.

But that life-changing impact does not happen by accident. It comes because in preparation for the great days, the great festivals, there are men and women who do the "pick and shovel work" of the Temple.

Does any local church "just happen to have" a good, effective, evangelistic, growing church school—a church school that is growing in numbers and also a school where persons are growing in the dimensions of their discipleship?

Does a church "just happen to have" an effective hour of public worship—an hour in which music, spoken word, and physical setting all combine to enable men, women, and children to feel and know themselves confronted by the living God? Does that kind of church service "just happen"? Or does it happen under the guidance and control of the Holy Spirit? Is such a service made possible in large part because there are many who give time, energy, and attention to the administration of details?

Our Bible chapters find David making assignments to persons who will assume day-to-day and service-to-service responsibilities for what happens in the Temple. Priests, Levites, musicians, and gatekeepers are assigned their regular duties. (See 1 Chronicles 23:4, 5, 28.)

In the New Testament we find the church with a three-fold division of service: interpreters of the word, servants of human need, and administrators. (See 1 Corinthians 12:28; Acts 11:27; 9:36.)

Do we as Christian disciples and as members of the church of Jesus Christ have a calling to find and to do faithfully little tasks in case the great, glorious moments might occur? I believe we do have such a calling and such a personal need. In my last full-time pastorate, a volunteer came every single Monday morning for three-and-a-half years to count the loose change from the previous day's offerings. Knowing without question that the volunteer would come and that the simple task would be done well released other persons in the church for larger duties. Another volunteer taught the first-grade church school class for twenty-one years without being absent a single time. My father-in-law sang in his church choir for fifty years!

The student book asks that we consider these questions: Does each of us have a role within the body of Christ? Do we share in one common calling to live responsibly before God and responsively to perceived human need?

Look again at the huge numbers of people declared by today's chapters to have been involved in the service of the Temple. How few names are recorded! Most of the people assigned to the various tasks did so in anonymity. Certainly history has no record of their individual role. It may be that way with most of us. But the integrity of our discipleship rests, not upon recognition, but upon fidelity to responsibility!

Reading these Chronicles chapters is valuable for the acquisition of historical facts and for gaining an historical awareness of the development and content of the religious life of the women and men of the Old Testament. There is a further value in reading these chapters to discern what they suggest for our instruction in righteousness; our training in sober, upright, and godly living; and our commitment to walking in the good works for which we are created in Christ Jesus. (See 2 Timothy 3:16-17; Ephesians 2:10.)

Is it enough for a Christian to be good? Each Christian must be good for something!

1 Chronicles 29:6-9—The Spirit of Cooperation

This section in the student book begins by listing several characteristics of the spirit of cooperation: unity, cheerfulness, cooperation, and willingness. Ask class members to suggest other characteristics and to list these suggestions on a chalkboard or on a large piece of paper. Then have someone in the class read aloud 1 Chronicles 29:6-9. What characteristics of cooperation are reflected in this passage?

Have the class think of projects in your local church that required a spirit of cooperation. Was such a spirit evident in these cases? Why or why not? Then conclude the discussion of this topic by listing on a chalkboard or on a large piece of paper all the roles of service that have been taken on by persons in the study group.

Close the session by asking class members to share new insights on 1 Chronicles 22–29. If time allows, list these insights on a chalkboard or on a large piece of paper.

Solomon son of David established himself firmly over his kingdom (1:1).

— 10 —

The Reign of Solomon

2 Chronicles 1–9

DIMENSION ONE:
WHAT DOES THE BIBLE SAY?

Answer these questions by reading 2 Chronicles 1

1. Where do Solomon and the assembly go to worship the Lord? (1:3)

   They go to the high place at Gibeon.

2. What important artifacts of the faith are at Gibeon? (1:3, 6)

   The Tent of Meeting and the bronze altar are at Gibeon.

3. What gifts does Solomon ask from God? (1:10)

   Solomon asks for wisdom and knowledge.

4. Why does Solomon want these gifts? (1:10)

   Solomon wants to govern the people well.

5. What does God add to these gifts? (1:12)

   God adds wealth, riches, and honor.

Answer these questions by reading 2 Chronicles 2

6. Why is the Temple to be so great? (2:5)

   The Temple will be great because God is greater than all gods.

7. What does Solomon see as the purpose of the Temple? (2:6)

   The Temple is a place to burn sacrifices to God.

8. What aid is the king of Tyre asked to give Solomon? (2:7-10)

   Solomon asks for skilled craftsmen and timber from Lebanon.

9. What is the name of the king of Tyre who helps Solomon? (2:11-12)

   His name is Hiram.

10. How will Solomon pay for this assistance by Hiram? (2:15)

    He gives Hiram wheat, barley, olive oil, and wine.

Answer this question by reading 2 Chronicles 3

11. What is put in the Most Holy Place of the Temple? (3:10)

    Two great sculptured cherubim, overlaid with gold, are placed there.

Answer these questions by reading 2 Chronicles 5

12. What artifacts of the faith are brought to the completed Temple? (5:5)

    The ark, the Tent of Meeting, and the sacred furnishings are brought.

13. Where is the ark placed in the Temple? (5:7-8)

    It is placed under the wings of the cherubim.

14. What is in the ark? (5:10)

    The two tablets of stone containing the Ten Commandments are in the ark.

15. What are the duties of the trumpeters and the singers? (5:13)

    They are to sing praise and thanksgiving to God.

16. When the ark is installed, what sign of God's presence is given? (5:14)

    A cloud with the glory of the Lord fills the temple of God.

Answer these questions by reading 2 Chronicles 6

17. In what city will God's Name dwell? (6:6)

    God's Name will dwell in Jerusalem.

18. What promise does God keep with the people? (6:14)

    God keeps the covenant of love with people who continue in his way.

19. Can the house that Solomon builds contain God? (6:18)

    The highest heaven cannot contain God, and neither can the Temple.

Answer these questions by reading 2 Chronicles 7

20. What actions will bring forgiveness and healing to the land? (7:14)

    Humility, prayer, seeking God, and repentance will heal the land.

21. What will happen if king and people are unfaithful to God? (7:19-20)

    God will remove the people from the land and reject the Temple.

Answer this question by reading 2 Chronicles 8

22. How long does it take Solomon to build the Temple and his palace? (8:1)

    The projects take twenty years.

Answer these questions by reading 2 Chronicles 9

23. For what purpose does the queen of Sheba think God has set Solomon over Israel? (9:8)

    Solomon will "maintain justice and righteousness."

24. What are the evidences of prosperity in King Solomon's day? (9:27)

    Silver and cedar are so common that they count for nothing.

25. How long does Solomon reign in Jerusalem over Israel? (9:30)

    Solomon reigns for forty years.

DIMENSION TWO: WHAT DOES THE BIBLE MEAN?

You as class leader, as well as those who study with you, probably have the feeling that we are currently engaged in plowing old ground in our Bible study. In our earlier study of Kings, we have covered the account of David coming to the throne of Israel, the repeated emphasis on the initiative of God in choosing this family for leadership, and the great splendor of the reign of Solomon.

What is to be gained, then, from further examination of this history? We may list several suggestions in answer to this question. First, we simply fix the outline of these important eras a bit more firmly in our minds. Second, we probe a little further in our understanding of these writings—Chronicles, our present concern, and Kings, which we recently studied together.

By probing deeper into these writings, we gain several significant insights. The Chronicler is writing history. This writer is looking back across a number of generations that have elapsed since many of the events he describes.

We know about this time lapse because in 1 Chronicles 3:10-24 reference is made to many generations of the royal family after Solomon. This passage, along with other internal evidence, leads some scholars to date the actual writing of Chronicles to 300 B.C.–250 B.C. In the Hebrew Bible these books (First and Second Chronicles) appear at the end of the third division of the canon: the Writings. This location suggests that they were the last books to be admitted to the Hebrew canon that was closed by the Council of Jamnia about A.D. 90. Closing the canon meant that from that time on no additional writings were admitted to the Hebrew Bible. The same process of canonization occurred with the various writings we now know as the New Testament.

From the history he surveys, the Chronicler draws lessons for the Hebrews of his own time. These lessons are pertinent to our times as well. The Chronicler writes salvation-history—history that describes a possible relationship between God and the people with assurance that when that relationship is right, the life of the people will be rewarding.

The Chronicler emphasizes that the well-being of the nation rests on its sincere obedience to the law of God and its faithful, purified worship of the Almighty. God is to be worshiped and adored because of the bounty of divine gifts, God's deliberate involvement in the affairs of history, and God's choice of this people for responsibility and for blessing. The people are called to an awareness that ultimately the affairs of the nations are the business of God.

Here and there, for varying lengths of time, individuals or foreign powers are permitted to assume that theirs is the kingdom and the power. But it is not so! To God belongs the kingdom—not just what is to come in eternity, but everything upon the earth in this present moment.

2 Chronicles 1. Remember that when the Hebrews first asked God for a king, it was in order that they might be like the other nations. (See 1 Samuel 8:5.) In Solomon's time the United Kingdom became like the other nations with a vengeance! The Chronicler places enormous emphasis in these records upon the wealth, the ostentatious living, and the military and economic power of Solomon. (See verses

14-17.) This frank rejoicing in material success is redeemed only by the spirit of Solomon in the beginning of his reign.

Solomon's prayer for wisdom and understanding (verses 8-10) can be the first major emphasis of today's study. The quality of mind and character exhibited by Solomon was much more than a desire for intellectual competence. It was the longing for penetrating awareness of the real issues of life, especially the life of the nation, coupled with an ability to choose the wise and sensible course for management of affairs. Though much later everything that Solomon acquired was to come under the judgment of the great prophets, here at the beginning of his rule Solomon is wise indeed.

The student book suggests that a possible interpretation of this prayer involves an understanding of "knowledge" as a mastery of facts and "wisdom" as a skill in the application of facts. We all know persons who know the right answers to many of life's concerns but who seem to have no skill whatever in applying those answers to the conduct of their own daily affairs.

Another redeeming feature in this prayer of Solomon is the reason he makes his request: "so that I may lead this people . . . this great people of yours." (See 2 Chronicles 1:10.) So Solomon's prayer is not merely a prayer selfishly asking God for things that will add luster to his name. At this moment Solomon's focus is on the life of the people over whom he rules.

2 Chronicles 3. This chapter gives us the details of the building of the Temple. Here we are reading a shorter version of what we already read in 1 Kings 6–7.

2 Chronicles 6. This was a magnificent scene, one surely designed to thrill the spirit, to touch the emotions, and to focus the political and spiritual loyalties of the people. Solomon acts as the father-priest of his people. He offers one of the most moving and memorable supplications recorded in the Old Testament.

The elements of Solomon's prayer of dedication include an emphasis on the "beyondness" of God, God's "over-against-us" stance in relationship to the world and this nation chosen in gracious love. (See Deuteronomy 7:7-8.)

God cannot be contained in the Temple or in the highest heaven (verse 18). God's dwelling place is beyond this earth (verse 21). Yet God acts and judges in the midst of the people (verse 23).

The actions and the judgments of God are intended to be life giving and life renewing in their impact. Thus forgiveness and restoration are among God's gracious blessings to be expected (verses 21 and 25).

Solomon recognizes the reach of God's love beyond the confines of the Hebrew people (verses 32-33) and emphasizes God's will for good and bounty and security in the daily life of the nation (verse 26-31).

In the most reverent sense we may say that the God Solomon addresses in this memorable prayer is a domestic deity. God is one for whom the daily life of the people is important.

God was not, of course, and is not today a domestic deity in the sense of being under our control. Rather, we are under God's control. There is no common human experience where God does not will to be the Lord and Savior of the people.

Our God is always one whose dealings with us—in judgment, in actions, in forgiveness—have a purpose. That purpose is always the same: that we might learn "the right way to live" (verse 27), that we might live out our years in deep reverence for God and obedience to the divine will (verse 31), and that through us God's name might be made known to all the people of the earth (verse 33).

2 Chronicles 7. Now Solomon's prayer of dedication is finished, and the Temple is consecrated to God. There is a total extravagance about Solomon's offerings as the house of God is dedicated (verse 4). The people stand in the presence of God and give thanks for God's everlasting love (verse 6).

Fire and glory come from God at the conclusion of Solomon's prayer. The fire is to consume and thus to accept the sacrifices made, and the glory is to assure the king and his people of the divine presence in their midst. Fire is frequently a biblical symbol for the vital presence of God. (See Exodus 14:24; 1 Chronicles 21:26; Acts 2:3.) In the same manner clouds are often associated with the glory of God. (See Exodus 16:10, for example.)

Immanuel! God with us! That is the meaning of Solomon's dedication of the Temple. And it is a meaning desperately in need of appropriation by the church and the individual Christian in our own time. Our problem is not that God is not with us. Perhaps the difficulty is that in a world so filled with material goods, with vast military resources by various nations that do not trust one another, and with churches where institutional preservation often seems to outweigh ministry to human need, we have eyes but do not see. Perhaps we also have ears but do not hear.

DIMENSION THREE:
WHAT DOES THE BIBLE MEAN TO ME?

The Dimension Three portion of the student book is divided into three parts: "Knowledge and Wisdom," "The Scope of Prayer," and "Moral Expectations." You may not have enough class time to discuss all three issues. If not, ask class members which issue or issues they would like to discuss. Or, if the class is large enough, divide into three groups and have each group discuss one issue. Allow time at the end of the session for each group to summarize its discussion.

2 Chronicles 1:7-12—Knowledge and Wisdom

Twice in these chapters we encounter Solomon as a man of prayer. Here he asks that God give him wisdom and knowledge for the heavy task of governing the people. Later we will see Solomon in something of a high priestly role as he prays for the people who through the years will direct their prayers to the Lord in the Temple.

We are reminded that one greater than Solomon was also a man of prayer. (See Matthew 26:36; Mark 1:35; Luke 6:12; John 17:1-26.) Jesus did not hesitate to petition God for his needs and the needs of others. He did not think it unbecoming to intercede for the well-being of other persons. In like manner Solomon prayed very specifically concerning certain needs of those who would worship in this Temple. In the present passage, Solomon prays for wisdom and knowledge.

Ask class members to consider the difference between wisdom and knowledge. List characteristics of each attribute in parallel columns on a chalkboard or on a large piece of paper. Then have the class think about different situations when each of these attributes would be necessary or helpful. At what times is knowledge called for? When is wisdom necessary? Encourage group members to share and discuss specific situations.

2 Chronicles 6—The Scope of Prayer

You might want to begin discussion of this topic with a general introduction on the subject of prayer. The previous section dealt with Solomon's prayer for wisdom and knowledge. That prayer (2 Chronicles 1:7-12) was a prayer of petition. There Solomon prayed for the inner resources he knew he would need for his task of building the Temple.

Ask class members to consider and discuss the following questions about prayer: For what should we pray? For what do we pray? Can we pray about the sorrows and hurts that bring us awake in the midnight hours? Can we bring those whom we love, and those whom we ought to love, into the presence of God in the act of prayer? Is prayer a sign of strength or of weakness? Is prayer a sign of wisdom or of ignorance?

What prayers may we offer on behalf of our national leaders? Is it possible, in national and state life, to pray for

a person in authority without being in agreement with that individual on all programs and policies?

Whereas Solomon's prayer of petition in 2 Chronicles 1 was of a personal nature, in our present passage Solomon prays on behalf of his people. This type of prayer is called intercessory prayer. Here Solomon prays concerning the various ways he anticipates that his people will turn to the Temple in prayer.

After having class members discuss the questions in the student book, turn the discussion toward prayer concerning the church. When one joins a local congregation, membership vows usually include a commitment to uphold the church by our prayers. What a great Christian ministry could be ours if we fulfilled that vow! Ask what changes might happen in your church if for every word of criticism offered there was substituted a heartfelt prayer of intercession.

What prayers can we offer concerning the relationship of the local church to the outside world? Solomon prayed for the foreigner, and Jesus prayed for those who would believe in him through the ministry of his disciples (John 17:20). Ask the class members to consider what prayer they would offer for those who are outside the church. What is the difference between interceding for a person and trying to make that person behave as we behave?

2 Chronicles 7—Moral Expectations

Begin discussion of this topic by having group members consider what moral expectations God placed upon the people of Solomon's day. Have the class reread 2 Chronicles 7 and list the various expectations of God that are reflected in these verses. Next ask each group member to list God's expectations of him or her. What does God want us to be like? Then have class members compare and contrast the two lists. Ask for volunteers to share findings with the whole group.

Close today's session by having group members share any new insights they have gained from their study of 2 Chronicles 1–9. List these insights on a chalkboard or on a large piece of paper if time allows.

11

The Kingdom Is Divided

2 Chronicles 10–16

DIMENSION ONE: WHAT DOES THE BIBLE SAY?

Answer these questions by reading 2 Chronicles 10

1. Who succeeds Solomon as ruler of the United Kingdom? (10:1)

   Rehoboam succeeds Solomon.

2. In what city does Rehoboam have his encounter with Jeroboam? (10:1-3)

   The encounter takes place at Shechem.

3. What bad advice does Rehoboam follow? (10:10-11)

   He follows the advice of the young men to increase the burdens Solomon placed on Israel.

4. Why does Rehoboam reject the elders' advice? (10:15)

   Rehoboam rejects the advice to fulfill the word of the Lord.

Answer these questions by reading 2 Chronicles 11

5. What tribe joins Judah in remaining faithful to the house of David? (11:1)

   Benjamin remains faithful to David.

6. Why does Rehoboam not attack Israel under King Jeroboam? (11:4)

   God forbids brothers to fight against brothers.

7. How does Rehoboam fortify the territory of Judah? (11:5)

   He builds towns for defense.

8. Why do the priests and Levites of Israel come to Judah? (11:14-15)

   Jeroboam cast them out and replaced them.

9. How do the immigrants aid Judah and Rehoboam? (11:17)

   They strengthen Judah and make the king secure for three years.

Answer these questions by reading 2 Chronicles 12

10. What evil does Rehoboam commit? (12:1)

    Rehoboam abandons the law of God.

11. What king invades the city of Jerusalem? (12:2)

    Shishak, king of Egypt, invades the city of Jerusalem.

12. How long does Rehoboam reign in Jerusalem? (12:13)

    Rehoboam reigns for seventeen years in Jerusalem.

Answer these questions by reading 2 Chronicles 13

13. How long does Abijah, Rehoboam's son, reign in Jerusalem? (13:1-2)

    Abijah reigns three years.

14. Who wins the war between Abijah and Jeroboam? (13:15)

    Abijah and Judah win the war.

15. Who gives the victory to Abijah and Judah? (13:15)

    God gives the victory to Abijah and Judah.

Answer these questions by reading 2 Chronicles 14

16. When Asa succeeds Abijah, what kind of king does he prove to be? (14:1-2)

    Asa does what is good and right in the eyes of God.

17. What steps does Asa take to rid Judah of pagan religious practices? (14:3-5)

    He takes away foreign altars, smashes the sacred stones, and cuts down the Asherah poles.

18. Who defeats the Cushites when they attack Asa and Judah? (14:12)

    The Lord defeats them.

Answer these questions by reading 2 Chronicles 15

19. How does Azariah encourage Asa in his reforming efforts? (15:6-8)

    He assures Asa that God is with him and will reward his work.

20. How does Asa rebuke his grandmother's pagan religious practices? (15:16)

    He removes her from her position as queen mother and destroys her Asherah pole.

Answer these questions by reading 2 Chronicles 16

21. With what foreign king does Asa ally against Baasha, king of Israel? (16:2-3)

    Asa allies with Ben-Hadad of Aram.

22. How is this dependence on foreign kings received? (16:7-9)

    It is viewed as lack of reliance on God.

23. What is Asa's last mistake? (16:12)

    In his illness Asa seeks help from physicians rather than from the Lord.

24. How long does Asa reign over Judah? (16:13)

    Asa reigns forty-one years.

DIMENSION TWO: WHAT DOES THE BIBLE MEAN?

Background Information on 2 Chronicles 10–16

The content of Chapters 10–16 can be easily fixed in our minds. Our reading deals with (1) the breakup of the United Kingdom following the death of Solomon (about 922 B.C.) and (2) the first three monarchs of David's dynasty: Rehoboam, who reigned from about 922 B.C.–915 B.C.; Abijah, also known as Abijam, who reigned from 915 B.C.–913 B.C.; and Asa, who reigned from about 915 B.C.–873 B.C..

We should also keep in mind that we are reading the works of a writer we have identified as the Chronicler. Let us review briefly what we know about this author. This writer was a member of the staff of Judah's temple, probably a member of the priestly caste known as the Levites.

The Chronicler is concerned to interpret the past. His work, consisting of First and Second Chronicles, Ezra, and Nehemiah, was written at some time in the third century B.C. In Chapters 10–16, this author writes of events that transpired long before he himself came on the scene. In so doing, the Chronicler does what all historians do—he edits the material as he writes in order to set forth the view of history that he holds.

The Chronicler's view of history is that Hebrew history is religious history. This history focuses on God's election of this special people for a special purpose. Deuteronomy 7:6-16, though not from the pen of the Chronicler, sets forth a view that the Chronicler would have found totally congenial.

This religious view of history focuses on the affirmation set forth in 2 Samuel 7: "This is what the LORD Almighty says [to David]: I took you from the pasture and from following the flock to be ruler over my people Israel. . . . When your days are over and you rest with your fathers, I will raise up your offspring to succeed you . . . and I will establish the throne of his kingdom forever" (7:8-13).

God's special blessing rests on the dynasty of the house of David. It is that family, in the chosen city of Jerusalem and in the Temple itself, who will guide the establishment of the kingdom of God upon the earth.

Adhering to the one true God, maintaining the pure worship of that God, and steadfast commitment to the law of God bring blessing. Unfaithfulness to God brings disaster.

2 Chronicles 10–11. Here we have the first major disaster. All the tribes except Judah and Benjamin rejected the house of David in the person of Rehoboam. From our perspective, the kingdom divides because of Rehoboam's ill-advised decision to continue, and perhaps increase, the costly expansion programs of Solomon.

Prior to the division of the kingdom, Rehoboam travels to the northern city of Shechem to be made king. He was already recognized in Jerusalem as king. Why then did he make this trip to Shechem?

We may assume that he wished to identify himself as fully as possible with the ancient traditions associated with this place. At Shechem, Abraham built an alter to the Lord as he came into Canaan (Genesis 12:6-7). Jacob bought land and erected an altar to God at this place (Genesis 33:18-20). At Shechem the tribes, under the leadership of Joshua, became a confederacy. Here also Joshua was buried in the land Jacob had purchased (Joshua 24).

Thus for Rehoboam, son of Solomon, grandson of David, to establish his kingship at Shechem was to appeal to the holiest memories of the Hebrew people. It was a brilliant strategic maneuver. However, his next major act was not wise. Rehoboam arrogantly rejected the people's rightful request for an easing of the burdens Solomon imposed. That program of forced labor, military service, and heavy taxation was to be continued and increased!

Rebellion flared, and at Shechem the kingdom was divided. The United Monarchy began at Shechem, and at Shechem decay set in.

The rebellion is led by Jeroboam, who once had charge of forced labor in the northern provinces during Solomon's reign. (See 1 Kings 11:26-28.) There he was associated with an abortive plot to overthrow Solomon. When that effort failed, he fled to Egypt and was given political asylum by Shishak, king of Egypt (1 Kings 11:29-40).

Now Jeroboam has returned. About 922 B.C. he is proclaimed king over the ten northern tribes. From now on these tribes will be known as Israel (or sometimes Ephraim, since Jeroboam came from that tribe).

The Chronicler's view is that this division did not happen without the knowledge and concern of God. Indeed, God was responsible. However, God did not permit Rehoboam to attempt restoration of national unity by means of force. The divine seal of approval was not given for civil war. (See 2 Chronicles 11:1-4.)

2 Chronicles 12–13. The Chronicler's view of history is succinctly demonstrated in 2 Chronicles 12:1-14. The decay in the national life of the Hebrews was at its root a moral and spiritual failure.

Rehoboam, once his rule is firmly established, turns away from God. His people follow him (verse 1). As a result of this infidelity, the people are attacked by Shishak, king of Egypt (verses 2-4).

A spokesperson for God, Shemaiah the prophet, speaks to the king and princes of Judah who repent and humble themselves before God (verses 5-6). After seeing this repentance, God decides to withhold the total disaster that might have come upon the land. The people will not be destroyed, but they will experience some punishment "so that they may learn the difference between serving me and serving the kings of other lands."

The downward movement of the Divided Kingdom is further symbolized by the necessity for Rehoboam to use bronze shields where Solomon had used gold (verses 9-10). Verse 12 is characteristic of the Chronicler's view of history.

Abijah, Rehoboam's successor, does enter into war with Jeroboam. Second Chronicles 13 records Abijah's victory. With an army half the size of the rebellious Israel, Judah claims its right relationship with God as a powerful ally.

Jeroboam is put to flight, and he dies in 900 B.C. Abijah lives on and reigns in prosperity until 913 B.C.

The Chronicler has no doubt that this triumph results from Judah's special relationship with God. Jeroboam, in the Northern Kingdom, had proven himself pagan at heart and hostile to the rightful priesthood. (See 11:14, for example.)

Abijah and his kingdom, Judah, find their great strength and superior power in their fidelity to God. In the joy of their right relationship to God, they make the bold claim that a fight against them is a fight against the Lord God! (See 2 Chronicles 13:10-12.)

2 Chronicles 14–16. Abijah goes the way of all flesh. Fortunately, he is succeeded by Asa his son, who will reign over Judah for forty-one years. (See 2 Chronicles 16:13.)

The tone of Asa's reign is set forth in the very beginning of the account: "Asa did what was good and right in the eyes of the LORD his God" (14:2). Why does the Chronicler portray Asa in such a favorable light? First, Asa destroyed the many evidences of infidelity to the God of the Hebrews. (See 2 Chronicles 14:3-5; 15:6, 16-17.) Also, Asa challenged the people of Judah to keep the law and the commandments of God and to seek after God. (See 2 Chronicles 14:4; 15:12-15.)

Asa's reign was primarily one during which Judah was at peace with the surrounding nations. Second Chronicles 14:1 says, "In his days the country was at peace for ten years." Second Chronicles 15:19 tells us there was no more war until the thirty-fifth year of Asa's reign. At that time, and with that particular political and geographical setting, two brief military campaigns in a forty-year period constituted an enviable record!

Although the overall assessment of Asa's kingship is favorable, the Chronicler does point out that there were imperfections in Asa's character. Read, for example, the comment in 2 Chronicles 16:12 about Asa's foot disease. This comment has no real meaning for us unless we note that in those days medicine and magic were often confused. Here the Chronicler is telling us that at the time of his approaching death, Asa's faith wavered and he turned to forbidden practices for aid.

Second Chronicles 15:1-15, and especially verses 12-15, call for special comment. We may look on verses 12-15 with envy as they represent a genuine national revival of religion. As Christians we will perhaps stumble at verse 13, since it suggests conversion by force rather than by persuasion.

However, we cannot avoid noticing the intensity of the commitment to seek God. Even at this long historical distance, we may rejoice with the people because "they sought God eagerly, and he was found by them. So the LORD gave them rest on every side" (2 Chronicles 15:15). We are reminded of the words of God through Jeremiah, "You will seek me and find me when you seek me with all your heart" (Jeremiah 29:13).

The student book suggests that these chapters contain at least three emphases: (1) "Chaos in the Land," (2) "A Covenant of Salt," and (3) "God's Work in the World." According to the student book, all these emphases reflect the larger issue in these chapters of a national and individual response to God. You might want to have the class discuss this larger issue as well as the three emphases treated in the student book.

For the Hebrews, who did not have our modern emphasis upon individuality and personality, what happened to the nation happened to the men and women who comprised the population. What happened to certain key individuals (the king, for example) in a sense created the destiny of the people as a whole.

Although we may not think in such terms today, the essential truth of that close relationship between rulers and people is relevant for us. In some ways, the goodness of a people, when it is present, can percolate upward to those in authority. When good people are in authority, something of their vision of truth and honor slips downward into the common life of the people.

Thus when we read of Judah's inconsistent response to God's call and when we read of the uneven response of the three kings in 2 Chronicles 10–16, we may learn something of value. We can learn that in all the affairs of human existence, there is always present an intermingling of good and bad. Ask class members to consider how this combination is reflected in our society, in your church, and in each individual.

2 Chronicles 10:12-19—Chaos in the Land

These verses narrate in concise terms the division of the United Kingdom. Rehoboam, son of Solomon, was largely responsible for this unfortunate event in the life of God's people. The Chronicler tells us that Rehoboam "did not listen to the people." (See 10:15.) As a ruler, Rehoboam effected change.

The student book concentrates on the feelings that must have been aroused in the people under Rehoboam's leadership. Their kingdom has been divided. There was chaos in the land. The Chronicler tells us that Israel has "been in rebellion against the house of David to this day" (10:19). Use the questions in the student book to help the class discuss how changes on the national level affect us today.

We read in later verses that Rehoboam did try to achieve stability in the land for the sake of the people. Read aloud 2 Chronicles 11:5, 11-12. These verses show us Rehoboam's earnest desire to improve the life of his people.

Ask class members what value they place on making life good for other men and women.

2 Chronicles 13:1-7—A Covenant of Salt

Abijah and his people had, from their viewpoint and certainly from the viewpoint of the Chronicler, ample basis for claiming the favor of God. From their perspective there was little or no room for doubt that God was with them. The people had no reason to question the correctness of their affirmation that their battles were God's battles.

The student book asks the class members to consider the idea of a personal covenant between individuals and God. In class discussion, stress both the positive and negative aspects of such a covenant. Ask class members to think about the times they have felt that God let them down.

The student book asks class members to consider what basis we have for assuming that we have a similar covenant with God. Where do we get assurance of God's presence, grace, and aid? We have to answer in specifically Christian terms. We answer in terms of God's coming among us in the person of Jesus Christ. What evidence do we find in the person of Jesus?

First, we have proof positive of the scope of God's love for us. (See John 3:16.) Second, we have proof positive that when our lives are headed in God's direction, then in all the circumstances of life God is at work with us to bring good out of ill, light out of darkness, and life out of death. (See Romans 8:28.) This is a bold affirmation and often requires faith and trust in the ultimate goodness of God.

Consider with the class whether this kind of faith affirmation has any practical, tangible meaning for the common experiences of daily life. Ask class members to share experiences when dark clouds proved to be the prelude to light, hope, and joy.

2 Chronicles 14:1-8—God's Work in the World

Asa, in his own life and in his reign over the people of Judah, illustrates our view that life is so often a mixture of good and ill. He was a man of courage, a man of zeal. He did sometimes need reinforcement, and on occasion he did fall short of what the Chronicler sets as a goal for the kings of Judah. Do we not also fall short of what others expect of us?

To begin the discussion, have class members review the account of Asa's reign (Chapters 14–16). Have the students list in parallel columns on a chalkboard or on a large piece of paper the positive and negative comments the Bible makes about Asa. Then lead the class in a discussion of Asa's qualities and how they are reflected in each of us.

Close the session by asking class members to share any new insights they gained in their study of 2 Chronicles 10–16.

All Judah brought gifts to Jehoshaphat, so that he had great wealth and honor (17:5).

12

Judah's Kings

2 Chronicles 17–26

DIMENSION ONE: WHAT DOES THE BIBLE SAY?

Answer these questions by reading 2 Chronicles 17

1. What are the virtues of Jehoshaphat who succeeds Asa as king over Judah? (17:3-6)

   He seeks out God, rules wisely, and opposes the Baals.

2. What kind of teaching mission to Judah does Jehoshaphat sponsor? (17:7-9)

   He sends officials, priests, and Levites to teach the law of the Lord.

3. What peoples bring tribute to Jehoshaphat? (17:11)

   Some Philistines and Arabs bring tribute.

Answer these questions by reading 2 Chronicles 18

4. With whom does Jehoshaphat make a marriage alliance? (18:1)

   Jehoshaphat allies with Ahab.

5. What does Micaiah say that God has done? (18:22)

   God has put lies into the mouths of the prophets.

6. Jehoshaphat escapes at the Battle of Ramoth Gilead, but what happens to King Ahab? (18:28-34)

   He is wounded and dies at sunset.

Answer these questions by reading 2 Chronicles 19

7. How does Jehoshaphat do the work of an evangelist? (19:4)

   He goes to the people and turns them back to God.

8. Why are the judges appointed by Jehoshaphat to be careful in their work? (19:7)

   God is impartial, is above bribes, and does no injustice.

Answer these questions by reading 2 Chronicles 20

9. Whom does Jehoshaphat trust when he does not know how to defend Judah? (20:12)

   Jehoshaphat's trust is in God.

10. What is the Chronicler's assessment of Jehoshaphat as king and as a person? (20:32)

    He does what is right in the eyes of the Lord.

11. Is everything in the reign of Jehoshaphat precisely as God wishes it to be? (20:33)

    No. The high places are not removed, and the people's hearts are not set on God.

Answer these questions by reading 2 Chronicles 21

12. What does Jehoram do when he comes to the throne? (21:4)

    He kills his brothers and some of the princes of Israel.

13. With what words does the Chronicler record the death of Jehoram? (21:20)

    Jehoram died with "no one's regret."

Answer these questions by reading 2 Chronicles 22

14. Who is Jehoram's successor? (22:1)

    Ahaziah succeeds Jehoram.

15. Who counsels Ahaziah in doing evil? (22:3)

His mother counsels him to do wrong.

16. Who seizes the throne after the death of Ahaziah? (22:10-12)

Ahaziah's mother, Athaliah, seizes the throne.

Answer these questions by reading 2 Chronicles 23

17. Who leads the rebellion against the queen? (23:1)

Jehoiada leads the rebellion.

18. What rightful heir to the throne does this rebellion establish? (23:3; 24:1)

Joash, son of Ahaziah, is made king.

19. What is the covenant that Jehoiada makes between the people and the king? (23:16)

The king, the priest, and the people will be the Lord's people.

Answer this question by reading 2 Chronicles 24

20. What happens to Jehoiada's reforms after his death? (24:17-18)

The king and people return to the worship of pagan gods.

Answer this question by reading 2 Chronicles 25

21. What does Amaziah, son of Joash, do when he comes to the throne? (25:3-4)

He kills his father's assassins but does not kill their sons.

Answer these questions by reading 2 Chronicles 26

22. How long does Uzziah reign over Judah? (26:3)

Uzziah reigns for fifty-two years.

23. From what illness does Uzziah suffer as punishment for his pride? (26:21)

Uzziah suffers from leprosy.

DIMENSION TWO: WHAT DOES THE BIBLE MEAN?

Background Information on 2 Chronicles 17–26

Chapters 17–26 in today's study cover the reign of seven monarchs in Judah. We cover the 130 years from the accession of Jehoshaphat in 873 B.C. to the death of Uzziah in 742 B.C.

These chapters tell a story of greed, family strife, and distress for the land of Judah. Time is running out, the kingdom and the house of David are playing out, and the end is in sight. That end will not come until 155 years later when, in 587 B.C., there is a second deportation of the people of Judah to Babylonia. We will read of that event in the closing session of our study of the works of the author known as the Chronicler. (See 2 Chronicles 36:11-21.)

Though the general course of events is downward, from our perspective there are elements of hope and light scattered all through these years and this record. We find ourselves examining the pattern of good kings and bad kings, faithful rulers and faithless rulers, that by now is very familiar to us. We read again that when ruler and ruled, king and people, walked in the ways of God, there was peace and well-being in the land. (See 2 Chronicles 17:5; 23:21; 26:5.)

When the monarch and the masses, the royals and the commoners, walked in rebellion and turned from the God who had established them as a nation, there was personal and public disaster all through the land. (See 2 Chronicles 21; 24:15-27.)

These chapters record seven monarchs who ruled in Judah during this period.

Jehoshaphat reigned twenty-five years in Jerusalem and "did what was right in the eyes of the LORD" (2 Chronicles 20:31-32).

Jehoram reigned eight years in Jerusalem, and "he did evil in the eyes of the LORD" (2 Chronicles 21:6, 20).

Ahaziah reigned one year in Jerusalem and "did evil in the eyes of the LORD" (2 Chronicles 22:1-4).

Athaliah made herself ruler at the cost of all the royal family of Judah except Joash, who was rescued by his sister (2 Chronicles 22:10-12). Athaliah held the throne for six years.

Joash had the throne restored to him and as long as Jehoiada the priest lived "did what was right in the eyes of the LORD" (2 Chronicles 24:1-2). After Jehoiada's death, Joash and his people turned from the Lord. They were defeated by the Arameans; and, in the end, Joash was murdered by his servants (2 Chronicles 24:17-27).

Amaziah reigned twenty-nine years in Jerusalem and "did what was right in the eyes of the LORD, but not wholeheartedly" (2 Chronicles 25:1-2). Under Amaziah, Judah was grievously defeated by Israel (2 Chronicles 25:20-24).

Uzziah, the leper king, reigned fifty-two years in Jerusalem; and "he did what was right in the eyes of the LORD" (2 Chronicles 26:3-5).

From the many events recorded in these chapters, we will take the following to examine in some depth:

(1) the reign of Jehoshaphat, whom we shall call Judah's "teaching king" (Jehoshaphat reigned from 873 B.C. to 849 B.C.)

(2) the work of Jehoiada the priest and the restoration of the throne to a rightful heir, Joash (These years are from 842 B.C. to 800 B.C.)

(3) the reign of Uzziah whose name, at least, is more familiar to most of us from the reading of Isaiah 6 (Uzziah reigned from 783 B.C. to 742 B.C.)

2 Chronicles 17–20. Many details are given here that call for exposition. Let us focus on those passages that, in describing the work of Jehoshaphat as king of Judah, cause us to give him the title "the teaching king."

We find these verses in 2 Chronicles 17:7-10 and in 2 Chronicles 19:4-11. The latter passage illustrates Jehoshaphat's concern for the quality of administration in his kingdom. But we will suggest that this passage represents a continuation of his concern that his people should know the law of the Lord (2 Chronicles 17:9).

First, let us look at the passages that tell us several positive things about the character of this king. "His heart was devoted to the ways of the LORD" (2 Chronicles 17:6). "He went out again among the people . . . and turned them back to the LORD" (19:4). "He walked in the ways of his father Asa and did not stray from them; he did what was right in the eyes of the LORD" (20:32). These verses ascribe to Jehoshaphat courage, action, and integrity. These are desirable qualities for any ruler of any people in any time!

Some of Jehoshaphat's actions were directed toward the constant struggle to free the religion of Judah from pagan thoughts and practices. The persistence of the pagan fertility religions as an insidious attraction for the rulers and people of Judah and Israel is amazing! Here again we read of royal efforts to stamp out the pagan places of worship and pagan images (2 Chronicles 17:6). Jehoshaphat was not totally successful; no one ever seemed to be. (See 2 Chronicles 20:33.)

Jehoshaphat also directed other efforts toward establishing efficient justice in the land. (See 2 Chronicles 19:4-11.) In his administration he distinguished between affairs that we would today call secular and those we might call religious. (See 2 Chronicles 19:11.)

Yet other energies of Jehoshaphat were devoted to what we might call a religious revival in the land. He was one of the few kings, if not the only one, who used the many princes of lesser rank than himself in the royal household (2 Chronicles 17:7-9). He made the princes, the priests, and the Levites move out from their comfortable positions in Jerusalem into "all the towns of Judah" to teach the law of God. Jehoshaphat was a worthy ruler for the chosen people of God!

2 Chronicles 23–24. In studying the work of Jehoiada the priest, we examine the influence of a religious leader upon one who, in our terms, would be considered primarily a secular leader of his people. We must remember that for this people in this day there was no thought of separation of church and state, either in structure (as our American constitution provides) or in relationship (as certain voices are calling for today).

From Saul to David to Solomon down to the encounter of the prophets with Jehoshaphat and Ahab (and beyond), those who were called to speak for God had easy access to the king.

Jehoiada was a politically involved priest. He took the leadership in wresting the usurped throne from Queen Athaliah and placing upon it the rightful heir and descendant of David—Joash. (See 2 Chronicles 22:10-12.) In taking this action, Jehoiada was the human instrument in giving Judah another one of the kings it so desperately needed, one who "did what was right in the eyes of the LORD" (2 Chronicles 24:2).

Joash continued doing what was right as long as his mentor and benefactor, Jehoiada, was present to lend his support and to bring his influence to bear. Unfortunately, Joash was unable to stand for the right when it became necessary for him to stand alone (2 Chronicles 24:17-18). Here is another example of a king who follows bad advice. (See also 2 Chronicles 10:6-19.)

The reign of Joash ended in defeat for his nation and in shameful death for him (2 Chronicles 24:23-35). He had given permission for Zechariah, the son of the man to whom he owed his throne, to be killed because of his pronouncement of God's judgment. (See 2 Chronicles 24:21.) Perhaps Jesus had this incident in mind when he spoke of Jerusalem as a city that stoned the prophets. (See Matthew 23:37.)

When Joash dies, we have an example of a man who came to great privilege and responsibility on the shoulders of others. But his sense of indebtedness fades away, and in the end he repeats many of the crimes against which his own enthronement was a protest.

2 Chronicles 26. Uzziah is the king whose fifty-two-year reign is most remembered by an event that transpired in the year of the king's death (Isaiah 6:1). We might wonder if amid the pageantry associated with the death and burial of a king, anyone noticed a vision of a young prophet. The centuries have witnessed that the vision of Isaiah was of more significance than the funeral of King Uzziah. Very often what makes the headlines is not, in the long run, the event of greatest meaning. However, we must not overlook the fact that Uzziah was significant for the people over whom he reigned for so long.

Under the leadership of Uzziah, Judah peaked in terms of economic and military power. He brought into Judean control that area known as the Negev. He also gave attention to the development of agriculture. We are told that he had large herds and "loved the soil" (2 Chronicles 26:10).

We read that Uzziah "sought God during the days of Zechariah" (26:5). The Zechariah mentioned here is not the person whose name is associated with the Old Testament prophetic book. This Zechariah is one of those persons whose names are little more than footnotes in history but who through some relationship, some kind of influence exerted, have carried significant weight.

What do we know of this Zechariah? Almost nothing. But we do know of the person whose life he influenced—Uzziah.

Uzziah, like every person, was not without some fault or failure. "After Uzziah became powerful, his pride led to his downfall" (2 Chronicles 26:16). We must remember the Chronicler's conviction that the ritual for the worship of God was of vast importance. Thus when Uzziah tried to overstep the bounds of his role as king and take over the role of the priests, no one—the priests, the people, or Uzziah himself—was surprised at the immediate calamity that resulted.

Verse 21 tells us exactly how King Uzziah's pride leads to his destruction. He is stricken with leprosy and suffers with it "until the day he died." Those who suffered from leprosy were considered impure and were forbidden to enter the sanctuary.

DIMENSION THREE: WHAT DOES THE BIBLE MEAN TO ME?

In the three portions of today's assigned Bible chapters chosen for special emphasis, there are at least these lessons for Christians who are heirs to this great religious tradition and this Hebrew history.

(1) Jehoshaphat was remembered for his contributions in the areas of teaching and administration. In what sense would we consider that God favors the administration of persons who govern in accordance with the divine goals? What do we consider to be the goals for which God labors in our time?

(2) What do we, with our special Judeo-Christian heritage, believe to be the proper relationship of church and state? What "political priests" can we identify among us today? What is our reaction to such persons?

(3) Is there always in men and women, in nations, and in movements of people a mixture of good and evil? Is there always some unconsecrated area of personality and character that lurks to trip us up and keep us just outside the goal of perfection?

These are tough questions. Neither time nor wisdom will permit the class to answer such concerns in full or to the satisfaction of all. But as the disciples of a Lord who has instructed us to love God with our minds, we cannot consider ourselves freed from the obligation to think.

Indeed, one of the richest of all meanings of the Bible for us in our time is the freedom and the obligation of Christians to be thinking persons. We do not question for one moment the utter importance of "heart-love" for God.

But that recognition does not permit us to down play the call for "mind-love" of God as well.

2 Chronicles 17:7-9—Mission in the World

We consider our first questions listed above as we review the highlights of the reign of Jehoshaphat. Quickly survey Chapters 17–20 to list the things Jehoshaphat did that the Chronicler, our historical writer, saw as harmonious with the mind of God. These accomplishments might include (a) developing military strength, (b) rejecting pagan gods and pagan worship practices, (c) teaching the people to know the law of God, and (d) providing for efficient administration of justice in the land. (See 2 Chronicles 17:1-9; 19:4-7.) Ask class members to think about and discuss how these accomplishments reflect the mind of God.

As we read of Jehoshaphat's reign, we sense that he felt required by God to perform a mission in the world. Could we expect that if such a spirit dwells in the minds of modern rulers of modern nations, they will have the favor of God resting upon them? Why or why not?

Ask class members to consider what goals they believe God has in mind for America in our time. List these suggestions on a chalkboard or on a large piece of paper. Then ask the class to consider whether such goals could be met through a teaching mission like the one described in Second Chronicles. How would they describe such a teaching mission?

To begin this discussion, suggest the following elements that might be included in a teaching mission:

(1) the call to justice and resulting peace within our country's borders

(2) the call to an international role for our nation as peacemaker in the affairs of other nations

(3) the call to demonstrate that "liberty in law" provides the best framework for the fulfillment of human hopes and dreams

(4) the call to sacrificial love and service for the last, the least, and the lost within our own land and beyond our borders

2 Chronicles 23–24—Church and State

We consider our second question in light of Jehoiada's political action in leading the revolt against Athaliah and putting Joash on the throne of Judah. Can we say that the question of who will sit upon David's throne was none of the business of the priest? Should Jehoiada have prayed and comforted people spiritually and left political questions to other persons? Use the class discussion of these questions as a background for considering the larger issue of church and state.

Ask class members to list issues that we encounter today involving both religion and government, church and state. You might want to choose one of these issues to discuss in more detail. (The student book mentions abortion as an example.) Try to keep the discussion centered on the relationship between church and government and not on arguments about the issue itself.

One final question: Does the American doctrine of separation of church and state mean that the Christian community cannot address national affairs? Does it mean that Christians must, if they address national affairs at all, make no effort to influence the governing process and the governing bodies? If not, then what does this doctrine mean in the lives of Christians today?

2 Chronicles 26—Pride Leads to Destruction

The introduction to Dimension Three asks whether each person has a flaw, such as pride, that keeps him or her from achieving perfection. The answer seems obvious in light of this history, of all the history we have read in First and Second Kings and First and Second Chronicles, and in light of our own experiences.

We all have the mixture of good and evil that characterizes King Uzziah. Christian men and women know that whatever the progress made in spiritual growth and maturing discipleship, there is more within us that needs to be offered to Christ for his cleansing, healing touch. Have the class suggest other character flaws, aside from pride, that keep us from perfection.

Close the session by having class members share any new insights they have gained from today's lesson. List these insights on a chalkboard or on a large piece of paper if time allows.

13

Hezekiah and Josiah

2 Chronicles 27–36

DIMENSION ONE:
WHAT DOES THE BIBLE SAY?

Answer this question by reading 2 Chronicles 27

1. What is Jotham's attitude toward the Temple? (27:2)

   Jotham never entered the Temple.

Answer these questions by reading 2 Chronicles 28

2. What three sins does Ahaz commit? (28:2-3)

   Ahaz makes cast idols, burns incense, and sacrifices his sons.

3. What do the Israelites do with their captives? (28:8-11)

   They send the captives back.

4. In his distress, what does King Ahaz do? (28:22)

   He becomes yet more faithless to the Lord.

Answer these questions by reading 2 Chronicles 29

5. What is the Chronicler's assessment of King Hezekiah? (29:2)

   King Hezekiah "did what was right in the eyes of the LORD."

6. Where did the order for the worship in the Temple come from originally? (29:25)

   The commandment came from the Lord through the prophets.

Answer these questions by reading 2 Chronicles 30

7. What great feast does Hezekiah invite Judah and Israel to attend in the restored Temple? (30:1)

   Hezekiah invites them to the Feast of the Passover.

8. What does Hezekiah promise the people if they will keep the Passover? (30:9)

   He promises God's compassion, grace, and mercy.

9. What attitude does Hezekiah regard as more important than ritual cleanness? (30:18-19)

   A desire to seek God is more important.

10. How long has it been since Passover was kept so well in Jerusalem? (30:26)

    It has not happened since the time of Solomon.

Answer these questions by reading 2 Chronicles 31

11. Does Hezekiah's revival of religion reach beyond Jerusalem? (31:6)

    Yes. It reaches all towns of Judah.

12. What offerings do the people make? (31:6)

    They offer tithes of herds and flocks and "of the holy things dedicated to the LORD their God."

13. What do Hezekiah and the princes do when they see the offerings? (31:8)

    They praise the Lord and bless the people.

14. How does the Chronicler summarize Hezekiah's attitude? (31:21)

    Hezekiah "worked wholeheartedly."

Answer these questions by reading 2 Chronicles 32

15. Why does Hezekiah believe Judah can be strong and of good courage against Sennacherib? (32:7)

    The one with the Lord God is greater than anyone with Sennacherib.

16. What is the great offense of Sennacherib's servants? (32:19)

The servants speak of God as no different from other gods.

17. What is the flaw in Hezekiah's relationship with God? (32:24-25)

He is proud in his heart.

Answer these questions by reading 2 Chronicles 33

18. What happens when Manasseh comes to the throne? (33:1-2)

He does "evil in the eyes of the LORD."

19. What occasions Manasseh's conversion and return to the Lord? (33:11-12)

The king of Assyria takes him captive to Babylon.

Answer these questions by reading 2 Chronicles 34

20. How does Josiah bring reform to Judah before he discovers the Book of the Law? (34:3)

He destroys the high place and idols.

21. What great discovery does Hilkiah the priest make? (34:14)

He finds the Book of the Law in the Temple.

22. What response does Josiah make to the reading of the Book of the Law? (34:31)

He makes a covenant to be totally faithful to God.

Answer these questions by reading 2 Chronicles 36

23. What kings after Josiah are taken into exile? (36:4-6, 9-10)

Jehoahaz, Jehoiakim, and Jehoiachin are taken into exile.

24. On what note of hope does Second Chronicles end? (36:22-23)

The exiles will return from Babylon.

DIMENSION TWO: WHAT DOES THE BIBLE MEAN?

Our final chapters in this study of Kings and Chronicles provide us with an excellent summary of the message of the writer of these books. We have identified this writer as the Chronicler, who was the author of First and Second Chronicles, Ezra, and Nehemiah.

The Chronicler's message has these principal emphases:

(1) The pattern of Hebrew history is clearly outlined. Good kings, faithful to God and sensitive to God's requirements, come to the throne and much good is found in the life of the nation. Evil kings, unfaithful to God and openly disdainful of divine expectations, come to the throne and much evil comes upon the nation.

Thus Jotham (as regent from 750 B.C. to 742 B.C. and king from 742 B.C. to 732 B.C.) did right in the sight of the Lord. He was followed by Ahaz, who did not do right in the eyes of the Lord. From 735 B.C. to 715 B.C., this man was ruler of God's chosen people. (See 2 Chronicles 27–28.)

Of the eight kings that follow Ahaz, only two, Hezekiah and Josiah, are recorded as men who did what was right. All the others, even the eight-year-old Jehoiachin whose reign lasted three months and ten days, are described as evil.

(2) The cumulative effect of evil leads to the final ending of the kingdom. In the last chapter of Second Chronicles, we are exposed to two very crucial ideas. First, God does not easily or quickly surrender the divine intention to mold this people into a nation where moral and spiritual values prevail (2 Chronicles 36:15-16). This people, the Hebrews, were chosen for God's purpose by the free act of God's love.

Second, in this steady downward movement there is always the possibility of a springtime of renewal. As Hosea says when he pictures the relationship between God and this people as a marriage relationship, "I am now going to allure her; / I will lead her into the desert, / and speak tenderly to her.... There I will ... make ... a door of hope" (Hosea 2:14-15).

The Chronicler saw this renewal happen quite literally in the days of Hezekiah (2 Chronicles 29–30); for the Lord "took care of them [Judah] on every side" (32:22), and Hezekiah "succeeded in everything he undertook" (32:30). Our writer saw it happen in the days of Josiah (2 Chronicles 34–35). During all his days the people did not turn away from God.

If we take an overview of the course of events in 2 Chronicles 27–36, we see a pattern of the nation's life emerging. It was a time of conflict with external foes. (See 2 Chronicles 28:16-18, for example.) It was a period of relative stability in the royal house. The kings who reign from Jotham (Chapter 27) to Josiah (Chapters 34–35) averaged nearly twenty-five years each as ruler. With the passing of Josiah the powers of national decay and defeat are accelerated, and the remaining four kings occupy the throne for an average of five-and-one-half years each.

This period was a time when the word of God was present through the prophets. "The LORD, the God of their fathers, sent word to them through his messengers again and again. . . . But they mocked God's messengers, despised his words and scoffed at his prophets" (2 Chronicles 36:15-16). We are reminded of Jesus' statement in Matthew 23:37.

Oded, a prophet in the time of Ahaz, prevented the men of Israel from destroying two hundred thousand Judean prisoners of war. (See 2 Chronicles 28:8-15.) We only meet Jeremiah indirectly in these chapters, but these are the years of his ministry. He prophesied from approximately 626 B.C. to 585 B.C.

(3) The Chronicler is aware of God's tenacious love. The story of our books (First and Second Kings, First and Second Chronicles) ends on a note of tragedy but with a glimmer of hope. The sun sets on Judah, yet there is the promise of sunrise. For this promise people will endure weeping for a night, but rejoicing comes in the morning. (See Psalm 30:5.)

The kingdom that began with such bright hope and promise in the reign of David and his successor, Solomon, comes to an end. Israel (the Northern Kingdom) earlier ended in about 721 B.C., and Judah comes to an end in 587 B.C. The Temple is destroyed; the people enter a fifty-year Babylonian captivity. (See 2 Chronicles 36:20-21.)

But in 538 B.C. there comes an edict from Cyrus, king of Persia, who has overthrown Babylon. The Hebrew exiles are to return! It is on this note of return that the next study begins. (Compare 2 Chronicles 36:22-23 with Ezra 1:1-4.) In the end, divine love continues to call us and to provide us broad room in which to make proper response.

2 Chronicles 28:8-15. This is one of those great moments in the Old Testament when actions on the part of a pre-Christian people, as our Hebrew faith ancestors were, come very close to reflecting the mind of Christ. We have earlier encountered such an experience when Amaziah kills those who assassinated his father, Joash, but does not kill their sons. Amaziah was returning to the law of Moses. He was rallying to the principle of individual responsibility for evil. The idea that children might be punished for the faults of their fathers is also rejected in Jeremiah 31:29 and Ezekiel 18:1-4.

In 2 Chronicles 28:8-15, Oded the prophet persuades the Israelites not to take revenge on the people of Judah. The prophet taunts the Israelites with the thought that they too are sinners and have no need to bring heavy punishment upon sinners such as the men of Judah. The student book suggests that in this action of Oded and the Israelites, we Christians find Christlike actions on the part of persons who had not yet heard of Jesus.

2 Chronicles 29–32. Of the many events recorded of the reign of Hezekiah, from 727 B.C. to 698 B.C., we have chosen to focus on two: (1) Second Chronicles 30:18-20 provides an insight that does not depreciate the value of ritual preparedness for the worship of God but points out the great importance of the mind, will, and purpose of the worshiper. (2) Second Chronicles 31:2-19 shows the peo-ple making offerings for the support of the clergy as well as the clergy being expected "to distribute portions to every male among them and to all who were recorded in the genealogies of the Levites" (verse 19).

In addition to these two events, two famous prophets lived and worked in Israel during Hezekiah's reign. The prophet Isaiah started his ministry when Ahaz was on the throne and completed it approximately two years before Hezekiah's death. The prophet Micah also lived in the time of Hezekiah. The presence of these two men would have made Hezekiah's reign notable, but the passages we are looking at add meaning to his reign for our lives as Christians today.

Second Chronicles 30:18-20 emphasizes inner spirit over outward ritual actions. There is a fitness to come into the presence of God that has little or nothing to do with rite and ceremony. This fitness, which is either within us or not within us, is a fitness of intention, of desire, and of purpose. As Christians we must bring faith and intention in mind, will, and heart. This attitude is close to the "more important matters of the law" of which Jesus spoke (Matthew 23:23).

We do not know the precise nature of the sanctuary's rules of cleanness mentioned in verse 19. However, we may assume that these rules included the necessity to partici-pate in the blood sacrifices. (See 2 Chronicles 29:20-24.) These rules probably also included the kind of elaborate descriptions of clean and unclean acts found in Leviticus 17–23. Many of these laws in Leviticus are moral. For example, we find injunctions against child sacrifice and a commandment to "love your neighbor as yourself" (19:18).

Other rules for cleanness, if we take them at face value, seem to have little relation to the quality of a person's relationship with God. The great breakthrough of Hezekiah is to see that God is more concerned with the worshiper's inner attitude than with outward appearances.

Let us look now at the verses that suggest the types of gifts given by the people for support of the clergy (2 Chronicles 30:2-19). The verses also suggest much about the tone and quality of life of the professional leaders in the church.

For the Hebrews, the concept of devoting oneself to the Law of the Lord (31:4) involved deep, intense, and consis-tent study of the written word. As the years went by, the concept came to mean more and more of what we know today as scholarly Bible study. Here a student wrestles not only with the biblical text but also with the accumulated insights and understandings of those who have preceded in a serious attempt to come as close as possible to the core message of the passage.

Keeping oneself holy had a double meaning, a meaning symbolized by the mixture of ritual and moral command-ments in Leviticus that we have noted above. It meant keeping oneself in a state of readiness for conscious entry into the presence of God. Such a state of holiness was, and is, a noble ambition and one that our clergy today might do well to consider.

Second Chronicles 32:30 notes that Hezekiah was renowned for his improvement of Jerusalem's water supply. More specifically, Hezekiah was responsible for the construction of what we now call the Siloam Tunnel. This tunnel connects Gihon, a site outside the city wall, with the Pool of Siloam, located inside the wall. Hezekiah's tunnel was about 1,700 feet long.

2 Chronicles 34–35. Here is another great moment in Hebrew history. The reform period of Josiah has drawn the attention of many devout Bible scholars. A number of questions must be asked about this event. Among them are (1) Why was the Book of the Law lost? and (2) What was this book that Hilkiah the priest found and that created such a profound response in the king and in the people? We have addressed ourselves to the second question in our earlier study of 2 Kings 23. You might wish to review that discussion now. (See Lesson 5.)

We cannot really answer the first question. What we do know is that this book was recovered when workmen were repairing and restoring the Temple. We may speculate that the book had been cast aside, with a good many other precious things devoted to the worship of God, during the reigns of Manasseh and Amon. (See 2 Chronicles 33.)

The response of Josiah and his people to this book is more important than the details of its discovery. That response was one of repentance (34:19) and renewal of the covenant with God, "to follow the LORD and keep his commands . . . with all his heart and all his soul" (34:31).

Then follows Josiah's cleansing of the land from the abominations of the pagan gods. We must not think these pagan places of worship and these pagan symbols were just another way of worshiping God. They threatened the moral and spiritual insights of the Hebrew faith. They were associated with male and female prostitution, with the burning of children as sacrifices to the gods, and with the denial of the most important tenet of Israel's faith—the oneness of God. (See Deuteronomy 6:4-5.)

2 Chronicles 36. The Chronicler seems to know that his story is ended. The events covered in this last chapter are only lightly touched. It is as if the writer is anxious now to get through with the tale, to close the book, and to get on with the rest of his task.

DIMENSION THREE: WHAT DOES THE BIBLE MEAN TO ME?

The student book portion of Dimension Three focuses on four topics: "The Limits of Compassion," "God's Covenant," "Clergy and Laity," and "Love or Justice?" In addition to these topics, you might want to have the class discuss Josiah's reform. (See the section entitled "Religious Reform.")

2 Chronicles 28:8-15—The Limits of Compassion

This episode in Second Chronicles has no parallel in the Books of Kings. It is surprising to find a story in Second Chronicles about the Israelites. We have noted elsewhere that since the Chronicler believed that only the people of Judah were the chosen people of God, this author paid very little attention to the Northern Kingdom, Israel. Here, however, we read about Oded persuading the men of Israel to have mercy on their captives, the people of Judah.

Earlier in this chapter (verses 1-4), we read about the great wickedness of King Ahaz. He worshiped idols, burned incense at pagan altars, and even sacrificed his own children to pagan gods. The writer leaves no doubt that Ahaz deserves harsh punishment and that his people should be punished as well (verse 6). Yet the people of Israel are persuaded not only to spare their captives but also to clothe them, feed them, anoint them, and carry them back to Jerusalem.

The student book emphasizes the compassion of Oded and the men of Israel. Ask the class members to consider the situations in their lives and in the life of the church that call for compassion. When has compassion come easily? When has compassion been difficult to find? Who are the Odeds in your life? in your church? in the world today? After the class members have discussed these questions and the questions in the student book, relate the idea of compassion to the parable of the good Samaritan. (See Luke 10:25-37.)

2 Chronicles 30:18-20—God's Covenant

Read the material in the student book for comments on this section of today's Bible reading. Then have the class discuss the idea of covenant and what it means in their lives.

The student book stresses inner spirit over outward ritual as proper preparation for entering into covenant with God. What constitutes proper preparation for entering God's presence? Is it ritual readiness? Or is it a deeper, inward orientation of mind and spirit? Refer group members to Psalm 51:16-27 and Philippians 4:8-9.

2 Chronicles 31:2-19—Clergy and Laity

This passage emphasizes offerings made by the people. It deals also with the goal of those offerings. By implication, the passage deals with the character of life expected of professional leaders of the church.

The student book asks several discussion questions. You might want to have the class discuss the following questions as well: (1) What do we believe to be the real purpose of the ordained minister or pastor? (2) Why do we have such a person assigned to our congregation? (3) When do we think the pastor's salary has been earned?

For Protestant Christians a basic tenet of faith is commitment to the priesthood of all believers. What differences can and do exist between the clergy's quality of life and the quality of laypersons' lives? Should only the professional clergy be responsible for the law of God? Do school teachers also have this responsibility? Why or why not?

2 Chronicles 34–35—Religious Reform

The contrast between the religion of the Hebrew people and the religion of the surrounding nations was the contrast between morality and immorality. One people burned theirs own sons in sacrifices as a means to gain favor with their gods. The other circumcised their sons as a token and symbol of their becoming, by God's grace, living members of the people of God.

The reforms of Josiah also represented a striving for unity among the Hebrew people. The emphasis upon Jerusalem as the one proper place for the true worship of God was a political and national move as well as a spiritual one. It was a means of unifying the people.

Now let us ask ourselves, *Do we wish people to become Christians? Do we care if they ever become believers in our Lord? Why is it important that persons become committed Christians?*

Ask class members to discuss this proposition: There is not sufficient moral difference in the life of church members and those who are not church members to justify an appeal for church membership. If time allows, have the class spend time discussing what might constitute a religious-national reform for America at this time in history.

2 Chronicles 36:17-23—Love or Justice?

Recall that the Book of Second Kings closes on a note of hope. In Second Kings that hope is for the return of the royal house of David to sit upon Judah's throne. (See 2 Kings 25:27-30.) Second Chronicles likewise closes on a note of hope. However, here the hope is that the Temple, the very center and spring of Judah's life, will be restored. In that Temple men and women will not find David in the person of his descendant. Rather, they will find David's greater treasure, the presence of David's God. There they will pay tribute, not to the royal house, but to the God whom David adored and served.

The student book suggests that in this passage, as elsewhere in the Bible, hope outweighs the judgment of God. Love outweighs justice. The student book asks what evidence of hope exists in our present society. Is it a hope for the maintenance and continuation of structures? Or is it a hope for something deeper? If so, what? Do we hope for a continuing discovery and renewal of the dreams of liberty and equality? How can the structures be changed through which that dream is implemented while the dream remains the same?

How do love and justice balance in the church? Is there something finer and more significant to our church than its present building and organization? How could the outward forms change but the essence of the church remain the same?

Close the session by having class members share their new insights on 2 Chronicles 27–36. Allow some time at the end of the session for review of Kings and Chronicles.

EZRA, NEHEMIAH, AND ESTHER
Table of Contents

About the Writer

The writer of these lessons on Ezra, Nehemiah, and Esther is Dr. Brady Whitehead, Jr. Dr. Whitehead is an ordained United Methodist minister. He is a member of the Memphis Annual Conference.

INTRODUCTION TO EZRA

*by Linda B. Hinton**

The Book of Ezra continues the history of Israel begun in 1 and 2 Chronicles. Chronicles, Ezra, and Nehemiah were once one book. Second Chronicles 36:22-23 is duplicated in Ezra 1:1-3, indicating that the two were once part of the same book. In Hebrew, Ezra and Nehemiah were grouped together under the title *Ezra*. *Ezra* is a variation on a Hebrew word that means "help." Jerome, a fourth century Italian theologian, was the first to name the second part of this book *Nehemiah*.

The same type of Hebrew and the same literary style dominate all three books. They share an emphasis on worship in the Jerusalem Temple, on the purity of the Jewish community, and on devotion to God's law. All came from the hand of the Chronicler who wrote between 350 and 250 B.C.

Ezra and Nehemiah record the history of the Jews from the exiles' return to Jerusalem (536–432 B.C. or 398/97 B.C. depending on the date given for Ezra's work). They tell of the restoration of the Jewish community in Palestine—the rebuilding of the city wall and the Temple, the renewal of the covenant, and the expulsion of non-Jews from the community. Some of this history is also found in the apocryphal Book of First Esdras.

Ezra and Nehemiah are our best history of the Jews from 538–432 B.C., despite the fact that the Chronicler omitted information on the period from the completion of the Temple (515 B.C.) to Nehemiah's return (445 B.C.). The prophetic books of Obadiah, Malachi, and Joel give us our only glimpses of this period in Jerusalem before Nehemiah and Ezra arrived. The prophets Haggai and Zechariah report the rebuilding of the Jerusalem Temple (520–515 B.C.).

The Chronicler's sources of information for this history included biblical books, Temple documents, and biographies and autobiographies of Ezra and Nehemiah. The royal letters in Ezra 5:1-6 and 7:12-26 were written in Aramaic, the diplomatic language of the day.

The content of Ezra may be divided into two parts: (1) the return of the exiles and the rebuilding of the Temple, Ezra 1–6; and (2) the work of Ezra, Ezra 7–10 (concluded in Nehemiah 7:73–10:39). To be chronological, the story of Ezra's work could be read as follows: (a) Ezra's journey to Jerusalem (Ezra 7–8), (b) Ezra's reading of the law (Nehemiah 8), (c) the rejection of all foreign wives of Jews (Ezra 9–10), and (d) the renewal of the covenant (Nehemiah 9). To the Chronicler, the religious significance of the events was more important than their exact sequence in time. In Chapter 4 of Ezra, the Chronicler places material belonging to the time of Xerxes (486–465 B.C.) and Artaxerxes I (465–424 B.C.) between material from the time of Cyrus (550–530 B.C.) and Darius (522–486 B.C.).

The Chronicler says that Ezra arrived in Jerusalem "in the seventh year of King Artaxerxes" (Ezra 7:7). The Chronicler also says that Nehemiah arrived in the twentieth year of the reign of Artaxerxes I, 445 B.C. This writer treats Ezra and Nehemiah as contemporaries, inserting part of Nehemiah's story (Nehemiah 1–7) into Ezra's story (Ezra 7–10; Nehemiah 8–10). However, in Ezra 9:9, Ezra gives thanks to God that the Temple has been built and Jerusalem's walls restored, indicating that Nehemiah's reconstruction work had been completed.

Some ancient manuscripts indicate that Nehemiah returned first. This would mean that Ezra came to Jerusalem in 398 B.C. during the reign of Artaxerxes II (404–358 B.C.). Today there is no general agreement on whether Ezra preceded Nehemiah or followed him.

We know little about the man Ezra. He was a scribe and a priest. His story is told in the first person (Ezra 7:27–8:34; 9:1-5) and in the third person. He brought to Jerusalem from Babylon a copy of "the Book of the Law of Moses" (Nehemiah 8:1). This book was probably the Pentateuch (Genesis–Deuteronomy). Ezra helped to establish the Pentateuch as the authoritative rule for Jewish faith and practice in the postexillic Jerusalem community. For this he is known as the father of Judaism.

Ezra is credited with reinstituting the laws for worship and religious ceremonies and festivals. He was alarmed at the presence of foreign women (and their gods) in Jewish families and he demanded that they be expelled from the community. He stood in the prophetic tradition by applying in practical terms the prophets' call for a renewal of service to God.

Devotion to the law could and did lapse into legalism. However, Ezra's work helped keep the Jews from being absorbed into the prevailing culture. His exclusivism helped create a worshiping community out of which would spring modern Judaism and Christianity.

---

*The writer of this Introduction and the Introduction to Nehemiah and Esther is Ms. Linda B. Hinton. Ms. Hinton received the Master of Theological Studies from the Candler School of Theology, Emory University. Ms. Hinton is also the author of *Ezekiel and Daniel* in this series.

— 1 —

The Exiles Return

Ezra 1–2

Several books have been attributed to Ezra. The names (or the numbers) of these books have caused confusion. Whereas the question may never arise in your class, it would be well for you to have the matter clear in your mind in case it does.

The books of Ezra and Nehemiah were originally one book. They were still together when the Septuagint, an early Greek translation, was made in the third and second centuries B.C. In the Septuagint, Ezra–Nehemiah is called *Esdras b* and the apocryphal book we know as First Esdras is called *Esdras a.* The book known as Second Esdras had not yet been written.

By the time the Vulgate version (a Latin translation) was made by Saint Jerome near the end of the fourth century A.D., Ezra and Nehemiah had been separated from each other, and are called in this version First Esdras and Second Esdras respectively, while the books that we know as First Esdras and Second Esdras in the Apocrypha are called Third Esdras and Fourth Esdras. (The Vulgate was immensely influential, and became the authoritative version for the Roman Catholic Church.) Portions of Fourth Esdras circulated separately, and became known as Fifth Esdras and Sixth Esdras. At the time of the Protestant Reformation, Martin Luther dropped Third and Fourth Esdras from the Bible, and referred to Third Esdras as Nehemiah because of the opening words of that book.

The confusion created by all these terminology changes exists today. Therefore, when we speak of First Esdras or Second Esdras, we need to indicate which First Esdras or Second Esdras we mean. In this study we shall refer to the biblical books as Ezra and Nehemiah, and to the apocryphal books as First Esdras and Second Esdras.

DIMENSION ONE:
WHAT DOES THE BIBLE SAY?

Answer these questions by reading Ezra 1

1. What Persian king makes a proclamation? (1:1)

   Cyrus makes a proclamation.

2. What does Cyrus say God wants him to do? (1:2)

   God wants Cyrus to build a temple at Jerusalem.

3. What does Cyrus allow the people of God to do? (1:3)

   The people of God are to go to Jerusalem and build the temple of the Lord.

4. What does Cyrus say the Jews who remain in Persia are to do? (1:4)

   The remaining Jews are to assist those who are returning by giving them silver and gold, goods and livestock, and freewill offerings for the temple of God.

5. Who rises up to return to Jerusalem? (1:5)

   The heads of the fathers' houses of Judah and Benjamin, the priests, the Levites, and everyone whose heart God has moved to go up to Jerusalem.

6. What do those not going to Jerusalem give to aid those who are going? (1:6)

   They give them articles of gold and silver, goods, livestock, valuable gifts, and freewill offerings.

7. What does Cyrus bring out to give to those returning to Jerusalem? (1:7)

   Cyrus brings out the articles belonging to the temple of the Lord that Nebuchadnezzar had carried away from Jerusalem and placed in the house of his god.

8. To whom does Cyrus have Mithredath give these vessels? (1:8)

   Mithredath gives them to Sheshbazzar, the prince of Judah.

THE EXILES RETURN

9. Where do the people go when they return to Judah? (2:1)

   They go to Jerusalem, and each person to his or her own town.

10. What category of people does Ezra enumerate first? (2:2)

    Ezra enumerates the men of the people of Israel first.

11. What group of people does Ezra enumerate next? (2:36)

    The priests are enumerated second.

12. What is the third group Ezra enumerates? (2:40)

    The Levites are the third group.

13. What other groups does Ezra list? (2:41, 42, 43, 55)

    The singers, the gatekeepers of the Temple, the Temple servants, and the descendents of Solomon's servants are listed.

14. What is different about the people Ezra mentions next? (2:59)

    They cannot prove whether or not they are Israelites.

15. What happens to those who claim to be sons of the priests, but cannot prove they are? (2:61-62)

    They are excluded from the priesthood as unclean.

16. The governor says these priests may eat the holy food when? (2:63)

    These priests cannot eat the holy food until a priest can consult the Urim and Thummim.

17. Why do some of the heads of families make freewill offerings? (2:68)

    They make offerings so they can build the house of God on its site.

DIMENSION TWO: WHAT DOES THE BIBLE MEAN?

None of the information found in Dimension Two of this teacher book is repeated in the student book. By becoming familiar with this material, therefore, you may add to the students' knowledge, either through lecture or by being prepared to answer questions that may arise.

Of course, you will need to be familiar with the material in the student book too.

Ezra 1:1-4. The proclamation of Cyrus is found in 2 Chronicles 36:22-23 and 1 Esdras 2:1-7 as well as here. The proclamation is found in a slightly different form in Ezra 6:3-5.

Ezra 1:1. Ezra gives God the credit for stirring up the spirit of Cyrus to allow the Jews to go home. So also does Second Isaiah (Isaiah 44:28; 45:1, 13).

Jeremiah's prophecy that Ezra refers to is either (a) the defeat of Babylon (Jeremiah 25:11-12), (b) the promise of a return to Jerusalem for the Jews (Jeremiah 29:10), or (c) the rebuilding of the city (Jeremiah 31:38), or perhaps all three.

Ezra 1:3. We know from Cyrus's own writings (on what is known as the Cyrus Cylinder) that he allowed the captives of other nations to return to their homes too.

Ezra 1:4. The meaning of this passage is not absolutely clear. "Survivors" would seem to mean all those Jews who had survived the ravages of Nebuchadnezzar (2 Chronicles 36:20), and had survived the captivity in Babylon. In that case, all the Jews would be returning to Jerusalem, and "the people of any place" who were asked to help finance the trip would be the Babylonians. But why would Cyrus require the Babylonians to finance the Jews' trip? And why would the Jews return to Jerusalem? Some had prospered while in Babylon as Jeremiah had advised them to do (Jeremiah 29:1, 4-7). And the prospect of starting all over in Jerusalem would not appeal to them. Probably, therefore, the wealthy Jews who were staying in Babylon were asked to help finance the trip of those poorer Jews who were returning to Jerusalem.

Ezra 1:6. The Hebrew expression here translated *assisted them* is more literally translated as *strengthened their hands* (as in the King James Version). The term usually means *gave encouragement to.* See, for example, Isaiah 35:3-4 and Nehemiah 6:9.

Ezra 1:8. The student book identifies Sheshbazzar with Shenazzar, and this identification is probably correct. If so, Zerubbabel would be Sheshbazzar's nephew. Some believe, however, that Sheshbazzar is to be identified with Zerubbabel. This is for three reasons: (1) Both Sheshbazzar and Zerubbabel are depicted as the leader of the people (Ezra 1:11; 3:2). Sheshbazzar drops out of the picture after Chapter 1 and Zerubbabel is suddenly the leader with no introduction or explanation. (2) Both men are given credit for having laid the foundation of the Temple (Ezra 5:16; Zechariah 4:9; Ezra 3:8; 5:2). (3) Both men are spoken of as the governor of Judah (Ezra 5:14; Haggai 1:1, 14; 2:2, 21).

The probable explanation of this confusion is that both men led groups back to Jerusalem, but at different times. Both men worked on the Temple and both men served as governor. If we are correct in identifying Sheshbazzar with Shenazzar, then he would have been fifty-nine or sixty years of age when he returned to Jerusalem in 539 B.C. Work began on the Temple about 520 B.C. Both he and his younger nephew, Zerubbabel, could have laid the foundation, and he shortly thereafter could have turned over the governorship to Zerubbabel.

Ezra 1:9-11. The New International Version follows the Hebrew text in which the number of items listed does not match the total given, meaning that there must be at least one error. First Esdras 2:13-14 (one of the books found in the Apocrypha) gives totals that do match.

NIV

30	gold dishes
1,000	silver dishes
29	silver pans
30	gold bowls
410	matching silver bowls
1,000	other articles
5,400	total given

First Esdras

1,000	gold cups
1,000	silver cups
29	silver censers
30	gold bowls
2,410	silver bowls
1,000	other vessels
5,469	total given

Ezra 2:2-35. A large number of non-Jewish names for those who returned to Jerusalem are listed here. The name *Bigvai,* for example, is a Persian name. *Pahath-Moab* is a Moabite name, *Azgad* is an Edomite name, and about half of the remaining names are Babylonian rather than Jewish. We may be sure, however, that each person's ancestry was checked carefully (Ezra 2:59). Giving their children Babylonian names while the Jews were living in Babylonia and trying to stay on the good side of the Babylonian officials seems like a natural thing to do.

We are not certain whether *Senaah,* (Ezra 2:35) is a family name or a geographical name. There is a *Hassenaah* mentioned in Nehemiah 3:3, and this may be the same name. On the other hand, Ezra 2:35 lists an unusually large number of descendants for it to be a family name. Therefore, some scholars believe *Senaah* is a shortened form of the name of the city *Magdalsenna.* There are also other names on which scholars disagree as to whether they refer to families or villages.

In Ezra 2:7, notice that descendants of Elam are listed, and the descendents of "the other Elam" are listed in 2:31. Since we know of only one Elam, and since the numbers given for each are exactly the same, we cannot help wondering if Elam was not accidentally listed twice. Perhaps someone, noticing the error, inserted "the other" before the second mention of Elam. We cannot be certain.

Ezra 2:40. The Levites began as full-fledged priests, and only gradually did their station diminish. Eventually, however, they came to be thought of as servants or assistants to the priests (Numbers 3:5-9; 1 Chronicles 23:28, 32). Levites might serve as judges and officials (1 Chronicles 23:4; 2 Chronicles 34:13), as scribes (2 Chronicles 34:13), or as teachers of the law (2 Chronicles 35:3; Nehemiah 8:7, 9). They might be singers or players of musical instruments (1 Chronicles 15:22; 23:5; 2 Chronicles 34:12; Ezra 3:10-11). They could be gatekeepers (1 Chronicles 9:26; 23:5; 2 Chronicles 8:14; 23:4; 34:9, 13; Nehemiah 12:25; 13:22) or cooks (1 Chronicles 23:29). They could be charged with the responsibility of cleaning the courts, the chambers, or the sacred things vessels (1 Chronicles 23:28), preparing the sacrifices (1 Chronicles 23:4, 31), or carrying the ark (2 Chronicles 35:3).

The student book lists two possible reasons why so few Levites returned from Babylon. Still a third reason might have been because of the menial tasks they were required to do.

Ezra 2:41. David had named Asaph, Heman, and Ethan as singers (1 Chronicles 15:19). Only the sons of Asaph returned to Jerusalem. Asaph is given credit for having written some of the psalms (Psalms 50, 73–83).

Ezra 2:42. The author of Psalm 84:10 says, "I would rather be a doorkeeper in the house of my God than dwell in the tents of the wicked." One gets the impression from this statement that the job of gatekeeper was not a very lucrative one.

Ezra 2:43. The list of Temple servants contains a high percentage of non-Jewish names. This may indicate that captives of war were made Temple servants. In a similar way, Joshua made the deceitful Gibeonites "woodcutters and water carriers" (Joshua 9:23, 27). On the other hand, it seems strange that Ezra would go to such lengths to make an accurate list of foreign slaves. Perhaps the most we can say for sure is that the Temple servants performed a vital function in the Temple.

Ezra 2:63. The governor directs that those excluded from the priesthood were not to eat the holy food until a priest could consult the Urim and Thummim. It is interesting that it was the governor rather than a priest who made this ruling. Just which governor is meant is unclear, though 1 Esdras 5:40 says it was Nehemiah.

Certainly there were plenty of priests around. "A priest," therefore, probably means a high priest (1 Esdras 5:40).

Exactly what the Urim and Thummim were is not known. They were used to determine God's will (for one example, see 1 Samuel 14:41). They were small enough to be carried in the breastplate (Exodus 28:30; Leviticus 8:8). They were probably the same as or very similar to the ephod (1 Samuel 23:9-12; 30:7-8). In any case, these persons were not to perform the priestly duties until it could be determined whether they were qualified to do so. And this was to be determined by consulting the Urim and Thummim.

Ezra 2:64. Here the writer gives the total number of persons in the assembly as 42,360. This number is greater than the sum of the various groups listed previously. It probably includes some persons who were not mentioned before. The actual total number of people is 29,818. The actual total of the corresponding list in Nehemiah is 31,089 and the total of the corresponding list in First Esdras is 31,600. However, all three lists say the total is 42,360 (Nehemiah 7:66; 1 Esdras 5:41).

DIMENSION THREE: WHAT DOES THE BIBLE MEAN TO ME?

Ezra 1:1—The Lord Stirred Up Cyprus

The first issue raised in the student book is whether God can or will use non-Christians to accomplish the divine will today. It is important for us to remember two things here. First, God has used nonbelievers in the past. God's use of Cyrus is a good example. Another example is God's use of Assyria in Isaiah's day.

> Woe to the Assyrian, the rod of my
>   anger,
> in whose hand is the club of my
>   wrath!
> I send him against a godless nation.
>   (Isaiah 10:5-6)

Yet the king of Assyria did not know God was using him. He thought the whole thing was his idea!

> But this is not what he intends,
>   this is not what he has in mind.
> his purpose is to destroy,
>   to put an end to many nations.
>   (Isaiah 10:7)

The second thing to remember is that we cannot put God in a box. We cannot make decisions for God. God can work whenever and with whomever God chooses.

Ezra 1:3—The Long Journey

The second issue raised in the student book concerns our willingness, or our lack of it, to make sacrifices in order to do God's will. So much popular religion today (including most of what we see and hear on television) promises us earthly rewards (from peace of mind or a good feeling inside, all the way to monetary rewards of a promotion on the job). That is a far cry from the sacrifices Jesus asks of his disciples.

Ezra 2:59-63—-The Purity of Heritage

The third issue has to do with the purity of heritage. It will be important for you to help the students see that the issue is not racial or national. The purity that was required was religious and theological. Both the Old Testament, in such passages as Isaiah 49:6, and the New Testament, in such passages as Acts 15:7-11, emphasize the universality of God's love.

Be sure to have the class consider the question of how exclusive or inclusive your church should be. Should any restrictions be placed on who may worship in your sanctuary? Why or why not? What about membership in your church? Should anyone who wants to join the church be allowed to do so? Or should there be restrictions on church membership? Should those who join the church go through an intensive training period first? Should they be required to believe certain doctrines or to behave in certain ways before being accepted into the church? Why or why not?

These are questions on which sincere Christians disagree. There may not be one right answer to any of these questions. But they are all questions that we need to think about. You will do well to save some time for the class to discuss them.

Close the session by having class members list the most interesting facts they learned today. Then ask the class members to indicate which issues they have discussed that might have the most effect on their lives.

And all the people gave a great shout of praise to the LORD, because the foundation of the house of the LORD was laid (3:11).

2

Rebuilding the Temple

Ezra 3–4

DIMENSION ONE:
WHAT DOES THE BIBLE SAY?

Answer these questions by reading Ezra 3

1. When do the Israelites gather in Jerusalem? (3:1)

   The Israelites gather in Jerusalem in the seventh month.

2. Who directs the people in building the altar? (3:2)

   Jeshua and Zerubbabel direct the people in building the altar.

3. Whom do the people of Israel fear? (3:3)

   The Israelites fear the peoples around them.

4. What offerings and sacrifices do the people offer? (3:3-5)

   The people offer burnt offerings for the Feast of Tabernacles, the daily burnt offerings, the regular burnt offerings, the New Moon sacrifices, sacrifices for the appointed sacred feasts, and freewill offerings.

5. Are the people able to offer their sacrifices to the Lord before the Temple is completed? (3:6)

   Yes, the people offer sacrifices even before the foundation of the Temple is laid.

6. From where do Jeshua and Zerubbabel have cedar trees brought for the construction of the Temple? (3:7)

   The cedar trees used to build the Temple come from Lebanon.

7. When does the work on the Temple begin? (3:8)

   The work begins in the second month of the second year of their coming to the house of God.

8. What persons are appointed to have oversight of the work on the Temple? (3:8)

   The Levites twenty years old and older are appointed.

9. What do the priests, the Levites, and the people do after the foundation of the Temple has been laid? (3:10-11)

   The priests come forward with trumpets and the Levites with cymbals. They sing, giving praise and thanks to God. The people shout and praise God.

10. Who weeps while others are shouting for joy? (3:12)

    Many of the older priests and Levites and family heads who had seen the first Temple weep.

Answer these questions by reading Ezra 4

11. Who approaches Zerubbabel and offers to help build the Temple? (4:1-2)

    The enemies of Judah and Benjamin offer to help.

12. Why do the enemies say they want to help build the Temple? (4:2)

    They say they want to help because they worship the same God.

13. Is the offer accepted? (4:3)

    No, the offer of help is refused.

14. What do the people around the Israelites do next? (4:4-5)

    They try to make the people of Judah afraid to build and they hire counselors to frustrate the people of Judah.

15. What else do the people around do to frustrate the people of Judah? (4:6)

The people of the land lodge an accusation against the people of Judah to Xerxes.

16. What do the enemies do during the reign of Artaxerxes? (4:7)

They write a letter to Artaxerxes.

17. What does the letter say? (4:12)

The letters says that the people of Jerusalem are rebuilding the city, restoring the walls, and repairing the foundations.

18. What will happen if the people are allowed to finish building Jerusalem? (4:13)

The people of Jerusalem will not pay taxes, tribute, or duty, and the royal revenue will suffer.

19. What proof of the accusations does the letter offer? (4:15)

The letter says that records in the archives will show that Jerusalem is a rebellious city.

20. What does Artaxerxes find when he searches the records? (4:17-19)

The records show that the accusations are true.

21. What does the king do then? (4:21)

Artaxerxes issues an order that all work on the city should stop.

22. What do the enemies do when they receive the letter from Artaxerxes? (4:23)

They go immediately to Jerusalem and force the people to stop building the Temple.

23. When does work on the Temple begin again? (4:24)

Work begins again in the second year of the reign of Darius.

DIMENSION TWO:
WHAT DOES THE BIBLE MEAN?

Ezra 3:1. Notice the similarity between this verse and Nehemiah 7:73–8:1. In each case a solemn ceremony is about to take place (the institution of the religious ceremonies here in Ezra, and the reading of the Book of the Law of Moses in Nehemiah.) In each case the ceremony

happens in the seventh month. In each case "the Israelites" are in "the towns" or "their own towns." In each case "the people" or "all the people" assembled "as one man" either in Jerusalem or before the Water Gate. Notice, too, that the seventh month always has been religiously significant for the Jews (Numbers 29; Leviticus 23).

As we noted in the last lesson, there is confusion concerning the dating of some of the events in the Book of Ezra. The author here speaks of the seventh month, but of what year? The only year mentioned thus far is the first year of Cyrus (1:1). Does the writer mean, then, that the people who left Babylon in 538 B.C. gathered at Jerusalem when the seventh month of their return came? Probably so. But in 3:8, Zerubbabel is mentioned as one of the leaders who began the work on the Temple, and Zerubbabel did not return to Jerusalem until later (Haggai 2:1-2; Zechariah 1:1; 4:6-10.) The author apparently has the facts confused, and believes Zerubbabel returned with the first group. (Remember that this passage was written more than one hundred years after the event.)

That the people gather as one man may mean nothing more than that they are all together. Or it may mean they come together in one accord, for a common purpose. Probably, however, it goes even deeper than that. The people are there to restore the relationship that once existed between them and God. Therefore, this is a solemn occasion, demanding a renewal of loyalty on the part of the entire community. This renewal can come about only if the people are together.

Ezra 3:2. The student book mentions that Jeshua's name is listed here before that of Zerubbabel. As stated there, Zerubbabel receives top billing in every other instance where their names appear together (Ezra 2:2; 3:8; 4:3; 5:2; Nehemiah 12:1; Haggai 1:1, 12, 14; 2:2, 4). Zerubbabel definitely seems to be the more important of the two in the Book of Haggai. Not only is Zerubbabel mentioned first each time, but he is also singled out in Haggai 2:20-23 as chosen by God. Haggai also elevates Joshua (or Jeshua), however. He never refers to Joshua simply as one of the priests, as Ezra does, but always as "the high priest."

In the Book of Zechariah, Joshua receives more attention than Zerubbabel, the latter being mentioned only in Zechariah 4:6-10. Zechariah never calls Zerubbabel "governor" (or any other title, for that matter). But Haggai regularly refers to Zerubbabel as "governor of Judah."

Ezra states that Zerubbabel is the son of Shealtiel. Zerubbabel is usually referred to in that way (Nehemiah 12:1; Haggai 1:1, 12, 14; 2:2.) In 1 Chronicles 3:19, however, Zerubbabel is listed as the son of Pedaiah, who is the brother of Shealtiel (1 Chronicles 3:17-18). Perhaps the writer either made a mistake, or Zerubbabel was reared by his uncle, and therefore came to be called his son.

Zerubbabel also could have been Shealtiel's son through the law stated in Deuteronomy 25:5-6. The technical name for this process is *leviration.* A levirate marriage is one in which a man marries his deceased brother's wife in order to insure that the brother will have a male heir. The first son born to the new couple is legally declared the son of the deceased brother. In a day when nothing was known of personal life after death, such arrangements provided a way to keep a man's name from being lost to history. No similar concern was shown for preserving the names of women.

Ezra 3:3. The people around come in friendship and help the returned exiles build their altar, as the manuscript (the *Codex Vaticanus*) quoted in the student book suggests. Why then does our text speak of "their fear of the peoples around them"? Perhaps the idea of aliens working on the altar was intolerable to the followers of Ezra. That is, from Ezra's point of view (as we shall see later), the people around them were not worthy to help build the altar. These people were interreligious and biracial. In Ezra's eyes only pure Israelites were worthy of worshiping at the altar, and certainly no one else could help build it! For those who shared these convictions the idea that the natives of the land helped to build the altar was intolerable. So, by changing a line in the manuscript, *friendliness* is changed to *fear*.

Ezra 3:4. The Feast of Tabernacles (*booths* in many Bible translations) gets its name from the fact that for seven days the people were to dwell in booths (or shelters) made from "palm fronds, leafy branches and poplars" (Leviticus 23:40-42; Nehemiah 8:15). The Israelites were to dwell in these "so your descendents will know that I had the Israelites live in booths when I brought them out of Egypt. I am the LORD your God" (Leviticus 23:43).

Ezra 3:5. The regular burnt offerings are the same as the "morning and evening sacrifices" mentioned in verse 3. These offerings are described in Exodus 29:38-42 and Numbers 28:3-8.

The offerings at the new moon are described in Numbers 28:11-15, and are referred to in Numbers 10:10; 29:6, and 2 Kings 4:23. We learn from 1 Samuel 20:5 that the king gave a feast on the new moon. Amos 8:5 tells us that no business was allowed on that day.

All the appointed feasts of the Lord are listed and explained in Leviticus 23.

The freewill offering is in addition to the other offerings, and is an expression of gratitude to God for one's prosperity or good fortune (Deuteronomy 16:10). It could be, for example, that some who made the long trek back from Babylon would want to thank God for the safe journey.

Ezra 3:6-9. Several features in this story remind us of the building of the first Temple. Masons and carpenters are employed as they were then (1 Chronicles 22:15). The people of Tyre and Sidon are employed in each case to bring cedar trees from Lebanon (1 Chronicles 22:4;

2 Chronicles 2:8). In each case they are paid in kind rather than in cash (2 Chronicles 2:10), and in each case they bring the cedar trees from Lebanon to Joppa (2 Chronicles 2:16). Both times the building of the Temple begins in the second month (1 Kings 6:1; 2 Chronicles 3:2).

These similarities have four possible explanations. (1) They happened by chance. (2) When the second Temple was built, Zerubbabel and Jeshua purposely followed the procedures used in the building of Solomon's Temple. (3) Ezra's account of the building of the second Temple was influenced by the earlier story. (4) The procedures used were customary, and it is not unusual that there should be these similarities. The class may want to discuss which of these possibilities seems most likely.

Ezra 3:8. An attempt to rebuild the Temple during the days of Cyrus was unsuccessful. It was successfully rebuilt during the reign of Darius. Zerubbabel and Jeshua were connected with Darius, but not with Cyrus. Ezra has confused the two attempts, perhaps even combined them into one account.

The Levites from twenty years old and upward are given oversight of the work of the house of the Lord. Some commentators believe the work of the Levites was limited to that done in the worship services. But there is no reason to doubt that the Levites had oversight of the construction of the Temple as well.

That the Levites as young as twenty years old were given oversight of the work is unusual. The customary age for such authority was thirty (Numbers 4:1-3, 21-23, 29-30, 34-35), although Numbers 8:23-24 does allow Levites as young as twenty-five to do the priestly chores. The Chronicler believes that the age of twenty for the Levites to begin their work was set by David (1 Chronicles 23:24-28; 2 Chronicles 31:17). But this writer does record the tradition that David numbered the Levites thirty years and older (1 Chronicles 23:2-3).

Several explanations may be offered. Perhaps the Chronicler knew of the tradition that David numbered the Levites thirty years of age or more. But the custom in his own day was to count them from twenty years of age, and he was eager to show that that custom dated all the way back to David. Or perhaps since so few Levites returned from Babylon (see Ezra 2:40, the smallest number in any of the returning groups), it was necessary to use the younger men. Or perhaps the age limit varied from time to time as the needs and circumstances dictated.

Ezra 3:9. In Ezra 2:40, where the list of returning Levites is given, the sons of Henadad are not listed. Some commentators believe, therefore, that this verse originally ended at the word *God*, and that the phrase about the sons of Henadad was added to make Ezra 3:9 conform with Nehemiah 3:17-18, 24. Another explanation might be that Henedad's name does not appear in 2:40 because he and his family had not been taken into captivity to Babylon, but had remained in Jerusalem.

Ezra 3:10. A number of manuscripts say that the priests stand up with trumpets rather than that they take their places with trumpets. First Chronicles 16:6 tells of another joyous occasion when the priests were to blow their trumpets. The priests also were used to sound the call to battle with their trumpets (2 Chronicles 13:12, 14).

We do not know where David gave directions for such a celebration. Second Chronicles 29:25 also says "in the way prescribed by David" in connection with the Levites having musical instruments in the Temple.

Ezra 3:11. The words *to Israel* are not part of the poem quoted (Psalm 136:1). The Chronicler knows this; he does not include these words when he quotes the poem elsewhere (1 Chronicles 16:34; 2 Chronicles 5:13; 7:3; 20:21). The words *toward Israel* were probably added later, perhaps by someone who wanted to make sure the reader would understand the true meaning.

Ezra 3:11-13. The weeping of the old men who had seen the first Temple is a weeping of sadness, not of joy. This much is clear. What is not clear is why there should be tears of sadness. The usual explanation, based on Haggai's words, were spoken before the reconstruction of the foundation was begun, when there was nothing there but the ruins of the former Temple. Furthermore, it seems that the new Temple is approximately the same size as Solomon's Temple. (Compare Ezra 6:3 with 1 Kings 6:2.) Perhaps the new foundation has even been laid on the old. Why, then, is there disappointment? The only possible explanation seems to be that this celebration, and therefore this mixture of sadness and joy, comes after the completion of the Temple rather than after the foundation is laid. Only then would the new Temple show itself to be of less splendor than the old.

The celebration must have been a sight to behold! Imagine, if you can, priests blowing their trumpets, Levites clashing cymbals, old men wailing loudly, and everybody else shouting with a great shout! No wonder Ezra says, "The sound was heard far away."

Ezra 4:1-23. The foundation of the Temple is laid in Chapter 3. We might expect Chapter 4 to tell the story of the completion of the Temple. Instead, we read in verse 24, "Thus the work on the house of God came to a standstill until the second year of the reign of Darius king of Persia." The purpose of verses 1-23 is to explain why the work ceased.

Ezra 4:1-3. The Samaritans are not enemies at the time they offer to help build the Temple. The gesture seems to be both friendly and sincere. They become enemies only after their offer to help is spurned.

Why do the Israelites reject the offer of the Samaritans? Because the Samaritans are a mixed-race people, a combination of Israelite blood and Assyrian blood. They are also a combination of Israelite and Assyrian religions. "We seek

your God and have been sacrificing to him since the time of Esarhaddon," they say. But do they also worship the Assyrian gods? Do they also sacrifice to them? Yes, they do. And Zerubbabel, Jeshua, and the other leaders in Israel are aware of this practice. And they are not willing to contaminate the Temple with foreign influences.

Samaria surrendered to Sargon II, king of Assyria, in 722 B.C. Shortly thereafter, the leaders and many of the people of Samaria were transported to other areas of the empire. Other people from various parts of the empire were brought to Samaria to live. These foreign people continued to worship their own gods, but began worshiping the God of Israel also. Eventually they intermarried with the Israelites who had been left in Samaria. The offspring of these marriages were both racially and religiously mixed. They are the people who later came to be called Samaritans (2 Kings 17:24-34).

Esarhaddon was Sargon's grandson. He followed the same practice as his grandfather. The people of Ezra 4:2 have been in Israel only "since the time of Esarhaddon."

The bitterness that begins with verse 3 continues to fester and to grow. We have a reminder of this hostility in the story of the woman at the well in the New Testament. (See John 4:1-42, especially verse 9.)

Ezra 4:4. The word *discouraged* does not capture the full meaning of the Hebrew. A literal translation is, "Then the peoples around them weakened the hands of the people of Judah." The expression *weakened the hands of* is a Hebrew idiom meaning "to discourage, frighten, or intimidate to the point of inactivity." (Nehemiah 6:9; Isaiah 13:7; Jeremiah 6:24; 38:4; 50:43).

Ezra 4:6-24. One gets the impression from reading this section that the only factor keeping the people of Judah from completing the Temple is the opposition of the people around them. When we turn to the Book of Haggai, however, two additional reasons, are hinted at—economic hardship and general apathy on the part of the people (Haggai 1:1-11). Ezra never admits these possibilities. For him, the only reason work on the Temple stops is because of the opposition from the Samaritans. No true Jew would lose interest in the project; he is sure of that.

Because of this bias on the part of Ezra, many Old Testament scholars believe Ezra purposely attributed to the early days of the project Samaritan opposition that did not arise until later. That was his way of saving face for the people of Judah.

What probably happened is that when the exiles first returned from captivity, enthusiasm ran high and the foundation of the Temple was laid. Times were hard, however, and people had to care for their own needs and their own families. Finally, all work on the Temple stopped and the Temple was allowed to continue to lie in ruins for another eighteen years. Then, in the second year of Darius, Haggai and Zechariah came on the scene. They both shamed the people for allowing the Temple to lie in ruins and inspired them to resume work on it. It was after this resumption of work on the Temple that the Samaritan opposition described in this section occurred.

Ezra 4:7. Notice that "the letter was written in Aramaic script and in the Aramaic language" and then "translated" (verse 18). In the Hebrew text the first two words in verse 8 are *in Aramaic*, indicating that what follows is written in Aramaic. The New International Version omits the words *in Aramaic* because the whole book is translated into English. But in the Hebrew manuscripts, the text alternates from Hebrew to Aramaic. Ezra 1:1–4:7 is in Hebrew, 4:8–6:18 in Aramaic, 6:19–7:11 in Hebrew, 7:12-26 in Aramaic, and 7:27 to the end of the book is in Hebrew.

Most of the Old Testament was originally written in Hebrew, and virtually all the New Testament was originally in Greek. There are a few Old Testament passages and a few New Testament words, however, that are in Aramaic.

Ezra 4:18-20. The words "powerful kings ruling over the whole of Trans-Euphrates" are an exaggeration. Even in David's heyday, Jerusalem did not rule the whole Trans-Euphrates.

Ezra 4:23-24. Probably the Samaritans not only make sure that the work on the house of God stops, but they also tear down the work that has already been done. It has been suggested that it is this destruction Nehemiah refers to in Nehemiah 1:3.

DIMENSION THREE: WHAT DOES THE BIBLE MEAN TO ME?

Ezra 3:1—One in the Spirit

Yours may be a church where oneness in the Spirit is commonplace. If your congregation is like most, however, you have found it difficult to get everyone to agree on anything! Yet, as the student book suggests, there are times when the whole congregation is unified. Sometimes the church will unite to complete a particular job in the church or in the community. Sometimes the congregation expresses a common emotion—shock at the death of a young person, or at a fire that destroyed the church building; sympathy for a longtime church member who has suffered a misfortune; or happiness for the good fortune of another.

The student book asks why it is so hard to get church persons to stand together on the great moral issues of the day. Let the group members list as many reasons as they can think of. Among the answers you get may be: an honest difference of opinion, vested interests (church members may own the liquor stores or the slum houses), a lack of

total commitment to Christ, or fear of what others may say or think or do.

Ask the class if anyone can remember a time when the churches of all denominations joined together in your community to combat some evil or to promote some worthy goal. What would it mean to your community if the churches regularly gathered together for such purposes?

Have the class read Luke 11:23. In what way does this verse speak to the discussion at hand? Now read Matthew 18:19-20. What additional light does this verse shed? Considering both of these New Testament passages, would you say Christ can accomplish his purposes even when some of his disciples are not faithful? Why or why not?

Ezra 3:2—Who Is a Man or Woman of God?

You may discover as the class discusses this question that there are differences of opinion about who is a man or woman of God. Some may think God calls only preachers. Some may think only of famous persons. But almost every congregation has in it one or more persons whose obedience to the call of Christ has been so complete that they legitimately could be called men and women of God.

As you think of the famous men and women of God, you surely will want to call to mind Mother Teresa of Calcutta, India, who has spent her life ministering to the poorest of the poor. Have the class list on a large piece of paper or a chalkboard all the women and men of God they can think of. Write beside each person's name the reason that he or she is included on the list.

Ezra 1–3—How Would You Feel?

The more the members of the class can put themselves in the places of the people in the Bible, and feel what they felt, the more they will understand and appreciate the biblical message. Ask them to list the emotions they might have felt had they been the Jews in Ezra 1–3. Some of the emotions they might list are

- delight and excitement at the thought of returning to Jerusalem;
- disappointment, shock, and outrage at the sight of the Temple in ruins;
- eagerness, determination, and joy at the rebuilding of the foundation of the Temple;
- frustration, anger, and discouragement as the work on the Temple is interrupted;
- pride, happiness, and satisfaction as the foundation is laid;
- dissatisfaction, sadness, and a sense of failure because the Temple was not as magnificent as Solomon's Temple.

Now ask the class members to list the emotions they might have felt had they been the Samaritans, the people of the land. Some of these emotions might have been

- eagerness to help build the Temple;
- frustration, anger, and resentment at being refused;
- spite, revenge, and determination to frustrate as a way of getting back at the Israelites.

Ask class members to recall times in the life of your own congregation when they felt one or more of these emotions.

Close the session by having class members share new insights into Ezra 3–4. List these insights on a chalkboard or a large piece of paper if time allows.

— 3 —

The Decree of Cyrus

Ezra 5–6

DIMENSION ONE: WHAT DOES THE BIBLE SAY?

Answer these questions by reading Ezra 5

1. What prophets inspire the people to resume work on the Temple? (5:1-2)

   Haggai and Zechariah inspire the people to resume work on the Temple.

2. Who tries to make the people stop working on the Temple? (5:3-5)

   Tattenai and Shethar-Bozenai try to make the people stop working on the Temple.

3. To whom do Tattenai and Shethar-Bozenai write? (5:6)

   Tattenai and Shethar-Bozenai write to Darius the king.

4. What does their report say? (5:8)

   Tattenai and Shethar-Bozenai tell Darius that the Jews are rebuilding the Temple in Jerusalem.

5. Who issued a decree ordering the rebuilding of the Temple? (5:13)

   Cyrus issued an edict ordering the rebuilding of the house of God.

6. What do Tattenai and Shethar-Bozenai ask the king to do? (5:17)

   Tattenai and Shethar-Bozenai ask the king to let the royal archives be searched to determine if this is true, and then to tell them what to do.

Answer these questions by reading Ezra 6

7. When Darius makes a search, what does he find? (6:1-5)

   Darius finds that not only had Cyrus made such a decree, but also that he had decreed that the cost should be paid by the royal treasury.

8. What does Darius command Tattenai and Shethar-Bozenai to do? (6:7)

   Darius commands them to leave the workmen alone and let the Temple be rebuilt.

9. What further decree does Darius make? (6:8-12)

   Darius further decrees that the work will be paid for out of the royal treasury, that the Israelite priests shall be given whatever they need to offer sacrifices, and that anyone who attempts to alter the edict will be dealt with severely.

10. When do the workmen finish the Temple? (6:15)

    The workmen finish the Temple on the third day of the month of Adar in the sixth year of the reign of Darius.

11. What do the people of Israel do when the Temple is completed? (6:16-18)

    When the Temple is completed, the people of Israel dedicate the building and set up the priesthood as it is written in the Book of Moses.

12. When do the Jews celebrate the Passover? (6:19)

    The Jews celebrate the Passover on the Fourteenth day of the first month.

13. Who is allowed to eat the Passover lamb? (6:19-21)

    Those who have returned from exile and those who have separated themselves from the unclean practices of their Gentile neighbors are allowed to eat the Passover lamb.

14. What emotions do the Jewish people have at this time? (6:22)

    The Jewish people are joyful.

DIMENSION TWO:
WHAT DOES THE BIBLE MEAN?

Ezra 5:1. Haggai is consistently called "Haggai the prophet" (Haggai 1:1, 12; 2:1, 10; Ezra 6:14). Zechariah is referred to here and in 6:14 as a "descendant of Iddo." According to Zechariah 1:1, however, Zechariah is the grandson of Iddo. Perhaps he is the son of Iddo in the sense of having received his inspiration from him.

Ezra 5:2. Where the NIV has "set to work to rebuild," the Aramaic text actually says "began to build." The NIV uses the word *rebuild* to account for the work begun by Sheshbazzar (verse 16) and because the verbal prefix translated *began* may be used without reference to time.

It is generally assumed that "the prophets of God" in verse 2 refers to Haggai and Zechariah of verse 1. The term could be used in a more inclusive sense, however.

Ezra 5:3. Apparently Tattenai was subordinate in rank to Ushtani, though each is called governor in the Babylonian records. Ushtani is not mentioned in the biblical records.

Possibly, Shethar-Bozenai's name was simply *Shethar.* Another Shethar is mentioned in Esther 1:14. If this is true, then Bozenai may be his title, or it may be a reference to a Persian god.

Ezra 5:4. We are not told here the answer to the question raised in verse 3. Instead, a second question is raised. The answer to the question of verse 3 is given in the letter Tattenai sends to King Darius (verses 11-16). We are never told the names of the men who are building the Temple.

Ezra 5:5. The elders of the Jews are the leaders of the Jewish community. They are roughly equivalent to the family heads mentioned in 1:5; 3:12; 4:2; and 4:3.

Ezra 5:7-8. The words *Cordial greetings* mean more than greetings. They mean "may the best always be yours."

The word translated *large* is of uncertain meaning. Recent discoveries seem to indicate that *huge* is not the proper meaning, since the word is applied to small objects. The word may refer to a particular type or shape of stone.

We are not certain what is meant by "placing the timbers in the walls." Some have thought this phrase refers to wood paneling. More probably, however, it refers to beams or rafters.

Ezra 5:11. "A great king of Israel" refers to Solomon. The account of the building of Solomon's Temple is found in 1 Kings 5–7.

Ezra 5:12. The Jewish people here accept the prophetic understanding of why Israel had fallen at the hands of Nebuchadnezzar. The prophets had always insisted it was because the Israelites "had angered the God of heaven."

Nebuchadnezzar did not defeat the Israelites on his own; God "handed them over to Nebuchadnezzar" (compare with Isaiah 5:26; 10:5-6).

Ezra 5:13. Some persons think the author made a mistake when he referred to Cyrus as "king of Babylon" rather than of Persia. What the author means, though is the first year Cyrus ruled over Babylon.

Ezra 5:14. Only here is Sheshbazzar referred to as a governor.

Ezra 5:15. The first part of this verse sounds as if the Temple were already standing, while the second part of the verse assumes that it is not. Probably the first part of the verse means "deposit them in the temple" that will be built in Jerusalem. It is almost as if the writer were saying, "These vessels go in the Temple in Jerusalem, so hurry up and get it built!"

Ezra 5:17. The last sentence of this verse implies that Darius could go contrary to the edict of Cyrus, even if it were found to exist. And no doubt he could. Who was there to prevent the king from doing what he wanted? Yet there was strong tradition among the Persians that no king's order could ever be revoked or even altered (Esther 1:19; 8:8; Daniel 6:15). Nor, probably, would Darius want to alienate himself from the Jews so early in his rule over them.

Ezra 6:1. "Issued an order" sounds public and formal. Perhaps "gave an order" is all that is meant.

Ezra 6:2. Media is referred to here as "the province of Media." Before being conquered by Cyrus in 550 B.C., Media had been an independent state. Ecbatana had been the capital of Media and continued to be used by the Persian kings as their summer residence. Its high elevation and cool breezes were a welcome relief from the heat.

Ezra 6:3. That a Jew would call the year 538 B.C. "the first year of Cyrus the king" is understandable. That was, after all, the first year Cyrus had been their king. It seems unlikely, however, that a decree ordered by Cyrus himself would be so worded. Cyrus had been a king for more than twenty years (since 559 B.C.)

The height of the new Temple is given, and so is the breadth. However, the width is missing. If the figures given are accurate, the new Temple is to be larger than Solomon's Temple had been. Some Old Testament scholars believe, however, that the measurements of the new Temple should be the same as those for Solomon's. Support for this view is found in the fact that the Syriac version does give the measurements as the same. (See 1 Kings 6:2 for the dimensions of Solomon's Temple.)

Ezra 6:8. Darius decrees that the cost of rebuilding the Temple shall be borne by the Persian treasury. Because this sounds unlikely, and because there is no record of its ever having been done, some believe this was not an actual part of Darius's decree.

Ezra 6:9-10. Darius also decrees that whatever is needed for the daily sacrifices shall be provided. No record exists that shows that this provision was made, but there are records showing a similar concern on the part of other monarchs. Darius probably would have ordered the same. Furthermore, as the student book points out, Darius has a self-serving motive for his benevolence—that they may "pray for the well-being of the king and his sons."

Ezra 6:11-12. Darius closes his letter with a dire threat to any who alter his edict. Such threats are not unusual at the close of royal edicts. And though the punishment seems severe, impalement was not unknown in the ancient world. Nothing in verse 11 would cause us to think it is not genuine.

However, verse 12 is another matter. First, warning has been given in verse 11; it is not necessary to make a second threat. Second, the "God who has caused his Name to dwell there" is a typically Jewish expression (Deuteronomy 12:11; 14:23; 16:2, 6, 11; 26:2). Third, while it is understandable that Darius would issue a warning about not altering his edict, it seems unlikely that a Persian monarch would pronounce a curse on someone who destroyed a Jewish temple. Many people believe, therefore, that verse 12 is not a genuine part of Darius's decree.

Ezra 6:14. One would expect to see the names of Zerubbabel and Jeshua here (5:1-2). Instead, the elders of the Jews are in charge of building the Temple.

The mention of Artaxerxes seems strange. We have heard of the decree of Cyrus (1:2-3; 6:3-5) and the decree of Darius (6:7-8), but all we have heard about Artaxerxes has been anti-Jewish (4:7-24). Probably someone added Artaxerxes's name later on the basis of such passages as Ezra 7:11-28 and Nehemiah 2:1-8.

Ezra 6:15. The Temple is completed on the third day of Adar. Yet, the third day of Adar in the year 515 B.C. is on a sabbath. Perhaps then, our passage lists the date of the first sabbath after the Temple was completed, that is, the first day the Temple was used.

Another explanation is that according to 1 Esdras 7:5, the Temple was completed on the twenty-third day of Adar rather than the third. This day would not have been a sabbath, and so would have been a work day. Many scholars believe that the twenty-third is correct, since it is more likely that twenty might be dropped inadvertently from twenty-third than that twenty be added inadvertently to third.

Ezra 6:16. In the parallel passage in First Esdras, it is implied that not all those who returned from exile helped rebuild the Temple (1 Esdras 7:6). That would be logical to assume, though our present passage implies the opposite.

Ezra 6:17. Twelve male goats are sacrificed as a sin offering. Sacrificing a goat is interesting in light of the levitical call for a young bull to serve as a sin offering (Leviticus 4:14).

Ezra 6:18. The priests and the Levites are stationed and are ready for the service of God at Jerusalem. So, too, are the gatekeepers, according to 1 Esdras 7:9. The Book of Moses contains no provisions for setting "the priests in their divisions and the Levites in their groups." Perhaps the author is referring to the consecration of the priests and Levites that is recorded in Exodus 29, Leviticus 8, Numbers 3, and Numbers 8.

With the close of this verse, the first Aramaic section of Ezra is completed, and the text is written in Hebrew again. (Refer to the teacher book on Ezra 4:7, Dimension Two, for exact references on which parts of Ezra are in Aramaic.

Ezra 6:20. This verse presents some difficulties as it now stands. It indicates that all the priests and Levites were clean. Then it says "they," these clean priests and Levites, "slaughtered the Passover lamb . . . for their brothers the priests and for themselves." Who are these fellow priests if all the priests are making the sacrifice? And why couldn't these fellow priests make their own offerings? There can only be one answer— they are not clean. Some of the priests and Levites are clean, and some are not.

The whole matter clears up instantly if the words *the priests and* are omitted at the beginning of the verse. That would mean that the Levites had purified themselves, and all the Levites were clean. Then it would say, "The Levites slaughtered the Passover lamb for all the returned exiles, for their brothers the priests and for themselves." Many Old Testament scholars believe this is the way the verse should read.

Ezra 6:21-22. The Passover meal was eaten, not only by the people of Israel who had returned from exile, but by "all who had separated themselves from the unclean practices of their Gentile neighbors." These persons would not be pagans, but descendants of those Israelites who had not been sent into exile.

The words *the king of Assyria* obviously refer to Darius. We should expect him to be called *the king of Persia.* Perhaps the old Assyrian Empire had been so dominant and overpowering that even at this late date the king sometimes was referred to as the king of Assyria. We know, for example, that the Assyrian records refer to Israel as *the house of Omri* even a century and a half after Omri had died.

DIMENSION THREE:
WHAT DOES THE BIBLE MEAN TO ME?

Ezra 5:1-2—How Important Is a Sanctuary?

It is important for a worshiping congregation to have a place to worship. No one would deny that. But where should that place be, and how much should be spent to build and maintain it? Sincere Christians disagree on their answers to these questions. Should the sanctuary (or, more correctly, the nave) be of the finest materials in order to show honor to God? Or should we worship in less expensive places, even in people's homes, and give to the poor what we would have spent on fineries? Have the class members discuss that issue. Encourage them to give reasons for their answers. Let them give as many reasons as they can think of on both sides of the issue.

You will want to introduce the suggested Scripture passages one at a time to make certain they have equal emphasis. The Luke passage emphasizes the temporal nature of a building. The Temple may be "thrown down," but the religion of Jesus will continue. In Matthew 19:21, Jesus says, "If you want to be perfect, go, sell your possessions and give to the poor." To whom does that command apply? Does it apply to congregations or only to individual persons? Or does it apply only to the one man to whom Jesus was talking?

Matthew 26:6-13 seems to imply that extravagance for the right reason is all right. "The poor you will always have with you," said Jesus. He seems to be saying, "You can give to them any time."

Deuteronomy 15:4-5 indicates that when the Israelites get to the Promised Land, "there should be no poor among you . . . if only you fully obey the LORD your God." However, Deuteronomy 15:11 gives a more realistic view. This verse agrees with Jesus, that "there will always be poor people in the land." You might point out to the class that rich and poor are relative terms. What is wealth to me may be poverty to you.

Point out that the emphasis in Matthew 26:11 falls on the second half of the verse. The woman's deed was commended because it honored Jesus, and he would not be there to honor very much longer. This saying of Jesus does not belittle the value of giving to the poor. The one who said, "I have compassion for these people; they . . . have nothing to eat" (Mark 8:2) would certainly want the poor to be cared for.

Ezra 6:6-12—Church and State

The question of the separation of church and state has never been settled. Some denominations and independent congregations refuse to accept any money from the government for any reason. Others eagerly seek large government grants for church-related colleges, church-owned elder care facilities, and many other institutions. What advantages are there to this practice? What are the dangers?

Mark 12:17 does not say that God has no claim on what is Caesar's. After all, everything belongs to God. Nor does it mean that what is Caesar's can never be used for religious purposes. The question put to Jesus has to do with paying taxes to a despised overlord; the question of the separation of church and state is not the issue at all.

Ezra 6:13-15—Religion and Politics

You have heard the saying, "Politics and religion don't mix." Have the class discuss what persons mean when they say that. Do the class members agree or disagree? For what reasons?

Groups all through the centuries have combined religious fervor with political endeavor. There were zealots of Jesus' day, the Inquisitors of the Middle Ages, and the Reformers of the sixteenth century. Ask class members to list additional examples. What about the Muslim fundamentalists who took over Iran under the inspiration of Ayatollah Khomeini? What about the Christian Coalition? In what ways do such groups do good? In what ways do they do harm?

Close the session by listing on a chalkboard or a large piece of paper any new insights class members have gained after studying Ezra 5–6.

Ezra . . . was a teacher well versed in the Law of Moses (7:6).

4

Ezra the Scribe

Ezra 7–10

DIMENSION ONE:
WHAT DOES THE BIBLE SAY?

Answer these questions by reading Ezra 7

1. When does Ezra arrive in Jerusalem? (7:1-8)

    Ezra the scribe arrives in Jerusalem in the fifth month of the seventh year of Artaxerxes.

2. What has Ezra set his heart to do? (7:10)

    Ezra has set his heart to study the law, to keep the law, and to teach the law to others.

3. Where will the people of Israel get the money to buy the animals and grain for their sacrifices and offerings? (7:14-18)

    Silver and gold from the king and from the freewill offerings of the people and priests will be made available to buy the animals and grain for their sacrifices and offerings.

4. What decree does Artaxerxes make to the treasurers in the province Trans-Euphrates? (7:21-23)

    Artaxerxes decrees that whatever Ezra requires of them they are to give, within certain prescribed limits.

5. What else does Artaxerxes tell the treasurers? (7:24)

    Artaxerxes notifies them that no taxes, tribute, or duties shall be imposed upon the priests and others connected with the work of the house of God.

6. What decree does Artaxerxes give to Ezra? (7:25-26)

    Artaxerxes decrees that Ezra is to appoint magistrates and judges to administer justice to all the people, that everyone should learn the laws of God, and that all who disobey the law of God and of the king will be punished.

7. What is Ezra's response to the decree? (7:27-28)

    Ezra praises God and gathers leading men from Israel to make the trip with him.

Answer these questions by reading Ezra 8

8. Who does Ezra discover to be missing? (8:15)

    Ezra discovers the Levites are missing.

9. What does Ezra do then? (8:16-17)

    Ezra sends some men to Iddo to have Iddo send him some attendants for the house of God.

10. What does Ezra do after Iddo sends attendants for the house of God? (8:21)

    Ezra proclaims a fast so the people might humble themselves before God and ask God for a safe journey.

11. Why is Ezra ashamed to ask the king for protection? (8:22)

    Ezra is ashamed because he had told the king that God would bless those who sought him and destroy those who forsook him.

12. What responsibility does Ezra give the leading priests? (8:24-29)

    Ezra tells them to guard the vessels, silver, and gold that have been given to the Lord and see that these vessels reach Jerusalem safely.

13. What do the people do after they reach Jerusalem? (8:33, 35, 36)

    The people weigh the silver and gold they had brought with them, make burnt offerings to God, deliver the king's orders to his satraps and governors, and assist the people and the house of God.

14. What sin have the people, the priests, and the Levites committed? (9:1-2)

   They have married the daughters of the neighboring people.

15. What does Ezra do when he hears this? (9:3)

   Ezra tears his garments, pulls hair from his head and beard, and sits appalled.

16. What does Ezra do after the evening sacrifice? (9:5)

   Ezra falls on his knees and prays to God.

Answer these questions by reading Ezra 10

17. What do the people do while Ezra prays? (10:1)

   The people gather around Ezra and weep bitterly.

18. What does Shecaniah suggest to Ezra? (10:2-3)

   Shecaniah suggests that the people make a covenant with God to send away their foreign families.

19. What does Ezra then do? (10:5)

   Ezra then rises from his prayers, and has the men of Israel take an oath.

20. What do the people of Israel decide to do? (10:10-14)

   They decide to let all who have taken foreign wives come at appointed times to make their confession.

DIMENSION TWO:
WHAT DOES THE BIBLE MEAN?

Ezra 7:1. We noticed in the second session that sometimes events in the Book of Ezra are reported out of chronological sequence. Therefore, when the author begins Chapter 7 with the words "After these things," we must ask the question, After what? In Chapter 6, Darius is king; in Chapter 7, Artaxerxes is. How much time, then, has passed between Chapter 6 and Chapter 7?

The question is not easy to answer. Ezra came to Jerusalem in the seventh year of Artaxerxes (verses 7-8), but which Artaxerxes does the author mean? There were three kings of Persia who ruled under that name. If Ezra came to Jerusalem in the seventh year of Artaxerxes I, as is sometimes assumed, that would be in the year 459 B.C., since Artaxerxes I ruled from 465 to 424.

However, it seems almost certain that Ezra did not come to Jerusalem until after Nehemiah did. Nehemiah came in the twentieth year of Artaxerxes I, around 445 B.C. Ezra's arrival in Jerusalem, therefore, must have been in the seventh year of the reign of Artaxerxes II. That would be in 398 B.C., since Artaxerxes II ruled from 404 to 358 B.C. Perhaps originally all of the Book of Nehemiah, except the Ezra chapters (Chapters 8–10), came between Ezra 6 and Ezra 7.

Ezra 7:6. Ezra served as both a priest and a scribe and is usually so designated (Ezra 7:11, 12, 21; Nehemiah 8:9). Some believe he also occupied an important position in the Persian government.

The "Law of Moses" may refer to the entire Pentateuch or Torah, the first five books of the Bible. Or the phrase may refer to a portion of the Pentateuch that Ezra apparently brought with him from Babylonia (verse 14).

Ezra 7:9. The first month is the month of Nisan. The first day of Nisan would be about the middle of our month of March. The fifth month is the month of Ab. The first day of Ab would be about the middle of our month of July.

Ezra 7:10. Ezra knows that studying the Law is not enough; one must also live the Law to be a faithful servant. Furthermore, it is Ezra's plan to teach the Law to others in Israel. The Law of the Lord that Ezra set his heart to study, do, and teach is the same as the Law of Moses mentioned in verse 6.

Ezra 7:11. This verse is written in Hebrew, and is the writer's introduction to the letter that follows (verses 12-26). The letter is written in Aramaic.

Ezra 7:12. The phrase *king of kings* implies that Artaxerxes was the most powerful king of all. The phrase was used of other kings at other times (Ezekiel 26:7; Daniel 2:37). In the Book of Revelation the phrase is used to refer to Christ (17:14; 19:16).

Ezra 7:13-16. The two purposes of Ezra's trip to Jerusalem are (1) to see how closely the people in Judah and Jerusalem are keeping the commandments of God, and (2) to take to Jerusalem the money that Artaxerxes and the Jews in Babylon had given for the Temple.

The seven advisers referred to in verse 14 are probably the king's most trusted. Persian kings often surrounded themselves with such advisers. (Compare "the seven nobles of Persia and Media, who . . . were highest in the kingdom" in Esther 1:14.)

Ezra 7:21-24. A literal translation of "a salt without limit" is *and salt which is not written*. Presumably the salt was not restricted either because it was available in quantity or because not much salt was required for the sacrifices.

"Whatever the God of heaven has prescribed, let it be done with diligence" is virtually giving a *carte blanche*. Usually a Persian king would not give such an order for the

Hebrew God, but Artaxerxes does not want to anger God. (Compare 7:23 to the words of King Darius in 6:10.)

"Taxes, tribute, or duty" must refer to three distinct taxes levied on the people (4:13). Many commentators have tried to explain the differences among them, but the truth of the matter is, we do not know.

Ezra 7:25-26. "The wisdom of your God, which you possess" is obviously a written document that Ezra carried with him, and is equivalent to "the Law of your God, which is in your hand" in verse 14. It undoubtedly was the Torah (the first five books of the Bible) or some portion of the Torah.

The magistrates and judges Ezra was to appoint seem at first to be given the power to judge all the people in the province Trans-Euphrates. But then their jurisdiction is restricted to only the Jews who know the laws of God. Notice that both the religious law and the civil law are to be obeyed, and punishments are mentioned—death, excommunication, confiscation of goods, and imprisonment.

The Jews continued throughout the years and centuries to stress that keeping the religious law was as or more important than keeping the civil law. When the two came into conflict it was the religious law that the loyal Jew felt obligated to keep. This sometimes resulted in punishment, persecution, or even war, as during the days of the Maccabees. (See 1 Maccabees 1:41-64 in the Apocrypha for a description of the conditions in Jerusalem in those days.) The same conflict between civil law and religious law is seen in the New Testament in John 19:1-7. According to the civil law, Pilate could find that Jesus had broken no law. But according to the religious laws of the Jews, Jesus ought to die.

With the conclusion of verse 26, we have come to the end of the letter of Artaxerxes, and the end of the Aramaic portions of the Book of Ezra.

Ezra 7:27-28. This section begins what is known as the Ezra Memoirs. These memoirs are in the first person, and presumably were written by Ezra very close to the time that the events being described actually happened. The Memoirs include 7:27–9:15, except for 8:35-36.

Ezra 8:15-20. When Zerubbabel made his trip to Jerusalem, only a small number of Levites went with him. (See the section on 2:40 in Dimension Two of the student and teacher books.) Now Ezra has the same problem. Later Jews apparently were embarrassed by this reluctance on the part of the Levites to make the trip and tried to make excuses for them. One excuse offered was that the Babylonian language was so similar to Hebrew that the Levites felt at home there and did not want to leave. Another excuse given was that the Levites, rather than play their instruments for the Babylonian king, had bitten off the ends of their fingers. And now, since they were married, they were no longer suited for service in the Temple.

Ezra lists the names of the leading men he sent to Iddo. Many believe some of the men are listed twice. For example, three men are named Elnathan and another is called Nathan. In addition, *Jarib* and *Joiarib* are probably two forms of the same name.

In spite of the fact that Ezra chooses men of insight, he tells them what to say. The text literally says, *I put words to say in their mouth.*

Verse 20 is the only place we are told that it was David who appointed the Temple servants to assist the Levites. Ezra apparently has a written list of their names, but he does not share his list with his readers.

Ezra 8:21-23. When Nehemiah had gone to Jerusalem, the king had sent army officers and cavalry to protect him (Nehemiah 2:9). Ezra chose not to request such protection, but to rely instead upon the protection of God. Some have said this shows Ezra had more faith than Nehemiah. Ezra, himself, admits that the reason he did not request aid from Artaxerxes was to save face. He had told the king that God would protect all that seek him. Ezra proclaims a fast and seeks protection from God.

Ezra 8:27. *Darics* were Persian coins, first issued by Darius I, who reigned from 522 to 486 B.C.

Ezra 8:31-36. The trip from Persia to Jerusalem is as follows: Ezra begins to gather men to go with him on the first day of the first month (7:9) of the seventh year of Artaxerxes (7:7). It takes three days to get all the people assembled at the canal Ahava and then counted (8:15). Procuring Levites for the trip, fasting, and entrusting the silver and gold and articles to the leading priest (8:16-30) takes another eight days. They then leave for Jerusalem on the twelfth day of the first month (8:31). They arrive in Jerusalem on the first day of the fifth month (7:9). After waiting for three days (8:32), the priests take the silver, gold, and articles to the Temple (8:33). Whether the sacrifices were offered immediately or the next day is impossible to tell. And how long it took to deliver the king's commission to the satraps and governors also is impossible to tell.

Ezra 8:31. "We set out" is literally, *we pulled up stakes.* That phrase is appropriate since they had encamped at the canal Ahava (8:15). God "protected us from enemies and bandits along the way," says Ezra, but what does he mean by that? Did God deliver them in the sense that no enemy attacked them? Or were they ambushed along the way, but God delivered them in the sense that no one was hurt and no silver or gold lost to the attackers? Either explanation is possible.

Ezra 8:32. The delay of three days is usually explained as a wait to allow the passing of the sabbath before delivering the silver, gold, and articles to the Temple. The frequency with which we find a delay of three days, however, makes us wonder if there was not some significance to a three-day waiting period, known to them, but now lost to us (Ezra 8:15; Nehemiah 2:11; Esther 4:16).

Ezra 8:34. Note the careful way the Temple treasures are counted, weighed, and recorded. The people had learned the hard way that priests can be dishonest too. After the priests of Jehoash's day had been caught pilfering the Temple money for their own use, the people began to take more precautions (2 Kings 12:1-8).

Ezra 8:35. The burnt offerings consisted of twelve male goats. Notice that all the numbers except seventy-seven are multiples of twelve. (First Esdras 8:66 says there were seventy-two lambs, once again a multiple of twelve.) Ezra tells us that these offerings are for all Israel, that is, for all twelve of the tribes.

Ezra 8:36. *Satraps* is a Persian term; *governors* is a more common term, used by Jews and Babylonians alike. The two words have approximately the same meaning.

Ezra 9:1. We cannot be sure that the events described here necessarily follow what happened in Chapter 8. The events of Chapter 8 occurred during the fifth month (7:8-9). The events of Chapter 9 occurred during the ninth month (10:9). What happened during that four-month period? According to Nehemiah 8:2, one of the things that happened was that Ezra read the Law of Moses to the people on the first day of the seventh month. The people then took an oath to obey God's laws (Nehemiah 10:29). The "after these things" of 9:1, then, may refer to the events of Nehemiah 7:73–10:39, rather than the events of Ezra 8. After all, it does seem logical that Ezra would help the people understand the law (Nehemiah 8:7) before he required all Israel to take an oath to obey it (Ezra 10:5).

The neighboring peoples were those whom the returned exiles found living in Judah at their return. Ezra lists eight such peoples.

Ezra 9:2. The concern over marrying foreign women was not felt in the early days of the Israelite people. Joseph, for example, married an Egyptian woman (Genesis 41:45). Moses married a Cushite woman. Though Miriam and Aaron spoke against Moses because of it, God made it plain to them that it was they who were wrong, and not Moses (Numbers 12). Boaz married Ruth, a Moabite (Ruth 4:10), and their great-grandson was David, the greatest king Israel ever had (Ruth 4:17). Only when foreign wives became a threat to the purity of religious practice were restrictions placed on who the people could marry (Deuteronomy 7:3-4; Judges 3:5-6).

Ezra 9:6. In this verse Ezra seems to be making use of a type of parallelism frequently found in Hebrew poetry. One line repeats the idea of the preceding line, but uses different words to do so. This technique is called *synonymous parallelism.*

Ezra 9:11-12. The commands that Ezra says God sent by the prophets do not come from any of the prophetic books. They come from one of the Books of Moses (Deuteronomy

7:1-5). Moses, of course, is referred to as a prophet (Deuteronomy 18:15; 34:10), though later generations make a sharp distinction between the Books of Moses (the Law) and the Prophets.

The student book suggests in the section on 9:6-15 that Ezra's questions of verse 14 may be directed more to the people around him than to God. Perhaps it would be accurate to say that this whole prayer was calculated to get maximum results from the people. The prayer is as much a sermon as it is a prayer.

Ezra 10:1. Ezra's prayer has just the effect he was hoping for—a large group of men, women, and children gather to him and weep. Presumably, these persons are in addition to those who trembled and gathered around him in 9:4.

Notice that with 10:1 the story is told once again in the third person rather than the first. We are now finished with the Ezra Memoirs. (See comments on 7:27-28 on page 401.)

Ezra 10:2. The student book points out that Shecaniah was not one of those men who had married foreign women. Some have thought, however, that he was the child of such a marriage. Notice that he is the son of Jehiel, and there is a Jehiel listed in verse 26 as one of the guilty persons. Surely, however, these are different Jehiels. If not, Shecaniah would be advocating that he, himself, along his mother and brothers and sisters, be ejected from the Jewish community.

Ezra 10:3. The solution of Shecaniah is harsh. It would break up families, cause heartbreak, and ignore human love. It assumes wives and children can be sent away at will. The situation was perceived as being desperate, and Shecaniah felt that desperate measures were called for.

Was the idea really Ezra's rather than Shecaniah's? The words "in accordance with the counsel of my lord" seem to suggest that Ezra had proposed such a solution. To say the very least, the plan met with Ezra's approval.

Ezra 10:6. This verse provides an important clue to the dating of Ezra. Ezra spent the night in the chamber of Jehohanan the son of Eliashib. Eliashib had been the high priest in the time of Nehemiah (Nehemiah 3:1; 13:28) and was in charge of the chambers of the Temple (Nehemiah 13:4). Jehohanan, his son, was high priest during the reign of Darius II. Assuming these are the same Eliashib and Jehohanan, this verse shows that Nehemiah came to Jerusalem before Ezra, and that we have Ezra placed in his proper chronological spot.

Ezra 10:13. Notice that the people themselves admit that they are guilty. This was not a tempest in a teacup, then, but a serious problem for the community.

Ezra 10:16-17. Presumably the family heads that Ezra selected are the same as the officials the people had requested be chosen (verse 14).

Ezra 10:18-44. The violators of the law are listed according to their status—priests first, then Levites, singers, gatekeepers, and finally all other Israelites. Seventeen priests are listed, six Levites, one singer, three gatekeepers, and eighty-four laymen. That is only 111 persons, a rather small percent in a community of thirty-five thousand or so.

Ezra 10:24. Ezra lists one singer and three gatekeepers as guilty. First Esdras 9:24-25, on the other hand, lists two Temple singers and two gatekeepers. Notice that no Temple servants are mentioned. Why not? We do not really know, but perhaps it is because they were foreigners themselves, and therefore outside the law.

Ezra 10:44. The last half of verse 44 is unintelligible in the Hebrew. It reads: "And there were from them wives and they put children." If we follow 1 Esdras 9:36, the meaning, if not the words, is clear—all the foreign wives and their children were put away. The reform was a success!

DIMENSION THREE: WHAT DOES THE BIBLE MEAN TO ME?

Ezra 7:26—Civil Law and Religious Conviction

If you did not use the Dimension Two material in this teacher book on Ezra 7:25-26, you will want to do so now. Refer the class also to Peter's words in Acts 5:29, "We must obey God rather than men!" What do these words contribute to the discussion in the student book?

Now have the class look at Romans 13:1-2. Do these words seem to be in conflict with Acts 5:29? Ask class members how they reconcile the two passages. When if ever, is it appropriate to disobey the law?

Ezra 9–10—Exclusiveness Rears Its Ugly Head

Ask the class members to explain what is meant by a course of action being the lesser of two evils. Ask them to name some times when it was necessary for them to make such a choice.

Perhaps Ezra and the nation of Israel were facing just such a time. The returned exiles were a very small group compared to the peoples who surrounded them. Pagan influence was all around. How could they remain true to their God and their religion if even members of their own households followed pagan practices? They therefore decided on the path of exclusivism.

Unfortunately, they chose to concentrate their efforts on the nonessentials of their faith—things like the food laws, the sabbath restrictions, and the rite of circumcision—while neglecting "the more important matters of the law" like justice, mercy, and faithfulness, as Jesus said (Matthew 23:23).

Ezra 9:6-15—Preaching a Sermon While Praying

Have the class look at some of the great prayers of the psalms: Psalm 51, for example, or Psalm 90. Then have someone read Matthew 6:9-13 and Matthew 26:39. What in these prayers is calculated to move human beings to action? Or are they genuinely addressed to God? Ask class members to suggest definitions of true prayer.

Close the session by asking class members to reflect on what new insights they have gained during this lesson on Ezra 7–10. If time allows, list these insights on a chalkboard or a large piece of paper.

INTRODUCTION TO NEHEMIAH

The Book of Nehemiah concludes the great history of Israel written by the Chronicler. First and Second Chronicles cover the time from Adam to Cyrus, king of Persia (536 B.C.). The Book of Ezra begins with the proclamation of Cyrus allowing the exiled Jews to return to their homeland. The Book of Nehemiah continues the story of the reestablishment of the Jewish community in Jerusalem into the fourth century B.C.

Ezra and Nehemiah were written as one book and were a single volume in the Hebrew Bible until A.D. 1448. The two were separated as early as A.D. 254 in Greek translations. Jerome, writing in the fourth century A.D., was the first to call the second part of the book *Nehemiah*. In Hebrew, *Nehemiah* means "the Lord has comforted."

The content of Nehemiah may be outlined as follows: (1) Nehemiah's return and the rebuilding of Jerusalem's walls, Chapters 1–6; (2) list of returning exiles, Chapter 7; (3) Ezra's reading of the Book of the Law, Chapters 8–10; and (4) Nehemiah's social and religious reforms, Chapters 11–13.

The Chronicler went to early biblical books and Temple documents for historical information. This writer may have used the Book of the Chronicles (Nehemiah 12:23) in writing Nehemiah 11:1–13:3. The Chronicler probably found Ezra's biography and Nehemiah's autobiography in the Temple archives and copied Nehemiah's story directly into his own work (Nehemiah 1:1-73, 13:4-31). This autobiography has been called one of the best historical documents in the Bible. It is the only complete autobiographical account of one person's career found in the Old Testament.

Nehemiah probably wrote his memoirs not long after 432 B.C. He may have placed his memoirs in the Temple as a memorial before God so that the Lord would remember Nehemiah's good works and assure him the "name" that he, as a eunuch, could not get through his children (Isaiah 56:3-5). The Chronicler interspersed Nehemiah's memoirs with material on Ezra (Nehemiah 7:73–8:8), with statistical lists, and with third-person reports of Nehemiah's social and religious reforms.

Before becoming governor of Judah, Nehemiah was cupbearer to the Persian king Artaxerxes I (465–425 B.C.).

The cupbearer was a eunuch who served as the king's wine taster and as supervisor of the king's apartments. This was one of the oldest and highest court positions in Babylonia.

In the twentieth year of Artaxerxes's reign, Nehemiah's brother reported to Nehemiah that "the wall of Jerusalem is broken down, and its gates have been burned with fire" (Nehemiah 1:3). In fact, Artaxerxes I himself had authorized forcing the Jews in Jerusalem to stop work on the walls (Ezra 4:23). Nehemiah was distressed, and secured permission from Artaxerxes to return to Jerusalem. In his request to Artaxerxes, Nehemiah does not specifically mention the broken walls. Instead he expresses concern for his fathers' burial places and the city gates.

Nehemiah returned to Jerusalem in 445 B.C. and was governor of Judah for twelve years (Nehemiah 2:1; 5:14). While governor, Nehemiah led the rebuilding of the city walls despite economic difficulties and vigorous opposition from the governor of Samaria. He instituted social reforms in the community. The population of Judah was rearranged and Jerusalem's population was increased. Sabbath observances were enforced and marriages between Jews and non-Jews were prohibited. Nehemiah participated in the renewal of the covenant between God and the chosen people.

Through these reforms Nehemiah tried to spell out how God's people were to express the ideals of holiness and righteousness in their daily lives. He saw his work as holy work, for the Jewish revival in Judah would have been impossible apart from God's guidance and support. Throughout his memoirs, Nehemiah expresses a deep abiding trust in his God. He often speaks of the hand of God guiding and defending him in his work (Nehemiah 2:8, 18).

The leadership given by Nehemiah and by Ezra was crucial in the survival of the Jews as a unique people with a distinctive faith. Ezra and Nehemiah helped to revitalize the institutions needed to keep the people and the faith together. The forces for assimilation into a larger culture were strong in their time and in the Chronicler's time. Yet, both Ezra and Nehemiah had a sense of Israel's corporate identity as God's chosen people. The Chronicler wrote the history of Israel as an affirmation of this identity.

The words of Nehemiah son of Hacaliah (1:1).

5

Nehemiah the Cupbearer

Nehemiah 1–2

DIMENSION ONE:
WHAT DOES THE BIBLE SAY?

Answer these questions by reading Nehemiah 1

1. Who does Nehemiah ask about the Jews still living in Jerusalem? (1:2)

   Nehemiah asks the men who come with Hanani about the Jews in Jerusalem.

2. How do these men say the Jews in Jerusalem are doing? (1:3)

   The men say the Jews in Jerusalem are in trouble. The Jerusalem walls are broken down, and the city gates are destroyed.

3. How does Nehemiah react to this news? (1:4)

   Nehemiah weeps, mourns, fasts, and prays.

4. What is Nehemiah's position in Persia? (1:11)

   Nehemiah is cupbearer to the king.

Answer these questions by reading Nehemiah 2

5. Who asks Nehemiah why he is sad? (2:2)

   King Artaxerxes asks Nehemiah why he is sad.

6. After hearing why Nehemiah is sad, what does the king ask Nehemiah? (2:4)

   The king asks Nehemiah, "What is it you want?"

7. What does Nehemiah request? (2:5, 7-8)

   Nehemiah requests permission to go to Jerusalem, letters from the king to assure him a safe journey, and a letter telling Asaph to give Nehemiah the timber he will need.

8. Who is displeased that Nehemiah has come to help the people of Israel? (2:10)

   Sanballat and Tobiah, two governors, are displeased.

9. What does Nehemiah do at night? (2:13-15)

   Nehemiah goes out by night to inspect the walls and the city gates.

10. What does Nehemiah say to the Israelite priests, nobles, and officials? (2:17-18)

    Nehemiah says, "Let us build the wall of Jerusalem."

11. What do the people say? (2:18)

    The people say, "Let us start rebuilding."

12. What do Sanballat, Tobiah, and Geshem say to the Israelites? (2:19)

    Sanballat, Tobiah, and Geshem ask what they are doing and if they are rebelling against the king.

13. How does Nehemiah answer them? (2:20)

    Nehemiah says that God will help the Israelites prosper and that they will rebuild, but the three have no historic right in Jerusalem.

DIMENSION TWO:
WHAT DOES THE BIBLE MEAN?

Throughout our study of Ezra, we have had the Book of First Esdras as our constant companion. Many times passages in First Esdras have enlightened, or sometimes corrected, the parallel passages in Ezra. First Esdras, therefore, has served us well in our attempt to understand Ezra.

Unfortunately we have no book that parallels Nehemiah all the way through. Only one section of Nehemiah (Nehemiah 8:1-12) is paralleled in First Esdras.

Nehemiah 1:1. "The words of Nehemiah son of Hacaliah" is the title for the book. (Compare with Jeremiah 1:1; Hosea 1:1; Joel 1:1.) The name *Nehemiah* means "the Lord comforts." We know of others with the same name—Nehemiah, the son of Azbuk (Nehemiah 3:16), and a Nehemiah who made the trip to Jerusalem with Zerubbabel (Ezra 2:2; Nehemiah 7:7). This cannot be our Nehemiah, since Zerubbabel went to Jerusalem in 520 B.C., and Nehemiah left in 445, seventy-five years later. We know nothing at all about Hacaliah other than what is in this one verse.

The month of Kislev is the ninth month. We are told that it is in the twentieth year of the reign of Artaxerxes. We notice, however, that the events of 2:1 and following, which happen *after* the events of 1:1-3, are dated in the month of Nisan, in the twentieth year. And Nisan is the first month of the year! Something, then, is wrong. Either 1:1 should say *nineteenth year,* or, as has been suggested by some, Nehemiah reckoned the years according to the Syrian custom of beginning in the fall.

Nehemiah 1:2. Hanani is called "one of my brothers." What does this mean? Is he a blood brother? a companion? a fellow Jew? or what? Some have concluded that Hanani was a blood brother to Nehemiah on the basis of 7:2.

We are not told in Nehemiah why the men were in Susa. Had they come for the express purpose of reporting the bad news to Nehemiah? Or did Hanani just happen to overhear the men talking? We do not know. One thing, though, seems certain. Hanani had not just come from Judah. He was already in Persia. Nehemiah's questions in verse 2 are not directed to Hanani, but to the men from Judah.

Nehemiah 1:3. "The province" is Judah, as in Ezra 2:1.

The meaning of the statement that the wall is broken down seems obvious until we realize that the English translation is really an interpretation. The Hebrew text says that "the wall is breached." That has a different meaning. Why do the NIV translators say "broken down" if the Hebrew says "breached?" Because (1) that would seem to be the correct meaning, and (2) the same Hebrew word appears in Isaiah 5:5, and there the meaning obviously is "break down" rather than "breach."

Nehemiah 1:5. The word *awesome* means "awe-inspiring."

Nehemiah 1:6. We can understand why God's ear would need to be attentive in order "to hear the prayer your servant is praying," but why would God's eyes need to be open? Probably the meaning is "to fasten your attention on." Or, perhaps the thought is that God could then see the plight of the people as well as hear their prayer. At any rate, the expression occurs several times in the Old Testament (1 Kings 8:29, 52; 2 Chronicles 6:20, 40; 7:15; Isaiah 37:17).

Some commentators believe Nehemiah's words, "I confess the sins we Israelites, including myself and my father's house, have committed," indicate that he was of royal blood. Also, in 2:3, he refers to Jerusalem as "the city where my fathers are buried." Jerusalem was the burial ground for all the kings. However, Jerusalem was also the burial ground for a number of other families. If Nehemiah were descended from David, however, that would explain his intense interest in how things were going in Jerusalem.

Nehemiah 1:7. Moses often is referred to as a servant of God. (Joshua 1:1, 2, 7, 13, 15; 1 Kings 8:53, 56; Nehemiah 1:8; 9:14.)

Nehemiah 1:8. The word God gave to Moses was both threat and promise. The word *instruction* makes us expect a direct quotation from the Law of Moses. But the words are not found in the books of Moses. The ideas are certainly there, but not the exact words.

Nehemiah 1:9. Return to me means "to repent." *At the farthest horizon* means "as far away as they can be taken." The place that God has chosen is Jerusalem (1 Kings 8:16, 44, 48; 11:13, 32).

Nehemiah 1:11. Nehemiah's prayer closes as it had begun, with a petition to God to hear (verse 6). The words *and to the prayer of your servants who delight in revering your name* may imply that others have joined in Nehemiah's prayer. Or, Nehemiah may simply be recognizing that many others must be praying for the people in Jerusalem.

"Granting him favor in the sight of this man" is confusing. What man is being talked about? In light of the next sentence, and in light of the story that follows in Chapter 2, the man seems to be King Artaxerxes. But why would Artaxerxes be mentioned? He has nothing to do with the prayer that is being prayed, unless Nehemiah is anticipating the events of Chapter 2.

That brings us to a solution, suggested by many, that may have merit. In 2:4, Nehemiah is talking to the king, and Artaxerxes asks him what request he has. Nehemiah's heart is in his throat as he answers the king, and he tells us, "I prayed to the God of heaven." Nehemiah tells us that he prayed, but not what he prayed. It could not have been a very long prayer, for the king was waiting for an answer. The suggestion of many is that these words in 1:11 may be the prayer Nehemiah prayed in 2:4. In this context, the reference to "this man" makes sense. Where it stands in 1:11, it hardly makes sense at all. Could it be, then, that Nehemiah's prayer in 2:4 accidentally got attached to his longer prayer of 1:5-11?

Nehemiah is cupbearer to the king. Two things need to be said here. First, this was a position of prominence. Tobit (the Book of Tobit is found in the Apocrypha) tells us his nephew served as cupbearer to Esarhaddon the king and was second-in-command. That Nehemiah, a Jew, rose to such heights is a tribute both to his ability and to the broad-mindedness of the Persian government.

Secondly, those who labored in the king's court, including the cupbearer, were usually made eunuchs. This was specially true for those who were allowed in the presence of the queen, and Nehemiah seems to have been (Nehemiah 2:6). Quite possibly then, Nehemiah was a eunuch.

Deuteronomy 23:1 says that eunuchs shall not "enter the assembly of the LORD." Perhaps if Nehemiah was a eunuch, some of the people resented the place of leadership he assumed in rebuilding the walls of Jerusalem (Nehemiah 3–6).

Some have suggested that Psalm 127 might have been written with Nehemiah in mind. Notice how well this psalm fits the situation. Verses 1-2 describe exactly the frantic building that took place under Nehemiah's leadership, and verses 3-5 talk of the blessedness of having many children.

On the other hand, many of the Jews appreciated Nehemiah's leadership and were more open minded about the place a eunuch might have in the assembly of the Lord.

Nehemiah 2:1. Assuming that 1:1 should read, "in the month of Kislev in the nineteenth year," the events of 2:1-8 would be four months later. The probable reason for the delay is expressed in 2:2. Nehemiah was afraid. Or perhaps the delay was because Artaxerxes spent the winter away and has now returned for the spring months.

The words "when wine was brought for him" perhaps should read "before me." That is what the passage says in the Septuagint, a Greek translation of the Jewish Scriptures. That translation seems to fit better with the next words, "I took the wine and gave it to the king." The meaning may be, however, that the wine is sitting on the table before the king. Nehemiah takes it up and pours it into the king's cup.

Perhaps sadness was showing on his face and Nehemiah was not aware of it. He had thought he was doing a good job of hiding his true feelings. This may explain his fear.

Nehemiah 2:6. The parenthetical statement "with the queen sitting beside him" seems to serve no purpose in the story. But perhaps the idea is that the mere presence of the queen made Artaxerxes more genial and more generous in his response. If so, Artaxerxes was neither the first man nor the last to display his better self when in the presence of the queen.

Nehemiah 2:8. We do not know anything about Asaph, the keeper of the king's forest. Since *Asaph* is a Jewish name, some have thought the king's forest might be located in Israel. That, however, is unlikely. Solomon had imported cedar from Lebanon when he had the Temple built (1 Kings 5:5-6; 2 Chronicles 2:8-9, 16) because he wanted to use only the finest lumber available. The cedars of

Lebanon had continued to be prized (Ezra 3:7). So the king's forest is probably located in Lebanon.

Nehemiah plans to use the lumber for the beams for the gates, the wall of the city, and for his house. When Nehemiah speaks of the house he will occupy, is he talking about just a house for himself, or is he speaking specifically of the governor's residence? We know that Nehemiah served as governor of Judah for twelve years (5:14). And if the dates of 2:1 and 5:14 are both correct, he began his governorship immediately upon his arrival from Persia. Was it worked with Artaxerxes in advance, then, that Nehemiah should be governor of Judah? And, if so, does Nehemiah expect that the house he is building will be the official residence of the governor?

Nehemiah 2:9-10. The governors Nehemiah encountered are the ones named in verses 10 and 19. Verse 10 seems out of place. It would be more appropriately placed in verse 8 after the words, "the king granted my requests."

Nehemiah names his enemies by name, just as Ezra does (Ezra 4:7-10). These men are greatly displeased because their power and authority would be weakened if Nehemiah is successful. Judah has been a weak province, but if Jerusalem's walls were rebuilt, she would again become almost impregnable. In that case the center of power in that section of the Persian Empire almost certainly would shift from north to south, leaving the status and power of Sanballat and his cohorts severely crippled.

The words *had come* should be translated *was coming.* Nehemiah has not reached Jerusalem yet. He encounters these men on the way, and does not get to Jerusalem until verse 11.

Nehemiah 2:13. The Jewish people were never squeamish about the names they gave to persons or places. The Dung Gate was the gate through which the excrement of their animals was taken to the garbage dump. As the student book indicates, all other garbage was taken out that same gate to the same garbage disposal. That disposal place was the Valley of Ben Hinnom. In earlier days, the Valley of Hinnom had been used by the devotees of the pagan god Molech as a place to burn their children in acts of worship (2 Kings 23:10; 2 Chronicles 28:3; 33:6; Jeremiah 7:31; 32:35). In Nehemiah's day, a fire was kept burning in the Valley of Ben Hinnom as a way to dispose of the garbage. By the time of Jesus, *Gehenna,* the Greek word for Valley of Ben Hinnom, had become a symbol for hell.

DIMENSION THREE:
WHAT DOES THE BIBLE MEAN TO ME?

Nehemiah 1:4—Mourning for Jerusalem

Ask the members of the class to be honest with themselves as they answer the question posed in the student book. We can understand it when a father laments over the death of his son, as David cried out in anguish over the death of Absalom (2 Samuel 18:33). And we can understand it when Jesus weeps at the death of a dear friend (John 11:35-36). But how many of us are distressed to the point of tears at the sins of our people?

Nehemiah 2:4—Praying at Critical Moments

The answers to the questions posed in the student book are not as simple as they may seem. Most of us treat God as a divine bellhop. When we get into a crisis situation we tap the bell, and expect God to come running to our rescue! Is that what Nehemiah was doing?

The Apostle Paul's advice was to pray constantly in any and all circumstances (1 Thessalonians 5:17-18; Romans 1:9; 2 Timothy 1:3). Is that was Nehemiah was doing?

Perhaps it would be helpful to count how many times we find it recorded in Nehemiah's book that he prayed. That might tell us whether Nehemiah was genuinely a person of prayer, or whether he prayed only in crisis situations (1:4, 5-11; 2:4; 4:4-5; 5:19; 6:14; 13:14, 31).

Now, the hard question: What about us? Are we men and women who pray without ceasing or are we persons who pray at critical moments only?

Nehemiah 2:10-20—The Faith to See It Through

Again the questions posed in the student book require us to be painfully honest with ourselves. It might be better not to try to discuss the questions raised in Dimension Three. Maybe they are too personal. Each person in the class might read the Dimension Three questions, then listen to you share with them the material below on the biblical concepts of faith. Then they can reflect on their own lives, their own faith, and their own commitment. It might be helpful to have them write out new commitments they want to make. These new commitments will be made in private, of course, and shared with no one except God.

Close the session by asking persons to share new insights on Nehemiah 1–2.

So we rebuilt the wall till all of it reached half its height (4:6).

— 6 —

Restoring the Wall

Nehemiah 3–5

DIMENSION ONE:
WHAT DOES THE BIBLE SAY?

Answer these questions by reading Nehemiah 3

1. Who is the high priest in Nehemiah's day? (3:1)

   Eliashib is the high priest.

2. Does the high priest help rebuild the wall? (3:1)

   Yes, Eliashib does help rebuild the wall.

3. What are some of the types of groups doing repair work? (3:2; 3:3; 3:17)

   Family groups, territorial groups, and professional groups are used to repair the wall.

4. What is different about those from the household of Shallum who work on the wall? (3:12)

   Shallum's daughters work on the wall.

Answer these questions by reading Nehemiah 4

5. How does Sanballat feel about the wall being rebuilt? (4:1)

   Sanballat is angered by the news that he ridicules the Jews.

6. What does Tobiah say? (4:3)

   Tobiah says if a fox runs across the Jews' wall, the wall would fall down.

7. For what does Nehemiah pray? (4:4-5)

   Nehemiah prays that God will turn the taunts of Sanballat and Tobiah back upon them and that they will be plundered in a land where they are captives.

8. What groups plot to fight against the Jews? (4:7-8)

   Sanballat and Tobiah, the Arabs, the Ammonites, and the Ashdodites plot to fight against the Jews.

9. What do the Jews do then? (4:9)

   The Jews pray and they put a guard out day and night.

10. What does Nehemiah tell the people? (4:14)

    Nehemiah tells the people not to be afraid, to remember the Lord, and to fight for their families and homes.

11. What precautions does Nehemiah have the people take? (4:16-18)

    They are armed while they work, some keeping one hand on their weapons while working with the other hand.

Answer these questions by reading Nehemiah 5

12. What three complaints do the people have? (5:1-4)

    They do not have enough food, they have had to mortgage their property, and they have had to borrow money to pay the king's tax.

13. How does Nehemiah rectify the situation? (5:11-12)

    Nehemiah castigates the nobles and officials who are taking over the people's property, and makes them swear to give it back to the people.

14. How long is Nehemiah governor of Judah? (5:14)

    Nehemiah is governor for twelve years.

15. How is Nehemiah different from the former governors of Judah? (5:14-15)

    He does not accept the governor's food allotment nor does he lay heavy taxes on the people for his own benefit.

16. What prayer does Nehemiah pray as he remembers his years as a governor? (5:19)

Nehemiah prays, "Remember me with favor, O my God, for all I have done for these people."

DIMENSION TWO:
WHAT DOES THE BIBLE MEAN?

Chapter 3 of Nehemiah interrupts the story that is being told in order to tell us about the repair and rebuilding of the wall. The story left in Chapter 2 is continued in Chapter 4.

Nehemiah 3:1. The Tower of the Hundred probably had military significance, and perhaps can be identified with the fortress of the Temple mentioned in 2:8. Fighting units were sometimes composed of one hundred men (2 Samuel 18:1), and that may be the significance of the name of this tower. Even in Jesus' day, the Roman centurion was the commander of a hundred men.

Nehemiah 3:2. Zaccur was not a common name. The name appears more frequently in Ezra and Nehemiah than in all the rest of the Bible. Yet each time the name appears in these books, Zaccur has a different father (Ezra 8:14; Nehemiah 3:2; 10:12; 12:25; 13:13).

Nehemiah 3:4. Meremoth works here and again in verse 21. Similarly, Meshullam works here and again in verse 30. Meshullam is also mentioned in verse 6 but he is apparently a different man. A different Zadok, son of a different father, appears in verse 29.

Nehemiah 3:5. The men from Tekoa come from the little village whose brightest star had risen some three centuries earlier (Amos 1:1). The citizens of Tekoa seem to work as hard as any. "Their nobles would not put their shoulders to the work" is translated in other versions as "neck to the work." The metaphor comes from the farmland, where the necks of oxen are put in the yoke of the plow.

Nehemiah 3:7-8. Melatiah appears only here in the Bible. The province Trans-Euphrates is the province of Aram. *Uzziel* is a common name, but *Harhaiah* is found only here.

The Broad Wall is mentioned only in the Book of Nehemiah. It seems fairly obvious what the Broad Wall was, but it is difficult to know where it was, or why it was broader than the rest of the wall.

Nehemiah 3:9. "Half district of Jerusalem" is curious. Rephaiah is ruler of half of Jerusalem, and Shallum is the ruler of half the territory outside of Jerusalem, assigned to be governed by Jerusalem. That seems to be the intended meaning.

Nehemiah 3:10. Harumaph means "split nose." Probably his nose was flat down the middle. *Harumaph* may have been a nickname, but it could have been his real name. Hebrew parents were sometimes almost brutally honest in naming their children.

The part of the wall Jedaiah repairs is opposite his house. The same is true for others (verses 23, 28, 29, 30). Perhaps Nehemiah believes the workers will be more keenly interested in seeing that the sections of wall near their own houses are done correctly.

Nehemiah 3:12. This is the only place where we are told a man's daughters helped repair the wall. Usually each man's sons helped. Perhaps Shallum had no sons, so specific mention is made of the work done by his daughters.

Nehemiah 3:13. Hanun must have brought several of the inhabitants of Zanoah with him, for they not only repaired the Valley Gate, but also repaired five hundred yards (approximately a quarter of a mile) of the wall.

Nehemiah 3:14. Malkijah is the son of Recab. There was a Recab of old from whom the Recabites came. These Recabites were a disciplined group who followed a strict set of rules, one of which was complete abstinence from wine (Jeremiah 35). It would be interesting if Malkijah were descended from that Recab since Malkijah is the ruler of the district of Beth Hakkerem, and *Beth Hakkerem* means "house of the vineyard."

Nehemiah 3:15-16. The king's garden is mentioned in 2 Kings 25:4; Jeremiah 39:4; and 52:7. The "House of the Heroes" undoubtedly has some connection with the mighty men who were David's warriors (2 Samuel 10:7; 16:6; 23:8; 1 Kings 1:10). Perhaps David had a special residence for his most valiant warriors.

Nehemiah 3:23-30. Either Benjamin and Hasshub lived together, or the word *house* should be *houses*. Neither Palal nor his father Uzai are known to us. They only appear in the Bible here. The living quarters of Meshullam is unknown to us except here.

Nehemiah 3:32. One of the evidences we have that the books of Ezra and Nehemiah used to be one book instead of two is that the Masoretes (a group of Jewish scholars who very carefully copied their Scripture) placed a note at 3:32 indicating that this was the middle of the book. Obviously 3:32 is not the middle of the Book of Nehemiah. A little arithmetic shows, however, that there are 343 verses from Ezra 1:1 through Nehemiah 3:32, and 343 verses from Nehemiah 4:1 through 13:31.

Nehemiah 4:1-5. The story left hanging in Chapter 2 is now continued. Notice that Chapter 2 closes with Sanballat and Tobiah, along with Geshem, deriding the Jews and asking,

"What is this you are doing?" Nehemiah responds with a prayer.

The fact that Sanballat is saying these things in the presence of the army of Samaria shows how seriously he is considering military action as a way of stopping the Jews. His concern when he asks if they will sacrifice is not clear. The observance of their religious rites would have been of little concern to Sanballat. Besides, they had already been offering sacrifices for some time. Perhaps the meaning is, Do you think they would be doing all this if all they had in mind was to offer sacrifices?

Tobiah's remark was intended to be sarcastic, and undoubtedly received a lot of laughter. We cannot be sure of his exact meaning, however, without knowing whether he made his remark in the hearing of the Jews. If only Sanballat and his associates heard the remark, Tobiah would seem to be serious in thinking the Jews were incapable of building a secure wall. If, however, his words were said in front of the Jews, a part of his intent may have been to discourage them by exaggerating their incompetence. (See the similar situation in 2 Kings 18:26-29.) There is nothing in verses 1-2 that would indicate Tobiah was standing where the Jews could hear him. On the other hand, Nehemiah seems to have known about the taunts in his prayer recorded in verses 4-5.

Nehemiah 4:6. There must be many shouts of joy as the last breaches in the wall are repaired, and the wall reaches all around the city from the ground to the middle of it, or, to half its height.

Nehemiah 4:9. Nehemiah is a religious man, but he is also a realistic man. The time has come to do more than just pray. He prays, but he also sets up a guard to watch for possible enemy attacks. One is reminded of our Lord's words to his sleepy disciples in the garden of Gethsemane—"watch and pray" (Matthew 26:41; Mark 14:38).

Nehemiah 4:12-13. Many of the Jews do not live in Jerusalem itself. They come into the city by day to help build the wall, but return to the surrounding areas at night. Some of these men who lived by the Samaritans are told ten times that Sanballat and his forces are planning a surprise attack on the Jews.

The text does not actually say it was Sanballat who planned the attack, but the author of the Book of Nehemiah obviously considers Sanballat the leader of the enemy forces. We may feel confident, therefore, that it is Sanballat and his allies who are meant. Nehemiah therefore doubles his efforts at protecting his people. Now he not only has a guard to watch, as in verse 9, but he actually stations people with swords, spears, and bows. He will not allow Sanballat to kill them and stop the work.

Nehemiah 4:15. Something has been left out of the story. In verses 10-14, Nehemiah prepares his people for a surprise attack by their enemies. In verse 15, we are told that since

"God had frustrated it [their plan]," Nehemiah and his people "returned to the wall, each to his own work." We are not told how the enemies' plans were frustrated.

Nehemiah 4:17. "Those who carried materials" may have been those who brought the stones to the wall, or they may have been those who carried the mortar. In either case it is difficult to see how they got much work done if with one hand they held a weapon.

Nehemiah 4:18. Nehemiah had the man who sounded the trumpet stay with him. There must have been more than one trumpeter, however. Presumably there were trumpeters stationed at various points along the wall, for the people were instructed to rally to the place where they heard the sound of the trumpet (verse 20). If there were only one trumpeter, such instructions would not make sense. He could not be at all places at all times, and the wall was close to a mile and a half long. Were the enemy forces to attack the opposite side of the wall from where he was, how would he know it? And how much damage could they do before he arrived to sound the trumpet?

Nehemiah 4:22. When the times got critical, Nehemiah ordered every person to spend the night inside the city limits. That would (1) give the people more protection at night, (2) assure Nehemiah that the workmen would be there and ready to begin work early in the mornings, (3) provide safety for those who otherwise would have to journey alone outside the city walls, and (4) prevent any of the men from defecting to the enemy or leaving Jerusalem without permission. Nehemiah mentions only the first two of the reasons.

Nehemiah 4:23. The words *each had his weapon* is an attempt on the part of the NIV translators to make sense of an unintelligible text. What the Hebrew actually says is, "each his weapon the water." But the translation has no meaning. Commentators have suggested various renderings for this text, but none is better than, and most not as good as, the reading found in the NIV.

Nehemiah 5:1-19. Once again the story is interrupted. We are told now of some of the internal problems that Nehemiah has to deal with, but it is almost certain that these events did not occur until after the wall was completed. Several considerations lead us to this conclusion. First, the conditions described there would require a longer time to develop than the time that the people have been working on the wall (6:15). Second, the famine mentioned in verse 3 fits the conditions prevalent in Chapter 13, several years after the wall was built. Third, given the urgency of the task of completing the wall—men sleeping with their clothes on, working with one hand and holding a weapon in the other—it does not seem likely that Nehemiah would take the time to hold a great assembly in order to bring charges against the nobles and the officials. And fourth, it is evident from verse 14 that Nehemiah is writing this after the thirty-second year of Artaxerxes the king. The entire twelve years of the first term of his governorship have passed. The conditions and the problem here described, therefore, occur some time after the wall has been completed.

Nehemiah 5:1. The words *the men* may simply refer to the poor. Or they may refer to those who were left in the land as opposed to their Jewish brethren, who had returned from exile.

Nehemiah 5:4. This verse is the only indication we have that the Persian kings levied property taxes on their subjects. However, we do not find it surprising that they did.

Nehemiah 5:7. The Jewish law permitted the exacting of interest from non-Jews, but not from Jews (Deuteronomy 23:20; Exodus 22:25). When Nehemiah says to the nobles, "You are exacting usury from your own countrymen!" he is saying to them, "You are not obeying God's law!"

Nehemiah 5:11. Nehemiah demands that their fields, vineyards, olive groves, and houses be returned to them. Only in this way could these people pay their debts and buy back their brothers they had sold into slavery (verse 8).

The additional requirement of returning "the hundredth part of the money, grain, new wine, and oil" that they have been exacting of them sounds strange. Repaying such a small amount does not seem just, nor would it be economically helpful to those who were oppressed.

Nehemiah 5:12. Nehemiah is not content just to take the word of the nobles. He requires them to take an oath in the presence of the priests. People had gone back on their word before (Jeremiah 34:8-11). To swear in front of the priests was the ancient equivalent of putting one's hand on the Bible to take an oath.

Nehemiah 5:13. Several of the prophets used actions to dramatize their words. (See, for example, Jeremiah 27:1-15; Ezekiel 5:1-2; Isaiah 20:1-6.) Nehemiah is here following in that tradition.

Nehemiah 5:14-19. Only in this passage and in 12:26 are we told that Nehemiah was governor of Judah. Notice, however, that Nehemiah is definitely the person in charge. There is no hint anywhere that Sanballat or anyone else is challenging his authority. The episode with Sanballat must have been only in the early years, then. This passage was written much later when the memory of Sanballat's plots against Judah had faded. At this time other matters were occupying Nehemiah's mind.

Nehemiah 5:14. Nehemiah is governor "from the twentieth year of King Artaxerxes . . . until his thirty-second year." It was in the twentieth year of King Artaxerxes when Nehemiah left Persia for Judah (2:1), and it was in the

thirty-second year of Artaxerxes that he returned (13:6). He therefore served as governor the entire time he was in Judah.

The food allowance of the governor that Nehemiah refused to extract from his people is alluded to in Malachi 1:7-8.

Nehemiah 5:15. Who were these earlier governors that Nehemiah talks about? Sheshbazzar served as governor of Judah (Ezra 5:14). Does Nehemiah mean him? Zerubbabel served as governor of Judah (Haggai 1:1). Does Nehemiah mean him? If so, these are Jewish governors soaking their own people. If, however, Nehemiah is referring to former Persian governors of Judah, the practice of laying heavy burdens upon the people would be more understandable, and from his point of view less reprehensible. Foreign rulers were expected to rule harshly, but it was laid down in the law that "you must not rule over your fellow Israelites ruthlessly" (Leviticus 25:46).

Nehemiah 5:16. "I devoted myself to the work on this wall," says Nehemiah. Nehemiah is not listed in Chapter 3 as one who worked on the wall. But all of Chapter 4 gives the impression that he is right in the thick of things. At the very least he is present when the work is going on (4:18, 20). He sleeps with his clothes on to be ready to use the weapon in case of attack (4:23); and if he is including himself in the "we" of 4:21, he did, indeed, help to build the wall. Perhaps he did not assign himself a specific section of the wall to repair so he could be free to go where needed.

When Nehemiah says, "We did not acquire any land," he may mean that he did not take land from the people as the nobles had done. Or possibly he means that he did not acquire any land at all while he was governor.

Nehemiah 5:17-18. Included in those whom Nehemiah feeds are (1) Jews, (2) officials, and (3) "those who came to us from the surrounding nations." The word *Jews* undoubtedly refers to the poor Jews who could not feed themselves, perhaps because of such conditions as those depicted in 5:3 and Chapter 13. Likewise, "those who came to us from the surrounding nations" would be poor and would have no means of supporting themselves. It is more difficult to understand, however, why Nehemiah would also serve free meals to the officials.

The amount of food Nehemiah says it took to feed these people is enormous! Just how many persons Nehemiah fed each day is impossible to say, but one estimate is that this amount of food would feed six hundred to eight hundred persons. "In spite of all this, I never demanded the food allotted to the governor," says Nehemiah. And the reason he does not is because the servitude was heavy upon the people.

Nehemiah 5:19. Then, sure in his own heart that he deserves a reward for all this, he prays, "Remember me with favor, O my God, for all I have done for these people."

EZRA, NEHEMIAH, AND ESTHER

DIMENSION THREE: WHAT DOES THE BIBLE MEAN TO ME?

Nehemiah 4:4-5—For What Should We Pray?

Nehemiah is not the only one in the Old Testament who prays imprecatory prayers. (An imprecatory prayer is one designed to bring a curse upon, or hurt to, the one being prayed about.) See, for example, Jeremiah's prayer in Jeremiah 18:19-23. See also the cry of the psalmist in Psalm 137:7-9. Nor is this attitude unknown in the New Testament. When the Samaritans would not receive Jesus, James and John wanted to know, "Lord, do you want us to call fire down from heaven to destroy them?" (Luke 9:51-56). Such an attitude is very common and very understandable. It seems to be a natural instinct to want to get revenge when someone has harmed us or humiliated us.

But the question raised in the student book is, Is such a prayer fit for a Christian? We may feel that way sometimes, but is it appropriate to pray that way? If we feel that way, and do not pray that way, are we being honest in our prayers?

Consider another fact. You and I have two thousand years of Christian heritage behind us. We have been taught from our earliest days to love our enemies, to turn the other cheek, to go the extra mile (Matthew 5:38-44). Yet we still feel the bitterness of resentment when we are wronged. Nehemiah lived four centuries before Jesus did. Shall we, then, condemn him? "I won't say capital punishment is right," said a friend of mine, "but when you have a thirteen-year-old brother die at the hands of muggers, you can understand why people feel that way." Then he added, "Don't condemn those who believe in capital punishment till you have experienced that." Is Nehemiah's prayer appropriate or isn't it? Why?

Also, Nehemiah was so sure that he was doing the will of God that anyone who opposed him was by that very act opposing God! "They have provoked *you* to anger before," he says (See note for 4:5, italics added). In that same spirit the writer of Psalm 139 is sure that God will be pleased because "Do I not hate those that hate you, O LORD? . . . I have nothing but hatred for them" (verses 21-22). What persons or groups take this attitude today? What are the dangers in this attitude?

Have the class consider the above questions and all the questions in the student book. Is this prayer by Nehemiah an appropriate model for the Christian of today? Why or why not?

Nehemiah 5:7-8—Love Your Neighbor

When Jesus said the second greatest commandment is, "You shall love your neighbor as yourself" (Matthew 22:39; and Mark 12:31), he was quoting from Leviticus 19:18. In Leviticus, the term *neighbor* refers only to fellow Jews. Jesus expands the word to include anyone who needs assistance (Luke 29:37).

What implications does Jesus' new definition of *neighbor* have for Nehemiah's concern that the Jews not exact interest from their fellow Jews (their neighbors)? Is it wrong for banks to charge interest on personal loans? Why or why not? Is it wrong for an individual person to charge interest on a loan? Why or why not?

Nehemiah 5:12—Taking Oaths

Have class members discuss the student book questions. Here are some additional questions to consider. Does it strike you as odd that in a court of law one is asked to take an oath by placing a hand on the book that says, "Do not swear at all" (Matthew 5:34)? Should Christians take such oaths? Why or why not?

Close today's session by having class members share new insights on Nehemiah 3–5.

7

The Census

Nehemiah 6–7

DIMENSION ONE:
WHAT DOES THE BIBLE SAY?

Answer these questions by reading Nehemiah 6

1. What do Sanballat and Geshem do when they hear Nehemiah is completing the wall? (6:1-2)

   They send word to Nehemiah to meet them on the plain of Ono.

2. Why does Nehemiah refuse to go? (6:2-3)

   Nehemiah refuses to go because he knows they intend to harm him.

3. Of what does Sanballat accuse Nehemiah? (6:5-7)

   Sanballat accuses Nehemiah of planning a rebellion, of wanting to become king of Judah, and of appointing prophets to proclaim that he is king.

4. What does Sanballat threaten to do? (6:7)

   Sanballat threatens to tell the king that Nehemiah wants to have himself proclaimed king of Judah.

5. Why does Sanballat send this letter? (6:9)

   Sanballat sends the letter to frighten the Jews so they will not complete the wall.

6. How does Nehemiah reply to Sanballat? (6:8)

   Nehemiah replies that there is no truth to Sanballat's accusations.

7. What does Shemaiah tell Nehemiah to do? (6:10)

   Shemaiah tells Nehemiah that they should go to the Temple and lock themselves in because Nehemiah's life is in danger.

8. Why doesn't Nehemiah follow Shemaiah's suggestion? (6:11-13)

   Nehemiah does not follow Shemaiah's suggestion because he will not flee to the Temple to save his life, and he knows that Shemaiah has been hired by Tobiah and Sanballat to intimidate him.

9. What prayer does Nehemiah then pray? (6:14)

   Nehemiah prays that God will remember the evil things that Tobiah, Sanballat, Noadiah, and the others have done to him.

10. How long does it take to complete the wall? (6:15)

    It takes fifty-two days to complete the wall.

11. What do the enemies of Judah do when the wall is finished? (6:16)

    They are afraid, and loose their self-confidence.

12. Why are some persons in Judah bound by oath to Tobiah? (6:18)

    Some in Judah are bound to Tobiah because both he and his son are married to daughters of the men of Judah.

Answer these questions by reading Nehemiah 7

13. Who does Nehemiah put in charge of Jerusalem? (7:2)

    Nehemiah puts Hanani and Hananiah in charge of Jerusalem.

14. How does Nehemiah protect Jerusalem? (7:3)

    Nehemiah orders that the gates be kept shut and barred until late in the mornings and that guards stand watch.

15. Why does Nehemiah decide to take a census of the people? (7:5)

    God puts it into Nehemiah's heart to take a census.

16. How many people are in the whole assembly? (7:66)

The whole assembly numbers 42,360 plus servants.

DIMENSION TWO:
WHAT DOES THE BIBLE MEAN?

Chapter 6 resumes the story of Chapter 4. Some lapse of time is evident, however, since Chapter 4 ends with the men sleeping with their clothes on in order to be ready either to go to work or to go to battle. Chapter 6 begins with the wall completed except for putting the doors in the gates.

Nehemiah 6:1. The rest of the Jews' enemies would be those listed in 4:7. The words *up to that time* show that the account is written sometime after the events being described. Notice that here we are told that the doors were not yet in the wall, but Chapter 3 indicates that the doors were rebuilt and put in their places simultaneously with the repairing of the wall.

Nehemiah 6:2. The Hebrew text does not say "let us meet together in one of the villages on the plain of Ono." It says, "Let us meet together in Hakkephirim in the plain of Ono." *Hakkephirim* may be the name of a village. If not, we do not know the meaning of the word.

Nehemiah 6:5. What is meant by an "unsealed letter" is not clear. Perhaps the letter was written on a clay tablet, and there was no cover over it. That may be true, but it is difficult to know why that should receive special mention. An unsealed letter may have had significance that was understood then, but is lost to us today.

Nehemiah 6:6. Jerusalem already had a reputation as a city that had risen up against kings in the past (Ezra 4:19). Artaxerxes would surely not allow a situation to develop that might lead to that again.

Some four centuries later, when Pilate was trying to decide "what shall I do then with the one you call the king of the Jews" (Mark 15:12), the words that convinced him that he had no choice but to hand Jesus over to be crucified were these: "If you let this man go, you are no friend of Caesar. Anyone who claims to be a king opposes Caesar" (John 19:12-16). Kings get upset when one of their subjects proclaims himself king!

Nehemiah 6:7-8. Sanballat possibly was not lying when he said, "It is reported . . . that you and the Jews are plotting to revolt . . . and you are about to become their king and you have even appointed prophets to make this proclamation . . . 'There is a king in Judah!' " Ahijah the prophet was behind the revolt of Jeroboam (1 Kings 11:29-31). Elisha instigated the rebellion of Jehu (2 Kings 9:1-13).

Both Haggai and Zechariah had said Zerubbabel would sit on Judah's throne.

In Haggai 2:20-23, Haggai speaks of Zerubbabel as "like a signet ring" for God. A signet ring bore the seal of the king, and that seal guaranteed the authenticity of any document coming from the royal house. Zerubbabel was to be God's signet ring. He was to be the guarantee that God was behind it when the kingdoms of the nations were overthrown.

Zechariah 6:12-13 proclaims that the Branch shall "sit and rule on his throne." *Branch* is a Messianic term. That Zerubbabel is meant here can be seen by comparing this verse with 4:9. Zerubbabel was the one who began building the Temple and he, says Zechariah, "shall also complete it." Joshua, the high priest (6:11), will not rule, but will be the priest by his throne.

Quite possibly the hopes of the Jewish people had risen to that pitch again. The suspicions of the nations had probably been aroused anyway. Nehemiah himself, however, had no such designs. He was doing the job he had been sent to do, nothing more (2:5-6). He denies the charges emphatically.

Nehemiah 6:9. When a person's hands "get too weak for the work" that person has become discouraged and demoralized to the point of being unable to function efficiently. When a person's hands are "strengthened" that person has a new spirit of determination to get the work done. Sanballat tries to bring about the former; Nehemiah prays for the latter.

We have become accustomed to Nehemiah's short prayers at critical moments along the way. We are not surprised, then, to find another one at this point. Perhaps, however, what we have here is not a prayer at all. Both the Septuagint and the Vulgate read, "And now I strengthened my hands." If the two versions are correct, the meaning is that Nehemiah determines to finished the task with new vigor.

Nehemiah 6:10. Shemaiah is the grandson of Mehetabel. The only other Mehetabel we find in the Old Testament is the wife of Hadar, an Edomite king (Genesis 36:31, 39; 1 Chronicles 1:43, 50).

What does it mean to say "Shemaiah . . . was shut in"? Various meanings have been suggested. Perhaps he was confined to his house because of some cultic or physical impurity. Perhaps he was pretending to be a hunted man as Nehemiah was, and so had to stay home. Perhaps he was symbolically confining himself in order to dramatize his words. All of these suggestions, and others, have been made. But we really do not now why Shemaiah was shut in.

Perhaps when Shemaiah tells Nehemiah that his enemies are coming to kill him at night, Shemaiah means this night. Shemaiah would have to get Nehemiah to the Temple on a specific night if Tobiah and Sanballat were to be able to carry out their evil intentions against him.

Nehemiah 6:11. You will remember from our discussion of 1:11 that Nehemiah was probably a eunuch. If this is true, then here is another reason why Nehemiah could not meet with Shemaiah within the Temple. Eunuchs were not allowed near the altar (Leviticus 21:16-24).

Nehemiah 6:12-13. Where the NIV says, "And I realized that God had not sent him," the Hebrew text says, "And I understood . . . that a not-God had sent him." This is a strong condemnation and emphasizes the contrast between a divine commission and a human one.

Nehemiah 6:14. Noadiah is mentioned only here. What she did to, for, or against Nehemiah is not recorded. The name appears in Ezra 8:33 as a masculine name. Significantly, perhaps, Noadiah is called a prophet rather than a prophetess in the Septuagint. Prophetesses were not unknown in Israel (Judges 4:4; 2 Kings 22:14), but they were rare.

One ancient manuscript has a variant reading here. Instead of "who have been trying to intimidate me," this text has "who were giving me warning." That reading transforms Noadiah and the rest of the prophets into those who were helping Nehemiah, in contrast to Tobiah and Sanballat who were seeking to harm him.

Nehemiah 6:15. The month of Elul is mentioned in the Bible only here. It is the sixth month, and corresponds to our August-September.

How could such a long wall have been finished in only fifty-two days? Josephus says in *Antiquities of the Jews* that it took two years and four months, and many are inclined to accept Josephus's report as being more accurate. Several considerations, however, make the time of fifty-two days more plausible. First, Nehemiah had his people well organized so that each could work at full potential all the time. Second, Nehemiah instilled into the people a sense of urgency. So they were willing to work long hours and at great personal sacrifice. Third, the harassment of Sanballat and Tobiah made the people all the more determined to finish. And finally, there undoubtedly were large portions of the wall that needed only minor repair. That would explain why some people had such a long portion of the wall to repair (3:13) while others had but a short piece (3:21).

Nehemiah 6:16. The meaning of the NIV text is clear, but there are other possibilities. The NRSV reads, "And when all our enemies heard of it, all the nations around us were afraid and fell greatly in their own esteem." According to that reading, the nations felt inferior to Judah. The Hebrew text, however, is ambiguous at this point. "Then they fell much in their eyes," it says. *They* could refer to *our enemies.* And if so, it was Sanballat and Tobiah who "fell much in their eyes." The Jews were able to build the wall in spite of everything Sanballat and Tobiah could do. And as a result, these two men lost prestige among the nations,

or "fell much in their eyes." Many believe this to be the intended meaning of the text.

Notice that it is not only Nehemiah and the Jews, but also the other nations, who recognize that "this work had been done with the help of our God."

Nehemiah 6:17-18. Tobiah had married into one of the families of Judah, and apparently it was a family of no small stature and influence. As a result, many of the nobles of Judah carried on an extensive correspondence with him. The Shecaniah whose daughter Tobiah married may be the Shecaniah whose son helped build the wall (3:29), but we cannot be sure. Shecaniah's father, Arah, is undoubtedly the Arah mentioned in Ezra 2:5 and Nehemiah 7:10.

Not only had Tobiah married into a Jewish family; so had his son, Jehohanan. Jehohanan had married the daughter of Meshullam. This is the same Meshullam who had worked on the wall (Nehemiah 3:4, 30).

Nehemiah 6:19. "They kept reporting to me his [Tobiah's] good deeds," says Nehemiah. Tobiah's name means *goodness of the Lord.* Nehemiah is here making a play on words. They spoke of the good deeds of (the) goodness of the Lord! How ironic that Tobiah should be named *goodness of the Lord*! How wearisome to have persons constantly speaking of his good deeds!

We have come now to the end of the interference of Sanballat and Tobiah. We hear nothing more of them until we get to Chapter 13. (The Tobiah of 7:62 is a different man.)

Nehemiah 7:1. The mention of the singers and the Levites sounds strange here. Usually the gatekeepers, the singers, and the Levites are listed together when we are talking about the gatekeepers of the Temple (verses 43-45). But here the Bible is speaking of the gatekeepers of the city gates. We cannot help but wonder if someone, seeing the gatekeepers mentioned, did not add the singers and the Levites out of a misunderstanding.

Nehemiah 7:2. There has been much speculation that perhaps *Hanani* is a nickname for *Hananiah*, and that Nehemiah turned over charge of the city to one man rather than two. The singular "he" and "man" in the rest of the verse would lend credence to that view.

God-fearing people are those to whom the holiness and righteousness of God is so real that they would not dare to live contrary to God's laws.

Nehemiah 7:3. The Hebrew text does not say, ". . . while they are still on duty." It says, "while they are still standing." To whom does the word *they* refer? The NIV appears to be correct in assuming that the gatekeepers are meant.

The words *some at their posts* imply that assignments were made by hours and by place. Apparently Nehemiah is just as meticulous and methodical about this as he had been about building the wall.

Nehemiah 7:4. Beginning with this verse (or perhaps with 7:73) we leave behind the first portion of the memoirs of Nehemiah, those portions of the book written by Nehemiah himself. We are told here that "the houses had not yet been built," yet in verse 3 we are told that the some guards stood "near their own houses." One or the other seems to be in error.

Nehemiah 7:5. The concern over the small number of people living in Jerusalem seems to have been the matter that was weighing on Nehemiah's heart when God told him to assemble the people to be enrolled by genealogy. Nehemiah needed to populate his capital city. Many of the people who had come back from Babylonia had settled in Jerusalem. We have plenty of space here, he could say to them (verse 4), and our gates are tightly secured (verse 3). The census seems to have been the first step in determining who the people were, and where they were now living.

The words *who had been the first to return* seem to imply that this list was only of those who came to Judah in that first group led by Sheshbazzar. (See the section on Ezra 1:8, page 386.) The words can be translated, however, as *previously.* In that case, we may assume that the list is composed of those who returned to Judah at various times.

The return seems to have taken place in at least four stages: a group led by Sheshbazzar came when Cyrus was king (538 B.C.); a group led by Zerubbabel came when Darius I was king (520 B.C.); a group led by Nehemiah came when Artaxerxes I was king (445 B.C.); a group led by Ezra came when Artaxerxes II was king (397 B.C.).

Nehemiah 7:70-72. As indicated in the student book, Nehemiah 7:6-73 is virtually identical to Ezra 2:1-70.

Ezra 2:68-69 says the people "gave freewill offerings toward the rebuilding of the house of God on its site." That was the project dearest to Ezra's heart. Nehemiah 7:70-72 says the people "gave to the treasury for the work." The term *work* is used consistently in Nehemiah's book, both as a noun and as a verb, to refer to the building of the wall, the work dearest to Nehemiah's heart. The only exceptions to this are Nehemiah 10:33; 11:12; and 13:10, where the term is used of the priestly functions in the Temple.

DIMENSION THREE: WHAT DOES THE BIBLE MEAN TO ME?

Nehemiah 6:3—When Is a Lie Not a Lie?

Does a good tree bear bad fruit? Or a bad tree bear good fruit? No, according to Jesus, it does not. The good person produces good, and the evil person produces evil, "for out of the overflow of the heart his mouth speaks" (Luke 6:43-45; Matthew 7:15-20). Does that statement mean that the good person never speaks an untruth?

A basic and elemental truth seems to be that goodness is best served when we use good and honorable methods to achieve it. Yet, are there circumstances where telling the truth would be hurting the cause of goodness? How does one decide when it is legitimate to "fudge" a little on the truth? Or is that never acceptable for the Christian? Are you willing to allow someone else to decide that for you? Or does each person decide it for himself or herself? Or has Jesus already decided it for all of us? If so, what did he decide? And how do you know that is what he decided? And how do you respond to those who also are followers of Christ, but who understand Jesus' teachings differently?

Nehemiah 7:2—Leadership Qualities

Notice that the men Nehemiah selected were men "of integrity and feared God more than *most* men do (italics added). Does that mean there were others who had greater integrity and feared God more than those he chose? And if so, were these not the only two qualities he was looking for? Are there some people who have integrity and fear God but who would not make good leaders? Who are they? Which is more important in a leader—to have integrity and fear God or to have unmistakable qualities of leadership? What kind of a person would be your ideal leader?

Close the session by asking class members to share new insights they have gained from their study of Nehemiah 6–7. If time allows, list these insights on a chalkboard or a large piece of paper.

— 8 —

The Book of the Law

Nehemiah 8–10

DIMENSION ONE:
WHAT DOES THE BIBLE SAY?

Answer these questions by reading Nehemiah 8

1. Where do the people gather? (8:1)

   The people gather at the Water Gate.

2. What does Ezra read to the people? (8:1, 3)

   Ezra reads the Book of the Law of Moses.

3. How do Jeshua and the others help the people? (8:7)

   Jeshua and the others help the people understand the law.

4. What do the people do when they hear the words of the law? (8:9)

   The people weep as they listen to words of the law.

5. Why do the Levites calm the people? (8:11)

   The Levites calm the people because this day is sacred.

6. What do the people discover God has commanded them to do during the feast of the seventh month? (8:13-14)

   They discover God has commanded that they live in booths during the feast of the seventh month.

7. What do the people do then? (8:15-16)

   The people gather branches and make booths for themselves.

8. How long do the people keep the feast? (8:18)

   The people keep the feast for seven days.

Answer these questions by reading Nehemiah 9

9. What do the people do on the twenty-fourth day of the month? (9:1-2)

   The people separate themselves from all foreigners and confess their sins.

10. In his prayer, what does Ezra say their forefathers did? (9:16)

    Their forefathers became arrogant and refused to obey God.

11. How does Ezra say God responded to the disobedience of the forefathers? (9:17, 20)

    God was gracious and compassionate and did not desert them.

12. How does Ezra say the people responded to these new acts of grace on God's part? (9:26)

    The people remained disobedient and rebellious.

13. What does Ezra say God did then? (9:27)

    God handed them over to their enemies, but rescued them when the people cried out.

14. What does Ezra say God finally did? (9:30)

    God finally handed the people over to the neighboring peoples.

15. Does Ezra believe God has been just? (9:33)

    Yes, Ezra believes God has been just in dealing with the people.

16. What does Ezra say is the plight of the Israelites today? (9:36-37)

    Ezra says the Israelites are slaves in the land God gave them to enjoy, and the harvest goes to the king because of the sins of the people.

17. What do the people do now, and what do the leaders, Levites, and priests do? (9:38)

The people make a binding agreement, and the leaders, Levites, and priests affix their seals to it.

Answer these questions by reading Nehemiah 10

18. What do the people pledge to do? (10:29)

The people pledge to follow the law of God and to keep all God's commands.

19. What laws do the people pledge to keep? (10:30-31)

The people pledge not to intermarry with the neighboring peoples, not to buy merchandise or grain on the sabbath or other holy days, and to forgo working the land and cancel debts in the seventh year.

20. How do the people pledge to support the work of the Temple? (10:32-37)

The people pledge to give a third of a shekel annually, and to bring in the wood offering, the firstfruits, the firstborn, and the tithes.

21. Where are these offerings to be taken and kept? (10:38-39)

These offerings are to be taken to the priests and Levites, and stored in the storehouse.

DIMENSION TWO: WHAT DOES THE BIBLE MEAN?

As we begin Chapter 8, we might well wonder if we are still in the Book of Nehemiah. We have been reading about Nehemiah, the wall, and opposition from Sanballat and others. Now, all of a sudden, we are back to the story of Ezra. What has happened?

Two solutions may be offered. Verse 9 gives one of them. According to that verse, Nehemiah was there with Ezra. Yet as we saw in Lesson 4, Ezra and Nehemiah were probably not contemporaries. Nehemiah came to Jerusalem in 445 B.C., Ezra in 397. The statement in verse 9, "Nehemiah, the governor," therefore, is considered to be a later addition to the text.

The other solution is to recognize that this portion of the Ezra story has been transposed from its original place (probably immediately after Ezra 8) to where it now stands. Scholars do not agree as to why this transposition took place, but that it took place is almost universally accepted.

Nehemiah 7:73. The seventh month is sacred. The Feast of Tabernacles (booths) (Leviticus 23:33-43) takes place in the seventh month, as well as it being a month of rest and atonement (Leviticus 16:29-30; 23:23-32; 25:9). Four holy convocations are also held in the seventh month. (See Numbers 29:1-39, especially verses 1, 7, 12, 35.) The ark of the covenant also was taken to the Temple in the seventh month (2 Chronicles 5:1-7). And now, once again, the seventh month is selected for a solemn gathering of the people.

If the events of Chapter 8 follow immediately after the events of Ezra 8, as seems probable, this assembly took place only two months after Ezra's arrival in Jerusalem (Ezra 7:7-10). The reason Ezra came to Jerusalem was "the study and observance of the Law . . . and to teaching" it to others (Ezra 7:10).

Nehemiah 8:1. All the people of Israel gather before the Water Gate. The Water Gate is located on the eastern side of the wall close to the Gihon Spring. A large open area is there that often is used for large gatherings.

Ezra is usually referred to as "the priest, the scribe" (Ezra 7:11, 12, 21; Nehemiah 8:9). Here he is called only "the scribe," perhaps because the function he will now perform, reading the Law, is a scribal task, and not a priestly one. However, in verse 2 he is called "Ezra the priest."

The people seem to know that Ezra has the Book of the Law of Moses, and that he will read it to them. This book was the law of God that Ezra had brought from Persia (Ezra 7:14). It undoubtedly was a portion of the Torah or Pentateuch, the first five books of the Bible.

Nehemiah 8:3. Ezra reads aloud to the people from early morning until noon. Ezra probably had some help in reading from the Law (verses 7-8). And surely it must have been welcomed help! From early morning until noon is a long time for one person to read aloud.

Notice that here (verse 3) Ezra "read it [the book] aloud," yet it is not until verse 5 that we read that Ezra "opened the book." The author is probably stating in verse 3 that Ezra read, and in verses 5 and 6 is giving a more detailed and dramatic description. Or these verses could be two accounts of the same event.

Nehemiah 8:4. Thirteen seems to be an odd number of men to stand with Ezra as he reads. Having seven on each side of him has symbolic value, since the Jews regarded seven as the perfect number. Having six on each side, for each of the twelve tribes of Israel, would also be symbolic. But six on one side and seven on the other seems strange. Perhaps the name Meshullam should not be included. Meshullam is the last one mentioned on Ezra's left, and the Hebrew name *Meshullam* means "on his left."

Nehemiah 8:8. Ezra probably read from the Hebrew, and the Levites translate the Hebrew into Aramaic, the language of his people. Later in the life of the Hebrew people

THE BOOK OF THE LAW

this practice became a weekly event. The Torah was read in Hebrew in the synagogue, and translated into Aramaic for the understanding of the people. The later rabbis looked back upon the event described here in Nehemiah 8:8 as the beginning of that practice.

Nehemiah 8:9. The words, *then Nehemiah the governor,* should be omitted here. The words, *and the Levites who were instructing the people,* also probably should be omitted, since the verb *said* is singular in the Hebrew.

This day is holy to the Lord because the first day of the seventh month is the day of the Feast of Trumpets (Leviticus 23:23-25). No trumpets are blown, no burnt offerings are made, and none of the other requirements of the day are met. So this cannot be a celebration of the Feast of Trumpets. What makes this day holy to the Lord is that on this day the law of God is read (8:8).

Nehemiah 8:10. Choice food is the NIV's rendering of Hebrew word *fat,* meaning the fattest meat. Sweet drink could be any sweet drink, but the Vulgate reads, "wine mixed with honey."

Nehemiah 8:13-15. On the second day only the leaders of the people meet. They are the ones who need to be the real experts in the details of the Law.

In Leviticus 23:40, "palm fronds, leafy branches and poplars" are mentioned as the materials out of which the booths are to be made. Poplars are not mentioned here, but palm and other shade trees are, along with olive, wild olive, and myrtle. Why the lists differ is not clear. Perhaps this passage reflects the practice current in the day it was written.

Nehemiah 8:16. The people build booths on flat roofs. At that time, the roof often served as a place to entertain guests or sleep when the night was pleasant.

Nehemiah 8:18. For many scholars the story of Ezra ends here. The only reference to Ezra in Nehemiah 9–10 is in 9:6, and there only in the Greek text, not in the Hebrew. But other scholars believe Nehemiah 8–10 rightfully belongs between Ezra 8 and Ezra 9.

Nehemiah 9:1-38. The sudden and strange shift in the mood of the people has caused many to believe that Chapter 9 is out of place. Some want to put it after Chapter 10 of Ezra, since both of these chapters deal with putting away foreign wives. Others would leave Chapter 9 where it is, but move Chapter 8 to the end of the book. Each of these solutions shows the confused state of the text of Ezra and Nehemiah.

Nehemiah 9:1. As the text now stands, "the same month" refers to "the seventh month" (8:2). If the people began the celebration of the Feast of Tabernacles (booths) on the fifteenth of the month as the Law requires, and kept the feast for seven days (8:18), then the feast ended at the close of the twenty-first day. The next day, the twenty-second day of the seventh month, the people held a solemn assembly (8:18). Apparently they had no assembly on the twenty-third day, but were called to assemble again on the twenty-fourth.

If, on the other hand, Chapter 9 belongs after Ezra 10, as many believe, then "this month" refers to the first month. In that case, the sequence of events would be as follows: first, assembling at Jerusalem on the twentieth day of the ninth month (Ezra 10:9); second, examining individual cases, beginning on the first day of the tenth month (Ezra 10:16); third, completing the examination on the first day of the first month (Ezra 10:17); fourth, the assembly described on the twenty-fourth day.

Nehemiah 9:3. Grammatically, *they* has Israelites as its antecedent. Probably, however, *they* refers to the Levites of verse 4.

"A quarter of the day" is three hours according to Jewish reckoning. The assembly, therefore, lasted six hours, probably from 6:00 A.M. until noon.

Nehemiah 9:4. Perhaps the stairs leading to the platform Ezra spoke on are what is referred to here. This would lend strong support to the view that this platform was not built just for this occasion, but was a frequently used old platform with a special set of stairs for the Levites. (See the student book for the section on 8:4.)

Nehemiah 9:5. Eight Levites are named, but only five of them are the same as those named in verse 4! Surely, however, these are the same men.

Nehemiah 9:6. As is pointed out in the student book, Ezra's name does not appear in the Hebrew text. However, the words *and Ezra said* appear in the Septuagint, the Greek translation of the Old Testament made in the third century B.C. Obviously the prayer is by someone, and the Septuagint attributed the prayer to Ezra. That seems unlikely, however, for during the period of Persian domination the people did not live in the way described in 9:36-37. The Israelites were not slaves under the Persians.

The Persian kings had freed them from captivity and allowed them to return to their homeland. The Israelite attitude toward Persia was one of gratitude, not hostility. Ezra would be grateful toward the Persian government (Ezra 7:6, 11-27). The situation described in Nehemiah 9:36-37 sounds more like the Greek period of Israel's life (after the time of Ezra). The Greek rulers demanded the rich yield of the land, and caused the people distress.

Nehemiah 9:8. The covenant referred to is found in Genesis 15:18-21. However, the nations listed here do not coincide with the nations listed there. Nehemiah's list is closer to the lists in Exodus 3:17, 23:23; and Joshua 24:11.

Nehemiah 9:11-13. Three times in three short verses the author of Nehemiah changes the theology of the story he is relating. Exodus 15:5 says, "They sank to the depths like a stone." Our author gives God a more active role: "You hurled their pursuers into the depths, like a stone" (verse 11). Exodus 13:21 says, "The LORD went ahead of them in a pillar of cloud." Our author says God led them, not in a pillar of cloud, but "with a pillar of cloud" (verse 12). Here God is external to the cloud. In Exodus 19:20-21, God descends to the top of Mount Sinai, calls Moses, and speaks to him there. In Nehemiah God descends to Mount Sinai, but speaks to the people "from *heaven*" (italics added) (verse 13). We are witnessing the development of Jewish theology.

Nehemiah 9:14. The special mention of the sabbath among the Ten Commandments reflects the concerns of the day (13:15-22). This emphasis on the sabbath continues until Jesus' day (Luke 13:14).

Nehemiah 9:16-17. The term *stiff-necked* was used when an ox decided not to go in the same direction as the plowman. The ox stiffens his neck to resist the pull of reins. The term came to be used for any rebellious or stubborn person and is applied frequently to the Israelite people (Jeremiah 7:26; 17:23; 19:15; Nehemiah 9:29).

The story in the Book of Numbers does not say the people actually appointed a leader to take them back to Egypt. It simply says the idea was discussed among them (Numbers 14:4).

Nehemiah 9:21. During the forty years of wandering, the Israelites' clothes did not wear out and their feet did not swell (Deuteronomy 8:4). The rabbis also had an answer for what happened to the children's clothes, though it is not found in the Bible. The clothes of the children grew with their bodies, "like the shell of a snail."

Nehemiah 9:22. The victory over Sihon, king of Heshbon, is described in Numbers 21:21-26; the defeat of Og, king of Bashan, is related in Numbers 21:33-35. These battles were long remembered and celebrated because the Israelites had fought against great odds.

The Hebrew text says God divided the people "according to a corner." The meaning of that phrase is not clear. The NIV translation, "allotting to them even the remotest frontiers" attempts to make some sense from the context. Presumably, what is meant is that God determined the boundaries for all the kingdoms.

Nehemiah 9:25. Notice the similarity between this verse and Deuteronomy 6:11. Notice, too that "fruit trees in abundance" remained in the land. The deuteronomic law expressly forbids destroying fruit trees when warring against a land (Deuteronomy 20:19-20).

Nehemiah 9:26. To "put your law behind their backs" is, as we would say, to turn their backs on the Law.

Killing prophets is an especially heinous crime, since the prophets were chosen by God to bring the people to repentance. This crime is despised by God's faithful and referred to often in the Bible (1 Kings 19:10; Matthew 5:12; Revelation 16:6.)

Nehemiah 9:27-28. The *deliverers* God sends are called *judges* in the Book of Judges. God has to send many deliverers because the people kept sinning.

Nehemiah 9:29. God warned the people through the prophets. Notice that here God warns them "to return to your [God's] law," whereas in verse 26 it was "to turn them back to you [God]." The distinction may seem slight, but the earlier verse sounds more like the God of the New Testament. (See 2 Corinthians 5:19, for example, where Paul says that in Christ God was reconciling the world to God, not to the law.)

Nehemiah 9:30-31. God speaks through the prophets. (See Zechariah 7:12 and 2 Peter 1:21 for similar statements.) But when the people keep refusing to obey, God gives them to the "neighboring peoples." The author must mean the Babylonians, for that was Judah's ultimate punishment.

Nehemiah 9:34. Even kings, leaders, and priests have disobeyed God. Many of the prophets could be added to this list (Micah 3:5-7).

Nehemiah 9:35-37. As indicated earlier (see the section of 9:6) the situation described here sounds more like the Greek period than the Persian. The Greeks made virtual slaves of the Jews, and had power over them. (See 1 Maccabees 1:33-50 in the Apocrypha.) If this prayer does come from the Greek period, then it could not have been prayed by Ezra.

Nehemiah 9:38. In the Hebrew text this verse appears as the first verse of Chapter 10. We do not know exactly what this verse means. The Hebrew text says nothing of making a binding agreement. It says "we are cutting support." Furthermore, there is no verb in the Hebrew to say what the leaders, Levites, and priests do. "Affixing their seals to it" is simply an impossible reading. The verse serves as a bridge between 9:37 and 10:1, and doubtless this was its original intention.

Nehemiah 10:1-39. This chapter is probably out of place. The editor of Nehemiah saw the chapter as concluding the events of 9:1-37, and wrote 9:38 to bridge the two. But Chapter 10 has little or nothing to do with Chapter 9. Possibly Chapter 10 is the conclusion to Chapter 8. Most Old Testament interpreters, however, believe Chapter 10 should follow Chapter 13. Both 10:30 and 13:23-27 deal with not marrying foreign women. Both 10:31 and 13:15-22 deal with not buying or selling on the sabbath. Both 10:35-37 and 13:31 deal with offering the firstfruits; 10:37-29 and 13:12 deal with paying the tithes. Sealing the agreement not to do all these things would logically come after the reform measures taken by Nehemiah in Chapter 13.

Nehemiah 10:2. The name of Eliashib, the high priest, is missing (Nehemiah 3:1; 13:28).

Nehemiah 10:28-29. "The rest of the people" are those who did not sign the covenant. This group, of course, made up most of the people, since only the leaders signed it. The very small children are excluded from entering an oath, because only those who can understand it are required to do so. To enter into a curse is to call for God's judgment if you fail to live up to your oath. The leaders apparently took such an oath earlier.

Nehemiah 10:32. When the Jews first returned from exile, the Persian government supplied them with money to take care of their Temple needs (Ezra 6:3-4, 7:15-24). But now it was time for the people to take over this responsibility.

Exodus 30:13 commands that the Temple tax shall be half a shekel. In Jesus' day, the Temple tax is referred to as the *two-drachma tax* (Matthew 17:24-27) which is the Greek equivalent. By the time the Gospel of Matthew was written, the Jewish Temple no longer stood, but the Roman government continued to collect the tax. In all these cases, both before Nehemiah's time and after, the Temple tax is half a shekel.

Some believe Nehemiah began the Temple tax, and that a third of a shekel was the original amount. Later the amount was raised and not until after the tax was raised was the command to pay the tax put into the law. That is why only the Nehemiah passage refers to a third of a shekel.

Another possibility is that long before Nehemiah's day the law specified half a shekel. But now the Jews had to use the Persian monetary system, and according to that system "a third of a shekel" was equivalent to the former half a shekel.

Nehemiah 10:33. The "bread set on the table" is literally *the bread of the row.* It is called this because of the command in Leviticus 24:5-6 that the bread be put in rows.

Nehemiah 10:34. The lots that are cast are the Urim and Thummim.

Nehemiah 10:39. Quite possibly the original words that concluded the Book of Nehemiah were "We will not neglect the house of our God." That would be true if Chapter 10 originally followed Chapter 13, as many believe. And what a fine ending to the book that would be!

DIMENSION THREE: WHAT DOES THE BIBLE MEAN TO ME?

Nehemiah 8:13-18
How Binding on Us Are the Bible's Commands?

Have the class members consider the issue as presented in the student book, and let them discuss the questions raised. Point out that there are many other commands in the Bible that we also ignore. Cite, for example, Deuteronomy 21:18-21 and Deuteronomy 25:5-6. Cite also the words of Jesus in Matthew 5:29-30 and Matthew 5:38-42. You might want to have someone in the class read these verses aloud. Should we keep these commands? Or are we correct in ignoring them or "spiritualizing" them? Why do you think so?

Nehemiah 9:29—Seek the Lord!

Most of what needs to be said here is contained in the student book. You might want to point out that the Pharisees of Jesus' day were experts in keeping God's law, but Jesus called people to himself (Matthew 11:28).

Nehemiah 9:31—What Is God Like?

Let the class members discuss the questions raised in the student book. Point out that some of the most beautiful passages on God's love found anywhere are found in the Old Testament. See Hosea 11:1-9, for example. See also Isaiah 40:11 and Psalm 103:1-5. The primary characteristic of the God of the Old Testament is love, which is shown in grace and mercy.

Close today's session by asking class members to share new insights they have gained on Nehemiah 8–10.

— *9* —

Nehemiah's Reforms

Nehemiah 11–13

DIMENSION ONE:
WHAT DOES THE BIBLE SAY?

Answer these questions by reading Nehemiah 11

1. How do the people decide who will live in Jerusalem? (11:1)

   The people cast lots to see who will live in Jerusalem.

2. How are the people who live in Jerusalem listed? (11:4, 7, 10, 15, 19, 21)

   The author lists the descendants of Judah and of Benjamin, the priests, the Levites, the gatekeepers, and the Temple servants.

3. In what two territories are the villages occupied by Jews located? (11:25, 31)

   The villages are located in the territories of Judah and Benjamin.

Answer these questions by reading Nehemiah 12

4. Who were the high priests from the days of the return from Babylon to this time? (12:10-11)

   The high priests from the return to Jerusalem to Nehemiah's day were Jeshua (Joshua), Joiakim, Eliashib, Joiada, Johanan, and Jaddua.

5. What celebration now takes place? (12:27)

   The dedication of the wall of Jerusalem now takes place.

6. What do the priests and Levites do before the dedication? (12:30)

   The priests and the Levites purify themselves, the people, the gates, and the wall.

7. How many large choirs does Nehemiah appoint to go in procession? (12:31)

   Nehemiah appoints two large choirs to go in procession.

8. In which direction do the two choirs go? (12:31, 38)

   One choir goes to the right and one choir goes to the left.

9. Where do the two choirs meet? (12:40)

   The two choirs meet in the house of God.

10. What takes place then? (12:43)

    The priests offer sacrifices and all the people rejoice.

11. For what job does Nehemiah appoint men on that day? (12:44)

    Nehemiah appoints men to place the tithes and contributions into storerooms for the priests and Levites.

Answer these questions by reading Nehemiah 13

12. What do the people discover as they read from the Book of Moses? (13:1)

    The people discover that no Ammonite or Moabite should enter the assembly of God.

13. What do the people do then? (13:3)

    The people separate from themselves all those of foreign descent.

14. What does Eliashib do for Tobiah? (13:4-5)

    Eliashib provides Tobiah a large room where the tithes had been kept.

15. What does Nehemiah do when he discovers this? (13:8-9)

Nehemiah throws all of Tobiah's furniture out of the room, gives orders to have the chamber purified, and brings back the equipment of the house of God.

16. Why does Nehemiah appoint treasurers? (13:10-11, 13)

Nehemiah appoints treasurers over the storehouses because the portions of the Levites had not been given to them.

17. What does Nehemiah do when he sees men working and selling their wares on the sabbath? (13:15, 17, 19)

Nehemiah warns the people, rebukes the nobles of Judah, has the doors shut at dusk, and sets up his servants to make sure no wares are brought into the city on the sabbath.

18. What command does Nehemiah give to the Levites? (13:22)

Nehemiah commands the Levites to purify themselves and guard the gates.

19. What does Nehemiah do to the Jews who had married women of Ashdod, Ammon, and Moab? (13:23-25)

Nehemiah rebukes them, curses them, beats them, pulls out their hair, and makes them take an oath not to intermarry with these people.

20. What summary of his reforms does Nehemiah give? (13:30-31)

Nehemiah summarizes his reforms as purifying the priests and Levites of everything foreign, assigning them duties, and providing for the wood offering and for the firstfruits.

DIMENSION TWO:
WHAT DOES THE BIBLE MEAN?

As we come to Chapter 11, we continue the story abandoned in Chapter 7. Most Old Testament interpreters think 11:1 connects directly with 7:73a, "And the rest of the Israelites, settled in their own towns." It seems more probable, however, that the genealogy of 7:56-71 is a later addition, and 11:1 connects directly to 7:5a, "So my God put it into my heart to assemble the nobles, the officials and the common people for registration by families."

Nehemiah 11:1-2. The leaders are undoubtedly the same as those listed elsewhere as the heads of the fathers' houses (7:70).

The lot was deemed sacred, and the determination made when the people cast lots was thought of as coming from God. Those selected by this method would feel a strong obligation to live in Jerusalem.

The men who willingly offer to live in Jerusalem probably take the place of some who otherwise would have to move there. The people bless those who spared them from having to go.

Nehemiah 11:3. "The provincial leaders" are probably the same persons as the leaders of the people in verse 1.

Nehemiah 11:4. It was the sons of Judah and Benjamin who were sent into exile in Babylonia, and it is they who now constitute the new Israel. One verse in the Old Testament (1 Kings 12:20) says that only the tribe of Judah remained loyal to the crown when civil war erupted at the death of Solomon. First Kings 12:17 says Rehoboam ruled over the cities of Judah, and does not mention the cities of Benjamin. And there are several places where "one tribe" is mentioned (1 Kings 11:32, 36).

The prevailing view in the Old Testament, however, is that Judah and Benjamin fought together, stayed together, went into exile together, and came back together to form the new nation (1 Kings 12:21-24; 2 Chronicle 11:1-12; Ezra 1:5; 4:1; 10:9; and here in Nehemiah 11:4). Perhaps the explanation is that at first only the tribe of Judah remained loyal to Rehoboam, but then Benjamin, too, gave allegiance to him.

Nehemiah 11:5. The Shelanites were descendants of Shelah, a son of Judah, the father of the tribe of Judah (Genesis 38:1-5). Athaiah of verse 4 also is a direct descendant of Judah, through Perez (Genesis 38:27-30).

Nehemiah 11:7. Since the meaning of verse 8 is not certain, Sallu is the only head of the sons of Benjamin we can identify with any assurance. His name appears in the Bible only here and in the corresponding list in 1 Chronicles 9:7. He is not listed among the Benjaminites in Genesis 46:21 or in 1 Chronicles 7:6-12.

Nehemiah 11:8. The meaning of this verse can only be guessed. The literal translation of the Hebrew reads, "and after him, Gabbai and Sallai, nine hundred twenty eight." The NIV assumes the number is followers of the two men named.

Nehemiah 11:9. The probable meaning is that Joel was the commander over the city, and Judah is over the second district of Jerusalem (Nehemiah 3:9, 12). Possibly, however, Judah was second in command

Nehemiah 11:11. This verse is exactly paralleled by 1 Chronicles 9:11 except that here Seraiah is the son of Hilkiah, while there Azariah is. In Ezra 7:1 Seraiah is the son of Azariah, who is the son of Hilkiah.

Seraiah (or perhaps Ahitub, though that is less likely) is "supervisor in the house of God," that is, high priest.

Nehemiah 11:12-13. "The work for the temple" refers to the priestly functions, not to physical labor.

Nehemiah 11:17. Mattaniah is a descendant of Asaph and therefore in charge of the songs of thanksgiving (Ezra 2:41; Nehemiah 12:8). Several of the psalms come from Asaph's hymnbook (see the titles to Psalm 50 and Psalms 73–83).

Nehemiah 11:19. Akkub and Talmon are the only gatekeepers listed here. First Chronicles 9:17 lists four, Akkub and Talmon being among them. In Ezra 2:42, six family names are mentioned, including Akkub and Talmon, as is true in Nehemiah 12:25.

Nehemiah 11:21. Ophel is the hill the original city of David stood on before the city was expanded by later kings. The word *Ophel* means "swelling or protuberance."

Nehemiah 11:23. What king is referred to here? Some believe King David is meant, since David is referred to in 12:24 as the one who originated the Temple ritual. But the reigning Persian monarch is the one referred to in the next verse. Persian kings often took an interest in Jewish religious matters, as we have seen from time to time in our study of Ezra and Nehemiah.

Nehemiah 11:24. The name *Pethahiah* is not a household word today, but he served an important function in his own day. He was an advocate for the Jews in the Persian court.

Nehemiah 11:25-36. The author now lists the towns other than Jerusalem where the sons of Judah and Benjamin live.

Nehemiah 11:26. This is the only place in the Bible where *Jeshua* is the name of a town. Some have wondered, therefore, if "in Jeshua" might not be a scribal addition to the text, indicating that all these towns are listed in the Book of Joshua (Jeshua and Joshua being the same name). Others, however, believe that the town that is called Shema in Joshua 15:26 was called Jeshua after the Jews returned from exile.

Nehemiah 11:30. The Valley of Hinnom was just south of Jerusalem, and served as the northern boundary of Judah (Joshua 15:8). Beersheba was the southernmost tip of Israel at her greatest expansion.

Nehemiah 12:1-26. These lists are apparently intended to supplement the lists given in Chapter 11. Jaddua is the last high priest mentioned in the Old Testament, and ruled during the time of Alexander the Great. These lists, then, are quite late. There is considerable evidence that the lists have been lengthened and modified from time to time. More than half of the names in the lists, for example, are missing in *Codex Vaticanus,* an important early fourth-century manuscript.

The list of priests (verses 1-7) should correspond with the lists in Ezra 2:36-39 and Nehemiah 7:39-42, since all of these are lists of the priests who came up with Zerubbabel and Jeshua. But this list is more than three times the length of the other two lists. The list of Levites (verses 8-9), too, should correspond to the lists in Ezra 2:40 and Nehemiah 7:43, but once again it is longer.

Nehemiah 12:8. This is the only place in the Bible where the name Judah is associated with "the Levites." Usually Judah is the name of a priest.

As in 11:17, Mattaniah is in charge of the songs of thanksgiving.

Nehemiah 12:9. Just what role Bakbukiah and Unni played in the service is not clear. Most commentators interpret this verse as referring to antiphonal singing. In 11:17, Bakbukiah is said to be the second among his associates, and we wonder if that has anything to do with his being opposite them in the service. In 12:25, he is named as one of the gatekeepers.

Nehemiah 12:10-11. These verses list a distinct group, the high priests. Unlike the other groups, there is no name of the group at the beginning of the list. Jeshua was the first high priest after the return from exile. The earliest date possible for him, therefore, is 538 B.C. A more probable beginning date for him is about 520. It is not known how long he served.

We do not know when Joiakim was high priest. The apocryphal books, Baruch and Judith, mention Jehoiakim and Joakim respectively as high priests during the Exile. But our Joiakim was high priest after the Exile. Joiakim is followed by Eliashib, who was high priest during the time of Nehemiah, about 445 B.C. We know nothing of Joiada except what we learn from Nehemiah 13:28, but that is enough to date him during the time of Nehemiah also.

"Jonathan" should read Johanan as in verse 22. Johanan was high priest in 410 B.C., as we know from extrabiblical sources, and was still high priest when Ezra came to Jerusalem in 398.

Of the dates of Jaddua we know nothing except that Josephus tells us Jaddua was a contemporary of Alexander the Great. Alexander died in 323.

Nehemiah 12:12-21. Here the author takes the list of priests in Jeshua's day (verses 1-7), and tells us who is the priest of each of those families in Joiakim's day. The two lists are basically the same, though the family of Hattush has dropped out, and there are several variations in spelling. The name Kallai in verse 20 appears only here in the Bible.

Nehemiah 12:22-23. Many believe these verses were not a part of the original text, but were inserted by a later hand.

The only use of the expression "Darius the Persian" that we have in the Old Testament is here. We find "Darius the Mede" in Daniel 5:31 and 11:1, and we are told that Darius was a Mede by birth in Daniel 9:1. There were three persons named Darius who served as king of Persia. It is not clear whether Darius II or Darius III is meant here.

Johanan is here called "the son of Eliashib." In verses 10-11, however, he is the grandson of Eliashib. Perhaps *son* should be read as *descendant.*

Nehemiah 12:24. Jeshua's name is usually first in a list of the chiefs of the Levites.

"Who stood opposite them" is the equivalent to verse 9. Once again the context makes the idea of antiphonal singing an appropriate interpretation.

The Chronicler believed it was David who had given the command about how Temple worship was to be carried out (1 Chronicles 25:1; 2 Chronicles 8:14). David is called "the man of God" here to emphasize that his authority in such matters came from God, and not from his position as king. But in 2 Samuel 7:1-7, David is not even allowed to build the Temple, much less to establish its order of worship.

There is yet another difficult phrase in this verse. What does "one section responding to the other" mean? The phrase has been interpreted as referring to the positions taken for antiphonal singing. But in all three cases (verse 9 and twice in this verse) we are not sure of the meaning.

Nehemiah 12:26. The days of Joiakim, the days of Nehemiah, and the days of Ezra are not simultaneous, but three separate sets of days.

Nehemiah 12:27. The Levites had to be sought because they were scattered throughout the territory (Nehemiah 7:73).

Harps hardly seem appropriate for the procession that follows. Perhaps the instruments were set in place before the procession began. Or perhaps harps were not as large then as they are today. Compare Isaiah 23:16, where the harp seems to be portable.

Nehemiah 12:30. Priests and Levites always purified themselves before participating in a service of worship (Numbers 8:21-22; 2 Chronicles 35:3-6; Ezra 6:20). The gates and the wall are purified to cleanse them of any contamination they may have suffered during construction. (See 2 Chronicles 29:15-19, where the Temple had to be purified from the contamination it suffered when King Ahaz was faithless.) The people, too, are purified before the dedication.

Nehemiah 12:31-43. Notice the symmetry between the "two large choirs," both in composition and in function. Each travels upon the wall, one to the right and the other to the left (verses 31, 38). Each group gave thanks as it went (verse 31). Each has a man of high rank following behind (verses 32, 38). Each company has in it seven priests named by name (verses 33-34, 41); each has eight Levites (verses 36, 42).

In each company are trumpeters (verses 35, 41). Each group walks around the wall, starting, apparently, at the Valley Gate. The first group proceeds south, and moves to the east side of the wall. The second group heads north. The two groups meet near the Temple. There they offer sacrifices and rejoice. So great was their joy that "the sound of rejoicing in Jerusalem could be heard far away."

Nehemiah 12:31. The "I" refers to Nehemiah. This is the first time since 7:5 that Nehemiah is referred to in the first person.

The leaders of the people gather on the wall. We do not know how wide the wall was at the top, but we do know that city walls were often quite wide.

Nehemiah 12:34. Judah and Benjamin are personal names here.

Nehemiah 12:36. The statement "And Ezra the scribe led the procession" must be a later addition to the text, since Ezra came to Jerusalem almost fifty years after Nehemiah did. We have seen before that such additions are not rare in the Book of Nehemiah.

Nehemiah 12:43. We cannot miss the note of joy in this celebration. Like the refrain of a musical masterpiece, the note is sounded with unmistakable clarity over and over again, ". . . rejoiced . . . rejoice . . . joy . . . rejoiced . . . joy."

Nehemiah 12:44-47. The system never worked as ideally as these verses would have us believe. If it had, Nehemiah's reforms would be unnecessary. Ezra would not have to call the people to repentance. We also find in the very next chapter of Nehemiah a description of several flaws in the system.

But if the system never worked quite this well, why does the author say it did? These verses probably were not part of the original text, but were added later to tone down what the text originally said about the negligence of the Temple and its services.

Nehemiah 12:44. "At that time" does not necessarily refer to the day just described. The phrase is used in the Bible in a way similar to once upon a time.

"The ministering priests and Levites" is literally, "the priests and the Levites who stood." Compare Deuteronomy 10:8 and 2 Chronicles 29:11, where the phrase *to stand before the LORD* means "to officiate in the Temple service."

Nehemiah 13:1. Once again we are not sure what day is being talked about. The law in the Book of Moses being referred to is Deuteronomy 23:3-5.

Nehemiah 13:2. This incident is recorded in Numbers 22–24, but that passage deals only with the Moabites, not the Ammonites. The verb *hired* is singular in the Hebrew, whereas the subject *they* is plural.

A curse was never actually pronounced. Balaam was sought out in order to curse the Israelites, but at God's bidding, he blessed them instead.

Nehemiah 13:3. The law in Deuteronomy 23:3 does not require that all those of foreign descent be separated from Israel. The ban is limited to Ammonites and Moabites and requires only that they be banned from Temple worship, not from the whole land.

Nehemiah 13:4. "Eliashib the priest" sounds as though he should be the same person as Eliashib the high priest. (See 3:1, 20; 13:28; see also 12:10, 22, where he is called simply *Eliashib*.) Many interpreters of the Old Testament believe it is the high priest who is meant here. But the description given here of Eliashib's work—"put in charge of the storerooms of the house of our God"—does not sound like the work of a high priest. Since Eliashib was a common name for a priest, it is probable that this was a priest of lower rank.

We are not told what the association with Tobiah is. The same Hebrew word is found in Ruth 2:20, and there it means a close relative. That is probably the meaning here, too, though there may have been some other way that Eliashib was connected with Tobiah.

Nehemiah 13:6-7. Artaxerxes was king of Persia, but it is possible that he, like Cyrus, assumed the title, king of Babylon.

The evil Nehemiah speaks of is the polluting of the Temple by letting Tobiah, an Ammonite, in it (4:3).

Nehemiah 13:8. Apparently Tobiah is not around as Nehemiah throws out all the household furniture.

Nehemiah 13:10. Because the Levites had not received their portions, they had left the Temple to work in their fields and the work of the Temple went begging. The Book of Malachi, written shortly before Nehemiah came to Jerusalem the first time, depicts the same situation (Malachi 3:8-10).

The Levites are forbidden by law to own property (Deuteronomy 18:1-2). Either they had disregarded the law, or, more likely, they had hired out to work in other men's fields.

Nehemiah 13:11. The words *the officials* are lacking in the best Greek texts. Without these words, the sense is that Nehemiah "rebuked" the whole people. That would make sense, since all the people were guilty. On the other hand, it does not surprise us that Nehemiah "rebuked the officials," since this seems to have been his usual practice when things went wrong (5:7).

Nehemiah 13:12. "All Judah" means the people of the entire land, including those of Benjamin.

Nehemiah 13:13. The duty of those Nehemiah appointed as treasurers over the storehouses was to collect and distribute the tithes equitably. The situation has been compared to that described in Acts 6:1-3.

We cannot identify with certainty any of the men whom Nehemiah appointed as treasurers. There were men of the same names who worked on the wall, but we cannot be sure they are the same men. We cannot identify with certainty their assistant Hanan, either, in spite of the fact that his genealogy is given.

Nehemiah 13:14. We have become used to hearing Nehemiah offer short prayers at strategic points in his life. We shall hear him do so three more times in the few verses left in this book (2:4; 5:19; 6:14; 13:22, 29, 31).

Nehemiah 13:15. Once again, the term *in those days* is indefinite. "I warned them" is literally, "I bore witness to them." The word is sometimes translated as *witness* in the Old Testament (Deuteronomy 4:26; 30:19), sometimes as *warn* (Deuteronomy 8:19; Jeremiah 42:19).

Nehemiah 13:17. Whether the nobles of Judah are engaged in the trading themselves, or simply allowing it to happen is not clear. At any rate, they of all people should have put a stop to it, so Nehemiah rebuked them.

Nehemiah 13:18. The obvious implication of this verse is that sabbath violations of the past are responsible for the present plight of the city. The more usual view is that all kinds of sin contributed to the fall of Jerusalem. A passage in Jeremiah, however, seems to agree completely with the point of view expressed here (Jeremiah 17:21-27).

Nehemiah 13:19. The purpose of setting his own servants over the gates is to make certain no one is bribed or threatened into opening the gates. Apparently it is permissible to go in and out of the gates as long as no wares to be sold are brought in.

Nehemiah 13:20-22. "Once or twice" would be one or two sabbath days. Nehemiah's threat seems to have worked.

Nehemiah's appeal here for favor is made "according to your [God's] great love," whereas in verse 14 it was based on his own good deeds.

Nehemiah 13:23. The words *Ammon* and *Moab* probably have been added to the text. Notice, for example, that only Ashdod is mentioned in verse 24.

Nehemiah 13:24. The wording of the King James Version makes it sound as if the children spoke a language that was half Hebrew and half something else. Almost certainly, however, the meaning is that half of their children, that is, those of Ashdodite mothers, spoke the language of Ashdod, while the other half spoke some other language. None were speaking Hebrew.

The Hebrew text does not say half the children "did not know how to speak the language of Judah." It says they "could not speak Jewish." We do not know what the language of Ashdod was at that time.

Nehemiah 13:25. We cannot help but notice the difference between Nehemiah's actions here and Ezra's reaction to the same problem in Ezra 9:1-5. Review the student book, Lesson 4, on Ezra 9:1-5 to refresh your memory on the meaning of pulling out one's hair.

Nehemiah first rebuked them and cursed them. Then he "beat some of the men and pulled out their hair." And finally: "I made them take an oath in God's name" that they would not intermarry with foreigners. Even so, Nehemiah never required as harsh a measure as Ezra did—that the men put away their foreign wives and their children (Ezra 10:1-5).

Nehemiah 13:26. The sin of Solomon referred to here is found in 1 Kings 11:1-11. The moral of this story is, marrying foreign women always leads to a corruption of one's religion, since the women bring their pagan religions with them into the marriage. If foreign women can make even Solomon sin, what chance do the rest of us have, then, to remain undefiled if we marry foreign women? That is the idea here.

Nehemiah 13:28. One case of a mixed marriage was particularly offensive to Nehemiah, and for two reasons. First, the guilty person was one of the sons (or perhaps the grandson) of the high priest. Second, this person had married a daughter of Sanballat, Nehemiah's old enemy. "There-fore," says Nehemiah, "I drove him away from me" and probably from Jerusalem.

Nehemiah 13:29-31. Sandwiched between two prayers is a brief summary of Nehemiah's work. The first of these prayers is an imprecation, similar to that of 6:14; the second is a plea for God's favor for himself, as in 5:19; 13:14; and 13:22.

DIMENSION THREE: WHAT DOES THE BIBLE MEAN TO ME?

Nehemiah 13:3—Christianity and Xenophobia

Have the class read the two paragraphs in the student book and answer the questions there. Help them explore their own feelings toward foreigners and those of other races. What specific things can you and those in the class do to improve the attitude of the people in your church and your community toward persons of a different national origin?

Nehemiah 13:25—When Others Disappoint Us

Have the class read this section in the student book. Help them be as honest as possible as they answer the question that begins the last paragraph. Let them give examples from their own lives or the lives of others. Compare Jesus' reaction to the woman taken in adultery (John 8:1-11).

Close the session by asking class members to share their new insights on Nehemiah 11–13.

INTRODUCTION TO ESTHER

The Book of Esther is named for its courageous protagonist. Esther was a young Jewish woman in Persia who rose from obscurity to become queen to Ahasuerus (Xerxes I). In this position, with guidance from her guardian Mordecai, she intervened to save her fellow Jews from a massacre planned by Haman, a Persian official. The Jews, instead of being destroyed, massacred their Gentile foes. From this victory arose the celebration of the Festival of Purim.

Esther's Hebrew name was *Hadassah* (Esther 2:7), meaning "myrtle tree." The name *Esther* was derived either from the Persian word for star or from the name of the Babylonian goddess *Ishtar*.

Set within the reign of Xerxes I (485–465 B.C.), the story of Esther could have been written by a Jew in Persia during the reign of Xerxes's successor, Artaxerxes Longimanus (465–425 B.C.). Some scholars place its writing in Palestine late in the second century B.C., reflecting the Jews' struggles against the Gentiles of the Hellenistic period.

The book makes no explicit mention of religion, and it is fiercely nationalistic. Later writers tried to correct this problem by adding prayers and other narrative material. These additions are now included in the apocryphal book *The Additions to the Book of Esther*. Because of its apparent lack of piety, both Christians and Jews were hesitant about including the book among the sacred scriptures. However, it was admitted to the Jewish canon in A.D. 90.

Esther is now in the section of the Hebrew Bible known as the Writings (the other sections are the Law and the Prophets). Each scroll in the Writings—Song of Songs, Ruth, Lamentations, Ecclesiastes, and Esther—is now read in Jewish congregations on special occasions during the year. Esther is the reading for Purim. The word *Purim* comes from *pur*, a non-Hebrew term meaning "lot." This name refers to the casting of lots by Haman to obtain the providential date for the massacre of the Jews. *Purim* is *pur* with the Hebrew plural ending.

One purpose of the Book of Esther is to explain the origin of Purim and to justify its continued celebration. Such an explanation was necessary because there is no basis for such a celebration in the Law (Pentateuch). The writer appeals to history to justify the festival. Purim is now celebrated on Adar 14–15, the twelfth month in the Hebrew calendar (February-March). From its beginning, Purim has been a time of feasting and drinking (Esther 9:19, 22). Mourning is prohibited. Gifts are exchanged and charity is given to the poor. The scroll of Esther is read in the synagogue. Purim is not considered a religious holiday. Celebrants were once advised to drink until they could no longer distinguish between "cursed be Haman" and "blessed be Mordecai."

This secularism may, in part, explain why the writer of Esther made no explicit mention of religion or God. In Esther 4:14, "another place" is regarded as a substitute for "God." The writer may have wished to avoid irreverence toward God and to remove the sanctities of the Jewish faith from association with such revelry. Even so, Jews have found a religious foundation in the book. Each development in the plot of Esther's story that some might regard as coincidence is seen as evidence of divine guidance and deliverance. The book as a whole is seen as proof of Israel's chosen position and indestructibility.

Some readers have criticized the vindictiveness displayed by the Jews in Esther's story. The writer of Esther claims that the Jews killed more than seventy-five thousand Gentiles (Esther 9:15-16). Long-standing persecution as well as their deep sense of being set apart by God could have contributed to such vengeance.

As persecutions continued through the generations, so did the popularity of the Book of Esther. Haman's downfall became a symbol of hope against anti-Semitism in any age. Esther has become known as the scroll in Judaism, second only to the Law.

As we have seen in Ezra and Nehemiah, the Jews became increasingly self-conscious and exclusive after the Exile. Esther reflects this self-conscious, aggressive determination to survive as a people. With such determination, Israel preserved her faith and her community.

— 10 —

Esther Becomes Queen

Esther 1–3

DIMENSION ONE:
WHAT DOES THE BIBLE SAY?

Answer these questions by reading Esther 1

1. For whom does Ahasuerus give a banquet, and for how long? (1:1-4)

   The banquet is for all his princes and servants, the military leaders of Persia and Media, and the nobles and officials of the provinces. It lasts for one hundred and eighty days.

2. After this banquet is over, for whom does Ahasuerus give another banquet, and how long does it last? (1:5)

   The king gives another banquet for all who are in Susa. This banquet lasts seven days.

3. Why does Xerxes become angry with Queen Vashti? (1:10-12)

   She refuses to display her beauty before the men at his banquet.

4. What does Memucan propose that Xerxes send to all the people in his kingdom? (1:19).

   Memucan suggests that Xerxes send a royal decree saying that Vashti could never again come into the king's presence.

5. What edict does Xerxes actually send to all the people in his kingdom? (1:22)

   Xerxes sends an edict written in each people's language saying that all women must respect their husbands.

Answer these questions by reading Esther 2

6. How does Xerxes decide to replace Vashti as queen? (2:2-4)

   All the beautiful virgins will be gathered to the harem in Susa, and Xerxes will select the one who pleases him.

7. Who is selected to be queen? (2:15-17)

   Esther is made queen in place of Vashti.

8. Why is Mordecai's name recorded in the book of the annals of the king? (2:19-23)

   Mordecai overhears two men plotting the king's death. He tells Esther, who then tells Xerxes. The men are found guilty and hanged.

Answer these questions by reading Esther 3

9. Who does Xerxes promote to second in command in the kingdom? (3:1)

   Xerxes promotes Haman the Agagite higher than all the other nobles.

10. Who refuses to bow down to Haman, and for what reason (3:2-4)

    Mordecai refuses to bow down to Haman because Mordecai is a Jew.

11. What does Haman want to do? (3:5-6)

    Haman wants to destroy all Jews throughout the whole kingdom of Xerxes.

12. What does Haman say in a letter he sends to the governors and nobles of every province? (3:12-13)

    Haman says that all Jews are to be killed on the thirteenth day of the twelfth month.

13. How do the people react to Haman's letter? (3:15)

    Haman and the king sit down to drink, and the people of Susa are bewildered.

DIMENSION TWO: WHAT DOES THE BIBLE MEAN?

Background Information on the Book of Esther

The student book points out the hesitation that some Jews and most Christians have had about the Book of Esther. Rabbis have questioned its value. The Essene community apparently did not include it among its sacred literature. (Esther is the only Old Testament book not found at Qumran.) The New Testament nowhere quotes or even alludes to it. Martin Luther said he was so hostile to Esther that he wished the book did not exist at all. For Luther, the Book of Esther "Judaized" too much and had too much "heathen perverseness."

On the other hand, the Book of Esther has been a favorite among many Jews. We have more medieval manuscript copies of Esther than we have of any other Old Testament book. And medieval Jewish scholars wrote more works about Esther than on any other book of the Bible except the Torah (the first five books). Esther is sometimes considered by Jews to be second in importance only to the Torah, and sometimes is placed above the Torah. For many Jews, Esther is a clarion call to protect their people from slaughter. The assumption is that Jews could survive without the Torah, but the Torah could not survive without the Jews.

A number of additions were made to the Book of Esther as it was translated into Greek. These additions were passed on from the Greek to the Latin, and eventually became part of the Apocrypha. The Protestant Old Testament, on the other hand, is based on the Hebrew text, and does not contain these additions. One major purpose of the additions was to correct the religious void in Esther. In the additions God is mentioned frequently, and Esther and Mordecai both pray long prayers.

The Book of Esther is almost certainly a Jewish short story, and not Jewish history. The story may be built around a kernel of history. But to read the book as literal history is to confront an unbelievable series of coincidences. These events work together to form a fascinating story, but they do not conform to the history of the times as we know it from sources outside the Bible. We shall observe these coincidences and non-historical elements in the book throughout Dimension Two.

Esther 1:1-2. Until about a century ago we had no evidence that would help us make a positive identification of Xerxes. Many guesses were made concerning who this king might be. Then, in the last quarter of the nineteenth century, inscriptions were found in which Xerxes's name appeared in three different languages. From these inscriptions it became clear that Xerxes is Xerxes I. Xerxes reigned from 485 to 465 B.C., and did indeed reign "from India to Cush."

The India referred to in verse 1 is Old Persia, including only the northwestern portion of the peninsula we know

as India today. Susa was the king's winter capital. Ecbatana and Babylon served as his summer capitals, while Persepolis seems to have been the location of his main palace where he spent five to six months of each year.

Esther 1:3. Persons have wondered why Xerxes would give such a lavish banquet, and many reasons have been suggested. This banquet has nothing to do with the story. It is at the next banquet, not this one, that Vashti disobeys her husband. Perhaps there was in fact an actual banquet of lavish proportions that the king gave in the third year of his reign.

The word *leaders* does not appear in the Hebrew text. Its appearance in the NIV is justified, perhaps, because it seems unlikely that the king would invite the entire army to his banquet.

Whenever Persia and Media are mentioned together in the Book of Esther, Persia is always mentioned first, except once (1:14, 18, 19). In the Book of Daniel, however, just the opposite is true. Media is always mentioned before Persia, and the Medes before the Persians, perhaps because during the time of its writing, Media was the dominant power (Daniel 5:28; 6:8, 12, 15; 8:20).

Esther 1:4. A hundred and eighty days is an incredible length of time for a banquet. However, compare the victory celebration in Judith 1:16 (in the Apocrypha) that lasted one hundred and twenty days.

Esther 1:5-6. "All the people" means *all the men.* The women are at Vashti's banquet in a different part of the palace (verse 9). "From the least to the greatest" refers to rank, not size. Both the important and the lowly are invited. White, blue, and purple are probably the royal colors (see 8:15). Archaeologists have discovered the remains of both the marble pillars and the mosaic pavement.

Esther 1:7. Each goblet is distinctive, different from the others. Such variety would surely show off the bounty of the king. It is interesting that whereas drinking and wine are mentioned as part of the banquet (verses 7, 8, 10), eating and food are not!

Esther 1:8. The meaning of this verse seems to be that each man could drink as much or as little as he pleased.

Esther 1:9. Some have wondered why the women would be at a separate banquet, since Persian custom did not demand it (5:6; 7:1). It is enough to say that the plot of the story demands two separate banquets.

Esther 1:10. "On the seventh day" does not mean on the sabbath. The phrase refers to the seventh day of the banquet. Only eunuchs were allowed to serve as household servants in either the queen's chambers or those of the harem.

Esther 1:11-12. When Queen Vashti refuses to come at the king's command, the king is angry. To put it bluntly, he is humiliated. Perhaps he had been bragging about his wife's beauty. He calls her to prove his boast, perhaps at the coaxing of some of his drunken companions. When she refuses, all the people present in Susa were there to witness it (verse 5). He could not allow her impertinence to go unpunished.

Why did Vashti refuse the king's command? Early commentators assumed it was because she was asked to appear before the men naked. Modern scholars point out that nothing in the text warrants this assumption. From a literary point of view, she had to refuse the king to set the stage for what comes next.

Esther 1:13-14. Although the term "wise men" normally means astrologers, that would not seem to be the meaning here. These wise men were versed in law. Xerxes does not consult the wise men at the banquet. He consults them later, when only the nobles are with him (verse 16). Notice that just as Artaxerxes had seven counselors (Ezra 7:14), so here Xerxes has seven nobles who have special access to the king. They are trusted enough to have daily contact with him and sit first in the kingdom.

Esther 1:17-18. The term "all the women" refers to all the women in the empire. By contrast, "the Persian and Median women" are the nobility, the wives of the king's officials. Apparently the contempt will be shown by the ladies, and the wrath by the king's officials.

Esther 1:19. "If it please the king" is the proper and usual way of suggesting a course of action to the king. The notion that a royal order may not be altered is found here, in 8:8, and in Daniel 6:8, 12, 15. In both of these books such a law enhances the stories being told. However, outside of these two stories there is no evidence for this practice.

Adding a touch of irony is one way to make a good story better. Our author is a master at using irony. Here is one example. Xerxes has been humiliated by Vashti. He deposes her in order to get another who is better (more obedient) than she. But the one he gets turns out to rule his life completely! And poor Xerxes never even realizes it because she always approaches him in deference!

Esther 1:22. Xerxes sends letters to all the royal provinces. Evidently, the Persian Empire had an excellent postal system. It has been compared to the Pony Express in early American history.

Esther 2:1-4. "Later" gives us no hint as to how much time has elapsed. The king evidently wants to reinstate Vashti as queen. But he is helpless in his desire because the royal order of 1:19 cannot be altered. His servants, to get his mind off Vashti, remind the king of the plan to bring beautiful young virgins to the harem (literally, *the house of women*) in Susa.

Esther 2:5. *Mordecai* is not a Jewish name; it is a Babylonian name. It comes from the Babylonia god Marduk. However, we know that some Jews took the name *Mordecai* (Ezra 2:2; Nehemiah 7:7).

Does this genealogy of Mordecai give us four successive generations, or the names of his father and two well-known ancestors of the past? Probably the latter. Shimei is known from the story in 2 Samuel 16:5-14 where his kinship to Saul is brought out. Kish was the father of Saul (1 Samuel 9:1-2; 14:51). Saul was the one who conquered the Amalekites, whose king was Agag (1 Samuel 15:5-8). Haman, whom we shall meet in the next chapter, and who is the archvillain of the story, was a descendant of Agag (Esther 3:1). So the purpose of Mordecai's genealogy is to set the stage for the conflict that follows. Not only are Haman and Mordecai enemies now; their families have been enemies for centuries.

Esther 2:6. The author explains why Mordecai is in Susa by telling us that he had been taken away from Jerusalem by Nebuchadnezzar at the time of the Exile. But this information only serves to confuse. For if Mordecai had been taken to Babylon in 597 B.C., then how old would he have been in the third year of Xerxes's reign, about 114 years later? Even if we say he was only one year old when taken from Jerusalem, and even if we say he was a full twenty years older than his cousin Esther, how could she, at 85, be such a ravishing beauty that Xerxes would select her over the other "young virgins"? Surely our author errs!

Esther 2:7. *Hadassah* is Esther's Jewish name. *Esther* is her Persian name. Taking a new name was the expedient thing to do, a way for captive peoples to win favor with their new government. Even today persons sometimes take on a new name when they move into a new culture for the sake of convenience. It is a matter of practicality.

Esther 2:9. Hegai takes delight in Esther. Perhaps Hegai knew the king's tastes, and knew she would be the one the king would select. Or perhaps he took a special interest in her because she appealed to him personally. In any event, he provided her with ointments and her portion of food. We are not told what her portion of food consisted of, but we may be sure it did not conform to the Jewish dietary regulations. Unlike Daniel, who found himself in a similar situation (Daniel 1:5, 8), Esther does not refuse the king's food.

Esther 2:10. Two questions arise in connection with Esther's hiding of her Jewish background. (1) Why did Mordecai see this secrecy as advisable, and (2) how did Esther manage to bring it off? The first question is never answered in the Scripture. Perhaps Esther could not have become queen had her Jewish heritage been recognized. We know from other sources that no one of any ethnic background other than Persian was eligible to become queen. In any case, the plot of the story demands that Esther's background be concealed until the dramatic moment.

The matter of how Esther kept her background secret is easier to answer, and of more concern to the Orthodox Jew. She could do so only by conforming to the heathen (non-Jewish) customs of Persia—eating what they eat, dressing as they dress, living as they live, perhaps even worshiping as they worship. But it seems strange that no one suspected her background, since Mordecai paid daily visits to see how things were faring for her (2:11).

Esther 2:11. How was Mordecai able to keep in touch with Esther after she had been taken to the royal harem? Four possibilities seem most likely. (1) Men were allowed brief contacts with the women, as long as they were supervised by the eunuchs. (2) Mordecai held an official position in the Persian government, and therefore was allowed special privileges. (3) Mordecai was himself a eunuch, and therefore allowed to enter the harem. (4) Mordecai did not actually see Esther, but was able to send messages to her through the harem attendants.

Esther 2:15. Apparently Hegai advised Esther well. He knew the king's desires, and she was willing to trust his judgment.

The statement that Esther won the favor of everyone who saw her is undoubtedly intended as a compliment. However, there is wisdom in the proverb, Beware of the one who has no enemies! In order to find favor in the eyes of all, Esther had to hide her Jewish heritage. That secrecy required compromising everything Jews held sacred.

Esther 2:16. Not until Xerxes's seventh year does Esther's turn come to go in to the king. That is four years after Vashti's banishment. Was Xerxes testing virgins all that time? That seems unlikely, yet the Bible offers no other explanation. Historians tell us that Xerxes I was fighting the Greek wars during two of those years.

Esther 2:18. We are not surprised that the king gave a great banquet to celebrate the selection of his new queen. Not only did Xerxes give a banquet, he also caused a *rest* as a part of his celebration. That is what the Hebrew says. The NIV interprets the phrase to mean he granted "a holiday." This may have meant that he gave a remission of taxes. Other translations interpret the Hebrew to mean he granted release to prisoners or release from military service.

Esther 2:19. We do not know why the virgins were assembled a second time. This verse and the verse that follows do little more than repeat what is said in verses 8-10.

Mordecai is represented as being at the king's gate often. Does that mean he was wealthy, and, not having to work, could sit leisurely at the gate? Does it mean he was a bum? Or does it mean he held some official post in the government? We cannot say for sure.

Esther 2:21. Bigthana and Teresh were two of the eunuchs who guarded the king's doorway. References to guarding the king's doorway are found also in 2 Kings 25:18 and Jeremiah 52:24. Probably the doorway to the king's living quarters is meant. If so, Bigthana and Teresh would have been two of Xerxes's most trusted guards. The Bible gives us no hint as to why they became angry at Xerxes.

Esther 2:22-23. Three unanswered questions come to mind as we look at these two verses. First, how did Mordecai hear of the plot to assassinate the king? True, he was sitting at the king's gate. But wouldn't two men plotting the assassination of the king be more careful than to allow their plot to be overheard by this man? Second, how did Mordecai communicate this plot to Esther? We dealt with this question in our discussion on verse 11. Third, why was Mordecai not rewarded for saving the king's life? Surely that must have been worth something to the king! The only answer we can give is a literary one. The story demands that Mordecai not be rewarded until later (Chapter 6).

Esther 3:1. The student book indicates that Agag indirectly became a part of King Saul's downfall. That story is found in 1 Samuel 15. But to get the full picture we need to go all the way back to the beginning of the desert wanderings, just after the crossing of the Red Sea. The first person to lead an attack against the people of Israel was Amalek (Exodus 17:8). Amalek finally was killed, but the bitter memory of him lingered. It was written in a book that God would utterly blot out the remembrance of Amalek from under heaven (Exodus 17:14).

In Saul's day Agag was the king of the Amalekites. Samuel sent Saul to punish the Amalekites for what Amalek had done to Israel back in Moses' day (1 Samuel 15:1-2). Samuel's instructions to Saul were that he was to utterly destroy the Amalekites. But Saul did not do that. He spared the life of Agag, the Amalekite king, and the lives of the best sheep and oxen. Therefore the Lord was sorry for making Saul king (1 Samuel 15:10). And that was the beginning of Saul's downfall.

For all of these reasons the Jews hated the Amalekites— Amalek was the first to attack the Israelite people; the Amalekite king, Agag, became a part of the reason for King Saul's downfall; and the Lord had commanded that the name of Amalek be blotted out of the memory forever. And for these same reasons, Mordecai did not bow down to Haman, and Haman was the enemy of the Jews.

Esther 3:3. The king's servants ask Mordecai why he does not bow before Haman. Why? There are four possibilities. (1) They were just curious. (2) They were afraid for his safety. (3) They resented his stance of superiority. (4) The plot of the story demands that Haman now become aware of Mordecai's defiance.

Esther 3:6. "He scorned" is literally, "he despised in his eyes." The idea is that Haman wanted to kill more than just one Jew. The only possible reason for Haman's delay in killing Mordecai is that the story demands it. Surely in real life Haman would take his vengeance on Mordecai immediately, even if he planned to kill all the Jews later.

Esther 3:7. "Nisan" is patterned after the Babylonian name for the corresponding month. The Jewish name for the first month was *Abib*. The month corresponds to our mid-March to mid-April. If we are now in the twelfth year of King Xerxes, then Esther is in her fifth year as queen.

Pur is not a Hebrew word. That is why the author has to explain that the word means "lot." They cast *pur* to determine on which day and during which month the slaughter of the Jews should take place.

Several commentators have noticed that 3:7 interrupts the flow of the story, and that verse 8 naturally follows verse 6. We shall have occasion to mention this again when we come to Chapter 9.

Esther 3:8. The Jews are scattered among the peoples in all the provinces of Xerxes's kingdom because of the Babylonian Exile. Notice that Haman says "your kingdom." Haman is the only person in the book other than Queen Esther herself (7:3) to speak to the king in the familiar second person. What Haman is saying to the king is this: "Mordecai disobeyed the king's command because he is a Jew. There are a lot of other Jews out there, and all of them may be expected to do the same thing. The best thing to do is just to exterminate all of them." We are reminded of the letter to Artaxerxes in Ezra 4:11-6.

Esther 3:10-11. The signet ring makes the seal that guarantees the document is from the king. It serves as the king's signature on legal documents. It is equivalent to a notary public's seal, the seal of the university imprinted on its diplomas, or the presidential seal used at the White House. The ring guarantees the authenticity of the letter or document. By giving Haman his signet ring, the king is giving him unlimited powers to do as he will. These, in fact, are his instructions: "Do with the people as you please."

Why would Xerxes turn a whole race of people over to Haman with no more information about them than that? He did not even know what people Haman was talking about! It seems equally incredible that Xerxes would refuse such a large sum of money—some have estimated the modern equivalent to be fifty million dollars—when Haman offered it. Here and elsewhere (5:3; 7:2-7; 8:3-8) the king seems to be very easily manipulated by those close to him.

Esther 3:13. Every thoughtful reader of the Book of Esther will wonder why the edict to slaughter the Jews was sent out eleven months before the date that the pogrom was to take place. Was it to give the Jews time to escape or to disown their Jewish heritage? Was it because it would take that long to get the message across the entire empire, and then set the pogrom into effect? Was it to increase the suffering of Jews by making them anticipate the slaughter for that long?

The best explanation is a literary one. Mordecai and Esther must have time to come to the aid of their people. Perhaps there is symbolism in setting the attack on the thirteenth day of Adar in the thirteenth year of the king. The Jews' fate is sealed on the day before they were to celebrate the Passover, the festival that commemorates their deliverance from Egypt.

Esther 3:15. The student book mentions the stark contrast between the consternation of the city of Susa, and the attitude of the king and Haman. However, perhaps this verse alludes to a practice whereby the Persian drank over a decision made while sober, and reconsidered when sober any decision made while drinking.

DIMENSION THREE: WHAT DOES THE BIBLE MEAN TO ME?

Should the Book of Esther Be in the Bible?

Have the class discuss the questions raised in the student book. The following facts may be of interest, or may enter into your discussion. (1) The probable reason Esther was given a place in the Jewish Bible was because it explained the origin of the celebration of Purim, as we shall see when we get to Chapter 9. (2) The *Additions to the Book of Esther* were a part of the Bible for all Christians for more than a thousand years—from the Council of Carthage in A.D. 397 to the Protestant Reformation in the sixteenth century— and continue to be a part of the Bible for most Christians today. (3) Contrary to what most Christians believe, the contents of the canon—that is, which books are to be considered a part of the Bible—are not fixed. The Church decides which books are to be considered the authoritative word of God. That is why the Protestant Bible differs somewhat from that of the Roman Catholic Church and the Orthodox Churches. (4) Modern objections to including Esther in the Bible are usually based on its lack of religious language and its low moral standards. But what about such verses as 1 Samuel 15:3 and Psalm 137:9? Shall we delete them, too? Or is God able to speak to us through the Bible in spite of such passages as these? (5) The Book of Esther is a vivid protest against the persecution of minority groups. Its only fault in this regard is that its author forgot that " 'It is mine to avenge; I will repay,' says the Lord" (Romans 12:19).

Esther 3:8—Treating People Who Are Different

The student book raises questions that encourage class members to think about their attitude toward those who are different. You might want to open the discussion by using the illustration that follows.

EZRA, NEHEMIAH, AND ESTHER

A friend of mine, who served in World War II, tells of seeing four soldiers pick up a fifth man by his arms and legs, and repeatedly butt the man's head against a tree trunk by swinging him back and forth. What was the man's crime? He was a Jehovah's Witness, and therefore would not salute the American flag.

How important is it that a person salute the American flag? How important is it that a person be allowed religious freedom to follow his or her own conscience? How tolerant are you of persons who are different? How tolerant should we be? Why?

Esther 3:15—What a Contrast!

If class members are hesitant to share personal experiences related to this issue, perhaps they could share some times they know of in other people's lives when the needy were turned away due to ignorance or apathy.

Another vivid contrast is found in Mark 10. Here Jesus and his disciples "were on their way up to Jerusalem" (verse 32). Jesus knew full well what awaited him there. He began to tell the disciples what was to happen to him. "We are going up to Jerusalem . . . and the Son of Man will be betrayed to the chief priests and teachers of the law. They will condemn him to death and will hand him over to the Gentiles, who will mock him and spit on him, flog him and kill him." But it all goes over the disciples' heads. "Teacher," they say, "we want you to do for us whatever we ask. . . . Let one of us to sit at your right and the other at your left in your glory." And there you have it! Jesus and his disciples walking down the road, he to give his life as a ransom for many, and they wondering what was in it for them.

Close today's session by asking class members to share new insights on Esther 1–3. List these insights on a chalkboard or a large piece of paper if time allows.

11

Esther Plots Against Haman

Esther 4–5

DIMENSION ONE:
WHAT DOES THE BIBLE SAY?

Answer these questions by reading Esther 4

1. What does Mordecai do when he learns about Haman's plan to destroy all the Jews? (4:1-2)

   Mordecai tears his clothes, puts on sackcloth and ashes, and goes about the city wailing loudly. Then he goes to the entrance of the king's gate.

2. What does Esther do when she learns about Mordecai's wailing? (4:4-5)

   Esther sends clothes to Mordecai, and sends Hathach to find out what is troubling Mordecai.

3. What does Mordecai ask Esther to do? (4:8)

   Through Hathach, Mordecai asks Esther to plead with the king for the Jews.

4. Why does Esther hesitate to approach the king? (4:10-11)

   Anyone who approaches the king without being summoned by him is subject to death unless the king holds out his scepter to that person.

5. What warning does Mordecai send back to Esther? (4:13-14)

   Mordecai warns Esther that if all the Jews are slaughtered, she and her family will be killed too.

6. What challenge does Mordecai send to Esther in that same message (4:14)

   Mordecai challenges Esther by saying perhaps she has come to the throne for just such a time as this.

7. What message does Esther send to Mordecai in return? (4:15-16)

   Esther tells Mordecai to gather all the Jews in Susa, and to hold a fast on her behalf for three days while she and her maids do the same. Then she will go to the king.

Answer these questions by reading Esther 5

8. What happens when Esther approaches the king? (5:1-3)

   The king holds out his scepter to her, and offers to give her whatever she wishes, up to half his kingdom.

9. What does Esther request? (5:4)

   Esther requests that the king and Haman come to a dinner she has prepared.

10. What does Esther ask for when the king repeats his offer at the dinner? (5:5-8)

    Esther requests that the king and Haman come to another banquet the next day.

11. What turns Haman's joy into anger? (5:9)

    The sight of fearless Mordecai at the king's gate turns Haman's joy to anger.

12. What do Haman's wife and friends suggest to him? (5:14)

    Haman's wife and friends suggest that Haman have Mordecai hanged on a gallows in the morning.

13. Does Haman have the gallows built? (5:14)

    Yes, Haman has the gallows built.

DIMENSION TWO: WHAT DOES THE BIBLE MEAN?

Esther 4:1-3. Apparently Mordecai has a reliable source of information at the palace. In 2:22, he learned of the plot of Bigthana and Teresh to assassinate the king, and here he learns of the plot of Haman to annihilate the Jews. Later we shall discover that he also knows of the king's private conversation with Haman (verse 7).

As the student book states, tearing one's clothes, putting on sackcloth and ashes, and wailing are all traditional ways of mourning among the Jews and other peoples of the ancient Near East. But these same acts are also used to express repentance, and to implore divine favor (2 Kings 19:1-4). Are these, then, religious acts on the part of Mordecai and the other Jews? Perhaps here the author's religion comes through, even though it is not explicitly stated. However, we need to remind ourselves that sackcloth could also be used to show humility and to beg for human mercy (1 Kings 20:31-32).

We do not know why no one could enter the king's gate clothed with sackcloth. Most interpreters believe it is because sackcloth is worn when mourning the dead, and anyone mourning the dead is ceremonially unclean. But this is only a guess.

Esther 4:4. This verse raises three questions in our minds. (1) Why did the maids and eunuchs tell Esther about Mordecai? (2) Why did she then offer Mordecai clothing? (3) Why did Mordecai refuse the garments? Questions 2 and 3 are answered in the student book. The issue raised by the first question is, Did the maids and eunuchs tell Esther about the situation simply because it was an item of interest? Or did they tell her specifically about Mordecai because they knew of the close tie she had with him? And if the latter, why did no one know Esther was a Jew, since Mordecai had made no attempt to hide his own Jewishness? (3:4). A fourth question we might ask about this verse is, Why had Esther not heard about the edict? Was she so isolated from the outside world that her maids had to tell her what was going on?

Esther 4:8. We are not told why Esther would need Hathach to explain the written decree to her after he had shown it to her. Perhaps Esther was unable to read Persian, or she may not have been able to read at all. Most women were not educated, and very few could read or write. The only verse in the book that even hints at Esther's ability to write is 9:29, and that verse certainly does not demand that interpretation.

Notice that Mordecai is now ready for Esther to reveal the fact that she is a Jew. For if she does not, the whole Jewish people might be destroyed.

Esther 4:11. The law to which Esther refers applies only to the inner court. The king could be seen from there, but could not be seen from the outer court. The purpose of the law was twofold: to protect the king from assassins, and to heighten the grandeur of the office.

The fact that Esther has not been called to come in to the king in the last thirty days has been interpreted as meaning that she has fallen into disfavor with Xerxes. Esther would not want the wise men consulted about another disobedient queen!

Esther 4:13-14. As indicated in the student book, Mordecai's words here may be seen either as a threat or as a bit of practical advice. We wish we could hear the tone of his voice as he gives the message to be taken to Esther. Basically, what he says is this: "Don't think your life will be spared just because you are the queen! If Haman has all the Jews killed, you can be sure that you will die too! And if you keep silent in order to protect your own life, deliverance will rise for the Jews from another place, but you will perish!"

From what place does Mordecai expect relief and deliverance to come? There are three possibilities. First, the words *another place* may be a veiled reference to God. Mordecai may be saying, "If you won't help us, God will!" Perhaps the author was remembering God's promise to King David long ago, "your kingdom will endure forever before me" (2 Samuel 7:16). And if so, his thought may have been that God would see to it that the promise was kept. So his words to Esther are, "If you won't help us, that won't mean the end for us. Relief and deliverance will rise from God!"

A second possibility is that by *another place* the author meant *a human agency.* Just as the Jews were able to establish a friendship with the Romans during the Maccabean period (1 Maccabees 8:17 in the Apocrypha), so also will relief and deliverance come now from another place.

The third possibility is a combination of the first two. *Another place* will be a human source of aid, but at God's prompting it will rise up to bring relief and deliverance for the Jews.

Why will Esther and her father's house perish? If the author means divine help in the above discussion, then he probably means divine punishment here. If so, Mordecai would be saying to Esther, "If you don't help us, God will save the Jews, anyway and will punish you!" Other possible interpretations are (1) that even if most of the Jews survived the slaughter, Haman would make sure he got her, or (2) that the surviving Jews would kill her for not helping them.

In Mordecai's next statement, the author's religious faith shines through. "Who knows," asks Mordecai, "but that you have come to royal position for such a time as this?" God is not mentioned, but what better statement of God's providential care than this?

But why would the writer so carefully avoid the use of the divine name? If he meant that God would send aid to them, why didn't he just say that, instead of saying help would come form another place? Perhaps for the author

God's name is too sacred to mention, and so he uses a substitute word. In a similar way the author of the Gospel of Matthew uses Kingdom of heaven where the other Gospel writers say Kingdom of God (Matthew 19:14; Mark 10:14; Luke 18:16.)

A second possible reason why the author avoids God's name could be because the Feast of Purim, which this book commemorates, is celebrated by the drinking of much wine. In fact, the tradition dictates that the Jews are to drink until they are unable to distinguish between "blessed be Mordecai" and "cursed be Haman!" In such an atmosphere, the author did not want to mention God's name lest those reading the story during the feast might inadvertently blaspheme God's name. A third possibility is that the Book of Esther is a book of wisdom. Wisdom books very seldom mention God, religious rites, or theological doctrines.

Esther 4:15-17. Esther is convinced by Mordecai's words, and she decides to go to the king. But first she makes an appeal to Mordecai, and through him to all the Jews in Susa. We do not know how many Jews there were in Susa. But there must have been quite a few, since they will later kill five hundred of their enemies in one day (9:12) and another three hundred the next day (9:15).

We can hardly believe that Esther would request that the people fast on her behalf without also asking for their prayers. These two religious acts often accompanied each other in both the Old and New Testaments. This is another example of the author's careful omission of religious language.

The fast did not last a full three days, for it was on the third day that Esther approached Xerxes (5:1). It is interesting that Esther has her maids fast also. These were not Jewish maids, but maids in the Persian court (2:9).

"If I perish, I perish," says Esther. What lay behind those words? Was this a resignation to the inevitable, or was it a selfless and courageous act of daring? Perhaps it was a little of both.

Esther 5:4. Why did Esther delay her request of the king? She had him in the proper mood, and he had promised to grant her request "even to the half of my kingdom" (verse 3). Why didn't she ask him at that time to spare her people? The author wants to exalt Mordecai at Haman's expense before Haman's final humiliation occurs.

The other question that arises out of this verse is why Esther would want Haman at the banquet. How could she ask the king to counteract Haman's edict with Haman sitting at the table with them? The writer probably wants to exalt Haman so the contrast with his fall will be greater.

An interesting accident of writing occurs in this verse. The initial letters of the words *let the king and Haman come today* (the literal Hebrew text), when written in Hebrew, are *YHWH*, which is the Hebrew word for *Yahweh*, the divine name. Some ancient manuscripts emphasize this by writing these initial letters larger than the other letters. Some interpreters of the Bible have wondered whether this was an intentional act on the part of the author. Probably it is nothing more than a literary accident.

Esther 5:7-8. If we can read between the lines, it seems as if Esther almost made her request of the king, but then stopped short. "My petition and my request is this," she says, but perhaps losing her nerve, she only invites the king and Haman to another banquet the next day.

Esther 5:9. Mordecai is now back at his familiar spot at the king's gate. This means that he is no longer dressed in sackcloth (4:2). Even Haman's edict to have all the Jews killed has not humbled Mordecai. He still "neither rose nor showed fear in his presence."

Esther 5:10. Apparently at this point Haman still thinks it unwise to harm Mordecai, for he restrained himself. Why is he reluctant to harm Mordecai unless he can do so in a pogrom against all the Jews? (3:5-6). Is it because Mordecai has popular support? (Compare Matthew 26:55, where Jesus' popularity with the people apparently prevented the elders and chief priests from arresting him in broad daylight.) Or does Haman restrain himself because Mordecai is a court official? The author never tells us, and may not have a reason other than that the plot of the story requires that Mordecai be left unharmed.

Esther 5:11. Haman's riches were many if he could pay ten thousand talents of silver for the slaughter of the Jews (3:9). A large number of sons was considered a great blessing (Psalm 127:4-5). According to 9:10, Haman had ten sons, but according to Jewish tradition he had 208 sons in addition to these ten.

Esther 5:14. The original Hebrew measures the height in cubits. A cubit is the distance from the elbow to the tip of the middle finger, generally about eighteen inches. Fifty cubits high, therefore, is about seventy-five feet high. The only possible reason for having gallows that high would be to express the hostility felt toward the one being hanged. The fact that Haman could not hang Mordecai without securing the permission of the king may support the theory that Mordecai held a minor position in the government.

DIMENSION THREE:
WHAT DOES THE BIBLE MEAN TO ME?

Esther 4:11-16—Undaunted Discipleship

An ancient coin had on one side a picture of an ox plowing a field. On the other side was a picture of the same ox being offered as a sacrifice. The inscription on the coin said, "Ready for Either."

That is the way it is with the Christian. Being Jesus' disciple does not automatically mean persecution and death, but it may. And the Christian is called upon to be ready for that. On the other hand, our calling as disciples of Christ may be to a long life of service, and we are called to be ready for that too.

One other thought. To say, "Lord, I am ready to go with you to prison and to death" (Luke 22:33), does not mean I shall then have no fear. It is not the fool, but the disciple who is faithful in spite of fears.

Esther 5:11-13—This Does Me No Good

Let the class discuss the questions raised in the student book. You might want to discuss a passage like Matthew 18:21-22 in this connection.

Esther 5:14—"Merrily, Merrily on High"

The questions in the student book do not have right and wrong answers. They are rhetorical in nature. In other words, the questions in the student book just pose the problem. It will be up to you to ask the right questions to keep the discussion going. Here are a few questions that might help.

(1) Have you ever made the statement, "There is nothing wrong with this . . . that a few good deaths wouldn't cure?" If so, what did you mean by this statement? Were you serious, or were you kidding?

(2) What problem exists in your church that seems to have no easy solution? Are your motives always pure when you desire (or resist) some change in your church?

(3) How could you become an effective change agent or reconciler?

(4) Where could you compromise in order to bring about a peaceful resolution to a problem? Where could you never compromise? Why do you feel that way?

And finally, there is the old Abraham Lincoln story about his political cronies who were urging him to destroy his enemies rather than being so kind to them. Lincoln's solution was as profound as it was simple. "Do I not destroy my enemies when I make them my friends?"

Close the session by having class members share new thoughts and insights on Esther 4–5.

So they hanged Haman on the gallows he had prepared for Mordecai (7:10).

12

Esther Intercedes for Mordecai

Esther 6–7

DIMENSION ONE: WHAT DOES THE BIBLE SAY?

Answer these questions by reading Esther 6

1. Why does the king have the royal chronicles read to him? (6:1)

   The king has the royal chronicles read to him because he is unable to sleep.

2. When the readers come to the place where it is written that Mordecai warned the king of the plot against his life, what does the king ask? (6:3)

   The king asks how Mordecai was rewarded for this deed.

3. When told that Mordecai has never been honored, whom does the king ask how he should be honored? (6:6)

   The king asks Haman.

4. Whom does Haman think the king wants to honor? (6:6)

   Haman thinks the king wants to honor him.

5. What honor does Haman suggest? (6:7-9)

   Haman suggests that the one being honored should be robed in a royal robe, sat upon a horse that the king himself has ridden, and led around the city by a high official.

6. Whom does the king say is to be honored, and who is to lead him around the city? (6:10)

   The king says Mordecai is to be so honored, and Haman is to lead him through the city.

7. What do Haman's wife and friends tell Haman when they learn of his humiliation? (6:13)

Haman's wife and friends tell him that since Mordecai is a Jew, then Haman will not prevail over him, but will fall before him.

Answer these questions by reading Esther 7

8. What does Xerxes ask Esther as he and Haman are dining with her? (7:2)

   Xerxes asks Esther what petition she would make to the king.

9. What petition does Esther make of the king? (7:3-4)

   Esther asks that she and her people be spared their lives.

10. What does King Xerxes do when he learns that Haman is the one plotting to kill all the Jews? (7:7)

    The king rises in anger and goes into the palace garden.

11. What does the king see as he returns to the banquet hall, and what does he think is happening? (7:8)

    The king sees Haman falling on Esther's couch to plead for his life and he assumes that Haman is molesting the queen.

12. What order does Xerxes then give? (7:9-10)

    Xerxes orders that Haman be hanged on the gallows that Haman had built for Mordecai.

DIMENSION TWO: WHAT DOES THE BIBLE MEAN?

Background Information on Esther 6

Coincidence and irony! We have spoken before of the author's delight in these two areas of storytelling. But here in Chapter 6 we are besieged by them. Why is it, for example, that Xerxes was unable to sleep on this particular night? What a coincidence! And why would he have the royal chronicles read to him? How was it that his readers just happened to read that portion of the chronicles which told about Mordecai's deed? Why did the king seek advice about how to honor Mordecai? How did it happen that Haman entered the outer court at just the time Xerxes was looking for someone to advise him? And why does Haman assume the king wants to honor him? If any one of these coincidences had failed, the story would have taken a different turn.

And talk of irony! At the very moment Haman was plotting Mordecai's death, the king was planning Mordecai's honor! Haman arrives early the next morning to request Mordecai's hanging, and because of that very fact ends up as chief architect of Mordecai's celebration! Haman assumes that he is the one the king wishes to honor. He therefore proposes the most lavish honors, which are then heaped upon his archenemy, Mordecai! The noble prince Haman thinks should lead the procession and announce the high honor turns out to be Haman himself, who must lead the procession for Mordecai! And the friends, who along with his wife suggested to Haman the plot to kill Mordecai, now are described as "advisers." They tell Haman that any encounter he has with Mordecai will lead to his downfall, not Mordecai's!

The author is a master storyteller! Every detail of the story is carefully planned to lead to surprises that are unleashed at just the right moment. The ancient rabbis, of course, had a different explanation. For them, the story of Esther was not fiction, but history. And for them, these coincidences were not coincidences at all. They were the hand of God. The outcomes of Haman and Mordecai were determined not by chance, but by providence. And as for the irony—well, that's just the way God does things. The one who digs the pit will be the very one to fall into it (Proverbs 26:27).

The chronicles (The RSV calls it the "book of memorable deeds") was the kind of book every king kept. It highlighted the most important accomplishments of his reign, but also included other events of significance.

Esther 6:4. Either Haman comes to the palace in the middle of the night, or Xerxes does not sleep all night! Haman stops in the outer court, since the law prevented his entering the inner court without being summoned (4:11).

Esther 6:6. The Hebrew word translated *delights* denotes a strong urge. It is the same verb as that used in 2:14 to describe the king's longing for one of his wives.

"Haman thought to himself" literally translated is *he said in his heart*. These words were used by early rabbis to prove the divine inspiration of the Book of Esther. How could the author know what Haman said to himself, they reasoned, unless he were inspired?

Esther 6:7. Any suggestion made to the king was prefaced by, "if it pleases the king" (1:19, 3:9; 5:4, 8; 7:3; 8:5; 9:13).

The fact that Haman does not do so here has been attributed to his overconfidence. However, it might just as easily be due to his excitement.

Esther 6:8-9. Haman recommends the deeds that would bring the highest honor to the recipient, little realizing that by so doing, he would bring the greatest disgrace upon himself. The actions that Haman recommends are similar to the honors accorded Joseph, the son of Jacob, upon his elevation to second in command in the land of Egypt (Genesis 41:39-43).

The royal crown set upon the head of the horse has troubled some commentators, who think the crown should have been placed on the head of the rider of the horse instead. Both Assyrian and Persian art, however, picture the king's horse as wearing a crownlike head ornament.

Esther 6:10. Here is the turning point of the story. Until now, Haman has had cause only to rejoice. True, Mordecai the Jew irritated him, but he was about to get that little problem taken care of. He is now ready to receive, or so he thinks, the greatest honor yet bestowed on him. But here in this shattering verse 10, he receives the news that he is to do to Mordecai all that he had thought would be done to him! The leaf has now turned over. It will be Mordecai's turn to taste honor, and Haman's turn to know the pain of humiliation.

The story is so skillfully told that no additions could improve it. But the ancient Jewish rabbis could not resist the temptation to add even more drama to the story. When the king tells Haman that he is to lead Mordecai through the open square of the city, another source document, the Targums (Aramaic paraphrases) have Haman ask, "Which Mordecai?" The king answers, "Mordecai the *Jew.*" But Haman still feigns ignorance. "There are many of that name among the Jews," he says. Then the king answers, "I mean the one who sits in the king's gate." At that, Haman cries out, "I ask you to slay me rather than impose this duty on me." But the king answers as if he had not heard Haman's cry. "Make haste," he says, "and omit nothing of all you have said."

The question is raised by almost every interpreter of the Old Testament. How could Xerxes now honor a Jew after having just recently given Haman the authority to annihilate all Jews? The answer is obvious. Xerxes is unaware of the identity of the people Haman plans to exterminate. Haman told the king that "a certain people . . . do not obey the king's laws" (3:8). He never told the king who they were, and the king never asked.

Esther 6:12. Mordecai receives his high honor at the hands of Haman. But when it is all over, he returns to his usual place at the king's gate. It is not now, but only after he is discovered to be Esther's cousin, that Mordecai is elevated in the king's court (8:1).

Esther 6:13. Haman's friends (here and in Chapter 5) are the same as his advisers. Notice that the advisers tell Haman, "Since Mordecai . . . is of Jewish origin, you cannot stand against him—you will surely come to ruin!" A lot of good that information does Haman now! Why couldn't they have told him that earlier, instead of suggesting that he have gallows built to hang Mordecai on? They knew then that Mordecai was a Jew. Why this sudden change in their picture of the future? It can only be because of Haman's shift of fortune.

Esther 6:14. Some have assumed that since the king's eunuchs arrived and took Haman to the banquet, Haman either had forgotten the banquet or in his grief he had let the time slip up on him and was late for it. But neither of these assumptions is correct. It was customary to send servants to escort guests, particularly when the guests were of importance. This custom still prevailed in New Testament times (Luke 14:17). And to have "hurried Haman away" is to recognize his importance, not to chastise him for being late.

Esther 7:2-3. The Persian custom was that after the banquet food was eaten, the guests continued to lie on their couches drinking wine. At this point Esther does not know of either Mordecai's honor or Haman's humiliation. The king would not have told her, since he did not know of her connection with Mordecai. Nor did he know that Haman was humiliated by bestowing the honor on Mordecai. As far as Esther knows, Haman is as powerful as ever, and she has no way of knowing how the king might respond to her request.

Esther 7:5. The Hebrew text begins this verse, "Then King Xerxes said, and he said to Queen Esther." The NIV smoothes this over by using only one verb phrase. The King James Version smoothes it over by reading, "Then the king Ahasuerus [Xerxes] answered and said unto Esther the queen."

"Who is he?" the king asks. Xerxes is completely unaware that Esther is referring to the deal he had struck earlier with Haman.

Esther 7:6. "Enemy" is a common term for Haman in this book (3:10, 8:1; 9:10, 24).

Esther 7:7. Why does Xerxes go into the palace garden? The author does not tell us, leaving the door open for much speculation. Perhaps the king wanted to work off his anger, to avoid having to look at Haman whom he now despises, to take time to think about his decision, to keep from having to condemn Haman whom he still calls his friend, to get a breath of fresh air, or to work off the natural restlessness of anger. Once again, however, the literary reason seems to be the real one. The author is setting up the scene recounted in verse 8.

The wrath that now fills Xerxes may be caused more by a realization that he has been duped than by the concern he has for the Jews.

Esther 7:8. Haman falls in fear at Esther's feet. It is curious that he chooses to beg for his life from Esther rather than from the king. Perhaps there is another bit of irony here, for that very choice seals his fate!

Falling at another's feet was a common way of expressing humility when asking a favor of someone (1 Samuel 25:24) or when expressing awe or admiration (Matthew 28:9).

Haman is falsely accused of trying to molest the queen. His present concern is personal safety, not sexual gratification. Esther knows that, yet she stands mute as the accusation is made. She wants this man destroyed before he destroys the whole Jewish population. Any accusation that will accomplish that—whether true or false—is good enough for her!

Why did the courtiers cover Haman's face? That was an act that signified the death sentence. The condemned person's face was covered before he was taken to his execution. We read of this custom among both the Greeks and the Romans. Although we cannot be sure such a custom prevailed also in Persia, it does not seem unreasonable to assume that it might have. So sure were the courtiers of the king's decision that they covered Haman's face even as the words left the mouth of the king.

Esther 7:9-10. "Harbona" is undoubtedly the same Harbona mentioned in Esther 1:10. Harbona's words provide an additional reason for executing Haman. He had gallows prepared for Mordecai, and Mordecai is the king's friend, for it was his words that saved the king.

Once again the king seems to be influenced easily by those around him. "Hang him on it!" cries the king, referring to the gallows just mentioned by Harbona. Irony continues to play its role. Haman is hanged on the very gallows he had constructed for Mordecai. And the gallows are located in Haman's house.

DIMENSION THREE: WHAT DOES THE BIBLE MEAN TO ME?

Esther 6:6-11—Sealing Our Own Tomb

Have the class members read the paragraph in the student book, and answer the questions there. You will probably not have difficulty finding enough embarrassing situations to discuss!

Esther 7:4—How Much Is a Human Life Worth?

Let the class members discuss the questions posed in the student book. Then have them discuss the following. If it was wrong for Xerxes to condemn a whole people to death because they did not obey the king's laws (3:8), would it be wrong today for the United States to make its foreign aid conditional on another country's acceptance of our laws and standards? Why or why not?

If it was wrong for Xerxes to condemn a whole people to death for ten thousand talents of silver, would it be wrong for the United States to make war against another country to protect our oil rights? Why or why not?

Now have the class think about another issue. Throughout the history of the United States, the use of tobacco has been a personal individual issue. But during the last twenty years, the negative effect of smoking on both the smoker and anyone nearby has been proven. A loud and angry debate has been enjoined about whose rights are greater: the smoker or the health-conscious nonsmoker. Whose rights are greater? Who determines the greater rights? Who determines the balance of health, economic, and rights issues? How much is life worth?

If you have time and courage, you might also introduce the abortion issue for discussion.

Esther 7:9—A Loyal Servant or an Opportunist?

The student book concentrates on the idea of taking delight in others' adversity. After group members reflect on this aspect of the issue, have them discuss the following questions.

How loyal should a person be to his or her boss? If you know your employer is acting in an illegal or unseemly manner, what should you do about it?

To whom does our highest loyalty belong? What does a verse like Acts 5:29 mean for us in our world?

At the close of the session, have class members share new insights they have gained during their study of Esther 6–7.

Therefore these days were called Purim, from the word pur *(9:26).*

— 13 —

The Feast of Purim

Esther 8–10

DIMENSION ONE:
WHAT DOES THE BIBLE SAY?

Answer these questions by reading Esther 8

1. What does the king give Esther, and what does he give Mordecai? (8:1-2)

   The king gives Esther Haman's estate, and the king gives his own signet ring to Mordecai.

2. What does Esther plead for from King Xerxes? (8:3-6)

   Esther pleads for Xerxes to write an order revoking the slaughter.

3. What authority does Xerxes give Esther and Mordecai? (8:8)

   Xerxes gives them the authority to write a decree on behalf of the Jews in the king's name, and to seal it with the king's ring.

4. What privilege does Mordecai grant the Jews in his letter? (8:10-12)

   The Jews are allowed to gather and defend themselves, and to kill anyone who attacks them, and to plunder the property of their enemies.

5. How do the people of Susa react when Mordecai walks among them? (8:15)

   The people of Susa react with joy and gladness.

Answer these questions by reading Esther 9

6. What do the Jews do all the thirteenth day of Adar? (9:1-2)

   The Jews gather in their cities to attack their enemies who seek to hurt them.

7. Why do the nobles and satraps and other royal officials decide to help the Jews? (9:3)

   The nobles, satraps, and administrators decide to help the Jews because they fear Mordecai.

8. How many men do the Jews slay in Susa on the thirteenth day of Adar? (9:6-10)

   The Jews slay five hundred men plus the ten sons of Haman.

9. What does Esther now ask of Xerxes? (9:13)

   Esther requests that the Jews be allowed to do again tomorrow what they have done today, and that the ten sons of Haman be hanged on the gallows.

10. Do the Jews of Susa continue to slay men on the fourteenth day of Adar? (9:15)

    Yes, the Jews of Susa slay three hundred men on the fourteenth day of Adar.

11. Do the Jews of other provinces of the kingdom slay men on the thirteenth of Adar? (9:16)

    Yes, the Jews of other provinces slay seventy-five thousand people on the thirteenth of Adar.

12. What do the Jews in the other provinces do on the fourteenth day of Adar? (9:17)

    On the fourteenth day of Adar the Jews in other provinces rest and feast with joy.

13. When do the Jews in Susa rest and feast with joy? (9:18)

    The Jews in Susa rest and feast with joy on the fifteenth day of Adar.

14. What does Mordecai instruct the Jews to do in a letter he writes? (9:20-22)

Mordecai instructs the Jews that they should celebrate every year on both the fourteenth and the fifteenth day of Adar.

15. Why are the fourteenth and fifteenth days of Adar called Purim? (9:24-26)

These days are called Purim because Haman had cast the pur *(lot) to determine the day the Jews would be destroyed, but his plot came upon his own head.*

Answer these questions by reading Esther 10

16. Where can more information about King Xerxes be found? (10:2)

More information may be found in the book of the annals of the kings of Media and Persia.

17. Why is Mordecai popular among his fellow Jews? (10:3)

Mordecai is popular because he seeks the welfare of his people and speaks for the welfare of all Jews.

DIMENSION TWO: WHAT DOES THE BIBLE MEAN?

Esther 8:1. Why is King Xerxes able to give the estate of Haman to Queen Esther? It is not his to give, is it? Obviously it is, but why? How did he get it? Ancient historians tell us that a criminal's possessions reverted to the king when the criminal was executed. On the other hand, if "the estate of Haman" refers only to his place of dwelling, then it may be that the king furnished a residence for his grand vizier.

Mordecai comes before the king. He has now joined that select group who saw the king's face and sat first in the kingdom (1:14). The reason is not because he had saved the king's life; he has already been rewarded for that. Mordecai may now approach the king because Esther had told the king what he was to her (cousin, guardian, and solicitous parent).

Esther 8:2. The removal of the signet ring from Haman undoubtedly preceded Haman's execution, but we are not told about it then. Giving the ring to Mordecai means that Mordecai is now the grand vizier of the kingdom. The grand vizier (or prime minister) was the one who actually ran the kingdom, thus leaving the king more time for leisure. That is why the grand vizier needs the signet ring.

Esther 8:3-4. At this point Esther goes back to her request of 7:3-4. The king has been sidetracked by his anger at Haman, and has never done anything about her request.

But when does this scene take place? Has Esther once again risked her life in order to plead for her people (as in 5:1-2)? She had, indeed, if she has once again approached the king without being summoned by him. And it is certainly possible to read the story in this way. But it is also possible that the NIV has incorrectly made verse 3 begin a new paragraph. Possibly Esther and Mordecai are still with the king when she falls at his feet and pleads that he retract the edict of Haman. If so, holding out the golden scepter to Esther had a very different meaning from the meaning it had in 5:2 (4:11). Here it would seem to be a signal for Esther to rise.

Esther 8:5-6. Esther prefaces her request with four conditional clauses. "If . . . if . . . if . . . if . . . ." The first two of these we have heard from her before (5:4, 8). The last two conditions are new.

Esther must have known that an edict written in the name of the king and sealed with the king's ring could not be revoked. Yet she asks anyway. "How can I bear to see the destruction of my people?'

Esther 8:7. The king reminds Esther and Mordecai what he has done for them already. The thought is not that he has done enough for them and they should not be asking for more. Rather, the king is saying that these things will show his friendly disposition toward the Jews and his readiness to do what he can to help them.

Esther 8:8. The king is as unconcerned about the welfare of his subjects here as he was in 3:11. But the story demands that there shall be a battle on the thirteenth of Adar. So the king has no choice but to allow Esther and Mordecai to write an edict. This will become clear to us when we reach the last half of Chapter 9.

Esther 8:9. Trivia enthusiasts may be interested to learn that this verse is the longest verse in the third section of the Hebrew Bible. The first section of the Hebrew Bible is the Torah; the second section is the Prophets; the third section is the Writings. Included in this third section are eleven books (thirteen, the way Christians count them). In all of these books—Psalms, Proverbs, Job, The Song of Songs, Ruth, Lamentations, Ecclesiastes, Esther, Daniel, Ezra-Nehemiah (which for Christians are two books) and Chronicles (which for Christians are two books)—there is no verse longer than Esther 8:9. For another piece of trivia, look back to Lesson 6 on Nehemiah 3:32, page 410 in the teacher book.

Esther 8:10. This verse has an unusual word. The word translated *fast horses* is not the usual word for *horse*. The word appears in 2 Kings 4:28 in reference to Solomon's swift steeds and again in Micah 1:13, where it refers to the steed that pulls the chariots. Apparently this is a particularly strong and fast horse.

Esther 8:11. At first the edict sent out by Esther and Mordecai seems meaningless. All it says is that the Jews could defend their lives against "any armed force of any nationality or province that might attack them . . . [on] the thirteenth day of the twelfth month, the month of Adar." If this decree had not gone out, would the Jews have simply allowed themselves to be slaughtered without a fight? Some have said Haman's earlier edict implies that the Jews are to submit willingly (3:13). But the truth of the matter is, Haman's edict does not say anything about how the Jews are to react. It is simply an edict saying the Jews are to be slaughtered. Furthermore, if Haman's edict had said that the Jews were to submit to death willingly, then that edict could not be revoked, for it was sealed with the king's ring (3:12).

The edict is not meaningless, however, for its purpose is more psychological than instructional. It is intended to bolster the courage of the Jews and to dishearten the enemies of the Jews. That it had both these effects may be seen from 8:17 and 9:3.

Esther 8:15. Mordecai's large crown of gold was not the equivalent of the king's but the author intends us to understand that it was impressive! It probably was not the entire city of Susa that celebrated, but only the Jews. There would have been from non-Jews, however, the cheers accorded any head of state.

Esther 8:16-17. Verse 17 mentions that "many people of other nationalities became Jews." Some have wondered whether those persons did not just pretend to be Jews. Probably, however, the author intends this to be a genuine shift in their allegiance. This is a part of the grand reversal that is taking place.

Esther 9:1. Beginning in 8:13, and repeated here, the Jews suddenly have a lot of enemies (9:5, 16, 22). Before 8:13, the only enemy of the Jews that is mentioned is Haman (3:10; 7:6; 8:1). He will continue to retain that label (9:10, 24), but he is joined now by many others.

Once again the author makes use of irony. The Jews were to have been slaughtered on the thirteenth of Adar. Instead, those who were to have slaughtered them were themselves slaughtered on that very day. And once again the author studiously avoids mentioning any divine assistance.

Esther 9:5. This verse clearly states that the Jews do not limit their actions to self-defense. They go about slaughtering and destroying their enemies, and "did what they pleased to those who hated them."

Esther 9:10. We do not know why the Jews did not touch the plunder. This must be an important point, however, since it is mentioned three times (verses 15 and 16). Perhaps the writer wants to emphasize that the Jews engage in this slaughter only to protect their honor, and not for any

personal gain. Or perhaps he is remembering that the downfall of King Saul began when he took some of the spoils of his attack on the Amalekites (1 Samuel 15:9-11, 19). See also the student book and especially the teacher book, Lesson 10, on Esther 3:1.

Slaying the ten sons of Haman was undoubtedly a step toward blotting out "the memory of Amalek from under heaven" (Exodus 17:14; Deuteronomy 25:19).

Esther 9:13-19. The problem of Esther's ethics in requesting a second day of slaughter is discussed in the student book. If the event is considered as historical, there is no defense for her request. From a literary point of view, however, the second day of slaughter is necessary. The author must have a reason to give the readers for the fact that the Jews hold the fourteenth day of the month as a day for gladness and feasting, whereas the Jews of Susa hold the fifteenth.

Seventy-five thousand seems to be an unusually high number of casualties sustained at the hands of the other Jews. It does not seem possible, either, that a monarch would allow such wholesale slaughter of his people. Very few major wars would have cost him that dearly!

Esther 9:20. Some scholars have inferred from this verse that Mordecai was the author of the Book of Esther. The things that Mordecai recorded, however, were probably the events connected with the recent battles.

Esther 9:20-32. The student book points out that the main purpose of this section seems to prove that Purim is a legitimate festival, and that it should be observed by all Jews. Purim is not prescribed by the Pentateuch. In fact, the Pentateuch knows nothing of the festival. Jews normally did not observe festivals not prescribed in the Pentateuch. It was necessary, then for the writer to prove that Purim should be kept.

The student book also points out that some Old Testament interpreters believe 9:20-32 was written by someone other than the writer of the rest of the book. There are three main reasons for this view. (1) the purpose of the writer seems to be different (see the first paragraph in the student book). (2) The language in this section is different enough from the language used earlier that it seems probable that this section comes from different hands. (3) In a number of places 9:20-32 seems to contradict the earlier story.

- In 9:19, some Jews observe the festival on the fourteenth day of the month while others observe it on the fifteenth. In 9:21-22, on the other hand, the Jews are enjoined to keep the festival on both these days.
- In 9:24-25 the king does not know of Haman's plot to destroy the Jews. In 3:8-11, however, the king knows about the plot from the beginning.
- In 9:25 the king orders that Haman be hanged because of Haman's plot against the Jews. But in 7:8-10, Haman

is ordered hanged because of his supposed molestation of Esther.

- Haman and his sons are hanged together in 9:25, whereas in 7:10 and 9:14, Haman is hanged first, and his sons later.
- In 9:22 and 9:31 fasting, lamenting, and sending gifts to the poor are part of the festival. In 9:17-19, these customs are not mentioned.

For these three reasons, then—the shift in the writer's purpose, the different styles of writing, and the differences in the details of the story—some think 9:20-32 was written by someone other than the writer of the main story. However, we must also keep in mind that the plot of the story, even from the very first, leads to the establishing of Purim. This purpose is achieved in 9:20-32. One way to solve the difficulty is to say that the same person wrote both. In 1:1–9:19, the writer is the author, whereas in 9:20-32, the writer is a borrower from another source. Perhaps the book of the annals of the kings of Media and Persia was that source (10:2).

Esther 9:22. It was entirely appropriate that Mordecai added sending gifts to the poor as a part of that festive occasion. That element of Purim lasts even to today.

Esther 9:24. The Hebrew word for *ruin* is very similar to the name *Haman.* So this verse might be an intentional play on words.

Esther 9:26-28. When we get to 9:26, we find out why *pur* is mentioned in 3:7 and 9:24. It is to let us know where *Purim* got its name. Apparently the festival existed, and was observed by the people, but there was no command for it or sanction of it in the Pentateuch. Therefore, this writer wants to explain why the festival exists, why it is called *Purim,* and why all Jews should continue the festival throughout every generation.

The letter mentioned in verse 26 has been thought by some to refer to the Book of Esther. Actually it refers to Mordecai's letter of verses 20-22. The "all who join them" (verse 27) are those who had declared themselves Jews (8:17).

Esther 9:29-32. Though there is some confusion in the Hebrew text, the NIV is probably right in assigning this letter to both Queen Esther and Mordecai. They write to confirm "this second letter concerning Purim," but what second letter do they have in mind? So far, Mordecai has written the only letter about Purim that we have (9:20-22). The word *second* is probably a later addition to the text. Many of the ancient versions do not include this word. The fact that a second letter had to be sent would indicate that some of the Jews, at least, were reluctant to observe the directives of the first letter. The fact that Queen Esther co-authored the letter would indicate that some teeth were needed in the command. Apparently it worked, for the writer tells us that the command of Esther fixed these practices of Purim.

Esther 10:1. Why does the writer mention that King Xerxes lays a new tribute on the land? That does not seem like an item of overwhelming interest for the readers. Does the writer want to add a touch of reality to the story? Or was there an actual tax levied at this time? We do not know. Some scholars speculate that the king levied new taxes to compensate for the loss of the ten thousand talents of silver offered by Haman. Others, taking the story as historical, believe the purpose of the new tax was to help the king recoup his losses in his war with Greece. But the writer's purpose here may be literary. Esther and Mordecai have been rewarded for their accomplishments. Now King Xerxes, who also played a significant role in the liberation of the Jews, must be rewarded too.

Esther 10:2. As we read this verse, we are reminded of the same conventional expression used over and over again in the books of Kings and Chronicles (1 Kings 11:41; 2 Kings 1:18; 2 Chronicles 25:26). The writer has mentioned these annals before (2:23; 6:1). It is interesting that a full account of the high honor of Mordecai is written in the book in addition to all the acts of power and might of Xerxes.

As was mentioned earlier (see the teacher book, Lesson 10, on Esther 1:3), whenever Media and Persia occur together in this book, Persia is always first, except in this one instance (1:3, 14, 18, 19). Probably, Persia is mentioned first because at the time of the writing of Esther it was the dominant power in the double kingdom. Media is mentioned first here because reference is made to a historical document that listed Media first, since Media was the dominant power at the founding of the double kingdom.

Esther 10:3. The one who was next in rank to the king was the real ruler of the kingdom. We can infer this from 3:12; 8:2, 9, 15; and 9:3-4. But we are told explicitly in Tobit 1:22 that the one who was second to the king was keeper of the signet ring and in charge of administration. Tobit is one of the books in the Apocrypha.

Mordecai's elevation to second in the kingdom was undoubtedly the high point of the book for the writer. The Jews were to have been slaughtered, but instead they came out on top. But followers of Jesus are more likely to think that the best thing in the book is Mordecai's seeking the welfare of his people. That is a fine closing to the book.

DIMENSION THREE: WHAT DOES THE BIBLE MEAN TO ME?

Esther 9:13—Getting Even Is Never Enough

Have the class members read the material in the student book, and discuss the questions there. Point out that most of us are never satisfied just to "get even." When someone wrongs us, our natural impulse is to go the person one better. But then that person wants to go us one better, and an unending spiral of evil is unleashed.

Jesus saw the folly in this pattern. "You have heard that it was said, 'Eye for an eye, and a tooth for a tooth.' But I tell you, Do not resist an evil person" (Matthew 5:38).

" 'Lord, how many times shall I forgive my brother when he sins against me? Up to seven times?' Jesus answered him, 'I tell you, not seven times, but seventy-seven times' " (Matthew 18:21-22).

"If you love those who love you, what reward will you get?. . . . And if you greet only your brothers, what are you doing more than others? . . . Be perfect, therefore, as your heavenly Father is perfect" (Matthew 5:46-48).

What message does Jesus have for us in these statements?

Esther 9:1—Unconscious Influence

The student book emphasizes the influence that each of us has on others, sometimes without even realizing it. But Haman was not just an ordinary citizen; he was second-in-command in all the kingdom. Ask the class: Do persons in power have greater influence then the rest of us? If so, what responsibility does this place on them? Do you think a person in power is more likely to use his or her influence for personal gain or for public welfare? Why? Discussion of these questions will lead naturally into the next section.

Esther 10:3
Power, Corruption, and the Shield of Faith

Have class members read the material in the Student book, and discuss the questions there. Then have someone read Ephesians 6:13-16. How will putting on "the breastplate of righteousness" and taking "the shield of faith" protect us from temptation? How will taking these actions keep us from falling into sin? Why was Mordecai able to resist the corrupting influence of power?

At the close of today's session, ask class members to share any new insights they have gained from their study of Esther 8–10.